David & Gail,- journey!
Enjoy the journey!
Keep on Pedaling
Peace

KT-495-366

# CYCLES OF A TRAVELER
True Tales of Voyage, Discovery and Synchronicity

authorHOUSE®

*AuthorHouse™ UK Ltd.*
*500 Avebury Boulevard*
*Central Milton Keynes, MK9 2BE*
*www.authorhouse.co.uk*
*Phone: 08001974150*

*First published by AuthorHouse 8/4/2010*


*ISBN: 978-1-4520-5023-2 (dj)*
*ISBN: 978-1-4520-2635-0 (sc)*


*This book is printed on acid-free paper.*

# CYCLES OF A TRAVELER

True Tales of Voyage, Discovery and Synchronicity

## Table of Contents

Dedication and Thank You.................................................iii
Author's Note ...........................................................vii
Introduction; Life's Too Short ..........................................x
Preface; Where It All Began .............................................xiii
Maps.....................................................................xv

## Chapters

### Cycle One; Motorcycle Days
### -Awakening the Passion-

1.  The College Dream Realized ..........................................2
2.  An Unlikely Encounter ............................................. 12
3.  P.S. 106 – Teacher becomes Student ............................... 26
4.  Pushing the Limits ................................................36
5.  A Lucky Break......................................................54
6.  Baptism by Fire – Finding My Path ................................70
7.  The Road to Japan – Not Exactly as Planned.......................94

### Cycle Two; Leaving on a Jet Plane
### -Discovering the East-

8.  Kenji and the Watch ..............................................120
9.  Mom and Aunt Mary Come East .....................................140
10. Striking a Delicate Balance .....................................145
11. Christmas, New Years and New Beginnings .........................153
12. Tasmanian Devils to Kiwi Hospitality ............................176
13. An Unexpected Respite in Oz......................................190
14. Healing Old Wounds, Creating New Ones............................196
15. The Camera ......................................................206
16. The Disappearing Rainforest .....................................213
17. Tour of Duty ....................................................229
18. The Mantra ......................................................247
19. Entering Moscow .................................................271

## Cycle Three; Land of My Ancestors
### -Rediscovering My Roots-

20. Returning to the Familiar .........................................302
21. Hitting the Ground Running ....................................308
22. A Walk across Tunisia ............................................320
23. Scared in Morocco .................................................356
24. Back on Track in Europe .........................................368
25. Finding Lost Relatives ............................................378
26. Illiterate in Greece .................................................384
27. A Turkish Experience ..............................................403
28. Pedaling behind the Rising Curtain ...........................434
29. From Prague to a Plan .............................................446
30. Ian, Olives and *Retsina*..........................................457
31. Different Wavelengths..............................................467

## Cycle Four; A Collision Course
### -America and Australasia Revisited-

32. Crossing Spokes, Crossing Wires..............................482
33. A Route Altering Root Canal....................................486
34. Northern Mexican Angels .......................................500
35. The Letters ..........................................................514
36. A Subtle Shift in Gears ...........................................531
37. China's Destinies ...................................................546
38. Our First Date .......................................................572
39. The Rutted Roads to the Invisible Border.....................590
40. Saying Goodbye in Chengdu ....................................602
41. The Three River's Gorge ..........................................611
42. Slow Trains, a Fast Plane and a Big Change..................617
Epilogue ...................................................................645

### PHOTOS

Chris's Bike................................................................vi
Author and Family......................................................viii
Cycle One.................................................................103
Cycle Two ................................................................286
Cycle Three...............................................................470
Cycle Four................................................................628

# Dedication and Thank You

This book is dedicated to everyone I ever spoke to; those who inspired me, frightened me, made me question. There are so many people that stand out in my mind, who were invaluable in enabling me to find my path. It's impossible to list them all here, but thanks for the help! Especially.......

My mother, Anna; I only know now how hard it must have been not to tease me with any guilt about going out to explore. Your deep spiritual beliefs have seen you through, and although we do not always see eye to eye, we respect each other's path. Thanks for the prayers, crying quietly, letting me explore with an open mind, and not making me feel guilty.

My father Joe; although only there for my first seventeen years, your struggle to find yourself, be a good parent and husband didn't go unnoticed. Over thirty years later, now raising my own children, I can understand more of what you were all about. Thanks for making mistakes and being human enough to show them. I still learn from them daily.

My cousin Richard; although you never lived beyond your eighth birthday you always remained in my mind. We were the same age when you sat on my brother's bike in our backyard and said, "I feel like I can see the whole world from this bike seat – it's so high up." The very next day – your birthday – a drunk driver ended your life too swiftly while riding your new bicycle. I nearly fulfilled those words spoken in my backyard. Your death made me face relationships, loss, and mostly forced me to forge a relationship with your mom, my Aunt Jenny. There were lots of bumps along the road, but it showed me how we can all be there for each other even though our roads vary. Thanks for coming to Australia Aunt Jen!

My mother-in-law Margaret; when your twenty-five-year-old daughter called from China to tell you she was going to cycle into Tibet with this guy from The Bronx, you respected her choice and, in what must have been a difficult phone conversation, asked, "Is he nice?", and stood behind her decision from afar. For that among much other help and support throughout the years in our chaotic semi-nomadic lifestyle, I am grateful.

My wife, Angie; although not a natural nomad like myself, you have put up with *our* thirteen years of moving around, until we found our small place to stop for the moment! For many other things too many to list here, you have been behind me. Our love and mutual respect has grown from that moment we met in China, and on our wiggly road since. We have helped each other to find deeper strengths as individuals, parents and a couple. Also, for the too many hours of editing, proofreading, drawing small-scale maps and making sense out of my written words, I am deeply grateful; it made the whole process of writing and remembering that much better.

My children, Louis and Francesca; nothing can replace the deep learning about ourselves that our children force us to do – thanks for the help. To feel unconditional love was made possible by your births, and it grows every day we're together. I also appreciate the patience you both had watching daddy write his book instead of playing as much as I could have.

My brother Larry; thanks for being the calm side of me I always strive to be. In the midst of the craziness you smile and bring smiles to others, something well-needed in this world. I'm also grateful for you taking me into the older crowd at an age when most older brothers run as far away from their younger siblings as they can. Many of those connections helped me immensely along my way.

My sister Nancy; you always made me feel welcome in your house (or backyard) when I showed up on my many two-wheeled adventures over the years with various friends, and at all hours of the night. It meant a lot to me, and the warm bed and love was always a comfort.

Aunt Mary and Uncle Lou; you were always like my second parents at our home in The Bronx. I felt more like a member of a small loving community made possible by sharing that space with our two families. I look back on my childhood and adolescence fondly because you were a part of it. I also enjoyed sharing some of my travels with you both.

My many travel companions along the way; some I'm still in touch with, others I haven't seen since those times we shared together. You have all brought something to my life, and I can only hope the feeling is mutual. Unfortunately a few have left this world too early; Phil, Charley, my cousin Bobby and Chris, our paths crossed for a reason, and all of the memories make me glad for the time we did have.

iv

*Dedication and Thank You*

Elphie Quinn, my young artistic neighbor; thanks for the sketches. You didn't feel up to the task, but your lovely artwork shows you most certainly were. *

Sandy Anthony; for countless hours of proofreading, input and helpful hints along the way, your advice and enthusiasm made what was enjoyable also fulfilling.

Sebastian 'Bas' Pot; the feedback and crash course on book formatting helped me immensely.

All the authors of all the books I ever read; I now have an idea of how hard it is to get from an idea, an abstract thought or real life encounter down to the written word. Thanks for taking the time to share your insights with the wider world.

The list can go on, but I hope the book itself can get across the essence of what I feel. Thank you everyone; family, new friends, old friends and friends I haven't met yet, because we are all part of the tapestry of each other's lives. I've enjoyed reminiscing in my stories, but look forward to what lies ahead and take the experiences as they come.

*All sketches printed with permission. elphietquinn@hotmail.com

# In memory of Chris:

Too bad we didn't get to do our trip together this time around. *

*\*No Truth No Justice* – By Audrey Edwards
Chris's story as told by his mother
www.watersidepress.co.uk

# Author's Note

I have written this book over a period of time using my journals, articles and other scribblings I have done as references. The origins of the book were many short stories, and through the writing process these stories slowly merged and hopefully became a representation of those years in a continuous flow. Every person, place and event in the book is real. Some characters may have amalgamated in my mind over the years, but everyone mentioned is, or at least was, flesh and blood. I used the actual names for most people and places, but changed some. Only when writing did I realize, although I met many people, quite a few of their names were the same. I tried my best to differentiate those characters in other ways, and apologize for any confusion.

All of my coincidental encounters along the way are also authentic. The historical, political, religious and environmental issues I came across over the years were the backdrop of my travels. I attempted while writing to check on their accuracy, and keep the book truly informative in the same way I learned small details along my journey. I ask forgiveness if I did not get everything exactly correct; my intention was to share my choices, philosophies, and experiences with you, the reader. The setting of my travels on this fantastic planet we call Earth is just the icing on the cake. I can only hope the stories entertain and make you think. Most importantly, my hope is that we can all get together and realize that it is truly one world, and we all affect each other. None of our decisions or experiences stay tucked away neatly on a shelf; they gather, meet and shape our beautiful world. Life has many stories, points of view, and realities; this book is representative of mine.

I have never been able to turn back from the path I fashioned for myself, and the world helped to always push me further. My mother always said, "Joseph, you should write a book." I didn't take her maternal pride too seriously and never set out on my travels to do so. Luckily I kept journals, and mom kept my letters, so when I finally decided to take her advice, I had something to refer back to.

Writing about thirteen years of my life in a (sort of) condensed book was a very difficult, yet enjoyable task. We all fall into patterns, and to see my own emerge in these pages was an interesting exercise of discovery. Of course it's difficult to cram thirteen years of life into a book; I had to pick and choose certain events, people and places that stood out from the rest. It's not to say those not mentioned didn't make an impact, they all did, but 42 chapters could have easily turned into 420 chapters if I didn't give myself a self-imposed deadline – my mother's 80th birthday.

I'm glad I had the time to write and rewrite the pages you are about to read. I've separated the book into four sections or 'cycles'. I felt they were all new phases; read it more like four books in one cover.

I'm happy to share those years with anyone who reads on from this page. I hope the stories can touch you in a small way, and help you appreciate our world in a big way. Enjoy the ride!

Thanks, Joe Diomede*

Author Joe Diomede and Family: Angie, Louis & Francesca

*To make comments, share your own story or just get in touch visit: www.cyclesofatraveler.com

"When the student is ready,
the teacher will appear."

— Buddhist proverb

"Not all who wander are lost."

— J.R.R. Tolkien

"To the bicycle tourer, one minute's realism
is worth an hour's imaginings."

— James E. Starrs

# Introduction; Life's Too Short

I was riding my bike along the riverside with my seven-month-old son behind me rocking gently in his bicycle trailer. The Chateau was just becoming visible over the trees. The Loire Valley is absolutely beautiful this time of year, I was thinking to myself; the September lighting gorgeous glinting off the wide smoothly flowing river just to our left. The poplar and plane trees throwing long shadows across our path and the crisp evening air gave a clarity of vision you never experience in the heat of summer. What could be better?

A man and his son were riding with me as I pulled my small child along. I was talking to the young man's father and at one point he turned to me and asked, "So how is it you were able to live here with your wife and son for the past six months without working? Did you get leave from your job?"

The father was in his late-fifties, his son in his mid-twenties. This had been their first vacation together. They were enjoying their holiday, but were both sad it was ending in two days. The elder had a high-pressure job that kept him busy nearly fifty weeks a year; the younger was entering into a career that sounded most likely to repeat the pattern. The tone of the question seemed almost pleading for my answer to be an inaccessible one, like I won the lotto, or was born into millions.

"This opportunity came up to house-sit for a friend in exchange for working on the house, so we have no income at the moment."

He looked at me strangely; no income was a foreign idea. "How do you manage?"

I replied, "Try to be creative, grow what we can, we don't own a car, and stay local."

"Not a bad place to stay local," he laughed, "I paid nearly three grand for the privilege of pedaling locally for a week." I think he saw the surprise on my face, and then added, "Before airfare!"

"Wow!" was all I could come up with and then continued, "I've lived most of my single life without a steady income – traveling, working and exploring. When my wife and I were offered this situation, we thought, 'Life's too short', and grabbed at the chance to live in France and see just which way our new path as parents would lead us. We're all bound for the same ending ultimately. At a young age I decided I'd try to carve out my own unique way through life. Luckily I married a woman who agrees."

The elder of the two became silent, trapped in his thoughts. His son looked more comfortable with such ideas; he unconsciously nodded as a smile came to his face.

A week, I thought to myself, as we pedaled gently up the tree lined road which leads to the small village of Villandry where the Chateau famous for its incredible gardens dominates the landscape. Wow, seven days. That's all!

I've had the pleasure of meeting so many remarkable people in my life, many having taken different paths inspiring and helping to lead me to where I am today. When I was younger and taking to the road across America on motorcycle I noticed that the people who made the greatest impression on me were the ones who had taken charge of their lives and often made choices that were unconventional or risky. I was open to talk and learn from these people. When I started traveling further afield, witnessing how people lived in other countries, and what true poverty was, my eyes were truly opened, and my life changed forever.

I remember going to an 'AA' meeting. I had friends who were suffering and wanted to be there for them and share their world. At one particular meeting I listened as a fifty-six-year-old man told his story of addiction and how at sixteen, against his better judgment, he started to drink to fit in, then smoke, then snort, skin pop, mainline, and the course of his life was shaped. Forty years later he was still fighting those same devils, and he said one thing that has always stayed with me: "Every weak decision made me weaker, but when I made the occasional strong decision, it made me stronger." It struck a chord with me, and has always remained as a premise in my life. I enjoy trying to make the strong decisions.

Beginning my travels I read a book named *The Teachings of Don Juan.* The lead character was a Yaqui Indian from northern Mexico. His student was Carlos Castaneda, the author, who was seeking wisdom. The older man likened death to a panther always stalking, waiting to pounce on us around every corner. To me he wasn't advocating living life in fear, but saying, "Live your life bravely, go out and face it, make decisions live by them, change your job, move house, start that small business you always wanted to, just make sure you are alive. You never know what could happen tomorrow, the ultimate purpose of life is to consciously live each moment."

I read many other life-changing books as I started out on my own journey of discovery as a young adult. I met many people rich and poor, the basic difference was not the amount of money or material goods these people had, it was how they viewed life. I like to think of my life as a work in progress, as I hope everyone does. When we think we are immortal is when we lose a grip. We are not immortal; the panther is there.

To live consciously is a difficult task, one that gets easier and easier as we live life more mindful of our decisions. We do not live on an island,

and no man is one. I'm not special. I'm just a guy from The Bronx fumbling through life like everyone else. I'm sure that my dad's untimely death had lots to do with my choices as did my eight-year-old cousin's, and my friend's fourteen-year-old daughter's. Read any given news item in the paper on any given day. These should empower us to be strong, not scare us into being weak.

My choices as youngster, college student, traveler, husband and father have been riddled with mistakes, but as the Buddhist saying goes, "What is good, what is bad? Need we ask these questions?" We live out our days, make our mistakes, hopefully learn from them, and then move on.

The stories in this book cover a thirteen-year period of my life as I searched and finally found not a path, but a starting point to cut my own small track in the woods. Bob Marley sang out, "None of us can stop the time." True, but we can enjoy the process of moving through it. That process can be a beautiful one, and I hope that you enjoy moving through some of these short snippets of time with me.

N.B.

I needed to pick between American and The Queen's English with spelling, writing and colloquialisms, so chose, and tried to stay true to my natural voice, American.

I also do not refer to only one system of measurement with distance, so miles and kilometers are interchanged, as it felt natural. (1 mile = 1.6 kilometers, 1 meter = 3.28 feet)

# Preface; Where It All Began

The bicycle came into my life in much the same way as it does most American kids – under the Christmas tree – though I embraced it perhaps more than many of my friends.

As pre-teens, my best friend Billy and I would go down to Boyd Avenue to visit 'the bicycle man'. Nowadays he would probably be feared by parents, but he was just an eccentric old man with a backyard filled with old bikes and parts. We would spend hours there rummaging through everything to make our bikes better or go faster.

At thirteen I had my first job delivering meat for a local butcher. Of course, the bicycle was the delivery vehicle and I was forced – without much arm-twisting – to cycle all over my neighborhood every day after school, delivering meat and occasional sacks of laundry for the small laundromat next door. The perfect job!

By the time my friends were growing out of their childhood romance with bicycles, I was still hooked. A timely break up with my girlfriend when I was sixteen left me with a little money which I'd been saving for her birthday gift. Instead, I got in touch with 'Puerto Rican Phil,' a cycle courier who was a friend of my older brother. He got me my first real quality bike. It was not as well-known as the ubiquitous, American-made, 'Schwinn Varsity' or 'Continental', it was from Japan – a 'Bridgestone Kabuki' – and coincidentally cost about the same amount of money as I'd saved for the gift. I quickly became known for showing up everywhere on my bike; it was my freedom machine.

The next spring I participated in a large organized bicycle event in New York City – a thirty-six-mile ride around all the five boroughs of New York – *The Five Boro Bike Tour* – the second of what is now an annual event. That day I and 10,000 other New Yorkers had a great time. Since I had no friends that I knew of who wanted to join me, I did it with two older men, husbands of my mom's work mates.

The enormity of the bike ride and being swept up with 10,000 other bike enthusiasts only served to fuel my own fire of bicycle obsession. It was fantastic I thought as I looked around. The sound of the whirring wheels and the tinkling of bells enthralled me. People chatted easily as they rode, profiting from the freedom from engine noises and fumes. All of this I found exhilarating, serving to strengthen the belief forming within me that the bicycle equals liberty.

At one point during the ride I pulled over to look for my two cycle companions from whom I'd become separated – a futile exercise – it felt as if I was watching all the inhabitants of New York City cycle past me in a blur of orange safety vests.

When I'd finally realized it was unlikely that I'd meet up with my original companions George, whom I knew vaguely from the neighborhood, pedaled up and said hello. We talked a while and decided to ride together into Staten Island. From that day on George and I became good friends, and we started on some of our own cycle adventures.

One particular trip sticks in my mind; George passed by my house after dinner and asked if I wanted to go for a ride. With no idea where we were heading we took off into the hot sticky New York summer evening. We cycled west to the Hudson River and then headed north.

At one point I turned around and couldn't see any sign of George. I started cycling back and then saw a Carvel Ice Cream shop lit up in the darkness with the silhouette of a bike leaned on the window and there was George tucking into a cool ice cream. He calmly said, "I shouted, but you didn't hear me. I figured you'd notice I was gone at some point." He was right, and we both enjoyed a well-earned ice cream.

I then realized we were close to my sister's house – about forty miles from where we'd started. We wound up making it there past midnight. We fell asleep in her backyard in a screened-in tent and awoke to the aroma of freshly cooked pancakes and hot coffee. My nephew was about two and a half years old then, with a new-born sister, and over the years they got used to 'Crazy Uncle Joey' – a tag that would stay with me for many years to come – showing up and sleeping over on many two-wheeled adventures.

My older brother Larry had many friends who were influential in my life. One character among them was Kevin. When I was seventeen we went off on a one-week camping/canoeing trip which turned into a two-week adventure verging on the ridiculous; a broken-down car, hitching a ride on a small airplane and being dropped off on a lakeshore with 100 miles of rivers and lakes between us and civilization. That trip awoke in me a love of the unknown and pure, unadulterated adventure.

When I was eighteen my brother's friend Jack introduced me to the world of motorcycles. From the back of his bike I got hooked into a new mode of transport, and a desire to cross America was born.

Jump ahead to end of August 1983; I had just graduated university, and, along with Gary – a college buddy – we were ready to head out across the country, my dream of a two-wheeled long tour was finally coming to fruition. After a weekend of partying, we folded away our college degrees and pointed our motorcycles west on a warm August Monday morning. Two Bronx boys heading out on their poorly packed bikes with their cheap camping equipment, up for whatever America would throw at them.

# MAPS*

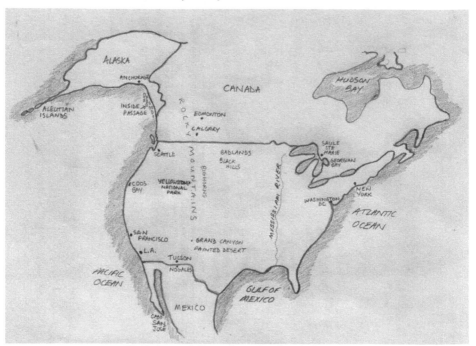

U.S.A. and Canada – Cycles 1 & 4

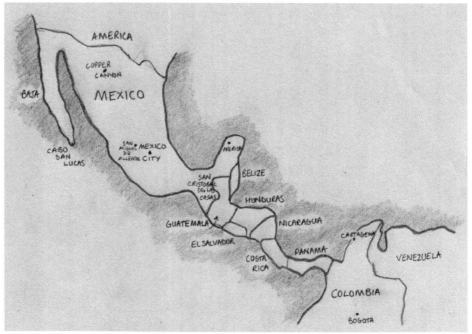

Mexico and Central America – Cycles 1 & 4

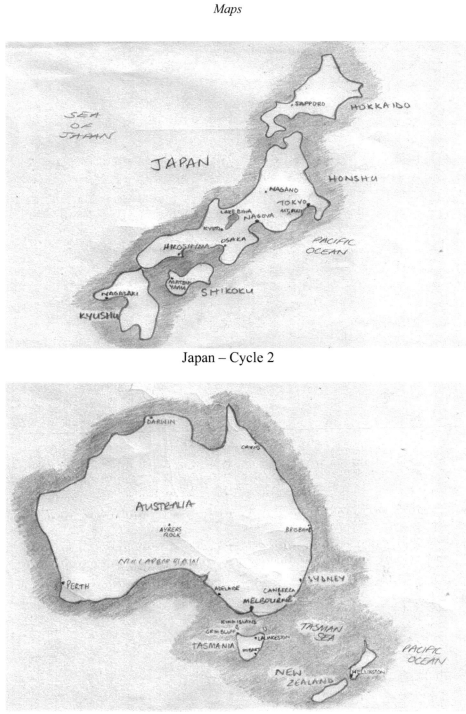

Japan – Cycle 2

Australia and New Zealand – Cycles 2 & 4

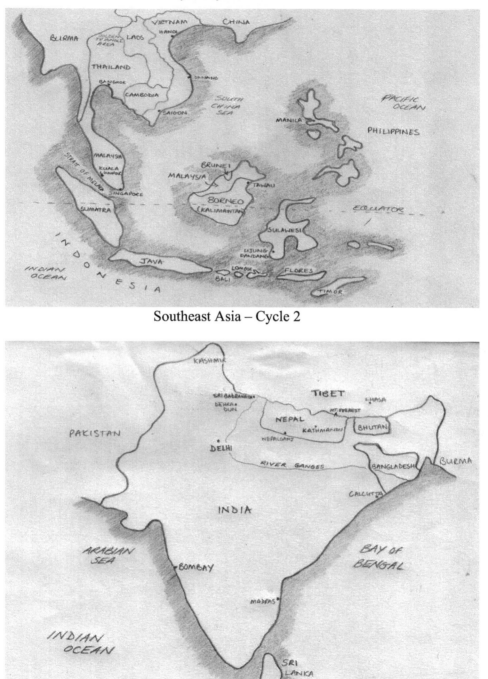

Southeast Asia – Cycle 2

India and Nepal – Cycle 2

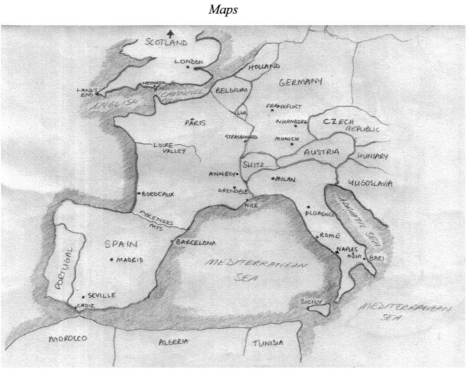

Western Europe – Cycle 3

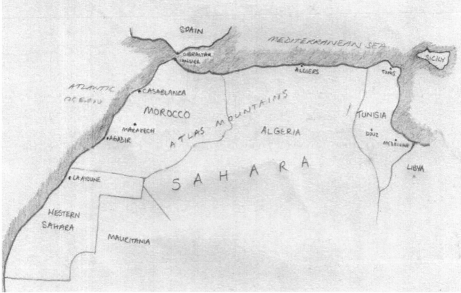

Northern Africa – Cycle 3

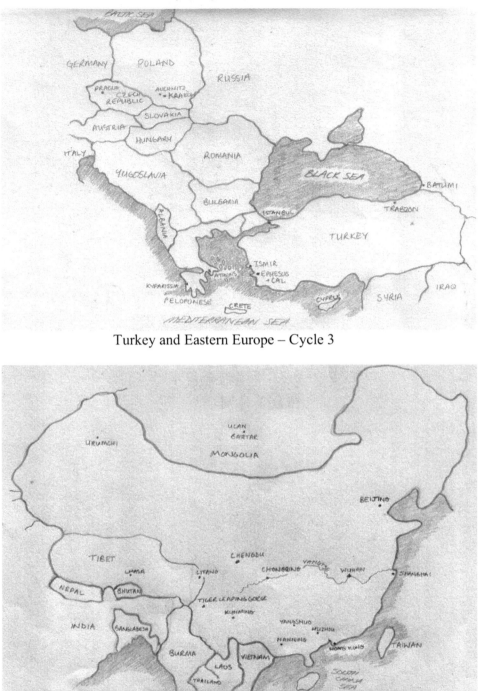

Turkey and Eastern Europe – Cycle 3

China and Tibet – Cycle 4

SYNCHRONICITY: the coincidental occurrence of events that seem related but are not explained by conventional mechanisms of causality

# CYCLE ONE; Motorcycle Days
## -Awakening the Passion-

# The College Dream Realized

The wide brim of the Wyoming State Trooper's hat shaded his face already half-hidden by his dark sunglasses, and his Midwestern drawl elongated his words. This gave me a few more seconds to formulate how I was going to try and wriggle out of this sticky situation. I took advantage of the moment to strip out of my rain gear.

"How fast do you think you were going son?"

"Uh well, at a guess about fifty or fifty-five miles per hour?" I answered feebly.

"Actually, sixty-three. Do you know what the speed limit on this here road is?"

"Um, uh, fifty?" I replied again trying to sound apologetic and clueless at the same time. The fact of the matter was I had no idea what the speed limit was, forty rang some sort of bell.

It was a tiny ribbon of road heading out of the Black Hills of South Dakota. The morning had started in our campsite with a light drizzle so we had donned our wet weather gear for the first time since Ohio, and headed out. As we left the Black Hills behind us, the snaking of the road gave way to a more open vista and the straighter roads just pleaded to be accelerated into. The sun had broken through in a cloudburst and the rays brightened the day as a sign welcomed us into Wyoming. I was lost in the moment and found myself speeding west. Gary faded in the rearview mirror and the next time I glanced into it my heart sank as I saw the blue flashing lights of the State Trooper who now stood in front of me. He took off his sunglasses to reveal his steely blue eyes, flashed a broad smile and replied, "Twenty-five miles per hour."

He let the words linger in the air between us as the realization sank in. The expression on my face was honest as I did the quick math and thought to myself, man, I'm screwed.

"Twenty-five?" I said this time genuine astonishment in my voice. "I had no idea, wow, I really had no idea." I was lost for words, and truly shocked at how low the speed limit was. To be honest, I had assumed I was a bit over the limit. I then went on to explain. "Actually officer, we started out in rain this morning, the sun came out as we entered Wyoming, and it was very exciting to be heading west. This road's so beautiful it's difficult to go that slow. My friend and I are heading to California."

Nearly on cue Gary pulled up, a few minutes behind me, which wasn't great for my argument as he was on the same road, and it would seem he had been obeying the speed limit.

"You know, that's going to cost you about a hundred and fifty dollars," the State Trooper added.

I gulped, and again spoke the truth. "Man, that's going to really kill my budget, we've been camping out at night, we just graduated college, and were hoping to make it to California."

Was that sympathy that flashed across his face? I wasn't sure. He adjusted the brim of his hat and put his shades back on.

"Good to see two young American boys doing something interesting, I see lots of foreigners round here; they don't speak any English – gets pretty frustrating. You take care now. Watch this road, the speed goes up and down for the next thirty or so miles. Have a good trip."

He gave me a nod and got back into his car. No ticket, nothing, plus he had actually warned us about upcoming speed traps. I couldn't believe my luck. Gary, who was waiting on the fringe peeling off his rain gear, came over.

"What was that about?"

"Speeding," I answered.

"I saw the sign," he said. "I tried to flash you, but you were gone. Great road man. Did'ya get a ticket?"

I smiled and walked over to my bike, "Unbelievably, no. I was going thirty-eight miles per hour over the limit! He liked our story, and said something about us being American and speaking English." We both shrugged, re-mounted our bikes, then pulled off into the Wyoming sunshine, being very careful to obey the speed limit signs from then on.

Such was the experience of our continental crossing shaping up. People were nice, and although the well-meaning warnings from friends back in New York about speed traps had been validated, our first experience with one had turned out to be positive. We had found a human side.

The first few days of our trip had been spent finding our feet on the road. The first night camping with my brother Larry and his friend Lou was wet, but quite nice. We ate under the overhang supplied by the campsite to avoid getting drenched. Lou wasn't a big camper but Larry was an adventurous soul who had done many a road trip with his friends. Being five years my elder his influence was strong. The fact that I was even on a motorbike was due to his friend, Jack. Now here we were, him saying goodbye to me for a change. It had been his idea to follow in his car and camp out for the first night, and I was more than happy he'd suggested it. I think he was reliving some of his adventures through his little brother and was happy that we were heading out to California. He had lived there years before but had moved back to New York after our dad died – a small thread to Larry's other possible life. We feasted on a huge breakfast in a diner after packing up our wet camping gear.

3

"Have a good trip little brother," he said. Was that a tear in his eye? "Enjoy the journey, not just arriving."

Wise words from my then twenty-five-year-old brother, "Of course we will, lots to see between here and there." He knew that all too well from crossing the continent on a Greyhound. Hopefully we'd take longer than three days, and have more adventure than could be had on a bus. "Thanks La, love ya."

"You too Joe. Take it easy Gary, watch the girls out there – they'd love to catch a coupla Bronx Boys!" we had a good laugh at that. A big embrace for both of us was in order and an awkward handshake from Lou – a man of few words.

"Don't worry Larry, the Midwest girls don't have a chance." Gary added.

A last check that we had everything, rain gear donned, final hugs in the diner parking lot, then we kicked our motorcycles to life.

We followed each other to the sign for 80 west then with a toot and a wave Larry and Lou turned off to head back over the George Washington Bridge. Our wheels were heading west, and spinning fast. We rolled through Pennsylvania and into Ohio under dark, wet skies, our adventure nothing yet but wheels kicking up spray from the black tarmac, but above those clouds, we were heading into the sun. The rain continued until we decided to take shelter for a while beneath a highway overpass. Trucks roared by in clouds of mist as they passed leaving us cold and wet. The romance of the road trip seemed far from our reality at that point, huddled silently beneath gray concrete with the constant drone and hiss of traffic speeding through the fine film of water covering the highway. Camping that night didn't appeal – as a matter of fact, nothing seemed very appealing at that point. I could still feel the excitement of what lay ahead lurking in my gut, but I looked over to Gary wondering what was going through his mind.

When we became friendly in my last year of college, Gary didn't have a motorcycle, nor did he know how to ride. As I spoke of the possibility of heading across America by motorcycle, Gary became interested. When I bought my bigger bike for the trip, Gary and I rode to Albany just for lunch. It was a fine spring day, and Gary was hooked, much in the way I had been on the back of another bike. Gary owned a beautiful Cougar car – quite sellable – so sell it he did, bought a motorcycle and taught himself to ride over the summer. Caught up in the excitement we would watch the movie *Easy Rider*, not letting the ending put us off too much. Now here we were; no sunshine in sight, sitting under an overpass, the spray of the passing truck wheels creating huge moving wet clouds behind them making us shiver. Did he hate me for talking him into this crazy idea? I wasn't about to ask.

Our first day out from New York had been fine, but the weather had turned while we were in the campsite, and it hadn't let up the whole day. I walked over to where Gary was taking shelter from the rain. We both stared at our bikes leaning on their kickstands on the shoulder of the road. Gary looked at me and said, "I guess we should get going." I nodded in agreement, and off we went into the relentless rain.

We crossed the border into Ohio and at about six in the evening we saw a cheap hotel. I couldn't stop my hands from shivering as we signed in. After long hot showers and a change into dry clothes we walked out towards a diner. The sun was just visible – the weather possibly breaking. We smiled at each other. A big meal was in order. Walking back, looking at the setting sun we had a good feeling we would be dry the next day. Sure enough we woke the next morning to glorious sunshine and the feeling that maybe this wasn't such a bad idea after all. We enjoyed good weather for the rest of the journey, except for that short drizzle in The Black Hills.

Crossing the Mississippi River was quite a big deal – we truly felt California-bound. The call letters on the radio stations even changed. It was another something I learned on the road, and I'd graduated with a degree in Mass Communications! East of the Mississippi radio stations started with a 'W', west of the Mississippi they start with a 'K'. I didn't remember learning that in school – it wasn't earth shattering or life changing, but just another small detail of American life that I found curious.

After putting in lots of miles, camping was a great way to end the day. We cooked mostly over open fires, chatting into the night under the stars. Whereas many motorcyclists tended to use two-way radios to communicate while riding, our equipment was as basic as it could be. We communicated through hand signals and nods of the head during our days on the road. It was mostly at night that we had the chance to catch up with how each other was feeling or talk about the beautiful scenery or the crazy trucker who had passed a little too close. It was during these talks that I got to know Gary better.

He had been a friend from college. We'd met working on theater projects, but whereas I was involved in the acting, he worked backstage and had a flair for the technical side of things. He knew that was where his talent lay and it probably gave him more of an idea of where he was heading in his life. I was still on a search. This meant that I was free to immerse myself in the experience simply for the worlds it was opening up to me, but Gary, although enjoying it, was suffering a little from homesickness and the life he'd left behind.

I had brought a radio/cassette player with me to listen to the occasional local radio or the music compilation tapes which another college friend, John Clemente – or 'Johnny C' as he was always known in our circle – gave to me as a good luck gift. Some nights we would put on the familiar music of our college days, look up at the star-studded skies and enjoy the strange juxtaposition of it all.

The long vistas stretching to the horizon soon gave way to the rolling, dry, desert-like scenery of the Black Hills where Lincoln, Jefferson, Washington, and Roosevelt were carved into the scenery. Soon after that we met our friendly State Trooper, but then the roads flattened out again – though not for too long. Something loomed on the horizon; The Bighorn Mountains. Being the first real mountains we'd crossed at first I thought they were the Rockies. When I naively asked the gas station attendant how it felt waking up to the awesome view of the Rockies every morning, he smiled, wiping his hands clean to accept my money and said, "Couldn't tell you son, these here are The Bighorns." I paid him for the gas, felt like a fool, and climbed back on the bike. Gary heard what I said and was laughing, glad that he wasn't the one to ask the foolish question.

On the other side of the small range we stayed in a town called Tensleep, Wyoming. It sat on the western edge of the mountains. I started to understand the romantic draw of being a cowboy; the beauty of the area was nearly overwhelming. It was in Tensleep that I witnessed admiration for a bull rider win over an unfortunate underlying, and sometimes plainly open, racial prejudice that runs often too deep in America.

The bars were allowed to stay open all night on the weekend of the rodeo. I figured I would go out and have a drink with the cowboys – the ones who were supposed to give us trouble because we were from New York. Gary was exhausted, and decided to stay back and read but my desire to socialize won out. When the cowboys found out I was from The Bronx, the beer flowed, not the fists.

It was a lot of fun, but the scene changed briefly as a drunken guy staggered out of a bar to where I and a few locals were having a laugh outside. The drunk pointed to a black guy in a cowboy hat across the street, and blurted out vehemently, "Is that a nigger?" We all ignored him. Then almost shouting he said again, "Is that a nigger?"

One of the cowboys I was with turned and quietly said, "He's a bull rider with the rodeo."

The drunkard just slithered off mumbling, "Oh."

This was one of the most interesting things I'd witnessed on the trip so far – something about that whole exchange intrigued me. I had a lot to learn about my fellow Americans. Growing up in New York there was racism, but it felt different to what I had just witnessed. I couldn't explain it. It dawned on me though that if Gary and I were a darker color, or spoke a different language; maybe our trip would have been different. It was a sad, sobering thought.

Our first experience in an Indian Reservation wasn't what I thought it would be. I didn't know exactly what I had in mind, but after entering and stopping into the shop which sold cigarettes and alcohol and looked more like a neglected Bodega in the South Bronx, I was disillusioned. The native people looked less like a proud nation of people, and more like a bedraggled mess shunted away from the crowds and put off into the corner to sulk at the loss of what was once their beautiful land. I was sure, or at least hoped there was more to the reservation than we saw, but I had read and heard much about the alcoholism that was rife on Indian Reservations, not so much the fault of the natives, but due more to the inappropriate way in which they had been treated. I knew intellectually that my grandparents had come from Italy to America at the beginning of the twentieth century, and were not part of the history affecting the native people, but on the other hand, I felt maybe we were all in some way implicated in the mistreatment of our fellow human beings. We were too excited crossing America for the first time to consider this for long, and when we left the official borders of the reservation, I let the situation slip from my immediate thought. One day the scene would return to the forefront of my mind.

We were aware that the continent was whizzing by – we were trying to heed my brother's advice, but the riding was the journey and we were enjoying every minute of it. Our first real view of the Rocky Mountains stretching from south to north across the horizon was awe-inspiring. We had waited days to witness it. We had been impressed, and even fooled by the Big Horns, but once we set eyes on the Rockies it simply took our breath away – they first appear as a bump, then as a dark shadow. We sped faster and faster west until there it was, unmistakably reaching for the heavens, the great mountain range we had only ever seen in pictures. Soon we would be riding on the roads that would take us deeper into their natural wonders.

The trip was awakening my love of nature, freedom and travel – riding on traffic-free roads, around the many lakes, across the wide rivers, camping under the starry skies were what really was inspiring me. Next stop, Yellowstone National Park.

The mountain roads climbed for miles. Our bikes leaning and banking into the contours of the landscape – we were in the Rockies! In the Yellowstone Lodge we met young people our age working there for the summer season, Europeans hiking on the wooded paths, and in the cool evening air, small crowds gathering around to watch 'Old Faithful' shoot its steam towards the star studded heavens. The black sky with billions of twinkling diamonds shining down and the wide white smear of the Milky Way spread across the center of it all – breathtaking. We were very far from home now, and we knew it. We had ridden our bikes here from the streets of New York, not an amazing feat, but for me it was the college dream realized.

It was as if a small seed was taking hold, a tiny imperceptible change in my view of the world. 'How much more was possible?' The night skies, the wild life, constantly in awe of the natural beauty we were surrounding by, made me feel a small part of a much bigger picture – my small seed being somehow nurtured. We saw bison, deer and caribou in the fields next to us as we rode and watched eagles flying overhead. We were like two kids in a candy store. We had made this happen. We were here because we both had made a decision to do it. All this beauty was here to witness for anyone who wanted to come to its greatness. All that was needed was the want to do it, and the follow through to accomplish it. This was all right on our doorstep. What was waiting further beyond? I fleetingly wondered, before pulling myself back into the moment, and what great moments they all were. We were actually crossing America.

Arriving in California was emotional for both of us. The obligatory photos were taken of two sunburnt, matted-haired Bronx Boys, with huge smiles, and shining eyes. I hadn't learned my lesson yet on following traffic rules. I thought bikes should abide by slightly different rules of the road than cars. In Wyoming I had been lucky, but not with The California Highway Patrol.

As I was riding the hard shoulder in some traffic north of San Francisco, I was pulled over by a figure from my TV-watching youth; a CHiPS officer. Unfortunately the story about trying to make it to California didn't hold the same weight once we were there. He was friendly, and feigned interest in our trip, but the forty dollar fine was handed to me with a smile all the same, payable by mail. Like before, Gary pulled up after the fact, obeying the law once again. It's true that riding on the hard shoulder can't really be explained away. I was asking for trouble, and although it was a financial blow, the romantic side of coming face to face with one of my childhood TV hero figures, complete with knee-high leather boots, dark shades and a fully dressed Harley Davidson, half made up for it.

My Aunt Mary and Uncle Angelo welcomed us when we arrived in Oakland California after crossing the continent in ten short days. We'd had a wonderful experience but we could have taken more small roads. The motorcycle riding itself had been what the trip was about, plus we'd had each other for company, which had been good for both of us. The speed and maneuverability of the bike was what had drawn me to it at first. Now it was the freedom of travel and the open roads that had me fully hooked.

I got to know all my relations in the Bay Area. My cousin Auggie had paved the road before me. He and his friends who were teenagers in the early seventies had made it to the doors of all my cousins out here. My brother was the next wave, making it by Greyhound bus. Now here were Gary and me on our motorcycles, another contingent of the crazy New Yorkers just continuing the tradition. We took BART into San Francisco. At first I thought we were meeting a friend, but found out, much to everyone's laughter, that BART is an acronym for The Bay Area Rapid Transit – the New Yorkers had arrived! My relatives treated Gary like he was family, and after a week or so in the Bay Area, we took off to ride the coast road down to Los Angeles.

Things were moving quickly; we were enjoying it, but were still moving at a New York pace. It was setting the scene for future crossings; I would eventually learn to slow it down a bit, but this trip was about crossing America and getting to Los Angeles California, and we did.

In Los Angeles Gary and I went our separate ways. He had no desire to stay in the city area, he had friends further south and he continued on to meet them. I stayed in L.A. to see what would transpire there. If America was a melting pot, L.A. was the microcosm of the macrocosm. There were people from all over the States living in the small apartment building in Venice, California where I was staying while trying to find work; stone masons from Idaho, musicians from Michigan, and even a child actress. L.A. was such an interesting contrast to New York – so different in lifestyle, and with the Pacific Ocean out your door, it was quite beautiful. It was my first time west of Pennsylvania and walking on the boardwalk of Venice beach felt so exotic; Muscle Beach, Hollywood, Santa Monica – these place names brought to life. There was also something about having arrived overland that made it special to me. My brother and cousin had lived out here a few years back, and it was great to meet some of the people that Larry and Jen both knew.

I'd met up with a friend of Jen's called Neil in a *sushi* bar where he ordered two *miso* soups. I was raised on an Italian-American blend of food and *sushi* had not made it to my table before. I ate the *miso* soup not wanting to look like a boy from The Bronx with no worldly experience, which was basically what I was. I ate it quickly, and thought it was disgusting. Neil mistakenly took that to mean I liked it, and ordered another. I got through it somehow, little knowing I would one day live in Japan and grow to love the stuff.

9

I also met up with a woman who was in the movie industry – another acquaintance of my cousin Jen. We met early in the day, she lined up some cocaine and we were snorting lines before I'd even eaten breakfast – definitely not my normal morning routine. Then we got into her Porsche and drove down to the Main Street Café to eat. Sitting next to me, bleary-eyed, was Rod Stewart, sipping what looked like a Bloody Mary. I felt out of my league, but this was L.A. It seemed a hazy dream, but enjoyable at the same time.

Riding up Topanga Canyon through Malibu was fantastic, it all felt surreal but I was actually feeling that maybe life in a big city would be easier in one I knew better. As new and exotic as it all felt, I was starting to realize that maybe living in L.A. was not on the cards at that moment in time. I enjoyed the vibe, but missed New York. I had been in New York my whole life as a student, maybe there was a different world waiting for me if I went back now. I knew my trip had been formed by all the people in my life; my brother, my cousin, my parents, my father's untimely death; there were many reasons I had wanted to head out to California. My dad had been waiting to live the life he always wanted until he retired, but died at age fifty-seven before ever making those changes. I felt I didn't want to put anything off until later. I knew it was possible to get sucked into a life I didn't want, and years later ask the question, "How did I get here?" Something inside was pushing to the forefront of my being. Like the skin of an onion I was peeling back the layers and this first trip had only peeled back the brown, hard, outer skin.

Gary had had his reasons for coming west as well. He had friends from his old neighborhood in The Bronx who had moved out a few years back. They lived further south and Gary was thinking of making a permanent move too – while I partied in L.A. he stayed with his friends in Orange County.

It had been a few weeks since we spoke when I decided to call Gary, not sure what his plans had come to. When I found out he was also planning to return to New York, but was going to sell his bike and fly back, I came up with an alternate plan. Our money was running low, the eight hundred dollars each that had felt like a fortune when we started out was reaching its limits, but I suggested we ride back together across the southern states. His instant response was, "When?" Not one for procrastinating I said, "Monday?" It was now Friday. I said goodbye to L.A. and headed down to meet Gary. We spent the weekend with his friends, and with another small send off we were off into the face of the rising sun, heading back east.

We were looking forward to getting back. We didn't tell anyone in New York about our plan figuring we'd surprise our friends and family. The ride back was just as beautiful, but the scenery quite different. We rode along the southern rim of the Grand Canyon, like two insignificant insects crawling along this vast 200 mile wide gaping colorful chasm. The Painted Desert with its colorful reds and pinks was fantastic. The pastel colors actually did make it look like someone had painted this part of the world. I thought of how this land had not changed since the beginning of time. No matter what atrocities might have occurred between the white Europeans and the natives, this land's beauty was moving. The Petrified Forest in Arizona was fascinating – the ancient trees turned into stone over thousands of years were mind-boggling. I was discovering a love of nature, and realized that my education and all the books and photos you could see would never be a replacement for the real thing. Our whole return journey was an added bonus. We were pretty broke now, and in Indiana we caught two full days of constant cold rain. We shivered the rest of the way east, never quite getting rid of the chill of those two miserable days.

Our equipment was just not good enough to keep us in comfort through the extremes of weather and distances we were covering. Nonetheless, we were greeted by the beautiful autumn colors of western New Jersey; it was far more welcoming than any red carpet could have been. The splendor of the views from the road was familiar, but exquisite in its natural wonder all the same. This was literally our backyard and the 'Welcome to New York' sign should have said 'Welcome Back'. Even though our whole journey only took a little over two months, we came home feeling like we had accomplished a great thing.

It was to be the first and last crossing for Gary, but for me it had awakened a love of travel and let me realize that in life there were always doors open to you, it was just a matter of walking through them. One of the highlights of the trip for me was having time to think and be alone on the bike. I was given some great books to read on the journey. I read Robert Pirsig's *Zen and the Art of Motorcycle Maintenance* but it was beyond me. I enjoyed reading Carlos Castaneda and Jack Kerouac too; I was always drawn to a spiritual search of some sort, and I re-found my love of reading on that trip, especially in the tent at night.

The first trip across America was a success – at twenty-one years old it filled me with ideas and showed me an America I never knew existed. The unknown, I felt strongly, was not something to be feared, but embraced. My second trip started taking shape with my ears still buzzing from the first whirlwind tour across the continent – the moment I arrived back in New York I decided I would do it again. This time I would slow it down and change the route a little; being alone I would be free to go any which way I desired.

# An Unlikely Encounter

Heading out alone across America by motorcycle sounds like a daunting thing to do, especially at twenty-two years old, but with the previous year's experience under my belt I felt more confident. I worked as a bartender and a land surveyor for that year between trips, and although I enjoyed my year at home, I knew the money I was saving was for another journey across America. Looking at a map, I thought that highway 2 across the upper peninsula of Michigan across the Border States with Canada looked quite nice. I was never one for doing too much forward planning, and that seemed enough. I had the camping equipment and the motorcycle, and so enjoyed my year in New York knowing I would once again be on the road.

My time back in New York was fine, I had probably drunk too much alcohol – getting a job in a local bar didn't help – and lots of good times were had. I got to work with and know better some friends from the neighborhood; but I also realized we were all on our separate journeys.

The scene in the local bars on 'The Avenue', as White Plains Road was known, was quite good. You could bar hop and within six blocks the bars varied so that there was always something which would suit your mood. One bar had a pool table, which changed the vibe a bit, the other one darts or a television playing sports; it was a typical Bronx scene, and my friends were colorful, many of us now into motorcycles, and nearly everyone I hung out with had gotten at least one tattoo – I had three. I wouldn't trade a moment of my time in The Bronx and deep down I still consider myself a boy from The Bronx, even though my travels have taken me far from those nights on The Avenue drinking in *Donovan's* or *Bill and Bob's*.

We would sometimes head down to Manhattan for dancing in the clubs; *The Bottom Line, CBGB* or *The Mudd Club*, rock concerts in *The Garden*, as Madison Square Garden was known. Cocaine and marijuana were easily found, as were other drugs, mostly hallucinogens like acid, THC, or mescaline. We didn't always depend on drugs or alcohol to enjoy ourselves, and my friends and I were not drug addicts by any means, but we were all in our early twenties and now had money because we were no longer students. Most of my friends could handle the drugs we were using for pleasure, but I had also seen some friends and acquaintances go down paths that were hard to get back from. Unfortunately I also knew of young lives lost to overdoses – one friend's girlfriend fell off a roof to her death while high.

Seeing the delicacy of life, and experiencing the diversity of lifestyles right at my doorstep in America, I knew I wanted to taste more of the road, and less of the mind-altering enjoyment drugs and alcohol had to offer.

The other job I had which drew me away from the bar scene was working for a Civil Engineering company – RBA. My friend Ernie got me the job – four ten-hour days a week, perfect. The best part about the job was learning about something new. I also had the pleasure of going off to upstate New York to spend entire days walking through fields and farmland with a chief surveyor, mapping out the area for one of our contracts. It was allowing me to get more in touch with the outdoor side of myself which had been nudged awake on my first journey across America. Sometimes the forested areas were so thick with undergrowth we needed machetes to cut through – I used to let my mind drift, and try to feel what it might have been like to be doing the same not even a decade before in a far-flung place called Vietnam. I had been too young to be drafted, but through my brother's and cousin's friends, I had always listened to stories in awe. I could not imagine what it had been like, but once in a while swinging my machete to cut through the thicket to find our next point on the map, I would try and conjure up some of those feelings I had felt while listening to veterans talking of their fear. I wasn't obsessed with the war in a romantic way, just intrigued on a deeper level that someone just like me would actually have been in a life or death situation, where my only real fear was a mosquito bite, or a scratched arm.

I knew the job – although interesting – was only a means to an end. Ernie had his degree in engineering and a more obvious career path. We had been friends since childhood but our paths were diverging. We had motorcycles in common since he had recently bought one, and I was helping him to learn to ride, but on many other levels, we were slowly drifting apart, politically, socially, and financially. I knew my friends were all going to find their paths, but I felt much of my search was not going to be in New York or its environs.

My boss at the engineering company was in his forties and he wanted me to remain in New York and train to stay on in the company. After spending a week together in upstate New York we got to understand each other on a deeper level and he knew I'd soon be gone. When I finally told him I was leaving after being there ten months, he just nodded and said, "Enjoy." He had ridden motorcycles, had done some long-distance touring, and must have seen in my eyes that that side of my life was far from over.

The previous year Gary and I had met people from all over America – people old and young doing things with their lives. The bartending job had opened my eyes wide – I served men old enough to be my father who were still using alcohol and the bar scene as their main source of life outside their jobs or homes. I knew that my days of drinking just for the sake of it were slowing down. I had already stopped smoking pot and the other more expensive drugs were taking too much fuel out of my motorcycle's gas tank so they were starting to slip away as well.

The small abstinences were letting me see and think more clearly. On the occasional Saturday not waking up under the dark cloud of hangover, I would be full of energy; I would rise early, get on my motorcycle, and keep the vision of another cross-continental trip alive and well, until it eventually took flight.

So here I was, on the road once more with California as my destination – for now I knew I wanted to head towards route 2 in Michigan. I would make sure the general direction was west, or in this case northwest. If needed, I would consult a map, but I was so excited to be on another long-distance open-ended journey I often didn't. I was into the smaller roads and had no one to agree or disagree with about direction or where we would stay. Now I was on the other side of the border – Canada – and had piloted the bike to a dead end. I didn't know how I was going to go around the very large expanse of water I found myself looking at – The Georgian Bay. Time for the map. I noticed a small thin dotted line tracking its way across the light blue on the map and after hunger led me to a small diner, the helpful waitress told me about the ferry. I found out the crossing times, eager to get to that small thin peninsula in Michigan which had looked so intriguing back when this trip had turned from a vague idea into a real plan.

On the ferry I met two people who would be significant in my life for various reasons. The first guy must have been about forty-five or so and had just been through a divorce. A couple of his friends were going through similar situations. We had a nice long chat – he said he was one of the lucky ones because there were no kids involved. He told me of friends who had been through bitter custody battles, forced to pay extortionate lawyer fees on top of all the other bills of divorce, child allowance, alimony etc. His divorce was still raw and he was wary of what lay ahead, but he had a lot of time for this young guy just starting out on his own path of discovery. He seemed not to be bitter, but willing to impart some of the wisdom he had gathered as he trundled along his path of life. He talked mildly of a lot of the mistakes he had made, and why they were not bad, but something to learn from. He had come out the other side of his encounter with some money in his pocket as he had sold everything he had from his car to his couch. He had kept his camping gear, toiletries, and bought his dream motorcycle, a BMW R100. Now he was finding himself on the small roads of northern Ontario and had some good tales to tell of his last few months on the road. I enjoyed telling him about my university

14

days, my father's death and how it changed my view of life, my first cross-continental ride and whatever else I had to offer. He appeared to be genuinely interested and told me to take as much time as I needed in my search for meaning, myself and whatever else I was looking for. I always remember something he said to me, "As soon as you think you are there, is when you have to look deeper and realize how much further you have to go." I didn't quite understand it then, but pondered its implications time and time again. I now feel that the essence of those words were that the human condition is in a constant state of searching, and the gray areas of existence are more complicated and ever-present than you think.

Unfortunately we were going different ways when the ferry docked so our time together sipping a coffee on the Chi-Cheemaun heading northwest was all we would have together to tell our tales. Our conversation made me realize how important it is when we talk to people, and how powerful our words and ideas can be. It also helped me value every day we walk the earth as our physical journeys on this planet are very short. No matter how brief, I was glad for our time together.

The other person I met on the ferry was Frank Westerlaken. He introduced himself with a strong handshake saying his full name almost formally. Paul and I had said our goodbyes already when Frank and I met on the other side of the boat. We were heading in the same direction, me to Saulte Ste. Marie Michigan, and him to his grandparents' on the Canadian side of the same town. He asked if I would be interested in coming over for dinner. "Sure," was my short answer – not many home-cooked meals come your way traveling alone crossing the continent. As we disembarked, Paul gave a toot and a wave as he leaned off to the right, north-bound. Frank and I did the same as we banked left heading south.

It was only a forty minute ride to Frank's grandparents' house where I was welcomed graciously and seemed almost to be expected. It was about five p.m. or so and dinner was cooking on the stove, so we sat down for a chat and had a nice hot cuppa. Frank's grandmother was telling us about how just about a week earlier Frank's brother, John and his friend had stopped by on their way across Canada by motorcycles. John was on a Kawasaki GPS and his friend was on a BSA. Now that was an interesting combination of bikes. An old British classic bike from the sixties coupled with a Japanese café racer. We spoke about my cross-country trip the previous year, and I was sure they would have a great time. She talked about their approximate route, and where they were hoping to wind up. Her tone and the glint in her eyes made it obvious she was reliving her motorcycling days when she and her husband had ridden around the U.S. and Canada. We had a scrumptious roast dinner but as the days were long I was keen to roll out some miles. Shortly after dinner I continued on

15

towards the border of Michigan and let Frank catch up with his grandparents. He was only there for a short visit before returning to the small satellite town of Brampton, near Toronto, where he worked. I smiled when he told me he was a policeman – his formal introduction and strong handshake made more sense.

I would have made it nice and dry to my campsite on the American side of the border, but for some reason the border guard decided I was trafficking drugs or something else illicit. He asked me to unpack my whole tank bag, then my saddle bags. My beautiful sunset was quickly clouding over into a blackness that smelt like rain. Re-packing everything was a pain, especially because after he was satisfied I had no illegal substances, he left me on my own, uncovered, as it started to rain. He went back into his small heated box, and I and all my gear were unnecessarily getting wet. The whole border check took a little under an hour. After packing I was left feeling angry and resentful about the whole thing. I headed on to my campsite which was about fifteen minutes away and, as I pitched my tent, I contented myself with the fact that I was on my way across America on my motorcycle with unknown adventures spread out before me. Okay, I was wetter than I should have been, but in ten hours or so Mr. Borderguard would be in his box looking for the elusive drug trafficker or smuggler of Canadian Jewels while I would be once again heading west with the sunrise reflecting in my rearview mirrors, my feet kicked up on my highway pegs, dipping and leaning into the twists and turns that highway 2 would offer up to me and my bike.

The morning had shaken off any rain that had come throughout the night and the sky was a brilliant orange. I imagined the sun rising over the New York City Skyline. What a different world I was in right now and a whole different headspace; a few weeks ago I would have been walking to work on Broadway, now I was holding open my throttle with a wide grin just knowing that nearly all of this beautiful continent was still laid out ahead of me. I yelled a quick good morning to Mr. Borderguard, knowing he was probably just waking up somewhere putting on his uniform safely out of earshot.

The Upper Peninsula of Michigan is undulating, forested and known for its mosquitoes. Many lakes dot the countryside, and although still a part of the States, it feels more a country on its own or part of America's northern neighbor. The roads are quiet and sometimes I wouldn't encounter a car for hours at a time The people I met were more the shotgun on the gun-rack type, but I never felt threatened in any way, just about a million miles from New York City!

One day it was just about noon when off in the distance I saw what I thought to be a motorcycle. I cracked the throttle to catch up with it. When

I finally did, it was two locals out for a ride and they were slowing down to pull into a diner. When they saw my bike all loaded down, they motioned me to join them. I wasn't ready to stop for lunch, but as I'd tried so hard to catch them up, and now they were inviting me in, I figured I might as well.

The diner was bustling with a full lunch crowd getting ready to eat. When it came out that I was from New York City – The Bronx even – the local motorcycle boys were quite interested and I must say they asked some bizarre questions. I put it down to living in a very secluded part of the world in very rural surroundings, not pure racism, although I must say when they asked me how it was living with "all the niggers" in New York City, and were they as bad as the "fucking Indians" out here. It made me feel uneasy, but all questions were asked in a normal tone sitting at the counter of a crowded diner, and no one seemed to think that any of the words being used were out of place. I briefly thought of the bull rider in Tensleep not even a year ago. I know the same conversation could not have happened as openly in a New York City diner without quite a few eyebrows being raised or even worse. I tried my best to answer their questions without offending them, but I also tried to be true to myself and not feed into their pre-conceived ideas. Hopefully I confused their world a bit, and maybe opened a small chink in their thinking.

After a big lunch and a little insight to the local mindset, I left feeling that our world needed to get together and realize that people are people, and although varied cultures, foods, music, religions, philosophies may appear to differentiate us, it doesn't mean they should define us. We are all first and foremost human beings. We have more in common with our fellow humans than we are willing to admit, and whenever I need to bring myself back to reality, I remember a phrase that in its simple gruffness is so true: "In a hundred years we'll all be dead," a sobering thought. When you really think about it, we are sharing the here and now with people who are shaping our current world. We all have power in our thoughts, words and actions, and if we all decided to get together and realize that no past or future or prejudice has any control over us, we could all change the living moment in a second. Although we all have these strange definitions about who we are, our nationalities, our beliefs, at the end of the day, no matter what we believe, the physical forms we now inhabit will all return to dust. We're not separate; we are all on this earthship together – a speck of dust clinging on to the life-giving heat and light of a nondescript medium-sized star swirling out in the vastness of unthinkable space. All of these thoughts went reeling through my head as I rolled out across highway 2 on a small peninsula on the gigantic continent of America.

My second ride to California was shaping up nicely. I had already met some interesting people, and the time on the bike gave me space and time to allow my head to swirl with all these new philosophical thoughts. I did not have a fancy bike with music, my camping gear was bought in a department store called Caldors, and I'd never heard of hi-tech clothing, just my leather jacket bought on Orchard Street for seventy-five dollars, and a few pairs of Levis 501 jeans. I didn't even have a small windshield. It was me, the wind in my face, and the open road.

My conversation with Paul was still fresh in my head. I could still see his huge smile as he told me of how he had been up in northern Ontario for a few weeks camping and his love for motorcycle touring was infectious. Not that I needed to be infected with that love of touring, but it was nice to meet people who shared your interests, or should I say passions.

My trip across the northern Border States was taking on its own special shape. I'd had nice weather so far. The wettest I got was that day at the border. I was even able to find a soft spot for Mr. Borderguard, especially now that I'd had some time to rethink, and enjoy the simple pleasures of being on the road. I was enjoying the freedom to go left or right when I wanted, to stop anywhere I pleased, to camp or stay in a small hotel. I enjoyed sitting on the side of the road sometimes and just staring at the birds or the butterflies. I would write in my journal or read a book. I think back and realize how few people in our western world of absolute craziness ever get time like that. My time was even more special because it was real, true open-ended travel. I did not have a job waiting for me back home, or a job to go to. My choice to go across America by motorcycle at age twenty-two for the second time was something that was possible because I had a family. I knew in the back of my mind I could always go back to New York. My mom's house was also my house. The ability to do that is almost unheard of for many people in our society, let alone the world. I somehow just wanted to absorb anything I could with my travel. I wasn't afraid to be afraid; I wasn't scared to put myself out there. That was all made possible though because I had friends and family that gave me that strength.

All of these thoughts were not conscious at the time back in 1984. I was on a search. I wanted to experience humanity. The humanity in that diner was not evil; it had just never been exposed to anything else. I was forming my own philosophies, as I was reading others. All my chance meetings were little doors into new spaces. I loved walking through those doors and exploring all that wide open space.

My motorcycle headed west, my throttle cracked open and the cool mountain air was sweeping down the plains to meet me straight in the face at seventy miles per hour. Mountains are always places to feel majesty and insignificance at the same time.

Glacier National Park is inspirational! The Rockies are full of places that make your jaw drop. At the same time, on a motorcycle you are in awe, but also in control of a powerful machine. With the flex of your wrist you power into turns, scrape your pegs as you dip and dive on the mountain roads. The higher you get, the thinner the air, and the colder it gets. The roads become more challenging; winding and looping back on themselves and your adrenaline begins to flow, heightening all of your senses as you become alert to everything around you. You pass that campervan on a blind curve that is crawling up the mountain roads – it is a risk, but your ears are tuned in, your eyes peering around every corner somehow through the wooded roads – you make choices. It's incredible. You're alive; everything you own is on your bike, everyone you know is thousands of miles away; you, your machine, and your mind are melting into the surrounding beauty. You tingle; miles slip by without you realizing that you're going too fast. You're passing through the mountains too quickly, the experience just takes you along and you are lost in a different world, your thoughts are all focused on the now, and when you eventually do stop, you realize what life is like just being absolutely lived in that supreme wonderful moment. In that same moment you realize how insignificant you are, we are, and even those mountains are. If our planet is a small speck floating in space, these mountains – even though awesome in their magnificence – are an even tinier speck. But at the moment they overwhelm, they encompass my every thought; they make me wonder at the endless beauty of our planet, our universe, and ourselves.

Reality snaps back in. I get a tad nervous when my mind is lost in these thoughts while my body is somehow controlling a motorbike on difficult mountain roads without my conscious effort. Somehow, the human brain manages to do both. The riding becomes second nature and the mountains put me in a different world. My second long-distance trip on a motorcycle is starting to change me. I'm seeing things differently and becoming more awake as a person. My twenty-two years as son, friend, student, New Yorker, American etc. are all starting to challenge me. What am I? What are these definitions? Are they significant? Do they change with every move I make? As I withdraw from these definitions simply by not being active in them, I start to identify less and less with them and reduce – or should it be increase? – myself back to simply being human and recognize my link with all of humanity. I'm really using my motorcycle as the machine to take me on an adventure in other directions.

The many glaciers of the national park makes you sit and wonder at our planet's constant changing. These rivers of ice recede and sometimes advance. You would think it impossible for such masses of frozen water, miles long, to actually be moving, but constantly moving they are, after all, wasn't the Hudson valley formed much in the same way? I've heard it said that the human body is made up of seventy-five percent water, is it just a coincidence that so is our earth? Are we indeed the truest microcosm of the macrocosm? We are also in a constant change, the only constant in life is change, we cannot stagnate even if we wanted to, the planet we are hitching a ride on for our short physical journey shares our cells, and we its. As I passed through all the inspiring scenery it awakened in me a feeling of kinship, to respect nature is to respect ourselves.

My time in the mountains was intense; the riding keeping my senses in tune, my mind and thoughts being challenged every minute, philosophies coming to the fore from a deeper place I had no control over. The campsites nestled in the folds of the landscape, gorgeous mountain scenery, starry nights, wildlife, and the winding roads, of course, spectacular. When I left the Rockies I felt changed once again, just like the previous year. I laugh at myself humming the tune to John Denver's, *Rocky Mountain High.* I feel almost corny to myself, but I'm beginning to understand the words that much better.

I'm trying to slow it down a bit, but once again am approaching the west coast quite quickly. One more mountain range separates me from the Pacific Ocean. Although looking at the map, the crashing waves of the coast are still a thousand miles off, I was happy about that.

Which way to go? There are many choices. Drop in a southerly direction? Continue due west? I'm not sure. I let the road decide, the weather, gut feelings.

Last year Gary and I entered California from the west. Maybe I'd like to enter from the north this time. I heard the Oregon coast is beautiful. Not being absolutely sure where I was heading added to the excitement. I had no idea where my journey was taking me. I feel though, I'm just scratching the surface. The one thing I'm fairly certain of is that I'll stop in the Bay Area; it's becoming a ritual to visit my relatives who live there. I had never been on a commercial airplane at that point in my life, and it was to be my second trip to California from New York, although I wasn't there yet. At a small junction in the road I made the decision to head due west, to the coast of Oregon before heading in a southerly direction towards California.

The weather had been dry, but man was it hot! I was in the high desert of eastern Oregon. I knew that once I crossed over the mountains I would then again be in rainforest type area, then over to the coast. I would usually start to look for a place to camp around sundown.

I enjoy riding at dusk, but it makes setting up camp feel rushed. I found a small road leading into a forested area – it looked like a logging road, so I decided I would camp the night there. I set up in a clearing of trees. The sun set in a spectacular fashion as I pitched camp, gathered wood for a fire and made my pit for cooking. I walked up to  higher ground where I could watch the vibrant pink and red sky dulling itself into a less vivid, but no less beautiful, indigo and blue filtering through the thin branches of the pine and spruce woodland. I knew the next day I would be riding towards the place where the sun was now setting, and that the Pacific Ocean was somewhere beyond that, but still out of sight.

Camping rough was always a delight, and I was glad to have not polluted my brain with many horror movies. I'd seen a few, but my mind did not normally race with the paranoia created by the over zealous movie industry. I knew that the small noises I heard in the night were just the animals I was sharing the woods with. I stayed up to watch the stars and contemplate everything I had experienced so far on my journeys. I decided that no matter what happened to me, I had at least taken lots of time to explore, and was looking forward to many more adventures ahead, and probably in a day or two I would be crossing the final range which would once again bring me within smelling distance of the Pacific Ocean!

Sometimes I would take out the tapes Johnny C gave me, put on my headphones and listen to the familiar music while writing in my journal or just gazing up at the night skies. I enjoyed having the tunes once in a while and it would transport me to a good party, one of the bars on The Avenue with my friends and even the times when Gary and I listened to the same music on our trip the year before; a small connection to a different world from where I now was.

The hot dry roads of the eastern part of Oregon gave way to a small steady climb up through the Coastal Ranges. The arid landscape of the high desert flashing past me in various shades of yellow and brown made for a beautiful ascent, but once over the final pass I was shocked by the way the scenery changed instantly and dramatically. The speeds I was traveling at probably accentuated this perceived change. It was suddenly green, lush and almost cool. The rainforest-like scenery was mind-blowing; majestic, with magnificent trees and an unimaginable variety of shades of green.

There was a buzzing in my head but it wasn't coming from the speed of the bike or the adrenaline coursing through my veins. It was a nearly imperceptible light tingle and my whole being felt as if there had been a shift. The seed which took root in the Rockies last year was starting to sprout. I felt I slipped into a groove, and my life was starting to spin its own unique web. The feeling remained with me until I fell asleep in my tent that night.

The next morning I awoke early, the familiar rustle of my sleeping bag comforting me as I remembered the tingle from the day before, the majestic beauty all around, accompanied by the something happening inside all felt good. I savored my small breakfast in the jungle-like setting of the forest, smiling at the endless possibilities which lay ahead.

The miles rolled by, and the Pacific was getting close. The first glimpse is always special, especially when coming across overland. You have crossed a continent, behind you is the Atlantic, with all that land mass in between; now you must get used to the sun setting over the water, not rising from it.

I pulled into a small town and a Dairy Queen came into view. Mmmm, a nice cold ice cream would be great. So I stopped in and watched as they mixed all the ice cream and chocolate chips and whatever else went into the icy cold *Blizzard.* I sat alone on the table savoring it – I did not treat myself often to these delights, it would be too tempting to have them all the time, and I would be fifty pounds heavier at the end of my journey. As I was about to walk out a young mother with two children stopped me and asked if that was my motorcycle out front. I told her that it was and we fell into a deep conversation. I felt that it was Paul and me again. It was wonderful that in such a short time since our chance meeting on the ferry across The Georgian Bay I felt so much had happened to me. On my first trip across the continent, I'd read my first Carlos Castaneda book, *The Teachings of Don Juan,* along with *On the Road* by Jack Kerouac, which were both given to me as going away presents. On this trip two Richard Bach books; *One,* and my favorite, *Illusions*, found their way into my saddle bags as well. Pirsig's classic – *Zen and the Art of Motorcycle Maintenance* – had made it across again, and I was still trying to grapple with its meaning.

Lots of deep thoughts and nights alone to contemplate had left me feeling I had more insight as to where I was heading. This young woman on her own search and I sat for nearly an hour talking. She was married, and sounded happy in her marriage, but confused about life. I think the two young children at the table with her probably brought wisdom beyond her age to her as well. She not only was a young woman, but a mother and a partner, it's a lot to be when you were barely just twenty. As we spoke, I noticed an older couple at the table next to us looking up and listening; they just smiled at us and nodded. Our conversation ended on a nice note, and we said a warm goodbye to each other. I wonder if she ever thinks of that conversation like I think of mine and Paul's.

I kicked my waiting motorcycle to life. The more I rode the bike, the more I wanted to ride it, but felt I wouldn't mind some company. On this trip I had not hooked up with anyone going the whole way across, I would run into the odd motorcyclist here and there, mostly locals. The most riding I had done with anyone was with Frank Westerlaken. That was a long time and lots of miles ago. There was a long stretch to San Francisco.

I was still enjoying myself, just feeling I wouldn't mind putting up a tent with someone else and share the road with another bike.

I pulled out of town and passed a gas station, about a mile later something said to me, "Go get some gas." My bike didn't have a big tank, and I couldn't remember when I last put gas in, so it wouldn't hurt to top up. I dipped into a u-turn and went back to the station. I filled up, paid, threw my leg over the bike, kick-started it, and was just about to pull out when I heard what I took to be a motorcycle engine, no, actually two.

I waited for them to appear, and from the sound of the engines they sounded like fast bikes, maybe just some locals out for a ride. As the sound drew nearer, it was obvious by the downshifting and groans of their slowing engines they were pulling in for gas. They pulled into the station and I was interested to see two loaded bikes. I thought ah, some travelers. One bike was a Kawasaki GPS and the other was a BSA. Could it be a huge coincidence? I remember Frank's grandmother saying they were heading to British Colombia. This was Oregon, not too far to make it impossible. I nodded at them, and they both smiled at me. I casually walked around to the back of their bikes to see their license-plates. Ontario! No way, I was thinking, it couldn't be. So I waited until they filled up went over to the guy on the Kawasaki and said "John?" he looked at me quizzically. Remembering Frank's firm handshake and formal introduction I then said, "John Westerlaken?"

He looked really confused now and checked his jacket as if looking for a clue to how I had known his name, "Do I know you?" he asked.

"Well actually no" I said, "but I had dinner with your grandparents and brother a few weeks ago!"

"What? Where?" was his startled reply.

I explained the whole story and we all stared at each other in amazement. "Where you headed?" I asked them.

"California somewhere," was their answer.

Nothing else was needed to be said. They paid, nodded at me and I at them. We all smiled. "Let's go" was what we all said with our bodies. So off we headed. I was laughing out loud to myself as we rode off. No amount of planning could have gone any smoother, nearly 3,000 miles from his grandparent's house! I now had some riding partners to head into California with, and hopefully they were glad to have a new friend to chat with at night by the campfire.

The new dynamic was welcome; it was nice to be sharing the road with a couple of other guys who enjoyed riding as much as me. You could tell that they had been riding together for a while; the way their bikes appeared to communicate, the fun they had chasing each other. It took me a while to fall into their style of riding, but we all liked similar speeds, and even

23

though their bikes were more racy, and mine more a street bike, the luggage we all had evened things out a bit.

We camped out together in a State Park and the next day we would see the Pacific Ocean, me for the first time this trip. What a beautiful sight it was, made even more so by the weeks of anticipation and the perfect weather we were having. The clearest of blues with the sun glinting off it made the thought of a swim irresistible so we headed down to the beach and enjoyed the majesty of the earth's largest ocean.

Something about California evokes certain emotions. Probably blame it on pop music, or the sixties generation, but it still carries a mystique with its name. When we reached the border we took the obligatory photos – all excited to have made it. That night we celebrated with a large campfire-cooked meal under the stars, and a few icy-cold beers.

The next day found us entering another legendary area – Highway 1, one of California's most beautiful and scenic highways! It hugged the coast and at some spots was downright scary! The switchbacks getting to the coast were a bit hairy, and the sheer drops to the sea were absolutely breathtaking.

We camped out and swapped stories and sometimes just had a real good laugh at the sheer impossibility of our meeting up. The next day was more gorgeous coast-hugging riding. The cooking at night was something we all liked to do while camping. We camped out near Point Arena, which was billed as the closest place on the continental forty-eight states to Hawaii. It was a hippy enclave, but didn't have a good place to pitch a tent. We wound up in a KOA (Kampgrounds of America) campsite a few miles up the road, laughing at the folly of winding up in this family-orientated camping institution complete with swing sets, televisions and screaming kids. We bought a few beers, pitched at the furthest point we could from the commotion, and talked until we babbled from tiredness. We then collapsed into our tents for some well-needed sleep.

The next morning we made ourselves some strong coffee, then packed up our bikes and headed off on what would be, although we did not know it then, our last day of riding together.

Their money situation needed sorting out and they had to find a bank. We headed to Santa Rosa but got separated, and hadn't made a contingency plan. We didn't know exactly where the bank was. I was just following them, but a traffic light started the problem, and we lost sight of each other. I looked around for their bikes, but there was a lot of traffic, and I had no reason to be there. I didn't worry too much; they had each other and we'd had a few days of excellent company, riding, and camping together. I thought it was quite cool to lose each other as easily as we found each other. We had met and shared some special moments of camping and exploration together, and then just like that, we were all on our separate paths again. The natural chain of events just happened and our unlikely encounter ended in much the same way it began.

When I got to the Oakland/Berkeley area for the second time by motorcycle, it seemed more like my cousins were expecting me than surprised at my unannounced arrival. I enjoyed getting to know my west coast family better; Mary, Angelo and their sons – Joe and Bobby – who were married with kids of their own. Their families became my west coast comfort zone; it would feel like a small homecoming. Judy and Yolanda – my cousins' wives – always threw their doors wide open to their itinerant cousin from New York. Their young children slowly growing accustomed to my face and strange accent. Arriving there now was becoming a ritual of sorts, and remained so for the next couple of years.

My life was changing in New York, but I was making other connections – my life on the road was showing me other sides to everything, even my family. My west coast cousins were so relaxing to be with, and their lifestyle, although similar in an Italian American way, was very different to their New York counterparts. My Uncle Angelo had married Mary, a woman with Mexican American blood as had Bobby, so that introduced a whole different culture into the family.

San Francisco, *The City on the Bay*, is a wonderful city – its wide boulevards, sweeping vistas, and rugged physical beauty – is so different to New York with its narrow streets, and towering skyline looming over you at every street corner. It was nice to get to know New York's distant cousin on the west coast. I like to say that San Francisco is probably America's finest city, while New York is America's best city. I'll excuse myself if I'm prejudiced, and do not mean to hurt anyone's feelings. My second trip across the continent had been a success, and what lay ahead was more of the great unknown.

# P.S. 106 – Teacher becomes Student

Now my appetite was whetted. I felt like a veteran. I'd had a cold and beautiful ride coming back home for the second time. If things had worked out in the west that would have been great, but as it happened I was walking the streets of New York once again. That was fine too. I wanted a change. What I was looking for was a mental space where I fit in. My friends were settling into lives that I did not want to fit into and I needed to find my own space. The second trip across America was starting to give me an idea of where I wanted to be. The term I like to use is 'in the groove'. That chance meeting with John and Louis in Oregon had felt right, as had that talk with Paul. I didn't want to talk about mortgages or the future. I didn't want alcohol or anything that numbed my mind to rule my life. I wanted to be part of the now. I craved experience. I loved to shatter pre-conceived ideas about people and places. I was realizing I could love New York and not have to live in it all the time. I could dip in, do work that I thought was challenging and go off for more adventures. I wanted to be on the road!

After a few weeks back and meeting up with my old friend John, I confused my want of travel and adventure with his future plans and nearly ended up on his path instead of mine. I was in New York, nearly flat broke, still looking for a way to continue to travel when in walked John who I had been to elementary and high school with and we had remained good friends ever since. John was always a straight A student whereas I was usually not one for the books and had to work that much harder to keep up my grades. John was going to the city to take the officer's test for the navy. I wasn't working yet, and thought I would join him. Somehow we both got the test handed to us. I explained I was not there for the test, but the recruiter asked me a few questions, and said I should give it a go.

John aced the test, and I just missed officer candidacy by ten points. I was assured that if I decided to brush up on the math, I could re-take the test, even if I went in as an enlisted man first. I thought I was a good salesman, but he was very good – I left there with an appointment to see my local recruiter.

John and I went out to lunch, and talked about the navy. He seemed happy in his decision; mine was not so much a decision, but something to fulfill my need for adventure.

The recruiter I met with saw I was ripe for the picking, and before I knew it, I was heading to Brooklyn for my physical and to find out what the navy had to offer.

My good friend Stan was trying to talk me out of it; he and I had worked together the previous year and we had gotten to know each other much better. My mom said I wasn't cut out for the navy because of my questioning personality, and thought I would find it hard to put up with all the structure and hierarchy of the armed forces. My recruiter saw that I was looking for something and adventure was what he sold me. I would be traveling the world; I would be making a difference. I bought the whole sales pitch – nearly.

In Brooklyn I had taken the written tests and physicals, passing all with no problems. My tattoos were a focal point of some ridicule for the naval or army officers asking us to pee in jars step on scales fill out forms and whatever else we had to do that day. It was kind of weird and I was lost in a reverie. I discovered after a few hours that I would be getting on a plane to the Great Lakes in January. I would be in boot camp there, and then I would get my training as a medic – the navy was offering me a future as well as adventure. Something though, was not feeling correct. I had always questioned things and my cross-country trips had opened a new world to me. John and I were on different paths – what the heck was I doing? Was I blindly following John into a future in the navy?

Stan's voice rang in my head, "What're you fuckin' crazy? You in the navy!" Then he would burst out laughing.

Sure I thought I was partying too much, and wanted to curb my alcoholic intake. Then I thought of Ritchie, another friend who had joined the navy after high school. He'd had a slight problem with drugs then. The navy cured his slight problem that was for sure – he was a full-blown drug user after four years in. My mom said to me, "Are you sure Joseph? Four years is a long time. Remember how you and your dad always butted heads?" I did remember that. I'd never been great at following orders that didn't always make sense to me and I had always driven my dad crazy by my constant questioning of everything. That was four years ago though. John and I were good buddies and he was joining.

I was walking down the hallway with the papers in my hands, behind a few other guys from the neighborhood whom I'd never met before, and with whom I didn't have much in common. Our footsteps echoed on the shiny tiled floor like another part of my own brain trying to get through to me. I started to hear the voices of Stan, my mom, my brother and other friends questioning this as a good move. I thought of John and realized that maybe we were on different paths after all. We probably wouldn't even have that much to do with each other after joining up as he was joining as an officer and I was starting from the very bottom. I was starting to seriously doubt what I was doing walking down the halls of some dreary military institution in Brooklyn. I was last on line – all the other guys signed the dotted line, and were heading down to swear in. The navy didn't waste any time. I got to the counter with my recruiter to my left, and an officer in front of me handing me a pen. I looked at these two and thought of my cross-country trips, my college days, and all my experiences in life. These men were not the type of people I would ever choose to hang out with. Now I was about to sign up to four years of their company.

I looked up at the officer, "Have I joined the navy yet?"

"Just sign here son, go downstairs, swear in," was his curt reply.

Something about the "Son", reminded me of a certain State Trooper, "Yes, I know that, but as of this moment, am I in the navy? Have I made any commitment to join the navy?" I repeated.

A look came over his face, and it wasn't pretty, "No son, you haven't. You just need to sign these papers, go downstairs, and swear in."

I looked at both of them and repeated myself once more, "So I haven't joined the navy."

A cold stare was his answer.

I then slid the sheets of paper back across the table, put down the pen, and said, "I'm going to think about it."

The officer behind the desk had gone a certain shade of purple and was looking quite agitated, "Son, the navy has given you a physical, you have a seat on a plane, and you are headed for medic candidacy school."

I now was feeling relieved and even a bit cocky that me and these two didn't have a future together, "Thanks for the physical, but I'm going to think about it first."

Now my recruiter chimed in, "If you aren't signing up, I'd normally give you a token and let you catch the train home."

He'd given me a ride down to Brooklyn and was due to be dropping me back after we'd all done the tests and signed the forms. There was no way he was going to change my mind back to joining up for four years in the navy by threatening me to find my own way home and I think he knew it. I just looked at him. "I'm still gonna think about it, I'll wait here for the others."

The officer nodded at him to get the others going, and I sat in a waiting area. While I waited for the other three to swear in for the next four years in the military, I wanted to scream for joy. I could not believe I'd come so close to joining the navy.

I was called in to three different officers' cubicles in that time to tell me what the navy was offering me, and how civilian life didn't offer me half those options. Every small encounter just made me surer than ever of the choice I just made. I couldn't wait to get home, have a beer with Stan, and tell my mom who was probably praying at the moment.

The car journey back was silent and the atmosphere was not particularly friendly. It was a long drive from Brooklyn, and I had never felt so lucky in my life.

My mom was overjoyed, and Stan and I got very drunk – we made a date to have a party on January 24$^{th}$ as well – the date of my plane to boot camp.

Now an alternate plan was starting to formulate in my head. Get a job. I found work with a florist as a means to an end. I had worked there before, as had Johnny C. We stayed friendly after college; his tapes a constant companion on my previous two trips across America. He loved music and had a nice voice. Although he was at a loose end after college, he always pursued his passion of singing in accappella groups. I liked the fact he always stuck with it, and even had a hit tune played on local radio stations at Christmas time, a real celebrity! In the florist, he made the arrangements, I delivered them – it was a means to an end for both of us.

I became quite friendly with the people in the funeral parlors to whom I would deliver flowers quite often. On a delivery one day I happened to walk into the wrong door. The mortician was at work with a cadaver. I excused myself, and back-stepped quickly but he called out to me, "Joe, come back, close the door behind you."

I did, and there was the body of a man in his sixties or so laid out in front of us.

"Have you ever seen this before?" he asked.

"No actually. Is it alright that I'm in here?"

"Not really, just talk quietly."

Then he pulled back the sheet, and there was the body. For some reason it had been emptied of all its internal organs. He then snipped a suture that was holding his skull cap together, pulled the skin off the skull, and removed part of his cranium. I was feeling apprehensive thinking I was going to see the gray matter, but to my surprise, there was a pair of pajamas shoved in. He saw my surprise, smiled and said, "He must have been a real sleepy head."

"What was that?" I asked in amazement.

He put his finger to his lips, then went on to explain that the body had been totally cleaned out at the hospital, and his job now was to get it ready for that night's viewing. He described how with make up and other aids he would make the corpse look like he was just sleeping.

I left the room with a bouquet of flowers presumably meant for the man I just saw. I walked past the small office where a man in a black suit was talking to two women. They looked like a mother and daughter tearful in grief. I put the bouquet down as they walked out of the office, and we nearly walked into each other, I apologized, and then realized they were

29

crying for the body I had been examining just a few minutes before. It was another kind of spiritual awakening for me. My dad had been on a table just like that a few years back. My mom's calm had been surprising to me – of course she'd cried, but she knew my dad was at peace. I thought how wonderful it is to believe in something other than life being so linear, and death being so final. I was glad to have been raised with some faith in the unknown. Even though I'd left the church's teachings, it had opened my mind for the possibilities that death was not a definitive ending; it was possibly a new beginning. Those women were not crying for that cadaver, they were missing his essence, his words, his being dad or husband. Of course they would miss his touch, that is our human side, the physical is much of what our earthly existence is about, but in that small room, and with the few experiences I had so far in my life, I was finding deeper meaning in everything, even a brief moment in a mortician's office.

My path was taking me somehow to a deeper me, and I was glad I hadn't walked the path of the navy. I'm sure it's a great thing for many people, and I hoped John would get what he wanted out of his time there, but for me, I wanted to share the few things I had learned with a wider audience. So I found myself applying for work in a field I'd never thought I had a calling to.

While working in the florist, Johnny C and I took a test to see if we could be schoolteachers for the N.Y.C. Board of Education. The process was not long or too involved. New York City was in dire need and at that point the fact we had a heartbeat and a college education meant we were more than qualified for the job; a little scary to think that I was going to be forming young minds. How many people selected were suited to be classroom teachers? Was I? I would soon find out.

In January 1985, I started subbing in different schools around The Bronx, which means being called in the morning to go into a school that needs a teacher for the day. The phone calls kept coming from the navy every Friday at dinnertime. I finally told them I was a schoolteacher now and to please leave me alone. They finally believed me and my name must have been crossed out because the phone stopped ringing on Fridays.

After a month or so of subbing, I found myself in P.S.106 in a fifth grade permanent position at a school in The Bronx. The P.S. stands for Public School, all the New York City schools are identified by numbers which make them sound more like prisons than schools. It was the area I did all of my work anyhow but it was going to be a challenge. I had the lives of thirty-three nine and ten-year-olds in my hands from February to June but I didn't know where to begin, or how to go about it. I was thrown in cold.

I turned to the Assistant Principal, but received no help from him. As a sub it's easy; you go in for the day, stick to the lesson plan if you want and, as long as you keep the kids under control, it doesn't matter too much. Now things had changed, and changed a lot. There were lesson plans to write, tests to grade, and homework to check. I was in deep. "I can do this," I told myself. So I went about doing it.

I wasn't what you would call a 'by the books' teacher. That was okay. I wasn't receiving any help, and as far as the school administration was concerned, they had a teacher for a classroom of kids. A sad situation, but we all were in for an adventure! An adventure it was. I slowly found out all the reasons these kids had no teacher from mid-term. Their teacher had broken her wrist, and was out for a few weeks. She had been teaching a long time and was due to retire. She did not want to return to this class because it was one of the worst behaved classes of her career. She had connections in the union, and was able to take an early retirement by stretching out her medical problem. So now in walks twenty-three-year-old, bright-eyed, bushy-tailed Joe, fresh into the world, a couple of cross America trips burning in his blood, and ready to change the world of these poor inner city kids.

I had been to Catholic schools all the way through high school. Discipline, uniforms, respect, and sadly, fear, kept things pretty much in line. You didn't mess with the nuns in grade school, and definitely not the brothers in high school. A month ago was my first step into a public elementary school and the scene was quite different. I thought since these kids would be my full-time students till the end of term, I needed a way to show my authority. When I was growing up, each day before class was out, the nuns would clap their hands and each student had to sit silently and fold their hands together on the desk in front of them. When I first told my new students that this would be our method before lunchtime they looked at me as if I had three heads.

"Whaddya think this is Catholic school? We ain't doin' that."

"Uh oh," I thought, "I might have pushed this too far." I realized I couldn't show any sign of weakness though and knew I couldn't back down now.

"Yep, that's right," I continued confidently although inside I wasn't feeling quite so courageous. "No one leaves until everyone's hands are on the desk folded."

The kids gradually all began to fold their hands on their desks, some of them muttering resentfully. After a minute or two there was only one kid, Quincy, left with hands unfolded, staring at me defiantly. It was a battle of wills and once he realized that he didn't really have any option and some

31

of the other kids started grumbling at him that they were missing their free time, he slammed his hands down on the desk, folded.

"Okay. Let's go." I said immediately and they were out the door and running. Maybe it was a good start, maybe not. Time would tell.

You couldn't touch the children in any way shape or form. Staying after school had to be done with notice to the parents first, and even a simple exercise in discipline like writing the times tables fifty times was considered corporal punishment. I do believe I bent some of the rules.

The first week I called all the parents and introduced myself to them. I explained my position, and briefly how I got there. They sounded relieved their children had a teacher who cared. Second task at hand was to make the switch from substitute teacher to full-time teacher. That was difficult. I had to make the change. I was supposed to be their sub for a two-week period and following lesson plans and checking homework had been lax on my part. Now I had to switch mid-flight and become Mr. D. their fifth grade teacher. It took about a week to undo some of the things I had established in the first two weeks. Of course when I told them their teacher would not be coming back, they all of a sudden became very sentimental for her. The teacher they forced into early retirement became their favorite teacher, and they missed her sorely. I could never be Mrs. Hawker. That was true, I couldn't, but this is where we were, and we had to move on.

I had absolutely no poker chips to play with. They were so bad they'd had their spring trip withdrawn and that's a big thing when you're in fifth grade. I approached the person in charge of such things and told him I was planning a trip in the spring and asked what I needed to pull it off. "A miracle," he said and laughed, then told me what else I needed; at least four parental volunteers and the class had to get itself on the good side of the administration. I had my work cut out for me. At least now we had something to look forward to, something to pull together as a class to achieve. So we set about trying to accomplish the goal. I sent letters home with every child fishing for some volunteers. These kids came from broken homes; stepfathers, no fathers, working moms, absent moms, so the task was never going to be easy, but we scraped together a list of possibilities. Getting on the good side of the administration was fairly easy, and basically up to me. If I was giving good results, and telling good tales about my students, that was half the battle. The other half was keeping my kids out of major trouble. That was going to be a bit more of a challenge.

The first weeks went along quite well. I brought in photo albums of my cross-country trips, and every Wednesday afternoon was dedicated to a geography game we used to play with our parents on long car drives. It broadened these children's horizons, we had fun, and it even showed many of the kids places that they themselves were from. U.S. and world geography was not on the official teaching curriculum for fifth graders, but hey, we all liked it and by the third week, if I gave the kids any free time, many of them were poring over maps, atlases or my photo albums. They started to ask questions about the longest rivers in the world, and about place names like Yellowknife, Northern Territories in Canada. I knew it could not be all that bad. The last hour on Fridays was dedicated to an in-class talent show. I also got various friends; Larry, who was a city cop, Tommy, a firemen, and Ernie from RBA, to come in and speak to the students. It was going well. Not smoothly, but well.

My second week in the school I remember going into the teacher's lunch room for my lunch break. I sat down, the new face among the crowd. When the other teachers heard the class I had taken over, they started saying how bad this one was, or what a terror the other one was. After that I tried to limit my time in the teacher's lunchroom. I'm a firm believer in creating and working off a good energy and that the reverse is also true and I did not want to hear about all the awful traits of the kids. I started having lunch with the students, or alone. It was much more enjoyable, and kept me focused on the positive side of the teaching experience. It's true that I did have some tough kids in the classroom. One named Jason was labeled 'The Terror'. He was living up quite nicely to his given name. I tried turning the tide. I found out he played Little League baseball. One evening I took my motorcycle and showed up at his game. I didn't go over to his dugout; I just let him notice I was there. He turned and saw me at one point and I saw him almost blush before turning to one of his teammates saying, "Oh snap, that's my teacher." The next day I put Jason's team standings on the board. The class was interested, and didn't realize he played. That, I believe was a real turning point in Jason's attitude, maybe even the class.

There were many small stories, victories and losses in those five months. I learned valuable lessons as did the kids. We got to go on our school trip with another class and their teacher – nothing special or exciting, just down to Pelham Bay Park for a day of sports, running around, having fun and them just being kids.

I was able to work with two students who were probably going to be held back, and pushed them into trying harder to pass. Dexter and Davie thought it was cool to flunk the year and get put back. I already had kids in the class who had been put back two years which is the maximum amount permitted. Once a kid is in a class with other kids two years younger than themselves they tend to completely stop caring about succeeding in their studies and fail all the exams that come up. I didn't want that fate to befall either of these two kids who were pretty intelligent. I spent time talking to them explaining that the choices they made now could impact the rest of their lives. When I saw them scribbling and doodling over the multiple choice exams, I gave them a little extra time and encouraged them to fill in the answers correctly. I was starting to understand how much emotional work goes into teaching children. I enjoyed it, but when I got home, I was exhausted.

The class was also given a Ukranian girl, Nadia, who didn't speak a word of English. She was just casually dropped into the classroom one day. The kids were awful to her – so bad that one day I sent her out on a mission to the principal's office. I then had a long talk with the class. They were all immigrants, some Puerto Rican, Dominican, Jamaican, Korean, Haitian, etc. I tried to make them remember how it felt when they first came to America, could not speak properly, and did not know anyone. After that they eased up on her and one of my vivid memories is the day she put up her hand to come to the front of the class and fill in a part of speech that was missing from the sentence on the board. The whole class applauded and her face was shining with pleasure. The class grew together a little in a way that I couldn't explain. Yes, I definitely broke many of the rules and I probably wasn't the greatest teacher of many of the subjects I was expected to teach, but I was thrown in cold and had to make it up as I went along. I even promised one girl called Tania a motorcycle ride if she pulled all her marks up above 85%. I got her parents' consent first and she worked hard to succeed. On the last day of school I took her on the back of my motorcycle all the way up out of The Bronx into Westchester County. She had grown up in The Bronx and couldn't believe the big houses and backyards we were passing. It was like a different world to her and I like to think that it was one of the more exciting things to happen to her during that school year. Unfortunately getting off the bike her exposed calf touched the hot motorcycle exhaust pipe. Maybe that small burn mark reminds her of that day.

I think the most valuable lessons learned that year were that we can all 'do hard'. I did it, the kids did it, and all it took was some determination, and the want. There were many stumbling blocks, and a few students who made my life difficult the whole time, but that's life. The kids even got used to folding their hands before lunch. My Friday afternoon break-dancing sessions were popular with the kids – probably not the administration although I did become friendly with some of the teachers. I received some help here and there and once in a while someone would stop by to give a hand or ask if everything was okay. I even started eating in the teachers' lunch room more often and realized that I had been too quick to judge all the negativity. I understood it more, and learned to respect those who had taught for thirty or more years. I took on a job and a responsibility that year, and tried my best to do my best for those kids. It would be great to write of a fairy tale ending and of the kids that went on to become famous and successful in their fields. The truth is that I have no idea of what happened to any of those kids. I just tried to be fair and give them a break and the benefit of the doubt whenever I could.

After completing the school term, I knew that I wasn't ready to spend the rest of my life as a teacher just yet but felt ready for another extensive motorcycle ride. I'd been toying with the idea of riding to Alaska, but it scared the heck out of me. Just looking at the map would make me break out into a cold sweat. Although after taking on the responsibility of thirty-three lives, and doing pretty well, I now felt up to the challenge.

# Pushing the Limits

Pushing the limits was what it was all about. It was usually my own boundaries that I was stretching but this time I was talking about my motorcycle as well. It had crossed America four times by now. It was a street bike not actually made for long-distance touring. No windshield and a kicked back cruiser set-up, but it was all I had. I loved that bike, and it had been a trusted companion for all my other journeys. My original equipment was still holding up from that first trip, although its limits were also being stretched. The past five months thrown in cold to a classroom of thirty-three students and getting through it had shown me what you could accomplish. It had been a great experience, and I was learning more and more through all my travels that I could get through the tough times and come out the other side a stronger person. I was learning that everyone has the potential to rise to a challenge. I was being pushed onto a path, and the excitement in my gut was so mixed up with fear, uncertainty and every other emotion that I knew I was ready.

July 1st 1985 I set out. My first stop was at Ernie's parents' summer house in Connecticut. I spent two nights there, and we had a good time drinking beer, eating and reminiscing. I was still apprehensive and Ernie and his girlfriend Nancy could see I was a little nervous.

He asked, "Why are you doing this if you're that nervous?"

I said, "That's exactly why I'm doing it."

"What're you trying to prove?" Nancy prodded.

"Maybe, that it can be done, that I can do it, or maybe nothing, just a challenge."

"You've crossed America four times now, why so nervous this time around?" Ernie asked.

I pulled out my map and showed them the road ahead, 5,000 miles to the border of 'The Last Frontier', "That's why I'm nervous, but it feels good."

"Just hang out here for a few weeks, then head on home," he joked with me. I probably appeared to be drifting to Ernie. He was still working for RBA which was not a bad thing, he could see clearly where he was headed; Nancy would be his wife, and civil engineering his profession. I, on the other hand, was still on the road with no end in sight. My future even seemed foggy to me, but it always got clearer when I pulled away on my own and faced myself, and my fears. Sure it was almost a tempting idea – friends, beer and motorcycles, but no, I was being pulled.

What was I proving? I didn't feel I was trying to prove anything, just taking up a personal challenge and exploring more of the continent of my birth – I wanted to know North America before I traveled abroad. I felt that one day in the future I would be exploring foreign lands. More imminently though, Alaska beckoned; heading north was going to be tough, but I needed that push. My friends didn't understand and in a way, neither did I. It was time for me to go.

I broke the bonds of comfort and was glad I had no more goodbyes – they make it much more difficult. Explaining was nearly impossible – I was doing this because I was scared. I was doing this to push the limits of myself, my motorcycle, my cheap camping gear. What was my drive? Why did I have this yearning at a young age to always push my limits? Was it my dad's untimely death at fifty seven years old? My cousin getting killed at eight? I can guess and make assumptions, but mostly it was just because it felt right. Whenever I came back from a trip I felt stronger as a person. I saw my path clearer, and felt connected to the more spiritual direction that my life was taking. I felt in control of myself and knew I had to do it. If I didn't it would weaken me and every decision after that would weaken me more and more, until I would have given up – the tortured man at the AA meeting.

I had decided on Alaska because it looked like the furthest point I could ride to overland. If I wanted a challenge then this was definitely it. There was something about Alaska: the wilderness, the vastness, The Last Frontier, I wanted to meet people, see the great northern part of the continent, but most of all I wanted to see if I could make it. After setting off, I was the most anxious I'd ever been on any of my journeys thus far.

The nights were hard – I was faced with myself then. After leaving Ernie and Nancy I was even more confused; I cried in my tent, I could not even eat dinner. I went up through Vermont, camped out on the Fourth of July, and had to drag myself out of the tent to watch the fireworks. "Why are you doing this? What are you trying to prove?" Those questions would come back in the quiet evenings. I would ask myself and come up with blank answers. Confusion filled my nights. In contrast, the days on the motorcycle were great. It was the only known. I loved riding that bike. I knew it so well. Finding beautiful roads, scraping the pegs as I leaned into turns was what I knew, and why I chose to travel by motorcycle. After a few more days alone I started feeling more settled. It was like I had come through some sort of barrier; I had pulled out of my comfort zone and was forging my own way ahead. I stopped looking at the map and freaking out. I was open to the adventures the road would throw at me. I was in Canada now, and crossing the border was like the final decision made. As America receded in the distance behind me, so the voices of fear and uncertainty in my head faded until I was feeling really good.

On the tail end of my first week I was riding through the outskirts of Montreal when I spotted another guy on a motorcycle ahead of me. I pulled up next to him at a traffic light. I had an instantaneous good feeling. I asked him if he knew where there was some good camping. "Follow me," he motioned. I followed him right to an apartment building parking lot where he lived. Bob was his name. I introduced myself, and he asked where I was headed. When I told him Alaska I got the same reaction from him that I would get from most of the bikers I would meet along the way. I never realized when I had made the decision to ride to Alaska that it was a dream of so many long-distance motorcyclists. It was obviously the same for Bob now as a distant look passed across his face followed by the faraway words, "Alaska by motorcycle, it's always been a dream of mine." He snapped out of his split-second funk, smiled and said, "This is where I live, I have a great map upstairs, and maybe you'd like a cold drink."

We went upstairs and started talking. He was an American who had moved to Montreal a few years back, his wife was French-Canadian and they had met while he was on a cross-country motorcycle trip of which he had many fond memories.

The cold drink turned out to be a beer. Instinctively I knew I would not be riding anywhere that night, so I took him up on his offer. He produced a photo album, and we looked at familiar pictures for both of us. He kept on repeating how lucky I was to be heading to Alaska.

One beer turned into another and as the sun began to fall lower in the sky, I said, "We'd better look at those maps, I need to get a tent up soon."

He waved his arm, "Don't worry, we'll have dinner together here."

His wife then arrived home and Bob introduced us. Her name was Julie.

"I saw the motorcycle with the New York plates and all the gear in the parking lot and somehow figured Bob had something to do with it," she laughed.

Julie was very friendly and we decided to order out for pizza. I explained briefly how we met at the traffic light, and that I was looking for a campsite. She nodded, and in her nod, I recognized that she also knew that camping was not on the cards for me that night.

We ate pizza as the sun got lower and lower in the sky. She had to leave to teach an aerobics class. I said goodbye to her and thanked her for her hospitality. She smiled and left to go teach. I made one last ditch attempt to ask Bob about camping and he said that I was more than welcome to sleep in the spare bedroom. I took him up on his second kind offer. We decided it would be best not to leave my stuff on the bike all night, so we went down, unpacked the bike, and hauled my trunk and saddlebags upstairs.

Bob enjoyed the exercise – it reminded him of his days of traveling on the bike. We threw the stuff in the bedroom, broke open another beer and started sharing travel tales. When Julie arrived back she smiled and said, "I knew you'd still be here when I got back." We all chatted for about an hour or so more until Julie decided it was time for her to get to sleep. She had a long day ahead of her and so did I. Bob seemed reluctant to let it all end. I think he was still holding on to the road. My gut feeling was that he was not finished with his long-distance motorcycling. Julie gave me a warm hug and said goodbye. She had to leave early in the morning. Bob told me again how jealous he was. We shook hands, and we all went to sleep. This is what the road was about for me – chance meetings, trust, and nights of friendship.

The next morning I woke up to the ultimate of trust; a note on the kitchen table; "Had to go, have a great trip, send us a postcard when you arrive, cereal is in the cupboard," then an address scribbled at the end. I was amazed and gladdened at the same time that they could leave a stranger in their home in that way. We'd had a great night, and the morning was even better because of the wonderful feelings it instilled in me of the beauty of people. I ate a bowl of cereal, anxious to get on the road. Lugging the bags down the few flights to the small parking area, I was thinking of Bob and Julie, their kindness, their hospitality to a stranger, their sincerity and mostly how wonderful and refreshing it is to know that many people still trust others.

All the road signs were in French now and I really felt as if I were in a foreign country. I'd probably had one too many beers the night before. The motorcycle helped to blow the cobwebs out of my head. My journey was beginning. I felt I was more than ready, and the feeling that I was doing the right thing was washing over me. I looked forward to the nights of camping and writing in my journal. I had passed one of the major stumbling blocks, fear. I had faced it, and looked it in the eye. Now I had conquered it once again. I felt stronger for it, and the miles were slipping past me on the Canadian roads. French signs and kilometers per hour, I was heading to Alaska!

The next couple of days were excellent; great weather and nice camping. I rode on a stretch of highway known as 'The Terry Fox Memorial Highway'. He was a man who had faced fear and death. He was dying of cancer, having already lost a leg to it when he decided to run across Canada. He didn't make it all the way across. I came across a memorial to him and looked at his likeness in a running pose, complete with prosthetic leg turned towards the west as if to say, "I'm not looking back, I'm heading west!"

I met another motorcyclist in the western part of Ontario. We rode for two days together and even splurged on a cheap hotel so we could shower and have a bed each, camping every night is great, but the occasional bed is also nice. He was nice enough, but there was something that put up my cautious radar. I couldn't put my finger on it, but I didn't leave my wallet around while I took a shower. It was something in the way he spoke, his attitude towards life, and others. I sensed a lot of anger towards the world. On a certain level I could relate to that, but it permeated the atmosphere. We rode well together and it was nice to have company, but I didn't want to cross Canada with such a negative vibe. About four in the afternoon on the second day we pulled over for a snack and I knew I did not want to camp that night with him. That's the beauty of meeting someone on the road, you can't hurt their feelings too much if you say goodbye, or decide to stay put for the night. He was on a tighter schedule than I was and was chalking up the mileage as the days were very long in mid-summer in mid-Ontario. I said I was going to check out a provincial park not too far from where we were but he wanted to put at least five more hours of riding in, all due west. We said goodbye, thanked each other for the company, and wished each other luck. He was heading for British Columbia too but I was pretty sure we would not meet up again. I was glad for our meeting and time together but at the same time I was relieved he didn't think my idea to camp out was a good one.

On the road all you have is your instincts. People are constantly inviting you into their lives, to put up a tent in their backyard, have a meal together, or even travel together. You have to learn when to say no, and when to accept. This instinct is something I believe we all have, but it gets lost on package holidays and in everyday life where we find ourselves in situations that are often fairly predictable with many decisions having been taken out of our hands. Most of our day to day choices do not often allow us to hone our instinctive skills and when they do, it is often a media-induced response of fear that takes over rather than our own primal systems of danger avoidance. Stepping into the unknown, and being out there for months at a time forces you to tap into these depths of yourself lying dormant. I guess growing up on the streets of New York had allowed me to develop a feeling around what was not a good situation to be in, but here on the road I felt myself becoming more in tune with these feelings than ever before.

It worked out well that I headed north and stopped early that day. The park was gorgeous; heavily wooded with pines and spruce as well as deciduous trees, and the camping spots were secluded. I put up my tent that night the earliest of the whole trip, and walked through the woods. I enjoyed the solitude and peace of the woods and it gave me time to think in a different way. It wasn't the trancelike state that riding can induce although I loved that and the way it allowed me a way into myself and a kind of meditation for hours and hours. This different action of walking and the silence apart from the crunch of my own footsteps was something I probably never gave myself enough chance for. I tried to remember to take more time for smelling the roses in the future.

A late start the next morning was my insurance to myself that my riding partner from the day before was well and truly ahead of me. Not that I was worried, I just wanted to give him his space, and protect mine. The next few days were long days on the bike, and as I rode I mentally made a list of people who would love to be on these empty beautiful roads with nothing to do but ride and think. The list was getting long when I looked up at the sky and realized the sun was finally beginning to set.

I was putting a lot of daily mileage on the bike. I would get up with the sun, have breakfast, pack, and ride. I would stop in an interesting town if I passed through one; have a mid-morning snack in a diner somewhere; eat lunch when I felt hungry or the sun looked at least midway through its daily circuit. Then I would ride until I felt it was getting near dusk before looking at a map to decide where to camp. There were privately owned campsites or the provincial parks to choose from. If not, there were plenty of beautiful spots on the roadside as well. I always carried enough food for at least two meals. I looked down at my odometer and I could not believe the mileage I was chalking up. I knew the roads were sometimes straight and flat, and the miles would slip easily by, but I was nearing five hundred miles that day with lots of stops. I was putting up my tent in a campsite thinking it was probably about eight-thirty when I asked a young girl who was camping with her family if she knew the time. "Ten forty-five" she replied. I could not believe it! That was why I was putting on so many miles. I hadn't taken into account the fact that I had come quite far north in mid-summer. I was heading to the land of the midnight sun, and had never put two and two together. I was getting up with the sun, and going down with the sun, but there were nearly eighteen hours of daylight between those two times. I laughed at myself.

I went to the building to pay my fee for the night. When I wrote down my address on the registration form, the ranger looked up and said, "Wow, I don't think we've ever had someone here from The Bronx, New York before." I was taken aback, normally used to surprised responses, silly questions about guns, drugs, violence etc. Thank You Hollywood! But this was almost approaching star status. Sort of like, "Robert DeNiro is staying here tonight!" I went with it and asked him if he was serious. He was – I guess it was a small campsite in the middle of rural Manitoba so there wouldn't be too many New Yorkers passing through. Maybe a few people from The Dakotas, but The Bronx? Not many.

He was a nice guy and asked genuine questions about growing up in the big city. He was impressed that I was riding my motorcycle alone to Alaska as he didn't think city people liked doing that kind of thing. I told him I was an oddity, not understood by my friends or family. I enjoyed the traveling very much, but I had to push myself out of my comfort zone many times to reach the stage I was currently at right now. He agreed that it was tough to break patterns and that it was too bad that more people from the big cities didn't make it to small places in rural Manitoba. He grew up in a large town, but always had the desire to be in the trees which were never far away growing up in central Canada.

The next morning I awoke to another beautiful day. The weather had been fantastic so far and the riding good, although in the plains it tended to get monotonous sometimes. No curves, no mountain peaks looming, just flat road stretched out before you. Then again, it was yet another lesson in how travel imitated life. Those plains seemed endless, but they did end. When they did, you wound up in the mountains. The roads would start to swoop and curve, the snow peaks would stretch towards the heavens. The plains would be a memory, a special beauty unto themselves, but for me, traveling by motorcycle, they were something to cross to get to the mountains. The beauty of the mountains came with their price too, the changeable weather, the cold evenings camping 8,000 feet above sea level. But even those carried their reward. The starry nights in the mountains are the most spectacular light shows you'll ever see. Nothing, for me, puts life into better perspective.

Saskatchewan rolled by, I tried rigging up my headphones under my helmet to listen to music, the famous Johnny C tapes still shoved in my tank bag, but it didn't work that well. I was stuck with my mind drifting off and enjoying the sound of the engine. I had to settle for the occasional music at campsites, or at lunch breaks – the familiar tunes or a local radio station were welcome diversions, especially in the plains; but Alberta was approaching.

Alberta was the mountain province; the Canadian Rockies loomed. As I crossed into Alberta, there were dark clouds on the horizon. I rode on, deciding not to don my wet weather gear yet. It was a little game I played with myself. I always had the idea that putting on your waterproofs invited the rain to come. All travelers have different philosophies about that. I met a guy who would go to the hassle of putting them on at the slightest chance of rain, because he swore that it would then never rain. Anyway I motored on into the damp smell of rain and it soon became apparent that getting wet was inevitable. I told myself I'd stop at the next available spot to put on the waterproofs. In a few miles such a place came up. I pulled over and started to rummage through my bags. The one-piece quality rainsuit that I had splurged on before leaving New York had gotten slightly buried because I hadn't had any use for it yet. I finally found it and was slipping into it when I heard the engine of another bike pull up and stop.

A big smile from another loaded motorcyclist as he said, "I was delaying putting on the rain gear, but it looks like we're gonna get wet!"

I laughed and agreed. He was friendly and after we were both suited up he asked where I was headed. I simply said, "West."

He said, "I'm heading for Calgary."

"I don't think I'll go that far west tonight," I replied, "but let's ride together in the rain for a while anyhow." He nodded and shrugged his shoulders in agreement.

The rain came, and with the proper gear on it's always much better than it looks. You see people on motorcycles in the rain and think, oh that poor guy. It's actually almost meditative with the tapping of the raindrops on the helmet. You are also so concentrated on the road and handling the motorcycle, that time goes by quite quickly. Stopping is worse than riding through the rainstorms. When you stop, you fall out of that groove and all the little spots that might have gotten wet now feel wet and cold. If it's still raining when you want to continue, getting back on is that much harder. So we just rode on and on. We glanced at each other and smiled through our helmets. Time and miles were slipping by. It was fun having a riding partner. There is something nice about riding with another bike. Even though you are on separate machines, there is a connection. You share the road, you share the rain, and you do feel as if you are almost on the same motorcycle at times.

A break in the rain was coming. The sky had that beautiful color of late afternoon with the black clouds moving off, and the sun wanting to come through. We pulled into the parking lot of a diner. We didn't even have to motion to each other to do it. We just pulled in like we had planned it; like we knew it was coming up around the next bend in the road. Stripping off the rain gear we both smiled and said, "That was fun." He then said, "A hot drink sure would be very welcome." I agreed.

The diner was small and cozy. We finally introduced ourselves formally; his name was Pierre and he was French Canadian. He was going to visit some friends living in Calgary and I was more than welcome to join him. We had ridden so far in the rain that Calgary was only about seventy miles off by now. After getting to know Pierre over a cuppa, I decided what the heck, this is the next adventure so we enjoyed the next hundred miles once more riding without speaking and enjoying the wordless connection that comes from many miles on a bike and a comfort at the handling of your own machine like it was almost a part of yourself.

Calgary was a nice large town nuzzled in the foothills of the Rockies. The town was heaving with activity as the rodeo was in town. It was called, 'The Stampede'. The townspeople were all out and about in a sea of cowboy hats and the smell of warm stone and earth wet with rain filled the air. We rode through the streets looking for the address. Pierre had just finished his three-year stint in the Canadian Air Force and was here to catch up with his buddies who had moved out west. One of them was the manager of an apartment building, the building we were now looking for. You could feel we had left the prairies. The high peaks were not visible, still about a hundred miles away. There were definite bumps on the horizon though, and the road approaching the town was starting to feel different. Another ride across the plains was over.

We found the apartment which was in a small building. Three of Pierre's friends were waiting and glad to see him. They didn't hesitate for even a second to shake my hand like they were expecting me as well.

His friend, Scott, who managed the building asked, "Are you two too tired, or would you like to come to a party on the outskirts of town?"

We were hungry, and a party sounded like food and a few beers. "Let's go," Pierre said.

Scott then threw the key for an empty apartment in the building at us. "Put your gear in there. That'll be your place for the weekend." It was a carpeted two bedroom apartment. We couldn't ask for more. We unpacked quickly, had a quick wash, and jumped in the back of a pick-up truck for a crisp drive to a party. Not a bad reception, and quite different to any expectations I'd had when I woke up that morning.

Expectations were like that; if we could only start living in the moment all the time we would find that the day will unfold, events will happen, and doors will open. The trick is walking through the doors and accepting what life has in store for you in that particular moment. Samuel Clemens, otherwise known as Mark Twain, once said, "Apparently there is nothing that cannot happen today."

The drive was beautiful and yet it was a strange feeling to be moving along faster than walking speed on something that wasn't a motorcycle. We were heading out into the countryside. It was hill country, the sun was still up, but slowly sinking low, the reds, pinks and oranges merging with the residual clouds of an earlier rainstorm that had left the road with a thin covering of water, the wooden fences damp, and the unmistakable earthy smell after a rainstorm in the countryside. Before us the land spread out far and wide, cattle dotting the huge, seemingly endless paddocks.

We heard the party long before we arrived. There was music blasting, and nothing to hold the noise from drifting far in the crisp evening air. It was going to be a cool, clear night. We pulled up closer to what looked like a parking lot for pick-up trucks. We parked among them. We were truly out west!

Inside a huge hangar were lots of people amongst whom we arrived unnoticed. Pierre and his friends made a bee-line for the cooler of beers and I followed. Then I searched out some food. As I did I started to meet people. I only had to open my mouth before they asked, "You from back east?" When I said, "Yes," they assumed Toronto – when I told them New York, as always, it was an eyebrow raiser. "New York, how the hell did you wind up here?" I would launch into my story about motorcycling and meeting Pierre. Some were drunk already, others well on their way. I was then handed a beer, "Because I had balls riding my bike all the way to Calgary from New York," is how it was delicately put by one bearded big guy wearing a cowboy hat who I wouldn't want to mess with.

The night was just getting under way, and the five of us were pretty much the only ones from back east. We became known as the, 'DFE s'. It was a term of endearment, and I was not going to argue with a barn full of cowboys anyhow. DFE stood for, Dumb Fuckin' Easterner. We took it as it was handed to us, and proudly played up the city boy routine. I felt like the guest of honor all night getting introduced as Joe from The Bronx. It was a fun evening and I ate and drank more than I had in quite a while. The party went on and on and we stayed until the wee hours. Eventually we crawled towards our pick-up, and remarkably found the correct one. By the time we left, I'd had lessons in throwing a lasso, worn about seven different cowboy hats, and had a blue ribbon pinned on my leather jacket for winning a drinking competition known as, *The Boat Race*. Our team of DFE's won! We beat the cowboys on their own turf in a drinking game, earning us some respect and maybe even got the "F" dropped from our term of endearment.

I must say, I was more than glad not to be riding anywhere that next day. My head was pounding and I was officially hung over. A breakfast with strong coffee helped a bit, but walking in the fresh air of Calgary did much more to clear my aching head. We spent the day wandering around town and going from coffee shop to eating establishment talking, drinking coffee, and eating. What a perfect spot Calgary was. With the buzz of the rodeo in town, people were everywhere. The coffee shops were all full, and everyone was in a good mood. We met up with some of the cowboys from the night before, some good natured ribbing went on, and the day passed much in that way. The vibe was great – small town meets cosmopolitan city meets the cowboy. There were lots of cowboy-booted men and women, but it was real here, not just a fashion statement. I'd never considered cowboy hats sexy until I spent a day walking around Calgary. The women looked great in their blue jeans, cowboy boots and hats. Some of the men from the rodeo were wandering around town too. You could hear mumblings of "he's a bull rider," which reminded me of another rodeo in Wyoming, "he breaks broncos" etc. The words "bull rider" were almost whispered. Unfortunately, tickets were sold out, so we never got to see those men and women at work.

That night we went out to a local bar. I slowed down my beer intake, and did not get involved in the rounds of shots that started happening with Pierre and the boys. I was slowly starting to enter a new phase of my life. I was reading books about spiritual journeys, starting to explore some Eastern philosophies, and the more philosophical the reading material was getting, the deeper I was tapping into myself and the less I felt the need to alter my state of mind for the sake of it. I was still only twenty-three years old, and drinking was so much a part of the socialization process that it was hard to avoid and at that point a part of me was still enjoying it, but I was feeling stronger in myself. I was starting to feel that I could be accepted in circles without drinking and that night was the first of many where I was able to say, "No thanks, I want to be fresh in the morning if I'm going to ride," order water or a soft drink, and not feel any pressure to do otherwise. No pressure from them, and none from me. I felt as though it would be tougher, but I learned that night that people respect a strong decision. If I had said, "Well maybe just one beer and a shot, I really shouldn't...," I would have been drinking all night again with the boys. I just made the decision, and they said "Okay," and continued without me. *Every strong decision makes you stronger.* I thought back to that meeting.

The next morning Pierre woke up feeling very much the same as I had the day before. I, on the other hand, felt fresh and ready for a ride – once again the desire to wake up clear-headed far outweighed the want to do shots at the bar. Pierre was heading north to see his sister who lived in Edmonton. I was heading west but north too so I decided I would rather meet Pierre's sister and her family in a place called Edmonton than go to Lake Louise in Banff – supposedly one of the most picturesque places in the Rockies. It was another direction that was slowly becoming clearer – although loving the natural beauty – for me it was just as interesting to get on an intimate level with the people I came in contact with. We rode the whole day with a nip in the air under dark gray clouds. It never did rain, but it was not the best day on the bike. For Pierre, nursing a hangover, I expect it was far worse.

His sister lived in a small house with her two kids and husband. It was simple and plain. Edmonton pulled back away from the mountains, and where Calgary had that feeling of something happening, the mountains coming, diners, cafés, and young people looking happy; this place had a feeling of industrial – I'm here because this is where the factory is. I was glad I came. The contrast with two days in Calgary was worth it. I found out that Edmonton was home to one of the largest shopping malls in the world and it made perfect sense.

After leaving Pierre's sister's house and thanking them for a nice evening, I said my goodbyes to Pierre and headed west. Decision time was coming, and coming soon. That night I slept in Jasper national park under a starry sky in the Rockies. I loved the mountain roads and for me the day just flew by. It was fun, and you had to ride and control your bike all over again. In the plains you just rested on the throttle enough to stop yourself from falling over, here you leaned into the road, read the painted lines and instinctively knew how far over to get. When the pegs started to scrape on the road, it was a feeling and a sound that got the adrenalin going and reminded you how alive you were, and how close you were to that road whizzing by right under your feet. There is a two paragraph passage near the beginning of *Zen and the Art of Motorcycle Maintenance* that describes it perfectly.

*"You see things vacationing on a motorcycle in a way that is completely different from any other. In a car you're always in a compartment, and because you're used to it you don't realize that through the car window everything you see is just more TV. You're a passive observer and it is all moving by you boringly in a frame.*

*On a cycle the frame is gone. You're completely in contact with it all. You're in the scene, not just watching it anymore, and the sense of presence is overwhelming. The concrete whizzing by five inches below your foot is the real thing, the same stuff you walk on, it's right there, so blurred you can't focus on it, yet you can put your foot down and touch it anytime, and the whole thing, the whole experience, is never removed from immediate consciousness."*

Along with other realities, I was also now in bear country. With bear country came all the warnings and horror stories. You had to sift through what you wanted to believe was real and what was just another 'Urban Myth', take your chances, be careful with your food and share the mountains with the wild animals that have lived here long before we arrived proclaiming National Park status and putting up tents. The stars were beautiful. The night was chilly, and I was zipped into my bargain-priced Caldors sleeping bag to try and stave off the cold. (I would one day actually have quality camping equipment but that was years away.)

The next morning I awoke all in one piece – no bear attacks, and my food hanging in the tree was untouched. Today would be the day I would come to a split in the road and make the big decision if I would ride all 800 miles to mainland Alaska on the Alaskan-Canadian Highway – 'The Alcan' – as it is affectionately known, or would I head due west to the islands and utilize the boats on the 'Inside Passage'. That decision would be made when I approached the sign.

I was nearing Alaska, but it was still a long way off. I never realized how far 5,000 miles actually was. When you hit the Canadian Rockies you think, well I'm almost there. Not quite, there was still nearly 1,500 miles to go – a long way on highway 97 – the Alcan.

The decision was not all that big a deal in the end. I had built it up in my mind that I would be stopped on the side of the road looking at the sign trying to make up my mind but it was a lot easier than that. I was cruising along when a road sign approached with two arrows, one pointing to the right saying, 'Highway 97 Alaska', the other pointing straight saying, 'Ferries'. I simply leaned into the bike and veered off right. I said out loud, "Alaska, here I come!" A wave of emotion swooped over me all at once after passing the sign and I had the clear vision of all those people I had met along the way who said it was their dream to ride to Alaska, or asked for a postcard. There were many; sometimes it would be an older fella who used to ride, or a young rider met in a truckstop, Pierre, my students, and of course friends and family from New York. I still remembered the emotion in Bob's far-away look, nearly a plea to do it because he hadn't, but I knew that in his voice was the voice of someone who was not finished with his travels, he would do it one day, and Julie would be with him. Theirs was that relationship of two individuals growing as a unit of one and respecting each other as people. I know it's a lot to tell from one night, but it's just one of those feelings you get being with certain couples. A postcard would definitely make it back to their apartment in Montreal.

I looked over the map, and decided to skip the town where highway marker mile one would be. The Alcan is all about these highway markers, from Dawson Creek, British Columbia to the frontier with Alaska all marking the miles so far. I noticed a road that cut through a section of forest on the map. It looked like an excellent piece of road and I was not in the mood for a town. I had enough fuel in my belly and gas in the tank of the bike, although from now on, I would never pass up another gas station. I couldn't take the chance of running out. My bike was getting old, and I have always asked a lot more from it than it was built to do. Now I would treat it kindly, and feed it often. I could get about 260 miles to a full tank – there would probably never be that big a stretch between stations, but better safe than sorry, I was getting up into the middle of nowhere.

That night I camped out under the stars. It was a beautiful night, and I must admit that here, as opposed Yellowstone or Glacier National Parks, I felt that I was the intruder, completely dwarfed by my surroundings both physically and mentally. The bears and wild animals really ruled the roost. This un-trafficked road was just a tiny winding path cutting through the forest like a loose black thread lying across an immense pristine carpet of wilderness. This was a part of the world far away from the cities of Canada, and the U.S. I was feeling like the city boy once again. For the first time in any of my cross-country travels, I felt I had entered a new league and I was now playing for the 'Majors'.

My tent and I survived the night. I looked at my bike that I used to ride back and forth to college in The Bronx, and laughed. I said to it, "Well here you are, on the way to Alaska, how do you feel?" I think we both felt the same – overwhelmed, but up to the challenge. We had both made the commitment, our equipment was maybe more suited for less challenging terrain but we would make it work, and together as a team we would cross the border into Alaska. I had a feeling deep down inside that it was going to be fine, and both man and machine would achieve what we set out to accomplish.

The next major event was crossing into the Yukon Territories. It was getting stranger and stranger. It felt that I should not be spending money to eat, but trading in gold nuggets. Dawson City, Yukon – a sleepy town of 500 people – was just a little north of where I now was on the Klondike River. Gold fever had swept through in the 1890's and men with little or even no knowledge at all about living wild, flocked up to the area. The population swelled to 300,000, all searching for the illustrious metal which was seemingly abundant in the Klondike. Nearly one hundred years later things had shifted back to a more normal pace of life here in the far northern throws of the continent – the occasional prospectors made it north, but the Gold Rush of nearly a hundred years ago had subsided. Now here I was, probably coming under the same description of having little or no knowledge of traveling in such wilderness, but I was trying and, as I was soon to find out, was not alone.

I stopped into a diner for some breakfast that morning, and heard some interesting news. My waitress inquired where I was from, and where I was heading. As I told her she interrupted saying, "Oh about three days ago a guy on a bicycle ate here from New York. He was riding to Alaska too." I had met one other cross-country cyclist in 'The lower forty-eight' as the states were known up here, but New York to Alaska. Wow! I would be sure to meet him unless he happened to be pulled off the roadside eating when I passed. I calculated that I would probably catch him later on that day. I didn't know it then, but I would be meeting my future.

A few hours later deep in The Kloane Ranges, I saw something in the distance moving slowly up the hill; at first it appeared to be a car, then as I approached, it looked like a motorcycle. When I was nearly upon him, I realized it was the lone cyclist and I pulled up next to him. There I was shivering in my leather jacket, and there he was sweating with the effort of the climb.

I said to him, "You must be from New York."

He looked back and said, "How did you know?"

I said jokingly, "I could tell by your riding style."

He looked quizzically at me then I laughed. I told him the story about the diner. As it turned out he was from White Plains, New York, not far from The Bronx. We chatted but it was tough for me to ride at his speed, and I guessed not very pleasant for him to talk and ride up hill. All I could think of at the time was how miserable he must have felt. We complimented each other on our decisions to do what we were doing; he said I was brave riding all the way on a motorcycle. I quickly countered that he was the brave one on his bicycle. He tilted his head in a laugh as we wished each other luck, and said goodbye, companions in some way on our route north. It was too bad that it was not later in the day or we might have camped together. He creeps into my mind occasionally as now I can understand him so much better, having pedaled many long miles.

Later on that day I was in Norseman, Yukon Territories. I decided I didn't want to camp so booked into a small hotel. I was eating in a diner when an older gentleman came over to my table and asked, "Do you ride a Yamaha motorcycle?"

I said, "Yes, Why?" I was waiting for him to say it fell over in front of the hotel or something similar.

"Just wondering if you would mind sharing the cost of the room with a fellow motorcyclist?" He then introduced himself as Charlie, and he was heading up to Alaska as well.

"No problem," I said, "that would be great. Just tell the lady at reception."

I continued eating and a few minutes later Charlie walked in and asked if he could join me. I said certainly. He ordered food and we got to know each other. He was sixty-eight years old and was heading into Alaska. He had no camping equipment, and hadn't set out to ride all the way to Alaska, it, "just kind a happened," he said.

He had been a motorcyclist his whole life, and now was riding a nice big Honda Shadow, much like mine, the only difference being a small windshield. We woke up that morning to a third motorcycle parked next to ours – a fully dressed Harley. Ed then appeared out of his room. We all

50

introduced ourselves, and decided to ride out of town together and see what happened.

What happened was I rode with Charlie and Ed and gained close to a century's worth of motorcycling experience that they shared between them. Their stories of crossing America in the fifties and sixties were fascinating – what a different place, no major interstates – small town America was alive and well back then. The Alcan reminded me of the America which has been lost in many ways to the franchises and fast food chains.

We met two other motorcyclists heading up to Alaska on enduro type machines. They bought the bikes just for the purpose of doing this trip. Their idea was to get rid of the bikes in Alaska and fly home once they made it. I could not imagine the return trip without my faithful Yamaha. I could see why they came up with that plan though. The Alcan was a notorious highway that got tougher the further you went. The road surface deteriorated as the scenery became more wild and stunning. This was unfortunate as your eyes were definitely needed to watch where you were riding. The road was only half-paved, and those sections were full of what are called 'frost heaves'. This is a phenomenon caused by the extreme weather in winter causing waves or heaves in the road. Cycling on the Alcan deserved all your attention, all the time. Whereas on the paved roads of Canada and America you could easily chalk up 400 miles on a good day and feel like you did other things besides just ride, here we were averaging about 150 miles per day, and were exhausted at the end of it. All along the way you would hear stories or see the outcomes of mishaps; broken axles on the campervans who did brave the journey, flat tires and the occasional story of a motorcycle getting caught in a rut and flipping over reached our cars, but the three of us survived without misfortune.

Ed was an interesting character, a retired commercial airline pilot who put over 50,000 miles on his Harley every year. He has probably ridden every secondary road in the lower forty-eight! He was on his way to visit his niece in Anchorage. To add to his persona, he did all this with a colostomy bag to irrigate every night. When I bartended in The Bronx for a while, I served many locals who did nothing after retirement except drink and wait to die. Ed was an inspiration.

We had a great time motoring up the Alcan together through Canada heading to Alaska. What an experience! We were raced once by wild horses, and a mother black bear and her cub ran across the road just in front of us necessitating an abrupt pull on the brakes. Rustles in the trees and dust being kicked higher up on the hillsides provided us with glimpses of deer, a family of moose grazing a hundred or so feet nearly out of sight of the road, more bear, mountain goats, caribou, and the sky – when not black and threatening rain – was the deep blue only found far from the smog of cities. Birds of prey circled above like tiny dots in the sky, but the occasional swoop down showed their true size to be jaw-droppingly big. The rivers we crossed were sometimes gray and silty, which baffled me until I found out it was glacial runoff, not pollution. It made me feel better to think these raging wide rivers were bringing well-needed minerals to the verdant fields, rather than run off from the ever-expanding Alaskan oil industry which, although bringing financial wealth to many Alaskans, was also doing irreparable damage to the natural beauty and wildlife of America's largest, and by far, wildest state.

The landscapes, no matter which way I turned my head, were scenes straight out of photo books I normally only saw on coffee tables. The Matanuska and Mendenhall Glaciers were the highlights for me. I remember one day just watching small ice falls break off the glacier and splash into the water, the ice so cold it was blue in places. I remembered Glacier National Park and its beauty, thinking of the Hudson Valley being formed by a receding glacier in the Ice Age. Now for the second time in my life I was up close to glaciers on my motorcycle and it brought to life the knowledge of the valley I grew up near and the river I saw so often when crossing the George Washington or Tappan Zee Bridges on the same bike. Here I was now far from those bridges and that familiar valley, soaring past a river of ice just off to the left, all my geography and topography lessons now making more sense. Seeing that glacier up close was worth a thousand words. I could picture the ice moving slowly down the valley, dragging the earth with it. It was happening right in front of my eyes. You could see and feel the frozen torrent, its path through the mountains visible. The mouth of the river was there but it just looked like a huge mass of ice ending in the sea. Later in the journey, on boats through the Inside Passage, we would sail past the glaciers feeling as if we were on one of the frozen planets of our solar system.

We did not camp at night, but shared cheap road-side hotel rooms. That was fine with me. The knowledge we were sharing was incredible and the comradeship between the three of us was something truly special. The black skies pierced with a galaxy full of twinkling stars were becoming harder to catch sight of the further north we traveled. They would undoubtedly come out, but only for the briefest of times between dusk and sunrise, usually too late for any of us to stay up to see. If I was awoken by a call of nature I would glance up at the night sky and be nearly moved to tears by the overwhelming feelings of awe, satisfaction, accomplishment, and mere beauty of it all. I was on the road with two men old enough to be my grandfather, and interesting enough to forego camping for a few nights. We would sit out in front of the hotel room till late in the evening and watch nature's version of *The Late Show* – an almost unending sunset. We were from three diverse parts of the States; Charlie from rural Illinois, Ed from Pennsylvania, and me the youngster from New York City and we all had stories to tell. We rode, enjoyed the scenery, and learned about each other.

I remember it almost as clearly as if it were yesterday. We were on a beautiful stretch of road in The Yukon territories as a big wooden sign approached reading 'ALASKA', with a map of America's largest state drawn beneath that one big name. It was a great feeling and a wave of emotion swept over me. What a privilege to be with these two veteran motorcyclists fulfilling their dream. I was a twenty-three-year-old New Yorker on the border of Alaska, all the doubts, fears, and anxieties gone. I was re-entering America thousands of miles from home, I had traversed the continent, and was at The Last Frontier! The otherworldliness of the Alcan all behind me, the strange towns which felt like they stood still in the 1800's lost in time at mile 41 or mile 242 was a strange world, but here I was. I had pushed the limits, both mine and my bike's, and we made it. We still had far to go to get to Anchorage, but the longest leg of the journey was over. I'd accomplished it without abandoning my original plan and had motorcycled over 5,000 miles to a place in my head that I'd never been to before. The latest frontier was to be the beginning of many others I would cross in my life; physical, mental and spiritual ones.

We all shook hands, took snapshots, mounted our steeds and headed down the road to Anchorage scraping our pegs, letting the sparks fly, and feeling the cold breeze coming off the Mendenhall Glacier to our left.

# A Lucky Break

Anchorage was a well placed city for the outdoorsman. At sixty-one degrees latitude, the sun was barely setting at one a.m. to rise again less than two hours later. This meant lots of daylight hours in the summer for the outdoor activities that were everywhere; hiking, kayaking, mountaineering, and more. I saw hot air balloons taking off at eleven in the evening from where I sat looking out across the Cook Inlet to the Kenai Peninsula. I could imagine the archipelago of the Aleutian Islands gently sloping away to the southwest extending its one arm out to embrace the Bering Sea and keep it safe from the northern reaches of the mighty Pacific, drawing it back in to the body of mainland Alaska. Was that all just outside the door of where I was now sitting in this warm and friendly house?

I had been made welcome in the home of Ed's niece. We were eating fresh fish caught on those same Aleutian Islands by the Aleuts, the natives of that harsh land jutting out into the sea. Looking out over the Gulf of Alaska on the other side of the Aleutian 'arm' the scene was magical and brought home to me how far I had come; five thousand miles northwest and twenty degrees latitude further towards the Arctic Circle than the city of my birth; the same country but a different universe. For Alaska, Anchorage was a metropolis: for a New Yorker it was more like a small town. I enjoyed a well-needed rest at Barbara's house for a few days but I soon knew it was time once again to be on the road and to head south.

Heading north out of Anchorage meant retracing a lot of our steps back to the Yukon Territories in Canada and then south back into Alaska to Skagway where you could catch boats through the Inside Passage. This strip of America's most northerly state consisted of a narrow band of coastal mainland bordering Canada. There are hundreds of small islands hugging this coastline where it is possible to travel on the ferries that make up the mass transportation system for the inhabitants – very different to the IRT Line of the mass transit system I was used to. With my inferior camping equipment and my street cruiser motorcycle, I had decided that heading further in to Denali State Park or Fairbanks wasn't on the cards this time around. I was weary of being cold all the time and my motorcycle had already gone above and beyond its limits. It was doing well so far and even the road to Skagway was not going to be easy – lots of the same rutted dirt roads we had been on already, plus a few more. My cheap tent had done me proud and, although not used much lately, it was starting to show its limits.

My cash situation was okay, but if I was going to make it back to New York I was going to have to be a bit more creative; after all, I was at least 5,000 miles away, and the back tire of my motorcycle had been badly worn down by the Alcan Highway. Now we would be heading back to another notorious stretch of road to get to Skagway. What a great name for a town.

We had seventy miles of rough road to tackle after we crossed the border at a place called Beaver Creek, Yukon Territories, the cold breeze of the now familiar glacier this time in our faces. After two more days of riding we headed back into Alaska once again towards Skagway.

The Diomede Islands in the Bering Strait – the waterway separating the Russian Bear from the American Grizzly – always made me curious as we shared a common name. America purchased this far away land of ice, snow and oil fields from Russia in the late 1800's, it later gained its statehood in 1959. Little Diomede and Big Diomede Island now became separated by nationality – one turning American overnight. Families no longer able to see each other, centuries-old traditions of fishing and celebrations on the many islands abruptly coming to an end because of a division of land made in an office thousands of miles from the reality of the Bering Strait. It was too far to head to now, but made me think of all the unmentioned casualties of our silly political games that affect so many lives – too many cast-offs in history – their stories never told, but many of us get caught in the middle, wanting nothing more than to get on with our lives.

Back on the rutted, unsealed roads of this tiny strip of America tucked up somewhere near the Arctic Circle, we finally made it to Skagway. About a hundred years previously many others might have felt the same feeling of accomplishment in making it to this same place. The only way to Skagway back then was over the 3,500 foot Chilkoot Pass, a long difficult path leading up and over the mountains. Tens of thousands would make their way over that pass, some even dying while chasing that elusive soft, yellow metal called gold. I made my comparison with those prospectors; I was also in search of something on my journey – it wasn't as solid as gold, but it seemed to be nearly as elusive. Here I was, on my third cross-continental trip, trying to find that special something that would feel right. I didn't know yet what it was and almost envied the prospectors of a century ago – when they panned for gold, they knew when they hit the right part of the mountain or the river – the mother lode. Would I be so lucky? Would I know when I had found what I was looking for? I could only hope so, and since it was nothing material but something more ethereal, it would be that much harder to hold up and say, "Here it is, I found it!" I was confident that one day, somehow I would find something that made more sense but for now I was still enjoying the journey.

Our ticket allowed us to get on and off the boat system as much as we wanted. They were well-used by the locals living on the Inside Passage and there were always a regular service ferrying people up and down the waterway. We saw a cruise liner or two every so often on the wider stretches of open sea, but not many. A whale came within a stones throw of the boat which made everyone on board excited – even the locals, for whom I presumed seeing these majestic mammals of the sea was more common. Although seeing its magnificence parting waters so close to the ship made me realize how difficult it would be to get used to such an awesome sight.

In Juneau we met an Austrian couple of about thirty years or so who were on a long motorcycle tour for their honeymoon. Theirs was a rugged off-road machine which they shared. They had aluminum box-type saddlebags and were on a tour of The Americas. They had started in Florida about seven months before and had ridden their bike to Prudhoe Bay, the most northerly point of Alaska for which they had needed to get special permission from the military. The road sounded a real nightmare; where I had seen the occasional black bear, they had seen grizzly. They had quite a lot of luggage, a big tank bag, and, in true European form, wore full leathers all the time. Their trip was now hopefully going to take them to the southernmost tip of South America in Tierra Del Fuego, Argentina! I wondered about a trip like that – one heading south instead of north – and stored the possibility away like a squirrel hiding his nuts for winter.

Eddie and Charlie would be heading back east after hitting the mainland and I was still planning on heading to California. After Juneau we parted ways after exchanging addresses, and for years beyond that day we kept in touch. We all agreed it made sense for me to search out more adventures. I traveled and camped with the honeymoon couple for a few more days. Their way of traveling would not have suited Eddie or Charlie in this phase of their lives. I knew they'd done their share of roughing it back in their day. It was even tough for me; after cheap hotels and staying in a house in Anchorage, I was now thrown back into the hard reality of my tent once again. Despite the lack of creature comforts, though, I realized I'd missed it.

We slept out on the docks, and explored the more rural parts of the Inside Passage. We had a great time under the stars in the evening eating good food, and sharing the occasional beer. As summer marched on and we headed south, we were able to see starry nights once again before midnight. My street bike which I was squeezing as much as I could out of was not up to the tough terrain their bike was built for. They were planning some tougher off-road travel and camping on the next island. I went straight on through to Prince Rupert Island, but when we parted ways I

56

asked them to keep me informed of their trip, which over the next two years they did conscientiously. I lived their adventures with them through their letters over the years, but since have lost contact with Hans and Ursula.

Leaving the last island, Prince Rupert Island, was quite strange after days of the routine of embarking and disembarking boats to make my progress south. I headed east briefly and crossed a bridge which put me back on the mainland of Canada. Everything was more familiar now. The roads were not the rough roads of the north, and the weather was milder. I had never heard about the fruit-growing areas of British Columbia called The Okanagon Valley until this trip, but I was eager to check out this large verdant valley – it promised some beautiful motorcycle riding, fresh fruit, and great camping. The area even smelled fruity and did not disappoint!

How great it was to be on nicely paved roads again. I was blessed with the weather, even in Alaska and the Inside Passage it had been relatively dry. The Okanagon was beautiful; the roadside was full of stands selling delicious fresh fruit, green rolling hills, and the north-south road was a beauty. The days were still the longer days of summer, even though the longest day was well past. The Okanagon River was flowing off to my left, the sound of it rushing drowned out by the engine of my bike. When I stopped to have a picnic or a drink, I would lie down in the grass just gazing up at the blue skies and fluffy cumulonimbus clouds that accompanied me down the valley. The air was clear and clean, the roads were smooth, and almost too soon I found myself heading to the border-crossing with Washington State.

Being back in the lower forty-eight was welcome and familiar. The green money, road markings and highway systems I had become so used to over the past five continental crossings on my trusty Yamaha 850 Special gave comfort, almost like I was home, but not really. Home lay a few thousand miles east. The Cascades were a pleasant range of mountains. Being summer, there was lovely weather, and again it was quite dry. There were lots of incredible roads where it was easy to slip into that different state of consciousness, realizing hours later that miles had been covered. The only thing that was worrying me in the back of my mind was my back tire. The long road from New York to Alaska had taken its toll – I'd put it on new before I left but now it was badly worn. I'd have to take care of that soon as it was the only thing stopping me from fully enjoying the roads.

Washington State is beautiful, tucked up in the western corner of America bordering its northern neighbor. The small ribbon of road heading west out of the mountains was a dusty brown color and the mountains slowly faded from view out of my rearview mirrors. In a strange way I missed riding on busy roads weaving in and out with the cars, but a big city would have jolted me too quickly out of my state of mind and I was not ready to break that spell. I had been in nothing but small towns, villages and country roads – even Juneau, despite being Alaska's capital city, was still a small town. Over the past two months I had been riding under big skies, not city skylines. Wild life and rutted roads were what slowed me down, not traffic jams and pot holes. On the other hand, I was tempted towards some big city riding to see if I hadn't forgotten what had always come so easily.

A couple of more days crossing Washington State over the Colombia river, and seeing Mt Rainier in the distance was a perfect welcome back to the picture-perfect American northwest. I was nearly on sensory overload. Looking at a map, there was so much to explore; The Colombia River gorge, numerous mountains, the Yakima River, the Straits of Juan de Fuca and more, but not at the moment. I was enjoying the riding and soon found myself on the outskirts of Seatac.

I hit the traffic slightly after rush hour with light still in the sky, and I fell easily into riding amongst the traffic. It came back surprisingly naturally after being on such empty roads for so long. I was not thinking of where I would stay that night but just enjoying the ride. All of a sudden, another bike passed me in my lane, it was a couple on a loaded bike, not an off-road bike like the one I'd left a different world ago in Alaska, it was more a street bike or cruiser. They beckoned me to follow them with a toot and a wave. We played a sort of motorcycle tag weaving throughout the traffic for what seemed just minutes, but actually was more like half an hour. Time just slipped by, dusk turned into night, the other motorcycle put on their directional and the passenger gave me a wave to say, "Follow Us."

It was intriguing; we hadn't said a word to each other, but their license-plate let me know they were from Wisconsin, and mine let them know I was from New York. I followed them into a gas station, and we both filled up. Our helmets came off and we saw each other for the first time. A familiar Midwestern accent began our conversation.

"Hi, I'm Wayne, this is Ellen, I see you're from New York."

"Yup, my name's Joe, looks like you two are packed and quite a long way from home as well."

"Actually, we've been traveling for about three weeks – we're on our honeymoon." A proud smile came to Wayne's face, and Ellen who had been silent till then, chimed in with, "Yes Wayne here picked me up on the way; we got married in Vegas."

I looked surprised, and before I could say anything, Wayne cut in and said, "Ellen loves joking around. We *are* on our honeymoon, but didn't get married in Vegas. What about you?"

"I had my wife with me too, but hit quite a big bump in the Cascades. Haven't seen her since." I looked at Ellen, the joker, and we all laughed.

It came out they were mostly camping, as I had been since meeting the Austrians, and we decided that none of us would mind getting a room. We struck up an instant bond, and re-mounted our bikes to search for a cheap hotel to spend the night. I seemed to be on the honeymoon tour.

When we found the place I said, "Should we get two rooms?" Assuming I would get a single and them a double, but the budget mindedness of all of us won out, and we wound up sharing a double room. I felt funny, and asked, "Are you sure? After all you are on your honeymoon tour."

They both laughed and Ellen said, "We've been on the road about a month, we're childhood sweethearts, so the honeymoon, as they say, is over!"

I chuckled as well. They were a likable couple, I told them about Hans and Ursula and how I was used to being the odd one out.

As motorcyclists our enjoyment came from riding on the empty roads, coupled with the camping. For me it fulfilled the need to get lost in the beauty of where I was, and to wander off in my mind. In the evenings I enjoyed winding down with an occasional walk to calm down the buzz in my arms and legs after long days in the saddle. Stargazing by a campfire was a nice pastime too, but alone I found I did not sit out as much as crawl into the tent and read. Meeting people was always nice, and in all my journeys so far, I had met the right people at the right time. Wayne and Ellen were much the same in that they loved the riding, and it showed. Their bike was well looked after, and they had chalked up an impressive amount of miles on their way west from Wisconsin.

It felt wonderful to be clean. Free camping and washing in lakes and rivers was great, but a hot shower, ahhh! I even managed to find some relatively clean clothes. The pizza we ordered in was the first I'd had since that night with Bob in Montreal. It brought back that fond memory, and we too chatted till late in the night when sleep came quickly and easily to all of us.

Wayne and Ellen were both school teachers, and since I had done some teaching we had some stories to swap. They were enjoying themselves, and we were all inspiring each other on different levels. Going to Alaska was too big a trip to tackle in their minds, but I feel any trip is too big unless it is taken just a step at a time, just like life. They took any small road they could find, and chocked up loads of miles. They loved motorcycles, and their enthusiasm for their trip was so catchy that I decided I would get my rear tire replaced the next day so I could remove any of the apprehension I was feeling about riding. I wanted to get back to total enjoyment of my days on the road. Their time was getting short, and they were starting to head back east. The next morning we splashed out on a big breakfast in a diner before saying goodbye. I had a mission to find a shop for my back tire.

The shop I found on the outskirts of Seatac was nice and clean and the workshop was quite big, but there was a strange energy that made me feel ill at ease. There was no way to put a finger on it. I could not fault the service I received in the front shop, but still, when I left my bike and went off to get a hot drink, something about the vibe was trying to get my attention. I got back an hour or so later, and the shop assistant told me my bike was ready out back. I paid for the tire and installation then went to get my bike. When I went out back, the feeling became really strong. I noticed a big grease smudge on the tank then smiled at the mechanic who I assumed had done the work and thanked him. He looked up without making good eye contact and I instantly got a chilly feeling. I walked the bike out of the workshop, and decided I would take a closer look at the work done.

I had taken the rear wheel off my bike a few times so was familiar with the way things should be tightened. I looked down to the rear axle nut, and noticed that the cotter pin which goes through the rear axle and nut as an added security against the wheel nut vibrating loose was not there. I felt the tightness of the nut with my fingers and it felt tight, but I decided to give it a check with my tools. I dug out my spanner and was shocked that it tightened a full turn until all the holes were lined up again. I went back to the workshop and told the mechanic about the missing cotter pin. He grunted something incomprehensible as he handed me a cotter pin with his greasy hand. I said to him, "You know, I'm traveling a long way and that could have been potentially pretty dangerous on a fully loaded bike." He didn't appear to care so I put the cotter pin in, bent it in place, packed my tools and bike and was nearly shaking with a mixture of anger, fear, uneasiness, and indecision. Should I tell the owner, manager, or whoever those people were in the front shop? I didn't know what to do. I just wanted to get out of there and go over my bike with a fine tooth comb. I did not feel deep inside that he would have tinkered with anything on the bike, I just felt he was either a burnt out, or very pissed off mechanic, not a devious person who would cut my brake line or something like that, but who knows? The energy he gave off was strong, even permeating the front of the shop where he seemingly never entered. I just wanted to give the work he did a good check over, and put my mind at ease.

I rode my bike cautiously to the parking lot of a supermarket, and parked out in the back. I took off my trunk bag, un-strapped my other things from the backseat, and checked all the brake lines, nuts and axles for both wheels. I wiped the grease stain from the tank and was satisfied that all was fine. I shook off all the bad energy, took a breath of fresh air and repacked my bike. I reminisced on how this bike and I who had done so much together found each other just six or so months before my first trip with Gary. The motorcycle I thought I had conjured up in my mind came to me in what I'll call, for lack of a better word, a coincidence.

When I knew for sure I was crossing the continent on a motorcycle, I felt my first bike – the Honda 550 – was too small for the job. I had seen a Yamaha 750 Special, but felt 200 cc bigger wasn't big enough. An 850 would be perfect. I thought I saw one somewhere – a red bike would be nice, but the right bike was more important. I looked around, but all I found was the Special 750 or 650. I would widen my search for other bigger bikes in my price range – between $1500 and $2000.

One day my friend Audrey and I came back from a ride into the cafeteria at Lehman College where I attended university. We sat at a table with a few friends, and came in carrying our helmets. Another friend Lisa was there. She saw the helmets and commented on them. She was into motorcycles too. I mentioned to her I was looking for a used bike so if any of her friends were selling one to let me know. She then said, "Well my boyfriend Bobby is selling his bike. He just got his third speeding ticket."

"What kind of bike is it?" I asked.

She replied, "A Yamaha Special." My ears perked up.

"What size?"

"I think it's an 850," she said.

I looked at Audrey as if to say "are you playing a joke on me?" I then said, "I suppose it's red."

She said, "Well, not fire engine red, but a burgundy red."

"Nice joke Audrey," I laughed.

Lisa looked genuinely confused and Audrey said, "I swear, I didn't say anything to her." I asked Lisa to find out more details and let me know the next day.

I couldn't believe it, my dream bike landing right in my lap. The next day Lisa let me know it was an 850, it had never been down, and he wanted $1,850 for it, firm. He was heartbroken to have to sell it and I nearly bought it sight unseen. That night I was over his house shaking hands on the deal. What a bummer for Bobby, but a lucky break for me.

When that negative energy attempted to pollute our trip I was glad that I had acted on my original instinct and checked everything out. Now, after repacking and getting lost in those memories, I felt all was back to normal. I decided not to go back and say anything. I'm not sure it was the right or wrong thing to do, but I must say, it was partially a selfish decision based on self preservation. I wasn't sure what the mechanic might do if I got him

61

in trouble or fired. The people in the front shop saw me check my wheel and go back into the work area – maybe that was enough.

I let the late morning's unfortunate encounter slip away. I decided to tap more into the positive energy of the breakfast with Wayne and Ellen, and the road ahead. Plus now, I had a meaty new back tire on the bike. I gave it a pat on the side wall, spoke some nice words to it, and filled it in on the upcoming adventures. I even had a quick feeling of remorse for not saying goodbye to the tire that took me to Alaska, and leaving it in that workshop, but decided I was getting a little too attached to my equipment, or basically just losing my mind!

The movement towards California did me good. I was ready to get there and stop for a while. This trip had been long, physically taxing, and full of meetings with inspirational people. I wanted to have time to ponder everything I had experienced. There were, however, still some adventures and lessons awaiting me in Oregon, the one state left between me and California.

I got into mile-eating mode as I headed towards Oregon, which I entered on a main road, but quickly decided to get over to the smaller roads hugging the coast. The miles were slipping by quickly. I had newfound confidence in my back tire, and was glad that I had replaced it – even with the awkwardness involved. I camped out a few nights with the majestic roar of the Pacific in my ears. I stared out across the Pacific, pondering the last few years of my life, then I took a deep breath, and headed south.

I met a guy called Gary traveling in a small pick-up truck at a lookout point on the Oregon coast road; he was about my age, on a solo trip from his native town of Little Rock, Arkansas. We got to talking and wound up eating a very late lunch together. I had only ever met up with other motorcyclists before. It wasn't out of any ill feelings towards other modes of transport, but it just made sense. Motorcycles could weave in and out of traffic, plus it was easier to tell a loaded motorcycle from someone camping in a car or truck as the baggage on a bike is more obvious. Despite our different travel modes, however, Gary and I struck up an instant friendship so we decided to see if we could travel together for the remainder of the day, and camp out together that night.

Gary had a desire to check out some of the sand dunes in the area about 100 miles south of us at Coos Bay. It sounded like a good place to meet up so after lunch I straddled my bike, Gary climbed into his truck, and we both headed south. For a while he was right behind me, but then a slow car and a truck got ahead of us. My bike was far easier to maneuver around both vehicles and head off on the empty road ahead. My throttle hand gave a twist and I was off, the fresh sea air sliding up my leather jacket sleeves like a natural coolant under the hot summer Oregon sun.

The miles slipped away – the road sometimes hugged the coast, and then the ocean would disappear for long stretches of road. As I approached Coos Bay, the sand dunes were becoming more apparent, and I would stop in amazement and look at the miles and seemingly endless miles of dunes. I thought Jones Beach out on Long Island in New York was a long walk to the beach over what we would call 'The Dunes', but these were the real thing. I had no idea that they existed on such a big scale anywhere else than the Sahara Desert.

I arrived first, and much to my surprise Gary was there quite soon after me. He was as impressed with the majesty of the dunes as I was. We both had never been to sand dunes before and the smell of the salty air with the sea birds flying overhead were the only reminder that the ocean was not too far behind these huge mountains of sand. We decided that we would find a campsite and rent some dune buggies the next day.

It was that night where the difference between the two modes of transport became apparent. Whereas all my gear had a certain place, Gary's camping gear and other items were just tossed into the back of the truck. It wasn't a mess, but there seemed to be unending space. Plus I was windblown, a little chilly, and worn out from the long day in the saddle. The one thing that both Eddie and Charley had recommended in Alaska was a small windshield and I decided that that would be my next purchase for the motorcycle when I had spare money. I set my tent up quickly, and put out my sleeping bag and sleeping mat to air out. My sleeping bag wouldn't hurt with a wash, but that would have to wait until I was in California. Airing it out would have to do for the time being. We got to the campsite with more than enough time to start a fire, and let the embers settle in for a nice hot cooking fire. We set out our food to cook, and where the bad energy I'd felt in that shop a few days ago was so apparent, the good energy that we were creating in our small campsite was tangible as well.

Gary was taking the whole summer traveling and camping. He had been to the far north of Canada, but not into Alaska. He enjoyed being alone, and his small truck ensured him his solitude. When I told him of all the people I had met and traveled with since leaving New York he seemed to be amazed. I was drawn to motorcycle travel because it afforded you the best of both worlds; as much solitude as you wanted, but at the same time the openness for someone to come and talk to you – and evey so often – a traveling companion. Gary had met and stayed with lots of interesting people, but his bigger interest was Mother Nature. He knew his birds, trees and insects inside out. He enjoyed doing lots of backwoods hiking and camping, but besides the odd hitchhiker now and again, this was the first time in months he had met someone and then made a plan to meet up down the road. It was nice that we both felt comfortable enough with each other. I had mostly been fortunate with the people I hooked up with on the road, and Gary was yet another interesting person. It felt nice to be fine-tuning my instincts – being able to sense bad or good energies when I came across them.

With the fire building up embers, we gathered more firewood, and by emptying our bags we realized we had enough food for a feast. It was about eight in the evening when we started to cook. I was feeling the fatigue of a long day in the saddle, but I was also quite hungry. Gary was easy to talk to. He enjoyed the company of people, even though a lot of his trip was solo. He was into the idea of renting out dune buggies the next day together. It sounded great especially after seeing the dunes up close. Coos Bay was littered with places to rent the machines, and we would check out what was on offer. We ate a great meal under the Oregon stars, but a mist drifted in and quickly enveloped them as we were washing up our dirty plates. It must have been about ten or eleven by the time I zipped into my sleeping bag; the sunlight was the next thing I remember seeing.

Gary was up already, he had a cooking fire going and the smell of coffee wafted through the tent door as I unzipped it. "Good morning Joe, sleep well?"

"Yes, what about you? Sleep at all?"

He laughed, "I'm an early riser, but I've only been up about half an hour."

I got dressed, and woke up into a proper breakfast; coffee, bread, boiled eggs, and even a bowl of porridge. "Wow, you've had a busy half an hour!" A better breakfast you couldn't find anywhere.

Still sipping our hot coffees we broke camp and headed to a nearby dune buggy rental place. I wasn't to know that today would illustrate my recent philosophical thoughts about never knowing what was in store.

The dune buggy riding was fantastic. I couldn't believe how far you could go without hitting the ocean. I didn't see water at all. Even from the top of some of the high dunes, all you could see was more dunes.

Dune buggies always have roll bars, because dune buggies can roll quite often, as mine did. Most also have straps around the steering wheels for your hands to strap into. Mine didn't, but it had a net. The reason for the straps and nets is to keep your hands inside the vehicle when it rolls – the instinct is to put your hand out to stop it, a silly thing to do. One time my instincts got the better of me – I put my arm out to stop the roll – and before I could pull it back in, it was too late.

The x-ray showed the wrist was broken in three places. Luckily these were the days before insurance companies ruled our world, and you could walk out of an emergency room without having to re-mortgage the house. For seventy-five dollars I saw a doctor, had an x-ray, and was casted up to the elbow of my right arm. My throttle arm! Hmmmm, now what? Gary and I looked at each other and tried to come up with a plan.

I happened to spot a motorcycle repair shop and came up with an idea in my head that I would be able to ride my motorcycle to California anyhow. Gary thought I was crazy, but nonetheless, he rode my motorcycle to the shop, and I drove his truck. When we got there, the owner was quite a nice guy, and when I explained what I wanted done, he thought it was possible – crazy – but possible. I liked him!

Brewer, the owner was about sixty years old or so and his right arm was lame from a stroke. Perhaps this had given him a sense of what was possible when one side of your body is handicapped. Together we managed to change my throttle over to the left-hand side of the bike and, with the use of a thumb-activated throttle which is used on quad bikes, I thought I could make it to San Francisco. It would mean my left hand now had to activate both the clutch and the throttle as well as steering, and braking could only be done with the right foot activating the rear brake. It was only 700 miles! If the accident had happened after a fifty-mile ride, I guess I wouldn't have had to dream up a way of continuing, nor would I have been in that 'anything's possible' mindset, but I had gotten tough on nearly 6,000 miles and obstacles were simply challenges to be overcome. Gary and the owner of the shop were both thinking I was nuts but were giving me the benefit of a very big doubt! To me the options were clear. I was just not going to leave my bike and get on a bus.

Gary had to help me strap my helmet on and I had to find a position I could maintain by leaning my casted arm on the tank bag. We took off down the road heading towards Highway 5, and after a few miles I began to adjust to the new riding method and arrangement. The twists and curves of the coast road were beautiful; I remembered them well from my previous two trips although the concentration needed to ride the bike in this new style changed the experience a little. We went about seventy miles of twisty roads leaving the coast for the interior. Fortunately the weather was good and I was slowly getting used to riding my bike in this awkward way. Gear changing was tricky but I gradually mastered it, and my thumb quickly got very tired from holding down the lever to keep the throttle engaged.

We skipped the idea of camping; setting up a tent would have been a nightmare. Gary was fine with that. He had to help me unload my bike; we got a small room with two beds, and ate in a diner. What a difference to all of our plans. Like water though, we went with the flow. Gary didn't mind changing his route a little, although we would have to part company the next morning. I think he was more curious as to how it would all work out. I knew I would have to ride 700 miles the next day in one shot as there was no way I could do all the loading, unloading and taking on and off of my helmet without Gary's help. The prospect of 700 straight miles wasn't filling me with joy. At least I had my new tire!

The next morning Gary had to help pack my bike and it was a great learning experience for him; everything in its place and no room for just throwing the extra bit of this or that in. Luckily my tank was full, so once I was on my bike I didn't need to get off until a fill up – about 260 miles or so.

I had to blank out the pain in my thumb, and the pain killers I was given for my wrist were never used. I just got on highway 5, stayed in my lane, got lost in thought, and tried not to think about 700 miles, but of exit signs, and much smaller distances. It seemed like ages later when I made it through the first tankful of gas. Putting my tank on reserve was a tricky business – too risky to do while moving – so as soon as my engine spluttered, letting me know I was getting low; I had to pull over to the shoulder, flick up the tiny levers under each side of the gas tank with my left hand, and switch to reserve. My first fill up on my own was difficult, I was trying to not draw any attention to myself as I was not sure if what I was doing was illegal, but didn't want to find out. I undid my helmet, filled up and paid. Then realized I couldn't get my helmet re-strapped. Luckily there were no helmet laws in the states of Oregon and California back then, so I was able to shove my helmet on the back and continue with the next third of the trip.

It was hard going. I was able to block out the pain in my thumb and wrist, but simple things like wiping my dripping nose while moving was too dangerous. I had grown a full beard by now, and it provided something of a sponge for absorbing the mucous. I had to pass through a border control for fruit between California and Oregon, but luckily they didn't care about a motorcyclist with a broken arm, and a sodden beard. I decided to top up the tank; both mine and the bike's, and stopped at a diner. I made it to the bathroom to wash my beard and face before greeting anyone that day – I don't think I would have been such a pleasant sight otherwise! I had to reset my odometer to keep track of the miles, but I had made it to California. I even worked up the nerve to wave to a passing motorcyclist with my casted arm. I was becoming more confident, and when I hit 500 miles done with still plenty of daylight, I was able to count down miles happily.

The highway was pretty straightforward. When I made it to the familiar hilly streets of Oakland and Berkeley manouevering was more challenging; traffic lights, hills, stop signs, and pedestrians. I was glad to have had 700 miles of experience in my new set-up before arriving.

In my quick change of plans I realized I hadn't even called to warn my relatives I would be there. They knew vaguely I was on my way out once again, but that was all the contact. So when I knocked on the door at about seven p.m., looking quite a sight I'm sure, along with the broken wrist, my Uncle Angelo opened the door and looked at me. His first words were, "You didn't come by motorcycle, did you?" I just nodded back at the pavement in front of the house – there was my old faithful. He just shook his head and said, "You are crazy you know," then shouting, "Mary, put out another plate, Joe's here."

I felt like crying with relief. How good did that sound? I'd made it. Not exactly the way I would have wanted to enter California for my third time by motorcycle, but against the odds, and maybe somewhat riskily, I overcame the obstacle thrown in my path, and here I was. The broken wrist was not only a physical challenge, but a defining moment in my travels up to then.

I chose to stay put in California while healing. My bike stayed in the north with my family – to be picked up later on after I healed – while I headed south. My cousin Jen was now living back there. It happened that we would live together for a bit. We grew up in the same house in The Bronx – she and her brother Auggie were more like brother and sister than cousins, her parents more like second parents; it was the extended Italian household, and here it was again. Unfortunately it was the imminent break up of her marriage that offered the opportunity for us to get to know each other on a deeper level, but we both helped each other over a rough period, and before I knew it, I was immersed in the Spanish-speaking world of southern California.

The company Jen worked for was going bankrupt fast. It was 1985 and computers were becoming more popular, but not such a household item as they are now. I had missed the whole computer thing in school and had managed to graduate university with a degree in communications without ever seeing or working on a computer and now I was working for a small computer company.

Since I spoke the second-best Spanish in the small office, I was elected to hire the workers that used to hang out on Wilshire Boulevard looking to earn some money. I worked alongside two guys from Guatemala most of the time, and they were really intriguing me with stories of that country. My arm was healed now, but I did not feel like embarking on a motorcycle journey. I was feeling that my mode of transport needed to be more fluid.

My funds were seriously low, so I had to expand my horizons in the small company which was quickly going under and somehow or another I wound up replacing motherboards in computers for them. This was after a crash course in the office, so now I understood why the company was going under. They were a great bunch of people, but just badly managed. I did enough work for them to have earned some money, but it looked like I needed to find a new job, soon.

I came up with the idea that I would now try to join the Peace Corps. I realized after talking with the recruiter that, if I was honest with myself, I was just looking to the Peace Corps as another means to travel, just like I nearly had with the navy. I saw it clearly while riding my bike back from the office. I needed to fund my own experiences. I had to rely on my own abilities, not ride on the back of organizations, no matter how noble I tried to make them sound. I needed to find another job. I started looking for work the next day.

In L.A. it was easy to be surrounded by the casual drugs and drink that I was coming to think of as a waste of my time, money and life. I decided a good way to test what my relationship was with both of those small vices; so I gave up drinking alcohol and using casual drugs for six months. This little challenge served a dual purpose; it firstly tested my inner strength, and secondly, saved me quite a lot of money. I was learning quite quickly how much cash those habits could consume, no matter how infrequent. I also had put on some weight having the broken wrist. All that eating in diners and riding my motorbike nearly all summer didn't help matters much either. When I stopped drinking alcohol, that weight just slipped right back off my midsection. I learned a lot from those six months.

I wound up working in a music shop in West L.A. It was a fun job close enough to Hollywood so a lot of stars shopped there. We were under strict rules not to ask for autographs, or hassle any of the celebrities coming in. I helped Vanessa Redgrave find albums she liked and sold albums to other familiar Hollywood faces, but the day Bruce Springsteen came in I was out to lunch and my friend Ken was working the register. When I came back from my break, there was Bruce looking very uncomfortable sitting in his black Vette in the parking lot, waiting for something, then out runs our manager, Ed – the one who was strict about the 'no autograph' rule – ripping off the plastic from Bruce's latest album and thrusting it through the window for him to sign. Two sets of rules going on there, I laughed to myself. Ken told me he hadn't been able to help himself either, and had quietly asked Bruce for his autograph after he bagged up his purchases. Ken was a struggling musician, and he told Bruce how he was inspired by him, Bruce gladly signed him a nice autograph which said, 'Ken, Good

Luck, Rock On, Bruce Springsteen'. I wonder what he wrote on Ed's album cover. Of course we all never saw it.

Besides the odd brush with celebrity, I met a woman called Carina there who I dated for a few months. She was a transplant out there like most others I met. She was from the Midwest, her twang reminding me of my various crossings through the hinterland. We began a relationship that was great on many levels, but I knew that my desire to travel and further explore was calling me. We had a good time together; went up north to visit my relatives, spent lots of time on the beach in Santa Monica, took long motorcycle rides, but when I was leaving, I somehow knew, she would not have been interested in coming. I brought it up briefly, but she didn't feign any interest. It was almost a relief. This was my search, and heading south alone felt what I needed to do.

After having saved a few hundred dollars, I once again tore myself away from a comfortable situation. I left the life I had created, but just knew, like my first time in Los Angeles, that it wasn't for me. What I was looking for was somewhere else. People started to ask me what I was running from. In the beginning of my travels I was. I was running from myself, but on the last voyage when I left New York in tears heading to Alaska alone, I knew I was no longer running from anything. I felt more like I was more running *to* something and that I deeply needed to head to Mexico and see where it would take me. Lots of signs were showing me I should go. Even though Carina and I were getting along well, we were on different paths, although we enjoyed walking down each other's for a short time.

The other signs were not so easily ignored. The Guatemalan men I was working with in the now bankrupt computer firm were a great influence to open my mind about heading south, plus one American guy – Reuel, who also worked there – had a Mexican wife and was pushing me to head down to Mexico because he thought I would love it. There was also John Maier. He was ready to pack up and leave L.A. altogether, and had an idea of traveling by bicycle throughout parts of Asia; we had many long talks about cycling, motorcycling, and exploring other countries. The computer company was gone now, but the seeds it planted in my head were beginning to sprout.

Then walked in Crazy Tom; he was a friend of Jen's, an unusual guy and an intense individual, but he owned land in Cabo San Lucas at the tip of the Baja Peninsula, and needed his vehicle transported there – a hundred bucks in it for me, plus transportation for my first two weeks in Mexico – I didn't hesitate to walk through that open door. After all that transpired since that day on the dunes I had to question which my true lucky break was.

# Baptism by Fire – Finding My Path

The first day in Mexico was tough, all the warnings reminiscent of the first time I set out to cross America ringing in my ears – advice that rang with fear of the unknown rather than that of true experience. I was quickly learning that many people's lives were completely driven by fear. The toughest thing for me was leaving the known comfort zone, and the first night I found myself lying alone in a seedy hotel in Ensanada thinking, "What the hell am I doing?" I was confused once again as to what I was actually trying to achieve. I was driven to go further, looking for understanding of myself and the world, but at that point I felt I was losing sight of the big picture. Or perhaps I was finally just getting a glimpse of it? I wasn't sure of anything except that the only thing since graduating college that filled me with inspiration was my travels. I felt that discovery of myself and the wider world could only be positive and was driven to look further, go deeper.

After a few days driving Tom's *VW Thing*, which was a cross between a jeep and a car, with the somewhat prophetic personalized license-plate reading *YBNORMAL*, I began to feel more settled. Carina and the last romantic, tearful night we spent with each other kept appearing in my head to upset and confuse me, but I kept heading south. In my greatest moment of self doubt I found myself sharing a table with three fellow travelers. I heard them speaking English and had invited myself over to join them. They were friendly and welcoming and asked about me and what I was doing. I ended up blurting out how I wasn't sure that I had done the right thing by leaving my girlfriend behind. They looked at me and said, "If you really loved her, and she you, either she'd be here, or you there." They were the words I needed to hear at that moment to confirm what I was doing was the right thing as I immediately felt lighter and more carefree than I had since leaving. The next day I was able to begin to enjoy things without doubt crowding into my head too much.

Before delivering the vehicle for Tom, I was determined to pick up a hitcher. I had been warned that this was too dangerous but I had learnt not to take on other people's anxieties. I knew I had to extinguish the seeds of fear that had been planted before they were allowed to take root and become real for me. I picked up a young Mexican kid on his own, and was able to take him right to the door of his parents' house. He was one of the many illegal workers that make it over the border to work in *El Norté, Los Estados Unidos* – the country of my birth. He spoke some English but we communicated by slipping in and out of both languages.

When we arrived at his family's small house the slight detour I had taken was made well worth it to see the warm embraces and kisses thrust upon him from his little sisters and brothers when they opened the door. His parents were incredibly grateful to me for delivering their son safely back home, and I was a little embarrassed at the amount of praise I was given for simply giving the young guy a lift. I was invited in for a cold drink and to stay to eat and wasn't allowed to refuse. Miguel, my hitcher, apologized for not being able to offer me a place to stay but I wouldn't even hear of it. I felt bad enough stopping over for dinner.

The meal was a simple affair; a scrawny chicken, rice and beans and plenty of hot sauce but the warmth of the company more than made up for anything lacking on the table. I wanted to get going and leave Miguel to his family. I asked if he knew of a place for me to stay, and he insisted on coming with me to find it. We went out to Cabo San José, which was not far, and Miguel found a cheap, clean local place for me to spend the night. The price was quite reasonable, and I think Miguel must have known the man, for it felt more like the local price I was paying. I wanted to drive him back home, but he insisted on finding his own way. I wished him luck with getting back to the States, and told him to enjoy being with his family. He gave me a big smile, but his eyes showed a little heaviness of the two worlds he lived in; a small town boy in his village on the Baja Peninsula, and his other life as a *wetback* – a Mexican illegal worker doing itinerant work in America always looking over his shoulder waiting to be found out. His family loved their son, but the money he made working in California was more than his entire family could earn in Cabo San José, so Miguel's life was to be lived in that murky world. I was glad to have helped in my small way, and even happier to shatter another illusion of fear.

The Baja was a beautiful way to start my journey in Mexico. It still holds the feeling of California and gradually becomes more and more Mexican as you go further south. The peninsula is a wonderful place. Once you break the reaches of the infamous border town of Tijuana, and get just past the beach town of Ensenada, you feel like you have broken contact with California. The desert scenes were beautiful with sandy beaches stretching out as far as you could see dotted with small idyllic fishing villages. Sometimes I would sit on the eastern side of the peninsula, staring out over the 'Sea of Cortes' knowing that the mainland of Mexico was just across that strip of water. I once witnessed a few fishermen on a boat not much bigger than the row boats you could rent out in City Island back in The Bronx come back with a haul of hammerhead sharks. It made me think twice about taking a swim, but greater than the worry of sharks was how the whole scene felt so foreign to me. The humanity was the same as the life I had left behind; the familiarity of people's actions and their

71

interchanges with each other, but the backdrop of scenery, language and lifestyle was so vastly different from anything I had ever experienced before that I was beginning to tingle through my whole body. Familiarity and foreignness co-existing within me gave me a strange feeling, one of expansion and possibilities. I held the vision of Miguel's smiling family and it made me feel sad that borders had to exist; I wished we could all figure out a better way.

Before making it to Cabo San Lucas I did get stopped by machine-gun-carrying *Federales* – Mexico's national police force – at a checkpoint. These were the officers I had been warned about – all crooked and bound to rob me. I had no doubt there were crooked policemen in Mexico, but I had nothing to hide in the car, and tried not to come from a place of fear. I communicated in Spanish, which was improving, and was sent off with a wave. Fear, I was learning, was something that you cultivated; staring down fear, and not accepting it, was also something you had to nurture.

After delivering the vehicle and spending a couple of nights in the American enclave known as Cabo San Lucas situated at the tip of the Baja Peninsula, I was ready to get to the mainland of Mexico. I now had no car, and was at the mercy of buses, trains and boats. I was new to these modes of travel being so used to having a motorcycle, and having always been in an English-speaking country. Although my motorcycle journeys had been challenging in themselves, I had never yet left America or Canada. But now here I was on a boat heading to the mainland of Mexico.

On the crossing I met some locals from Topolobampo, the town where the ferry docked. They were friendly, as were most of the people I was meeting, and I stayed in that town for two days meeting up with them a few times for dinner and conversation. My Spanish was improving but I cursed myself for not having been a better student. I was buzzing on being 'South of the Border'. With a bus ticket in hand I would soon be much further south.

It was 1986 and The Soccer World Cup was taking place in Mexico. It made me realize what a different life we lived in America; most of the world was glued to their television screens to follow the progress of the 'football' (as the rest of the world calls it) tournament that happens every four years, but in 1986 back home not many people that I knew had even heard about the World Cup.

One very long bus ride later I was bleary-eyed, but well and truly in the heart of Mexico. I probably wasn't as well-rested as the spare driver of the bus. After the first breakdown we all had to disembark and when we did, they opened what I thought was the luggage hold underneath, but lo and behold out climbed a driver from what looked to be his sleeping quarters. I was amazed. It was the middle of the night, and at first I thought I was seeing things incorrectly, but on the long overnight marathon journeys the spare driver slept underneath. What an excellent use of space. When we got on the bus once again, I felt sorry for the driver being shut away under the bus for the night, but after the twentieth hour of shifting awkwardly in a small seat trying to get comfortable, and possibly get a few winks of sleep, I was ready to crawl underneath and beg to share a place to stretch out in. I was quickly adjusting to my new modes of transport, and beginning to enjoy them, even with all the discomforts. With at least one more breakdown, we finally made it to San Miguel de Allende.

I decided to look up the family of Reuel. It was a good lesson in perception. Reuel was convinced that his wife's mother hated him for taking his daughter away so he had given me their address, but told me maybe it was better not to mention his name. They ran a guest house so it wouldn't be difficult to say I just happened upon their place. The town was full of artists and retired Americans stretching out their budgets, living alongside the locals. I was always led to believe that the world waited on lines in American embassies to be let in to the country where the streets were paved with gold. This was the first time I had met Americans making conscious decisions to live outside of their native land. Some were political or financial refugees, some were artists, some students, and some were just doing what they could to try and live a more fulfilling life. They all had varied lives and were walking paths different than any I had encountered in the U.S. I was intrigued to meet these people who had somehow seen a world outside the ones they had grown up in and chosen to step into it.

I found Reuel's in-law's place with the help of a local who knew the street. I remember it clearly to this day, *Numero 5 Calle de Guadalupe*. I knocked on their door and asked if they had a room, they did. I was shown into the kitchen and the woman who had answered the door bustled around getting me a cold drink and chatting amiably. I felt a bit of a fraud sitting there letting her think I had just by chance found her place. I was looking around the room when I happened to notice a stack of mail sitting on the table. The letter on top had an American postmark and the return name and address; Reuel Frankel. I now felt compelled to tell the truth. When Maria José came back with the cool drink I pointed to the letter, held my breath briefly, and then just came out with it, "Reuel is my friend, I worked with him in California, he told me about your place." After that, it was all smiles and I was treated like a king; how wrong he appeared to be.

I cooked one night for the family which turned out to be quite an amusing affair. I used to watch my mom make pizza, but the dough was bought in the local pizzeria, and the other ingredients were bought from local supermarkets, bagged and ready to go, so when Maria and I went to the local outdoor market where most of the world's population shops, my ignorance came beaming through. We had to buy everything fresh, even some of the spices. The dough I made with the help of the daughters; willingness and a lot of laughs seemed to be the right ingredients and it all turned out okay. The sauce was a little more challenging but I somehow managed to rustle up something respectable from the tomatoes we had bought; maybe I had absorbed some of mom's talent by osmosis. I somehow produced a huge homemade pizza and it was a hit. Luckily it was much bigger than I bargained for; it had to be put out on two large cookie sheets. It was just as well, for when dinnertime came, kids and adults appeared out of the woodwork making fifteen hungry appetites instead of the seven I had planned for.

What a great meal! No stress, and whether it was through kindness, hunger or genuine enjoyment, that pizza disappeared quickly. Reuel's mother-in-law had two more daughters living at home, and I think she had me picked out for one of them. At that point I would have had to admit to running from something, and that was her daughter Maria. She was nice enough; pretty with the classic beautiful big brown eyes of the Mexican people, but I hadn't come to get married. We spent a few fun days, went out dancing, and despite lots of flirting going on and even a little kissing, I escaped unmarried. My Spanish was improving greatly so I felt ready to head further south. Next stop, Mexico City.

At the bus station I met an English guy called Jason who knew Mexico City as he was doing business there. It was nice to have someone to talk to on the long bus journey and we decided to room together at a cheap place he knew. On arriving we found the hotel not far from the *Zocalo* which turned out to be an excellent place to stay in the heart of the city. It was an incredible mix of people, rich *Mestizos* – those of mixed European and Indigenous blood – mingling with impoverished Indians from small villages or the shanty towns on the limits of the city. On one hand the buzz of a city that was hosting the internationally famous World Cup and on the other beggars and utter poverty. The contrast was mind-boggling.

What an incredible experience – Mexico City at the time had 16,000,000 inhabitants – to share the streets with so much humanity was nearly beyond belief. The *Zocalo* – a huge square in the middle of this overcrowded city – was the largest open area in the Americas. Ongoing protests were happening, and it looked as though people permanently lived there in makeshift tents. Mexico City – or *DF* (*Districto Federale*) as it is commonly known – suffered from the worst air pollution in the world, and it was known for birds to drop out of the sky dead. Children had to walk to school well after the rush hour in the morning for fear of developing pollution-induced asthma.

About twenty-five miles from the city was *Teotihuacan* – an archeological site with two large pyramids – one for both the sun and the moon. It was believed to be one of the largest self-contained cities in the Americas 2,000 years ago; the people had mysteriously vanished and left behind the abandoned site including the 'Avenue of the Dead' and other dwellings, but not much else to help modern man explain their existence and sudden disappearance.

The pyramids were stunning in their beauty, and awesome in their otherworldliness. I climbed to the top of both and was exhausted at their summit then quickly blown away by the enterprising young kids selling postcards and fake 'archeological' artifacts they had somehow managed to trudge up to the top. I wished I had their lungs and entrepreneurial spirit.

I also went to watch a bullfight – not my preferred way to pass the time, but intriguing nonetheless. I found out I was in the world's largest bullring, and then proceeded to watch seven bulls being taunted, teased and slaughtered. It wasn't what I'd call a fair fight. When the *matador*, literally 'killer' in English, finally came out – his slight body regaled in a colorful costume with the tell-tale red cape draped over his forearm – to face the exhausted, frustrated animal after at least twenty minutes of chasing, poking and prodding by the *picadors*, I was nearly relieved for the bull's imminent demise. The overheated animal now had seven or eight bobbed pointed arrows protruding from his bloodied flanks, and the *matador's* fun and games began. Deftly handling the red cape he occasionally brought the poor bull to its knees as it mustered every last bit of energy to seek revenge on his final nemesis. When the sword finally found the bull's heart the crowds went crazy – the *matador* was a hero. If he missed the target the bull suffered even longer and the *matador* wasn't awarded the crowning trophy – the bull's ears. Cutting off the ears was considered the prize for a good, clean, skillful kill. What a non-fitting ending for such a majestic beast.

The pageantry involved and the colorful costumes worn by the *picadors* and *matadors* were splendid to see. The *matador's* use of the red cape was exhilarating, but I couldn't help siding with the bull – which actually provoked loud cheers when it jumped out of the ring or nearly gored one of its tormentors. Cheering for the bull though was tantamount to cheering for the Christians against the lions – much like the bulls, they didn't have a chance. For all the costumes, colors and energy that went into the killing, the red blood-stained earth was still the image burnt into my mind's eye as they dragged the fatally-wounded victims away. I couldn't conceive that this archaic blood sport was also popular throughout Latin America, areas of Spain, Portugal and France too.

To appease our obvious sensibilities to the brutality of the whole scene, the person sitting beside us let us know, between his shouts of *olé* and cheering for the *matador*, that the meat would be served up in the local schools for food. Probably better ways to kill the animals, but slaughter houses weren't a barrel of fun either I assumed. I was baffled by the sheer lust for blood, but then I was in a bloody part of the world where even Jesus on the cross in the churches was depicted with more blood trickling down his face and body then I ever remembered seeing.

I went up the Latin American Tower – the tallest building in Latin America – to try and see through the haze of the city. It was all so new to me; coming from New York I felt at home in a big city, but combined with the foreign culture, I was overwhelmed. The streets filled with traffic and bustling with activity, pyramids on the perimeter, bullfights in the center, shouts and conversations all around me in high-speed Spanish scrambled my brain and I once again felt that unidentified feeling of expansion into a world of 'otherness'. It was all here, existing just as I was seeing it now, during my youth growing up in The Bronx. How much else must there be to see? I couldn't wait to explore more.

I was in some strange way enjoying being confronted by humanity in all its devastation, and its differences. I felt it shift something inside of me. It seemed a more real representation of the world we lived in somehow. Here I was, in a land sharing an American border, able to come the whole way on bus. Although I spent time in poor areas of New York City and went to many parties in the South Bronx during my university days, nothing I had seen compared to the poverty which was now staring me in the face and the difference in culture right on my doorstep in North America's largest city. I was starting to question other things about my life and lifestyle – slowly realizing how much more I had to learn.

Politics had always intrigued me in a small way; Vietnam, Watergate etc. were the backdrop of my and everybody else's childhood who grew up in the late sixties and seventies in America. At twelve I was campaigning for John McGovern for president. I always questioned the status quo, church doctrine and authority, much to my parents' chagrin. I enjoyed shattering pre-conceived ideas and finding my own way. Even the lessons of 'Three Mile Island' in my last year of high school and the whole nuclear debate hadn't awoken me as much as seeing a small protest in Mexico City. University, motorcycles, and too much partying had put to sleep some of those other sides of me. My dormant, ever-questioning self was now re-awakening.

The dispute, when I probed further, was due to the fact that none of the workers in the McDonald's where the demonstration was taking place could afford to buy a meal in the establishment with the pittance they were paid. Speaking to the young man holding up a sign and chanting something I couldn't quite make out, hit a chord deep inside. Everything else was just another news item or story in a newspaper. There was nothing like coming face to face with injustice, and seeing this large corporation taking advantage of its workers in that way made me think and begin to understand. I thought how important it was to try to put faces to the news flashes or articles, if not we become numb to our world's realities.

I was on my way to the train station when I witnessed the protest and all these thoughts were spinning round in my head as I arrived there to be confronted with another inconceivable scene. It was a different world to the city streets I had just been walking on; crowds everywhere, people carrying what looked like their lives around in bundles, women with three, four or five children in tow, begging. I couldn't make out who was traveling, who lived right there in the station, or where the ticket office was. I finally figured it out after stepping over people, children and small livestock and somehow managed to buy a ticket for Oaxaca.

It was a fourteen-hour train journey to Oaxaca amongst chickens, pigs, heat, and people selling all sorts of delicious foods at the train platforms. The food had a small resemblance to the Mexican food I had eaten in America, but this was slightly different. The ingredients available were more restricted to areas – the Mexican food in America was more of a mélange but here the food was regional. Just like any food making it to a melting pot like America, the ingredients available are different, and there is no way a menu of food can represent a country as big as Mexico. I tasted *molé* sauce for the first time in Mexico City and on the train journey I had a chicken and *molé* sauce that tasted nothing like that first chocolate spice sauce I'd had. *Molé* is a varied sauce that has up to twenty-four spices and chili peppers in it – it takes three days to make and a lifetime to perfect. I could not find a burrito anywhere, but tostadas, smothered in guacamole, and bags of avocado were easy to find. Mexico was a feast for the palate, as well as every other sense, and I had never seen anything like it. Humanity was bursting out all over. Poverty confronting me at every turn, but so were smiles. I didn't know what to think. I just sat, observed, conversed, wrote in my journal, and soaked it all in.

Once in Oaxaca I searched out a hotel on the outskirts, grabbed a quick nap amongst the cockroaches – something I was learning were more prevalent here than in the New York restaurant scene – and a lukewarm shower, then headed to the main square to greet Oaxaca and see what was in store for me there. I met up with a bunch of American hippies who were an interesting group of sixteen or so; men, women and kids all traveling together. We sat on the square and talked about many things. The square was alive; musicians busking, kids with bare feet begging, foreigners strolling around, delicious smells coming from the different food stalls. I was hungry and decided to brave the street food. I had no idea how long I would be down here and to be overly-cautious about food would get boring. Anyway, the food looked good and I liked supporting the small guy. I tried to pick a clean stall and was joined by one of the people from the group of hippies I met who all enjoyed eating from the street sellers.

They were American by birth, but had been traveling in Latin America for more than a year. They questioned corporate America, and although were not vegetarian they always supported the smaller food places. If living in a place for a longer period of time they would only eat meat they had raised and slaughtered themselves. We talked about slaughter houses, hormones, animal rearing in commercial enterprises, and the devastation of rainforests in South America because of large corporations selling hamburgers. I thought of my brief trial at being vegetarian during college. It hadn't been easy – I really hadn't known what to eat although my mom tried to help me out but struggled knowing what to cook. It didn't last long, but now I was being faced with the effects of eating meat, and the repercussions of not questioning one of the most basic things we do, nurturing our bodies. My eyes and ears were open, and I was listening.

During our conversation on the outskirts of the lively square in Oaxaca, I realized that choices we make do affect the wider world. They were sharing the streets with me right now. In America we were taught to become happy consumers; keep the economy going, don't question where your food comes from, how the cattle are reared, who makes the cheap plastic toys your children play with, etc. just get into debt, and continue on the treadmill which keeps corporate America ticking over. Brady's long beard, bright eyes and passion was infectious. The night passed quickly with us deep in conversation.

Brady invited me out to the house they were staying in. I decided to walk there the next day, and take him up on his invitation to lunch. On my way there I ran into my first encounter with a corrupt police officer who tried to take advantage of his uniform. I was walking past a checkpoint for trucks, but as I walked by, I was beckoned over with the wave of a gun by the police officer manning the post. Okay, I thought to myself, you've done nothing wrong. The conversation took place in Spanish, and went something like this.

"Hello *gringo*, you're American?"

"Yes officer, I am." I had a small backpack with my camera and a light jacket in case it got colder in the hills around Oaxaca. I had already been walking for about an hour by this point.

"Open your bag please, Americano." He was already making me feel uneasy.

I opened my bag, and he and his friend, who was not in uniform saw my camera and lens. "Your passport please."

For some stupid reason I hadn't brought it with me. I wasn't used to traveling in places where I even needed a passport. "It's back at the hotel."

Now his eyes brightened a bit, "You go get your passport, and I will hold your camera here until you get back." His friend, who sat silently looking red-eyed, just smirked.

Yeah right. I may have been new to traveling in foreign countries, but I wasn't an idiot. I thought quickly, "I'm an American citizen and don't need to carry my passport with me." Now I took some liberties with the truth. "I'm visiting my uncle who works for the U.S. Embassy in Mexico City, and don't want any trouble." I felt that maybe some link with someone in authority might scare this guy into dropping any funny business – I was desperate not to lose my camera. Remarkably, at that point, a car pulled up a few yards away, and I noticed it was a taxi. "And there's my taxi." I said without missing a beat.

I took my backpack, walked over to the taxi, jumped in the back seat and said, "Go, go! I have *pesos*, just head that way." The police officer began walking over to the car, and I said once again, "Please just go, I will pay you." He looked at me, and the officer approaching, and must have decided I was the better bet. He took off, and I looked back at the officer who just turned on his heels and headed back to his small booth. I was shaken up as the taxi drove on and I asked him to stop about a mile away. I was getting close to my turn off according to the hand-drawn map Brady had given me. I handed the confused driver a few hundred *pesos*, said, "*Gracias.*" He smiled, pulled a u-turn, and drove off.

As I stood watching the taxi disappear in the dust, I was suddenly caught in an incredible hail storm. The hail stones were as big as golf balls. I ran to take shelter under a tree, shivering and wondering what on earth could happen next before I made it to my destination. I was still thrown off kilter from the whole interchange with the police officer, but was very glad not to have lost my camera.

Finally arriving at the commune, I was warmly welcomed and we soon got to talking. I discovered that they had just come from Dangriga in Belize and their stories of that country intrigued me. Oddly enough Brady's son's name was Reuel and I told him how I was here in Mexico by the prompting of a person I worked with who had the same name. Being a not so common name, we both took that as a sign that our meeting was meant to be.

I relaxed into their company; enjoying the conversation and my first experience of a true commune. Some of the kids were products of the trip. I was so happy seeing a young baby in a sling breastfeeding, thinking about all the experiences that that youngster was already having. We ate a beautiful vegetarian meal cooked from local produce bought in the market the day before in Oaxaca. I told them about my encounter with the officer, and explained why I was a little nervous to walk back the same way. They told me of the local bus to Oaxaca and I opted to return that way instead of walking, which also gave me an extra hour or so to stay with Brady and his extended family.

My stomach was tender from sampling the street food, my body was tired from overnight train journeys and twenty-four-hour bus rides, my head was reeling from trying to get to grips with a foreign language, dealing with corrupt officials, my level of comfort was pushed to its limits in the cheap hotels amongst the tiny insects and occasional small rodents I shared my rooms with, plus I was overwhelmed by the poverty right on the border of America, but I absolutely loved it. I felt more a piece in the bigger jigsaw puzzle of our world, not the separate one called America. I felt a connection, a kinship or solidarity with the rest of humanity that I had been separated from, and I wanted more. There was a richness here I was slowly finding. It was not a richness in monetary terms, but a richness of culture, family, life lived in the squares at night, children and parents together, music, food. It was all served up with smiles and a sincerity that was quickly fading in the big supermarkets, fast food places and seven days a week shopping of home. The emphasis here was on quality, not quantity. For me, that was wealth.

After Oaxaca, I made it to a place called San Cristobal De Las Casas, in the state of Chiapas. The *mestizo* population which had been dominant so far was the definite minority in Chiapas. The simplicity and kindness of the indigenous people was heart-warming. The poverty did not take away the joy that emanated through their dark brown expressive eyes. It was a combination that I had been taught was mutually exclusive and it felt foreign and wonderful to me. In San Cristobal I met travelers and people from all over the globe who were living there. Some had opened restaurants or small hostels; others were working with the locals in different ways – teaching English, working with the homeless, or just simply raising awareness to this part of the world. It was a different version of San Miguel, but again, people were living lives that they had chosen. Every restaurant had a vegetarian option. The few conversations I got into with American dropouts, traveling Europeans or locals, all brought up the same point; personal choices make a huge difference, the struggle here was not much different than the struggle in Tibet and elsewhere in the developing world, even America had its closet full of skeletons. I had witnessed the squalor of that quick visit to an Indian reservation while on my first crossing of America with Gary which prompted me to read, *I*

*Buried My Heart at Wounded Knee,* learning about broken treaties and trust betrayed. Although I had not gone through another reservation on my consequent trips; possibly trying to avoid the reality, not to see the inevitable. Well, like it or not I was faced with it all quite candidly now, and I was ready to understand what it meant.

I sat silently and took it all in. I was listening to ideas that I had only just touched on previously. Now I was learning – up close – the other truths which existed, the page twenty-seven column two in the free press. It took me too long to find the lesser known stories, but I blamed myself for that. The struggles I was now witnessing were right on the same continent where I grew up, the same land where I stared in awe of its unending physical beauty from my motorcycle seat. Being in these small villages made the discussions at parties, or debates on social injustice of my college days jump back to life and somehow take on a deeper meaning. It was my best social studies class ever, and nothing compared to the jump I was about to take.

I met an American named Gary and a Frenchman called Richard and we all took a hike together on the outskirts of San Cristobal. Gary was a photographer, who was trying to create a small postcard business to help the Guatemalans affected by the ongoing civil war. His stories of that country pushed me into heading to the embassy to get a visa so I too could go there. I left the Guatemalan Embassy feeling like a real traveler. I was so new to all of this, now here I was with a visa for a country in Central America!

What little I had heard of Guatemala by that point in my life didn't prepare me for the reality. Although my time in Mexico had started the process, the country and region of the world I was about to enter would change how I saw myself, my country, my life, my friends, family and even my existence for ever. For me it seemed unbelievable that I had come down mostly by bus. A road to *El Norté* existed – no airplanes, if you wanted you could walk. The first time when Gary, Richard and I stepped out of the back of that pick-up truck, Gary said to this naïve twenty-four-year-old, "Get ready for your life to change as you now enter the third world!" He couldn't have been more right; those few steps crossing into Guatemala left my head spinning. It was like the moonlanding commentary – "One small step for Joe's body, one giant leap for his consciousness."

People in colorful traditional dress, big smiles on their faces, dark-skinned and open, their facial features obviously more akin to Native Americans than my European features, greeted me and I was thrown into a world where I felt like an intruder. Was I an American? What was an American? Were these descendants of the ancient Mayan culture more connected to the North American continent than I would ever be? Guatemala taught me so much about myself, and the part of the world I thought I knew so well. I couldn't stop myself from wanting more. I met European travelers, Australians, Americans. I learned things about my country's jaded past, assassinations, military coup d'etats, puppet leaders replacing democratic elected presidents, civil war, all in the name of democracy, or dare I say freedom? In reality, all for the almighty protection of corporate interests. I was learning all too quickly that I had been raised in a bubble and had only ever been taught from one perspective.

The decade of the fifties, I was learning, was a conundrum. In America it was hot rods, *Happy Days*, and the prosperous years after the Second World War. It was the exponential growth of the American suburb during which America's thirst for the bigger and better had been nurtured. As Americans at home were nicely wrapped in their blanket of freedom and democracy, a certain senator McCarthy was making some people uncomfortable, demonizing anything that went against that grain, pointing the finger at so called 'communists'. History would show us it was a misguided witch-hunt. In Guatemala the American corporate-backed communist witch-hunt showed a different, even more sinister side – the ousting of a democratically elected leader – Jacobo Arbenz – which threw the country into a state of civil war for nearly four decades, but re-instated the United Fruit Company, an American corporation which stood to lose land and money if Mr. Arbenz succeeded in transforming Guatemala's economy. The population had not recovered, and the wounds were still open.

The fifties saw the newly formed CIA in America wielding its strength, experimenting with new forms of torture and military coups. Not only was Central America its new experimental ground, another leader in Iran was 'replaced' with The Shah – a man who brutally ruled there for a quarter century. The repercussions of this came back to haunt America with quite sensational headlines in 1979 – *The Iran Hostage Crisis*. I had dutifully joined the masses screaming out "Free the Hostages" or "Fuck Iran" having no idea of America's complicity in the whole situation.

Nationalization, protection of mineral and other natural resources, and possible transformation of the poorer countries of the world stood in the way of unbridled western capitalism which was on the rise. Communism was a big scary word, and worked well in getting public opinion behind many disasters, in the beginning of the sixties, Vietnam being the next.

I would see throughout my travels that the fifties, sixties and seventies for the world at large had been a human rights disaster. The seeds planted in Central and South America, the Mid-East, The Congo, Northern Africa and Indo China would all come back slowly to bite back and once again trick the world into thinking that events just spontaneously happen – it is one of the biggest lies ever perpetrated. Every action has a reaction, and none of the problems we face in the present are surprises if you just look back in history. I had been led to believe that people in other countries were different from me; from an American. I had found something here – just a few hundred miles south of the American border – that I had been zooming across America on my motorcycle to find.

In Guatemala I visited some much-visited Mayan ruins, but it was in the little known places in the highlands, the village of Nebah where I saw sights that still stick in my mind. Nebah consisted mostly of widows and children after all the men of the village died in atrocities carried out by government troops to stamp out 'communist' sympathizers. That hazy word once again. Could you substitute 'Freedom Fighters' for 'communists'? Would the founding fathers of America have been called communists because they fought against the colonizing powers? Nonetheless, I was still greeted with smiles and gorgeous scenery at every turn. I was too distracted by it all to stay put and start volunteering or do something on a more altruistic level. I was still on a crash course in life; my funds were running very low and my health was suffering a bit, but I was confronted with so much that I felt cheated. I felt like I hadn't been told the whole story; hadn't been allowed to make up my own mind. Did I want to be part of the system that chewed up and spat people out under the guise of freedom, democracy or free markets? Was our system somehow failing if so many on our planet were still suffering? Hadn't we fought wars to end suffering? If I was rich as a direct result of others' misery, there was something wrong. I had not been given a choice; I was automatically signed up at birth, and then shown only one side of the story. Again I blame myself for not digging deeper sooner, but now I had my spade.

On Good Friday I stumbled upon a colorful ceremony, which like many, had come from Spain. The locals were on their knees from sunrise decorating the streets with an *alfambra* (carpet) of beautiful, intricate designs made of sawdust. The time consuming effort was done as everything else seemed to be done in Guatemala, from the heart. Then at three in the afternoon, the local priest followed by a huge entourage of followers carrying heavy depictions of 'The Passion of Christ' on their weary shoulders would stride up the street reducing the artwork to piles of colorful dust in their wake. The local people lucky enough to carry this burden through the streets also had to pay for the privelege. In a land where hard work was a way of life, and poverty the norm, on one of the few days people did stop plowing the fields, or carrying their large sacks to the markets to sell their wares or foodstuffs, surely the church could harness all the energy and man-time in much better ways. The procession slowly wound its way through the narrow streets sending me off in thought. The colorful hand-woven clothing and small cowboy hats worn by the men jolted me back to the reality of where I now stood.

Another church-related stop was in a small village called Chi Chi Castenango, where there was a Catholic church. Inside it was not at all what I would have expected. There were no pews, and it was full of smoke from burning candles and incense, normal for a church, but that was where the similarity ended. Where the pews would normally be there were photos of people and strange looking idols. Surrounding these were little braziers with burning incense sticks or candles. I looked around in amazement wondering if I had been correct in assuming that his was really a church. I walked back outside to confirm that, yes, it was a Catholic Church. After all there was an altar. I started speaking to an older man who was sitting outside in his traditional dress. He spoke Spanish, but his native tongue was one of the many indigenous languages spoken throughout Guatemala. I asked about the strange set-up of the church and he went on to explain that on Sundays the chairs are moved in and the priest comes to give his sermon. The older people are allowed to pray to their gods; the god of maize, or a sun god – they even put curses on people who have done them wrong – but on Sunday it is the Christian God and Jesus who are praised from the altar.

He went on to explain that in due time when the older generation dies out, the gods and idols will be replaced by Christian Saints, the Virgin and crucifixes. The younger people would slowly forget their old religions and ways, and magically everyone would be a Christian. He had seen it before, and this was one of the few churches left in the area that still allowed the practice of praying to other gods. I struggled internally between the knowledge that Christians and missionaries can do good, but I felt that other countries were entitled to develop their own belief systems. Was this the true role of religion, to create a system of good and bad, right and wrong, my religion and your religion? It didn't feel correct. Has much changed since the time of the colonizers? Christopher Colombus sailed for the cross, and history has not been so kind to his memory, millions killed in the name of Christianity, and mostly for the material wealth found in this part of the 'New World'.

My questioning of organized religion began when I was sixteen – for me I felt clearly that something couldn't be right when it prevailed through bloodshed or deceit, and then call itself an instrument of God. In highs chool I met Father Bob and he turned me on to spirituality. He allowed me to see things in a different light; he didn't adhere to the strictness of church doctrine and his belief in Jesus came from a more human perspective, not punishment, fear and guilt. For the first time I saw the whole Bible story in a different light; I was allowed to find out where the story fitted into my life, or indeed if it did. I then heard Father Bob was in trouble with his superiors from the church for his radical views. After that I left the church. I couldn't believe that the one person who had been my connection to a spirituality that felt real inside of me had been excommunicated. I knew then that organized religion was not my path, but now I was questioning more and digging deeper into my being and frankly it scared me. The stakes were much higher now. I had been thrown into a world I somehow knew existed on a deeper level, and subconsciously had been searching for, but now that I'd found it, I could not hide it away. I had broken bread with these people hidden from history, I had laughed and smiled with them, fallen in love with the beauty of their countryside, looked into their deep brown eyes, played with their children, enjoyed their hospitality. It meant I would have to be open-minded, willing to accept that nothing is perfect, and realize being part of the solution is a lot more difficult than being part of the problem. It made me question what exactly it meant to be a responsible American and to accept that the suffering of these people and my lifestyle were intertwined.

My journey took me to a place named Panajachel, which was dominated by a volcano and a lake named 'Atitlan'. It reminded me – in its dominance of indigenous people – of San Cristobal in Mexico, although topographically it was vastly different.

Panajachel wasn't an easy place to get to; a steep, unpaved, pot-holed road wound its way down to the small village on the shore of the large lake. The hilly shores of the lake rose abruptly into the surrounding volcanoes. You could walk around the lake, find a place to block off some of the hot sulfur volcano-fed water, and then sit for hours in the soothing curative waters away from the rest of the world. Boat rides across the lake would bring you to villages cut out from the jungle with a few basic places to eat and stay. People in colorful, traditional dress, little girls weaving, the foliage, no cars – it was hard to believe you were on the same continent with shopping malls, large cities, airports and all the mod cons of life. You were easily transported away in time and head space.

Panajachel had a few restaurants; some owned or run by locals, others by foreigners. Having met up with Richard again it was here that we found ourselves surrounded by the local weavers and I decided to buy a few hundred friendship bracelets. I had no idea what I was going to do with them but it was a fun hour or so making deals with the little local girls who made their living braiding these colorful trinkets. I wound up buying over 700 of them after getting caught up in the moment. We both had a great laugh with the young girls and I thought maybe I could sell them in New York at a flea market and that it would somehow open up conversation about the part of the world I was now in. It was fun buying them but in the end I wound up traveling with them for years afterwards and giving them away to people I met, which worked just as well. All of my friends and family had at least one tied around their wrist, and knew where they came from. I'm not sure if I had more fun giving them away or buying them.

A scene I witnessed for the first time in Guatemala, but one that would constantly repeat itself throughout my travels later in life, put into perspective a household chore I had seen my mom doing all my life: the laundry. In The Bronx nearly every house had a clothesline in the backyard. My mom would hang out the washing on a line which was strung from my bedroom window to a pole at the end of the back garden. I never questioned owning a washing machine, didn't everyone have one? Everyone on my block did, that was for sure. Now though, as I was waiting for a bus on a crossroads aptly named *Quatros Caminos* or 'the four roads', I thought I heard laughter and kids playing.

Intrigued, I climbed a small hillock behind me to get a better look and at first I thought there had been some sort of accident. Clothing was strewn about everywhere and the place was crawling with women and children. Had one of the many overloaded trucks tipped over and thrown everyone out all over the road? Maybe the laughter was screams? I quickly re-adjusted my brain, took in the scene and chuckled at myself. It was indeed laughter; laughter of naked children playing in a small muddy river. The colorful clothing fanned out across the fields was drying laundry, and in the river were the women of the village, their traditional dresses hoiked up around their knees, some with tiny babies on their backs, knee deep in muddy soapy water hand washing the family laundry; smiles, laughter, and banter permeated the magical atmosphere. Where there were normally great expanses of green, now there were vibrant reds and burnt oranges, peacock blues and luminescent yellows. This non-sequitur added to the calm chaos of it all. The women were bent over large stones, pounding and wringing out the water. Once the item of clothing was clean to an acceptable degree, a small child would help spread it out to dry. It completely challenged my perception of a simple task. Another humbling experience, but like the hundreds of women I would pass in Mexico and Guatemala on their way to the market places, carrying heavy loads, baskets balanced on their heads and young ones on their backs, it was done with a feeling of community, and where the male seemed to be absent from many of these labor intensive tasks, the women had a bond between them borne of the toughness of their common station in life; a common thread in my travels – the hard-working female and the absent male. Sometimes the absent male was dead due to war or other atrocities, perhaps other times the males were at work in factories or out of sight. It was a puzzle, but made me appreciate the way that women keep life going. Although there were many differences between the rich west and the poorer developing world, the quiet female holding life together seemed to be a common factor.

Marco and Esther were a couple I met in Panajachel. They had just visited Cuba and I was jealous – as an American it was difficult to fly to the forbidden island country and sworn enemy to America. I learned, once again, another side to that story from Marco and Esther; not everyone in Cuba was launching themselves onto boats heading to Miami. Life was vibrant there, people were happy, the music and life on the streets reminded them of Mexican villages and although the cars were old and the poverty apparent, that certain non-material richness still existed. Maybe, I mused, that was the real 'enemy' to corporate America, or unfettered capitalism at large, the ability to be happy without every single material trapping. How damaging would that be if the word got out, or indeed had the word got out already and what I was hearing about and witnessing first-hand was simply brutal damage control? Was it just a strange coincidence that the wars and targets always seemed to be the poorer nations?

One of the most influential conversations I had in Guatemala was with an Australian guy I met named Alan. We traveled together for a little while, but one night over a couple of beers in a bar in Panajachel, he mentioned he was heading to Japan to teach English saying he had heard it was easy to find work, and the pay was great. He had been on the road for two years, worked in ski lodges in the States, and was going to learn Spanish in a town called Antigua, Guatemala. I hooked up with him and we went on together for a week. We had clicked. My ears pricked up on hearing his tales of travel and finding work along the way doing different jobs. It all sounded like a great adventure and I tucked the information away in a recess of my brain.

Guatemala was a strikingly beautiful country as well as having great cultural, religious and political interest. Volcanoes, lakes, coastline and mountains all made for wonderful scenery. The beaches I made it to on the west coast were black sandy beaches from volcanic ash. The further east towards Belize I went, the country turned into a whole different place more similar to the West Indies in my mind. The colonization of this part of the world, and movement of people from other colonized countries of Africa to work on the plantations or in the European owned silver mines changed the face of what Central America once was. Colonization, another loaded word.

Juxtaposed to those realities were the physical beauties, and the legacy of the Mayan culture. It was such an intelligent and deeply spiritual culture, the pyramids in the jungles of southern Mexico and Guatemala were awe-inspiring, and built with such precision that in certain times of the year, usually the solstices; shadows serpentine their way down the steps of the pyramid, the number of steps being 365! Yes, the Mayans had a precise calendar as well. Interestingly enough the Mayan calendar ends in 2012.

It made me wonder how a culture could be so tuned in with the celestial skies, the equinoxes, and the solstices a thousand years ago. We have lost so much of that connection in our modern day world. I'm not romanticizing and saying the culture was perfect – far from it I was sure. Had slave labor built hose wonderful pyramids? How much inter-tribal warring went on? They also lived with their humanness, that same genetic difference which separates us from other animals also puts us at odds with ourselves. It's just that the older cultures seemed to realize that humanity and the earth we live on is in a symbiotic relationship with the heavens – common thread shared by many of the indigenous populations of the world, those populations which are being marginalized and 'globalized' slowly out of existence. That symbiotic relationship, I thought to myself, is something we have forgotten about in the west and are, with medical precision, removing it where it still manages to exist.

Eeking out my fast-dwindling funds I did manage to make it to Belize and even Dangriga. Belize was another interesting place – a small country once known as British Honduras. Some British hardware of war was still apparent, as were the half-British babies to be seen everywhere. Belize felt more like I pictured Jamaica to be rather than a small country on the Central American Isthmus. The 'Hummingbird Highway' was little more than a dirt track in places, but it was the major north-south road in the country cutting through the deep lush jungle. Belize had not yet hit the radarscope of the diving world, the untouched *Quays* (Keys) were popular with travelers and Belize's future was about to change, but for the moment, it was a world lost in the past. Its Capital, Belize City had open sewage running in the street, the main road was a dirt track, and the natives were friendly, poor, and spoke a patua and pigeon English, the latter harder to understand than Spanish. The film *The Mosquito Coast* had recently been filmed there, and many people were happy to tell me they'd met Harrison Ford. I couldn't wait to see the film, and thought what an appropriate name. I was lucky with the mosquitoes, and although bitten a lot, I covered up at sunset, and never wanted to take anti-malarials. I survived with nothing more than annoying scratchy bumps.

I continued back up into Mexico, and would have loved to explore more of that diverse country, but I was feeling ill from too much street food, and from my calculations, I had just enough money to get to California, then to New York on my motorbike, but I needed to travel fast – a relative term on Mexican buses. I explored a little of the Yucatan Peninsula and was finding Mexico such a mix of cultures, ancient, and modern. The beach resorts such as Cancun were a world of sumptuous luxury unto themselves, while right on their doorstep was the contrasting world of peasant living, and destitute poverty. On the other hand, a half-day bus ride from the same resorts brought you to exquisitely preserved ruins stunning to explore with marvelous names such as Pulenque, and Chichen Itza.

Merida was the capital of the region, and as it turned out a great place to buy hammocks. I had never heard of the famed hammocks before, but they were beautifully woven, and I suddenly became an expert on different materials, double weaves, triple weaves, and all things having to do with hammocks. As many of the places I had visited had hooks for hanging your own hammock, I wound up buying one. It was a great bonus. I hooked it up to the wall of my small hotel, and what a great place for an afternoon *siesta*, a read of a book or to write in my journal. That evening I was feeling happy with myself; I was traveling in a beautiful country, my language skills were improving greatly, and I had found a place where I felt I wanted to be inside my head. I even now had a vague plan, teaching in Japan.

I befriended a group of people in a restaurant. It started out with a young woman flirting with me; we got to talking, and she and her friends began telling me they were on a journey to America. I was naïve to many things I was quickly finding out. My street smarts had got me through a few sticky situations so far, but I had never heard of the world of *coyotes* – not the animals, but the 'guides' who made their living getting people across the border with America for a large fee, often people's life savings. As I sat chatting with my newfound friends about my travels and a little about theirs, a man with an air of authority came over and very sternly asked one of the young men at the table who I was. He was obviously known to the group who all began to look a little uneasy. The man looked to be close to fifty, with a paunch pulling his tucked-in shirt tight across his skin. He had the swarthy looks of a local with a moustache and heavy eyebrows. His expression was fierce and his demeanor was threatening. A shouting match developed in rapid-fire Spanish but the situation was under control so I decided that, as I appeared to be the cause of the problem, I would excuse myself from the group. I went to my table, and ordered dinner. The man came angrily over to me, and rudely pulled his chair up next to mine.

"You are traveling alone *gringo*?" he said in a harsh English with a heavy accent which reminded me too much of the bad guys in the Humphrey Bogart movie *Sierra Madre*.

I wasn't sure what tack to take; he made me feel instantly nervous, and his energy was threatening. "I'm eating alone, and would like to keep it that way." I said.

"Why were you asking my clients so many questions, *gringo*?"

I ignored his nasty intonation on the word *gringo*, and registered the word 'clients' he chose to use. I glanced over to the table where young woman who had been flirting with me looked away quickly and shyly, as if she had been scolded by her father. My instincts told me that this was not a man to mess with, and he was not a tour bus operator. I answered, "They were asking me lots of questions, and we were just talking about New York."

"You are from New York? Do you have your passport with you?" I knew he was no official, and I was not breaking any laws even if he was.

"Yes I have a passport, and I'm from New York." I was not enjoying our encounter.

"May I see your passport, and have your address in New York?" he asked.

This conversation was getting strange, "No you may not see my passport, nor have my address." I had a little confidence as we were in a public restaurant, and was very glad not to have met this man in a back alley.

"You are staying in this hotel, no? I know what room you are in."

I felt sure he didn't know what room or hotel I was in, but unfortunately he had guessed correctly, I was staying in the hotel attached to the small restaurant. Keep control of the fear, don't show any if possible. "What does that matter to you?" I asked.

His reply was icy cold, "*Gringo*, if I find out you are working with U.S. customs, I will come into your room tonight and slit your throat. So show me your passport."

Man, this guy looked like he meant it. The situation had become clear to me; this was a guy who was being paid to get the group of people illegally across the border into the U.S. He thought I was an undercover officer from the U.S. customs coming to bust him. I was definitely not going to show him my passport, which was stuffed in a money belt under my trousers at the moment. I continued trying not to shake with fear, "I do not work for U.S. Customs, I do not know what you are doing with those people, nor do I care. I'm not alone, and am staying in a hotel in the middle of town." I felt really threatened and was wondering how I could leave the restaurant unnoticed by him.

"*Gringo*, these people have paid me a lot of money, no one will stop them from reaching the border." He then added, "Not you or the U.S. fucking customs."

I felt he believed I didn't work for customs now, but I was still nervous in his company, and I already foresaw a sleepless night ahead. I added, "I don't want to stop you or them from reaching America. I would like for all of you to reach America safely, move there, work there or whatever you want to do. I was talking to them because they called me over to their table."

"Okay *gringo*, good night." He then got up, walked away, and no one at the other table even looked my way.

What had started out as a good night had quickly gone bad. It was the first time I'd felt so threatened in my travels, and, like the man who replaced my motorcycle tire, his bad vibe lingered long after he was gone from view.

I wished I hadn't ordered food already, but it turned out to be a good thing. I ate, even though I was not feeling very hungry anymore, and by the time I had finished and paid my bill, the people on the other table were leaving. I had not seen where the *coyote* had gone, but I was still unsure if he might be waiting in the shadows. One of the girls came over to my table, probably volunteered by the group because of her command of English. She was fighting back tears as she said, "I am sorry that he was so mean. We are from Guatemala, and have paid a lot of money to go to *El Norté*, please don't stop us from getting there." She walked away, and I did not know what to say, so opted for saying nothing. I felt sure the *coyote* must have gone for her to have come over. With my bill paid, I took my chances and left.

I kept the key for my room out and quickly went to my room, glancing over my shoulder with visions of someone following me behind; I half-expected to feel a heavy hand clamp down on my shoulder as I fumbled to put the key in the lock, but I made it into my room, slamming the door shut and breathing a sigh of relief as I leant back against it in the safety of my room. I locked the door and crawled into the bed without turning on a light, brushing my teeth or even peeing. I shivered fully clothed under the covers for a while, looking up at my hammock swinging above me and wondering if I could get up the courage to move before the morning. As the night ticked on I got braver; I went to pee, but decided my teeth could wait. I put a table in front of the door and finally let myself fall asleep. The sun woke me up, and although the dawning of the new day is always a cleansing of sorts, I was quite happy to remain in my room and eat some fruit I had in my backpack.

I stayed in Merida another night assuming the *coyote* and his clients would have moved on. I walked the streets and tried to shake off the ill feelings of the previous night. I met some charming ladies making fresh corn tortillas – the staple food of the region – which, fresh and warm made a simple, yet delicious lunch along with some ripe green avocados. The people of the Yucatan Peninsula were as warm as the climate. I was glad to stay another night and fell back into good thought patterns reflecting that even though the world is a good place, and my travels had put me in contact with so much positive energy, it never hurts to keep your wits about you. I did not want to come from a place of fear, and I made sure that the episode with the *coyote* did not change my perspective on being open with people. If anything it helped me to hone my instinctive radar for trouble.

I was far from *El Norté* myself and there were many places I would have loved to have seen, but I would have to save that for another time. I never would have dreamed that the few hundred dollars I made in the music shop would have funded three months of traveling in Mexico, Guatemala, and Belize. I decided to stop in San Miguel de Allende to break up the many long hot bus rides. Every bus had a spare driver sleeping comfortably stretched out in the place I now coveted in my mind, the small enclosed under cabin. I am sure it wasn't luxury by any stretch of the imagination, but on the long rides scrunched up in my seat for more than twenty hours at a time, my imagination was getting flexible! After San Miguel, and one more stop in Topolobampo, it was pretty much a bee-line for the border with San Ysidro, California.

After making it to the border-crossing, I hopped on the least expensive bus heading to L.A. I was the only non-Hispanic person aboard. Somewhere north of San Diego, we were stopped and U.S. customs got on. They wanted to see everyone's papers. The officers were intimidating with their sunglasses and wide-brimmed hats. They even made me nervous and I had nothing to hide. A young guy was taken off the bus, a look of defeat on his face. Everyone else sat stock still and no eye contact was made with anyone else. The custom's officer looked coldly at me and checked my passport. The sweat on my brow was obvious, but he handed my passport back and glanced around the bus again before getting off. After we set off again I could feel the tension dissolve. After a few miles the bus was up to speed and heading to L.A. I lay my head back against the seat and watched the countryside passing, all the time thoughts running through my head of my hitcher Miguel, the *coyote* and all his clients, and the poor kid who'd just got taken off the bus. It was an odd game to play. Realistically everyone in America knew that without the immigrant workers fruit would be ridiculously expensive to eat. Who would build the fences in the rich suburbs, work in the restaurants, and add more color to that tapestry known as America? The game, for whatever reason, had to be played though, and as long as it was, the dream of *El Norté* would burn in the eyes of people born on the south side of the border.

Those short three months had allowed me to see everything in a new light. My motorcycle experiences had merely paved the way for the path which now lay ahead. I had met travelers, I had learned things about my country's dark past, and its present. In short I was shown a world where everything I grew up learning and thinking and feeling was thrown into question. I briefly thought of that short encounter with the navy again and how remarkable life was. If I had joined my perspective would have been so different. I would still be me, but that path would surely have led me through experiences to a different version of myself.

# The Road to Japan – Not Exactly as Planned

I finally made it to L.A. and my motorbike. I then limped back to New York, nearly flat broke, my insides riddled with Central American parasites, my head buzzing from all I'd seen, and those I'd met. I had just enough money to make it back with the fastest crossing I'd ever done. I sat on the bike for 500 miles a day and crossed from Los Angeles to New York in six days. I was now, once again, one of the world's poor, but being lucky enough to be born on the right side of the border, I had options, a place to live, and a plan. My family and friends were delighted to see me and me them, but some were worried because I was so thin that it may have been more serious than internal parasites. I knew it was just that. I even saw the exhalation of relief that I was probably done with 'that travel thing' and would be ready to settle down. I was enjoying being back and bided my time to tell them of my next move.

I'd kept in contact with John. The navy, so far, was working out great for him. Our paths had definitely diverged, so we agreed to disagree on some subjects, but our history together was strong, and he had asked me to be in his wedding party. At the time I'd been living in California and declined, but as it turned out I got home just before the big day. John's dad was clearly angry with me as he felt I should have been in the bridal party. I went to the wedding as a guest remembering the night John met Regina in the Irish pubs we used to frequent in the west Bronx. I was glad to see him marrying Regina, and now embarking on a career as an officer in the navy. My life was heading a different way into quite an unknown future – now that my health was on the mend I was looking and feeling better. After a year away from home I had some catching up to do.

My Swiss friends Marco and Esther came to visit New York, after just having left Mexico and Central America. They passed through on their way home where I was glad to be able to extend some hospitality to them. It was always nice giving back. They also validated some of my stories about Guatemala for my friends and family who had listened to my tales and nodded in all the right places, but even then I could see that it was hard for some people to comprehend – Central America, Cuba, it was all too foreign. What did I really expect? It had been our own personal experiences. It was difficult, my past with my family and friends were what had formed me, and intellectually I knew that they were all on their own paths of discovery. I tried to enthuse about the political side of my travels and make my experiences real for them, but I knew I was too headstrong and it was still too raw.

If you haven't looked into the widow's eyes, heard the children's laughter, or touched the poverty as we'd been privileged to, it's difficult to have empathy. Thankfully that's not always how it works and we listened to each other's views, though eventually the subject would change – the things Marco, Esther and I spoke of were just another news item, and definitely not a headline. Fair enough, the lives my friends and family were leading and their worries were getting harder for me to grasp too. I brought some awareness to my little corner of New York about the small forgotten places; giving away my bracelets helped, but I still had a lot to learn. I needed to let go of expectation, and respect the path everyone was on. For my passionate self that was a very difficult task. I saw the tears well up in my mother's eyes when I threw my passport on the floor in frustration saying, "How can I call myself an American after all the lies and deceit our government is involved in? I don't even know what an American is, or what I am."

She replied, "But my father came here to give us a better life, he only wanted an education for his children and a better standard of living. He had nothing to do with Guatemala or Mexico."

I knew in those words she was right. There are so many layers to a human being – to being an American. I wanted and needed to know more about this world. Much to my mom's chagrin, I said I would be saving enough money for a plane ticket to Japan, to head there and teach English. Just another crazy idea, but I was serious. It was August and I was planning on walking the streets of Japan come January. Nothing was going to get in my way, or so I thought.

With plans, I was learning constantly, it was best not to make anything too concrete. "Better to bend in the wind than break in the breeze," as the Zen Buddhist saying goes. Revisit and adjust when necessary. I needed to keep my fluid feeling alive, but I also had to live in the present. When I got back from California in the last throes of summer I got reintroduced to Noemi – a girl I had known for a few years – and we started dating.

Noemi had ideas for traveling and we'd had loose plans to meet up in Europe before I headed off to Alaska instead – life put us on a collision course once again. As we got more and more involved I was torn; on the one hand I was enjoying our relationship, on the other I was still determined to head to Japan. The larger problem was that she was carving herself out a career as a nurse in a local hospital, I was becoming a traveler and the two professions didn't exactly complement each other. As we got to know each other better though, I discovered she still wanted to travel.

She had been born in the Philippines but had moved to New York as a five-year-old with her family. After nursing school she'd traveled a bit, and the previous year she and her best friend Kathy, my future sister-in-

95

law, had traveled in Europe together, but Noemi had always wanted to cross her adopted country – America. She and another mutual friend had an idea to do just that in the late spring. However, the other girl, Andrea, was getting involved with a boyfriend and everything was getting muddled up. With Christmas approaching I had not yet purchased any plane tickets and there was a slight danger of losing sight of the bigger picture. I kept delving back into those feelings I'd had when I was in Guatemala – the reasons I travel, how much more I felt I wanted, no, needed to learn.

My spark to travel was kept alive by a small but nearly constant influx of people I had met in Mexico and Guatemala showing up in New York; Marco and Esther, Friedl, the young medical student from Austria whom my mother took an instant liking to because of his blue eyes and romantic accent, two other New Yorkers named Brian and Mike whom I met up with in New York City, and even half of the Brady clan from Oaxaca made it to an apartment in The Bronx before heading out to Europe to continue on their journey.

My two lives were converging. My friends and family in New York were meeting some of the people who were beginning to shape me as a traveler, and my traveler friends were coming to the place and seeing the place and people who shaped me as a person. It somehow made it all feel more real.

I attempted once again to be a vegetarian, remembering what Brady and I had spoken about in Mexico. It was difficult getting the right foods because no one else I knew was a vegetarian, but I tried. My mom made meatballs with soya, or from turkey. I was dabbling, but determined to try and watch where my food came from.

I started teaching again. I liked kids, but was still sure that it was not to be my career. I made sure I remained a substitute teacher this time, as the flexibility fit in with my lifestyle better. This time around I wound up working mainly in two schools and made friends in both. In one school I worked with handicapped children and it added a whole new dimension to my appreciation of the here and now. Some of the children were born handicapped; others' disabilities were the unfortunate results of accidents. Everything on my path was showing me the same thing over and over again; life was a gift, health was something not to be taken for granted, so I embraced the two even more. I started to walk down some alternative paths of eating, and looking at traditional western medicine in a different light. My tiny bit of traveling so far had shown me the way we lived in the west was only a small percentage of how the world functioned – there were other ways to live, eat, and take care of your body. I felt I had grown and become a better teacher; I enjoyed my few months subbing around The Bronx and felt I brought more life experience to the table. I had several chances to take on a full-time position but stayed firm in my mind; I was still heading to Japan but now with Noemi in the picture it was just a matter of how exactly I would put that idea into practice.

On Christmas Day I asked Noemi if she wanted to cross America with me in the spring on the back of my motorcycle, then head to Japan after making it to the west coast. I'm not sure any of us expected this to happen, but it all worked out. Andrea was more involved with her boyfriend Charley now, and they were forming vague plans to cross America themselves. Noemi was getting fed up with the local hospital, and a cross-country trip on the back of a motorcycle then heading off to Japan sounded a pretty good idea. The only one who wasn't too pleased was Noemi's dad. There were a few reasons for this, the first few were obvious; taking his eldest daughter away from New York, on a motorcycle no less, her quitting her job and heading into an unknown future with me, the traveler didn't fill him with delight either. His greatest misgiving, however, was that his father had been killed by the Japanese in World War II and he hadn't been able to let go of his animosity towards that country. I couldn't blame him for that, and anyway it took the emphasis off me as public enemy number one. As time went on though he came to terms with his daughter jetting off to Japan but wasn't happy about the long motorcycle trip. I unfortunately climbed back up to concern number one so we just stopped mentioning the motorcycle leg of the journey at family functions.

We planned to leave in late May, as did Charley and Andrea. By this point, my friends were getting pretty sick of throwing me going away parties, but now there were three more people involved, so it was the excuse for having another good send off. For a different approach we all headed to a campsite in western New York State and spent a weekend camping together. Fun was had by all and when we headed south on Monday morning we all waved goodbye; our friends back to New York, Charley and Andrea heading their way, us on ours.

Another cross-continental trip by motorcycle but this time with a passenger – a new adventure, something my motorcycle and I were always up for. We tried to vary the route west by heading south first, then heading into the sunset. We zigzagged a lot more than I ever did before, went much slower, and covered lots of ground. Noemi was petite and I sometimes wondered if she could be having as good a time as me being stuck behind someone she couldn't see over or around but she insisted she was having a ball. We fell into a good groove camping. I would set up the tent and she would collect the firewood. We traveled well together, and stopped by to visit some friends and family we had along the way. We looked up Gary, of dune buggy fame, in Arkansas.

Gary and I had kept in contact since that day on our dune buggies. He was glad to see me and to meet Noemi. He showed us around Little Rock. We both experienced – for the first time – Walmart. Sam Walton, the founder was from Arkansas. Walmart was not as big as it is now, at the time it was still busy taking over the small towns of the south. As we passed it Gary asked if we wanted to go in, it was becoming famous for its reputation of being so big, and turning its founder and original investors into very rich people. We walked in, and I immediately didn't like it. It felt overwhelming and something didn't sit right with Noemi or me about its vibe.

Gary was telling us how it had spread out through a few states in the south but the exponential growth didn't sit right with me, especially after my last trip in Mexico and Central America. I didn't like the business plan. I remembered what was spoken about in a tiny restaurant in San Cristobal, a year ago, and I was glad that my money, and my choice not to shop in places like that, has not helped their worldwide domination. I still felt attached to the little guy.

Besides Walmart, Gary showed us around some of the nicer parts of Little Rock and we took a hike on the outskirts of town in a natural setting. It was nice seeing Gary in his home environment – still the outdoorsman.

We jogged northwest across the country, crossed the Rockies near Taos, New Mexico, and headed to Mesa Verde National Park in Colorado. We swerved a little out of our way to Yosemite; I could always go to that park and not get bored of its magnificence. John Muir had the right idea to preserve the beauty, it was his influence which pushed Teddy Roosevelt to preserve Yosemite and several other North American natural treasures – giving them National Park status, and what a place Yosemite was, El Capitan jutting towards the heavens – calling out to the hearty, risk-taking climbing fraternity, the waterfalls, camping, the feeling you were miles from anywhere while not actually being too far from San Francisco. Unfortunately, when it was founded as a National Park, the Native Americans were forced out of its borders. It was thought the city people wanted nothing to get in the way of their view of their ideal of 'Real Wilderness'. What a beautiful country, I kept thinking to myself. We just needed to pull together more as a small community in a larger world, rather than a larger nation in a world made for our convenience.

Traveling along the beautiful roads and meeting the people always filled me with hope that it was possible; as a nation, and as individuals we needed to embrace the philosophy that less is more, small is beautiful, and our world is large enough for all of us to benefit from what it has to offer.

To try and make a small personal contribution to those ends I tried to make conscious decisions around most things I did and was still attempting, as well as I could, to be vegetarian. It was hard watching Noemi bite into juicy hamburgers while eating a grilled cheese sandwich, but it was a challenge to try and keep to it. The political reasoning behind it was probably futile anyhow. Who knew where the cheese and eggs I was substituting for meat were coming from? Laughingly, I was eating tuna (somehow fish wasn't meat for me then) which was probably far worse for the world at large, but I was still learning, and there was no harm in the self restraint exercise anyhow.

I tried to fit in some new sights for myself, but also wanted to show Noemi some of my favorite spots from previous trips. In doing this we clocked up nearly 9,000 miles crossing America, such a difference from my solo journeys. It was nice to see it all from her perspective; the absolute vastness of the middle of America, the grandeur of the Rockies, the verdant greens of the Coastal Ranges, plus there was one more place I needed to visit. It meant a lot to me, and since Noemi had heard so much about it, we headed out to the dunes of Oregon.

We were heading back to Coos Bay to thank Brewer, the old fella who had helped me alter my bike after the dune buggy crash. We pulled up in front of his shop and leaned our loaded bike up on its kickstand. He was still there, his lame arm hanging lifeless, as he worked on a bike with a tool in his good hand. When I took off my helmet he took a double take.

"YOU! I can't believe it! When you pulled away from here I felt awful, I was sure you were a gonner!"

I just smiled and said, "Hello Brewer, well I made it! Just rode back to thank you for helping me out."

He shook his head at the memory, "I must've told the story of you pulling outta here on that bike to my whole family. I must say, I wasn't sure I did the right thing."

I realized then I probably should have written him some form of note to let him know I was alive. I clapped him on the shoulder, "Oh, you did the right thing, don't worry about that. I had to come back to say I don't know what I would've done if you hadn't helped me out."

With that he offered us a free dune buggy rental each for a few hours. We took him up on the offer, but I insisted that the dune buggy have hand straps, we all laughed.

Another crossing of America was under my belt, and Noemi had a great time. We packed quite a lot in, and still hadn't lost sight that this was just leg one of a much longer exploration. As we rode down the coast towards California, I kept glancing over my right shoulder looking out across the Pacific – would we really both soon be living on a small island country called Japan thousands of miles across that vast ocean?

Any cross-country journey was not complete without a stop at Mary and Angelo's. They were always welcoming, and it was great to stay put for a few days. Noemi had some family out in The Bay Area – we visited them, and swore them to secrecy that we had come out on a motorcycle. I think Noemi's dad had figured it out by then, but we all played the game anyhow.

After a few days in the Bay Area, it was time to head down the gorgeous coast once again to L.A. Before leaving though, we needed to buy some plane tickets to Japan – after all, that was the whole point.

There were very cheap direct flights to be had if we booked a month in advance and we decided it was best if I flew out first. Noemi would stay behind with relatives and do some nursing work. We heard you could earn good money in Japan, but we also knew it was quite an expensive place to travel. I would do the leg work; locate a city or town that felt right, get a place to live in, find work. We would have plenty of time to explore Japan once we were living there. With blind optimism it never entered our mind that it wouldn't work out so we took advantage of the month we had before I flew to Japan – first down to Los Angeles to visit Jen, maybe search out some other friends and relatives, then off to Mexico and Central America.

We took a different route through Mexico, but of course had to stop in Mexico City, which had unfortunately suffered a devastating earthquake since my last visit. We stayed in the same place where Jason and I had stayed a year previously, but the devastation was obvious – over 10,000 people had died and everyone in the city was affected in some way or another. Buildings stood half-crumbling yet still inhabited; it was yet another rude awakening to the poverty of the world.

Walking the streets of this magnificent, overcrowded, polluted urban sprawl, my love affair with travel was getting stronger. The destruction from the quake served to open my eyes wider and realize how every moment was precious. Just one year ago at least 10,000 more people were alive walking the city streets, and in a moment they were gone, as were some of the buildings that housed them. How long did we all have? Our existence was surely fleeting.

The future was exciting, but the power was all in the moment. Yet I still couldn't wait to be walking the streets of Tokyo trying to find work while stepping into the complete unknown and unfamiliar.

In Mexico it was a good feeling to know somewhere so different more intimately. The long bus rides were sometimes tedious, and I laughed at Noemi's reaction seeing the spare driver released from his moving basement apartment, and chuckled as she also started to covet its tiny possibilities of comfort. At least together we were able to take over two seats and almost lie down. We headed down to Guatemala overland, our

100

main destination being the country that changed my reality forever. A month felt like a long time to travel, but with slow trains, broken down buses, and the *mañana* mentality, it seemed too short. Noemi was eager to see the country I spoke so highly of – and I was keyed up to show her.

Guatemala was as beautiful as I remembered it and the land crossing just as overwhelming in its other-wordliness as it had been a year previous. I repeated the words Gary said to me when I first entered that country, and watched as Noemi took it all in.

Unbelievably, I saw some familiar faces in Guatemala. I spotted one guy who had been in the same place the year before asking the same questions. He turned out to be a writer for a guide book and I asked him if he traveled out to all the places he wrote about. "Not all of them," he told me, "but I try and do a yearly road trip to check up on the bigger towns and city information." He was a nice guy and his real interest was butterflies. Writing the guide book allowed him to spend time catching, collecting and observing these colorful insects – I put that in my mental notebook as a small anecdote about guide book information.

Noemi and I decided to do the one thing that I hadn't done the year before: taking the bus from Guatemala City to Tikal. It was eighteen hours of hell, but worth it. We met up with some other travelers on the *gringo* trail, and shared the nightmare journey together. The road could not have been worse on top of the fact that the bus was made for small people. Noemi was perfect at just five feet tall, and I managed okay at five foot ten inches but we both felt bad for a six-foot-something couple we met up with sitting with necks cricked for the entire journey.

Tikal is astounding. It is a testament to how big the Mayan culture was before it mysteriously disappeared. The jungle has slowly taken over this once central city of the Mayans, but the little that has been uncovered stretched throughout the jungle. We explored the pyramids, the ancient sports fields where the winner of the game was sacrificed to the gods – that we both found a hard one to swallow. I don't know if I would have tried my hardest to win that match. As we walked under the brilliant green canopy to explore on our own, we were followed by the other inhabitants of the jungle; the monkeys. They were cheeky companions, sometimes throwing down a branch, and always keeping an eye on us.

The ruins were in great repair, and archeologists were constantly uncovering more and more of this marvelous place. It was possibly the center of the Mayan culture at its peak. As buildings, roads, and temples were constantly being uncovered all over the Central American Isthmus, the mystery of the Mayan culture was also growing. The jungle was unforgiving, and anything left uncared for would be swallowed up by its natural hungry will to constantly expand. It's a constant battle to keep back the growth, and again one of life's conundrums – should we let the jungles do what they do best, supporting boundless nature, tribal ways of life, and giving so much biodiversity to our planet? Or do we explore, and uncover the mysteries, minerals, resources and other richness they have to offer?

Leaving Tikal we decided to take the bus to a farm/traveler's respite called Phinca Ixobella run by two Americans who'd opted out of Ohio. It broke up the long bus ride to Guate, as the capital, Guatemala City, is known. It was a relaxing time in the jungle; good food, fresh fruit, yogurt drinks, ping pong tables, books to read, other weary travelers to talk to. Seeing how this couple had created a livelihood for the locals as well as a haven for travelers was inspiring.

Bret was the male part of the partnership, and his wife's name was Maryanne. He was a nice guy to talk to, knew a lot about the politics, and was trying to make a difference in this tiny piece of paradise. There were hammocks in trees if you so desired, small rooms, and also tree houses. You never paid up front, and just signed a book to keep track of what you ate or drank and paid when you left. You could take hikes in the jungle, or just chill out and prepare for the next leg of your journey north or south. We had heard there was a truck heading into Guate taking empty bottles from Tikal, and the small villages on the way. Flash floods and rain had stalled our journey by a few days already, and one bus was washed up in the floods, so the truck not only sounded more interesting, but it was going to be leaving two days sooner than the next bus. There was also the vague possibility that it would be more comfortable than the previous journey.

Noemi, Jim (another American), and I took up the truck offer and wound up sitting on top of the bottles, Jim playing his guitar, and for nearly ten hours we got bounced around in the hot humid air traveling through the lush green jungle with the bottles clinking beneath us – it actually *was* more comfortable than the bus!

We were tied to getting back to San Francisco for my flight east. After clanging and bouncing to Guate, we boarded a comparatively luxurious bus to the border of Mexico. Long arduous bus journeys were the norm, and we both missed the flexibility of having our own transport. For two months we'd had a motorcycle, now we were stuck on buses, and confined to a timeframe. I was slowly learning that time schedules, even though lax, did make you rush in the end. I liked the motorcycle, but even that mode of transport had its restrictions; gas stations, insurance, difficult side of the road maintenance, and all else that goes along with owning a motor vehicle. I felt a change of mode of transport was in the making, but wasn't quite sure what. In my mind I was still a motorcyclist but my ears and eyes were open to other possibilities. I just hoped I was alert enough to know it when it came my way.

Gary and Joe – On the Road!

Gary – 1983

The Grand Canyon

Louis and John – the chance meeting

Pierre and the DFE Crew

Charlie and Ed – we made it!

On the way to Skagway

Hans and Ursula – getting the bike started.

The altered bike throttle

Gary and his well-traveled pick-up truck

The broken wrist

Aunt Mary and Uncle Lou visit Jen (and me) in L.A.

Fishermen on the Baja with their catch – Hammerheads

A Mexican Archeological site

Jungle river transportation

Young weavers in Guatemala

Guatemalan girl in *Huipile* (traditional woven top)

The friendly faces of Guatemala

Richard surrounded by some bracelet sellers

The sawdust carpet and the locals awaiting the Good Friday procession

Alan – hiking in Guatemala

Typical men's dress in Guatemalan Village

Getting back from Mexico – a new path ahead.

Esther, me and Marco in The Bronx – on their way home

Noemi on the Yamaha – The secret crossing.

Noemi goes native – Guatemala 1987

Hitching a ride – Jim on the bottle truck, Guatemala

## CYCLE TWO; Leaving on a Jet Plane
## -Discovering the East-

# Kenji and the Watch

I looked down from the window of the plane knowing that, for the first time in my life, I was leaving the North American continent. I felt well-traveled, but now I was truly cutting my path. I was glad that Noemi wasn't coming yet. We weren't sure what lay ahead, but we both though it would be better if I arrived in Japan first. We had done a long cross-continental tour together; our month in Mexico and Central America had been short but filled with lots of long bus journeys, a boat crossing and a short plane ride – Noemi was glad for a small break.

A day mysteriously disappeared on the plane as happens when you cross the international time zone – going so far to the west it turns east – and it was midday when the plane touched down in Narita International Airport. A night's sleep had also been lost, but the excitement and adrenalin kept me going. I walked around the streets of Tokyo feeling as if I was in a dream. Tokyo! Even I was surprised that I had pulled this one off.

I decided I would be sleeping out in a park that night. Tokyo felt safe, it was a nice night, and I had a sleeping bag. So as dusk started to fall, my heavy eyelids followed. I was exhausted and my body was in need of rest. I searched out a bench, but just as I pulled out my sleeping bag a police officer very politely tapped me on the shoulder.

"Excuse me, it is too dangerous for you to sleep here, I will help you to find a hotel." I had looked at some hotel prices, and coming off the back of travel in Central America, they were quite frighteningly priced.

I shook my head, "Very expensive." My interloper continued to hold my gaze, and then I added, "*Too* expensive."

The train journey from the airport to the middle of Tokyo alone had been more expensive than three days in Guatemala including food, transport and a hotel! The Japanese *yen* was enjoying a strong exchange rate with the American dollar, even though I had several thousand *yen* in my pocket, it didn't amount to much in my own familiar currency. My policeman was politely insistent. I sighed and resigned myself to the fact there would be no peaceful park sojourn for me. It was a pleasant interchange nevertheless with no hint of aggression or annoyance, plus he knew of an inexpensive hotel. He drew a map for me, and insisted I would be much safer there. Who was I to argue?

I made it on foot to the said hotel and saw that the prices were cheap as far as Tokyo went. It was billed as one of the most expensive cities in the world at the time, so the equivalent of $30 U.S. was not such a bad price. I was really crashing now, so I paid the man at the front desk, and he gave me the key for room number 604.

Something about the hotel didn't add up through the fog of tiredness in my brain but I couldn't quite put my finger on it. I stepped into the elevator and it came to me suddenly that the building had appeared small for a hotel, surely far too small to have six floors. I didn't seem to have the necessary ability for problem solving so simply thought 'well the Japanese are not as tall as westerners.' I got into the elevator, found a button marked 600-650 and pressed it, then experienced a very fast journey up six floors – or so I thought. When I stepped out of the elevator I knew I was tired, but had to rub my eyes a few times to see if the sight was actually real. It just looked like, well like nothing I had ever seen before; two rows of tubes. Each tube had a small shade of bamboo in front of it, and they were stacked two high. There must have been thirty or forty tubes. I still didn't know what was going on when a shade was drawn open and a gray-haired Japanese guy popped his head out and gave me a weird look. It all clicked in; these *were* the 'rooms', but what was the key for? I looked to the opposite side of the rooms, and there were lockers, each locker number corresponding to a room on the other side. I was tired and starting to fade now so I found my locker number and got undressed as quietly as I could. I had no idea if every cubby hole was occupied by a person or not, but after shoving everything in my locker, I opened the shade of my room, and crawled in. My dad who had had a slight problem with claustrophobia would have been out the door, down the street and sleeping in the park. I chuckled to myself as I looked around my lodgings; a small molded tube made of white plastic, a tiny ledge which acted as a table was part of the design, a radio sunk into the wall, and a thin mattress on the floor. I struggled to put some illegible entry in my journal, hunching over my tiny table, minutes later I was fast asleep.

I woke up once in the night totally disoriented and it took a while to figure out where the heck I was. After I did work it out, I giggled again, and went back to sleep. The hotel was wide awake at quite an early hour the next morning. Contrary to what I would have thought, the hotel was full of men in business suits. It was known as a 'Businessman's Hotel'. Hotels being expensive in Tokyo, these offer a *sento* (public bath house) on the top floor, and a cheap price. You have your private room, and if you are a working-class businessman, it makes quite a lot of sense. I decided to forego the Japanese bath house as the urge to get out into sunshine, stretch my arms and breathe in some fresh air was greater than my need to be clean. It had been quite an experience. It inspired me to find an English language bookshop so I could somehow or another locate a traveler's place to stay in Tokyo.

The sleep had renewed me; I felt just about whole again and was up for an adventure. I walked around wondering if I should be pinching myself –

I could not believe I was walking the streets of Tokyo. I bought an underground ticket, and hopped on the train system lurking below. The crowd's homogeneity blew me away. Subways in New York were such a mix of races and colorful clothing but here the overriding color of hair was black, the eyes dark brown and the suit color gray. Of course there were other people and different colors dotted here and there but the overall impression was so strange to me. I spotted a westerner who looked like he knew his way around; he did not have a backpack and was dressed in a casually neat way. I thought he might be a temporary resident of Tokyo. I made my way over to him and, as we waited for the train, I tried to look for a clue as to what language he spoke. Nothing to give that away, but he didn't look Spanish or Italian. Swedish was a possibility, but I then stopped playing the game with myself and just asked, "Excuse me, do you speak English?" It turned out he did, but I could hardly understand a word of it. He was from England somewhere, but with the noise of the underground and all the beeping and buzzing I would become used to from my time in Japan, I was lucky to understand half of what he said. I grinned and hoped he didn't require a reply, and then asked if he knew of a bookshop where I could buy some English books. He understood me which was a relief, and told me the name of a bookstore called 'MeidiYa' or something along those lines.

The Japanese characters were indecipherable for me, but luckily most everything was written in *Romaji* – the phonetic writing in the Latin based alphabet westernizing many words. It meant I was able to pronounce things and find shops but remain clueless of what things actually meant. He told me the train stop I needed, and that I would be able to see the shop when I left the station. We boarded the train, my backpack, although quite small, still proving to be in the way on the crowded cars. My English friend somehow slithered deeper into the bowels of the train and I lost sight of him.

Getting off where I was supposed to and walking in wide-eyed wonderment, I found the bookshop, and in it a guide book of Japan in English. I wasn't about to spend a small fortune buying it, but found the pages marked cheap places to stay in Tokyo, and noted a few details in my journal.

My second night in Tokyo I found myself in a crash pad for travelers and alternate type businessmen. These were blue-collar workers who were happy to mix with foreigners and sleep in a dorm style room. It was great fun for me. My first night in Tokyo had been memorable, but I didn't fancy sleeping a second night in a tube! This place was also much cheaper.

One of the Japanese residents of the crash pad took a liking to me. I often gravitate towards eccentric people so we hit it off fairly easily. I assumed he was probably about sixty, with classical Japanese looks, but right from his first greeting I felt there was something deeper behind those soft, sloping brown eyes and his glowing face. Kenji was his name and he would slowly reveal that depth to me over the next few days.

He was quick to laugh, an infectious laugh complete with a wide open mouth and a slap on his knee – anyone lucky enough to experience it could not help being drawn into its energy. His smile was friendly, but there was something more to it; although a genuine smile, it told of a hard life lived.

He took me out for a dinner of eel, rice, and sake. It was a fun evening as Kenji pointed out much of my naiveté on Japanese etiquette. I sneaked a quick glance at the bill, and could not believe how much this total stranger was spending on taking me to dinner. We talked about what I was doing in Japan, and my reasons for coming etc. He was curious about my travels and when I wanted to ask about his life he gently steered my questions back around to me. I wasn't sure if it was just another technique to re-direct the focus of my question about his family, but he glanced down at my wrist and registered its lack of a watch.

"You don't own a watch, Joesan?" he asked.

My mind instantly flashed to the time when Gary and I were preparing to go across America, getting ourselves psyched up by watching *Easy Rider*. I always loved the scene when Peter Fonda looks at his watch, the camera then pans in and, in a real sixties movie montage effect, makes a big scene of him un-strapping the watch and throwing it in the dirt. I have never been a watch person; there's always enough watch-wearing people to ask the time, and that's always a good way to meet people, or force otherwise strangers into saying hi, and literally give you the time of day. So for me not wearing a watch was normal. Kenji though, had different ideas. I told him about *Easy Rider* and the opening scene but he wasn't too impressed. I then told him my public clock theory and the 'making contact with other people' idea as well, all to no avail. We got in late that night warmed by *sake* and a good meal, and I thought our watch conversation was over.

The next morning I decided to visit our hostel's *sento*. Now I was in more need of a bath than a stretch of my arms. All the shy Japanese men were there with their towels in the appropriate places. I spotted Kenji, we said good morning and he asked me if I had had any breakfast. I told him no, not yet, but I didn't want him spending another small fortune on a meal for me. He assured me of a cheap breakfast, and so I agreed. First though, a bath.

I went on to nearly breaking every *sento* rule there was, and there were a lot. Luckily Kenji was there to talk me through. I almost just climbed into the steamy hot bath with the others, much to the chagrin of everyone else. Kenji brought me over to a smaller bath and showed me how to wash off the dirt, then he said I could hop in. It was a sizeable tub but a few laps were out of the question! You just let yourself relax in the bath with the water washing over you. It felt so relaxing and comfortable and I enjoyed a good ten minutes of soaking. Of course, getting out was a more complicated affair than simply jumping out and rubbing yourself off with a towel. You now need to wash the water of the public bath off your body. So after throwing on a few more buckets of water and chuckling at the other Japanese trying to sneak a few surreptitious stares at the tattoos on my arm, back and leg, I was ready to eat.

We got dressed and were ready to face another day on the streets of Tokyo. It was early morning, and the stores were just opening. If you have never walked into a Japanese department store at opening, you haven't really lived. The doors swoosh open, and you are greeted by hundreds of men and women in store uniform, bowing to you with hands respectfully joined at the chest saying "*Irashe masen*" which means welcome. Ah, I thought laughing, finally the respect I deserve! Kenji and I then retreated into the basement where there was a magnificent and beautifully presented display of food, and near every food counter, free samples. We picked our way methodically through almost all of them. Fish, rice balls, *tofu*, free tea – you name it, it was there. We ate to capacity, then went to the bread section and bought a small loaf of bread and an iced coffee, taking the elevator manned by a young Japanese girl giggling behind her hand and giving a running commentary on the delights awaiting us on each floor on our way up. As the doorway opened out onto the rooftop, I was amazed to see a garden with benches, and in this particular instance, a human-sized maze as well. We chose a bench overhung with very beautiful purple blossoms, and, washing down our free samples, admired the commanding view of Tokyo.

I slowly learnt more about this quiet person with the infectious laugh, and as we looked out over the city of Tokyo from our bird's eye view, I became the listener in a fascinating story about his earlier years.

Kenji had grown up in a small village on the outskirts of Hiroshima where his dad was a carpenter. They lived a simple life, and Kenji was the youngest of three children. The area was rural Japan on the main island of Honshu, and although life was hard, each village was a small vibrant community. The war years were difficult for young Kenji – his dad disappeared to fight in a war he did not know much about – a war which had already taken his uncle's life and two older cousins. Many of the males were gone from the villages, and life was getting more difficult. Then he told me of the hot August day in 1945 when nine-year-old Kenji and his friends looked out across the fields towards Hiroshima to see a large, strange mushroom cloud billow up towards the heavens above that small city. Everyone looked on in amazement as it just grew higher and higher then fell back into itself. No one quite understood what had happened. There was no clue that in that small instant they had witnessed 100,000 lives being exterminated. War-ravaged Japan in 1945 was a poor country, and news traveled slowly. Kenji had no idea he had just witnessed one of humanity's lowest points – at the time hailed as a great technological breakthrough – the atomic bomb.

The next day all of the high school aged children from the surrounding areas were called in to Hiroshima to remove rubble, search for survivors and do what needed to be done in the grave aftermath of that infamous August day. What happened slowly came to light, and they heard that another similar bomb had been dropped on Nagasaki, a town on the southern island of Japan called Kyushu. He remembers huddling around a radio watching his mother and people of the village sit uncomprehending, listening to the never-before-heard voice of their emperor, Hirohito, tell of Japan's surrender. Hirohito also explained the emperor was not a deity, just another human being. To nine-year-old Kenji this was all quite overpowering.

He went on to tell me that nuclear fallout and the diseases from radiation were also unknown at the time. Over the next few years Kenji, and many people his age who had not gone into Hiroshima to help, watched as their brothers, sisters, aunts, uncles, friends and neighbors slowly died from cancers and radiation-borne diseases. He told me of the occupation of the American soldiers. The children and adults were horrified waiting for the Americans to come and kill or eat them but they were always pleasantly surprised at the gentleness of the odd looking foreigners who seemed to have bottomless pockets of chocolate and endless smiles. Kenji thought to himself, could these be the same army that reduced two Japanese cities to rubble killing everything that moved? It inspired him to want to learn more about these strange people. He tried working with them, helping in any way he could. He became their liaison with the villagers, and quickly learned to speak English. He didn't understand why the American soldiers forced the Japanese women to wear shirts in the hot summer months, but there were many things he didn't understand about these tall peculiar *gaijin* – foreigners. The occupation ended in 1952, as the 'Peace Constitution' was transforming Japan – land reform and demilitarization seemed a good idea. Now sixteen years old, Kenji understood more and was pleased.

By 1961 Kenji's family had all but died. His family house was empty, and the people in his small village had all changed. It was no longer the village of his childhood memories, so at twenty-five years old he decided

125

to take to the road. He wanted to learn more about Japan. It struck me that I was now twenty-five on my own search as well. I also found it another coincidence that 1961 was the year of my birth, and the year of Kenji's re-discovery of life.

He started his new life in Tokyo and his English skills proved to be useful. The coming of the summer Olympics in 1964 was to put Japan on the world scene, and the western industrialization which had begun in the latter part of the nineteenth century was now to take a strong hold. The Olympics also proved to be lucrative for Kenji. He was once again involved with the Americans of his childhood, although they were no longer an occupying force. The Olympic events had provided many opportunities for an industrious person to earn money, and Kenji did – translating, selling Japanese souvenirs, cleaning the athletes' rooms. I could imagine his same smile, infectious laugh, and way with people opening quite a few doors. After a few years in Tokyo he decided to move on, his travels taking him to Hokkaido where he worked with fishermen, and collected and dried seaweed for money. The basic skills his father had taught him as a young boy helped him acquire the handy skill of carpentry – which came in useful at times. He moved around the small collection of Islands known as Japan for the following twenty years. Kenji had worked as far south as Kyushu and even spent time at sea on fishing boats. He thought losing the war had been what saved Japan from itself, but of course that loss was bittersweet.

Japan had a bloody history of occupation, annexing countries and war, but since 1945 Japan's focus had been diverted back to western-style industry and under the terms of the Peace Constitution Japan was not allowed to have a fighting army. Kenji found himself back in Tokyo by his mid-forties, and there his story grew vague. He never became one of the many robotic *salarymen* who were now all-pervasive in Japan, but seemed to have a little money in his pocket, and in his way, he'd found happiness. His voice trailed off, and a small sadness crept into his prematurely lined face – strange for a Japanese person, but then again Kenji appeared to break all the rules. Was there a love lost, or a child in his past?

We both felt the silence growing and once again Kenji brought up the fact I didn't wear a watch. He told me if I wanted to be taken seriously as a teacher I should. Japanese society was very earnest about such things, and in his opinion it would help my job prospects. He also told me not to buy one, but we'd discuss the matter later on that night. He bid me a good day, and we made a plan to meet up that night. I assured him I would be there on time, even though I did not have a watch. We both laughed and he disappeared into the throng of gray-suited, black-haired, watch-wearing Japanese.

126

I realized I had not even noticed if Kenji himself wore a watch. I assumed he did but I could not for the life of me conjure up an image of either of his wrists. His story had transported me to another place and time and I could not begin to feel what his life must have been like. To feel that losing the war was a good thing, but witnessing first-hand the devastation of that loss. I respected his integrity, and his life was a model for me; he did not wallow in the mire but picked up the pieces and carved an interesting path for himself. I was still curious as to what he did not tell, but of course that was for Kenji to decide.

My day went as usual. I stopped in tea houses, met up with a couple of fellow travelers from the crash pad, and we talked about the best parts of Japan to get work, live, or just explore. I saw some of the most bizarre vending machines I'd ever seen; you could get whiskey, beer, hot *sake* and rice ball snacks known as *oniguiri* from many of them found on the street. It seemed all too crazy, but what was crazy then became normal later on.

I came back later that night, and washed off some of the Tokyo soot and heat from my face and hands. Kenji was waiting for me at our previously arranged spot looking happy. We didn't speak any more of the past, but settled into an easiness now we both knew and understood each other that much better. I told him some of the thoughts I had about going to look for work outside of Tokyo. He thought it was a good idea, but I needed to have a watch. He then produced what looked like an old cigar box. In it was some cheap-looking jewelry and a few watches. He told me to pick one out for myself. I politely declined but he insisted that it would bring me good luck, and he would be very flattered if I would accept this small token of friendship and good fortune. I accepted and pulled out a rectangular face watch with a gold band. I strapped it on my wrist, and wore it every day I lived in Japan.

I didn't see much of Kenji in the days that followed. Tokyo was expensive, and I decided to head out to the smaller towns and cities to look for work. The day before I left I made sure to seek out and thank Kenji. He thrust his address into my hands and asked me to keep him informed of what happened to me in my search for work. He thought it was crazy just flying in on a whim to teach English, but he liked it. I assured him many foreigners did the same thing, and now was a good time to find work.

I left Tokyo and set out to look for two fellow travelers I had met in the crash pad who lived in a small village on the west coast of Japan. When I got to the village I realized that it was too small and I wanted more of a city environment. I also thought it would be nearly impossible for Noemi to find work there even if I did manage to get a job. I stayed a couple of nights and was shown around the place. It was nice catching these tiny glimpses of the country I would be calling home for the next little while.

Train and bus travel were eating into my funds, but I was confident I would find work soon so didn't worry too much about the shrinking budget; I hitchhiked which saved money and opened up a few interesting doors. I was relieved though, that Noemi had stayed in California and was earning some money there.

My trip into the countryside helped to crystallize the idea of what I was looking for: I wanted a small city environment with accessibility to countryside, and at least a pale blue sky, not one gray with pollution. It was time to look up Alan, the Australian guy who had planted this wild idea in my head in Guatemala. He lived in a city called Nagoya on the island of Honshu. According to its size on the map it looked like it might have what I was looking for in a city, so I hopped on a train and stayed in the youth hostel there before giving him a call. He was glad to hear from me, and we arranged to meet. He was living with his girlfriend Sue. She was English, and had a strong personality. Alan was a quietly spoken guy and Sue definitely wore the pants in the relationship, but she wasn't wearing them the night I showed up!

I had been invited to stay at their place for a few nights so I turned up with my backpack. When Alan answered the door, he was stark naked. I asked if I had caught him at a bad time but he said no, come on in. So I came in, and there was Sue, also dressed in her birthday suit. Now nakedness doesn't bother me, I kinda like it, but in this situation what do you do? Should I strip off and say, "Boy it's hot," or do I pretend not to notice, and stay dressed? I opted for keeping my clothes on for the moment and waiting to see where this was going. I was offered a cup of tea, showed where my futon would be, and we got to chatting. As things warmed up a bit, I felt I could break the ice about the clothing situation.

"So, is Nagoya always so hot?" I asked.

"Yeah, the summer can be quite muggy," Alan replied.

I then got to the point quickly. "Are you always naked in here?"

Sue's reply was, "Not in the winter, its bloody freezing!"

That was about it with no other comment on the state of undress that seemed the norm in their house. I asked if I could take a shower, and came out drying myself not bothering to get dressed. I got Sue's opinions on most things, with little nods from Alan. He was different than the first time I'd met him. Maybe having his girlfriend there or the fact that the last time we saw each other we were fully dressed in Central America made a slight change in the dynamic. Whatever it was didn't matter much and we had a pleasant time catching up plus they gave me a few good tips on finding some work.

In the middle of Nagoya was a place called 'The International Center' – a goldmine of information for foreigners. I wound up finding work in an

English Language school called Berlitz there and in the same center I saw a small, hand-written ad on the corkboard advertising under the heading 'Places to Live'. Noemi was due to arrive in two week's time and it would be nice if she could come into a place that was ours. Even if it was small, it would at least get us started.

The owner of the place we would call home – Andosan, as she became known to me – was a sweet old lady, and somewhat eccentric. The small hand-scribbled ad looking for people to stay in her *geishaku* – as to what that was I had no clue – was barely readable, and her English hardly decipherable. I gave her a call, and struggled through getting directions to her place to meet her that afternoon. I took the train up, and was met by my future landlady, permanently stooped over, like many other elderly women I saw, gray-haired and with a perpetual smile on her face. I'm not sure if it was just a nervous smile, but it was always there, even when, every week, no matter when I hung my laundry to dry, she would decide to burn her rubbish – plastic, rubber, or whatever else was around – directly beneath my clean wet laundry. I would run over and rescue my clothes from the black smelly smoke yelling, "Andosan" and she would cover her mouth and shriek with laughter saying *"Hena Geijin"* which translated into 'Crazy foreigner'. I used to shake my head in agreement – she was a crazy foreigner!

The place was a small room with *tatami* on the floor. *Tatami* is the woven straw or rush floor covering that is used throughout Japan. It is a permanent fixture and is one of the reasons that shoes are always removed at the door to prevent dirt entering and wear on the *tatami* mats that have to be replaced every ten years or so. There was a small kitchen area with sink, and a one-ring gas stove. The shower was shared with all the other rooms, which were mostly occupied by young students. We were to be the only non-Japanese living there. It was fairly quiet and surprisingly clean, except of course under the smokey drying line!

Now I had work, and for the moment a place for us to live. I was ready for Noemi to come on over, and she was excited to get to Japan as well. I wanted to call her, so I searched out a phone on the streets. There was a phone in the main area outside our room, but it was only able to dial within Nagoya. I was now able to put something to the test that I had come across on my way to Nagoya.

I decided, after leaving the west coast, to stop taking buses and trains and try my luck hitchhiking – which at the time this was a great way to get around Japan because the Japanese were obsessed with learning English. I had no problems securing lifts – which usually meant a stop at the driver's house, a hot meal, and a bed. All of this came at a small cost; an ongoing

English lesson for said driver and family. What a great opportunity to meet people.

One day I was at a truck stop hitching when I ran into a French guy called Pierre who was doing the same. A trucker picked us both up, and since Pierre spoke English, the driver was more than happy to listen to us talk while mumbling some new words he might learn. In our conversation, I casually mentioned that my girlfriend was still in America, and I wanted to give her a call, but it was far too expensive from Japan. He gave me a smile and said, "Well I have just the thing you need!" He then went on to explain about a magical number he had. I was pretty sure we were entering a shady area, but my ears were open.

I had been in California the year before when Paul Newman had published his calling card account number in a newspaper because of a fight with the then almighty AT&T and this sounded along those lines. Pierre proceeded to tell me a convoluted story about 'do-loops', big business, and free phone accounts.

"The number never gets billed to anyone," he assured me. "It's a created number that is stuck in a loop and no one is responsible for the bill." He nodded earnestly, "Really!"

"Okay, go on, I'm listening," I said with an echo from the driver, "Okay, go on, I'm listening." Pierre and I looked over at the driver's concentrated face and smiled.

"If someone was responsible, after a month or two the number wouldn't work anymore. Believe me, this account is just floating around in a computer, it is a gift from one of your country's biggest companies!" "A gift from biggest company," repeated our driver.

"So you're telling me that it's an untraceable glitch in the system?" I asked, very intrigued now.

"Exactly, the phone lines are there, the company makes billions, and people like us find some unseen crumbs on the floor, and benefit for a while. Give the number to as many people as you want, it might not last much longer."

I wanted to believe that no one would be charged, and it was this big do-loop caught in the computers of a faceless large monopoly. To allay any feelings of guilt that some poor sucker had had his account number stolen, I waited for a good reason to use it, and if it was still working maybe there was some truth to the elaborate story.

Now on the streets of Nagoya I found a phone booth, called Noemi, and the number worked. Noemi was happy to hear from me, and even happier to hear I had a job, and we had a place to live. I asked her to buy me some button-down shirts and a tie or two. Japan was expensive, and clothing was small!

130

As far as the magic number was concerned, it kept on working and became a lifeline for lots of people.

When Noemi arrived it was great to see each other after nearly a month apart, and all she had to do was find some work for herself. She had the cushion of the money she had earned in California, so we were pretty sorted. Now I had to figure out some kind of transportation to explore further and start to get back to some camping.

I met Bruno – a Swiss guy who was working for Berlitz – shortly after I began working there. He was a motorcyclist as well. He and his Japanese wife liked getting around and cutting through the traffic. Exploring the Japanese roads by motorcycle sounded like fun. We made a plan for the following Saturday to go to a used motorcycle shop so I could look for a bike. I had a paycheck coming soon, a place to live, and $700 U.S. left in my pocket. He thought this would be enough to get something with maybe a little to spare. In the back of my mind I was thinking of the bike which now languished in the garage of an aunt in southern California. I was so used to that Yamaha 850 Special and had covered many miles becoming half of a well-tuned team with it. The only touring I had ever done was on that bike. It required a certain style of riding as well as having a big engine. I would be getting a much smaller machine here. I would also be entering the world of insurance, etc. Bruno assured me it was no problem. With my International Driver's license and work visa, it would be no hassle. I figured what the heck, I wanted to have a mode of transport, I needed something to explore on, and motorcycling was what I knew best.

That Saturday Bruno picked me up in front of my small *geishaku*. I hopped on the back of his bike and off we went. Bruno obviously knew the roads and small streets of the area and took turns with the practiced ease of familiarity. I was trying to take in as much as I could as I was still fairly new to the city. All the shops passed by in a blur. I longed to have more time to take in the details of the journey. I couldn't twist my head fast enough to see what the street vendors were selling, or see the views of the distant countryside as it appeared from time to time through the high-rise streetscape. We were zooming up one particular street which was a little wider than the rest of the small streets we had been on when we hit our first red traffic light. While waiting for it to change I let my thoughts drift and allowed my gaze to wander over to a huge shopfront. There was an eye-catching window display showing bicycles – bicycles lined up, bicycles suspended, bicycles propped at quirky angles. The shop was so big I couldn't believe it was only for bicycles. I shouted to Bruno through our helmets and over the revving of his motor, "What's that shop?"

"It's the local bicycle shop," he shouted back, clicking his bike into gear as the light turned green.

"Wait, let's check it out," I said.

We pulled in to the parking lot. I took off my full-face helmet and was glad of the breathing space. It was a hot September day, and all the traffic was making it hotter.

"Do you know this shop?" I asked him.

"Yeah, my wife and family buy their bikes here."

"Do you have a bicycle, Bruno?"

"Just a '*mamasan*' for shopping." A *mamasan* bike was a traditional bike with step-through frame and basket. There were a few hundred parked at all the train stations at any given time.

We walked in and I nearly fell over in amazement. I was used to your standard bike shop like the one in the neighborhood where I grew up. You could have any bike you wanted as long as it was a 'Ten-Speed English Racer' as they were known. I hadn't been in a bike shop for a while and things had obviously moved on from those days. The owner's name was Yas Goto. He spoke a little English, and was very personable. I was transfixed by all the colors, shapes and models of bikes. The way they were all displayed made the most of each bike. I noticed one very beefy-looking bike hung on a wall peg. It was green with knobby tires and it reminded me of a motocross bike. I asked Yas, "What's that?"

"Oh that's a 'mountain bike', the latest style from America."

"Can you take it off the wall? I'd like to look at it closer." I was being drawn in by this odd, wonderful-looking bike.

He took it off and handed it to me. Despite all its beefy looks, it was pretty light. Then I looked at the straight handlebars and shifters; it was calling out to me. I looked at Bruno.

"Bruno, we're not gonna make it to the motorcycle shop – this is the direction my life's heading, bicycles!"

He raised his eyebrows. "Are you sure? You want to go to the motorcycle shop first?"

"I'm very sure," I assured him. "Thanks for the lift, see you on Monday." I got the feeling he thought I was foolish. He'd probably looked at the price tag of the bike I was drooling over, which I hadn't done yet. As Yas explained to me about index shifting, cantilever brakes and twenty-six inch tires I was getting more and more hooked. This forest green mountain bike, with the words ARAYA MUDDY FOX in white was beautiful. It was the only way I could describe it.

I took a small test ride in the parking lot as I watched Bruno pull out with the spare helmet now strapped onto his rear rack. He tooted and waved, moving out into the traffic as I was falling deeper in love. The bike felt like a motorcycle, looked like a mean machine, and handled wonderfully. It was nimble, and responsive, yet it felt like it could go anywhere. In my enthusiasm I never thought to look at the price tag, but how much could a bike be? So I rode back into the shop, and asked Yas how much the bike cost. When he told me, I was doing the calculations in my head and the first rudimentary calculation came out to be about $650 U.S. I thought, that can't be right, too many zeros. $65 U.S. definitely was not a possibility either. So I asked again; he told me the same price, and pulled out a calculator. We did the math and it was indeed the equivalent of $650.00 U.S. That gave me $50 U.S. to live on till my first paycheck. I gave a perfunctory look at some other bikes but the equipment was not nearly as nice. Yas threw in a few accessories to sweeten the deal on the green 'Muddy Fox'. I took out my traveler's checks and signed away the lot. We shook hands, and I laughed to myself thinking what Noemi was going to say when I showed up with no money and a bicycle.

I absolutely had no regrets from the beginning. I pulled out onto the streets, and it was incredible. The bike handled like a dream. The balance was perfect. I could brake with both feet on the pedals and even come to a complete stop for a few seconds before pulling away. I learned later in life how this is known as a track stand, and a well-balanced bike made it all that much easier to do. By the time I got home I had forgotten about the price of the bike – we were a team already. I stopped for a drink at one of the many street vendors that graced the Nagoya streets. I explored all the small streets and alleys between the shop and my house thanks to Yas who had given me a very detailed map of Nagoya. Now I had more time to see the things I had missed on the back of the motorbike and could slow up or stop whenever I wanted. I got home and was feeling high. I was so glad that the next day was Sunday. I was off from work, and could ride my bike and do some more exploring. I called Ernie in New York and told him how much I'd paid for the bike. He thought I was crazy. He, though, had never met my bike!

Life was interesting during those first few months; falling into a routine at work, meeting fellow travelers and getting some well-needed advice on living in this expensive country. One great piece of advice was shopping in the *gomi* – household large goods rubbish piles. What a great thing to know, and another side to this fascinating multi-faceted country.

Apartments were small and people needed to be creative with space. Japan was going through somewhat of an economic boom hence all the foreigners making lots of money teaching English. The flipside of this economic boom was that the Japanese had a strange obsession with 'Keeping up with the Joneses' – or 'Watanabes' as the case may be in Japan. If you went to the right neighborhoods on the night when the large household goods were thrown away, you could find just about anything. Many foreigners, me and Noemi included, bought nothing for our apartments. We furnished our place with an electric heater, small table, throw pillows, four futons to sleep on, stereo complete with turntable, two speakers and cassette deck, fan, some cheesy artwork for the walls, toaster, small cooker, and lots of other odds and ends. All in working order and free! We would go past on our bikes and rummage through. A Japanese person would not want to lose face doing something like that, but we had no qualms about it. I even passed a music shop on my way home, and slowly upgraded our stereo system with new and better components. I wasn't sure if this happened all over Japan, or still does today, but in 1987, rubbish rummaging was alive and well amongst the happy foreigners of Nagoya.

Our first real Christmas away from home was quite nice – being away from what could be overload in America let us enjoy a small quiet dinner with a few friends. Other than that, Christmas nearly passed by unnoticed. No one made too much of a big deal about it. Most of the foreigners we mixed with didn't have kids so that took quite a big chunk of the hype out of the picture, plus we were living in a non-Christian country. At first glance though, the Japanese seemed to embrace Christmas. There was Christmas music playing in shops, and I even saw a Santa Claus handing out something to kids in front of a department store, but when the 25th was over, it all just abruptly ended – decorations and music gone and business as usual the next day.

Cycling and teaching had pretty well taken over my life. I was slowly but surely finding my path and cycling had filled in that one missing piece. I fell in with a few guys who did lots of riding, and made friends with three others who had done quite a lot of cycle touring. It also showed me how sitting on a motorcycle for long stretches had taken away lots of my fitness. In the beginning I struggled to keep up with Phil and Gianni who would breeze up mountain roads leaving me gasping. I suffered through the weeks of feeling out of shape, and slowly saw the change in my strength until I was keeping up with them. It was a great feeling to find fitness levels I never previously had, then the cycle enjoyment exponentially increased. I was enthusiastically hooked now and turned a quiet guy we worked with – Chris – onto cycling. He read all my magazines, bought a bike, and quietly explored on his own. We became friends, but Chris liked to keep to himself. The rest of us did lots of exploring together.

In Japan my second attempt at vegetarianism came to an end. With the language barrier, I was getting nasty processed pork all the time which didn't come under the heading of meat. So when I said "*nicco nai*" – "no meat" – I got much worse, so decided for the present I would try to be mindful of what I ate, but put meat back on the menu. It was also nice to

134

try the food of the world, and if I was going to travel further in Asia, many local foods are based on local meat dishes, so my culinary experiences widened. Maybe one day I would be in the right place and time for a successful go at not eating meat or fish, but not yet.

Noemi wound up getting caught up in the whole bike scene as well, and she got her own custom built mountain bike that she was doing lots of exploring on. We were getting along fine and adapting to life in a foreign country. The money we were earning as teachers was pretty good, and if we lived frugally we could save a lot, even in an expensive country like Japan.

At one point though, something started to not feel right with our relationship. I couldn't pinpoint it, but one night when we were talking it sounded like Noemi thought this was a trip – a trip to me sounded like it had an ending. I didn't want to feel I was leading her down a path that wasn't shared by both of us. I really didn't feel, or could see at that time, an end to the travel. I was exploring the planet, and enjoying finding some of my true nature. I was feeling also, I will admit, enticed by the option of dating a Japanese woman. I was only twenty-five years old and many foreigners there fell under the same spell. In the end we both opted for an honest approach. It was better to confront any feelings head on and, ultimately, a much better way for us to move forward.

We decided to look for a new place for one of us. Whoever found a satisfactory place first would move out. She wound up finding a great small apartment, and we remained good friends. We still cycled together and saw quite a lot of each other.

From time to time I would glance at my watch and think of Kenji. We kept in contact, and when one of his letters arrived it was usually short and simple, written in an agreeable child-like English print. I was amazed though, that every time he wrote me a letter, it coincided with something I was going through, and he would help give me a glimpse somehow of an answer that lay inside of me. It was almost as if he was my guardian angel, although we never saw each other again after parting on that Tokyo street corner. His watch served me well, and who knows, it may have indeed brought me good luck. His letters and wisdom were simple and always made my tough decisions easier.

When it looked like Noemi and I were staying in Japan for a while longer, and we now even had proper work visas sorted out by our employers, my mom and my dad's sister, Aunt Mary, booked flights to Tokyo. My Aunt Mary was similar to my mom in the fact that she was born in Harlem, and had raised her kids downstairs from us in the same three-family house. My Aunt Mary's husband, Lou, was a radical guy politically, and he had retired young so he could spend lots of hours gardening, doing carpentry, and keeping up the house maintenance. Uncle Lou and Aunt Mary liked to travel, and had a little more time and money to do it with. They were not rich, but having grown kids who were married and gone, and two incomes, meant that they were able to occasionally splurge. Their trips were interesting too; they spent several weeks in Spain while Franco was still in charge. I think it rubbed my uncle's political side the wrong way, but they did it. They had kept in contact with their relatives on the coast of Italy, and had visited there as well. Now a trip to Japan whetted my Aunt Mary's appetite. Uncle Lou opted out as his travel days were slowing down, but mom and Aunt Mary were raring to go. They planned to come out in the summer of '88.

In February we had been in Japan about six months; I was getting fed up with teaching English, had a case of itchy feet, and some parts of Japanese culture – the all-encompassing work life of the *salaryman* and heavy drinking – were getting to me. I was thinking of quitting my job and heading off to other parts of Asia. The problem was that Mom and Aunt Mary had already booked to come and visit seven months later. I went through different scenarios of leaving and coming back to meet them in Japan; all of them too complicated. I never let them know of my dilemma. After lots of long talks with Noemi and other friends feeling the same stresses, weighing up different ideas, and a well-timed letter from Kenji, I decided to stay. Kenji's letter seemed to know of my dilemma without me telling him about it:

*Dear Joesan,*

*Life is hard and we must get past the tough parts. Japan has moved through many tough times in history, and I am sure we will again. Joesan, you have found a path you are on, stay on it, but do not think you will love every place you live in for every moment. On any search there are bumps, and we seem to be at a loss. It is those times we must not move and try to hear something in the silence of our minds. If we move on when our thoughts are bad, those bad thoughts come with us.*

*Enjoy your work, enjoy your mom's visit, Japan has much to offer you at this moment in time.*

*Yours truly Kenji*

It really felt that he read my mind. Kenji's letter was right, do not run, face your problems first, then make a decision.

The weather got better, the ladies' excitement was contagious, and in the end it was a great lesson for me as well. It was the longest I had ever been away from home at that point and I had hurt my back on a mountain bike ride for the first time in my life. It was an injury waiting to happen from the hunched-over posture riding my motorcycle for years. I was laid up for a week; it was quite scary to be in a foreign land not knowing how serious it was. It certainly felt bad to me; I even fainted once from the pain. In the end I searched out an acupuncturist and shiatsu masseuse. I decided not to go the mainstream hospital route. With exercise and stretching I was able to keep it in check, but it still rears its painful ugly head every once in a while to remind me I am not invincible!

Many foreigners in Japan thought getting drunk was the only way to spend their free time. It's not that I didn't enjoy going out to the bars, or never had an evening drinking. It was fun once in a while, but, I didn't want to turn it into a lifestyle choice. I thought back to the clear-headedness I was catching glimpses of when I slowed down or stopped drinking all together while touring in America. It reminded me of *Donovan's* back in The Bronx. I didn't want to depend on alcohol for my good times on top of the fact that a night drinking in Japan could easily cost fifty or a hundred dollars. The Japanese businessmen themselves were under enormous pressure to go out and drink until they were obliterated. It was another example of the duality of that intense culture.

Having the bike and meeting up with the circle of cyclists I got involved with, both foreign and local, truly saved the day. I worked with an interesting mix of people. I was once more thrown in with people who were living and traveling; Gianni, who traveled through India; Rob, who had cycled across Canada, America, Southeast Asia, China, and Pakistan; John who had sailed to the Canary Islands on a small boat, and spent months in Europe hiking; Neil, who was obsessed with crossing Tibet by bike, and had tried once to date; Phil, who was a great athlete, and would go anywhere on his bike; Stephan who spent all his spare time exploring southeast Asia, and the list goes on. Those who did nothing else but drink to oblivion in their free time quickly fell off the list of people I spent too much time with. Nagoya was surrounded by easily accessible countryside, and teaching English was more like a well-paid part-time job, so the time to explore was available; you just had to make sure you didn't become obsessed with making money every waking moment of your life. I got through my funk – maybe it had been the cold winter, maybe it had been the drinking, but on the other side of that tough time was nearly another year of excellent experiences in Japan. I was grateful to my mom and aunt's visit for having forced me to stay.

Together with the philosophical books I was reading and the way I was trying to live, it all fit in. I learned to get through lots of rough times by carrying loved ones where it really mattered, in my heart. I was learning that physical presence, although wonderful and irreplaceable, was indeed only one part of relationships, not only personal relationships, even relationships with cities, landscapes, buildings, and emotions too. My travels were teaching me so much and the lessons came in such various shapes and forms.

The summer was approaching, and I was now feeling great. I had begun teaching English in the bike shop where I had bought my bike and had started learning some bike mechanics. This too set a course for my life in many ways.

My bank account was growing and I wasn't trying that hard. I kept my weekends open so I could cycle and camp with friends. Noemi and I were still getting along fine, despite the change in our relationship. I never asked about her personal life, but Nagoya was a small place and our circle of friends even smaller, so we needed to be careful with each others feelings. I didn't always succeed but I was trying.

I dated a few Japanese girls and sometimes got caught up in messy situations because of the cultural differences. I realized that dating was taken seriously, and if things went further than casual dating, I had to be very careful. It was nice all the same, and it brought me in contact with a whole different side of the experience of living in Japan. I needed to be careful of not leading anyone down a path, so I kept that foremost in my mind. I wound up getting involved with one of my students, but she was heading off to America, and we dated up until the time she left. I was able to give her many cultural hints, and was also able to relax knowing that she was heading onto bigger adventures, and our few months together was exactly that. She was busy going to university, studying English, and keeping our relationship well away from her parents' radar scope, even though she was in her twenties. I understood, didn't take it personally, and it turned out to be perfect, because it stopped her from thinking we were heading into something more serious. It also kept me from feeling I was involved with someone I might wind up sending the wrong signals to. Right or wrong, I was still guarding my emotions, my travels and my single status very closely.

Mom and Aunt Mary were set to come out in August. They were flying into Narita, just like I had nearly a year before. Everyone thought, or assumed, I would go there to meet them. My mom was sixty, and my Aunt Mary sixty-three but they were both able-bodied and Aunt Mary had some experience traveling abroad. I thought about it, and asked them if they would mind making it down to Nagoya by themselves. I assured them that Japan was safe, and thousands of tourists do it every day. They were apprehensive, but agreed. I was relieved because it would have been a very long and expensive expedition for me, and secretly, I knew it would push them out of their comfort zones. I sent them all the train information they would need and Noemi wrote out the train station names. She thought I was being a little cruel and volunteered to meet them in Nagoya station when they arrived because I was going to be late cycling from the class I taught in the bike shop. Okay, maybe I was pushing it a bit to have them wait on the platform for half an hour.

# Mom and Aunt Mary Come East

Mom and Aunt Mary successfully negotiated the journey from the airport all the way to Nagoya – which meant changing trains in Tokyo, wielding their luggage across platforms and getting help from lots of locals. The two ladies from The Bronx took on the challenge and I had to put up with a few people thinking I was insensitive letting them do it on their own, but just ask Aunt Mary or mom what one of the highlights of their journey to Japan was, and they will reply without missing a beat that it was all the laughing and hilarity of making it to Nagoya station on their own. I wish I could have been there just to see it for myself!

They came with train passes for all three of us, and also with suitcases much too big to drag around from train to train and carry through the streets looking for places to sleep. After a few days in Nagoya, and letting the ladies adapt to a very different part of the world, I gave them both a smallish overnight bag each and asked them to pack a week's worth of clothing into them. They looked at me in disbelief, but I reassured them they wouldn't want to lug around those suitcases, and wearing the same clothes for a few days running would make life much easier.

In Nagoya two of my students had invited us into their homes for dinner. It was a kind gesture, and we were served traditional Japanese food. The two ladies were adventurous and ate *tofu*, *miso* soup, and raw fish all for the first time. I remembered my first introduction to *miso* soup not all that long before. It was funny to watch my mom force down this new food, and I chuckled at the role reversal of me making sure my mom ate all her food and didn't embarrass me in front of my students! All went well at both houses, and we were given a tour of their homes. One of the student's grandmothers was an artist, and both my aunt and my mom were given a signed calligraphy painting which was extremely generous. It also allowed my students to practice their English as well as showing the Americans how a traditional Japanese family interacts. It was also fascinating for me, because on a deeper level I was finding out about Japanese culture, and I even knew that in one of those households, the husband had no idea that the wife spoke English. It was intriguing to see that all was shown to be well and working smoothly, but just beneath the surface there could be a lot of disharmony. I didn't know their daughter, but I taught many stressed-out girls of the same age, cramming for exams, and keeping up their English, after living abroad for a year or two.

140

I enjoyed discovering the strange juxtaposition of the Japan that was presented to the world and the Japan that existed on the street. I knew it was my perception, but I also knew the suicide rates and divorce rates spoke clearly and loudly as well. Here we were in the picture perfect Japanese household; women in *Kimono* bowing in typical subservient manner, and of course the children being extra careful not to say too much or speak English better than their father. I was learning all the nuances of the Japanese language; the built-in discrepancies, the women's spoken language differing so much from the men's – one language separated by so many subtleties. Japanese was almost not a language of communication, but subjugation.

I was interested to observe my mom and aunt discover their Japan, and make their own opinions. My mother is an observant person, and we took long walks together at night when Aunt Mary sometimes decided to stay back and read. My mother picked up on much of what I was noticing, asking me if everything was as black and white as it appeared in the family household. I told her of some of my observations, but held back and waited for us to explore more of Japan, to see what she would pick up on.

Our first night traveling south we found a small *minshuku* – which was the Japanese version of a 'Bed and Breakfast'. The small room you were led to on arrival normally had a small table laid out with tea awaiting you. While you were out exploring, it was magically transformed into your bedroom by moving the table and laying out the futons on the *tatami* mats. Mom and Aunt Mary were quickly getting accustomed to taking their shoes off on entering houses and traditional restaurants. When I explained the reason it appealed to both their housekeeping and practical sides, but I also learned since arriving that in Japan the outside world and inside world represented two different energies and the taking off of shoes shed some of that energy and kept it outside. It was the small cultural differences which were the most fascinating for me.

The quaintness and simplicity of the *minshuku* tickled them both – they seemed to be enjoying their trip so far. Occasionally we found other cheap accommodation in the form of a western-style hotel but I drew the line at treating the ladies to a tube hotel, or the favorite amongst some of us when we were out cycling and didn't feel like camping, 'The Love Hotels'.

Love Hotels were a Japanese phenomenon. They were purpose built for Japanese men and women having clandestine love affairs. You never saw a person in the lobby as everything was electronically programmed. You paid your money into a slot, didn't receive a key, and followed the flashing lights to your themed room. Sometimes the themes were rather bizarre. These hotels charged hourly, but after ten or eleven in the evening you paid one low overnight rate. Rob and I would sometimes find ourselves and our bikes in a room decked out with leopard-skin sheets and bath towels. It was weird, but it was a shower, bed, and quite cheap. For my mother and aunt though, there was only so far I could push them!

We explored some small towns and bigger cities on the main island of Honshu. The *Shinkansen* or 'Bullet Train' as it is known whisked us to Nara, Kobe, Osaka, and Hiroshima. I remembered the first time stepping onto the platform in Hiroshima with Noemi – a strange wave of mixed emotions came over me – part of which was guilt at being an American. I thought of a nine-year-old boy named Kenji looking out over the fields and had to remember that the children cannot be held guilty for the sins of their fathers. Although it was not my father who flew the *Enola Gay*, it was his generation that saw that horrific moment in human history. I found it to be an almost eerie coincidence that the bomb which needed to be detonated 1,600 feet above the target city happened to explode above a church, a church which survived and stood as a bleak reminder of that fateful day; fenced off, its windows gone but the walls still intact, a testament to how we can be so cruel to each other. We, as a race, need to work much harder to respect, accept and even embrace the differences which give our wonderful planet its diversity. Organized religion isn't doing its job – as a matter of fact I remember a professor of mine in college once saying, "There is enough religion in the world to keep it at war." Standing in front of that church I almost cried. I knew that Japan was not innocent of its warring past – what country was? My mom and Aunt Mary felt overwhelmed as well, and I told them of my meeting with Kenji and his story. It personalized our trip to the museum in Hiroshima – a humbling experience for anyone.

The large Buddhas and wooden structures in Kyoto were marvelous for them to experience. The west coast with the cliffs of Tojimbo staring out over the Sea of Japan towards China was a glimpse of Japan at its most tranquil. The mountainous countryside was beautiful in any season, and as the train passed through all this beauty, my mom and aunt were surprised at the picturesque scenes flying past the window on this small island country.

It was so nice to see Japan through their eyes. It was good to have a laugh with Aunt Mary reading signs in bad English like the one in front of a hairdresser professing, 'FREE BLOWJOB WITH YOUR HAIRCUT!' or the *Pachinko* Parlor's sign asking the question, 'What hell is *Pachinko*?' *Pachinko* is a gambling game – a cross between pinball and slot machines where you can make money, and indeed, there are men who spend their lives doing just that.

One morning in a restaurant the ladies saw how rule-bound and inflexible Japanese society could be. There was a breakfast on offer –

different combinations of three foods all for the same price. It took a half an hour and the arrival of the manager just to switch the bacon of one plate for the sausage of another – something that is easily achieved in any American diner. This kind of confusion was quite common if you tried to alter anything from the exact way it was presented. I wondered why a whole culture could be this way and came up with my language theory.

In English you are given twenty-six letters, and from that group of letters you can experiment; put certain – perhaps incorrect – letters together and come out with the correct sounding word. You can start to read or write just knowing the basic sounds of most of these letters. The Latin based languages, and indeed most languages with alphabets allow you to achieve this to a modicum of satisfaction. In Japanese however you just have to memorize *kanji* or characters. The written and spoken language is mostly learnt by memorization. There are thousands of characters in the language, plus there is a grammar which comes in the form of *hiragana*, which help string together the characters, then there is *katakana*, which is the phonetic symbols for foreign words which have integrated into the language over the years. As foreigners we all memorized those fifty-seven or so symbols to navigate our way through menus.

Children at four or five and maybe even younger are just memorizing characters and speech patterns. The creativity of learning to sound out and figure out what words look like just doesn't happen, and that – I felt – had repercussions that would last forever. Along with a culture that was pretty much a feudal society up until World War II, and very much a male dominated society, it was confusing and difficult to try to peel through all the layers, especially as so much of it was kept hidden. As a foreigner it was understood that you would never comprehend the Japanese psyche. I had friends who were married to Japanese women, and even after ten years living and working in Japan, were none the wiser to the inner workings of the complicated family system. In Nagoya, arranged marriages were still common, and a girl from Hiroshima or Nagasaki was pretty much considered un-marriable for fear of mutations from nuclear fallout in the offspring.

Mom and Aunt Mary thought the way Japanese men treated their women reminded them of stories from the 'old country' – their grandfathers treating their wives in much the same way in 19th century southern Italy. An interesting observation which made me think back to how awkward it had felt on my first arrival, but now had become a familiar – yet frustrating – all-pervasive common backdrop of life on the street.

We took the smaller commuter trains to explore the satellite towns around Nagoya which were known for their pottery. Unfortunately I couldn't show the two ladies more of the life in the countryside that I was discovering on my bicycle – the tiny villages secreted away from the neon onslaught were like a whole different world again. Along with all the frustrations and pitfalls of language and gigantic cultural chasms, Japan also had a wonderful counterculture which my bike was helping me discover. To come across traditions, ceremonies and art forms older than modern-day America itself, was another realization of how young the culture of my own country really was.

It was also the first time for either of the ladies to spend time in a non-Christian country, me too for that matter. On a practical level it meant no mass on Sunday for the ladies, but to watch a collected 120 years of Catholic indoctrination being challenged was quite eye-opening for me. There we were, in a country of people with different religious beliefs happily living and treating us with kindness. For the two Catholic women, they were sharing their time with a whole society who – according to their belief system – would be condemned to an eternity in hell. It was the first time, I believe, that the blind faith and easy to say words were actually confronted with the reality they represented. It made for interesting conversation as the green fields, and mountains swooshed by our train windows, and the cutely dressed Japanese children would come up to us, point and say, "*Gaijin*."

Fortunately Noemi's apartment was bigger than my small *geishaku,* and Noemi kindly opened it up for us all to stay in; so mom and Aunt Mary spent the laste few days sleeping in a somewhat larger place, although still on the floor. The comfort of their beds awaited them several thousands miles and a world away from Nagoya.

Their trip came to its end and they were escorted to the platform of the train with a little more confidence this time heading back to Narita airport. We had all greatly enjoyed their visit, and I had them to thank for me remaining in Japan longer than I might have when I let all the frustrations of living in such a strange culture get to me, and in return they'd had an insider's look into Japan.

# Striking a Delicate Balance

By this time I was able to separate myself from the craziness, but as much as I was enjoying Japan – all the money I was earning, all the great cycling, the friends I was making – I still found it hard to live in the city of Nagoya at times. It was a place where the energy was, for me, soul destroying. I wanted to tell the young girls who cried in my classroom because they had spent a year abroad and now wanted to leave Japan but felt they couldn't, "You have options!" I wanted to yell, but then struggled with how much I could say to a fifteen-year-old girl from a culture I would never understand. I told myself not to interfere, but then when I would hear of another suicide because a twelve-year-old did not make it into the correct school or missed a grade I wanted to shake the parents and ask, "Were his grades so important? Did it matter what school she went to?"

Suicide rates in April rose incredibly among the young during test result time as there was so much pressure to go to the right school. It was an oppressive society, as are much of the driven Asian cultures where everything is based on results, education, and fitting into a certain box. There's a saying in Japan, "If a nail sticks out of the block, hammer it back in." Working or acting outside the norm was considered taboo. I wanted to run behind the counter at the ice cream shop and make the milk shake myself when the clerk wouldn't do it because they were out of milk, even after we handed her a fresh liter and asked her to charge us just the same. I wanted to tell my student who was newly married and working for a bank when we were out for a drink that he did not have to go to America for a full year without his new bride. I wanted to ask him to bring his wife out with him one night so I could get to know her better. When I was invited to his house for dinner, I wanted to scream when his wife served us in kimono, bowing in subservience, with a foundation of sickly white covering up her outdoorsy ruddy complexion. I knew he felt he was just doing the right thing, and if he didn't drink with the company boss or go to America to live in a dorm for a year there would be no way he would climb the company ladder. I didn't understand the system that gobbled up a large percentage of the population, and spat them out at the end of their lives unknown even to themselves. Yet on a trip I took to Hokkaido I met people living off grid – the sticking out nails – showing me that even in an overcrowded small island country like Japan, it is possible to tread your own path.

The heavy drinking helped me accidentally start a small side business that earned no money, but was never meant to. I used to cycle past a very crowded train station on my way home from work every day. The train stations were huge and usually filled with hundreds, maybe even thousands of parked bicycles outside. Many of the bicycles I would notice had different colored tags on them. I probed deeper as to what the tag system meant. The bicycle police would go to the stations and keep an eye on the parked bikes. If a bike was there without being moved for a week, it received a white tag; after two weeks it got a green tag, and past the fourth week a red tag. The red tag was the important one because the next day all the red-tagged bikes would have their locks cut, and would be trucked to the tip where perfectly good bikes languished in sorry heaps. That killed me so I kept a watchful eye out for the tags. If I met someone new at work or on a social occasion, I would ask if they needed a bike to get around town. I would then keep my eyes peeled for the green tag, when spotted, I'd let them know I could get a bike for them in a week or so. If no one was on the look out for a bike and there was a great bike with a red tag, I would go by and cut the flimsy lock myself and take it home. It was like *gomi* shopping, but more risky. It was fun keeping an eye out for the cops and learning the times they tagged and left the station. I wasn't stealing the bike; more rescuing it – it was a gray-area recycling of bicycles. I found a few excellent bikes, and one friend even took his back to Australia with him. I had a *mamasan* shopping bike as well, complete with step through frame and basket, why not?

The reason for this weird 'abandoned' bicycle phenomenon was mostly drunkenness. *Salarymen* were under lots of pressure, occasionally they would cycle to a different train station, get so drunk in a nearby bar that they would have to take a taxi home, and the next day have no idea where their bike was. I turned the drunkenness and high pressure lifestyle to a beneficial non-profit bike-finding service. Some people in Nagoya started calling me 'Bicycle Joe' because of my knack of finding the best bikes. I enjoyed getting people on bikes, and still do.

Japan was the microcosm of the macrocosm. Maybe I was letting it get to me because on a deeper level I felt that Japan represented the world system of capital gain for its own sake – throw-away society and high-pressure living for most of your life. The work-a-day life of the Japanese *salaryman* seemed unbearable, but how different was it from their American or European counterparts who were making their choices within a system that gives the illusion of free choice?

State of mind is very powerful – perhaps the most powerful tool we have – so it was important at that time I didn't allow myself to be overwhelmed completely. I came to grips with where I was and what was happening within me and realized that I had the power to change my perception. After that my time in Japan was very pleasant. I made several good friends, saved some money, and enjoyed one of the most marvelous experiences of my life. I even grew to enjoying wearing a watch. I think though that was because it was from Kenji. I would glance at it for the date every so often, and if some non-watch-wearing Japanese rebel asked me for the time on the street, I was ready. Sadly, that never happened.

Nearly all of my weekends were spent exploring the surrounding area on cycle forays into the countryside where a different side of Japan existed. We would stumble on festivals, be invited to parties, and spend pleasant weekends in the mountains just being in the forests camping. The bicycle was the key I had been looking for. It opened doors into Japan and allowed me to escape all that was going on around me both in a physical and a mental way. I tried to tune into the mysterious; a Buddhist temple in the middle of the woods, or a serene *Shinto* Shrine in the middle of a big city, a strange festival in a small village, boys playing a very familiar game of baseball on a field next to a rice paddy. The bicycle was taking me to places I could never have found on a motorcycle and it was slowing me down. We made it up to the snowline of Mt. Fuji – mostly carrying our bikes – and rode down the revered volcano. It was strange to come to Japan to re-discover a love of cycling, but it was the perfect place to do it.

I still loved the mountain bike I bought from Yas, but realized my frame was probably too small for touring. With quite a lot of umming and ahing I wound up selling my bike to one of my friends through the English teaching circuit. That bike had rekindled my love affair with non-motorized two wheels, now it was time to move on to the next willing owner. We all had been researching frame materials, and experimenting with different handlebar set-ups. Neil was the most creative with his designs, and Phil just stayed with his old faithful Nishiki mountain bike he brought from Canada. Rob was looking at new bikes too – his had lots of personality, which meant it looked road weary, and it was starting to show. I decided on an aluminum frame – the latest material being used for lightness. The bigger frame was more comfortable and welded in a factory where one of the Japanese riders we frequently cycled with worked, but, crazily, I bought the frame from America in order to save the equivalent of $400 U.S. on the price – including the shipping.

On those weekends in the winter when it was too cold to cycle, it was nice to stay in the city, meet up with other friends, catch the occasional movie, or head to a house party. I had gotten to know more of the nuances of the small city. Only in Japan could a city of five million be considered small. Through Akiko, my student/ girlfriend, we explored the quieter sides of Nagoya; parks to walk through, and quiet places to eat.

147

I was enjoying Japan now – the things that drove me crazy weren't dictating my choices. My cycling forays in the mountains of Nagano, the west coast, or night time rides to Nagoya Port were part and parcel of life. A two-week cycle-camping trip to the north island which began with an overnight boat journey transported me to a far removed from culture to the one I was getting used to on Honshu.

Visiting the *Ainu* populated areas of Hokkaido was a look into a different race and traditions of the mostly homogenous, Japanese islands – their ruddy-faced complexions reminding more of the *Innuits* of Alaska and Canada. Their outdoor lifestyle and bearded faces bore no resemblance at all to their fellow countrymen. Unfortunately their lives were set out on the margins, and some needed to squeak out a living from the tourist industry selling hand-carved trinquets, and having bears chained up in front of their stalls for the Japanese tourists to torment – a sad state of affairs all around. In the *sento* though, their prideful selves would emerge. They would compare their hirsuit body with mine, and be quick to point out they were not of the same bloodline as the Japanese. They worked the land and the seas too, and were definitely not heading to lives in gray suits. I felt a kinship with the dwindling population of the north, and enjoyed their company, and the fact that, although trying to be shoved out of existence, they held onto their pride, culture, and way of life made me happy.

Lake Biwa, or Biwako as it was known was one of the largest lakes in Honshu and was cyclable from Nagoya for a weekend away. The magnificent lake was beautiful, and there was something meditative about the water lapping hypnotically up on the shore. Living near the port of Nagoya allowed for us to cycle out in the evenings and stare far across to another land, and another life. I decided not to leave Japan for the whole sixteen months I was there. All my holiday time was spent exploring the other smaller main islands of Shikoku, Kyushu, and Hokkaido. Noemi and I did a lot of it together, and as a bonus of her being in Asia, her family came out from New York and went back to the Philippines for the first time as a family since leaving twenty years before.

I remember going through a small bout of doubt about what was happening in my beloved city, New York. Many students would come back from trips to New York and tell me of how they were robbed. The news that filtered through was only the bad news, a gun battle, crime rates rising etc. Seeing Noemi's family was a reminder that life was going on in New York as usual, but I do remember giving my friend Vinny a call asking him if it was safe to walk the streets.

"Vinny, have things gone completely mad there, is crime really so bad, is it safe to hang out in Central Park?"

"Joe," his deep Bronx accent soothed me, "what're you talking about? Of course it's safe, just like when you left."

"Thanks Vinny, I figured that, but all the news you hear is so bad, it seems all my students go to New York and get robbed."

Vinny laughed. He worked for the N.Y.C.Parks Department and was a real city boy. "Joe, you talkin' about the Japanese tourists who walk around with two thousand bucks worth of cameras round their necks walkin through neighborhoods I wouldn't go to? Sometimes I wanna rob 'em just for the hell of it." He laughed again, which made me laugh too. It was true, the Japanese made good targets and every story they told me left me wondering what they were doing in those places at night or why were they handing their cameras over to complete strangers on crowded street corners in Times Square or Harlem? Our short conversation brought me back to reality, and being away nearly two years at this point made me realize I was getting the perception that many people have of New York through the media and movies that thrived on sensationalism. I now understood why its reputation was so bad, and I was raised there!

Our time to depart was drawing near. Even the magic phone number had started to give some people problems. Noemi and I both had accomplished much, but now it was time to move on. I didn't want to wear out my welcome. I was ready, and so was she. As we remained friends the whole time there, even after our break up, we decided to leave Japan together. We handed in our notices to the schools we were teaching in.

Things were winding down. I was still finding the occasional bike now and again. I stopped *gomi* shopping since there was no way I was going to send any of the stuff home. What a bummer – it was the nicest component stereo system I ever owned!

I hadn't heard from Kenji in a while, but as I was getting ready to leave Japan he had been entering my mind quite a lot. I thought of our chance meeting in the crash pad in Tokyo, of the few letters we had written to each other over the past sixteen months, and how in his subtle way, he always made me feel calm. I would look down at that watch – which never let me down the whole time I was there – and smile. I dropped him a line to thank him for his friendship. I had no reply. I felt, though, that he was there, and somehow he knew. He was a special person, and he gave me a lot of strength. His generosity meant a lot to me, but now his watch, which was still strapped to my wrist, had served its purpose. In that short time in Tokyo, and through his few letters, he was always part of my life on that small Pacific group of islands – he became an unforeseen force for my time there. I wondered if I should give the watch away to someone else but decided no, it wouldn't be the same.

We were catching the train the next day, but we had another week in Japan before we made it to the port to embark on the boat to South Korea. Fortunately, a letter arrived from Kenji; I thought I'd save it to read on the train. Noemi and I had shipped our bikes to separate countries; Noemi's was on its way to New Zealand, and mine was heading to Australia. We would head to South Korea, spend some time there, buy plane tickets to catch up with our bikes, and continue our travels separately.

I sat on the train reflecting back on the past sixteen months in Japan; such an interesting mix of honesty and dishonesty, history and modern society, the sublime and the surreal. Japan's many dualities were at once paradoxical and fascinating. *Shintoism* and Zen Buddhism lived side by side in relative harmony – in the middle of a neon city like Tokyo you could find, just by turning a corner, a quiet solace in a Buddhist temple with the brazier full of incense sticks, and the quietness of a perfectly manicured rock garden. After hiking or biking in the mountains on a dirt road (which might be quite a few miles from any village), you would come across a vending machine selling *Pokari Sweat*, the Japanese version of a sports drink, and Coca-Cola. Hard-working people, who were only one generation from a war ravaged country, throwing out perfectly good household items just to be able to say they had the latest model.

The contradictions you confronted every day in the landscape, culture, and personal lives were always a challenge to my western mind. If you left your camera at a train station by accident and came back an hour later it would still be there; if not, it was sure to be at the lost and found. You could leave your backpack anywhere in a large department store in Tokyo, take off and wander for an hour or so, come back grab your pack and go. How interesting coming from a society where husbands and wives didn't communicate with each other, and children live in such secretive high stress that pushes them to dive in front of trains.

On the other hand the serene subtle movements of the traditional tea ceremony, the *koans* of the Zen Buddhist tradition, and the meditative sounds of the *Shakuhachi* flute, also had their roots in the small islands that produced the gray-suited *salaryman*, and the high speed *shinkansen* train. It had been an eye opening time for sure.

In the language school I worked in we had a struggle to change an unfair rule about men wearing earrings. We were dealing mostly with westerners within the hierarchy, but *they* were working within the Japanese system. One of the main arguments put forth was that we were the link between the Japanese and the wider world. We were teaching the Japanese to speak English, to do business in America, Europe, New Zealand and Australia, where earring wearing was a lot more common. Their argument was that we were in Japan, and Japanese did not wear earrings, especially *salarymen*. That was the whole point we thought; true, Japanese did not wear earrings, but *we* were not Japanese. Finally, through an ongoing dialogue, men who wanted were allowed to wear earrings, which was quite a large percentage of the foreign staff.

Tattoos were another story, and luckily mine were well placed; I could wear a short sleeved shirt and a pair of long trousers and they would not be seen. If exposed they would always attract attention, as only the Japanese Mafia – *The Yakuza* – normally had tattoos, usually fine works of art covering the whole of their back, not quite like my small separate pictures scattered in different places.

A few friends said jokingly, "Ah you are escaping the clutches of Japan." It was so true, there was a lure – the money was good and the work pretty easy. I knew some people who made quite interesting lives for themselves and had been there a long time. Japan had many more layers to explore more deeply if you desired; traditional pottery, music, art, Zen Buddhism, to name a few, but for us it now felt correct to be leaving.

Our friend Phil had frozen to death in Hokkaido on a cross-country skiing trip gone bad. He was a great guy and on many mornings turned me on to the mountain roads around Nagoya. His death, like any death, makes you look at what you are doing, and question it to make sure it feels right. Also a grim headline about a plane being blown out of the sky in a place called Lockerbie, Scotland, had just made the news. A lot of people would never have the choices we had right now.

Japan was a place much like Guatemala in that it showed me a lot about myself. It could have been a dangerous place – without a wide circle of friends, or family around who knew you well, you had to keep yourself in check. If you wanted to drink every night, have a different lover every night, and go off the rails, you could do so, easily.

I didn't always pass the test of being who I liked to be when I looked in the mirror. For a few months I was lured in, but woke up one day, feeling hung over, and realized this was not the path I had wanted to get on when I left Guatemala. Instead of leaving Japan then though, I knew from experience I had to leave Japan the person I wanted to be, not just run and take the person I did not like with me. So with the help of Kenji, my mom's and aunt's visit, bicycles, camping and having Noemi always stay a good friend, I stopped the things I didn't like. I changed all work so my weekends were free, and never took a job, no matter how financially appealing it was, that I didn't want to do. I needed those few months off the rails in the middle of my stay in Japan, just to see how easy it is to become who we don't want to be. It's a good feeling to be in tune with yourself, and now I felt ready to go. My bank balance was a lot bigger than I would have ever dreamed, yes it could have been even more, but then I wouldn't have had all those great weekends camping in the mountains, on the seaside, or enjoying a different side to the craziness that could be Japan.

I took a quiet moment looking at the landscape passing by the train's window to read my letter from Kenji.

*Dear Joesan,*

*I am sorry to take so long in replying. I was up in Hokkaido and did not receive your letter until I returned to Tokyo.*

*I am happy you are continuing on with your travels. Your time in Japan is over. Maybe we will meet again one day. If not, you know where to write.*

*Yours Truly, Kenji*

As usual, a timely letter, short, sweet, and to the point.

We were on the train to Shimonoseki sitting silently next to each other. Were we doing the right thing? So many people decided to stay and earn more and more money, some stayed because they genuinely loved Japan – again, everyone made their own decisions. We both felt that if we stayed any longer it would have been purely to make more money. Our relationship as a couple was over, but it was still confusing. We were young and now heading out of Japan together, but not really.

I looked down at my watch after folding Kenji's letter into my pocket. I was shocked – it had stopped working. The whole time in Japan it had kept time wonderfully. I was never late for an appointment and always knew the date. The watch was a true timepiece. I felt sad that it decided to give up the ghost, but then I thought what perfect timing. It had brought me luck, served me well, and fulfilled its promise – now our time together had ended. I looked at Kenji's letter again, '*Your time in Japan is over*' – it did feel right to be heading out of Japan. I was taking with me few possessions, now I was taking one less. I felt that it was Kenji saying, "Don't worry; you're doing the right thing, just follow your heart." I left the watch on for the last few days just to see if it would jumpstart back into life, but it never did.

We stood at the dock waiting for the boat to leave from Shimonoseki to Pusan in South Korea. I looked down at my watch, then into the pale-blue Japanese sky. I envisioned the camera zooming in on my watch, then me. I unstrapped the watch with its hands frozen at 7:22, and, probably just as smoothly as Peter Fonda did in *Easy Rider*, I threw the last watch I have ever worn down into the water and watched the few bubbles that rose to the surface until they disappeared

# Christmas, New Years and New Beginnings

Noemi and I spent Christmas in Seoul, traveling up from Pusan – South Korea's Port city in the south – by bus. When we found the place we were looking to stay we met some Londoners staying there and we all hit it off immediately. Christmas in this foreign land was not going to be a lonely affair, quite likely much the opposite!

The guest house was alive with travelers, some on holidays from working in Japan, Hong Kong or South Korea, and others just traveling around. After working in Japan for nearly a year and a half, it was nice to be in the travel buzz once again. Even though we were in Asia, South Korea and Japan could not be more different. South Korea was unbridled in its energy; the drivers were brash, people shouting at each other, fights nearly breaking out on street corners, whereas in Japan everything was so restrained and stoic that you never felt you knew what was going on inside. South Korea felt like maybe you knew too much and in some ways made me homesick for a good traffic jam in New York City!

Our guest house was a crash pad for travelers on a budget. We had gotten word of it from an American guy who was working in Nagoya and he had warned us not to mention we were coming from Japan – there was not a lot of love lost between the two countries. He had made the mistake of mentioning he was working in Japan when visiting Pusan and what had been a warm atmosphere in a small local bar turned quite frosty, to the point where he felt he should leave the premises. We were careful not to broadcast we had just left the 'Land of the Rising Sun', but obviously with other travelers it was quite an open topic.

We had a meeting in the guest house which brought back the encounter with the butterfly man in Guatemala – there was a guy there asking the same questions – I asked him what he was gathering the information for. As expected he replied a guide book – just filling in information on the places he couldn't make it to. He was living in South Korea with his wife and young child so it was difficult to get to every place he was writing about. This was now the second writer I'd met with a similar story. I felt it might be a bit misleading to the readers of those guide books, especially when some of the modern ones put forth quite strong opinions about things. Whose opinion were you actually getting? It was another first-hand collision course with reality. I'd never relied too heavily on guide books anyway, and since those two meetings, I remain aware that they are only written by a man or woman that I might not always agree with even in person.

There were many other travelers however, and they were full of valuable information. One of them let us know that although Seoul was a cheap place to buy plane tickets, Thailand was where you wanted to go for the best deals. Hmmm, an interesting twist, but maybe a last fun adventure for Noemi and me in Asia. We were heading off to different countries – our bikes were already en route – so a trip to Thailand would be brief. Summer was underway in Australia and New Zealand and we both wanted to get on our bikes. We were comfortable with each other, but since we knew we were not continuing on with our travels together, it felt odd at times.

Christmas became a party in the guest house – all the westerners going together to a restaurant, sitting around a huge table, sharing drinks, food and a lot of laughs. The *kimchi* – a traditional chili-hot fermented cabbage dish found everywhere in South Korea – warmed our insides, and cold beer chilled it off. We had even nick-named the subway system in Seoul *The Kimchi Express* because in the bitter cold weather the overcrowded hot trains were filled with the smell of garlic and *kimchi,* oozing out through the pores of the locals. It gave an interesting effect, especially the morning after our Christmas celebrations.

Our foggy heads also warranted a visit to a bath house – a nice hot soak would help wash away the overindulgence of the night before. The Korean version was a totally different experience to the Japanese one. Much as life on the street differed, so did life in the steamy bathhouse.

The male bathhouse experience began with immersion in a cold pool of water. You had to move into several different pools, each one warmer than the last, until the final one which was extremely hot – a constant movement from bath to bath, unlike the stillness of the Japanese communal hot soak. Afterwards, for a price, you could choose to have a massage, shave or a haircut as you desired, and the ambiance was that of a blend of massage parlor and hair studio. Toothbrushes were individually wrapped and given to you if needed, as were disposable razors. Hot showers with a powerful jet rounded off the experience nicely. It was like entering a quiet steamy world in contrast to the wintry streets of Seoul.

Noemi's and Sally's experience was quite different. Where the men's section had no kids, the women's was more like the mayhem of a playschool with unruly children of both sexes running around screaming and chattering. There were no haircutting chairs but you could shave your own legs if you'd dare to do so in public. A massage was available, but the pools were far from relaxing with kids splashing around in them. They wound up enjoying a soak in the water after two embarrassed mothers quieted down their children for the foreigners' sake, but the experience was nothing like our semi-relaxing ritual.

South Korea, like Japan, and much of the world, was a male dominated society, and right down to the bath house this showed through. Once again the woman took care of the children, and the female bath house was anything but a relaxing escape from it all – more tantamount to hard work.

Jezz and I emerged relaxed, our cobwebs massaged away and our bodies wrinkled and clean from our showers and bath. Despite the differences, Noemi and Sally managed to look relaxed as well, having enjoyed the experience. We said goodbye and exchanged addresses with Jezz and Sally – we would all stay good friends for years to come.

We found a ridiculously cheap flight to Thailand, and were off in two days. Seoul had prepared us slightly for the madness of Bangkok, but not totally. *Tuk-tuks* – a motorized type of transport resembling a rickshaw – were everywhere weaving in and out of the traffic. Their drivers seemed to be on a suicide mission but fortunately their missions failed, and somehow we made it to Kosan Road – the place to stay and buy our cheap tickets to Australia and New Zealand – alive.

Walking around the streets with Noemi was interesting. People assumed I had rented my companion to take me around and keep me company at night. Noemi was getting used to mistaken identities; crossing the States some thought she was a Native American, in Guatemala people spoke to her in local dialects, in Japan she had the problem of being mistaken for a Filipino prostitute and here she was taken for a Thai one. It was amusing sometimes, but frustrating for Noemi. It also showed that the land-crossing theories and migrations of people from Asia to the Americas could possibly be factual. Even we both found Noemi's similarities with the indigenous populations in Guatemala and Mexico to be striking.

After only a few short days in Thailand staying on Kosan Road, we had secured our flights. The detour had delayed our upcoming separation, plus Bangkok was colorful, crazy, noisy, and so different to our time in Japan. We both knew if we wound up traveling in Asia at any point in the future, Thailand would have to be explored further.

Noemi's flight was the day before mine and after she left I was suddenly alone and asking myself, "Is this the right thing?" I was on a soul search, knowing I couldn't keep a comfort zone around me in the shape of a girlfriend, a job, or whatever it was just so I would not have to feel the acute pain of necessary change. I felt that if I was to truly find where I was heading, I needed to always be honest. I was glad we left Japan together, but now also happy that we were able to go our separate ways. Now, for the first time in over two years, I was alone once again. It felt both good, and confusing. Noemi was also facing her own truths in New Zealand, undoubtedly going through her own confusion as well. Her bike was headed to a woman's house who was a cousin of a workmate in Japan, so at least she had somewhere comfortable to start from.

When I landed in Sydney I was without my bicycle for the first time in a long while. I had a couple of contacts in Australia; Alan in Melbourne, John in Western Australia, and Chris whom I had met at Berlitz and turned on to cycle touring. His family had emmigrated to Adelaide and Chris had insisted that it would be no problem to send my bike to their address and meet up with it there.

As I now stepped for the first time onto the soil of another continent, my bike was journeying alone on a boat heading to Chris's family house. I was facing New Year's Eve alone in a country where I could speak the language. Since being in foreign lands for a year and a half, I had forgotten the simple joy of easy communication and it took me a while to come down from the high of it. I was talking animatedly and at New York pace with the bank teller, the shop keeper and anyone else who would listen – it took a few strange looks before I realized that I was appearing more like a speed freak than a friendly stranger. I tried to tone down my approach and chuckled at myself.

I stayed in a hostel called 'The Pink House' in Sydney for a couple of days. New Year's Eve 1988 was a much quieter affair for me than Christmas 1988 in Seoul. I walked along Kings Cross, supposedly a bad area to be alone at night, but it felt strangely comfortable and I was far from alone, but not quite in Times Square. I was still feeling in many worlds, so much change had come pretty quickly – no job, no girlfriend, no bike, new country, new year, able to read or converse with anyone I wanted – it was nearly sensory overload.

Sydney is a stunning city in its geographical location; the Harbor Bridge, the ocean beaches, the Opera House, all looked exactly as it did in movies. Summertime was in full swing and everyone had shorts on from the mailman to the truck drivers. I had not seen so much blond hair since leaving Los Angeles. It was a perfect place to walk around, take in the fresh air, but at the same time walk the streets of one of Australia's biggest cities.

I knew my bike would be getting to Adelaide soon, so I made my way by bus from Sydney to Adelaide, anxious to start my solo bike journey in Australia. I had heard about the prevailing westerly winds, so my plan was to head out to West Australia by bus and cycle east. I could catch up with John whom I had met in the same crash pad where I had met Kenji. We had exchanged a couple of letters and he had told me to look him up if I was ever in Perth.

Chris's family was very welcoming and friendly although Chris himself was out touring in England on his bike, alone of course. His sister Clare and her friends were my contemporaries, so I met them and had a pleasant week as I waited for my bike to arrive. I learned about Christmas Crackers – an English tradition which the family took delight in showing me for the first time. I also, for the first time, and certainly not the last, found out how to do the washing up in a bowl, not earth shattering, but if done worldwide could save billions of liters of clean water from being repurified. My New York style of constantly running the water was making Audrey, Chris's mom, uneasy. These were the little clever things I could not wait to incorporate into my life, and tell my friends and family about when I finally made it back to New York – satisfyingly resourceful.

I also had a brief encounter with one of the famous Australian spiders, the big hairy, scary type. I was at a café in the beach area south of Adelaide enjoying the scenery, and still trying to come to grips with the fact that I was in Australia with some money in my pocket, nowhere to be, waiting for my bike to arrive from Japan. Life was feeling nice, my confusion fading as I enjoyed simply strolling along the beach. The sun was out, and as I ambled up the street, my head in the clouds, I noticed someone walking ahead of me with an interesting design on the back of his tee-shirt. I then noticed that the design was moving across his back – that cool a design I assumed it wasn't. I hastened my pace to catch up with him, excused myself in a hurried voice and asked if he had a pet tarantula. He looked at me quizzically and answered, "No," so I quickly brushed the rather large spider off his back onto the pavement. Everything happened so quickly that when the spider hit the ground with a slight thud and quickly scurried off, the confused fellow realized what it was all about. He just looked at me and said, "Thanks mate."

"No problem," I answered, "Just wanted to make sure it wasn't your hundred dollar pet before I smacked him off your back."

"Not my pet, I can assure you." He looked at the ground again, and shuddered a bit. He thanked me again and disappeared into the crowds.

I was a little freaked out by the whole incident, and hoped I didn't encounter one of those spiders in my tent or sleeping bag one morning. After a week of checking out the night life, eating curried kangaroo at a party, body surfing the waves of the Indian Ocean, flicking hairy spiders off people's backs, and meeting an interesting group of people in Adelaide, my bike finally arrived. I then bid farewell to my friendly hosts in Adelaide, the Edwards family.

The bus journey out west was long and excruciatingly painful as the back problem that had reared its head for the first time while living in Japan had now come to call for the second time. I made it to Perth, and spent one very uncomfortable night in a squishy youth hostel bed.

In the hostel I met an Englishwoman, Jean, who was also traveling by bicycle. She was working and saving for the next leg of her journey; from where we stood to Queensland – no lifts, no trains, just pedal power. The first leg had started nearly two and a half years ago. She and her boyfriend had quit their corporate law-firm jobs in Coventry, England, taken a ferry to Spain, headed on into Morocco, and spent a few months cycling in North Africa. Her boyfriend couldn't take it and wanted to stop. They flew home together from Algeria where she said goodbye to him, returning two weeks later to Algiers to continue solo on what turned out to be over two years of pedaling across the Sahara. Her bike had real personality. Racks welded out of steel to match her original aluminum ones after they had been crushed under the wheels of a truck; she told tales of riding on the crust of the hard sand. When I asked if she had ever been hassled being a woman alone in mostly Muslim dominated part of the world, she looked at me with her hard, steely blue eyes and simply said, "No." I wouldn't mess with her that was for sure! She had never seen her boyfriend again, and was thriving on her solo journey. She was looking forward to crossing the Nullarbor Plain, which I presume would be a cakewalk after two years riding through the sandy Sahara Desert. Meeting all sorts of travelers was a great buzz. I admired her determination, and even though I was new to cycling, I was hoping to be more flexible in my travels. I didn't want my bike to define me, or my journey – I wanted it to be an integral part of the exploration. I would see what happened.

I was feeling quite tender with my hurt back, and I was a little nervous about my first true solo bicycle journey of any great length. Even though I didn't aspire to travel like Jean the ex-lawyer, meeting people on journeys like hers would take the edge off of my nerves, and I would realize that once you are moving, you settle in and things sort themselves out.

I gave John a call the next morning. He was glad to hear from me, and with his directions I cycled to his house. He was a warm, generous guy, and when he saw me wince in pain, and hold my back he suggested I borrow his back brace. I declined but the next day went to search for help. I went into a chiropractor's office but somehow it just didn't feel right. He was trying to sell me on more visits, and when I explained I was on a cycle journey, he then said he could set me up with his colleagues along the way. I wasn't feeling inspired by my first visit. As I left the office I made another appointment with the young secretary, but wasn't sure I would keep it. As I walked down the road I passed a health food shop where I noticed an advert for an acupuncturist. The ad looked simple, and acupuncture was what had got me back on my feet in Japan. I took down his number and gave him a call as soon as I got back to John's. We made an appointment for the next day as my back was feeling decidedly worse since my visit to the chiropractor.

The acupuncturist worked out of his house – he had a bright smile, a genuine face, and must have been in his late sixties. He asked me to lie down and tell me the history of my back problem without worrying about the time. He then asked me to turn over, and inserted some needles. He then asked me to sit, put a needle in my knee, and I felt the pain release from my back. It was incredible. He noticed my shudder and said with a smile, "Not many people are open enough to feel that release." I told him I was very open to acupuncture, and had great faith in it. After what seemed like two or more hours he only charged me for a half an hour session since I was traveling and foremost he wanted me to get on the road. He then gave me the number of a friend of his who did deep tissue massage. He said I should give him a call, and come back for one more session of acupuncture after that.

His friend who did deep tissue massage was also an older guy, but his handshake nearly crushed my hand. Short of lifting me up and placing me on the table, we were into what would be an hour and a half massage. It was wonderful, but painful at times. He was also determined that the most important thing was that I be on my bike again. He only charged me for a forty-five minute massage, although I was there for nearly two hours all up. He said there would be no need for another session, and to wait another day or so before getting more acupuncture. I was walking much more erect now, and felt great. I booked in my appointment with the acupuncturist for two days time.

John was working night shifts in the gambling casino in Perth so we didn't see too much of each other, but when we did, he was interested in my progress as he also suffered from a bad back. We talked about Japan, and he asked me about Kenji, because he remembered that we spent a lot of time talking together. I told him briefly that we kept up letter contact, but had never seen each other again. He filled me in on Guatemala where he had recently been, and said he'd loved it as well. There had not been too many changes since I was there and he had found the people as captivating as I had. He didn't mention the history that had so much changed the perception of basically everything I knew up to that point in my life but said he was taken with the simplicity and the smiles. I smiled remembering that same feeling.

I was looking forward to my acupuncture appointment, but I think John was even more interested. He had seen me nearly hobbling a few days ago, and now he saw a vast change after only one appointment and a massage.

I called the chiropractor to cancel when I was sure I would not be going back. The secretary remembered me and somehow we made a date for dinner. I think my accent went a long way. The next day I just rested like the masseur said I should and when John came home I had made breakfast to show my appreciation for him opening his house to me. He was off night shifts in two days and suggested we go to the casino together so he could give me a good tour of the place. The next day I went for my acupuncture appointment. I was feeling much better now, and after that final treatment I was ready to go. Again he only charged me half-price, and was happier to see me so much better – a chance find, but those two men were the right people me and my back needed.

Dinner with Lisa was relaxing; to be in a foreign land but a known culture had a lot to be said for it. We both knew it was a casual date and talked and walked the warm balmy night away. The Australian accent is strong, and to be walking along with this woman speaking her accented English looking up at a backwards moon in the sky in the wrong seasonal weather felt perfectly normal because I could read all the menus in the restaurants, all the road signs, understand everyone around me, and knew that no matter what happened with Lisa and me that night, I would not be sending out mixed messages. It was a mutual attraction, and we were coming from the same headspace – such a difference to the last few months of my life. I felt relaxed with her, and hadn't realized how spending all that time in Japan had put me on edge in a casual dating situation. It was nice to feel light, and also a relief that my back was feeling much better as well. Lisa said she knew from when I walked out of the office that I wouldn't be coming back. She was glad when I called to break the appointment, and had been pleased when I asked her out to dinner.

John was shocked to see me so much better and took the numbers of both men and wrote them down in his phonebook. He was a skeptic on the acupuncture side of things, but I was living proof.

The casino was interesting as far as casinos go – they are not my thing, but it was fascinating to see the intricate security systems behind the scenes. We had a nice day and ate a great meal in the casino, but now that I was feeling better – I was raring to get on my bike. It was perfect having a house to stay in while I healed, and John was glad to be the one to help. He still wore the Guatemalan friendship bracelet I'd given to him in Tokyo.

I saw Lisa one more time – we star gazed, enjoyed being with each other, and I think because I was so relaxed in her company, she relaxed in mine. She told me she'd filed my folder away and not to worry about paying the balance for a treatment that had made me feel worse. I smiled and thanked her, and she answered, "No worries." I love that Australian saying, and still use it quite often. I enjoyed spending time with her and John – in many ways that time gave me the space to heal both physically and mentally. I felt re-adjusted to being back in the somewhat known, although I was approximately 13,000 miles from home. Now I could not wait to start on my first long-distance, open-ended bicycle tour.

I set off from Perth early the next morning, a wind in my face, but nothing was going to dull my excitement, I was on the road. Getting into Freemantle felt as if I had cycled into San Diego California; it was picture-perfect and clean with outdoor cafés dotted around, and most people had that healthy, I-live-in-a-lovely-place, glow about them. Freemantle had won some status since a local had won the America's Cup yachting competition. I am not one to follow such sports, but when someone heard my accent he insisted on showing me the boat that beat the Americans at their own game. It was a nice diversion, and it was early enough that I knew I would be able to do some more cycling that day to enjoy the weather, and feel the freedom of nowhere to be, some money in my pocket, and everything I called my own strapped onto a bicycle. I humored my tour guide and was drawn in by his enthusiasm. When we got back to the café, he bought us lunch, and was still talking about yachting. What could I do? He was buying, so I listened for the better part of an hour, and then I knew I had to be moving on. I liked Freemantle, but it was too upscale for me to want to stay the night.

That night I free camped on an estuary. I woke up early in the morning, and glanced over to see about fifteen or so kangaroos having a drink in the early morning light. I quietly packed up my tent, and basked in the perfection of that moment. The crunch of my bike wheels on the gravel road alerted them to my departure, but they didn't look too concerned.

The cycling, hugging the coast, was quite nice – when I was too hot I could jump into the ocean for a dip. I mixed up free camping with the occasional campsite for showers. My back was fine, not perfect, but was improving daily. I ran into two physical therapists, Marianne and Carmel, at a wine tasting place near Cape Leeuwin, the southwestern most point in Australia. We camped out together for five days, and they showed me some exercises and did some soothing massage to help put to rest some residual niggling pain. I couldn't believe my luck. They were out for a week of quiet away from Perth. We had fun exploring the area, sharing an onsite mobile home, and talking into the wee hours of the night while sampling lots of the local wine. So far the travel had been mellow, the cycling challenging, and my back pain was showing me that even a situation as bad as a hurt back could have a good side, and although my back was becoming my Achilles heel, it would also lead me to work in bicycle shops and be more attuned to people who wanted to ride bikes but be more upright and comfortable.

161

After leaving there I started, for the first time in Western Australia, to head east. I made it to a youth hostel in an area known as 'The Valley of The Giants', where the largest trees in Western Australia towered over me. I felt so small cycling through their magnificence and was glad of their shade. Cycling on a fully loaded bike with no real destination made me feel like this was it – the real thing.

I was realizing I needed to come to grips with a new language – one quite similar to my own. In one instance, a farmer whose land I was camped on asked me in for tea. I thought a hot cup of tea would be perfect before I started cooking my evening meal, but instead was served a full dinner, what a great accompaniment to the beautiful balmy night – quite a pleasant misunderstanding. *Yakka* was work, 'tea' was dinner, and 'mate' of course meant friend, buddy or anything along those lines. 'Bitchumen road', I learned in a funny interchange of total confusion which delighted the local farmer I was getting directions from, wasn't a street name, but a description meaning paved road.

In a place called Albany, I looked up John's parents and helped out on the family farm for a couple of days. It was good hard *yakka* and well worth it for the bed and the home cooked meals. I was expected because John had forewarned them of my arrival. They were sheep farmers, and at this point in my life I was eating meat again, so it was good to see everything that goes into rearing it, and I learned, first-hand, what *yakka* really meant!

I had opened a bank account in Australia when I arrived. I thought it would be easier than carrying traveler checks or money. The cash in my pocket was now dwindling and when I'd made it to a small village assuming there'd be a bank, I was proven wrong. I knew there was a bank fifty miles west, but I bypassed that town by taking a small forest road instead. I decided I'd hitch back to the larger town early the next morning.

I camped out and finished up the last of my food and woke to a bright, beautiful morning. I rode to town and asked if I could leave my bike at a gas station for a few hours. "No worries mate." I pulled on some trousers over my cycling shorts, locked up the bike, and stuck out my thumb. It wasn't too long before I was picked up by a logging truck. I hopped in, and he was heading right past the town I needed to get to.

We started to chat about the beautiful forests around the area. I told him I had cycled through some of those forests, and then he launched into his story about seeing a cyclist the day before on the twenty-five mile metal road through the forest not far from here – metal road being another term I learned the hard way meant small round stones about an inch or two deep making for awkward and extremely difficult riding. I asked him what kind of car he had and as he told me we both realized that we had seen each other on the metal road the day before.

"Was that you?" he asked astonished, then continued, "Me and the misses were coming back from a wedding and we felt bad for not stopping to offer food or a lift, but there was no room in the car, and not a crumb between us."

I laughed to myself, "No worries," I said trying out my new favorite phrase. I continued, "I had enough food, but man, cycling on a metal road is difficult!"

He then surprised me by asking, "You're not one of these Greenies who want to stop all the logging, are you?"

I felt a little lost for words and stumbled over a reply, "Well don't know if I'm a 'Greeny', but I like trees, and feel maybe clear-cutting isn't the best idea, I try and do my best to respect the environment."

He stopped me and said, "You know, actually I'm glad for the Greenies, I've been a logger my whole life, and I've seen some bad things done in those years. Sometimes the logging world can be too radical as well, and we need people on the other side to keep the whole argument in balance."

I was blown away. I didn't know if he was feeling guilt, or just coming to realizations in his later years, but it was good to hear it from someone like him, and the rest of our conversation was about cycling, Japan, and some of his travels abroad.

He dropped me in front of the bank, told me where to stand for a lift back, and said he'd put the word out on the CB that I was looking for a ride. I got to the bank, and thought just maybe it was no coincidence I was picked up by a logger. I put a face to the Greenies for him, and he put a human side to the loggers for me. We're all just trying to do our best. These 'coincidences' seemed to be cropping up all too often. I felt that maybe when you do cut a path, and follow through on the feelings which guide you from the inside, more and more of these chance meetings are out there.

I cycled on for a few more days just enjoying the time to myself. Now I was heading west and the wind was in my face – maybe my information was not altogether correct about prevailing winds – I started to think that it was probably better to just cycle in the direction that felt right, and take what came.

I was still new to cycling, and probably not as hardy as I could have been, but I was enjoying the experiences that came my way. On a long empty stretch of road between Esperance and Norseman I ran out of steam, and water, in a place called Grasspatch.

Grasspatch wasn't on my map – it was a pub, a few houses and as far as I could see, not much else. I noticed an abandoned house, and all the surrounding land looked like scrub, not great for camping. It was hot, and flies were a constant nuisance. I had even taken to eating lunch on my bike so as not to swallow flies along with my sandwiches. I went into the pub which was quite busy. It was near dusk, and I was going to ask if anyone minded if I slept in the abandoned house. As it transpired, no one would have cared, but I was made an offer by a farmhand called Paul – who heard me asking the bartender about the house – to stay at the farm he was working on. I gladly accepted. After a few drinks, and a celebratory round bought by the owner of a racehorse that had just won a local race, I was in with the locals.

I noticed a few local kids milling about my bike and touching it. I wasn't too concerned, but kids will be kids, and my life was on that bike. The bartender saw me go out and check the bike and she reassured me I wasn't in The Bronx, no one would touch my bike or equipment. As I left to throw my bike in the back of the pick-up truck, my heart sank – all three of my water bottles were missing. I went back to ask the bartender if she had recognized any of the kids. One of the guys at the bar said, "I noticed one of them, he looked like one of Trevor's kids." Now obviously that meant nothing to me, but it definitely did with the local population. The bartender apologized and said she'd somehow sort me out in the morning with some bottles. I told her it wasn't her fault, but asked what the story with Trevor and his kids was. She told me Trevor was a nasty piece of work, he had MS, was partially paralyzed, and liked to drink. His kids were pretty much the village troublemakers, and it wouldn't do to even try. I had a flashback to the classroom I was thrown in being told that the kids were 'bad'. I thought I would give it a shot anyhow. Paul looked at me with a raised eyebrow. "Good luck," he said as he pointed out the house. I wasn't looking forward to this but I was more curious than anything else and I really needed those water bottles.

When I got to the house I could see the strobe-like effect of the T.V. out of the window turning the darkness blue and white. I knocked on the door hard so they could hear me over the volume, when Trevor yelled out, "Yeah" I took that as, "Come in." So I did. I laugh to think of how I must have looked still in my cycling shorts, coming to plead my case for the missing water bottles to them.

I introduced myself then said, "Your sons and their friends were around my bike earlier, and I just noticed my water bottles are missing."

I was abruptly interrupted by Trevor with a can of beer in his hand, propped up by a few pillows on a dirty looking couch, the television still on, but the volume turned down. "Are you accusing my sons of stealing your water bottles?" Then, half-yelled across the room "D'you know anything about this man's water bottles?" A guilty, "We didn't do it, we didn't touch nothing on that bike of his," passed feebly through their pursed lips.

I cut in, "I wasn't accusing you at all, I just know you were around, and probably know all the other kids. I came here to ask for your help. Tomorrow I'm facing about eighty miles of hot hard cycling. Those bottles fit especially into my holders, and I'll need as much water as possible."

I then explained about my trip, and even Trevor looked interested, "You cycled all the way from Perth t'here?" he asked.

"Yep, and tomorrow will be a pretty bad day if I have to strap glass bottles to my racks. I would deeply appreciate it if your sons could possibly help me out, that'd be great." Even though it was a basic textbook getting the kids on my side plea, I did have faith in it, and thought maybe it would work. Trevor engaged me in a short conversation, and on leaving I just said to the kids, "If you happen to find out who did it, or find the bottles, just leave 'em near the front of the pub. I'll be getting some water there in the morning. Thanks."

I left the house and went back to the pub. "How was ol' Trev? Glad to see you?" Paul asked teasingly. I told him it didn't go too badly. The bartender said, "No worries, either way stop by tomorrow morning, and we'll have plenty of cold water for you."

Paul and I drove out with a few others in the pick-up truck – better known in *Strine*, as Australians call their colorful language – as a *ute* (pronounced yoot), short for utilitarian vehicle. After a basic meal of leftovers of some sort warmed up on the stove, I was asked if I wanted to go on a roo shoot (shooting kangaroos considered a nuisance to some farmers). I must admit it wasn't top of the priority list, but I thought oh well, it's all part of the Australian experience.

Two more farmers showed up and we all piled into the *ute* decked out with a powerful spotlight, shotguns and a high powered rifle. I was a tad uncomfortable with all the guns around amongst the beers and decided I wouldn't drink any more to keep my wits about me. We started driving out into the paddocks and came across a rabbit. I was handed a shotgun, and Paul said, "C'mon Yank, let's see what kind of shot you are!" I hesitated slightly and asked why we were killing rabbits on a roo shoot, the reply being that they fed the dogs the meat, and they were a menace to the farm. I was not used to shooting animals. As a matter of fact, I never had, but now the spotlight was on, the target running, and I found myself shooting at Peter Rabbit. I shot and unfortunately hit. Paul jumped out of the *ute*, picked the carcass up, and threw it in the back. The next thing we saw was a fox, and as it was running in zigzag motions under the spotlight, I was once again thrown the shotgun with the explanation that foxes weren't native animals, they were a menace, and the meat was good for the dogs as well. I didn't believe the last part, but I shot wide and thankfully missed the fox. My second shot caught it, but maybe didn't kill it, but another gunshot from the truck definitely finished Mr. Fox off. As Paul went over to get the fox, I did something which I'm sure broke every rule of proper gun safety – I put Paul in the sights of the gun. I thought how utterly bizarre guns were, you pull a trigger and something falls dead yards away – no eye to eye contact, just too easy. I thought of wars, drive-bys, and the other gun related problems the world faced. I'd killed two too many animals already. I put the gun down and knew I didn't want to kill anymore.

As we drove around the paddock, a shout of "ROOS!" was heard. The spotlight scanned the fields, and, in a scene similar to my first morning waking up on the road a few weeks back on the estuary, there were a handful of kangaroos grazing peacefully out in the field. The spotlight froze them in place, then I was handed a high powered rifle with a proper scope. "C'mon Yank."

I put the roos in my sights and they just looked back at me. I put the gun down and handed it back to Paul. He looked at me almost as blankly as the kangaroos in the light. I said, "Look, I've only been in Australia six weeks I'm not going to kill Skippy, I don't care how many fences he kicks down or what they're classified as." Paul shrugged his shoulders, took the gun, and took out two kangaroos before the others fled.

It was a situation I probably could have done without, but you can't undo an experience. I had killed two animals, got caught up in the adrenaline rush, and even had a human in my gunsights. The vision stays with me always, and I have never killed another animal since then. We got back to the farmhouse, where lots more beer was consumed, but I managed to slip under the radar to get away with just one more. As we all headed to sleep, I knew I had just experienced a side of life I was glad not to be a part of.

When I got back to the pub the next morning to start my ride across the dry hot landscape I was delighted to see all three bottles had mysteriously turned up and were sitting on the railing in front of the pub. I went in to fill them and there was not a little surprise on the face of the bartender from last night seeing my bottles had been returned. She filled them with some icy cold water which would quickly warm up to a tepid tea temperature, but it was wet! The whole experience of Grasspatch was fascinating on many levels. I was glad to have been there, but happy to pedal out of it giving Trevor and his sons, who were peering out of their front window as I pedaled past, a thumbs up and a big smile.

A few days of quiet cycling in the dryness and heat of the west was proving to be challenging. I needed to flag down a car asking for water, as all the water I started with disappeared quite quickly. I was ill-prepared for such hot weather cycling. I was not sure of my exact plan. The countryside had lots of options for free camping. I enjoyed pedaling in the late afternoons, as some coolness would descend – a respite from the daylong heat. I was on the outskirts of a small village and sat down to have a snack. I was just closing up my panniers and looking at the sky thinking I'd better get moving on the night's accommodation. Just then a cyclist with a guitar strapped on the back of his fully loaded bicycle pulled up and said, "Hi."

I returned his greeting and we started talking. "Which way you headed?" I asked him.

"Perth" he said.

There was something strange about his accent, it sounded as though he might have had a bit of French thrown into a northern American twang. I asked if he was French, but he said, "No, Quebecquois." Ah, that explained it I thought.

"Where you coming from?" I asked him.

"I've just come from Adelaide, the wind strong at my back for ten days. I used my tent as a sail; I couldn't sleep well at night thinking it might change direction. Which way you headed?"

"By the sounds of it into that headwind. Was it really pushing you for ten days?"

"Yeah, it pushed me and doesn't seem to be letting up. I wouldn't want to pedal into it, that's for sure." At least he was honest.

"I need to get some food and pitch my tent. You camping out tonight?"

"Normally I would, but I met a farmer who told me to meet him here. I'm sure he won't mind one more person – stay here and see what happens. Oh, by the way, my name's Craig." He thrust his hand out and we shook hands.

"Joe, nice meeting you Craig. Thanks for the invite. You sure that'll be okay?"

"Not sure, but I'd be surprised if it was a problem," he answered.

From what I had experienced so far hospitality was usually par for the course. The possibility of a bed and home cooked meal sounded pretty enticing but I didn't want to get my hopes up. "Okay, let's see what happens."

We chatted some more and I discovered that he'd started his travels a while ago with his girlfriend from Canada. Their idea of cycle travel was different; he was hardcore, and she was into the more gentle side of cycling and the occasional lift. Craig felt he needed to cycle every inch of the way on principle, whereas it sounded like his girlfriend didn't see it

167

like that. They talked about it, and decided that to remain friends they should split up and do their separate things. At the moment she was in New Zealand hiking, I told him of the coincidence that my ex-girlfriend was there cycling.

We got off the subject of girlfriends and travel and started talking about bike equipment. We were both touring on mountain bikes which were fairly new on the scene. Touring bikes with conventional, but sturdy racing tires were more the norm for travel. In Japan since purchasing my first mountain bike, then buying the new bike I was on, lots of tweeking and experimenting went on to come up with the newly formed hybrid mountain-tourer I was now straddling. The straight bars I first fell in love with had given way to drop handle bars for ease of changing hand positions and getting down out of the wind when necessary. I kept the shifters and had adapted them to fit the drop bars. I now had three racks and semi-slick tires which were more conducive to touring. In Japan our group was into mountain biking and touring and we found a frame builder who was willing to humor us on all our experimenting – new forks with longer rakes and braze-ons for low-rider racks, higher front ends etc. Since my first step into a bike shop only seventeen months ago, I had turned into quite a bike nut. When I told Bruno that this was the direction my life was taking, I couldn't have been more correct. Anyhow, Neil and I were the first ones of our friends who settled on drop bars with the mountain bike for touring. Since mountain bikes were still in their infancy, it was an unusual sight, and surprising that Craig also had a mountain bike with drop handlebars. We both spoke about the versatility of touring with a mountain bike, and how the drop handlebars combined the best of both worlds.

As we were talking bikes we heard a pick-up truck pull up. Out stepped a big burly guy with a thick Australian accent. "I see you found a friend. No problem, there's plenty of room at the house and plenty of food cooking on the stove." It was music to my ears, my discomfort about joining Craig immediately quashed.

We threw our bikes into the back of his truck and off we went. After about a ten minute drive into the dry fields on the outskirts of town we saw the farmer's house in the distance. It looked like it had just grown in the field – it was so much a part of the land. I had jumped into the back of the pick-up with the bikes and had time to reflect on people's different priorities and ways of traveling. I could see now how Craig's puritanism might have been hard for his girlfriend, especially since she was new to cycling, and they had started out together on the northeast corner of Australia, quite a long way and thousands of hard kilometers from where we now were.

As I took a hot shower I let my mind drift. I thought how Craig and Jean would hit it off – maybe he'd meet her in the hostel if she hadn't left by then – that would be an interesting match. I then remembered a novel I'd read before my first trip across America by motorcycle – *I See by My Outfit* by Peter S. Beagle. It was about two guys from New York going across America on scooters and had made an impression on me. The scooters had defined their trip and somehow themselves. I felt I was defined by my years traveling by motorcycle – a motorcyclist, a greeny, a logger, an American, a Mexican, a cyclist – who cares? There were already too many labels attached to people. I didn't want to live as a labeled anything, or be defined by a mode of transport. Craig and Jean's hard edge was fascinating, but I felt it also made them inflexible.

I then realized my time in Japan had not been only about cycling and teaching English, I had been exposed to some Zen philosophy, and was now seeing the beauty of the empty space, the non-defined me, the silence in between, the need to not have everything identified and categorized, the subtlety of bending in the breeze. I just hoped everyone – including me – was enjoying their chosen paths and leaving space for others to weave their own tapestries.

Stepping out of the shower in an old farmhouse and drying myself off with the smell of freshly cooked lamb filling the air, in our own room with two big beds, pillows, even a night table and reading light was, for me, the beauty of the bicycle, the pedal strokes didn't matter nearly as much as the connections it helped make happen. The small little luxuries and kindness that occasionally came your way were always appreciated at the end of a long day's ride.

Dinner was excellent; fresh lamb, carrots, pickled beetroot, a garden salad that was so alive I felt it might jump out of the bowl. What a feast, and most of it fresh. All the farmer's children were grown and gone and we were sleeping in what had been their two sons' room. His wife was of the hardy stock that farmer's wives seem to come from. He told us of his childhood growing up in Western Australia back in the thirties and forties. It was a whole different world. He camped on the land as a young lad of twelve or thirteen, and it wasn't strange for him to meet up with some of the descendants of Australia's original inhabitants. The Aborigines taught him to read the night skies, make fires without matches, and sleep out in the bush safe from snakes without a tent or any of the mod cons of modern day camping. He gave Craig and me a good recipe for 'billy bread' as he called it, basically an unleavened bread to go along with meals by the campfire. The way he spoke of the Aboriginal people of his childhood nearly brought tears to my eyes. I could tell he disliked the duality of being somewhat a part of the marginalization of the ancient race of intuitive people, but again he never would have had the life he had if his grandparents hadn't moved to Australia in the 1800's. What an intricate, confusing web we all do weave. He probably was about sixty-five years old or so, but I felt we were talking about a time way before the middle of the twentieth century. For me it was a history long gone from the environs of New York City; not even the oldest inhabitant of my area would have comparable stories with the American natives. There was no end to the stories he could tell, and Craig and I were riveted.

We prompted him and his wife to continue, but he was equally as interested in our stories. At first Craig told us of his adventures cycling across the Australian continent. His stories were also inspiring to me – he was hardcore, and I felt like a complete novice at long-distance cycling – which in comparison, I was. It had taken him months to cross the vast dry continent. He'd had some interesting meetings with Aboriginal people across the Nullarbor Plain.

One of the most bizarre people he'd met though was a Japanese guy who was rollerskating – with a huge pack on his back – across Australia. Having lived in Japan, I understood the psyche behind a lot of the obsessive Japanese travelers. As Craig described him, I felt I knew his personality, and was all too familiar with the society and the pressures that creates either *salarymen* who wear their gray suits and become one of the millions in 'The Japanese Machine', or the type who will do the absolute bizarre, those who turn so fully away from it all that they become obsessed in their quest for adventure. Craig's stories of his time rolling across Australia the past seven months were of picking grapes, pruning trees, sheering sheep, and lots of pedaling. My Australian adventure was just finding its feet, but I must say that both Craig and the farmer were more interested in hearing about life in New York City, rather than my few experiences so far in Western Australia.

It's a strange thing coming from New York, especially The Bronx. I feel the place sometimes far outweighs the person. Of course, I, the person, was shaped by coming from that place, but movies, books, and television put so many pre-conceived ideas in people's heads that it is difficult to explain that where I come from is quite different to that. My area of The Bronx was full of private houses rather than high-rise apartment buildings, and a lot of people had back gardens. The European influence in my area was immense. There was no typical Christmas dinner as I had neighbors from Ireland, Germany, Greece, and Italy, so the traditions reflected those roots. Yes, I did know drug dealers and people who were shot, overdosed, etc. but in a funny way, I never thought of my neighborhood as being rough – actually it wasn't. It only sounded rough when I tried to explain it to farmers who camped out with Aboriginals under the stars at twelve years old.

The television was humming in the background, I was vaguely aware of its presence as I was struggling to explain that my last job was teaching in a place called Co-Op City, an area of The Bronx that was built on a swamp in the late sixties; 320 acres of high density living, the largest of its kind in America, over 15,000 habitable units and over 50,000 people living in 35 high-rise apartment buildings. Make that clear to someone who lives in an area of the world so barren and vast that instead of counting head of sheep per acre, you count how many acres were needed to sustain one sheep!

The school I taught in was on the outer margin of this urban jungle. I tried to paint a picture that didn't make it sound horrible. Describing that to a person from rural Australia who had rarely, if ever, left its borders was getting me some blank stares. Even Craig – who was from Montreal, and had traveled far and wide – was rubbing his goateed chin.

All of a sudden, I thought I heard the news presenter saying something about "Rap music, break-dancing, and Co-Op City." I turned to look at the television, and there on the screen was the school I taught in. I calmly said to Craig, the farmer and his wife, "Well there it is." I couldn't believe my calm even as I said it. We all turned to the television and watched.

They were interviewing students of the schools I had been teaching in only two years previously! There were the occasional panning shots of the buildings, the parks within its borders, break dancers, and kids of all colors, shapes and sizes trying to get into the picture, as kids do when a television camera is thrust in front of them. It was not a piece on Co-Op City as much as a piece on world dance and music, and since New York was the birthplace of rap, there it was, Co-Op City, The Bronx. We all watched in utter silence as my descriptions were given life right there on the screen in front of us. It was quite a long piece I thought, and after the two or so minutes we all turned back and faced each other. I clapped my hands and said, "Well there you go, that was easier!" We all had a good laugh and could not believe what had just happened as the report segued into India and some form of dance which was popular there. I had a real inside chuckle to myself. The rest of the night continued with warm conversation and we all felt like we knew each other that much better at the end of it. It wasn't until I was lying in bed later with my mind drifting off to New York City schools, Johnny C still teaching in them, that I realized how incredible that unlikely coincidence really was.

Breakfast was a true farmhouse affair – all farm fresh produce right down to the milk. The bright orange-yellow yolks of the eggs looked like they had added pigment in them. The coffee was probably the only imported item on the table. The bread was fresh and although Craig was looking forward to heading west, and being dropped off at the same spot we were picked up so he could continue the last few hundred miles of his adventure, I had been lulled into a comfort zone, and could have spent more time with the home cooked meals, and fresh food on offer. I think I was not looking forward to a ride across the Nullarbor Plain into a potential strong headwind. I didn't have to make any decisions yet though. It was a sunny day with a light breeze at the moment. I took the lift back with Craig, not for any other reason than, in a reverse reflection of Craig's wishes, to avoiding having to pedal on the two kilometer long, bumpy driveway that led to the farmhouse.

I was enjoying the difficulty of cycle touring on other levels, but didn't feel the need to pedal every single inch of the way. My mental and physical strength were coming on quickly, but I wasn't ready to face down a 1,500 mile headwind alone. I was feeling good, but was still in my break-in period. My short trips in Japan were becoming distant memories, and I was slowly adjusting to the longer distances of Australia, and the subtleties of the changing landscape in a big arid country.

I arrived in Norseman and the wind was still blowing quite strongly in my face; the same wind which pushed Craig west was now threatening to fight me for the whole way back. I spent a night in Norseman not sure if I would cycle or hop back on a bus. I would let the wind decide. The next morning it was blowing just as strongly. I toyed with the idea of pedaling, but had nothing to prove; maybe if I had been a more seasoned cyclist the challenge would have intrigued me. I decided to catch the bus.

This bus ride was much better than the way west because my back was feeling normal, and I'd now had the wonderful experiences of over a month's cycling behind me. Although I knew Craig would not approve, I enjoyed the contrast. The bus driver was quite funny, and my seatmate – a young girl heading home to Sydney – was quite chirpy. As my mind had recently drifted to Johnny C, I thought about music; I no longer carried the bulky radio cassette player, but oddly enough had two of his tapes with me still. I'd nearly forgotten about them since I hadn't listened to them since living in Japan. Then an idea occurred to me, the bus driver agreed. So as the unfamiliar vastness of the Nullarbor rolled by, Johnny C's familiar musical taste filled the bus, and saved us from tedious elevator-type music.

The bus dropped me a two-day ride from Adelaide. I had been traveling in Australia for two months by this time. It was the end of February, and the weather was perfect for cycling. In Adelaide I stopped briefly to see if Chris was back, and he was. We caught up for a few days, and he told me about his trip. He made England sound idyllic for cycling. I wanted to see it for myself one day.

Chris and his family were soon moving back to England. Chris and I would see each other once more, ten months later in Melbourne. His life had a few more cycling adventures ahead, and his family seemed happy in their decision to move.

Now I was heading to Melbourne to catch up with Alan, this time on his home turf. We had become reasonable friends in Japan, and he had left Nagoya about six months after I arrived. He and Sue had had plans, and I was curious to see what had become of them. I was able to contemplate a lot on the empty roads, but now the vast expanses were beginning to get monotonous for me; headwinds notwithstanding, the hugeness of Australia was more than I bargained for on my first leg of this cycle journey.

I pulled into a roadside eatery/convenience store to benefit from a cool drink as the dry wind in my face was making sure that my throat was constantly parched. I camped the previous night enjoying the company of three Europeans from a small country called Lichtenstein, it was the first time I'd ever heard of the country. One of the threesome carried a small postcard with a map validating its existence, as on previous travels he'd come up with quite a few blank stares from many people like me. We had a good chuckle about that, as I had quite the opposite problem coming from New York. It was nice to have some company as I was getting weary of the long days in the saddle, the heat and constantly fighting the cyclist's invisible, but seemingly ever-present foe, a head wind. I was feeling I wouldn't mind a small break.

Melbourne was approaching slowly, but still many pedal strokes away. As I sat, luxuriating in the coolness of the drink, I noticed a bus schedule. It was nearing day's end and according to the schedule I could be sleeping in Melbourne that night. It was running an hour late which gave me time to disassemble my bike and put it in its travel bag. Fortunately the shop was also the bus depot. I decided to cut a few days off the cycling, opting for a four-hour bus journey. We would arrive in Melbourne at ten p.m – not the ideal time to arrive in a major city.

I boarded the bus and found myself sitting next to a Canadian guy. He was a little older than me and felt slightly out of beat. He was nice enough, but quite edgy about arriving in Melbourne so late. He was angry that the bus was now arriving at ten. Nine would have been perfect, but ten was just not right. We chatted about this and that. The Youth Hostel, he informed me, closed at ten.

As the city lights of Melbourne loomed up on the horizon I had a good feeling. I was looking forward to seeing Alan, who I was soon to have met up with in three very different parts of the world; Guatemala, Japan, and now his native town, Melbourne. I didn't call him or want to put him out when I knew the bus was arriving late – I'd call him the next day.

173

Our bus got in a few minutes before ten and my Canadian bus companion was off in a flash to the phone booth. He ran back to get his enormous backpack. I had to take a second look to make sure he hadn't grabbed my bicycle bag accidentally as his pack looked so unwieldy. I wondered what he could possibly have in there, as he had told me he wasn't even camping! Off he ran apologizing to me that there was only one bed left at the Youth Hostel and he'd called a cab because they were waiting for him to arrive. No time for pleasantries. Goodbye!

Bus stations are notorious for being on the wrong side of town but I didn't get any bad vibes as I pulled my bike bag off the bus, took a few deep breaths, and tried to get back into my head space. Putting the bike together is about a twenty-five minute job in the light of day so I figured I'd be pedaling out of the bus station before eleven. I slowly and methodically laid everything out, and enjoyed being reunited with my bike. I had a good feeling, and chuckled to myself when I thought of Mr. Canada running off like the Tasmanian Devil spending who knows how much on taxicabs and antacids.

It was a beautiful balmy night and I was now hanging my last pannier on my bike ready to pedal off. I asked someone the direction of Camberwell, the suburb where Alan lived. They said it was a long way off and pointed left. 'A long way off', I had learned from experience, could be anywhere from two to thirty kilometers, so I instinctively shrugged off the comment. For some odd reason, I decided to head off to the right. I asked the next person I saw if there were any parks around where I could put up a tent for the night. He assured me it would be dangerous if I did so. I'm not sure why he was so certain. Could it be because he was on the prowl lurking near bus stations close to midnight? I still was feeling unworried and felt it was all going to work out fine.

Pedaling along slowly I saw a guy on a bicycle ahead of me with a flowing shirt, a long ponytail and what seemed like a cool aura trailing behind him. I caught up and initiated a conversation. His personality was just as he appeared; cool, laid-back, and dare I say, hippyish. He saw my bags and asked where I had been, where I was heading, etc. He had just gotten back from Indonesia earlier in the year. Then he said, "Hey, you want to get an ice cream mate?" I replied that it sounded like a great idea.

I now found myself enjoying a refreshing ice cream cone with a complete, but very nice, stranger. How many lives ago was I sitting in a Carvel at midnight with my friend George on just such a night?

"Where ya heading mate?" he asked.

"Camberwell, I have a friend who lives there, but that's for tomorrow. Tonight?" I just shrugged.

174

He nodded and took a big mouthful of ice cream. "Camberwell's not this way mate, it's that way." He pointed in the direction I knew I should have been pedaling.

"I know but I wanted to get an ice cream first!" We both laughed. By now it was well after midnight and I was starting to realize I was tired.

"Where ya sleeping tonight? Need a place to crash?"

"That'd be great." I said. "You know of one?"

"I'm heading to a room I've been renting while looking for a flat. I finally found one and am nearly moved in. I'm heading back there now to pick up some a few things. Tomorrow I'm coming back with a *ute* to get my bed and stereo." I was following his story, but being tired and with his strong accent and use of slang, I wasn't sure if I knew exactly why he was telling me all that. Then he continued. "So if you don't mind a bed without sheets and a small room you're welcome to stay there for the night. My lease is up tomorrow."

"I have a sleeping bag. I was planning to put my tent up in a field but a room with a bed and a stereo sounds great," I said in appreciation.

"You can even have a shower if you want, mate. Might as well, it's all paid up till tomorrow. I'm sleeping in my new flat tonight. Just don't steal my stereo." He smiled.

"Nowhere to fit it." I smiled back.

We finished our ice creams and cycled to his rented room – my place for the evening. He took his bedding and shoved it in his rear pannier. He showed me where the shower and toilet were, grabbed a few more things, shook my hand and said, "Pleasant dreams." We never even exchanged names. I never saw him again, but didn't need to. Our moment was there and then.

After a hot shower I listened to a few tunes on the radio and spread out my sleeping bag on the small comfortable bed. I turned over, looked at my bike and smiled. Traveling was about everything; connections, bicycles, buses, trust and even ice creams at midnight!

# Tasmanian Devils to Kiwi Hospitality

After leaving my private room for the night, I made it to Alan's and stayed with him at his mom's place. We caught up on what had happened with us both since Japan. Alan had fallen out of his traveler's mindset and was re-adjusting to life back home. We went to the city and walking in the Dandenongs – the hills not far from Melbourne. The city had a nice vibe; it was small, yet the second largest in Australia. I wanted to explore it deeper, but not just yet. It was autumn and the weather was looking perfect in Tasmania, but winter would be closing in pretty swiftly. It still felt strange to be talking of the seasons back to front, as it was now March. I purchased my plane and boat tickets from a local travel agent to Alan's place to ensure my journey would continue; I was ready for more cycling. After our short visit we knew we'd catch up properly when I got back to Melbourne in a few months time. I was heading to the island state of Tasmania, and from there on to New Zealand. The short break with an old friend renewed my spirit.

The boat was rocking all night – the trip from Melbourne is known for being choppy. Luckily it was an overnight ferry so I slept through the roughest part of the crossing. When I woke the sun was breaking over Tassie, the term a lot of Australians (Aussies) like to use for Tasmania. Australian English is littered with shortenings of words, slang, and many phrases that make no sense at first, but soon become so normal. I waved goodbye to the dozen or so cyclists all setting off together. They were a nice bunch whom I'd met in Melbourne and we'd eaten together the night before, but their schedule was tight, and traveling in a big group like that didn't appeal to me. I wanted to explore this small island once known as Van Diemen's Land, floating in the open waters made up of the Indian Ocean, the Tasman Sea and the Bass Strait anchored just south of Victoria, Australia, slowly. I was sure there was much to see and I would have to cycle on the main roads sooner or later, but not just yet. Tasmania was definitely going to be a more manageable size for cycling than the vastness of the mainland. The west coast had a definite appeal; remote, rugged, maybe not many roads, but not 1,500 miles away.

I took a look at my map, and was getting ready to leave Devonport and pedal off west on the tiny road that wound off into the distance when I saw another cyclist looking at his map on the grass verge. I walked over to make sure he didn't need any help, and as I got closer I realised he was a fully loaded cyclist on a mountain bike. I said, "Hi, you alright, any bike problems?"

A Midwestern American accent came back at me. "No problems, just got off the same boat you did. I was waiting for the crowds to be on their way. I'm thinking of heading that way." He pointed west, the same idea I had.

"Actually the northwest looks intriguing," I said. "I'm thinking much the same – Sandy Cape, possibly Woolnorth."

He motioned me over to the verge where he was looking at his map. "That's just what I've been mulling over myself. I normally like traveling solo, but it's a small island, and there's only one road west. Since we're thinking alike, what about we pedal together?"

"Sounds good to me," I replied. His accent made me smile, it was so different to the Australian accent I had been getting used to over the last few months. It brought me back to my motorcycle trips. "Looks like the cars and bikes are all gone, and that road sure is calling."

"I'm Norman, call me Norm," he said, offering a strong hand to shake.

"Joe," I countered as we started making a move towards the bikes.

"I've been exploring just tiny bits of Victoria. My trip's nearly over, and Tasmania is my last stop, just decided two days ago to come on down, so I've no real plan, just following my nose," he added. We both seemed to have the same loose no-plan way of traveling; that was good.

We were both intrigued by the lack of roads marked on our map in the northwest heading towards 'Sandy Cape'. We cycled on our thin ribbon of road devoid of cars, trucks, bicycles, or anything. It was rather quiet for a road leading from the major ferry terminal. The ferry had been full, but nearly everyone had gone the other way. Norm and I got to know each other better as we cycled slowly along what seemed to be our own private road heading west. We had studied our map enough to know the few small turnings that actually did exist and we knew that ours should be coming up soon. We pulled into a small shelter which was buzzing with three or four locals putting up a map. It was a new tourist shelter that looked a little like a bus stop, but without a bus coming anytime soon.

We looked at the newly put up map, which had one of those big red 'X' markings that said, "You are here," along with the rest of that part of Tasmania. Norman and I both said at the same time, "Oh, we missed our turning." At that moment a hush fell over the small place. The people putting up the brand new map looked at each other, then over to us. There was a slight uneasy feeling for a moment until I broke the ice and asked, "Did we say something wrong?"

They all looked at us, and one of them said. "What did you just say?"

I repeated, "Did we say something wrong?"

"No not that, we all heard that correctly, but what did you both say just before that?" the tallest guy asked, not in an angry tone, but one of almost disbelief.

"Oh, that," Norm said with a smile, "we just said we missed our turn."

That didn't help matters any, and now they all looked at each other once again. "I told you someone'd notice," said a woman in her mid-forties who was up on a step ladder.

I explained further, "It's no problem, we both just realised according to your new tourist map that we just missed our turn."

They all sighed and the tall guy then groaned, "We thought that's what you said." It still didn't make sense that they would be so upset about two cyclists missing their turn, until the woman on the ladder explained. "The, 'You are here' X was a misprint. In fact you haven't missed your turn, it's a kilometre up the road, not behind you."

It came out that when they received the map from the printer they had realised the 'X' was in the wrong place but they had decided it was such a small road that no one would notice the difference and decided to put it up anyway. We were the first people to stop in the new booth with the map not even officially up yet, and we realised it was in the wrong place.

They laughed at the absurdity of it then Norm said, "Don't worry, we won't be typical of the people passing here using the map booth. We spent a lot of time on the boat poring over the map. We're thinking of enjoying some of the more remote spots, hopefully making it to Woolnorth."

One of them owned a kind of ski lift which shuttled people to the top of what was lovingly known as 'The Nut' – a small Tasmanian version of Ayers Rock. It was a big rock that jutted out of the earth in what was otherwise a very flat coastal area on the north shore of the island. The owner said, "If you do make it to Woolnorth, you'll be passing right by The Nut on your return trip. Stop by and get a well-deserved complimentary ride up."

We talked a while longer, and by the time we had finished our conversation, we noticed the woman on the step ladder started to take down the section of the map with the misprint. She said, "I feel we should change the mistake. After all, it is a tourist map, and no matter how small the road is, it's obviously been noticed, it just doesn't seem right, thanks fellas." She gave us a smile, then added, "Have a great trip, it's rugged on the west coast, but you'll love it there."

Our first meeting with the locals was an encouraging one, and we even helped out the local tourist board! We headed on to our first turning away from the coast and deeper into Tasmania.

Norm and I cycled well together; although fit, he had a slightly slower pace than I did. It didn't matter though. We chatted on the flats, and on the climbs I would wait at the top. He liked getting into his easiest gears and spinning away. I liked pushing a harder gear which meant I got there a little quicker.

The land was immediately rolling, green and beautiful. We cycled into a small village, and camped out in a local park. The local kids were very friendly and curious. We spent a good part of the evening showing them our gear and they were fascinated by the amount of stuff we could pack on our bikes. They were quite sweet in their innocence – some of them had never left Tasmania. They were curious about our travels, and why we were doing it, how did we like Tasmania, and all the usual questions of young curious minds. Although they all wanted a ride on our bikes, we opted to explain about the equipment, and showed them the gear system, which seemed to satisfy their thirst for taking rides.

Tasmania – population in 1989 only 450,000 – is the brunt of quite a few Australian jokes, the small/big, north/south mentality. It's the same the world over. The thing I find quite funny is that often those who are the brunt of the jokes are usually the nicest people, and quite unaware or even do not care about the jokes. The people here knew about the jokes, but didn't take it to heart. The many people we met who lived in and loved the place practically swore us to secrecy about its beauty and tranquillity. They did not want the word to get out because they knew they had a little jewel tucked away from the rest of the world.

We would be told by some people not to mention how great Tasmania was to anyone. They would put their fingers to their lips and say, "Shhh, it's our secret." Who cared about the jokes? I'd nod and gesture locking my lips tightly with a key then smile.

Norm and I headed out down to even smaller roads, and the surfaces deteriorated so that we had to push our bikes occasionally. The camping and the seclusion were fantastic. Norm enjoyed the task of building a fire to cook, and had it down to an art. He was a true Montana outdoor boy, and it showed. My learning all came from the road, but his oozed from his Midwestern pores. We made it to the seaside together and there we met abalone divers. They were a rough bunch but friendly. We struck up a conversation and ended up spending the evening together. As we cooked together over an open fire they told us about the dangers that abalone divers face and how they had either had close scrapes with sharks, or knew someone killed. We gained some respect with them because of the rough roads we had endured to get where we were. I sat back and enjoyed the ambiance of the chat and the cooperation required to work together to cook over the open fire and thought about the incredible differences between all the lives of the people we had been meeting here, and those I had met elsewhere in Australia. Had I been born in this part of the world, I could have been one of this crowd. Me, an abalone diver; the thought made me chuckle.

The next day the road got mildly better and we made it to a place called 'Grim Bluff' on the northwest corner of Tasmania. In yet another lesson of man's ability to inflict untold horror on his fellow humans, we learnt that this was the place where the last Aboriginals of Tasmania were chased to fall to their death in the late 1800's, mostly women and children. I thought back to my school years learning about 'Manifest Destiny' – the concept of the new European arrivals in America sweeping across that wonderful land because it was ordained by God. How misguided we all can let ourselves be.

Norm and I were enjoying the cycling even though the fillings were nearly being rattled out of our teeth. We camped out under a full moon, which enabled us to cycle and walk our bikes under its glow. It was utterly magical. By the light of day we knew the river that was accompanying us to our left was stained black from the tanin in certain leaves in the forest, much like tea stains water. We were told it was harmless to drink even though it was slightly off-putting, but while cooking by the light of the moon, the color of the water was not so apparent.

We finally made it back onto a paved road and eventually pulled into a proper campsite where I went into the office to pay for a pitch. We were filthy; the mud on our bikes probably thicker than the mud on our clothes. The biker's tan on our hands from the fingerless cycling gloves looked even deeper with the added layer of dirt on our fingertips. The man in the office was amiable and asked how we were enjoying Tasmania. I told him where we had come from, and realised that he didn't know we were cycling – the bikes were leaned on a wall out of view.

"Did you see the two blokes on bikes?' he asked me. "I heard there were two cyclists pushing their bikes up near Grim Bluff." I just smiled my muddy smile and watched the realization dawn on his face.

"Are you those two cyclists?" The surprise clear on his face. I nodded. "Well tonight's camping is on me. We don't get many cyclists coming up from the west coast, was it tough going?" We then fell into a conversation about our route, and he laughed, "Yeah, you're the ones who noticed the mistake on the map, are you going to head up to The Nut tomorrow?" I was now finding out how small Tasmania was and how quickly news made it even up to this little tucked away corner in the northwest.

I answered, "If the offer's still on we'll go up. We're more looking forward to a hot shower right now though!"

I think he then noticed how dirty I was, "Yes, oh yes, we have plenty of hot water, enjoy it. They changed the map you know. By the way if you didn't go to The Nut I think Bill would be offended"

"Believe me, we wouldn't miss it for the world but first hot water! Tomorrow, The Nut!"

I came out smiling and shouted to Norm that we were famous. I told him about the free camping, and then Norm said, "I just had the same conversation with a local who saw the muddy bike and asked if we were the two cyclists coming up from near Woolnorth. He invited us to stay with him on our way south and gave me two apples from his orchards." Then he threw me an apple. I proceeded to crunch into the ugliest, bumpiest, most deformed yet tastiest apple I had ever eaten in my life. We basked in the setting sun, baking the mud a little more deeply into our skin, enjoying our new-found celebrity status.

The hot shower was wonderful; shedding my mud layer I felt like I thought a snake must after it sheds its skin. I looked a few shades lighter, as did Norm. We decided to splurge on a meal and even a drink. We went to a pub which served both and being in a somewhat small town, we were quick to make friends, and we both probably had a bit too much to drink.

We made it back to our tents, and I slept like a rock. It was probably three hours later than our usual turning in time, but the next morning we paid for it. My head was tender but riding a loaded down bicycle soon blows out the cobwebs, especially in the face of a cool ocean breeze.

"Hey Bill, heard you finally got the new map," Norm said to the back of Bill. He turned and greeted us with a good solid handshake.

"Heard you two were boozing it up in the pub last night." I thought to myself, real small island. He continued, "Yep, we changed the map, the printer paid for it. Heading up?"

The chairlift blew away the final vestiges of the previous night's celebrations. It was a small tourist attraction; and we enjoyed the view from the top. We opted to walk down, and our cycling legs definitely had some unused muscles lurking behind those well-developed quads. It always surprised me that however cycling fit you get, a run or hike would expose the unused leg muscles quite quickly!

We thanked Bill with a wave as we headed to our bikes. He looked busy and gave us a smile and a wave back. Now, heads clear, we were off to explore more of Tasmania.

We met up with the orchard owner. He was a short man in his upper sixties but sprightly, and boy did he know his apples. Tasmania is famous for its apples, and this man had grafted all different sorts together on one tree. I thought he must have been some sort of tree elf. Norm had known about grafting but it was all new to me and I was blown away. It didn't take much in this environment; I was still learning so much about the natural – and the sometimes not so natural – world of gardening and growing food.

We were offered a night in his small house, and we accepted. He was a lonely guy, and his apples seemed to give him great comfort. I was hoping to get a few more delicious samples, and we sure did. That night we had a simple meal, and took a long walk around his orchard. Even though we did not cycle much, it was nice to keep him company for the day. It was heartwarming to see how excited he got showing us his grafted trees. I could have sampled his apples for a week. He explained that the ugly apples never made it to the supermarkets just because of their looks. Surely, I protested, if anyone tasted them, the looks wouldn't matter. He laughed at my naiveté and I then remembered the bigger supermarkets with their waxed apples looking so ordered – perfect and pristine – on the shelves. I just wanted to share the experience of these unbelievable tasting fruits with the wider world.

The next morning we squeezed in as many apples as we could into our panniers and headed off, finally in a south-easterly direction. Norm had more of a schedule than me, but it wasn't too strict. The weather was getting colder and I was timing New Zealand for the coming of winter, an interesting time to start a cycling tour. We headed to Cradle Mountain, and were able to cycle into the National Park. The camping was rough, and it was refreshing to be in a National Park that did not cater to the automobile. If you wanted to get to the Parks in Tasmania you had to be willing to rough it up a bit. There was lots of fly fishing going on, and Norm was fascinated to watch these fishermen do their thing. Norm had been known to do some fly fishing in Montana but it was all Greek to me.

When we got to Launceston Norm had to start speeding it up a bit. We spent two days together in Launceston which is known as the unofficial capital of the north even though the capital city of Tasmania is Hobart. We caught a movie, *Dead Calm*, starring a then relatively unknown Australian actress named Nicole Kidman.

We had our final breakfast together in a small café where we noticed information on a small hostel up in the forest somewhere below Launceston. I probed the café owner further; he wasn't too sure where it was, but a couple at the next table overheard me ask. They told us that the hostel I was looking for was about an eight kilometre climb on a small unpaved road in the forest. I needed to get there in daylight because it got dark quickly, but they said it would be well worth the effort. Norm was slightly jealous, but his time was running out. I, on the other hand, was looking for a place to chill out for a few days, and this sounded like the place. Norm and I said our goodbyes after breakfast and I watched him pedal off before turning to plan the next stage of the journey.

Getting to the forest hostel certainly was a challenge; the climb was arduous, and the road rutted, so I took longer than I had planned for and I was still pedaling as dusk was approaching. I must have looked quite a sight climbing at a snail's pace trying to use my 'mini-mag' light with its fast-fading batteries to show me the way. A mist was also descending to add to my visibility problems. A car drove past, then stopped. It had a few people in it who were staying at the hostel. They told me I wasn't too far, and they would have a cold beer waiting. That sounded great to me. I was sweating, and my light was not being a great deal of help. I nearly missed a handwritten sign saying 'HOSTEL' with an arrow pointing up a small track. The mist turned to drizzle, but I was so wet from sweat I didn't bother to put on a rain jacket. I finally made it well beyond dusk, and as I walked in I was handed a cold beer from Tim, one of a small group staying at the hostel, who was true to his word.

"If you promise to help cook dinner tomorrow night, there's a plate of food waiting for you," were his first alluring words of greeting. I would have promised to paint the place at that point and quickly agreed. I headed for a quick shower, before devouring my dinner. The rest of the night was spent mostly singing, laughing and having a 'few tinnies', as the Aussies call a few beers.

I knew instantly I would stay a few nights to make it worth while. There was some great hiking, and an interesting mix of Australians and Europeans, me being the only American just to round things off. The next morning I began to appreciate what a great place it was and how it had been well worth the climb in the dark. The weather was damp most of the time with its own microclimate because of the dense forest where we were situated. Hiking was breath-taking in both senses of the word. The green was so deep, I thought I would see everything green the rest of my life. The muscles Norm and I had awakened climbing down from The Nut were about to get put to use once again. Tim and I both wanted to explore the denser area of forest directly around the hostel. We had to cut our way through parts of the more impenetrable foliage. Most of the others were using the hostel as a base to explore the wider area around the north. Tim and I were slotted in for cooking detail that night. We chipped in for some food, and those who left to explore further afield in the car would bring it back with them on their return.

It was a relaxed hostel, not an official AYH or IYH (Australian or International Youth Hostel) so there were not many rules to abide by, and it was assumed that adults traveling would respect each other. There was a common room away from the sleeping area so those who did not want to stay up could easily go off to sleep. I had stayed in other hostels, or 'Backpackers' as some were called, and they were usually smoothly run.

On our walk in the forest, I also came into contact with leeches for the first time in my life, and Tim and I had to burn them off each other when we got back to the hostel – a different way to get to know each other! We cooked for twelve people that night, and the atmosphere was true Australian party time, and 'Vitamin B' (Victoria Bitter) was the drink of choice. It was fun to tip a few, knowing I was not cycling the next day, and I would probably just stick around, not hike or bike, just read a novel or write in my journal.

Leaving the hostel was much easier than getting there; a full descent without one pedal stroke. The ruts in the road made it difficult, but I was able to keep up a good speed, and trust in the sturdy wheels of my tourer; the converted mountain bike.

The rest of my time in Tasmania was spent cycling along at a slow enough pace to take it in and enjoy what the island had to offer in the way of hospitality, Aussie wildlife and empty, but challenging roads. I camped on small secluded lake shores, and in the green forests of Australia's forgotten southern state. A trick Norm and I learned was to let the wallabies – small kangaroos – lick the camping plates clean if we left them outside the tent at night. Perfect, just a quick rinse off in the morning and we were off!

One night in the mountains, I rode to a small nearby restaurant to eat. One of the cooks told me to stick around if I wanted to see a Tasmanian Devil. Wow, my vision of that particular creature came from the Bugs Bunny cartoons of my childhood; a crazy whirlwind character that entered like a swirling tornado, made weird noises and left things bare as he gyroscoped around them. That was about as far as my knowledge went on these mythical creatures, until I landed in Tassie and was enlightened. Now I would see one of these rare animals in the flesh and my childhood cartoon images would be shattered.

It was disheartening that the Tasmanian Devil – although naturally a nocturnal carnivorous scavenger rather than a hunter – was reduced to scouring the rubbish bins of the restaurant. The cook put out the food rubbish in a pile and this lone dog/cat looking creature came timidly out of the woods searching for suitable scraps of meat to eat. It was marvellous to see such a rare creature up close. Although not aggressive, the cook whispered to me as we watched from our vantage point – leaning out of the kitchen window – if you ever see one while camping make sure it doesn't feel trapped, they have powerful jaws, and could do a lot of damage if threatened. I didn't plan on cornering one any time soon. I rode home from the restaurant in the dark as the small crowd of us waiting for the show had had to wait until the sun went down.

Getting back to my tent was tricky; my flashlight's batteries were almost completely dead. I had no spare ones, and had to brush my teeth in the dark, hoping I wouldn't corner my nocturnal friend who might not be as amiable as my dish-washing wallabies.

Hobart was getting closer, and now I was looking forward to New Zealand. I had heard so much about the cycling there, and Tasmania had whetted my appetite for cycling in a smaller country. Even though it was part of Australia, Tasmania did not have that big spread-out feeling like it did up on the mainland. I was also curious if Noemi and I were going manage to meet up. It would be nice to catch up with her, lots had happened since Thailand. There was a possibility she would meet me in Christchurch.

In the airport leaving Hobart I met a French Canadian couple who were in big trouble with customs as they had overstayed their visa by six months. They were both taken into an office, and given a five-year ban on traveling back to Australia. The Aussies took their visas seriously!

The plane ride to New Zealand was relatively short, and the Canadian couple dramatically just made it on board – probably timed for effect by the customs agents just to press their point further. After alighting from the plane, I was met by a familiar face. Noemi decided to meet me and she'd already pitched a tent at a campsite not far from the airport – a very pleasant way to land in a foreign land.

We had lots to catch up on and our first night together was emotionally confusing. We had both been on our separate trips in the past few months and now here we were once again sharing a tent. We had to keep communication open, but traveling in such close quarters once again made us feel like a couple. It was strangely familiar, but also a tad dangerous for both of us. We knew it was going to be for a little while, so we didn't focus too much on the future and enjoyed what our trip in the South Island would bring.

The cycling in New Zealand was similar, but much more dramatic than Tasmania. This tiny country squeezed everything America had to offer in nature onto two tiny islands. It was late autumn and winter when we cycled in the South Island so it was cold. The people were so friendly and we were treated with so much kindness it was almost unbelievable. Noemi had told me that is how it was in the north, but it seemed even more so in the south.

By chance Noemi and I met up with the French Canadian couple I had met in Hobart airport. They had been on the road together for quite a long time. They were picking fruit in season, and now their plans to return to Australia were somewhat thwarted. When they told us the story of how they met, it sounded quite romantic.

He had been traveling on bike for a while in Europe, his now girlfriend had been in Europe too, but she was stuck on the trains and buses, and she was getting bored. One day she saw him cycling along from the bus window. She got off at the next stop, waited for him to pass, and flagged him down. He was startled at being flagged down by this complete stranger with a backpack on, but as coincidence would have it, they were both from Quebec. They started speaking with each other, and she invited herself to join him on his travels. They went to a bike shop in the small town they were on the outskirts of, and she purchased a bike. They had been together traveling ever since. They were a colorful couple and I could imagine Cecile flagging Michel down and inviting herself to travel with him. They had a few good stories to tell that night as we all stayed in a house of a friend of a friend that Noemi had tucked away in one of her panniers. Michel and Cecile were heading north to prune kiwi trees and Noemi and I were headed south; so we went our separate ways the next day.

I thought I'd come to grips with the funny type of English spoken south of the equator – *Strine* was full of colloquialisms – I had even incorporated some into my vocabulary, but when someone asked if we wanted to get some "lollies at the dairy" I had visions of muscling in on a few cows to get some weird New Zealand treat. Noemi kindly translated, "go to the deli to get some candy." Thank you became 'ta' as it had in Australia but it was more prevalent here – even used on road signs.

The weather was turning, but we had warm weather gear and were enjoying the empty roads as well as the open-ended style our now separate trips had become. So when I received a letter from my brother asking if I would be able to make it to his wedding in September, it threw me a bit. It was June, and I would be in New Zealand until August. I had no idea what was ahead, and flying to New York for a one-day party, even though it was my brother's wedding, would have changed things quite a lot. Luckily I had Noemi there to throw ideas off of as she was invited too – Larry was marrying her good friend from nursing school, Kathy. We both went up and down in our decisions, one day yes, the next no. It wasn't a cut and dried decision. If we had been interrupting a two-week holiday it would have been clearer, but we were both on a major world tour, traveling with a pretty open plan. Noemi's next stop after New Zealand was becoming clearer, and heading to New York was on the itinerary, but not just yet.

I spoke to my mom about it, and she understood my dilemma. Of course she would prefer all her children to be at her son's wedding, but she was seeing it from both sides, which was nice for me. I thought about it realistically; I would head back for the wedding, they would leave on their honeymoon, and then what? Would I fly all the way back to Australia, never mind the expense? I couldn't ask them to postpone their honeymoon so we could catch up, so the decision was hard to arrive at. In the end, I chose not to go back for the wedding, and Noemi came to the same conclusion. More and more family functions and friends' lives moving on without me in the picture would be the reality of my life if I chose the path I was on.

I was pretty good at keeping letter contact with my mother, but we found ourselves rarely near a phone. My mother's sister was not doing well in her battle with cancer. My close-knit Italian upbringing meant I was quite close with all my aunts and uncles. Aunt Ida was one of my mom's three sisters, and we were always close growing up. I used to think of my aunt once in a while and even wrote a letter to my Uncle Joe, her husband, letting him know I was thinking about him and Aunt Ida. I didn't know how bad she had gotten, but my memories of her were from nearly two years prior when she was seemingly quite healthy. So it was a strange phone call after being only on one-way communication for the past weeks. The only mail we had received was my brother's wedding invitation. When I finally was able to call my mom I found out my aunt had died two weeks previously, and was already buried. It was a lesson in the passing relationship we have with our earthly bodies. My aunt in my mind's eye was a boisterous woman with a loud laugh who got passionate playing pinochle whenever she got together with my mom. In fact, what Aunt Ida truly was had not succumbed to cancer at all, her body had, but her essence hadn't, it couldn't have, cancer was a disease of the physical body. Just like my cousin Richard or my father, the memories and the effects they had on my life, and the wider world was indelible. Death didn't scare me, and ever since that experience in the back room of the florist a few years back, I had a certain perspective on it. It was just one more reason, I felt, to live one's life to its fullest. I was learning that our life is much more than we can begin to realize, and we are all just more or less stumbling in the dark. Life and death, beginnings and endings, we are surrounded by their mysteries on a daily basis, but of course, the fact that I would never see my aunt again saddened me, and the loss to our family would be felt, but life didn't stop, and there was so much more life to be lived.

Back on the road, it was nice enjoying the added hospitality that cycling in the off-season afforded us. It was true heart-given hospitality in some of the loveliest landscapes you could ever wish to see. The hoar frost hanging on the trees, the crisp air, the mountain tops dressed in white, the normally green fields carpeted in a dusting of snow in the morning were all worth the extra layers of clothing we needed to keep warm on the bikes. The scenery changed much more quickly than in Australia, and the winter gave us the added benefit of seeing New Zealand and the Southern Alps in all of their beauty. I was glad I was pedaling; the heat you build up internally made it possible. I couldn't imagine motorcycling for any length of time in that degree of coldness. For Noemi the whole experience rounded her time off in New Zealand nicely. She'd had a lot of time on beaches in New Zealand's summer in the north; now, in the mountainous south, she had the winter.

We cycled together for nearly three months in all. It was good for both of us, but when I headed off to the North Island; she pointed herself towards Southeast Asia. I helped her pack her bike up and send it back to New York, and once again we said goodbye to each other in yet another foreign land.

Noemi had told me of hiking in Abel Tasman National Park, and we discovered the coincidence that she had actually been hiking with Craig's girlfriend about the same time I had met up with Craig in Western Australia. In the heat of summer up north, she said it had been almost impossible not to share the road with a cyclist. We both agreed that could be a good thing – sometimes. It was great to see Noemi in her own travel rythym. The cycling agreed with her, but she figured she would get a lot more out of traveling in South East Asia without it.

Her descriptions of Abel Tasman sounded beautiful. I wanted to check out the park, and heard there was a German guy renting kayaks on the northwest coast, not far from the park's entrance, so before I headed to the North Island, I searched him out. After a quick lesson of what not to do, I headed out to kayak around the northern tip of New Zealand's south island alone in the winter. Maybe a bit foolhardy, but who said I wasn't a fool, or hardy? It was a little scary going around the headlands, and I did wonder what on earth I was doing at times, but what a whole new perspective. It was exhilarating to be viewing New Zealand's coast from out at sea. Being new to the kayak was never lost on me, and kept me very alert. I always made sure I was in sight of the land, and got quite nervous when I had to ride the waves in towards the shore. I was still a land lubber, but always willing to try something new. It enabled me to get deeper into the Abel Tasman Park than I probably would have done alone on foot in winter, so I was glad of the experience. I made it to the inlets, and pulled my kayak well inland because I was told how high the tides could rise, and I did not want to find it floating off without me when I got back. The huts were empty and spoke nothing of the summer stories of overcrowded huts and people sleeping wherever they could find a space. I was completely alone for most of the time, but the last night two hikers walked into the hut I had chosen to stay in; Mark and Pauline. They were both from Melbourne and we hit it off immediately. I told them of my friend Alan, and how I would be flying back to Melbourne in a few weeks. They told me to look them up when I got there, and before I even made it back to Melbourne, I now had three friends in the city I would call home for a little while.

188

By the time I finally made it to the North Island, I only had two weeks left in New Zealand. With the weather having turned wet, sleety and icy, I decided to bus it to Lake Taupo; and was glad not to be cycling.

The geo thermal activity, geysers, and interesting lunar landscape around Rotorua promised cold walks and warm natural hot baths. The bus ride there was in white out conditions. In the nice warm hostel, by a big roaring fire, I met Marie and Kathleen – two Scottish girls. They said much of New Zealand reminded them of home and I thought one day it would be nice to see some of the countryside they described. Kathleen was living in Melbourne, and Marie was visiting her for a holiday. When I left for Auckland, Kathleen had given me her number in Melbourne and told me to call her if I needed a hand finding work or just wanted to meet some of her friends. I was heading to Melbourne with quite a list of friends.

# An Unexpected Respite in Oz

As I stood waiting for my bike I watched the other tourists and travelers seeking out their bags on the moving luggage belt. I was thinking of all the people I knew in Melbourne now and wondered if I would have time to catch up with them all. While drifting off in my head, a quirky-looking woman started up a conversation with me. Her name was Wendy. We spoke of our time in New Zealand – she thought the people were nearly as friendly as the scenery beautiful. We both were in agreement on that.

I told her about my cycling trip with Noemi, and she said, "That sounds like fun. Melbourne's a great city for cycling."

"Great, small cycle-friendly cities are always fun to explore." Remembering my brief time there a few months back. As we both looked at the empty conveyor belt she was beginning to get worried.

"I hope my bag made it on the plane, I barely did," she said with a nervous laugh. When my bike finally arrived through the two doors at the back of the room being wheeled by a customs agent, I was relieved; the possibility of a mangled wheel or worse sometimes niggled, especially in airports.

As I said goodbye and turned to go, Wendy asked, "Have you heard of a television show called *The Big Gig*?"

"No, haven't watched much t.v. in a long while. Is it Australian?"

"Yes, it's a comedy show; Jane and I are the presenters." She said motioning towards a tall woman standing quietly off to the side with her bag in hand.

She gave me a card and told me to call the studios and ask for her after I'd got settled in Melbourne – she'd get me a couple of tickets for the show. Melbourne was proving to be an easy place to meet people. They waved goodbye with things not looking too good for Wendy's baggage – the conveyor belt was still empty. As I strolled out into the fresh air, I reflected on her words; "When I get settled in Melbourne." Did she know something I didn't know? I wasn't planning on staying, I was just passing through.

After all the cycling and camping in rural areas, my desire for the city life was coming to the fore. Alan and I had a lot to catch up on, and the others I would fit in if I had the time. The one other person I had to see was Rich, the travel agent who had an agency near Alan's house in Camberwell. He'd got me the ticket to New Zealand flying in and out of four different cities. I had been told I would never be able to buy it that way as a round-trip fare. Rich secured it with no problems – I liked people who made the impossible happen.

Traveling with an open plan you realize that the world has other ideas for you, but you need to be able to accept these changes as small gifts. As I saw a pattern emerging in my life, these presents seemed to be around so many of the corners I hiked, biked and lived. The next one was down the street from Alan's house.

My mode of travel had well and truly changed, and it now felt right. I was enjoying the world of cycling, and the many options it brought with it. I smiled and remembered my chance meeting with the New Yorker on the way to Alaska. My headspace was now similar to what his had been, and what he had said to me about being brave on the motorbike hit me in a different way. On a motorcycle, you are free, and the power is fantastic, but depending on where you are, mechanical breakdowns or simple punctures could really be the end of a journey. Plus, as I learned with my rear-wheel experience in Washington, you are at the will of others. You can know a lot about motorcycle maintenance, but taking a tire off a motorcycle rim is quite a different procedure to taking one off a bicycle. Something about the ease and flexibility of a bicycle had been slowly getting under my skin.

I had not given up motorcycles or my love of them and still fondly remembered *Zen and the Art of Motorcycle Maintenance*. I knew these machines were just tools, and the real movement was on deeper levels, but the bicycle complemented the type of travel I was drawn to. It was caught in that in-between world of road vehicle and kid's toy. No insurance, registration, hassles at borders, but as I was learning, it could take you quite far, and could also let you enjoy other modes of transport too. It was a fluid way to travel, and basic maintenance could easily be done on the roadside; anything short of breaking your frame, or seriously buckling your wheels could usually be repaired without the need of a mechanic or a bike shop.

Another added bonus was freedom from gas stations, and instead of spending the money on gas, you could spend it on a different form of fuel; food. Big bonus! Plus it just plain slowed you down; it allowed you to hear the rush of a river, the call of a bird, or the truck lumbering up behind you. 300 or 400 mile days were things of the past, now I started seeing the places I traveled in small chunks of fifty to a hundred miles, and as I slowed down even more and started smelling the roses, I even chalked up days with as little as four miles.

It was good to see Alan again but there was a strange shift in our relationship. Where a few years back we'd met while I was still finding my feet and he was the seasoned traveler, I had now been on the road for quite a while, and he was back living with his mom after things had gone bad with Sue, and seemed to have lost his edge a bit. He was a personable guy, and a great traveler. He had had fantastic experiences that had made him interesting to talk with, but living at home with his mom was not easy after all those years traveling. It felt as though he had left a part of himself out on the road.

I planned to stay a couple of weeks – enough time to explore the city, try to see who I could, and get a flight to Indonesia, the country where Noemi had gone to after New Zealand, and from a letter I received it sounded like she was having some coincidences of her own. Now without her bike, she was taking buses and hitching on trucks. From the back of one of those trucks she spotted a westerner on a bicycle. A few days later she was walking back to her guest house when she noticed that same cyclist pull into the village. Since Noemi had been swept up into the world of cycling while in Japan she happened to notice the guy had drop handlebars on a mountain bike. When she mentioned this as an icebreaker in conversation, the cyclist was surprised she had noticed such a detail. As she was explaining how she knew, Craig stopped her and said, "Hi Noemi, I cycled with Joe in Australia." Noemi's reply was, "Nice meeting you Craig, I hiked with your girlfriend in New Zealand!"

The letter made Alan and I laugh, and reminisce about all the chance meetings we had shared over the years on our separate journies. It brought the spark back into his voice he had when I first met him. It was good to see he was still there, just derailed at the moment.

I was headed off to find my flight to my next adventure, but something different awaited. Once again I walked into the travel agent, which was known as 'Four Corners Travel'. A big mural of an African wildlife scene that had pulled me in there the first time still graced the window. Rich was an easy-going guy, and when I had been searching out the 'impossible to find' ticket he had just said "no problem" and found it. I walked in after my five months away and he remembered my name as soon as he saw me, poured me a cuppa and asked about the cycle trip. We talked about his last trip in Africa, and now that it was heading into Australian summertime, he would be getting busy. When I told him I wanted a flight to Indonesia, he asked me why I would cycle through a New Zealand winter, come to Australia with summer approaching, and buy a plane ticket to a country that is always warm. His logic threw me a little and I mumbled something about money and Indonesia suiting my budget better, plus I was also hankering to get back to Asia. He understood that part, but asked if I might want a break before heading back out on my bike. I had been on the bike now since I left Japan, so it had been nearly nine months.

"Do you like movies?" he asked.

"Sure, I love a good movie," I answered. It was a strange shift in the conversation I thought.

192

"Hold on, have a seat." I sat down and smiled at the young girl tapping away on her computer. I caught snippets of a phone conversation he was having…"Phil, I have a good friend here from New York, …Yes he loves movies, he's seen everything out in the past few years…sure, right,…tomorrow, …okay."

"What was all that about Rich?" I asked.

"My mate Phil owns the video shop next door, he owns three in Melbourne and he wants to meet you tomorrow."

I had walked into the agency for a plane ticket, and now was possibly walking out with a job.

Phil was a big man with a strong handshake and a loud voice. He liked Americans because they knew about customer service; he liked me because I was honest looking, and I did know a lot about movies. We shook hands on me working for him, and that was that. I didn't want to impose on Alan's hospitality too much longer and now it was time to find a place to live. I started working almost immediately in the shop nearest to Alan's house, but I had a bike, and the tram service was excellent, so I told Phil I could work in any of his shops if he needed. He needed me to cover in the Armadale shop for two days, not too far away, "And you'll be working with Jeff, you'll love him!"

I showed up at work, and Jeff was quite a character. We hit it off immediately. He was Jewish and reminded me of my few New York Jewish friends. Coming from an Italian New York family I can say that we have lots of dysfunction in common. I mentioned to him I was looking for a place to live. He told me about his friend John he used to work with as a teacher, but hadn't seen in a while; a single guy living alone who probably wouldn't mind the company, or the extra money. "Plus," Jeff added, "he's Italian like you!" I laughed to myself. Italians, Jews, Greeks – what we were didn't matter, but Australians, like Americans, held on strongly to their heritage.

I'd spent a lot of my college and high school years working in small retail businesses. What a great job; recommending movies all day and always watching one on the screen. For me the added bonus was that it was a great study of a huge cross-section of society. In a video shop you see everyone from teenagers to rich businessmen. It wasn't like going to your favorite restaurant, or café, it was a case of picking up a video on the way home from work or school at the most convenient shop. We had a good selection; everything from *RAMBO* to *Singing in the Rain*.

Work was an eight-hour day for us full-timers, and a few hours later, Jeff pulled me aside and said, "Joe, funny thing, 'The Luke' is here." I had no idea what he was talking about.

"The Luke, who's that?"

"John, The Luke, you know, with the house!"

"Jeff, what's his name, John or Luke?" I asked, confused.

"Oh, John, but we call him The Luke, short for his long Italian surname that you lot tend to have," and he smiled.

The Luke came in and Jeff was genuinely pleased to see him. They caught up for a while and I heard Jeff ask him what he was doing up in Armadale. He said he'd been meaning to stop in, and was passing so decided to see if Jeff was working.

As *Wall Street* played on in the background I stepped outside to meet The Luke and we all had a chat. He'd left teaching in a school setting and had taken a position teaching students living abroad by correspondence. I told him I'd been a teacher for a while in New York, and I can understand fully that decision. We both laughed – he seemed like a nice guy. We got around to the room and the house, and talked about price. I agreed then and there to take it. I fell into calling him Luke, or The Luke, and from then on that was his name. He was a little older than me and his personality was more cautious. I was listening to my inside voice and it was telling me this was yet another good situation. Luke insisted I see the place first although I said it wasn't necessary; if he was a friend of Jeff's, that was good enough for me. How bad could it be? It's a room in a house. I knew Luke would not be happy until I looked at it first, so I took this as a good thing, and we made an arrangement to meet up the next day before I went to work.

I packed the bike with the full intention of saying yes and leaving my stuff there. I met Luke in East Brighton which was where he lived. It was a small house on a street with lots of trees, not too far from trams, shopping and the cycle path into the CBD (Central Business District) of Melbourne. What a perfect location I thought. The house was a definite bachelor pad, but I'd seen a lot worse – I wasn't the neatest guy on the block either. I told Luke it was perfect and asked if he minded if I took my bags off the bike and left them in the room so I didn't have to cycle with them to work. He said it was no problem, and when would I get the rest of my stuff? I laughed and said, "When I buy it." Even though he knew I was traveling, he still couldn't get his head around the fact that all I had with me would fit on a bicycle. We had a good chuckle, and now we were officially housemates!

Work flew by that day with an ominous meeting at the shop. I was helping a woman out and we were talking about different films. I recommended *Dead Calm* that had just come out on video. As we were walking through the shop she asked if I was American. I told her I was from New York. She then she asked how I had managed to get a work visa. I muttered something about a mate, traveling, living, etc. She looked at me smiled and then said, "I doubt very much you have a visa, I work for immigration." I just kept on smiling, and wasn't sure where we were going with our conversation, then she quickly followed up with, "Don't worry, you're not in trouble or anything, I was only curious. I love this shop."

Traveling and working black go hand in hand. It supports a lot of jobs around the world. Harvest workers come to mind as one big black market economy that keeps the world eating, and till this day I'm not sure I ever met a fruit picker who was a legal resident of that country. I was confident there was no problem. By the end of the day I'd nearly forgotten about it, and I didn't see her then for nearly three weeks and by that time I was working nearly all my days in that shop and The Luke and I were becoming good friends.

While tidying up the shelves one day, I found a copy of the seventies movie *Jesus Christ Superstar* tucked away. I went to the computer to see it hadn't been rented out for quite a while. What the heck I thought, I asked Luke if he'd seen it, "Years ago mate." So I brought it home and we had a night watching the classic musical. Anytime I put it on in the shop I only made it half way through before someone would ask if they could rent it. I started a small trend!

Catching up on movies was a good perk of the job, plus I became quite friendly with the immigration worker; she even rented *Jesus Christ Superstar* – which she'd never seen. When she walked in after returning it, I was putting boxes back on the shelves. I saw her and smiled and asked her how she liked the film.

"Brilliant," was her reply. "How are you enjoying Melbourne?"

"Great," was my one word answer. If I was working when she came in, she always asked me to recommend a film; she liked my taste in movies. I was all too well aware of our first conversation. The game was being played, and my stay in Melbourne could have been much different if her personality didn't leave any room for those gray areas. The visa side of things was never referred to again so I felt secure in letting my mother make plans to come and visit in a few months time. My six-month visa was going to be used to its fullest, what I thought would be a two week breather turned into a welcomed, quite unexpected respite in Oz.

# Healing Old Wounds, Creating New Ones

Now mom was coming to Australia, when my dad died she was left a humble pension from the post office, so traveling the world was not a big option for this woman from Harlem who spent most of her time living, working and raising her children in The Bronx. I was glad to be an integral part of her exploration. This time she was coming with her twelve-year-old grandson, my nephew Denis, and her sister, my Aunt Jenny.

This visit had an extra special meaning for me. All visits from friends and relatives are nice, but Aunt Jenny lost her son at eight years old to a drunk driver. We were six months apart in age and always getting up to mischief together. Since that fateful day – Richard's birthday when she had let him out to play on his new bicycle – Aunt Jenny and I had had a strange relationship. I couldn't understand it when I was younger, but started to a little more as I grew older. Money had never come easy to her, especially as Uncle Frank had never come to grips with the death of his son, but now, nearly twenty years later, I was able to offer Aunt Jenny the realization of a lifelong dream as she had always had a fixation with Australia. The cost of the flight alone was off-putting, but if you added in hotels and everything else you would wind up booking through a travel agent in New York, it was nearly impossible. "Just book the flights," I said. "We'll figure out everything else from here." I was so excited to be a part of Aunt Jenny's dream that I knew we'd figure anything out. We'd rent a car from 'Rent-a-Wreck', stay local at Luke's for the time in Melbourne, and then head to Adelaide. As long as we saw kangaroos, some outback and spent some time together, we would all be happy.

The Luke – being a good Italian boy – had no problem with the upcoming visitors. We were getting on well; his family was the Australian version of mine – the immigration in the early part of the 20<sup>th</sup> century, the food, and all. He and I would get into long philosophical and religious discussions – he had more Catholic leanings than I ever did, so I knew he and my mom would get on well. We made plans to get out into some forest in upper Victoria State and visit some friends. John had some good, true-blue Aussie mates who would impress our visitors, especially if they really put on the *Strine*.

Landing at the airport in Melbourne would be easier for my mom than Japan had been. I couldn't think of any way to make it more interesting, and Luke insisted I borrow his car to pick them up. My mom nearly didn't recognize me at the airport; I was a lot darker than I had been in Japan, and my hair was long and tied back in a ponytail.

As much as I had changed, my twelve-year-old nephew was nearly unrecognizable. Had he not been with mom and Aunt Jenny, I would have walked right by him. It still took me a few days to get used to his changing voice and pubescent face looking all stretched and out of proportion compared to the child I last saw in New York. I think him being there helped a lot with Aunt Jenny and our long-awaited healing process.

We crammed all of us and their luggage into the car and off we went. The sleeping arrangements were going to be creative, but we would all have to cope. I booked time off work for the ten days they were visiting. We stayed local for the first couple of days, and I needed to get used to Denis's face, and strange voice. My life on the road was changing my place in the family. Not that I wouldn't be a part of it anymore, but I would be playing a very different role, and would be missing big chunks in between. I was okay with that. I was learning quickly that relationships were less about geography and more about where they are held in your heart. It made the times we met up all the more special, and now I was expanding the horizons of my extended family. My young nephew was getting to visit Australia because of me! I was starting to shed the frustrations that usually haunted me. I have always been quite intense and I didn't sit well with injustice, but now I was treading my own path, making my own discoveries, and finding my place in the world. When I left Guatemala I had been frustrated and feeling used, but now I did not feel held down by geography, family or anything – life was a gift, and I was slowly just tearing off the colorful wrapping paper!

My mom and Luke hit it off immediately – he reminded her of any one of her relatives back home – and although I was a grown man, she still looked at Luke, my roommate, as the man in Australia who was taking care of her traveling son. Since he was ten years older than me, mom put him in the category of older brother or sister, not peer. I had to forgive her; she was an Italian from The Bronx, and things fit into nice little boxes which made them easier for her to deal with. I was starting to help break the walls of those pigeonholes, but sixty years of upbringing is hard to change. I had only been walking the planet half that time, and trying to break my own ingrained habits and thought patterns was tough enough!

Everyone loved the house. It was a quaint old dwelling with a resident mouse, and pretty lopsided – completely different from the standard American home. The bedroom was perfect for mom and Aunt Jenny, and Denis was young and on a great adventure – the floor was cool. Anywhere would have been, he was in Australia! We took a walk outside for some well-needed fresh air after their long-haul flight from New York, their Thanksgiving Day literally having disappeared when they crossed into the next day over the International Date Line just west of Hawaii.

The area of East Brighton was a pleasant place for them to start their travels 'Down Under'. How great to be met at the airport, driven to a friend's house, stay with a close relative, and take it as it comes. I think that part was probably the hardest part for them to get used to. The 'take it as it comes' part was new to Aunt Jenny who usually traveled with an itinerary like many Americans of her generation.

Sleep came easily for them that night, and the first few days were spent just taking in Melbourne. I'd forgotten how everything would be so new to them. I'd been on the road for over two years at this point, so had to re-adjust to being around three familiar New Yorkers and try to see things through their eyes. My nephew didn't say much, but was obsessed with cars and a whole new continent of many different car-related differences – unheard of makes and models, steering wheel on the other side, driving on the left, etc. – kept him entertained without any extra effort on our part. Aunt Jenny and mom kept on mentioning how Melbourne reminded them of New York forty years ago. I wasn't sure if that was a compliment to Luke, but what could I do, they were their own people, and they had the right to say what they wanted. It was just mildly embarrassing sometimes when I felt it inappropriate to say such things with such fervor and excitement. It felt to me like they were implying that Melbourne was behind the times or quaint. My mom still had the ability to embarrass me in front of others – I think it's what moms do. Once I realized that people were entertained by her laughing, not understanding the accent, and pointing out everything that was cute, we had a good time.

We headed up to a deeply forested area in Victoria, funnily enough called 'The Grand Canyon'. It was a big canyon on the edge of some thick lush woods, and we were visiting friends of Luke's – Pat, Cheryl, and a couple of Pat's cousins who lived up that way. Maureen and Hazel, who were two Irish girls I had met and introduced to Luke, had also joined us. Pat and his cousins were great, real *Auckers* (Australians). My mom couldn't understand a word. Maureen and Hazel were from Northern Ireland, just to throw in another accent, and even my nephew Denis was getting embarrassed by how much translation was needed. We had a gentle stroll though the eucalyptus trees – known as gumtrees – with their gnarled and twisted trunks and branches with the undergrowth of tree-ferns and other lush, green, damp-smelling, low-lying plants. The car we rented from 'Rent a Wreck' did the job of getting us there which was good, as it was the trial journey before we headed off to Adelaide. After our walk we got a fire going so we could have a real Aussie Barbie – no shrimps though, actually, no anything except for food. We overlooked everything pertaining to plates of any sort, cutlery, drinking cups, you name it. I must admit I was still a bit rough from living on my bike for so long, so a hamburger on a bun in my hand was fine and some good Aussie sausage between some bread, no problem.

My Aunt Jenny came over and whispered in my ear holding in a giggle, "Joseph, do they use plates, knives or forks at Australian barbecues?" just as my mom said, "Okay, I'll set the table."

It was then we all realized we had brought the food and drink, and that was it. We all had a good laugh, and everyone went with the flow. Denis and I were probably the only ones who wouldn't have noticed if it hadn't been mentioned.

There were a few cold tinnies to be tipped, but when I reached for one, I realized I hadn't had a beer in a while, and with all the cycling in Australia and New Zealand, there had been lots of social beer drinking. After my short interval of giving up alcohol in L.A., I hadn't thought of the issue much in the intervening years. I didn't feel I had a problem in any way, even though in Japan I went through a time of drinking more than I should have, but now picking up the beer I thought I would challenge myself once again. It was in the places where drinking became more of a social necessity that I enjoyed stopping it altogether, because I felt it shouldn't have to be. I put the can down, and didn't say anything, and decided I wouldn't have a beer until New Year's Eve at midnight, nothing big, but an exercise in being mindful. Back at the barbie things were going well.

Mom and Aunt Jenny loved the Irish girls. The Australians were entertaining the Americans and putting on the *Strine* thicker than normal. They were so hospitable and even though translations were still needed, even after they turned down the slang, a great time was had by all. Despite not having plates and passing around any drinks we had in a bottle, we all had a first-rate time, and the surrounding countryside was beautiful. A walk in the lush green forest topped it all off quite nicely. No kangaroos though, Aunt Jenny wanted to see kangaroos, and I promised we would see some, but not yet.

On the way back our car failed part two of its first test, but luckily we were being followed by Luke and the Irish girls because the car broke down twice on the way back, and would not start without a push. It lived up to its name, but for a trip to Adelaide we deemed it not worthy. We would return the car when we got back to Melbourne, chip in a little more each, and rent from a more reputable car company.

Our first outing Down Under went off without too many hitches – just two car breakdowns and a barbie without cutlery. They were adapting to the day by day itinerary approach quite well. Denis had pointed out nearly every car that passed, and when he heard we were going to Adelaide he was over the moon as it was where the Australian Grand Prix, which I am sure he had watched many times from start to finish, took place.

With the more reliable rent-a-car secured, a map dug out of one of my panniers, and the packing pared down to a bare minimum, we were off to see some 'roos' and South Australia. Aunt Jenny was a tad disappointed we weren't going to Sydney, but I assured her that we would see a lot of outback on the way to Adelaide, and that it was a much smaller city also known as the 'City of Churches' which appealed to the ladies' Catholic streak. They were also both pleased that Denis would get to see the city of the Australian Grand Prix.

I had cycled on many roads like this one ten months previously. I remembered camping out at night, and seeing some wildlife from the saddle of my bike, but in a car it was just the world whizzing by at sixty miles per hour. The subtleties were gone. It looked even more boring than I remembered it. The initial excitement of a long-distance car drive even gave way to some mild boredom on Denis's part. I think what really got to everyone was the absolute vastness of it all.

I spotted a sign for an animal refuge center that no one else had noticed, so when I turned off the road in the middle of nowhere, I was asked where in the world we were heading. Luckily I put off the questions long enough to make it to the welcome sign. My mother smiled at me and asked, "Are we going to see Kangaroos?" I then felt I could say with confidence, "Yes!" Aunt Jenny was happy, and we all had a good laugh at having to see kangaroos in what was nearly a zoo, even in Australia. I explained my logic that if we saw them here, it would take the pressure off, and then we would all relax and probably see a few in the wild. The refuge turned out to be a hidden gem. We got to hold koala bears, saw wallabies, platypus, and all sorts of weird wonderful Aussie wildlife, and yes kangaroos! My mom whispered in my ear how wonderful that was – it made Aunt Jenny so happy. I smiled and over the seven days we'd spent together I felt old wounds finally healing between us. Having Denis there was certainly a bonus; she was enjoying his company, and he made her laugh with his car obsession. Even though life had dealt Aunt Jenny a rough hand, she always had a great laugh. I was what her son could have been at nearly thirty, and Denis was just about where Richard would always be in her mind, a child.

That stop was well-needed and took away some of the tedium. The next stop was at Policeman's Point for lunch. When Denis ordered spaghetti in our road-side establishment, I knew it would be spaghetti from a can poured out onto two pieces of toast. Now Denis, not having traveled, and growing up in an Italian American household, had different visions of spaghetti altogether when he placed his order. The two ladies knew better from Italian instinct to simply order sandwiches, so when the food came, everyone stared at Denis's plate and raised their eyebrows. I started to laugh. Denis asked me what it was while Aunt Jenny and mom were choking back laughter with watery eyes. I explained it was spaghetti on toast – a typical fast road-side meal – spaghetti on toast simply does not make it into road-side diners in America. I prompted him to taste it, but after one forkful he gladly traded me for my cheese and pickle sandwich with chips (French fries) on the side. He kept on watching me eat the spaghetti like I was eating the brain of a monkey in some far-flung Hong Kong restaurant. I assured him it was an acquired taste and not as bad as it looked. We had another good laugh, and at least the ladies were thoroughly enjoying the fact that you could get cappuccino nearly everywhere in Australia – a fact that made my mother very, very, happy.

With the day's amusement behind us, we plodded on through the dust and stayed the night on the outskirts of Adelaide. Getting into Adelaide early the following morning was perfect. The church bells were ringing as we dropped in from the backdrop of hills behind the city. I know it was not like seeing Sydney Harbour Bridge and the Opera house, but we were on a budget. I had some friends in town, and The Grand Canyon, kangaroos, spaghetti on toast and cappuccinos to the hearts content was just going to have to do.

Denis recognized Adelaide from the Grand Prix, and we got ourselves a place to stay within walking distance of the town center to spend our two nights in Adelaide. We drove down to the beaches and saw the beautiful southern sky. That night I pointed out the little I had learned about the different constellations to them. We were invited for afternoon tea at Chris's family's house which was a real English experience. Unfortunately Chris was away traveling but we all had a nice afternoon, and although the Edwards had lived there for nearly twenty years, they were still 'terribly British,' and I mean that in the nicest way. They filled us in on life in Adelaide and what Chris was up to these days now that he loved to travel by bike too. My mom enjoyed the afternoon tea, and Aunt Jenny and Denis looked like they were enjoying the biscuits. The middle class English accent was much easier for everyone to understand so no translations were needed.

Adelaide is a quaint city, surrounded by hills and not far from the ocean. We took a drive up into the hills north of the city, any thoughts of driving to Ayer's Rock quickly quelled by me telling them it would be about twice as far as we had driven already, on roads far more desolate. We walked along the beach south of Adelaide, and being late spring it was lovely and warm.

My nephew loved walking along the beach. Topless sunbathing was quite normal and I think the hormones were starting to divert Denis's obsession with cars in other directions.

The visit was deemed a success. Aunt Jenny and I definitely moved through an invisible wall. It was also great to be a part of Denis's first big travel overseas, and to show my mom and aunt another part of the world that neither would have been able to afford otherwise. On a personal note, it was great to meet up with family in the middle of my round the world travels. My mom was used to goodbyes with me by now, but tears always managed to well up in her eyes when she said farewell to her wandering son. The last two times we saw each other were strange though; instead of me leaving to travel, it was her leaving to go back to the familiar.

After leaving the airport terminal, I definitely felt a little odd myself; I was heading back to Lansdown Street to a life that was familiar, but then again not really. I knew that in a few months I would be once again on the road riding my bike through Southeast Asia, most likely never to come back to these circumstances, although I was also learning to never say never. I was driving away from Melbourne Airport feeling surreal. Could I say that all of this was a direct result of my first cross-country trip with Gary or a conversation about teaching English in Japan in a bar in Guatemala? In a strange way it was, but that was just proving to me even more how our lives and our choices truly affect everyone. Alan, in his small way, had unknowingly helped my Aunt Jenny fulfill her dream.

My remaining time in Melbourne was good fun. I met a girl from New Zealand named Denise and we dated for a while. She was keen on traveling and was heading out on adventures of her own, so we were a good match. Alan and I did some skiing and spent some time together. The break up with Sue had taken the wind out of his sails, but he knew he needed to get out there again and start dating. Living with his mom was a double-edged sword; on the one hand, it was saving him money, but on the other it was costing him energy living in someone else's space who had their own opinions on what he should be doing with his life. He knew he had his work cut out for him getting back on track so our talks were good for both of us. No matter what, we had interesting history together, and now *I* was maybe inspiring *him*.

New Year's Eve came and went and I didn't even have my beer. My not drinking alcohol was proving to be a challenge – mostly for others. When I ordered a juice or a sparkling water in a bar, the barman would balk and ask why I wasn't drinking. Sometimes it was quite comical, but it just fueled my desire to not indulge. I liked drinking on my terms, not society's.

Alan and I went to see Wendy Harmer and *The Big Gig* being filmed which was quite a good laugh. After the show we met her and she remembered us meeting in the airport. I told her she must be psychic, as I'd had no intention of living in Melbourne when we met. She just laughed and said, "Oh, am I? Well I wish I'd been psychic about my bag, I think it ended up going to Austria instead of Australia."

My friend John Cottle whom I'd worked with in Japan stopped by and stayed with us for a while. He was off to Tasmania and New Zealand on his bicycle, having stayed in Japan for a few more months after I'd left. He'd known Alan and Sue in Japan, so we got together and reminisced about the English teacher's life in Nagoya.

Chris came over from Adelaide and we all had a big barbecue at our house. I was getting ready to leave for Indonesia, John was heading off to Tasmania, and Chris and his family were making the move back to England. It was the last time any of us would see Chris but we didn't know that then.

"Hey Chris, we're gonna make use of your Russian language skills and do some cycling there one day, looks like it'll be possible now." The Soviet Union was crumbling and *Perestroika* and *Glasnost* were promising a new modern open country.

"I don't know Joe, I love the English countryside. You two sound like your idea of touring is much different to mine," Chris said with a smile.

"Wait a minute Chris," John interjected, "don't confuse me with Joe and Rob – those guys don't know when they're gonna stop, with those two it's some kind of mission."

"Whoaa there Johnny boy, what about your six months in Europe? Then Japan? Now where're you heading? Home? No... Tasmania, New Zealand and who knows where!" I had to defend myself and Rob, even though we were just about to meet up for an open-ended ride. Rob though, by anyone's standards, was pretty hardcore.

"You see? You two, or should I say three including Rob, are all on this insane undertaking to cycle the world, or die trying. You'll never settle down. I like the laneways of England, the gentle countryside, and a café for a cup of tea."

I glanced at Denise at the part about never settling down; feeling just a twinge uneasy knowing the truth in the remark, especially because my upcoming departure meant Denise and I were ending our short-lived relationship. I laughed though at his yearning for a cup of tea. How English.

Then John added, "Joey, how many years you been going now? Three? Four? Then what about all the motorcycling? Look, admit it, you're a travel junkie, and your bike is your needle."

"Ahhh, c'mon, you indulge a bit too much too."

Chris's quiet voice interrupted our discourse, "I'll meet you in the Yorkshire Dales for a gentle ride after you are all finished with the Himalaya, Andes, and Caucasus mountains."

"What about a cup of tea?" I asked.

"That goes without saying old chap," Chris teased.

"The Caucasus Mountains are out. We need your language skills for that part of the world! You're the linguist." Chris laughed when I said that.

"Okay, maybe, just maybe if you all survive the next few years, Russia opens up, and you still want to cycle there I'll think about it, let's keep in touch."

It sounded like a non-committal statement, but coming from Chris, was something to think possible. That's how he was; he went from slightly interested in our bike obsession in Japan, to heading off on his own bike with all the equipment he bought from reading the magazines I lent him. So maybe there was a Russian trip on the cards one day, complete with translator!

Denise was enjoying meeting all these travelers. She was nervous about beginning her journey, but meeting people who have done what you are planning to do makes you feel more at ease. I remembered that feeling from Guatemala. It was nice to see Denise relax into a conversation with Alan or John about working abroad, or traveling in different parts of the globe. It was also comforting to me. After nearly seven months living and working in Australia, I had to start pulling myself out of the comfort zone. I couldn't take any chances; I'd already extended my stay one month longer by legal means and I remembered all too well Cecile and Michel in Hobart airport. I didn't want to burn any bridges or get on any lists. I liked trying to fly below the radar.

Before I left I had one further thing I wanted to take care of, if it was possible. I had three tattoos and had been self-conscious of all the attention they attracted in Japan when I was sleeveless. Southeast Asia was where I was heading, and I thought maybe I would try to remove one of the tattoos on my upper left shoulder – a large black panther's face.

I decided to try a process called dermabrasion which was tantamount to shredding off layers of skin with a spinning wheel – much like you would use to strip paint off metal. The dermatologist performing the act wore what looked like a welder's mask which didn't exactly fill me with confidence. To say it was excruciatingly painful is a huge understatement, and halfway through I turned towards her to see the mask splattered with blood and pieces of my skin. After the first part was over I now had a pretty large open wound where the tattoo had covered my upper shoulder area. For the next two weeks I had to rub the wound with a dry gauze pad for fifteen minutes each day – not an easy task – I zoned out to MTV as I inflicted this pain on myself.

The final masochistic part of the process was soaking the finished product – my oozing skin – in acetic acid to help form the scab, while drawing the ink to the surface. I had to do the whole process twice, and even that wasn't able to remove the tattoo fully. However, now it was light enough to be able to cover it with something different one day after my poor skin got over the trauma of it all. The tattoo was just a scar from a bad decision made when I was younger, but with my chosen path of travel in foreign lands, I was self-conscious that tattoos had different meanings in other countries. I found out in an extreme way that sometimes we must just learn to live with our mistakes.

One night when the pain in my arm was keeping me awake I turned on the television to see Nelson Mandela walking out of prison a free man. I had memories of Ernie and me discussing Nelson Mandela in my college days, and the Specials' song that brought him into my conscious world. Now here he was walking out of prison after twenty-seven years of incarceration. I was filled with hope, and the throbbing in my arm somehow felt insignificant in comparison to his – and so many other people's – pain and suffering.

After all that had transpired Down Under, time was drawing near for me to go. I was back to my four panniers again. I needed to get into bicycle packing mode. I was still fairly new to it all, but now my camping equipment was much better than I'd ever had in America. I was traveling with two cameras, which seemed silly, because I was beginning to take fewer and fewer photos. I had the one camera I had traveled with and owned since I graduated high school, and the other was a small camera I had picked up in Japan. I was tending to use the smaller one when I did take a photo, but I still stuffed my front pannier with a 200 mm, lens, a camera body, a 50mm lens, and my smaller quality compact camera. I was over-packed, but wasn't too worried; I knew I would get rid of the clothes as I entered the heat of Southeast Asia. Even Johnny C's tapes, which lasted a good long time, didn't make the final cut, but I did mail them home instead of chucking them away.

Luke and I had become good friends; he had met my mom, and was planning to go to New York later on in the year. Another seven-month lesson in going with the flow had just been learned. It was just more proof of all the doors that can open and all the possible paths we can walk in our lives. I finally walked into 'Four Corners Travel' and purchased that plane ticket to Indonesia.

# The Camera

Incidents of synchronicity I was soon expecting at every corner – coincidences I was slowly realizing had a deeper spiritual essence about them, and we could turn them into life-changing experiences. Actually we could turn our lives around at any moment. The people we are put on collision courses with every day are also meeting *us*. When you start looking at encounters in a different way, life takes on new meaning, and the positive way we can affect everyone we meet has the power to change not only *our* world, but *the* world.

At the airport in Bali I was met by Rob. His six foot one, thin, lanky build with long, curly hair, clean shaven face and blue eyes stood in contrast to my more solid five foot ten and Mediterranean features of dark, bearded face with long hair. Interestingly, Rob had only one and a half lungs; half of one lung had collapsed due to a childhood illness but he never let that get in the way of his adventures. He was a good companion to hook up with; he had cycled in Asia a few years back with his then girlfriend, Sue. They had explored the Indonesian islands of Sumatra and Java, as well as parts of Malaysia and Thailand, together. Sue had opted out of going to China with Rob on his last trip – instead she headed to Japan to teach English and Rob met up with her after crossing the Karakoram Mountains from China and cycling down through Pakistan.

They were both teaching in Nagoya when Noemi and I came onto the scene. I met Rob at a party, and we became friends slowly, our love of cycling being a common bond. Rob was a funny mix; a loner sometimes, but sociable when he was in the mood. Over the sixteen months I was in Japan, we did some cycling and camping together in and around Nagoya's surrounding countryside. He left Japan before I did, and had just recently spent time in his native home of Canada. He caught up with family, and then spent some time panning for gold in the Yukon Territories. That's why I liked him; he was a quirky guy, and I knew cycling in Asia with him would be an adventure.

We stayed in Bali for a few days, and it was a perfect place to start our journey. It reminded me of the American frontier with Mexico where two worlds collide and have somehow reached a comfortable level of existence with each other. Although it wasn't a land crossing with Australia, it was close enough to be accessible, and the party atmosphere was apparent. The Balinese people hadn't lost grasp on their culture, even with the onslaught of tourism. In fact it was much the opposite; their Hindu beliefs showed through wonderfully in this predominantly Muslim country.

206

The colorful customs, generosity and the pride they took in the tiny gardens adorning their small houses made me smile. I remembered the name Bali from my university days as we had a dance teacher who taught Balinese dancing. I had no idea that it was a small Hindu island part of Indonesia. I thought it was a country in and of itself and had no idea where it was. Now, as I saw it again, and put two and two together I felt foolish for my lack of interest back then. I'd missed out on much in my years of formal education, but was now filling in the gaps!

We happened to be in Denpasar – the main city on this small island – for Balinese New Year. It was an unusual experience. On New Year's Eve no one was allowed out on the streets; dancers dressed up in costume, danced through the streets and made all sorts of noises to scare the evil spirits away. We had to remain in our rooms and were brought food and drink, with the compliments of the guest house. All guest houses did much the same. Pretty cool, I thought. The next day there was a party in the streets; food, dancing and colorful celebrations everywhere. There was a wonderful atmosphere and it was a great introduction to the warmth of the Indonesian people.

We were enjoying the Balinese people, and there were many ways to experience their culture. There was one 'attraction', however, that we both decided to give a miss. We'd met many people who would pay a guide a small fee, and they would take you to see a funeral. It was supposedly a wonderful ceremony; colorful, and more a celebration of life than a mourning of the dead. We were assured that the family didn't mind. If we had come across a funeral by chance we would have surely observed, and it was often the case traveling on the bike that we did stumble across many things that were astounding and more real than anything you could ever pay to see. I loved the philosophy of celebrating life at the funeral; it fit how these people lived, but we decided to forego paying a guide to take us there. We were witnessing enough on the streets to keep our senses alive, and I thought no matter how much I would not be offended if someone thought my father's funeral was a celebration, I probably would not have enjoyed a handful of tourists showing up to photograph the event.

We left Denpasar and decided to pedal east towards Lombok, Sumbawa and Flores – the lesser populated islands of the archipelago. Since Rob had been to Indonesia already, these smaller islands were unexplored for him. For me, it was all new.

Rob had kept his fitness level up in Canada as I figured I must have done cycle commuting for the past few months in Melbourne. I was wrong. The gentle commute and city riding did nothing to prepare me for the hills of Bali; I felt once again like the struggling, out of shape cyclist I had been in Nagoya. This time though I had a benchmark to check myself against – I had finally stopped gasping in Japan and felt more robust with every ride – so hoped the same would happen here. Rob was laughing at how much I struggled during the first few days or so. It spurred me on and surprised me at how out of my depth I felt. My leg muscles though, had good memory, and within a week I was struggling less and enjoying more. The roads occasionally threw challenges for both of us – coupled with extreme heat and humidity – but once again pushing through to better levels of fitness paid off immensely.

As we were cycling I started singing a song from *Jesus Christ Superstar*. Rob looked at me in surprise, "Why're you singing that?" I told him how the seventies film version had re-entered my life in Australia. "Wow, that's cool – I just watched it three or four times when I was back home. I love that movie."

We laughed at the coincidence and started singing the songs, but we could only remember a few lines here and there. We spent many an afternoon pedaling trying to remember the words to the songs so we wouldn't have to start humming after the third line.

We slowly pedaled through the smaller islands heading eastward, taking our time to acclimatize to the heat. We both sorely needed to brush up on our singing skills!

On Sumbawa we stayed in a guest house by the sea owned by a British woman who had married a local. It was a simple open plan structure, not much needed other than a roof to keep you dry in this part of the world – the stifling heat of day was blown away by the cool ocean breeze at night. It reminded me of the Phinca Ixobella in the jungle of Guatemala – you just signed a book for the meals you'd had, or drinks you'd helped yourself to, and paid in full for everything when you left. It was so nice to be part of such an honor system once again. They also had snorkeling equipment on loan – it was my first time to experience the undersea world, and the coast of Sumbawa was the perfect place to do it. The sea life was colorful, and there were plenty of little nooks and crannies to follow the marvelous colorful fish of all shapes and sizes into. Unfortunately I also unwittingly roasted my back a nice shade of lobster red.

That evening was yet another seaside experience I'd never heard of until then. There were tiny phosphorescent algae that would light up the sea luminous green in the evening darkness when agitated. We met some others staying in the hostel and all went down to the shore together. Not being a natural around water, it was a little unnerving for me to jump into the water in the dark, but I did it, and every time we moved the warm sea water around us turned a phosphorous green. Beautiful! One of the girls who came told me to bring an empty jar as I could use the collected algae from the sea water to light the way back that night. I dutifully collected the jar full of water ready to use nature's flashlight back to the guest house. I was walking along shaking the jar to get the algae to do their thing when I noticed giggles rippling around the others as I slowly realized my flashlight wasn't working. I was the brunt of a joke – the city boy was showing his colors much to everyone's delight. Then one of the others pulled me over to the side and confided that she had fallen for it the night before. They were a good group of people, and we stayed for a few days relaxing in the mellow environment.

We left and continued eastward opting to miss out on viewing the Komodo Dragon being fed. We both felt it was a tiny bit exploitive of the dragon, and if everyone who passed through expected the ancestor of the dinosaur to be fed a goat we were certain it wasn't good for the local dragon – or the goat population for that matter! Being cautious of our footprint and the wake we were leaving behind us was something we tried to be aware of, and it was difficult – like many things in life – to find, and then walk, that line.

I was slowly getting used to being in yet another different religious setting. It was my first time to be in a pre-dominantly Muslim country and Indonesia has the highest percentage of Muslims in the world. The call to prayer sounded exotic to my ears, and it hit me as strange that in Indonesia the religion could suddenly change from island to island. The island of Bali was Hindu, and Flores, where we were now cycling, had small enclaves of Christianity. These islands were once known as 'The Spice Islands' and still had a lot of Dutch influence which showed in the language as well as the numerous missions dotted throughout the countryside. The Dutch and Portuguese influence in this part of the world made for an interesting crossroads of religion, culture, language and history. As we headed further east, the riding was becoming challenging – long uphills and everywhere you looked a volcano.

One day we were exhausted and it was only just past midday. We had gotten up early and put in a lot of hilly miles. It happened to be Friday, and as it turned out, Good Friday. We had both forgotten that it was Easter week; being in a predominantly non-Christian country religious holy days often passed unmarked. As we were trying to find a place to sleep, we were told about a mission not too far from where we were – it was assumed we were Christians. We thanked them and wound up heading there, as it looked like that might have been the only place with a possibility for us to sleep. By the time we arrived it was about one-thirty in the afternoon. The priest spoke English and appeared to be genuinely glad to see us. He was a local by birth, but had been educated in Australia. He offered us some food, and we asked him if he had rooms we could rent. He said we were welcome to sleep in his storeroom where he could lay out some mats on the floor. One proviso was that we came to the church service at three. We thought, why not? It might be interesting to see an Indonesian Good Friday service, plus his manner was kind and not at all pushy. It also wasn't lost on us that our favorite film of the minute was based on the events which took place during this week nearly 2,000 years before.

The service was an interesting blend of local culture and Christianity. Our tiny priest had a big voice and looked very regal in his flowing purple robes. The local girls had beautiful voices and flowers woven through their long black hair. Much was lost on us because it was all done in *Bahasa*, the language of Indonesia. We only understood what was going on because we had both had a Catholic upbringing. After the service, the priest asked us what we thought of it, much like an actor asking about his performance. Both Rob and I said it was nice, and we fell into talking about different religions and cultures. Since it was Good Friday, and *Jesus Christ Superstar* had been on our brains recently, we asked if he had ever heard of that movie.

He nodded, "Yes I've seen it, but couldn't understand all of it because the singing was too fast. I'd like to understand the words more."

We told him about the coincidence about both of us watching the film after all those years, and he smiled saying, "Well, I have a copy here, and a video machine."

Sometimes, even though I was getting used to coincidences, and synchronous moments, the utter bizarreness would still catch me out. He continued, "If you wouldn't mind, could you watch the film and maybe write down some of the words to the songs for me? Dinner will be in two hours."

"No problem!" What impeccable timing.

So in a small sticky room on an otherwise little known island on the eastern edges of the Indonesian archipelago, Rob and I sat there forwarding and rewinding *Jesus Christ Superstar* so we could write down the words of the songs for a priest. Incredible! After completing our good deed – making two copies of the words – we shared a simple meal and handed a happy priest the words of the songs to our current favorite musical. The priest was delighted, and we couldn't believe we would be able to sing the songs in full after weeks of butchering and making up the words along the way.

As we pedaled out from the mission, with our own mission accomplished, we had some long hot climbs ahead of us. My eyes kept on being drawn to my over-packed front panniers; that big camera and lens resting there unused. What could I do about it? My camera had a history, I couldn't just hand it out to someone on the streets like I had all my extra clothing and sneakers which had been slowly given away since Bali. Mailing it home just didn't seem like a good option either. The camera had been a gift from my mom when I graduated high school; it went everywhere with me, I even studied photography in college on the strength of just owning a good camera and lens. After embarking on a lifelong travel career, my camera accompanied me on all my subsequent trips.

In Japan I had bought a used Olympus XA camera for a very reasonable price. I had never heard of this particular camera, but it looked quite nice – small with a lens of high quality. Now my Konica was looking quite bulky next to my tiny Olympus. I'd carried both cameras throughout Australia and New Zealand and had never considered cutting down to just the one. Photos had become less and less important to me. Contact with people was always my priority, and I began to realize that the bigger camera was starting to get in the way of that. Now in Indonesia I found myself with quite a lot of pannier space dedicated to cameras.

As we cycled further west trudging up the long hills in the tropical heat, our tires would stick to the road and our clothes would stick to us. We headed to a guest house further east in Flores someone had told us about in Lombok. They said it was nice and cool because it was so high up. They weren't kidding! We finally found the guest house which was a human version of a train junction for travelers coming and going from different parts of Indonesia. One group that was a good representation of just about every country in the English-speaking world entered the common room where we were sitting chatting. One of the guys looked really unhappy, and as I fell into conversation with the others, I asked one of his companions what was wrong. I was told that he was bummed out because his camera lens had broken on the last twenty-hour bus journey over the rugged Flores roads. I walked over and introduced myself to the guy with the broken lens. His name was David. I asked about his camera dilemma.

"I love taking photos," he said in a strong English accent of some sort. He continued, "Now I won't be able to take any until I get to a big city in Indonesia, or Singapore, at least a month away." He sounded very disappointed. I asked to see his camera and lens. He brought it out from his room. The mounting mechanisms for our two cameras were different. At first, I'd been thinking about maybe selling him my lens if it fit.

We'd been talking for a while when a realization came to me in a flash. I looked at the situation, and a smile came to my face. I started thinking to myself that I could easily solve two problems right in this moment. I disappeared into my room, came out with my trusty Konica and lenses and said to David, "This is your lucky day."

He looked at me confused then asked, "Are you offering to sell me your camera?"

211

I said, "Better than that mate, I'm giving it to you."

He balked and said, "No way, I don't even know you."

I explained further to him the irony. "Here we are, two people in this small guest house on this island in Indonesia – one unhappy because the camera he has is not working, the other unhappily carrying a perfectly good camera, but not wanting to use it anymore." I then handed it to him and said, "Here you go."

He looked at me not comprehending. He said, "Let me give you some money for it, I'll feel better that way."

"I'm not selling it or renting it to you. Think of it as a loan, with no expectations." He still looked confused, "Treat the camera as your own. Take photos with it, use it, love it, and if we meet again one day, you can give it back to me, or if it gets stolen, lost or broken, don't worry about it. Take me out to dinner in England if I ever come to visit you."

To me it made perfect sense. I didn't want it; he did. It had served me well for over a decade. The camera I nearly lost to a crooked official in Mexico deserved better than to be begrudgingly carried around in my front pannier. It needed to be used, loved, and appreciated. This was the man to do it.

That night I slept wonderfully. My camera had a new home, my mental load was lighter, and I now had some extra space to play with. There was also a happy man about to take loads of great photos in Southeast Asia with my well-traveled Konica. I had my Olympus in a small pocket of one of my bags taking up virtually no physical space and absolutely no mental space, which was way more important.

Is every person we meet a new opportunity to expand ourselves? When we get in tune with the lives we were meant to live these moments become more obvious, and it's up to us to act. My open-ended travel has let me act upon many situations that may otherwise have passed by unnoticed. It has been good training though, because in those times where I have stopped and worked, I was more attuned to the people and opportunities that were presenting themselves. I find the more uninvolved we become in the present moment the more passes us by. To not walk through these open doorways is a powerful statement thrown out to the universe. I'm learning that making decisive moves coming from the right place in our deeper selves usually has an outcome we can learn from which often will be beneficial, and that is the best conclusion we can want from any situation. Maybe that priest sings along to *Jesus Christ Superstar* as he walks to deliver his next sermon. It's a funny image to hold in my mind. Photos, they only capture images, material things only last for a period of time, but we have the power to remember, to visualize and to change people's lives with simple gestures.

# The Disappearing Rainforest

Cycling in Indonesia had been a wholly different experience to any of my traveling or cycling to date. Humanity oozed from every direction. The Indonesians were a very inquisitive people and if we stopped for a break from the midday sun as it was literally melting the roads, we would be quickly surrounded by curious men, women and children, just squatting inches away to stare at us and smile. The scenery had been fantastic, but sometimes the lack of personal space was hard to deal with. Giving away my camera had left me feeling good about the way it had all worked out and now with the words from *Jesus Christ Superstar* neatly tucked away and easily accessible we were ready to leave Flores.

I tried not to let my political side rear its head – I knew of the current president's rise to power in Indonesia, less a president than a military general carefully selected to lead Indonesia, with the help, once again, of the CIA. The sixties and seventies had been a bloody time in Indonesia, and Suharto replacing Sukarno had many eerie similarities to fifties style coups in Central America and Iran. Chile and Indonesia also had many things in common; Pinochet being the Latin face of Suharto in just about the same timeframes. I tried to see past it, but it was nearly impossible to turn a blind eye. How much of our world had been shaped by ruthless politics and greed? Yet, just like other parts of the world, smiles were the norm. I learned to realize that unjustness, unfettered capitalism, and brutal dictatorships were all part and parcel of life on the planet. I was aware of it as a constant white noise in the background. Sometimes it would affect my travels; but mostly we slipped between the cracks on our bicycles, exploring ourselves and small sections of our world. My awareness was growing, and first-hand knowledge was sometimes hard, but always welcome. I was trying to focus on my personal spiritual growth too. I was fascinated by world religions, customs and language differences – unfortunately learning languages didn't come easy but I always struggled to get a working vocabulary no matter where I was.

Rob was good at filling me in on many of the Muslim ways; how not to offend, and also how to make friends. He had learned quickly while traveling in many Muslim countries that the first words of greeting are normally, "*Salaam Allaaikum.*" It is a greeting loosely meaning 'God is good', and goes a long way on meeting any Muslim. Also, I thought, it felt quite a nice way to greet someone, and evened the playing field when dealing with authorities or proprietors who were probably tired of dealing with travelers on a daily basis.

Such salutations were a thread that ran through many of the countries of the world – the appreciation of the presence of a deity or power beyond our humanness. For me it crosses religious and cultural boundaries, transcends churches, institutions, or political boundaries – a simple greeting that I feel links us on a deeper spiritual level. Small rituals like these I found fascinating; the placing of your hand over your heart when greeting someone was simple, but profound on a different level. Experiencing these customs was letting me realize that what Father Bob had awakened in me as a sixteen-year-old boy truly existed on the every-day roads of life. Humanity was connected and what fundamentalism or rules of doctrine tried to use for political or material gain could not change the fact that on a human level – right here on the ground in the small villages, the jungles, the towns and cities – people greeted each other with respect, and it was up to humanity to keep that connection alive. We had to try not to forget that the beauty we are surrounded with is not something to take for granted. Our earth is truly just one interconnected planet, and for every action there is a reaction, so ripples of kindness go a long way.

Customs and religion aside, life for Rob and me on our bikes in Indonesia was just about to get pretty close to heaven. The ride down to the coast of Flores was ahead of us and, as we had been climbing constantly for days, the downhill lasted all morning. The free-wheeling was exhilarating and I think one of the most memorable that I've ever experienced. I even gave a local man a lift on my front rack for about ten kilometers. He was afraid at first but gradually gained confidence and began to enjoy the ride. It certainly saved him a long walk. We sped along down the lush green jungle road, the constant breeze of free-wheeling blowing our hair back, cooling us down, and making us whoop and holler in near ecstasy. The locals thought we were crazy, but always smiled at the sight of these two freaks on their bikes leaning into turns on the tiny roads of their small island.

We finally made it to the coast and after gulping down some water and having a quick snack we walked over to the docks. With one or two well placed *"Salaams"* we made our way through a few official looking men in uniforms then talked ourselves onto a cargo boat heading to Ujung Pandang, Sulawesi (Celebes).

The boat trip was to be the longest crossing so far – we'd taken a lot of boats, island hopping east in Indonesia; Bali to Lombok, then to Sumbawa, finally Flores, but they were shorter trips between islands that were actually more like taxi services. The twenty-four-hour trip we had just secured for ourselves was going to be different. It was a 'proper' cargo ship, 'proper' in an Indonesian sort of way. It wouldn't pass any health and safety laws in America, but it floated and the rust on the hull didn't look too deep-seated. To be fair, it was well looked after, although the inside was quite basic. The captain's chair was tattered and torn, and there were no beds in sight. Not only did we have to sleep on deck, the crew did too. Luckily there was no rain in the cloudless blue skies. We had enough food for a crossing, and they were ready to set sail within the hour – perfect.

It wasn't a large boat, maybe fifty feet or so long with a mast and sail that I think was back-up. The engines were belting out fumes but we were not downwind of them, which was a blessing. We had eaten a bigger meal once we knew we had secured a crossing to Sulawesi. The crew was inquisitive, but after the novelty of the two long-haired foreigners with bikes sharing their ship wore off, their attention turned to more pressing matters, which was playing *carrum*, also known as Indian Billiards.

*Carrum* is a game along the lines of pool or billiards but played by flicking flat checker-like pieces across a smooth wooden board which was very well looked after and in impeccable condition compared to anything else within sight. I, loving games, got sucked in, as did Rob. Gambling for money figured in to the playing, but we escaped that part and just played for fun. It took a lot of skill to be really good at it, and the crew enjoyed a good laugh at how bad we were at first. We improved with practice and had some fun. The night drew in quickly and as the sun went down, our eyelids began to droop. Even though it had been a downhill ride to the coast, the heat and constant braking required a lot of energy. The rocking of the boat was lulling us to sleep, but the crew sprung to life playing *carrum*. It looked as though they could have played all night long and were still going strong when we turned in.

I woke in the middle of the night to complete silence except for the waves slapping the hull of our boat. With the engines off we were just drifting quietly. The crew must have finally turned in and now it was peaceful and calm. I could have been lulled back to sleep, but forced myself to get up and just take in the experience. There we were heading to another island on the Indonesian archipelago, the stars above us twinkling in the inky darkness, and the warm air and unfamiliar constellations reminding me that we were in the tropics on the south side of the equator. It was overwhelming to think that I had come this far in my life, both physically and as a person. I was still that same Joe who had had a desire to go across America on my motorcycle after university, yet here I was on a boat in the Sea of Flores, destination unknown, and had been away from any familiar surroundings for nearly three years. I felt privileged to be at this point in my life; I was happy in my choices, and at that precise moment in time, was glad to be floating in a calm sea heading towards another adventure. This trip was not in any way belittling my travels in America – quite the opposite. It was showing me even moreso how every journey, big or small needed a starting point. That motorcycle had been my first step, and if not for that first cross-country trip, that first dream realized, I might not be here. I lay down again, gazing at the stars. The hard bench underneath me felt almost comfortable, and soon my wandering thoughts gave way once again to sleep.

The sunrise was breathtaking, at first silhouetting and then highlighting tiny islands dotted in the sea. The day passed calmly and the crew fished for, and then cooked our lunch. We all ate together sharing stories as much as it was possible with our language barrier. We heard tales of the crew's other exploits around the Indonesian archipelago. They were a rugged bunch, and from the sounds of it, this boat was their home. They were all married, but that was all we found out. Spending time with their family never worked into any of their stories, we didn't even find out exactly which part of Indonesia they each called home. They were interested in our travels too, but our conversation was limited to *Bahasa*; the few words they knew in English were the typical "Hello, what is your name?" Quite amusingly when one of the crew heard I was from New York, he said, "Mike Tyson" and punched the air with a few jabs. I smiled and thought it funny that here on this cargo boat in the Flores Sea; Mike Tyson was an ambassador for my hometown.

We drifted on the sea all day, the engines off, with a good following wind so the sails stayed up. We were glad for the lack of fumes and with the ensuing peace the calmness and heat of the day rose up to encapsulate us. By nightfall we were pushing our bikes up the docks on yet another exotic part of the small chain of islands in this tiny country far away from New York City. This short twenty-four-hour crossing was to be a precursor to our next boat ride, but didn't quite prepare us for it.

A plan was vaguely forming in our heads; we would try to catch a boat west to Borneo. We cycled for a few days through the potholed roads of Sulawesi, and kept to the west coast of the island, hoping to find somewhere to catch that boat. Gradually the jungle scenery gave way to rice fields, then to small villages of houses seemingly hacked into the landscape, and built from the trees available.

The days were hot and humid, and even if we had managed to find a guest house with a shower – a rarity in those parts – we were sweaty and sticky before we had cycled for even half an hour. We got to a place in the road where there was an irrigation ditch that had flowing water in it. We stopped to wet our hot torsos, and suddenly, on this small empty road; people appeared from nowhere – incredible. They were farmers of the surrounding fields, so they closed off the irrigation ditches which were flowing under the road of the little bridge we were standing on. The farmer looked at the rising water and motioned that we could get in, it would cool

216

us down. We half-reluctantly immersed ourselves into the cool, slightly muddy water, but it felt wonderful. We sat down, and even though we looked a sight, we stayed in the water up to our necks for about ten minutes. We decided not to put our heads under, but it felt glorious to be immersed in the cool silkiness of the water. Besides the sea, it was rare that our bodies would ever be fully submerged. The locals were happy to watch us relax and cool off. As always it looked as if these people had nowhere in particular to go, and their raison d'etre was to cool us down.

We stepped out of the water carefully so as not to disturb the mud, which had apparently settled at the bottom. Our shorts and shirts were wet, but in the road-melting heat they would soon be crispy and dry. As we were putting our boots on, we noticed a dead rat floating in our small pool. When we pointed it out it elicited a few smiles. With sign language and some words, we all came to the conclusion that the rat had been living under the bridge and had been drowned out by the water gathering there. They all had a good laugh. Rob and I joined in, slightly fazed by having shared our bath with a dead rat. I was just glad I hadn't seen it while I was still in the water or I probably would have jumped straight out and made a fool of myself.

Later in the day we felt hungry and started to look out for somewhere to eat. The in-season menu seemed to be water buffalo intestine soup, which wasn't high on my list of favorite foods. Still, I looked at it as a necessary energy source – even if I would have preferred my mom's home-made eggplant parmesan it wasn't looking likely that anyone would have anything even closely resembling that tucked away in their kitchen. We soon came across one of the makeshift tents that served as food stops. These were always open and great places to meet interesting truck drivers or locals. We even met a local man whose grandfather had actually been part of a tribe which ate the brains of their rivals. Wow, how bizarre was this, a boy from The Bronx and a guy from Edmonton, Alberta, having lunch with someone who sat on the knee of a cannibal, and called him grandpa! We were further from eggplant parmesan than I had realized. At least human brain wasn't on the menu. He spoke some Hollywood movie English, and by now we had a passable vocabulary in *Bahasa* which was a simple language – grammar was not an important part of it, so it was easy to have basic conversations. We asked about the boats we were looking for, and he assured us that there were boats heading across to Kalimantan, which was the Indonesian part of the large island of Borneo.

Borneo consists of three countries; Indonesia, Malaysia, and oddly enough sandwiched in between the both, the host country to the richest man in the world at the time, Brunei. We hadn't met as many travelers here as we had on the other islands. On Flores the only other travelers we had

217

met were the people in the hostel; Bali had been full of mostly Aussies; in Sumbawa the unspoilt coastline and snorkeling pulled a few backpackers, but Java and Sumatra to the west of Bali were probably better traveled. Lombok was a small interesting island where the heavens decided to open up on us, but there was something wonderful about the lack of traffic we were encountering on these eastern islands. Although pretty wet, we had fallen off the beaten track.

The traveling was now logistically tougher because it happened to be the holy month of *Ramadan* – the beginning of the ninth month of the Muslim calendar – which was different to the Christian one. The fasting starts after sighting the crescent moon of the new month and the world we were in changed after that; it became hard to find places open that served food, except those road-side truck stops. In the Indonesian equatorial heat, no food or drink were supposed to pass your lips from sunrise to sundown, so that meant twelve hours a day, every hot day. There were ways around it, but for us the practicality was just finding food. Drinking out of sight was easier, and although we didn't feel obliged to fast, we also would not slug down our water or eat in front of someone who had to wait another six hours to do the same. The fasting, much like the Lenten fast for Christians, was to strengthen your faith, and honor God. I also found it interesting that, like Easter following the first full moon after the spring equinox, *Ramadan* was also tied in with the moon. Religions had a lot more to do with nature than I was brought up believing; even the Winter Solstice tied into one of Christianity's largest celebrations – the birth of Christ. When I traced the three dominant religions I knew most about – Christianity, Judaism, and Islam – they all led back to the Old Testament. Islam wasn't as different a religion as I had always been led to believe. Hospitality was also written into Islam, and along with our greeting, it had been an obliging religion to us two infidels so far.

The jungle was alive, and monkeys would follow along with us in the trees from morning to afternoon. The noisy cicada-like jungle insects would get ever louder as we approached and sometimes we could not hear each other even speak, or sing. We made it to the small coastal town of Parepare where two or three boats nosed lethargically in the harbor. We met someone selling tickets for the boat that was heading to Kalimantan Timur, a small island off Kalimantan, who reassured us we would be able to then hop on a small boat to Tawau in Malaysian Kalimantan. He seemed to know what he was talking about, and we thought the boat looked to be a reasonable size. After we bought the tickets – which we thought were cheap for such a nice boat – we were then led past that boat to another hiding behind it like a small child hiding behind its mother's legs. It was listing to one side in the water, the faded words *Nusa Inda* just legible on

218

its bow. We looked at each other and immediately decided to go back and buy some more food. This was going to be interesting. We cycled quickly back to the shop and bought a few more things to eat. Were we crazy? These were the boats you read about on page twenty-seven in the New York Times international pages – *Boat Sinks, Thousands Perish on a Vessel Meant to Hold 200.*

We strapped our bikes to the front of the boat as we looked ruefully across at the big tanker we had foolishly thought would be our transportation to Kalimantan. It took forever for the boat to get going, and we were now just two of the hundreds of others crammed on the boat. There were definitely no berths on this ship, and quite honestly, in New York I wouldn't have trusted it to get me from City Island to Long Island. Now here we were in for three days on this overcrowded beast. Three days sleeping on the floor didn't appeal, and it looked as though all the floor space was already taken anyhow. We found the captain – who wore no uniform – in the control room which looked pretty basic. It was adjoined to his room which did have a bed. Rob and I introduced ourselves, and, after the mandatory "*Salaams*", we somehow managed to bargain ourselves his bed. We offered him what was probably a large amount of money, which came out to about five dollars each but was well worth it. It was still *Ramadan*, but you are absolved from fasting if you are traveling, and as soon as the boat left the dock people began to eat – an exploitable loophole like Sundays during Lent. Some of the more devout would wait till sundown.

There was no going back now; the *Nusa Inda* was en route. There was no big fanfare, not even one streamer thrown to send us off. The boat just belched out a big black cloud and lurched out of the dock. This was going to be a long journey.

The captain's room had a door on it, but it was too stiflingly hot to close it. The one bed was small, and Rob and I slept top to toe, with our feet in each other's faces. The door could split in two like a stable door, and when we had just the top part open, people would come and visit, hanging their arms over the door as they ate their nuts and looked in at the two foreigners. We felt like zoo animals on display but we smiled and took it in our stride. We were possibly the first foreigners that many of these locals had ever seen as we were in fairly un-traveled parts now. After the third day or so we became less of a novelty as people got used to us. We got talking to some people, and found out that just about ninety percent of the boat's passengers were going to work in the rainforests. My environmentalist side was intrigued, and if and when we ever did get off the boat, we wanted to cycle through some of the remaining rainforests of Borneo.

For my first cruise I could have probably picked a better bed partner and more comfortable surroundings, but fate had decreed otherwise. It turned out to be seven days without a bath or shower, and the only toilet a hole in the floor at the bottom of the ship. Our food supply ran out on the third day, and the seas began to get rough. The clock in the captain's room was broken and the hands mostly lay limp at six-thirty. At one point when the sea was roughest, the hands were swinging freely from the nine to the three. It was not worth thinking about the state of the boat or how well it was holding up to the rigors of the seas. I tried to recall if I had seen any lifeboats strapped to the side. I thought I'd seen one lifejacket hanging somewhere, but amongst all the small livestock and people it would be nearly impossible to get my hands on it even if I could remember where it was. We were out at sea now, and as foolish as it may have been, we were stuck on the *Nusa Inda* until the end, which was hopefully when we arrived in Borneo.

From time to time we would go to the bow of the ship and say hello to our bikes. They looked out of place and abandoned clinging to the railing, but they were surviving. The ship's rice and bread also ran out, so somewhere north of the equator which we had just crossed – me for the first time in over sixteen months – the boat stopped. It was about four days into the journey and we were a mile or so offshore. The wrong shore though; still the coast of Sulawesi. A small dinghy left to replenish supplies. Rob and I had been sweating for days, and no water had touched our bodies in far too long, so we spontaneously jumped off the ship and splashed around in the warm equatorial waters. It felt great. One young kid joined us, but everyone else just enjoyed the show. It was salt water, but it was wet. After we climbed back in, we felt rejuvenated; the captain said we should arrive the next day, so we were hopeful. As we sailed on, we looked off to the side to notice that we were being escorted by dolphins. We heard someone say there were sharks around too, which might explain why people preferred to watch us swim, rather than join us.

The food brought back was for the crew as everyone else on the ship had enough to eat. People were kind and shared nuts with us. We bought the occasional bowls of rice from men who looked to be the cooks for the crew. Once or twice they even caught some fish off the stern and we were given some to eat by the captain. Finally, after six days, we pulled into the dockside of the small island of Kalimantan Timur – Timur meaning east. One last night on the ship, and the next day we would be back on land.

We were up with the sun, and immediately said goodbye to everyone. We unstrapped our bikes before noticing that Rob's tire was flat. Rob had a valve known as a presta valve for which the rim hole is smaller than the normal car-type valve known as schraeder, but the only spare tubes he had were the bigger schraeder type so did not fit through the smaller hole. What a silly oversight and carelessness on Rob's part. It meant we didn't even have the pleasure of cycling away from the port. Someone had played with the valve and broken it, so we couldn't get air into it. We limped to a place that looked like it might have a drill. We took off Rob's front wheel, and drilled a bigger hole in the rim, and just for good measure did the same in the rear. Now he could fit tubes with schraeder valves in, which were more widely available, and all that we had anyhow.

Now we were on the road again with no place to go. *Ramadan* was over, but in Indonesia, after *Ramadan* there is a festival called *Hari Raya*, which is a feast of eating all day, and celebrations that the fasting is over. It is a holiday, and on Kalimantan Timur, lasted for three days. Borneo – the third largest island in the world, home to the *Dyaks*, the tribal natives of the island, rainforests, long houses, jungle and baboons – sat a short boat ride away, but could we get there? Would we ever get to cycle on this mysterious island housing three countries?

We found a room in a small hotel, unloaded everything and spent that time cycling around exploring the island. We were greeted enthusiastically by everyone. Deeper inland was abound in wildlife, lizards of all sizes, monkeys, and insect life more akin to flying and crawling rainbows of colors. The few small villages we came upon seemed to be hacked out of the jungle; everything was built using local materials and when we pulled into these small snatches of other lives we must have looked like two aliens on our modern looking bicycles. It was a small island, so we just kept our room and did day trips.

We were stuck on the island with our next closest port of call being Tawau, Malaysia. We didn't yet have the official permission we needed to leave Indonesia. Finally, after the third day the visa office opened. The man working there was quite shocked when we appeared – we knew there were no other foreigners on the island, but we hadn't known we were there illegally. He had a gentle demeanor which, combined with his portly frame and kind eyes, made him look more like an uncle than a custom's official, but we knew he held all the cards. He seemed honest as he talked to us, and neither of us got the feeling he was looking for any *backshish* – a term meaning subtle bribery commonly found throughout most of Asia. He let us know that we would have to take a boat back to Sulawesi, then go to a bigger port town to get a ship to Malaysia. We told him we'd come over on the *Nusa Inda*, and that we'd rather live here than go back on that ship. He gawped, "You came on the *Nusa Inda*? That is the worst boat in all of Indonesia."

He thought for a few moments, his eyes flicking first to one then to the other of us. He must have taken pity on us because he sighed then said, "I will call Jakarta. I will try to get you permission to take the boat to Tawau."

It took two days for the permission to arrive, but when we entered on the second day, we were greeted with a smile as he handed us our legal paperwork to leave Indonesia. I could have hugged him. Property was probably cheap on Kalimantan Timur, but after six days on the island we were ready to go.

The boat ride took thirty minutes, and we were transported to a different world. Malaysia and Indonesia have many things in common, especially where we just stepped off the ship, but the attitude to foreigners was very different in Malaysia where no one even looked at us or our bikes. It was a relief to have breathing room.

There were two ways to head across to the other side of Kalimantan to our next big city destination, a place called Kota Kinabalu in the province called Sabah which encompasses the northwestern part of Borneo; we could follow the paved coastal road around the edge of the island taking in a famous orang-utan reserve, or cut through across the middle. We agreed the forest route looked the more exciting option and figured that to cycle along some logging roads through the interior might afford us some interesting insight to the world of deforestation. Our boat ride had put human faces and a human spin on a problem which is not disappearing. A bike ride might round out that first-hand knowledge nicely.

We spent a day or two in Tawau, walking the streets being blissfully ignored by everyone. Our celebrity status was gone. Malaysia seemed more of the current century – shops were everywhere and people reasonably well-dressed. From the place and situations we had just come from, especially the *Nusa Inda* experience, that thirty minute boat ride to Tawau seemed more like a time transport machine.

Our lives were just about to get interesting once again. We bought a good map of the island and saw the road we wanted snaking through the rainforest. It looked like it would be hard cycling though. We did have our tent and had crammed enough food into our panniers to last a few days. If all else failed, we assumed there would be logging trucks to beg food or lifts from. Water, we thought, would be easy to find in a rainforest! We headed out of civilization once again, and started off on a tarmac road which quickly disintegrated into a dirt track – fairly wide, but rutted and muddy. We looked at each other intuitively asking, "Do we really want to do this?" The smile from Rob let me know that he was more than ready. It was good to be cycling with him at this point in my life. Rob had been hardcore for a long time – cycling northern China and Pakistan back in the mid-eighties after crossing Canada alone in the winter had given him an edge that I hadn't fully developed yet, but my edges were being sharpened, and Rob was definitely part of the sharpening stone.

Experiences like the *Nusa Inda* and Indonesia in general were hardening, and in a strange way softening me. I was realizing that we lived in such a fragile world. I had experiences from New York to Belize, Australia and beyond and all these experiences humbled me as a person. All of the humanity I had met over the years was flesh and blood, just like me, my family and friends. Just because, by a quirk of fate, I was born in New York and someone else in Ujang Pedang doesn't make them less human. Unfortunately the power-hungry and megalomaniacs of the world would lead us to believe differently. I was learning from first-hand experience that every action made in New York or the rainforests of Borneo has a direct effect on all human life. I was now getting ready, unknowingly, for another humbling experience.

The road leveled out at a pretty bumpy, yet rideable state of affairs. We'd got an early start, and not so far out of Tawau we were in thick forest. Our wheels slipping and crunching on the stones were the only sounds we could hear. We would stop and listen to the sounds of the birds of the jungle, and occasionally see monkeys watching us and following at a safe distance. One truck had passed us on our first day and by lunch time I was feeling the undulating roads in my legs. We hadn't done so much cycling recently; the week on the boat had taken some of my hard-earned fitness away, but I'd win that back pretty quickly. Rob just seemed to keep his.

We were not sure what the night would have in store, but we had our tent and some food so we would be okay for the immediate future. At about three in the afternoon there was an abrupt change in the weather. We stopped to figure out what the noise was, and before we even had time to think, there was a sheet of liquid glass between us and we were soaked in a downpour like I had never experienced before in my life. Rob was nearly invisible to me standing only a foot or so away. I could not even see individual drops; it was as if someone had emptied an entire swimming pool's worth of water over us. It chilled us even though it was warm outside. Everything was drenched before we could even make a plan to seek cover under a tree or pull out a rain jacket, it was that sudden. We laughed at the wackiness of the situation, and looked at our road – which had resembled a dirt road a minute ago – now turned into a sticky sludgy mud. We made it over to a tree and huddled under it, finding little shelter. We wondered how long it would last, but we didn't wonder too long, and as unexpectedly as it had come, it stopped. The silence was deafening. The rain had been so loud and blinding that when it stopped we felt transported to a different place. We looked around at the muddy quagmire, our sodden bikes and selves, then up to the magnificent canopy above our heads and realized why we came. Here we were in one of the great rainforests of the world, and we were cycling through it. What a world, what a life, what a privilege!

After the sun filtered through the leaves we felt warmer and decided to move on. The road was nearly impassable now. I had fitted a pair of mudguards somewhere in Bali. They were cheap metal ones that didn't give much clearance, so it was almost impossible to move more than ten feet without having to clean the mud out so the wheels could pass through again. Rob was getting a good laugh at all this. He had sensible thick plastic mudguards that just slid off and on, and now they were neatly strapped on his rear rack. The guy in his bike shop had been thinking at least a bit. I had to disconnect the whole mudguard I'd painstakingly put on a month or so ago. Now with wet clothes, an immovable bike, standing shoe-deep in sludge, I was attempting to take it off. I was slowly slipping into impatience, the final straw being when I pulled at the mudguard and it came off gashing my leg – nothing serious, but enough to snap my patience. I bent it back and forth in a rage until it finally gave way and broke in two. I strapped it under a bungee on my rear rack, but as I went to mount the bike a ragged edge gave me another graze. By then in a mad fury, I took it off my rack and threw it out into the forest. It felt so good to yell at the top of my lungs, I think the mudguard took the brunt of the *Nusa Inda*, and any other travel frustrations that had been building up. Rob sat back and watched the show and after it had subsided I halfheartedly smiled and comforted myself in the knowledge that the mudguard was metal and would rust away pretty quickly in this forest. As we pedaled away, or tried to, I apologized to the forest for the temporary litter. I was also learning between experiences how important having the right equipment was. My bike had been a trusty friend for the last few years, and little did I know I was heading for a career in bicycle shops. All my equipment experiences and road-side maintenance was deepening my knowledge and respect for the simple machine which had become my chosen vehicle for exploring the world.

After my outburst, I was silent and so was Rob. My passionate New Yorker self was still alive and well. So, amongst the poverty, and cycling through a rainforest which was being cut down, a scraped leg and some mud had been the final straw for me. I laughed at the ridiculousness of it. That moment put things in perspective, and even in the midst of the bigger picture, my human side managed to focus on the trivial. We cycled on slowly and camped out under the forest's majestic canopy.

There were leeches about, and my first meeting with the tiny bloodsuckers in Tasmania was not to be my last. We found a place to put the tent, and enough dry wood to start a fire. We had dried from the rainfall, and night falls quickly in the forest. We had to check each other for leeches in the fading light. We were cycling with loose shorts on, and usually no underwear (to prevent chafing), and a leech had found himself a home on the tip of Rob's penis. As we burnt the leeches off each other with a match or a hot piece of wood, I let Rob know he was on his own with that one! It was quite comical to watch Rob, but I held the flashlight and tried not to laugh as he was being so tentative with the hot ember. After the mission was accomplished, we cooked a simple meal, and crawled into the tent, which wasn't getting used much at all, but when it did, it was well worth the little space and weight it took up.

After a fitful night's sleep in a very loud forest, we were ready for another day. Rob was an early riser, so he had a fire going, and I was just crawling out into a magnificent burst of morning colors. The oranges and reds of sunrise breaking through the green canopy, was all quite an extraordinary early morning show.

We cycled deeper into the forest and hadn't gone far when we heard the sound of a chainsaw. We stopped and watched as a small lone figure stood next to a tree which dwarfed him in size incredibly. In my mind's eye I saw the protected redwoods of California and the forest of giant trees I'd cycled through in Western Australia. The drone of the saw's engine, which was an assault on the ears, brought me back to the present, then came the cracking of the tree as the weight pulled it over. We were standing near the road, a far enough distance not to be crushed, but that tree fell so swiftly and with such force that the sound was almost creepy. The air rush from that tree being felled hit Rob and me in the face and body with such force I can still feel it till this day. I'm not sure if a tree falling in a forest makes a noise if no one is there to hear it, but on that day three of us witnessed a beautiful old-growth hardwood hit the forest floor, and I will tell you this, that sound should be heard all over the world, by every person who doesn't bat an eyelid when they read the news about rainforests disappearing at a rate of a football field a day. When you see it for real, it always stays real. There was silence for a few minutes before we cycled away not even sure we were ever seen by the man with the saw. As we got further away we heard the saw start up again, I couldn't bear to think about it.

We cycled on and decided we would try to keep track of the sun, and be more prepared for the onslaught of the afternoon rain. I was feeling stronger now, and the road was proving to be quite a challenge. The forest was alive, and when the more frequent logging trucks would pass us, they seemed to me more like hearses carrying corpses. It was hard to see these beautiful trees with so much life left in them and so much more oxygen to give to our earth being carried away to the western markets of the world for timber, furniture – or even worse – wood pulp.

Before the afternoon rains came we happened upon a logging camp. We weren't sure what to expect, but for being in the middle of the jungle they were pleasant and functional. They were simple, mostly wooden structures; basic rooms for sleeping and a couple of larger more communal buildings. We pulled in, and were greeted by a man who spoke very good English. He invited us in for a hot drink, and we gladly accepted. We knew that within the hour the skies would open up, and the sheets of rain would fall, so sipping a cup of tea was preferable to a drenching.

As it worked out, his name was Mohammed, but he told us to call him Mark. He was in charge of this camp and many of the operations going on in this part of the forest. He was a western-educated forester who'd had most of his schooling in Canada, where he'd picked up the handle Mark. We made small-talk for a while, talking about Canada, then he looked concerned and asked us if we were environmentalists out here to cause trouble. We were taken aback by the question, and appreciated the straightforwardness of the inquiry. We explained we were on a bike tour of Southeast Asia, and thought it would be interesting to cycle through the forest. He said he had never seen any cyclists on the road, and wondered why we weren't going to see the orang-utans. We smiled and told him about the boat journey and meeting many people who were coming to work in the forests, and although we were not working for an environmental organization, we did care for the environment. It struck me as funny that we normally referred to the two as separate entities – the environment and humanity – but I felt the 'environmental movement' was actually a 'save the humans' campaign because the earth would just shrug with a big sigh of relief and instantly start regenerating all the damage we caused if we finally brought on our own demise and ultimate extinction. Back in the logging camp though our host was a nice guy and listened to what we had to say with interest. He then went on to tell us that the rainforests in this part of the world were in danger of all being felled. He explained that his job in this part of the forest would last about ten years. After that, everything we will have seen and would see on our way would be gone. He must have seen the expression on our faces, and went on to explain that the west comes in and buys the wood, pays well for it, and gives his people no other options.

"Look around at all these people," he said. "They are from the Philippines, Indonesia, and Malaysia." He continued, "What does the west give them? Nothing. Development means Coca-Cola or turning their fields into factories where they can work for a pittance. Global greed often brings rise to fundamentalism, but here they have a steady income for ten years.

They can send money home, feed their children, keep their wives from working in factories, and even though it is a short term plan, ten years of guaranteed income can change a lot of people's lives."

Man he was erudite, and if his speech was practiced or not – maybe learned in logging school to combat the environmentalist movement – he hit the nail on the head. It was a hard line to argue with. I wondered what the Australian logger who'd given me a lift would have to say about it all. I also knew that we were in a part of the world where poverty was the norm, and income in any way was seen as a blessing. It was easy for the west to shake a blaming finger at all the trees coming down and the environmental devastation, but in the west we are good at creating situations that are nearly impossible to reverse. What could we do but nod? We didn't know enough, but I vowed that I would.

Was there an answer? Could the west offer anything better than sneaker and clothing factories, or chopping down trees? Are there sustainable solutions? Can we sit in our houses with central heating, cooking with organic palm oil which will be coming from these same forests in fifteen years, our cars parked in our garages and decry all the damage being done to our planet? The blame cannot fall on the same countries we ask to bear the burden of our material desires.

We were drinking tea on the veranda as the rain came down in sheets once again. We were made a kind offer to sleep in a room reserved for visitors. We ate in the dining room surrounded by smiling faces. Young Filipino women served us food, and our table was full of men who drove trucks, and cut down trees for their livelihood. The familiar clacking of wooden checkers hitting each other from the *carrum* game being played somewhere off in the distance brought a smile to my face. These men and women were all part of the same world I was raised in; playing games, eating food, talking, joking, and in the daytime, squeaking out a living. Their faces were as bright and inquisitive as those in all the small villages we'd cycled through. They were doing a job, and I do not think that any of them would have had a clue of what a fervor their existence was creating in places like London, California, and New York.

Mark let us know that the road we were on had a few more camps like this, and he would phone ahead for us to be able to sleep in a bed every night. We were never asked for a cent, and now when the trucks passed us we were tooted and given a friendly wave. The first and second day – before any one knew what we were about – perhaps people had been nervous that we were here to make trouble and take away their livelihoods. Now we were seen as two weird cyclists interested in what was going on in the place many of these people would be calling home for a while to come.

My mind was reeling – here we were cycling in a disappearing rainforest being treated like dignitaries; a bed every night, friendly waves, good food, and even, if we wanted, the occasional woman. We always accepted the former two, and declined the third, although it was admittedly tempting at times. The cycling in the forest passed in much the same way. If we wanted a lift, there was always that possibility. It was a strange feeling – for that week the people cutting down the forests were our friends, and even our guardians; when we had to camp out an extra night our awaiting hosts were even nervous that we had gotten hurt.

Once again, choice was coming to the forefront of my mind. In the west, we want palm oil, soy beans, and hardwood furniture, but all at the cost of destroying these mighty, diverse, life-supporting forests – the oxygen-producing lungs of our earth. Indeed, our choices *do* make a difference, kept running through my mind, as we pedaled beneath the awe-inspiring immensity of the overhead canopy of the beautiful rainforest, that has since, disappeared.

# Tour of Duty

We flew into Singapore which was like a breath of cool air in the midst of all the heat. It's a strange country which has embraced capitalism and modernity but in doing so has forsaken many other things. It was one of those places where you can relax, and recoup some energy for the next leg of your journey. Rob and I were now familiar with the words of *Jesus Christ Superstar*, and as we were heading down the road with Max – a nutty guy we had met at the hostel – Rob and I sang or hummed something from that soundtrack and Max cut in enthusiastically, "I love that play, I was just in a performance of it back in Amsterdam." He broke into a passionate and nicely sung version of the opening tune which we laughingly joined in with.

A few days later I was approached by a western girl who looked vaguely familiar. She said she had been traveling with David, informed me that he was enjoying the camera, and had taken lots of pictures. He had moved on to India and was heading back to England from there. It was nice to hear my camera had found a happy home.

Singapore was perfect to recoup some energy after our ride through the rainforest, where I picked up a bad chest infection, and Rob, a severe intestinal bug. The strong over-the-counter drugs we picked up in Kota Kinabalu and had been taking making our way to Kuching, while still in Borneo, had helped our healing, but we were aware they had also weakened our immune systems. So the sterility was somewhat welcomed. Air-conditioning seemed to be everywhere – it felt as if we were on vacation. After nearly a week though, it was time to move on.

Feeling rejuvenated, and our bikes given some needed maintenance, we headed for the border town with Peninsular Malaysia, Johor Baru. There was a line of cars leaving Singapore as it was illegal to leave the country with less than three-quarters of a tankful of gas because it was much cheaper in Malaysia, and lots of tax revenue would be lost – and they were actually checking!

Getting to peninsular Malaysia felt like we had gone back to Indonesia in some ways – it felt nice to leave the air-conditioning behind us. We cycled slowly north and stayed for a few nights in Melaka on the Malacca Straights – supposedly the busiest waterway in the world, with tankers full of crude oil. We heard many accidents occurred there, with minor oil spills being a weekly occurrence.

Rob and I were getting along fine, although our trip so far had been quite intense. We were both strong characters, and were in each other's space nearly all the time, so it was nice to get to the occasional backpacker circuit to lighten us up a little.

In Melaka we met a few others traveling, and in the food market one night I met a fellow New Yorker, we fell into easy conversation, and talked of what New Yorkers like to talk of the most – New York. For me the conversation was pure nostalgia because I had been away for so long. Rob never understood the love New Yorkers have for their city – he certainly didn't share that same affection for his home town of Edmonton. Even though I had spent a lot of my recent past leaving the city of my birth, I was still a New Yorker, and loved the place. It was nice having a light-hearted conversation about a familiar place in this foreign part of the world. The small encounters of familiarity were like a small refilling of the tank with energy. I was starting to feel that in the slightest way, I was running on reserve. Maybe three years had been long enough, but I was still enjoying the journey.

The cycling was challenging and we were buoyed up with energy after our Singapore R&R. We were putting in some miles now, and just keeping fit. Everything was new to me, but Rob was back on somewhat familiar territory having covered some of this ground a few years back with his then girlfriend, Sue. Although a bit blurry, the jungle scenery, small villages, and quick stop in Kuala Lumpur, were fascinating, but our next border was approaching quicly.

We entered Thailand on a land crossing with a big sign in English which outlined the rules of entry into the Kingdom of Thailand. 'You should be neatly dressed' and 'A man's hair should not touch his shoulders' were two of the many rules which were aimed at the hippies invading Thailand back in the late sixties and seventies. Fortunately it was an old sign, because on both accounts, Rob and I should not have been let in. We were being cautious about meeting and talking to strangers on or near the borders. Drug traffickers could be unscrupulous, and if we said too much about where we were heading it would not be hard to plant a cache of drugs on our bikes somewhere, have us unknowingly transport it over the border, then meet up with us later to retrieve it. It would not be the first time something like that was done – innocent people languished in prisons in Malaysia and many parts of the world for less. Caution was needed, and Rob and I would take to giving our bikes a pre-check before the borders – better being paranoid than becoming a victim of an avoidable situation which could ruin your life. It didn't mean we never spoke to anyone, but if the conversation was getting too specific, especially near a border-crossing with an unknown local or foreigner, we would be vague with our answers. With our long hair and bicycles we were already a target for overzealous border guards.

We didn't make any of the mandatory beach stops at Kho Samui or Pukhet. The roads were pretty busy and the small villages along the way were jam-packed – we could feel the crowdedness of Southeast Asia much more here than in eastern Indonesia. We were keen to get to Bangkok to see if the idea of visiting Vietnam would be possible.

With the car fumes assaulting our nostrils, we cycled through and made it to Kosan Road in Bangkok. Even I was familiar with the crowded street and its abundant guest houses. We looked around for plane tickets and visa possibilities – and being Bangkok – they were easily found with not much digging around. So once again, I found myself on a plane leaving the airport from this crazy city in the middle of Southeast Asia, but this time I was not alone heading to Australia, feeling unsure. Sitting next to me was Rob, and we were heading into a country that was part of the backdrop to my childhood, a place that had formed the politics of a generation, had given birth to the hippy movement, great music and the Peace demonstrations of the sixties – Vietnam.

I tried to feel the terror of being nineteen years old flying into this same airport only eighteen years previously, but I just couldn't. I remembered hacking through the forests in upstate New York letting my mind drift to Vietnam – now directly underneath the belly of the plane I sat in. I never dreamed then that I would actually be landing in the country that had made such a profound impression on me.

During my youth, as I had gotten to know veterans of that war, I thought I had some understanding of why some of my older cousin's friends were not able to function in the normal world without clinging onto a bottle of beer every day. Or the heroin needle being the only solace to be found in 1970's New York, when no one would listen to your tales of horror but for a few – one a nine-year-old boy listening in awe, amazement and fear. Tales of being carried over unknown shoulders to a helicopter as your rescuer is shot down dropping you within sight of the landing 'Huey', therefore saving your life and ending his. Of making a decision to shoot the Vietnamese boy running towards you screaming help; when your bullet hits his torso he blows up in a ring of shrapnel, smoke and flesh, again saving your life, and ending his. I now realized once again I could not conjure up any feeling of what it might have felt like in 1969 to be landing in Saigon – now known as Ho Chi Minh City, but always Saigon for me and the rest of my era.

My tour of duty was to be different – twenty years and a world of change later, and by bicycle. Vietnam was officially throwing its doors open and embracing the possibilities tourism brings. Visa problems, travel problems, language problems, and cultural problems – they all awaited us as we circled Saigon for the third time waiting to land. Looking down at the dense jungle that could be seen beyond the city limits, and the abandoned American aircraft sitting unused in the airfield made it more possible to bring myself back to 1969, and to conjure up images of my brother's and cousin's friends. I knew the stories, but I couldn't feel that fear, couldn't taste it in my mouth – the possibility that this might be the last time I ever walked off a plane in my life. No, I was landing with my bicycle, and our worst nightmare was red tape, not red tracer bullets.

Finally the plane landed and was taxiing on the runway. We alighted in the heat, expected now after all these past months cycling in Southeast Asia. Walking down those steps of the ancient aircraft felt different somehow – we were in Vietnam – 'The Nam' as it was romanticized in too many movies. What was in store we didn't know, but one thing we could be sure of was that our plan to cycle from Saigon to Hanoi was going to be tricky. We had managed to get a month-long visa but – we discovered getting off the plane – we were confined to a sixty kilometer circumference from the center of Saigon. I could smell a little rule-bending in the air.

Our bikes arrived and we watched them being rolled across the tarmac. They were wheeled into our hands, our visas validated and the month began ticking away.

Having our own transport once again saved us a lot of hassle getting into the center of the city. The roads were fairly empty and what little traffic there was consisted mostly of old cars and buses spewing out enough fumes to choke a horse. The endless scooters and pedal taxis became more apparent as we approached the center; a lot of people had their own vehicles of the human-powered kind. The airport was not far from the city center, and despite the subtle craziness, compared to Bangkok it was a pleasant ride, though the air was heavy, promising an afternoon thunderstorm. No problem – we would be housed in a hotel by then.

We were asked many times by the pedal taxis if we wanted a lift, which we found quite amusing. We would cycle alongside these pedal cabs and try to strike up conversation. We would even get in our drops and fake a bicycle race. A few would take up the challenge and we would charge alongside each other, the empty seats of the cab rattling and bouncing, it's protective canvas cover flapping and billowing with the wind as the driver pedaled as hard as he could despite his vehicle's weight and size. He would laugh, beads of sweat forming on his brow, trying to beat us. We would let him win and feign exhaustion, all laughing together as we began our process of falling in love with the beautiful Vietnamese people – the endlessly resilient nation who'd survived an extremely bloodied past.

The religious culture was an interesting mix of Confucian ideals, Buddhism, Christianity, and more. There was an exquisite mélange of food and even language – those old enough spoke French, some of the younger generation English, and of course the odd-sounding Vietnamese was the main language. It was miraculous how these people could have emerged from all of that still intact. Ho Chi Minh, who has stood the test of history as being much more like the revolutionary forefathers of America, and not the villain that the U.S. tried to paint of him, hung up on a word which would taint so much of that period – 'communism'. Vietnam's history, and indeed America's, could have been very different if market forces, greed, lies and deception didn't rule, but once again, I delve into areas I am no expert on, just someone stumbling through and learning that the lives we lead, choices we make and world we create is all of our own doing. We do not have to look far to see the beauty, and the more I travel and am permitted to see of this beauty, the more I shake my head in disbelief, and realize that maybe the Buddhist belief that this is all an illusion is true.

A small Vietnamese boy crossed my line of vision and snapped me back to reality with his captivating smile, dirty face, and deep brown eyes. I smiled back, and he shyly giggled, running and disappearing into the crowd. That smile, freely given, is filed along with some of the most wonderful treasures I have tucked away in a special part of my being. All those smiles collected during my years of travel make me realize that the small sacrifices to try and make this planet a better place are definitely worth it.

The streets, as in most of the developing world, were alive; food and drink sellers, hawkers of everything from goat's eyelashes sewn together for sexual pleasure, to half-hatched chicks in their eggs to be eaten. I didn't mind the French bread rolls with ants cooked into them that we were now being served up – that was not a delicacy as much as a problem of hygiene – but the semi-hatched eggs, no thanks.

We both tried a tiny taste of the snakes floating around in alcohol, a delicacy from somewhere in the Mekong Delta – not our favorite. We sampled lots of street fare, and, although there were a few things that Rob and I did not see eye to eye on, one thing we did agree on was food. As cyclists, food was fuel and we loved to eat; we enjoyed sampling the street food of the world – with some exceptions. There was always an increased chance of getting food poisoning or worse, but there were ways to minimize risks while still being open to the world's delicacies, at least some of them.

"Look at the whites of peoples' eyes," Rob advised me, "if they're yellowish they probably have jaundice which could mean hepatitis." We also looked for basic levels of cleanliness at the food stalls and hung back to see who the locals went to.

After satisfying our stomachs with chicken and a delicious spicy hot noodle soup, it was time to find a hotel. We rode in the cycle lane, which was made dangerous by all the pedal taxis, mopeds, and bicycles haphazardly criss-crossing and creating general mayhem. As a particularly enthusiastic rickshaw cut me off at top speed, causing me to slam on my brakes for the umpteenth time, I briefly wondered if I had had my final plane ride after all! We managed to make it to a hotel which looked to be the biggest in town. The top few floors were blown off, presumably one of the constant reminders of the violent departure of America and the final ending to the nearly thousand-year struggle for freedom. In many ways Saigon looked and felt as if it were suspended in time. Had the troops just left, or was it actually fifteen years since the fall of Saigon? Yes, it was definitely 1990, I was sure of that, the people seemed relaxed, although in our short month of cycling in Vietnam, it would be hard to picture these wonderfully beautiful people ever being stressed even back then, while three million perished in a war which was never meant to be won, or at any other time during their turbulent, slow crawl to independence.

In the hotel, we got to know the many prostitutes using two or three rooms of our hotel as their 'Place of Business'. We weren't interested in them for their trade, even though their beauty was apparent. We taught them games, English words, and even played jump rope together. Their bosses grew to not like us very much; we weren't making them any money, and the girls obviously preferred to spend time with these two weird guys who treated them as humans. Rob and I had other things on our minds as well – sort out that visa.

We visited the local police station which was the way you got most things done, but when we explained our situation and our plans the thick mud wall went up, and we started to realize that our trip in Vietnam was going to have to be within the environs of Saigon, unless we broke some rules. We didn't despair, but cycled out into the Mekong Delta. What a beautiful place it was – the tributaries fed nearly 4,500 kilometers away in the highlands of Tibet flowing through Burma, Cambodia, Laos and finally South Vietnam. The Mekong, which in Vietnamese is also known as the Nine Dragons because it breaks up into nine tributaries before it empties out into the South China Sea as it has done for millennia, supports hundreds of thousands of human beings that depend on its abundance for life. Unchanged by history, starting in one troubled land and flowing through many others, but nature just did its thing and would continue to do so despite all of man's best efforts to destroy it. From Saigon we couldn't explore all the way to the border of Cambodia, but we left early in the morning and pedaled for hours. We experienced some of the many floating markets, much like those in Bangkok, but not yet full of tourists. The exotic fruits from the orchards the Delta supports were mouth-watering to look at, and juicy and sweet to eat. There was enough fish for sale to keep small villages fed for years.

The life along the river seemed endless; the palm trees hugging the banks of the river and the muddy water lapping at the doorsteps of the bamboo huts made me nervous for the people living there as I thought of the high rainy season of June to September and the amount of water that could fall in just one day. The green rice paddies stretching on for miles appeared as a velvety cushion of lush grass, but we knew full well that underneath was waterlogged earth supporting this thirsty crop, and the possible lingering land mine.

We were being drawn into the captivation of Vietnam, as had so many servicemen before us who would try to convey it on their return from the war. It was hard to imagine landing here, probably the first time overseas for most of the young soldiers, to engage in a conflict that no one was quite sure about. To be in a place of such physical beauty, where the people were so gentle, and the topography stunning, while on a mission and in a state of mind to kill or be killed must have been mind-blowing. There was no wonder why so many turned to the bottle or drugs to try to make sense of it.

Vietnam was nearly unified in 1945, but with the help of the British, the French returned to their colonial position after the Japanese departed. The Vietnamese were separated, brother from brother, cousin from cousin, and even though Ho Chi Minh pleaded with the American President Truman for help, he was tragically ignored and the rift was prolonged for a brutal, thirty more years during which the hatred between the north and the south was fuelled.

The country made it through, and although growing pains were still apparent, it was at least united. It was so frustrating knowing that this beautiful country shaped almost like a spoon scooping up Laos, Cambodia and Thailand to its west while the warm waters of the South China Sea lapped at its east was just waiting for us to cycle along its roadways and meet its people, but a small piece of paper with the correct stamp on it barred our way.

The area around Saigon was interesting; the Saigon River was full of riverboats that were pulsating discothèques and fancy-looking restaurants which must have been heaving with GIs on their two-day furloughs. We would be stopped by smiling faces beckoning us in for a drink or food. Many spoke English, and as we would stop and talk to people, we would learn that many of the pedal cab drivers, floor sweepers or touts for restaurants, were educated men; some doctors, engineers and teachers, but when the Americans left in 1975, these men were left to fight their own battles. They would spend years in re-education camps, their old careers forgotten forever. Work for them meant menial low-paid jobs if they could be found; it was their punishment for consorting with the enemy. When the last helicopter flew dramatically from the embassy roof on that fateful thirtieth day of April, life would never be the same for hundreds of thousands of people both here and in America.

Rob and I also enjoyed lots of exploring at night, a habit we picked up in Japan. It was a great way to see the city in a whole different light, or darkness I should say. We would sometimes cycle until the street vendors were closing shop. It was a relaxing time to be on the street as the bustle and business of the day gave way to a calmer energy. The pedal cabs would slowly disappear, and the shroud of darkness would cover the city. The next morning would see Saigon awakening again to the fervor of a new day with touts selling anything and everything, but the cycle would once again complete itself and quietness would ultimately descend. It felt comforting to witness and be a part of it, knowing that these were the rhythms that keep the world turning. We would sometimes sit at a street-side café, sip a hot tea and watch the city go to sleep.

We soon discovered The Sinh Café – a western-traveler hangout, and it was there we met another American named Don, who was married to a Vietnamese girl. He had traveled through Tibet on a horse and wagon for six months before coming to Vietnam to chill out after spending "six of the loneliest, most wonderful, hardest months of his life." We met Twister, a Canadian rugby player who was there on a whim, and was just hanging out in Saigon.

Then there were two American girls from Colorado, Julie and Laura. They had been in Vietnam a little over a week and they too wanted to explore further afield. All their attempts were being met with red tape, and they were getting frustrated. Together we came up with a hair-brained scheme to get two bikes built for them so we could all cycle together. If procuring the visa was still a problem we would do it anyhow. We thought that it would be too difficult to get out of Saigon without being noticed so we planned to hire a truck and driver to drive us and our bicycles beyond our sixty-kilometer tourist visa limit and begin cycling north from there. We'd still try first for the correct documentation.

We went to the part of town which had a row of bicycle shops. Rob and I had been living and riding our bikes for a long time by now so we decided to pick out the equipment, from the frame to the wheels and gears, and have two bikes built so we could head out north together. We might look like a tour group and be left alone, especially if we were out of the city limits. We had no official way of knowing any of this, but we just thought it sounded good enough to give it a try. We had to wait for the bikes to be ready, so we took a daytrip to some of the tunnels in the Mekong Delta. It somehow didn't feel right climbing around these tunnels that had been used for war, the intricacy and seemingly endless work and ingeniousness of these underground mazes were incredible and paid tribute to how badly independence had been wanted and striven for. The area had now spawned a tourist industry which felt strange. It was, on the other hand, informative. I guess it was better for some of the natives to earn a living in a creative way, but there is a fine line to walk in these places – after all, the tunnels were built for the purpose of ambush and killing in a guerilla war. I just hoped that the line would be walked with integrity, and hopefully become an instrument to promote peace, not just another way to earn tourist dollars. History has a lot to teach us, but we're hell bent on repeating it more often than not.

In the Sinh Café I was approached by a young Vietnamese girl called Nha who said she had heard we wanted to cycle up to Hanoi. I asked how she knew, and she told me she was a friend of Don's wife. I thought I would listen to what she had to say. Her uncle was the commandant of one of the precincts in Saigon; she would take me to meet him the next day and see if he could help with our visa problem.

We met the next morning in front of our hotel, and we took a pedal taxi to the precinct. Her uncle was a big guy for a Vietnamese – I'm sure that after a hundred years of French colonial rule some European blood had seeped into the genetic lines of the usually smaller Vietnamese. He seemed genuinely interested in meeting me although, as it turned out, he couldn't do much about our visa problem, but was happy to talk to an American. He had fought alongside the Americans, which I thought was strange, because most of the people who had done that were sent to re-education camps, and were destined to do menial jobs the rest of their lives. I wasn't sure if his English or my translation of what he was saying was getting mixed up. Maybe he was telling me he had fought against the Americans! Either way, he was friendly to me, and his niece didn't say much during the whole meeting. We had cool drinks, and he asked me of our plans. I was careful not to say too much in case I was going to spoil the idea we did have and had already set in motion. I left with the feeling that the whole morning was orchestrated so he could meet an American, and our visa problem had never been on his itinerary. I thought about the chain of events in The Gulf of Tonkin – a lie about an American boat being sunk – which helped kick-start the whole American/Vietnam mess in the first place and wondered if I was getting involved in a little mess of my own. Was our visa problem even on Nha's mind? "Don't say too much to anyone," I kept thinking to myself.

When we got back to the hotel, Rob, Julie and Laura were at the café sorting out a van and driver for our departure. Nha and I went up to the room, and started kissing. She looked beautiful in her *Ao Dai*, which was the traditional Vietnamese long dress with two slits up the side. As she slipped out of it she looked even better! We started to kiss more passionately and as I was slipping past the point of no return I suddenly started thinking better of what I was doing and asked her how old she was. She replied that she was twenty-one (which was possible). With a break in the moment of passion she started talking about Don and how he'd married her girlfriend. I started thinking 'Whoa wait a minute here,' and realized that I was probably being very stupid just having her up in the room. I had broken my golden rule of travel in unknown cultures when just passing through, but fortunately it had not gotten too far and I was able to control all my other urges and calm the situation down. I explained how I was traveling with two other girls to Hanoi and I wasn't sure that it was a good idea for us to be here. With the heat of the moment past we left the room and walked to the café together. There were a few moments of feeling awkward, but then we fell into a conversation about her family, and how they ran a small restaurant on the outskirts of the city. I thanked her for all her help, and we had a hot drink at the café. Don was there and she went over to talk to him. Later on he came over to me and said that she was really twenty-one and just thought I was exotic looking. I smiled at the compliment coming from such an exotic looking person like her. She smiled at me, but I still felt better for not having let things go too far.

I met Rob and the girls later on, and they asked how things went. I told them we were still on shady visa territory, and asked how things had gone with them. They'd had success, and for a small fee we all had a van and a driver taking us out of the city to a place called CaNa when we were ready. It was further than we wanted to go by van, but it was near a beach where we could spend the night in a hut, and we would be well on our way north. All that was needed now was to check on the bikes.

We went to the street of bike shops late in the afternoon and were assured they would be finished the next morning. We knew we were cutting it fine, but it had to be, time was running out if we were to make it to Hanoi. We had already been in Saigon nearly two weeks. It had been a great time, and well worth every minute, but we were ready to head north – we had a lot of cycling to do, and Julie and Laura were yet another unknown quantity. Would they be up to it?

The back of the van was stuffed with us, four bikes, and baggage. We took turns sitting in front with the drivers. We bumped along the dusty roads for ages, but eleven hours and 180 kilometers later, we stumbled out of our diesel-spewing transport van and the sea view was worth it. It was great to be in a country that was not overcome by the tourist industry yet. If developed correctly it could be a wonderful place to travel. The scenery was beautiful, the food was good, and the people as honest as they were nice to look at. You would not know that this tiny country had been overrun, colonized, and occupied. It had proved its resiliency, and now we were hoping to explore its mysteries.

We unloaded, put our bikes in the hut, stripped down to our shorts and went for a refreshing swim. The afternoon was spent luxuriating in the crystal waters of the South China Sea finding it hard to believe we were in Vietnam. Unfortunately, those waters hide a thing of both beauty and danger – coral. I somehow sliced the top of my foot open on some of its razor-sharp protrusions. It bled a lot but it was a clean cut. I washed it out as best I could with water from my water bottle and applied a small bandage. It wasn't too serious, but coral cuts can be slow to heal.

The next morning we decided to leave early. The girls had strapped their backpacks – which were fortunately not too large – to the back of their bikes. Rob's and my bikes were lightly loaded as we'd left a few things back in Bangkok to pick up when we got back from Laos on our return flight. The girls' Czechoslovakian frames were adorned with Japanese components and put together in Vietnam – a pretty international package. The bikes were not bad quality, and although the sizes were not perfect, they were the smallest, best touring-style frames we could locate on such short notice.

We cycled away from our small beach hut, and quietly pedaled further and further from Saigon. Julie and Laura were grateful to us for helping them get their bikes built, and asking them to come on this adventure as they had been on the verge of leaving Vietnam without having left Saigon. Something about our plan sounded like it had possibilities to it, and if not, well even our little adventure so far had been interesting. They were both friendly and attractive and were friends out for a year's worth of traveling in Australia and Southeast Asia. They were adventurous and although no one decided in any way, we traveled as four friends with no romantic overtones which suited everyone just fine.

The first day of cycling was difficult for the two girls as Rob and I had a few miles in our legs. They were active girls, though, and in decent shape, so besides getting used to the bikes and cycling in the heat, their slowness was easily overshadowed by their willingness. There was a wonderful absence of vehicles on what was the main road traveling north. We met a few bikes ridden by locals and would occasionally be accompanied by boys and men on bikes asking questions as they rode along with us. Besides those few exceptions and the occasional bus and truck though, the road was ours. The coastline was literally and figuratively breathtaking, as with many coast roads it was an up and down affair. The glimpses of the blue sea and the marvelous cloud formations billowing up into the sky made a dramatic backdrop for our day's cycling.

The clouds truly were spectacular; huge cottonwool balls tinged around the edges with gold like something out of a Michelangelo painting.

After a few hours cycling we found a place to eat where the owners were surprised to see us. We must have made quite a sight; Rob and me with our long hair and beards; two pretty girls with bright white teeth and long flowing hair – one blonde one brunette – approaching on our bicycles out of the midday heat. Once again the openness of the locals' smiles and the willingness to accommodate us was almost unnerving. I started feeling ashamed that my country had helped wreak so much havoc on these wonderful people and their land. That night we had to sleep out, so we managed to find a small empty beach and tried to disappear off in a corner unseen.

The next day's ride was hot, and by midday we decided to stop for a few hours to allow the worst of the heat to pass. We started heading on a small road which looked as though it led to the beach, so we pedaled off the main road and passed through several small hamlets of simply-built dwellings. As we passed, a few children would shout hello, and gradually more and more children appeared. By the time we got to the beach the crowd behind us was big and it become pretty nerve wracking – we had to leave our bikes leaning up on an abandoned boat and climb up onto its rusting hull to avoid being crushed. It was comical in one way as all the kids wanted was just to look at us. We said a few preliminary words in Vietnamese that we'd taught ourselves, but mostly we stared and smiled at each other. Rob and I did some silly magic tricks we would do to entertain kids in Indonesia. Our audience slowly lost interest in us and a woman came over to help disperse the crowd so we could get back to our bikes.

The woman had a small child of about three clinging to her leg, and the older brother of about fifteen looked to be half-black. She came over and showed us a picture of a G.I., asking if we knew him – he said he would be coming back. I didn't know what to say; it was obviously his son standing before us, but what do you say, "Sorry, if he isn't dead, he's probably married and living in Alabama with a wife and kids, or strung out on heroin trying to cope with the things he has seen and done over here." I opted for the more simple, "Sorry, I don't know him." Rob, being Canadian, didn't harbor the same feeling about being here. I hadn't realized I carried so much guilt around with me about the war. Julie and Laura were younger than me and were too young to have friends affected. If they were going through their own personal feelings about the war we never spoke about it much. I kept my journal, and we were all enjoying the experiences laid out before us. The locals we met seemed to be telepathic or felt something in my energy, as they always directed their questions at me.

240

We asked the woman if there was anywhere we could find some food and were led to what looked like a house, but turned out to be a small eatery. Inside I notice a man slumped drunkenly at a table. The deep-set lines of his face and down-turned lips told stories of a tough past. We ordered our food while he just sat there glaring at us. As we ate our meal I felt his stares cut into me like laser-beams. His belligerence could be felt throughout the room, and the lady who ran the place seemed to be embarrassed about it. Finally the man broke the mounting tension with the words, "You American. Me V.C. I kill Americans," and he made a gesture of slitting a throat. I don't think I was ever so uncomfortable in my life. He said it again, half-rising from his chair, his eyes fixed on me, and as he did, I realized that not only were there Americans suffering alcoholism and emptiness after the war, the conflict had left its ravages on men here too, and here was one victim facing me now. He fixed his steely glaze on me, as if no one else was in the room. I knew that if he wanted, he could have killed me in one quick motion, but there was almost sadness in his eyes, not hatred. Maybe he was apologizing in some way. I don't know.

The woman serving us then escorted him outside. The ex-soldier threw me a hard look as he rose and exited. The woman, looking horrified, was waving her hand behind him, as if to say, "Never mind him, he's drunk."

Julie then said, "Man, he gave me the creeps, and I'm not sure why, but he had it in for you, Joe."

"Great," I said, "let's just hope he's sleeping it off somewhere." I forced a smile.

Laura added, "He was one tough looking guy, did you see his face? So taut, even though he was drunk, those eyes, man, they were like vacant holes, scary!" The owner returned and once again tried to pass it off lightly, making the motion of him being drunk to all of us.

Needless to say, none of us felt like sleeping out under the stars that night. The afternoon had spooked us all. It was incredible, though, to have finally experienced that fear I had looked for on the plane, and now I could perhaps empathize more with the young men and boys who had lost their youth and innocence as those wheels touched down. We pedaled on, and with the heat of the day fading, and plenty of daylight ahead, we made it to a big town where we could get a place to sleep. We had an early night, and sleep came easily.

The sunrise through the un-shuttered window was nearly blinding. My dreams had been strange and my mind could not help drifting back to young soldiers on both sides of the conflict now that a human face had been put to a Viet Cong soldier – not so long ago men were waking up in this beauty to kill or be killed. From the books I'd read, movies I'd seen, and talking to friends, the sunrise brought relief that the long night was over because much of the fighting in Vietnam took place under cover of darkness, or in the dense cover of the beautiful jungle. I wondered whether the soldiers were even able to notice the beauty around them in the face of the horrors they were going through. Either way I'm sure it was a terrifying situation, nothing in comparison to our small trials and tribulations on the road heading north. I kept all these views to myself and wrote in my journal a lot, but this small side trip to Vietnam was starting to mean so much more to me than I originally thought it would. It awoke in me feelings I had nearly forgotten I had along with the faces of those people I grew up hearing stories from. I wanted to heal some of the many wounds but how could I even begin?

We awoke with the bright, hot, sun and not a pounding on the door from the police. We were slipping through without the correct visas, our trick seeming to work. Our goal of Hanoi was getting closer. I kept thinking how difficult it must have been to be thrown here with a gun slung around your shoulder, not being able to trust the brilliant smiles and beautiful faces. We stayed in a small town that was big enough to have a place to stay, and with the progress we were making, it looked like we might even make Denang the next day. We had a few beers with dinner and were feeling quite pleased with ourselves. The exotic names all evoked memories, just saying we were probably going to make it to Denang the next day sounded too much like it couldn't be true. It was still surreal to me.

Julie and Laura were doing unbelievably well. They had never done a long-distance cycle tour, and here they were on bikes that were not the greatest fit for them, cycling on a hilly coastal road, playing a cat and mouse game with the police, with none of us truly knowing what would happen if we did get caught so far from the outer destination of our visa.

The next day we rounded a corner and saw a bus overturned. There were no skid marks, but the road switched back to climb higher. Then it all made sense; the bus hadn't skidded to where it lay on its side, it had actually fallen from the road above – a very horrible thought. We walked over to see the wreck up close, but it wasn't such a great idea – the smell of death lingered. The accident, we learned from a local man who was there poking around, had happened the day before and about forty people had died. The smell of fear and death was still strong and made all of us uneasy; my stomach was nearly pushed to the point of vomiting. The girls wisely enough did not come over for too close a look and opted to look out at the view, which was stunning.

Again, it was beyond belief. Was I creating these situations? It was slowly becoming a very intense trip accentuated by the dodging of the police. That day we cycled through a small village where there was an orphanage. We stopped for lunch, and Rob went over and started playing around with the kids, and then we all got sucked into a game of volleyball. The smiles on these kids' faces were bright and reached right up to their eyes. We played and I didn't notice for a few minutes the deformities they all had. Some were not kids, but were as old as thirty years old. We started to speak to one of the older people who had a good command of English and he told us that these young people, and even some of the people running the orphanage, had all been damaged by the chemical *Agent Orange* – created lovingly by American companies; Dow, Hercules and Monsanto to name a few. Some had been directly burnt by the chemical agent, and some had been born with horrific defects from any one of the other chemicals sprayed or used in some of America's darkest hours. I began to realize that this was just the reality of the country we were cycling in. Vietnam seemed to wear it well and incredible beauty lived right alongside these horrors.

We spent the whole afternoon there, and through someone at the orphanage, found a place to sleep that night that would not be a problem as far as registration was concerned. That was a bonus. We were slowly creeping north.

Denang would be possible if we cycled a short day, but that gave us the problem of registering too early, so we left the village a little later. We took our time meandering there on our bikes, but still arrived too early to register. It was hard not to stand out like sore thumbs on our fully loaded bikes looking very much not like locals. Denang was large enough to absorb a few foreigners, and although it was 1990 and Vietnam was not fully open to travelers, it was billed as 'The Year of The Tourist'. This was probably meant to be welcoming in some way or another, but it was not so easy for the independent traveler, especially on a bicycle. A few foreigners we met were paying a local 'guide' to travel with them so they could go by train. That way you could travel freely, but you had to pay for the guide's food, lodging, and other expenses, plus the guide would take you to only approved hotels, etc. which was the expensive way to go. We had briefly thought about that option, but it would have been complicated and our way – despite the possibility of not succeeding – sounded a lot more like an adventure. It was a bummer having to worry all the time if we stood out, or if the police would be meeting us in the morning, but considering as far as we had pedaled, coupled with our time in Saigon, we considered it a success already. Denang proved an easy place to find lodging, so we stayed two nights to explore its streets and open markets.

Out of Denang there was a village sizable enough to have a place to stay, but once again we were there too early to play the late registering game. We had all been feeling slightly off, and cycling in the high humidity of the rainy season was making us feel more lethargic. By the time we made it to the village we were all ready to stop, the memory of those smiling deformed orphans burning in our minds. They were so admirable. They held no apparent grudge, and again I felt my guilt must have been worn right out there on my sleeve. My government had done this to them. How could people sleep with themselves at night? I couldn't imagine being the people behind any of it. It had been a few days since we had been playing volleyball with their smiling faces and deformed bodies, but it remained clear in my mind. It was a lot more powerful than being scared to the marrow of my bones by the northern Vietnamese soldier, although that had made an impression also to say the least.

One day we met two young soldiers who were walking up the coast road. They weren't interested in paperwork or where we were heading, but were delighted to show us their AK47 automatic weapons and prompted me to hold one and take a photo with them. I didn't want to glorify their weapon, nor did I want to insult two soldiers armed with them, so I limply held it at my side for the photo. Rob was nervous that it might have been a ploy to get me to hold the gun so they could shoot us, and say we wrestled the gun from them. We were feeling ill, tired, and almost waiting to be arrested and turned back at any point. We wanted to find a place to sleep, lie down in bed, and wait till the rain passed so we could go out to eat. I also wanted to get somewhere I could take my boots off to air out my slow-healing coral wound. We all decided that a hotel was in order, and the time didn't matter. Sometimes confidence crept in allowing us to think we'd all make it to our destination of Hanoi.

We handed in our fake paperwork, and asked the woman if she would not hand in the papers to the police until the next morning, feeling a little guilty that we might be putting her in a difficult position. She was smiley, and gladly accepted the local currency, which on its own was slightly illegal. Although Vietnam had not been open for tourism for too long, they already had a two-tier pricing system, and the local price was far cheaper than the visitor's rate. The visitor's prices were in dollars which we did not have in small denominations. This was a mistake, but we did not think Vietnam would be as closed as it was proving to be, so we had no choice but to use local currency.

After a wash, a big rainstorm, and quick catnaps, we were all ready to eat. The drainage in the town left much to be desired; there were huge puddles everywhere, and the one in front of our hotel was nearly big enough to swim in. There was a small café that served food and none of us were sick enough not to eat. We all chose something safe looking then the two girls went back to the room while Rob and I remained and had a cool drink. There was a strange guy sitting at the table across from ours who kept staring at us. After we paid our bill and got up to leave, so did our new shadow. As we approached our hotel, he came up to us and asked us in broken English if we needed any help. We told him we were fine but he then insisted on seeing our passports. We lied and told him they were in our room. "Are you in the same room with the two girls?" he then asked. We were not too sure what his angle was. Did he want to meet the girls? Was he an official who had any right to see our passport? As he followed us into the small lobby, which had a table and some chairs, he then showed us some identification and asked us to get our passports and the two girls. This was getting weirder. We asked who he was, and he said he was a policeman, and he needed to do this for our protection. The second creepiest guy we'd met in Vietnam was here to protect us, hooray!

We went up to the room and told the girls, who were writing in their journals, what was going on and we all went downstairs not knowing exactly what to expect. We knew that we had made it as far as we had clandestinely. If this guy was the police, we could be in trouble.

When we got back downstairs there were four of them; at least it was an even fight! In the end, after about an hour of heavy arguing, our passports were taken, and we were under house arrest. The next day we were all put in a small soviet-era jeep with our bikes. Things could have been worse; we could have had things confiscated or been forced to pay a huge fine. As it worked out, we did have to pay a small fine and were then escorted all the way back to Saigon. We had pedaled half way and it had been incredible. The people, the scenery, and all the bits in between had been worth the abbreviated effort.

On the way down, we and the three police escorts had reached an understanding of sorts after a few strange hours of them showing their power, and us forcing them to pay for our lunch saying we were their captors. They did not enjoy this part, but it gained us some respect. Before making it to Saigon we had to sleep somewhere one night in transit, and the police chose a brothel to be our accommodation. We stayed in our room all crammed into two beds, and who knew where they stayed.

Back in Saigon we were told to buy an airplane ticket out of the country and we would have our passports returned. There was to be one more show of force before we were done with Vietnam.

The girls got nervous and headed off to the police station early. We must have gotten our signals crossed and waited on a corner for them to arrive. After they didn't appear we headed off for the police station, but we were very late, also unshaven and wearing shorts. The commander wanted to show off his power, so in the main waiting area of the precinct he berated us with such force and apparent hatred we thought that if he had had a gun he might have shot us – it was quite unnerving.

"You come to my precinct unshaven dressed like this (pointing at our shorts) and nearly one hour late! You have broken the laws of Vietnam, and you expect respect when you disrespect me in such a way?" He had everyone's attention now. He then threw open the door to his private office. "Come in here." We dutifully followed him in.

What happened next was unexpected. He slapped us on the back, let out a laugh and lit a cigarette. After offering us one each, and said in near perfect English, "You didn't make it all the way to Hanoi, but there is a big bike race every year from Hanoi to Ho Chi Minh City, maybe next year you come back and do it?" We looked at him and each other not knowing what to say, "Er, yes maybe." It was too bizarre. One minute it looked as though he could have killed us, the next he was slapping us on the back inviting us back.

Our flight took off. Our tour of duty was over. It was cut short by the people who insisted they were there to help us – the police – the only people we had unwillingly handed over money to, and been given an unwanted lift from. My thoughts then drifted back to the orphans and children disfigured from *Agent Orange*, my friends who had been here on their real Tour of Duty, and how they had been changed forever. I, too, had been changed; I had felt fear from the drunken ex-soldier we had met, experienced the smell of fear and death in the overturned bus, been captivated by the wonderful natives, but in the end, it was nothing compared to what others had experienced in this beautiful part of our world. We had been privileged to stay in Vietnam a little shy of a month. It was an intense time. We would much rathered have had our original itinerary of visiting Hue, the ancient seat of the King, and Phu Bai, where the French held out for their last and biggest loss in colonial Indochina, and entered Laos from Hanoi, but life had had a different plan.

The highlight of my trip to Vietnam though, came months later when I was back in New York. I was in *Donavan's* – my old haunt from years ago – where I saw Tommy, one of my cousin's friends who had survived Vietnam, but carried the war with him still. Tommy had never been the same since getting back from 'The Nam', his life a constant battle with drink and dealing with the horrors he'd witnessed. When I told him about our trip and what happened to us getting kicked out, he just looked at his drink, and laughing himself into tears said, "Imagine that, I tried for two fuckin' years any trick to get kicked out of Vietnam and it took you a month riding a bicycle to get thrown out." His distinctive laugh filled the bar as he shook his head. "Imagine that, you got kicked out after a month." He seemed to drift off to another place, and then pulled himself back into the moment, "What a great fuckin' story, a month on a bicycle, imagine that!"

# The Mantra

We were a little frustrated from the turn of events in Vietnam, but all in all, it had been a good try. It had been short but full of adventure, and the girls had had the experience of a lifetime for their first cycle trip. For Rob and me, it had turned our whole trip around. We were supposed to be in Laos cycling down towards Bangkok, but now were already back in Bangkok and not sure where to go. We headed up to the Golden Triangle around Chiang Mai and Chiang Rai up in the north of Thailand and rented a motorcycle for a few days. The sixty-mile-per-hour wind in my face was familiar, but I had made the switch to the slower pace of pedaling. The ease and self-sufficiency of bicycle touring had been in my life only a tad short of three years, but it had proven to be my preferred way of travel, although the faster speeds of the motorcycle coupled with the exquisite scenery was a good way for us to shed the disappointment of our deportation out of Vietnam while we formulated our next move.

With all the quick stops in Bangkok previously, on our return from the north we decided to stay in the big city a few days more. On Kosan Road we met up with the usual flurry of travelers coming and going from every direction. It was my third time there and at least that many times for Rob. Now we just wanted to relax – it was the ideal place for a traveler to regroup and let down his guard. We visited the Reclining Buddha, the Palace complex – which was vast – and luxuriated in the other-worldliness of the floating market – a burst of color and sound that challenged all of your senses; flowers of every description for sale, clothing, food, and vibrantly-colored fruit filling the small boats. The Chao Phraya River – the river Bangkok had settled on – came alive, its surface a writhing colorful serpent, much like the floating market in Saigon. Would Saigon look like Bangkok one day? There was a severe lack of tourism there, but here it was everywhere. Bangkok, though, carried it off well.

Gold flake on the temple roofs could be seen randomly dotted throughout the city, and it was startling to think, surrounded by so much poverty, how such extravagance could adorn the Temples expounding the teachings of the Buddha – literally meaning the Awakened One – who taught, 'The Middle Way'. What would he think about the opulence built around his teachings?

I thought it coincidental that Bangkok in Thai was, *Krung Thep,* which translated to 'The City of Angels', just like another city on the other side of the world that had helped me find the path to where I now was.

Both cities' had wonderful cultural sides to them, along with natural beauty, but lurking beneath the surface were reputations not so angelic; Los Angeles had its East L.A. gangs, drive-bys, and the Hollywood scene and all its trappings. Bangkok had Patpong road – well-known for its strip bars, pornography, prostitution, and general ambiance that anything was able to be bought or sold within its borders. The street was an entity unto itself, and the shows in the establishments made the topless bars of my youth look like a local family pub; women doing things such as throwing darts, shooting ping pong balls across the room, and even smoking cigars, but all done with a part of their body designed for vastly different activities!

*Tuk-tuk* rides were still the best cheap thrill to be found on the streets of Bangkok, and probably still safer than the other 'thrills' to be had. Leaving Patpong back to Kosan Road, we had yet another hair-raising experience in the back of one of these insane machines, complete with a suicidal driver.

My thoughts not being able to shake off the feelings a young soldier might have had during the Vietnam era, I walked around imagining how Thailand would have been a great place for R&R from the war zone; beautiful women, good food, exotic scenery, and nobody trying to kill you – a definite plus. The guest houses were cheap and cheerful; a bed, or two, or three, depending upon your budget, normally a shared shower which usually worked, and a maze of corridors with rooms randomly spread all over the one, two or three stories of the place you were in. It was a step above other places we had been in throughout our trip with either non-existent, or minimal plumbing. Bed-bugs were a problem everywhere – with that many travelers sharing beds, traveling in areas where washing is more a luxury than a given, its bound to have bugs of some description; cockroaches in Mexico and Central America, bed-bugs here in Asia, small and not so small rodents; everywhere!

Being able to watch a movie in some of the makeshift coffee houses showing a film was a highlight after being out of the loop for a few months. You would not run into many well-heeled travelers on Kosan Road looking for fitted sheets, air-conditioning, private bathrooms, etc. – those hotels were on the other side of town.

Thailand's population was just over 5,000,000 at the time – about the same size as Nagoya – but somehow Bangkok felt as though every single one of its residents were walking, driving like mad in a *tuk-tuk*, motorcycle, scooter, or badly tuned up car all on the same street as you. Nagoya however had a Japanese calmness about it, whereas in the Asian City of Angels, things were hopping.

After a few more days relaxing in all the chaos, Rob and I were ready to head further afield. Burma was out, the democratically elected new leader

248

of the country – Aung San Suu Kyi, a woman – was under house arrest, the military was in charge, and borders for the moment were closed to foreigners. The white noise of political upheaval had made it to the foreground once again, and helped divert us to our next adventure.

Rob had been to China and I had a desire to head there one day, but talking to people coming back from India and Nepal definitely tweaked my interest. Rob had never been either, so our decision was made.

We cycled from Tribhuvan International Airport in Kathmandu, Nepal, after pumping up our tires, which had been let down at the airport checking for contraband – more likely gold than drugs. It seemed the King's brothers had the heroin import business pretty well tied up. Just a few years back a scandal had exploded implicating the two brothers – or should I say princes – in Hinduism's only 'Kingdom'. One had fled the country because of the shame he brought to himself and his family, the other – basically untouchable because he was royalty – still hung around. Ah, the crazy world of Asia at it's highest (literally) and finest. We had heard of cyclists having their handlebars sawed in half by overzealous customs agents checking for drugs, smuggled art works or gold, so pumping up tires wasn't the worse thing we had to do. Landing in Nepal was like entering yet another different world.

The towering mountains around the Kathmandu Valley enclosed the high mountain kingdom of Nepal. It was chaotic, but nothing like Bangkok – Kathmandu having only a tenth of the population. There were Buddhist Temples, but they were different somehow; older and well-worn. More people were on foot, scooters were around, but if possible Nepal felt even poorer than where we had just come from, and life took on yet another pace of its own.

The *Karma Sutra* Temple in the middle of town was interesting – *The Karma Sutra* being the ancient sexual handbook well-known in the Hindu Religion. There were sculptures gracing the whole outside of the temple, the figures showing men and women in various graphic sexual positions. I tried to imagine that particular temple on Fifth Avenue next to St. Patrick's Cathedral and the idea made me laugh out loud.

We spent a few days in Kathmandu in what was now the off-season. This meant that the normal level of vigor to sell things or hire out rooms had subsided a little and, although there was an energy about the place, the hard buy and sell of the high-season was not apparent. We were able to chat with stallholders, owners of the countless galleries selling Buddhas and other Nepalese art forms, our mode of transport always curtailing an impulse to buy the odd trinket or two. The hoteliers didn't mind just passing the time of day with us rather than selling us a room to stay in. The cows didn't mind holding up traffic or sitting themselves inconveniently in front of shops. I had always associated India with sacred cows, but of course it made perfect sense in Kathmandu too. A book named *Man Myth and Magic* put forth a theory that the cow's importance for survival in this part of the world had led to its 'sacred' status; the cow's dung was used for heating and cooking, its strength for plowing fields, so the beast was a giver of life. Thinking back to the Hindu enclave of Bali, the theory, for me, made sense. The mild climate, lushness and abundance of fruits and vegetables on that small island didn't depend on the cow for survival; there were no large animals blocking the traffic, and they weren't elevated to a status of sacred. How interesting it all was.

Kathmandu was not our destination, just our starting point. It had decent food, and you could find apple pie, brownies laced with hash – a leftover from the days when Kathmandu was well part of the Hippy Trail – Bob Seger's song romanticizing the small capital city came to mind, *I'm Going to Kathmandu*. The ubiquitous yogurt and muesli was to be found quite easily and always went down well with our constantly iffy digestive tracts. Yak tea was on offer, but its rancid smell and taste were off-putting, so we opted for more normal-sounding brews. Hikers and climbers frequented the area, but we were content to look at Mt. Everest from a distance on the odd days it emerged regally from its shroud of clouds.

With the friendly people, the religious coexistence, and physical beauty of Nepal, you almost forgot about the underlying human rights problems that existed here as well. The Hindu religious code – *Manusmriti* – written 2,500 years ago, was still the code society adhered to in this mysterious mountain kingdom, what this meant was the caste (class) system ruled, and most people in power came from the upper castes. The lower castes were seen as lesser human beings. Torture in prisons was not all that uncommon, but again those in prison were usually from the lower castes, so the ruling upper castes didn't deem it a problem. The wider world did, but with royalty in charge, and Nepal being hidden high up in the mountains away from the limelight, it was hard to get this exposed. On the other hand – in the many dualities of our world – Hinduism also has as a core belief in compassion for all humananity. I don't claim a deep knowledge of the mess called religion, human character, and misinterpretation of Holy Scripture, but something seemed to be in conflict. Like many other religions the world over, there were problems, but the problems stemmed from our human selves. Hinduism's worst legacy, though, was the caste system, but the beginnings of what is now an entrenched, almost corrupt system wasn't always like that; its beginnings were based on fulfilling a talent or calling and working this into a serving of society and working together for the whole. Originally you may have been born into a caste, or family of artisans, but the possibility of moving out of that caste existed; now it is more akin to a privilege or birth defect you carried with you through this life.

We cycled south and west from Kathmandu, for some time cycling along a wide river being fed somewhere high up in the mountains – the Holy Bagmati River – which met up with the Holy Ganges in India. It was such a confusing part of the world; holy rivers, revered mountains, sacred animals, seemingly more gods than people, ancient rituals, tiny villages with no electricity, and dire poverty apparent everywhere – all this amongst the backdrop of the highest mountains in the world. The places we slept were so basic that our beds were just straw or hay covered by a sheet. The ever-present green coil that had been burning in every guest room and hotel we had stayed in along the way to keep mosquitoes away were a common link with the part of the world we had just left. Hopefully our days on the bike breathing in the fresh air was countering any negative effects these poisonous coils were having on our lungs. The constant damp and chill was slowly getting through to our bones. *We* were just cycling through, though. People had lived here well before we got there and would continue to do so long after we left. The kids were still smiling, and I shuddered to think what sort of beds or houses they were going back to if ours was the hotel!

In the damp mornings it nearly gave me chills watching the women washing their colorful clothing in the river, the vigorous thrashing on a stone reminiscent of another scene from my past. Here in the damp Kathmandu Valley though it didn't seem the clothes would ever dry. Some clothes were hung from branches, others spread out on the ground. I hoped for their sake and ours that the sun came out.

Once again, the cycling was splendid, and for all I was experiencing inside and out, I would not have wanted to be anywhere else. Rob had been home in Canada for the year previous to our meeting up where he had gone panning for gold in the Yukon in much the same area where I had met the long-distance cyclist from White Plains on my way to Alaska. I remembered pondering the gold rush when I was on my motorbike, thinking how out of place I was at the time in the wilderness of Canada and now here I was with someone who had recently panned for gold there, and we had just cycled together in the wilds of Borneo.

We were an odd duo. Rob, like me, was on a path that was taking him further from his comfort zones and his childhood upbringing in Edmonton. Where he was fresh, I was just beginning to show the signs of unraveling, not too much, but the intensity was tangible. The time away from home was my longest ever and the need for familiarity, while not overwhelming me, was rearing its head once in a while. Fortunately our mutual love of cycle travel kept us both somewhat sane. We were enjoying Nepal and every day brought us new insights.

Nepal was a gentle break-in to a different climate with much higher mountains, and a mild preface to the subcontinent of India. The Nepalese were welcoming with their open smiles and the physical beauty they lived amongst seemed somehow incorporated into their beings. The lack of material wealth and any other underlying hardships definitely did not make life easy, but it also didn't appear to define the people.

The rain continued on and so did we. We cycled past a small village called Lumbini, in the area known as Kapilavastu. Our ignorance came shining through when we found out it was the birthplace of Siddhartha Gautama – the twenty-nine-year-old prince who walked away from his future kingdom in search of enlightenment – more commonly known as 'The Buddha'. It was low key, and we could have easily cycled through it without knowing. Maybe we missed some of the hype, but I found the place was not commercialized at all, which was a good thing. Buddha trinkets were available all over Nepal and Lumbini was no different. I thought his birthplace was in India, but hey, you learn something new every day, although in the past few years it had seemed like every hour.

We hugged the border with India. There it was, off to the left, looming, calling to us, and waiting for our entry. Just the name of that country evokes all sorts of images: mysticism, upset stomachs, poverty, mountains, jungles, sword-wielding *Sikhs*, the Punjabi Desert, The Taj Mahal, sacred cows, traveling *saddhus* and more. After the otherwise mellowness of Nepal, we were ready to enter yet another unknown.

Our entry into India was a foreshadowing of what was to come. The weather worsened to a constant rain as we left the Nepalese foothills and headed southwesterly through the plains towards a small border-crossing at a town called Nepalganj. It looked straightforward – there it was on the map. A small road continued from Nepal into India, and so would we; simple.

After so many days of rain and damp clothes, we were happy to be heading into India. Even though we knew we'd be in the same weather zone, it was a change; in language, money and, hopefully, weather – something to look forward to, like a sunny day. We then planned to head back up into the mountains.

We left the Nepalese border-crossing and were stamped out of the country, our visas now void. As we sloshed across the hundred or so yards of no man's land between the two borders, excitement built up. We would soon be in India. At the border-crossing, the guard in the small concrete house looked at us strangely. He then informed us the crossing was only for Nepalese and Indians – he did not have the authority to stamp us in or recognize our visa. We looked back at the muddy strip of land behind us, and laughingly said, "Ah, home sweet home." We explained that our visa for Nepal was now void and we could not re-enter there. We had cycled too far and too long to go back five days to the next crossing. He had to let us in. He looked like a man who maybe didn't enjoy his job so much. We sloshed back together through the land that was neither India nor Nepal to the Nepalese checkpoint and the two border guards spoke heatedly, waving lots of arms. After a few minutes of this, the Indian guard looked at us, our long hair, wet beards and loaded bikes leaned together near the barrier. Maybe it was pity or maybe it was just exasperation but whatever it was didn't matter as he waved us on and said, "Just go. Go!"

We went. No stamp in our passports so we were now technically illegal in India – something to sort out when in Delhi, not to worry about now.

We cycled on to the small town of Nepalganj. The town was not pretty, but it did not offend. Foodstalls lined the roads of cinderblock houses and the whole town looked like an open air market, and smelled like little India on the lower east side of New York City! We were getting strange stares – like the inhabitants had never seen a foreigner. Admittedly the town was out of the way with the only road passing through leading to Nepal and was not, we knew from first-hand experience, frequented by western travelers. The stares were not unfriendly, just unnerving. In any case, now we had made it to our first Indian town, our first mission was to find lodging then a bank to change some money. We had tried and been successful at spending most of our Nepalese money as we knew we would lose a lot in exchange rates, so we only had a few Nepalese *rupia* in our pockets, traveler's checks, and some American dollars.

We found the only hotel in town, and secured a room. We had no money yet to give the owner, but he didn't mind. He seemed quite pleased to be the first man in Nepalganj to deal with these odd-looking travelers. On the way to the bank we tried to change some American dollars with the stallholders, figuring a black market economy probably thrived in India. They all looked at us and the funny green money we held out to them as if we were peddling dope. That was strange, we thought. Onward to the bank.

In the bank it was as if we were expected. The manager met us and asked us in perfect English to join him for a cup of tea. Over tea he explained that since no westerners came to this town or indeed this bank, he did not have the authority to accept U.S. cash or traveler's checks. Uh oh, we thought, now what? We asked if there was another bank that could. Yes, but it was fifty miles away. We left the bank, hunger now grumbling in our stomachs. We thought we would approach our hotel proprietor with the problem. He was quite unperturbed about our dilemma, even though it meant we did not have the money to pay him. Not only did he not mind, he took us to a food stall where he explained our problem to the stallholder. Within minutes, and with no protestations, two plates of food were offered to us. The rest of the day passed much like this. We ate two meals, drank tea, and slept in our hotel room. Admittedly nothing cost much to our minds, but that was not the point; these few *rupees* were someone's livelihood. We were now the penniless in India, and the natives were being very generous to us.

We woke the next morning to smiles, and the classic sideways gentle shake of the head associated with India. No one seemed too worried about our lack of finances, no one that is, except us. We decided to try a different ploy at the bank. We passed our friend at the stall and had some tea with *dahl* and *chapatti* for breakfast. At the bank we were greeted like old friends. More tea and pleasantries as we explained our new dilemma: not only did we not have any money, but we were now also in debt. The manager seemed to know this already, and explained that it had been many years since a westerner had been in Nepalganj and the people of the town did not mind helping us. They were flattered that we'd decided to cycle all the way from North America to their humble village.

The bank manager thought for a while before a smile illuminated his face as an idea came to him. He had to go to Delhi in a few days where he would be able to change a traveler's check. Until then he would give us the amount out of his own pocket. Unfortunately the smallest denomination we had was fifty dollars which was obviously out of his range. He turned and spoke to the people working in the bank and they all delved into their own pockets and began pulling out notes and coins, collecting enough money to exchange fifty dollars at a very fair exchange rate. Welcome to India we thought to ourselves. I laughed as I imagined the same scene happening in a bank back home. We thanked the bank manager and staff profusely then went to town to settle our food and hotel bills.

The morning was bright and dry, so we decided to pedal on. Riding through big deep muddy puddles reminded us that we would soon be riding in rain again. I was relieved that the cut on my foot from the Vietnamese coral had eventually cleared up before we got into such wet weather. We needed to get up into the mountains. They were not far now. We had enough Indian *rupees* not to worry for quite a while, and the Himalaya were beckoning us. The plains and rains would soon be a memory.

Coca-Cola was kicked out of India in 1977 by the then socialist goverment, it was now trying to come back, but market forces were failing to get in the door because of stubbornness. That stubbornness was all pervasive; the rain seemed stubborn, the culture seemed stubborn, the cows that sometimes chose the middle of the road for their afternoon *siestas* seemed stubborn. India, it seemed, did not want to let go of itself. Why not? It was wonderful to be in a place with a personality. It was once the richest country in Asia, but then enter the British Empire and, after raping the country for a couple of hundred years and finally being pushed out in 1948, India was left poor and in chaos. With that history I, too, would be stubborn and, to say the least, wary of yet another empire pushing itself down my throat. Could India hold back the market forces? The lure of capitalism is strong, and the propaganda machine behind it is big and powerful, but on these small roads drowning in puddles rather than traffic, the West, Coca-Cola and all that comes with it seemed to be part of another universe. India felt as close as we could get to leaving the planet without getting on a rocket ship. It was a breath of fresh air just to know that there were still places relatively unaffected by the onslaught known as progress.

The rainy season was making its mark. Sheets of rain would fall down from the haze in the sky every afternoon; one thing that definitely ran on time in India! Rain so thick it reminded me of the Malaysian rainforest. The puddles were as deep as wading pools and as large as football fields but the locals didn't seem to notice. The only difference in their movements was a hastened gait and plastic bags held firmly over their heads. The natives were dark-skinned with white teeth and dark brown eyes that would encapsulate you when they spoke, their heads would not stop moving when they talked, much like the dog with a spring neck in the back window of my brother's car. That slight back and forth shake of the head when they spoke was a constant reminder that we were in a different land – a land of political turmoil, poverty and happiness all surviving in harmonious instability and always accompanied by a smile.

Here we thought the caste system was more apparent than in Nepal; untouchables – the lowest caste – were doing the menial jobs, and many seemed to have a deformity of some sort, as if fulfilling their role in life with physical manifestations. *Brahmins* – the highest caste – usually filled the power and landowner roles, all born into their roles to remain until death released them. There were a few levels between the highest and the lowest, but as outsiders we were unable to notice the subtleties and daily interactions governed by the caste system, and it was all very confusing. Buddhism, which had many similarities to Hinduism, did not have a caste system and is more a philosophy than a religion, despite all the Buddhist temples of Thailand seeming to prove that to be wrong.

Life has many parallels, and I liked juxtaposing the microcosm to the macrocosm. Our planet works on a loosely based caste system too. The affluent west were the 'haves', our choices affected the wider world, helped pollute its waters, claimed a stake on its resources, and demanded cheaper and cheaper labor the world over. The poorer developing countries were the 'have nots', their resources were bought cheaply, their general populations never benefiting while the leaders got rich, and watched their own people die. Being born poor, or into a lower caste, was a debilitating deformity. As I was witnessing throughout my travels, colonization worked on these same lines.

When India was a British Colony, wheat imports nearly doubled in the late 1800's while famine wiped out millions (who weren't British). During that same timeframe of history, the Irish were faced with the potato blight and famine – Irish people were forced to leave their homes and their country, thousands starved to death, while again the British living in occupied Ireland wanted for nothing, and grain exports kept flowing from Ireland to Britain. The French in Vietnam, not to mention Northern Africa, The Dutch in Indonesia, The Americans in Central and South America – the list I was learning was very long.

Rob and I were now reading *The Baghavad Gita*, one of India's most holy books, as well as studying a book by Vinoba, who was Ghandi's spiritual successor in India. Along with everything we were witnessing first-hand, the whole package was quite an intense and heavy experience. I had been away from New York and any familiar surroundings for almost too long by this point; I was enjoying the traveling, but feeling the need to ground myself soon. Where was I going to fit with regard to my old life?

We woke up one morning, cycled out of town, turned a corner in the road, and saw a bump on the horizon. It reminded me of seeing the Rockies for the first time with Gary. The feeling was similar, but looking at my shirtless cycling partner on his loaded down bicycle, sweating into every pedal stroke rather than turning and seeing Gary in his leather jacket on his motorcycle jolted me back to this alien world I was experiencing. The mountains, though, kept that mystique. The Rockies were as mythical a range to me then as the approaching Himalaya Mountains were now.

We finally saw our goal. Images are conjured up in the mind from those two small words that label the most mystical mountains in the world. The shadows gave way to a definite outline and the pedaling became easier knowing we would be gaining altitude soon. That would mean leaving the rain behind as we crossed the watershed in the old British holiday resort town of Mussori. Our bodies felt strong and our minds were free, all the material things we needed for now being self-propelled to unknown heights.

After another day on the bikes we were truly in the mountains; it still was incredible to me how much ground we covered. The scenery was breathtaking and for a New York City boy to be cycling in the Himalaya

Mountains, passing turnoffs to places like Hemkund, a pilgrimage site for the *Sikh* religion, it was all very exotic indeed. We decided we weren't outfitted for the arduous hike and quite a long detour on the bikes, but met many *Sikhs* on their way to and from their sacred pilgrimage. Once we were pulled over by a vanload coming back from their pilgrimage/holiday who were in a state of euphoria after making it on their once in a lifetime journey to this place considered to be tantamount to heaven on earth. An impromptu party was had on the side of the road. We were also given a quick history lesson about a religion I previously knew very little about.

The *Sikhs* did everything as a devotion to god. They believed in equality of all mankind, denounced superstitions and blind rituals, and were open to all who wished to join them. Everything sounded so wonderful we felt a conversion was being attempted there and then with us. It seemed like a level-headed religion though – no caste system and, amidst a world where blind ritual and superstition were rife, *Sikhism* sounded quite grounded.

On a geographical note we learned that Hemkund was a high glacial lake surrounded by seven high peaks described in a famous *Sikh* poem. It was stumbled upon in the 1930's by a *Sikh* who was in the army – the lake fit the description in the poem perfectly and has since become a sacred site. After 1937 the paths to the lake were made accessible and word spread of its existence; now it was considered an honor to help clear the paths every year after the harsh winter receded so others could make it to its mythical shores.

The *Sikhs* were a hardy bunch, a common name being Singh, named after the tenth guru of their religion. It is a crossroads of Muslim and Hinduism, which emerged from a land between the two worlds, the harshness of the Punjabi Desert. The need to make their stand led to the uniform of the *Sikh*; the uncut hair, usually hidden under a white turban, the long beard, and always a sword at the ready. The sword over the years has given way to a symbolic sword worn around the wrist or elsewhere, but it is a reminder to the *Sikhs* of how they fought to keep their place in a part of the world where many religions flourished and sometimes clashed. Now having a world-wide presence in the millions and a living guru, the *Sikh* Religion, founded nearly 500 years ago, survived and indeed has flourished.

Other small villages were just blips on a map, some just seeming to be a tea stall, but tucked up and hidden away were simple dwellings made of stone or wood where people lived – human beings just like the ones living in Fifth Avenue penthouses!

Staying in towns with names like Dehra Dun – home to a small displaced Tibetan population like many such enclaves of these refugees from their homeland found in the Himalaya – was truly a privilege. The food was different than Indian food as were the customs, but the relationship with the locals was a good one, and religious tolerance the norm. These places of quiet calm and co-existence didn't warrant news headlines, but we were both glad to see their existence and briefly be a part of their energy.

Mussori was such a beautiful mountain village along the way that I almost felt like I was pedaling in a waking dream. The foothills were giving way to jagged peaks, the occasional meadow of Himalayan Rhododendron and other wildflowers, stunning in their repertoire of colors were a feast to our eyes. The lack of oxygen and occasional pain in the abdomen were well worth the trade off. There had been some landslides caused by all the rain, but they turned out to be a blessing in disguise. Although they posed a minor logistical problem in traversing them, once conquered by carrying our bicycles across, we had absolute traffic-free roads much of the way to a place called Sri Badrinath, home to one of Hinduism's holiest temples, and one of the mountain sources of the Holy Ganges River.

We were having an amazing time; the ten-day climb rising out of the soaked plains was tough on the lungs because of the altitude but our legs were up to it, and slowly the rest of our body was acclimatizing. Cycling next to rivers is never easy work. The road inevitably pulls up and away from the river, then heads back down, sometimes crossing the river, and, in the case of the road we were on, sometimes the river crosses the road!

Rob and I were on a spiritual as well as a physical journey. My mind was being opened to new experiences on a daily basis. I was being introduced to parts of myself I had never met before, and experiencing things that I had only previously read about. Many of the things I had experienced had never even entered the realm of what was known to me.

The experiences like the one in Nepalganj always nestled fondly in my memory, although now that we had been in the mountains for days, memories of all the mountain villages in Nepal, and the rainforests of Borneo were more vivid in my mind. The experiences in Vietnam would always bring many faces to my mind; the constantly smiling Vietnamese, and the tortured looks of friends in New York who'd had very different experiences there. My life was definitely changing; cycling in the crisp air, the snow peaks, the clouds drifting past torn open by jagged peaks reaching far up to the heavens – all were helping me to realize that anything was possible. To stay my path was not a crime – it would be a crime not to.

I had found a love of high altitudes from the Rockies to the Himalayas. I also discovered an affinity of finding a comfortable gear and spinning up hill for hours on end. Rob started our journey in great shape and we both just got better. It was nice to not be dragged down worrying about the days ahead pedaling – quite a contrast to the beginning of our travels in Indonesia when I was suffering in the saddle. I did covet Rob's lower gearing at times. I was still learning about bikes and equipment. I made a mental note to get a twenty-six tooth front chain ring for my 'granny gear' – as the lowest gear on the bike was known – in the future.

The contrasts of blue sky and dark stone, the soft green grass and the hard cold granite, the bird-life, the cold flowing rivers were our constant companions. The familiar leaves growing wild on the banks of the river made me smile, but here it was, in its natural environment – the female Indian hemp plant – better known in The Bronx by its Spanish name, marijuana. Its other nick-name made perfect sense now, *ganja*, of course, from the banks of the Ganges. Soon it became almost normal to be on an empty road surrounded by 20,000-foot-high peaks.

We turned a corner on our high mountain road with the mighty Ganges flowing off to the left. A rock outcropping made a natural tunnel as we cycled higher into a cloudless sky. We then saw three silhouettes, their shapes obviously those of men, but with the light of the sun it created an almost other-worldly sight. As they got closer, we saw the flowing hair and robes of the traveling *saddhu*. They carried tridents to use as walking sticks, and, as we passed, we waved at them and them at us, all five of us on a journey of seeking. My hair was flowing down my back, and my beard was bushy too, my bicycle was my trident, and although I had more possessions than they did, I felt a kinship with those three men. It was a moment that was timeless and irreplaceable. I turned to look once again at these three seekers as we cycled slowly past. Their eyes sparkled in the sunlight and their sunken cheeks, wild hair and matted beards made me smile. I looked at Rob and him at me. We shrugged and kept on pedaling onwards. It wasn't for about ten minutes until we spoke.

"Did we just pass three guys walking along with tridents?"

Rob laughed and said, "I think so!"

It was just that kind of place. Our realities had been so challenged that we sometimes were not even sure of the things we witnessed first-hand. It didn't help matters that we were reading *The Bhagavad Gita* every day and discussing the deep layers of meaning hidden within it. Being away from anything as familiar as New York pizza, friends, relatives, and western culture, gave me time to separate the me that I knew well from the me that was yet undiscovered and yet beginning to reveal himself.

That night we pulled into a small village. We ate in a small stall that you would not have expected the most delicious food to come out of, but somehow, this tiny ramshackle hut on the edge of a mountain road in the middle of nowhere produced some of the best *samosas* I had eaten, or have eaten since. The tea was a spicy milk *chai* that was all too familiar to us – its sweetness, almost undrinkable at first, now quite normal to our accustomed tastebuds. The next day was a gentle ride with sweeping vistas and the weather surprisingly pleasant. In the afternoon we came upon a small village not even marked on our map. We stayed there for lunch, and then were invited by some of the youngsters in the town to come with them on a long hike to visit their guru in the mountains. We decided that it was a worthwhile thing to do. We left our bikes where we'd eaten, and followed these young lads as they led us higher on small mountain paths.

The dexterity of these sandal-footed boys was remarkable, hopping like mountain goats from stone to stone and leaping and running as if the thin air was energizing them. We made it to a small, simple dwelling tucked away in the hillside. As we approached a thin, bearded *saddhu* came out of the doorway with the air of someone who had been expecting us. It was as if he knew that there would be two soul searchers arriving. He settled himself into the lotus position, smiled, and began talking to the youngsters.

They had brought him food, and kept him comfortable in exchange for discussions on the *Gita*, and some lessons in yoga posture work and meditation – a pretty fair deal for all involved. When the young boys were all settled and sitting in lotus, he looked at us and, in broken English, asked if we had come a long way. We explained about our trip, and where we were heading. He also spoke of himself and explained to us how he had lived in Bangalore for many years raising his family, and then left seeking knowledge. He spent twelve years living in a cave, and now he was here imparting what he had learnt about life and matters of the spirit. He then got into a position that I had never witnessed before. He expelled all the breath from his body then somehow moved the muscles across his abdomen in what looked like a living animal in his insides – I only learned later in life that this is like a massage of your internal organs, and in yogic circles called *nauli*. He then lifted all his bodyweight up onto hands before entering into a deep, meditative state. The boys sat with their eyes closed, and they all seemed to be together on a different plane. After about ten minutes, all eyes opened, we broke some bread together and had a very interesting conversation learning more about each of our individual life journeys. He was as curious about us as we were him. We talked about some of the parts of the *Gita* that had been confusing to us, exchanged ideas, and passed a pleasant few hours. We said goodbye and set off back down the mountainside. I never once worried about our bikes or belongings. I would not always be so carefree about every material possession I owned and my sole means of transportation, but there was nothing to worry about here, and we knew it, or should I say we felt it.

By the time we got back to the bikes, it was time to find a place to sleep. The proprietor of the food stall ran a modest place to bed down for the night – four walls, a tin roof and two lumpy beds. We had a cup of milky tea, the boys all disappeared back into their village dwellings, and we were left alone to contemplate what had happened that afternoon. Our tea stall man whipped us up a tasty dinner of *dahl*, some *chapatti* and a couple of greasy *samsosas*. This was followed by some creamy milk curd and a deep sleep high up in the crisp thin air of the Himalaya.

The next morning we could not wait to be on our bikes. We were still about three or four days from Sri Badrinath. There was one more sizeable town before we got there, after which we would be on the final ascent into the mountain-top village at the end of the road. It literally was the end of the road too. If you went a little beyond Sri Badrinath you found yourself on a highly disputed border road with Tibet, although the problem was with Tibet's occupying force, China. Welcome back to the realities of the political mess known as Asia. We were trying not to let ourselves get caught up in anything of this sort. We were minding our P's and Q's and staying away from anything that remotely resembled political conversation. I knew I could be drawn all too easily into that realm of things.

The next few days of riding were as before: beautiful scenic roads, the Ganges flowing always closely by so we could wash in its icy waters each morning. Rob's stomach was acting up a bit. Mine, for the most part was doing well. We pulled in to the last tiny village before Sri Badrinath, which itself is not a bustling metropolis.

Our town's amenities were the basic fare in these parts. Usually the room consisted of two beds, a table and a dim light. There were never showers or toilets in the room but there might occasionally be one in the building somewhere. Or, in many of the smaller places, the public toilet served what seemed to be the whole town. Matters of the toilet in India are very different than those in the west.

One particular night Rob and I had carried our bikes through a maze of tiny corridors to get to our room with two beds, one window – which in this case was our light source – and a small table. The usual routine was that I let Rob pick the bed of his choice. He would go through the same routine nightly, checking for bed-bugs, looking for tell-tale blood splattering on the walls near the mattress, flipping over the mattress, etc. The end result would usually be that I would awake unbitten and Rob's legs would be covered. I liked the ritual, and also smiled at Rob's morning grunts of disbelief that once again I was unscathed.

The cool of the evening was perfect for sleeping. The food we ate had not been the best, but we both had experienced worse. We woke with the sun, Rob going through his usual rant about bed-bug bites, but suddenly he looked at me, and with a knowing look, said, "I'm outta here. I'll meet you on the road out of town!" I knew the look, and the smell that preceded it, all too well. For even though my stomach was mostly behaving, we both knew when it was time to run to the toilet, or, when in India, just run and squat, and pronto!

"Okay, I'll be out in a few minutes," I called to his hastily retreating back. I started to slowly pack up, and then it hit me. Oh no, I'm not going to make it. I started rummaging around in my panniers frantically throwing out everything searching for a plastic bag I knew I had somewhere. I found it, and, might I add, just in the nick of time. It became my instant squat toilet. After thinking I was finished with my bag, a feeling of nausea came over me. I quickly untied the bag and vomited into it, and then another wave of diarrhea completed my morning toilet necessities. I felt remarkably well afterwards. I tied the bag, looked at the window and asked forgiveness to the gods as I threw out the bag into the dense trees. I finished packing my bike, carried it out through the maze, and reached the street. I cycled slowly away from town where the road was lined with men squatting down in their morning rituals. They all waved and smiled, and I smiled back. I saw Rob at the end of the line waiting for me, looking much less green and slightly satisfied with himself, and his perfect timing. We exchanged our toilet stories and pedaled off laughing with Rob yelling at the top of his one and a half lungs, "Ah, isn't it good to be alive and cycling in India!"

We both had some bread in our panniers. Dry bread was in order for the morning. At our next tea stall we would pull out the powdered baby food we carried, ask for a bowl of hot milk, and eat our somewhat stomach-friendly morning meal. We had found this to be the closest we could come to a breakfast of cereal before lunchtime when we would start with the onslaught of grease.

The road was absolutely picture perfect now. Rugged high mountains everywhere, the river raging next to us, crisp thin air, and the occasional bus passing us every couple of hours or so. Breakfast at our tea stall was quite satisfying and we treated ourselves with a double portion of baby food. We both felt remarkably better, although I would not want to guess at the havoc we were wreaking on our insides. It was a small price to pay for enlightenment, chuckle, chuckle!

Sri Badrinath was closer than either of us had thought. We cycled around a big bend in the road, and all of a sudden we were hearing what sounded like *sitar* music through a loudspeaker. We continued towards the sounds, and soon a big gaudily multi-colored building appeared on the horizon. It was quite unique in its appearance, and turned out to be the temple. Then we saw people on the big, chunky, black, Indian single-speed *Hero* bicycles, and a few beasts of burden. The music became louder and the distortion cleared. We had arrived. Its history was steeped in Hinduism – Lord Vishnu and Arjuna had connections with its temple, surrounding mountains and rivers. The characters we were reading about in *The Bhaghavad Gita* were coming to life along our journey.

Hinduism was full of deities and complicated stories and no matter how much we tried to delve into the historical tales, it always boggled our minds. With the help of Vinoba's book, we sometimes had a glimpse of clarity to the underlying philosophies, but the complications of the actual history, fact or fable, remained at a very long arm's length. After cycling the 300 or so kilometers to get here, it was interesting to know that the river Alkhnanada -which was the name of the river flowing through Sri Badrinath – merged with the Baghivathi River not far away to form the Ganges which we had followed all the way up to where we now were. Further on it would meet up with the Bagmati River from the Kathmandu Valley. The Ganges, with all its confluences and holy influences represented this part of the world perfectly. The religions merged and shaped each other, the rituals overlapped, the philosophies and people were similar, but they all melded into the one big great river which was the subcontinent. Even Jesus couldn't escape the mêlée; he was revered in India and known as St. Issa.

The town was not much to look at. The temple was the only building that looked like it was staying. Many of the stalls and other buildings looked like they had been thrown up quickly and could come down again just as easily. The bearded *saddhus* in their robes with their tridents, and alms bowls, the women in their flowing *saris*, made us feel as if we had just walked onto a film set. We searched for a place to sleep so we could park our bikes, and explore this fascinating village on foot. We found a windowless, damp, chilly room with two beds. Over our week-long stay here it became lovingly known as 'the cave'. Maybe we were trying to have our own unique cave experience in the mountains like the *saddhu* we had met days before.

We put our bikes in the room, and quickly set out into the cloudy waning daylight. We explored the town but did not see any westerners at first. I supposed the landslides had stopped a lot of the buses from getting up this high. We found a restaurant, and were both extremely hungry at this point. We sat down, and this was where we met the man who would become affectionately known to us as 'The Raj'.

He was eccentric, but that could be said about pretty much everyone we had met so far, including ourselves. The Raj, however, stretched our definition of eccentric – which was widening daily – even a little wider.

First of all, he wore crimson robes that he covered his whole body with, even his head, but not his face. He wore wooden sandals with soles made from two vertical pieces of wood to prevent him touching the ground. This, of course, would drain the energy from his body. ("Ah ha, that's what I've been doing wrong" I thought.) He never sat on anything without laying down a part of his crimson attire first and he spoke that perfect Indian English. His heart was in the right place, and he took an instant liking to us and an interest in our journey. He was also on a spiritual journey. His objective was world peace and he was concentrating all of his energies right now in northern India. He told us that we had arrived in Sri Badrinath at an auspicious time. He would meet us tomorrow for lunch and tell us more about it.

We wandered into the temple, had a look around the town, and I peeled off to find a small tea stall to sit and write in my journal for a little while. We would inevitably meet up sometime before dinner. My journal started to fill with lots of heady thoughts. I was entering dimensions to life unknown to me. It was wonderful and scary at the same time. I was getting nervous thinking about New York and life there. Would I ever fit in again? Did I want to? One of the marvelous things about life is that you can't unlearn something. You can choose to try and forget about it, but when you walk through doors knowingly you have to be willing to go on from that point and take everything you have learned with you. It was what we were doing on our cycle journey. We were trying to expose our unknown selves, and what better place to do it than in India? When nothing around you is familiar, it is easier to let the unfamiliar you emerge as well. Then, when you do go back to the familiar physical space, that unfamiliar you has no choice but to come with you, and therein lies the tricky part. Where do you go from there? How much of that unfamiliar person do you take with you and incorporate into your too-familiar ways of doing things? I think I was getting to the point where I wanted – even needed – to be surrounded by the familiar. I was so excited about the things I had learned over the past three years; now I wanted to see how much I was willing to take back with me, to embrace and welcome into my 'known' life. Could I do it, or would I just slip back into the old familiar patterns and ways of doing things?

The ominous meeting with the next day was very exciting for both of us. What did he mean that we had arrived at an auspiscious time? I slept fitfully that night. The cave was not the most conducive for sleep. It was damp and cold, but at least it was very dark as well. The next morning was clear, but I knew it would be clouding up after noon; it was the current weather pattern.

Baby food breakfast was actually growing on me. It also seemed to be the formula for keeping us pretty much healthy. I saw The Raj talking to a *saddhu* outside the temple. There he was sitting on his crimson colored head wrap so his energy would not be whisked away from him. He was sitting cross-legged, his imposing figure a great contrast to the very thin – almost sickly – figures of the traveling *saddhus*. The Raj certainly did not look undernourished. Rob and I walked over to him and asked if he was ready to eat some lunch. He said he certainly was so we headed to the restaurant and ordered a meal fit for three wandering souls.

We talked about many things. The Raj was a nice man. His sincerity mixed well with his dark brown eyes, big bushy beard and portly figure. You were immediately engulfed in his world of calm. His smile was contagious, and his laugh made you feel all was right with the world. His appetite matched him perfectly – to watch him eat a meal was like watching a form of art; not a morsel was dropped, his beard emerged crumbless, and he looked satisfied after every mouthful. In India cutlery is pretty much non-existent in the countryside. There is an art to eating everything with your right hand. Your hand forms a crane-like posture with which you scoop up the rice and whatever main dish you are having and hope you get most of it in. I hadn't mastered it, but I enjoyed the challenge.

After dinner we all had a sweet *lassi*, a yogurt drink common in India, and quite delicious. After our meal and our *lassi*, we ordered some tea, and now The Raj was getting excited. He started to tell us why this time was such an auspicious one. There was a gathering of *saddhus* happening in the village here to meditate together and put out vibes of peace and understanding into the universe. What a noble cause, I thought; glad to be an integral part of its energy. He told us to meet him near the outskirts of town after dark.

I always sit and wonder when I hear of travelers being robbed or even worse. Their stories are usually fraught with the most ridiculous of circumstances; "I met a guy who said he would get me a train ticket, so I gave him the cash and waited for him but he never returned"; "I was drunk in a bar on the outskirts of Puerto Angel in southern Mexico, and had to walk back alone to the place I was staying when I was robbed by three men," etc. I always tried to not get into compromising situations, or hand money to strangers in far-off lands, for the most part I had never been robbed in my travels, and the few things I lost while traveling were due to my own carelessness.

So I say all this about being cautious and streetwise, but we are just about to meet an Indian guy called The Raj on the outskirts of a mountain-top village in rural India at nightfall with our two passports, all the money,

265

traveler's checks, and identification we'll need for the next six months tucked inside our money belts, and nothing could have felt more right. The instant feel-good factor I described on first meeting The Raj is as close as I can come to how right that night's meeting felt. Rob and I never had a second thought about it.

We had been traveling and looking for something to try and help us to be calmer people. We had both vowed that for the time we were riding our bikes in Asia, we would be celibate – I slipped with Nah in Vietnam – celibacy was more a state of mind rather than just a physical abstinence; abstaining from sex didn't just mean the act itself, it was redirecting your sexual energy, difficult, but a challenge. We were reading the *Gita* and Vinoba to help us understand ourselves better. I was writing in my diary, and we were searching for some small foothold into the door of meditation. We knew that we were just touching the surface of the depths we wished to delve into, but we were trying. It seemed the less we outwardly searched and tried, the more came to us.

In the cave we talked about the imminent meeting. We couldn't tell from our windowless abode how dark or late it was. Neither of us had a watch, so every once in a while we'd walk to the front door of our dwelling to peer at the setting sun. The time was approaching and we were ready to go.

We began a circuitous route to the edge of town as the last rays of sunlight still gave their magical glow to the surrounding mountains. By the time we arrived at our meeting place we could see the outline of The Raj, looking – with his sandals and crimson robes – like some kind of strange movie extra.

When he saw us his eyes lit up and he motioned for us to get going. He seemed to be as excited or even more so than us. We walked around the outskirts of town. 19,000 and 20,000-foot peaks towered above our heads, the dusk throwing majestic indigo shadow forms against the darkening blue sky. We arrived at a door which appeared to lead into the side of a mountain, we could have easily walked past it if we hadn't known it was there. The Raj turned and in a hushed voice said, "Just sit quietly, and try not to disturb anything."

We opened the door and entered. The smell of human bodies mixed with a stale odor of smoke and damp assaulted our nostrils. To our accustomed senses it was a beautiful smell. It was the real smell of life. It wasn't chemical deodorants or aftershaves; it was pheromones, human smells, and the smoke of a fire to keep warm. It took me back to a primal state of mind. I looked around to see that we were surrounded by *saddhus*, the dim candlelight flickering off their matted beards. Some of the whites of their eyes were a yellow that would be considered sickly in the western world, but it was not the yellow of hepatitis, just a slight jaundice from malnutrition. It added to their mystique. Like their robes, calloused bare feet, and their tridents, it was part of the *saddhus'* uniform, quite different to the *Sikhs'*.

The room itself was alive. The walls were misshapen and seemed to be sweating and changing shape in the flickering candlelight. The space looked as if it had been hollowed by chisel and hammer then smoothed by thousands of hands feeling their way in the dimness to find a place to sit in lotus and convene with a higher consciousness. The walls and ceiling had the smoke stains of countless burning candles giving out just enough light but never too much. There was not a hint of the twentieth century to be found. No electricity, no gas ovens, radios, or televisions. We could have stepped through a corridor in time when the big wooden door groaned open and we stepped inside this precious space. Now we were here time didn't matter, it was just the moment. Whether it was 1990 or 1090 outside the door was of no consequence. All I was aware of were the thoughts swirling in my head.

The only sound was of slight light breathing. All were perfectly still, their postures erect – even The Raj managed this perfect position – then all eyes closed and off they went into their world. I felt out of place, like a hunched-back foreigner. I was uneasy at first and tried to make eye contact with Rob, but he too was in his own world and dealing with this in his own way. I would have to get comfortable. How I wished I had a mantra. I was so new to this. I couldn't even figure out a way to calm myself down. All of my traveling, cycling and reading could not help me here. I was out of my depth so I just closed my eyes. I felt all too conscious of the curve of my spine from years of badly positioned motorcycle riding, but I slowly began to relax into my body. My eyes felt closed, but not tightly. The buzzing in my head never went away, but subsided. Till this day I can not say how long we all sat there. The darkness was pure, the smell was real, and the energy was beautiful. Ten years before all of these men might have been working in big cities for large firms or some may have worked the land. Now they were here, the possessions of the material world cast off, sitting in lotus position near the roof of the planet all focusing on a peaceful world. Here I was, with the absolute privilege to be there, my life's path slowly changing forever. I opened my eyes and saw that bodies were beginning to move. My gaze met The Raj's, his eyes twinkled and he flashed me a smile. His expression said, "Pretty cool eh?"

Then I started to recognize other faces. The *saddhu* from the village with the young boys, the three men we had passed on the road and others were the men I had seen in various places in town. They all smiled, and nodded, and then we broke bread together in silence. My nature is to talk and at this moment I wanted to blurt out, "Wow that was unreal." I wanted to say something to acknowledge how wonderful I thought it all was but I learned a valuable lesson there and then; words were not needed. No words could describe what just happened, so why waste them? After a while, the Raj looked at us and nodded his head to say, "Let's go." We put our hands together in front of our hearts, slightly bowed our heads and said, "*Namaste*," yet another greeting we had learned, like the many around the world celebrating a higher essence in all of us, loosely meant, "The god spirit in me salutes the god spirit in you." Off we walked into the dark of the clear mountain air.

We didn't speak much at first. We let the moments slip by and the reality of what we'd experienced sink deeper into our beings. The Raj broke the silence when he asked us, "Well, what did you think?" All I could say was, "Intense!" Rob just nodded. I told The Raj how we had seen a few of these guys on the road up here. He told us that if you see them on the road, this is where they are heading. The Raj bid us goodnight, and Rob and I walked towards our own cave. We never ran into him again.

We talked excitedly about savoring the moment. We wanted to take it all one step further. Now more than ever I wanted a mantra and a way to meditate that didn't involve so much off-putting preparation. I knew so little about it and I needed someone to point me in the right direction.

The next morning we decided to leave our bikes in the cave, take my tent and hike higher up into the mountains above Sri Badrinath to camp out for a night or two. Neelkunt was a 19,400 foot peak that loomed over the town and was said to be a holy mountain. We wanted to get closer and sleep at its base.

The hike was relatively easy and it didn't take long to be out of sight of the village. As we surveyed the area it appeared as if we were in the middle of the mountains with no towns or villages for miles. We had in fact only hiked for a couple of hours. It was awe-inspiring. It felt as if borders had ceased to exist and in many ways they had. In this part of the world the nomad with his flock of goats or sheep moved freely through what political lines on a map call China, Nepal, Tibet and India. For the highland nomad in these parts, there were no passports or checkpoints, the animals were barter for food, the markets a source of income and social interaction.

We were excited to be at the foot of Neelkunt. The events of the previous evening were still giving me a tingle up my spine. I asked Rob if he felt the same and he did. We were at a point in our lives where change was wanted, even needed. We had both been traveling for many years at this point and people didn't always understand the traveler's mentality; no income, no jobs to go back to, just the freedom of the open road and the ability to explore the experiences life would throw in your path. I had always been asked what I was running from, but I liked to think of it more, as I said before, in terms of what was I running to. I wasn't hurting anyone, I was just not satisfied with an existence of school, work, retire, die. I had always felt there was more to it. I was not drawn in by the material comforts to the extent that I would let them rule my life. I enjoyed being in charge of my life and was happy to feel secure enough in myself that I did not need a new car, or high paying job to define who I was. This, though, did not sit well; every one needed a box to be put in, but I didn't have one. For an experience like the day before surrounded by life, the raw smell of it still in my nostrils, I would gladly be misunderstood by everyone I knew and loved.

Rob and I spoke about many things. I told him I was feeling the need to get somewhere known to see myself on a familiar backdrop. I had been away for a year before, a few months here and there, but those travels were in North America, and the experiences, although inspiring, had not challenged me nearly as much as these last three years. I was feeling the need to see if I was strong enough to put into practice this feeling I had tapped into. I was not quite ready to go though. I wanted my mantra, that one word to help me focus my mind.

We explored the surrounding area, and it was nice to be up in the fresh air, with our thoughts, a tent, and nothing else. We read some of the *Gita* and I think I was starting to get it. Not understand it fully, but I was appreciating some of its symbolism. I was starting to feel some solidarity with the main character Arjuna's fear and confusion. That night we slept well.

The next morning was clear and crisp. We had some bread for breakfast and heard animal bells off in the distance. I went and wrote in my journal, Rob also took himself off, and we both spent the morning in silence with ourselves and the mountains, not a soul to be seen for miles.

Our stomachs must have been on the same schedule as Rob got back to the tent about three minutes after I did saying he was starving. We sat in the tent to eat, but just a few moments later we heard a voice say, "Hello?" At first I thought I was hearing things. Then again, "Hello, may I come in?"

I unzipped the tent to see a *saddhu* with a dark black beard standing in front of the tent. "Sure," I said. He came in and was unfamiliar to us. He had not been there the night before, or at least not when we had been there. He had leathery feet and hands. We asked him if he would like to share some food with us.

He said, "Why not?"

We ate together in silence, and he glanced down and saw our copy of the *Bhagavad Gita*. He smiled, then wiped the crumbs from his beard and said, "You are needing to meditate, yes? Do not worry about so many things. To meditate you just must sit in silence and calm your mind. All you need to do is focus on a word or sentence. Do not make it so complicated."

Who was this mind reader? I said, "Yes, I want to meditate and clear my mind, but it always seems to be jumping around."

"I know it is difficult with so many things going on in the world. You both have seen much, you will see more. Keep your presence of mind, let go of expectation. This is a difficult task. There are many ways to meditate, but most importantly do not get caught up in the many things you must do to meditate. Sit in silence, focus on a word, any word, and allow it to calm your mind. It is that simple."

He smiled and thanked us for the bread. I unzipped the tent to let him depart then rezipped it. I looked at Rob and said, "Did that just happen?"

He grinned at me, took a bite of bread, and shrugged his shoulders. "I think it did."

I unzipped the tent again to see if I was hallucinating. A mountain mist had blown in, there was just a slight soft white veil draped over the area, and nothing or no one else to be seen. I came back into the tent. I was not given the specific word, but I had my mantra. I smiled and knew right there and then that slight figure of a man had just come into our tent and handed me my plane ticket back to New York. It was time for me to go!

# Entering Moscow

Flying directly to New York would have been unthinkable for me where I was mentally; the culture shock would have been too great. In any case, it was impossible from Sri Badrinath. We headed towards New Delhi, wending our way out of the mountains slowly. The trip was no less inspiring, and heading down was quite a thrill, but the excitement of knowing I was making a move towards the familiar made it all the better. My mantra of sorts tucked away in my mind, putting it to use would be the next challenge. We knew we'd be parting in Asia somewhere. We had shared an irreplaceable few months together. Rob decided he would put his bike on a bus and head on to some cycling further north after spending our last week together in India's capital city. I was headed to the familiar.

New Delhi was a good place to wind down, but being India, it was manic. We rode through crowded streets dodging cars, cows and trucks. On leaving the hotel, we quickly learnt to make a deft sidestep as the vultures shitting from the treetops in the small front courtyard made the doorstep their target. I could imagine them chuckling evilly to themselves as each new unsuspecting victim took a hit. Compared to the somewhat tame pigeon pooh that would be more the norm in a big city, what the vultures let fly were nearer small swimming pools in size. We even spied a small family of monkeys living amongst the chaos. Unbelievable! Only in India.

I needed to get special permission to leave India since we had enetered in that confusing manner without official stamps in our passports. It was easier than we expected, and with a long-drawn-out series of desks, papers being stamped, and nodding officials blowing through their nostrils, I had a small hand-written paragraph in my passport giving me permission to leave the borders of India. It was only a three-hour affair, but better than being held up at the airport.

After all the cycling with Rob, the experiences and everything that had happened in the last three or so years, it felt good to be heading towards home. My bicycle had been my only constant companion since leaving Japan and now even that was heading back to its new home in The Bronx, in three separate boxes. I now had only what could fit into a tiny backpack. From New Delhi I would be flying to Germany via a stop over in Moscow airport for just a few hours. Or so I thought.

The plane first touched down in Tashkent, U.S.S.R. – today, the capital of independent Uzbekistan. We were led off the plane by men in uniforms carrying guns and were escorted to a bleak, windowless room where there were coffee and biscuits waiting for us.

I looked around and thought to myself that this was about as close as I'd get to experiencing the slowly dissolving Soviet Union. As we were escorted back to the plane, I thought that this had to be the strangest airport experience of my life. I had a four-hour lay over ahead of me in Moscow and wondered if they would give us the same treatment.

Back on the plane I got to talking to a Russian guy and an American woman called Patty. The man was a local, so no problem with visas or the like for him, but Patty had had to go through an extensive process of booking expensive hotels, and receiving a letter of invitation from someone in Moscow before getting her visa. I definitely felt envious that she would be staying in Moscow for a week. As an American growing up in the cold war days, it was the forbidden fruit. The Russian *Intourist* hotels took full advantage of this and charged $110 U.S. a night for the privilege of staying there and they were the only hotels most foreigners were allowed to stay in. It was all a money-making sham, and, although I would have loved to have seen Red Square and walk around the forbidden streets of Russia's Capital City, I did not want to give in to the corruption that surrounded the whole process. I'd have to be happy with a white room in Tashkent, and whatever fun lay ahead in Moscow Airport.

The Russian guy advised Patty to buy a few cartons of cigarettes in the Duty Free shop as it was as good as, or even better than, *rubles*. For some reason, I also bought a carton of Marlboro cigarettes in the Duty Free, possibly in some secret hope that I would be bartering them on the streets for a meal. As the plane landed, a fog hung over the city. While we disembarked, Patty and I chatted and swapped travel stories. The only things I was carrying were a small red backpack, and a carton of cigarettes tucked under my arm.

As we chatted off the plane, this time we were not escorted by men in uniform. The Cyrillic writing apart, you might not have known you were in the heart of what once was the mighty U.S.S.R. Crumbling as it was, it held onto its aura, and Moscow still conjured up images of black Mercedes and KGB officers talking into their collars.

Once inside the terminal building there was all the usual hustle and bustle of an international airport; crowds holding aloft signs with the names of people they were hoping to meet, travelers pushing trolleys loaded with suitcases, families with toddlers getting underfoot, people staring up at arrivals and departures boards. I was still chatting and walking along with Patty. At a little past six a.m., with my plane to Frankfurt Germany leaving at ten a.m., I found myself stepping into a limousine with the rest of the group. I thought it was going to take us to the mandatory white room or a customs line – immigration maybe – but as the limo joined what seemed to be a highway, I looked at Patty and whispered,

272

"Are we out of the airport? What about customs?" She shrugged. I was stunned. I was trying to hide my surprise as we were dropped off in front of the expensive *Intourist* hotel where she was booked. I stood as discretely as I could until the check-in process was over, my brain flipping through the options of what I could do now I was actually in Moscow proper. I asked if I could have a wash in Patty's room, which was pure communist no-nonsense – small, dingy, efficient, and not quite windowless, but it somehow had a windowless feel to it. I took a nap on her floor for an hour or so, got up, had a wash before thanking her and heading out into the streets. So suddenly I found myself walking the streets of Moscow wondering what I could do in the one and a half hours before my flight left. Then I had a brilliant idea.

I flagged down a taxi, and for the price of a Marlboro pack he took me to the *Aeroflot* office which of course was open on a Sunday morning. I tried my luck and walked in while my taxi driver waited for me.

"May I change my flight to Germany to next week please?" I asked the woman behind the desk.

"Yes, if you have all the proper visas," she replied in her clipped, brusk English.

I was hoping she didn't notice the bead of sweat that instantly formed when she mentioned the word visa, but she couldn't have as she hadn't even looked up at me yet. I chanced my luck, "Of course I do." I tried not to move around nervously.

"What is the name of your hotel?" she continued, still not glancing up from her desk.

"The *Intourist* hotel in the center of town," I replied trying to sound convincing. The name of the hotel was in the Cyrillic writing, so I had no idea of its name or pronunciation. I was surely getting myself in too deep.

"Room number?"

Oh shit, she's buying the story, I thought to myself, and quickly said, "Sixteen Twenty-one." I remembered Patty's room number was fourteen twenty-one, and she was on the top floor. I didn't want to get her into trouble, but now I thought I'd blown it. For a split-second I saw her in my mind turn to me and say, "There are no sixteen story hotels in Moscow, you are lying," and then push the special red button for the secret police to come. Maybe my mind harbored memories of too many spy movies! In reality she did not flinch and finally looked up at me.

"Your ticket please!"

I somehow managed to calmly give her my ticket. She never asked to see my passport or visa. She then stamped my ticket in all the right places, and turned with a bored air to her next task never knowing that she had granted me the chance of a lifetime – to be in Moscow for a week.

"Thank you," I said, as I left the ticket office. If she could have peered into my mind at that moment, she would have seen a jumble of emotions; excitement, fear, accomplishment, confusion, but mostly nervousness. I had never been so nervous, not even when Rob and I faced the possibility of heading back to Sulawesi on the *Nusa Inda*. I had entered the Moscow underworld, visa-less in the land of endless paperwork, an American illegally walking the streets of Russia's Capital.

My taxi driver eagerly awaited the outcome as I had previously agreed that if I was able to change my flight, I would change some money with him. He was happy to hear of my good result and we headed off to his house. I didn't deal with many taxi drivers since I'd started traveling by bike, but the one thing I know is that they are usually in the know, and many of them are players, which was definitely true of this one. I had an idea of the black market price of the ruble and I also knew the official of eight was a joke. If you wanted you could probably get up into the hundreds, but I was more than happy with thirty-five to the dollar. I changed fifty dollars worth and had a cup of coffee with him and his wife. We didn't say much, exchanging mostly smiles and gestures. Then he dropped me off in Red Square.

I looked up at a public clock and realized my plane was now taxiing on the runway. Or was it? Had they held up the plane looking for me? An organized group of officers now moving swiftly through the cramped aisle, I had to shake the spy movie cliché soon, I decided. No, somehow Russia didn't seem to be that organized and a lot of the sinister preconceived ideas were already falling to the wayside. But now here I was standing in Red Square, no invitation, no hotel, and – as a plane thundered west overhead – no transport out for a week. No problem.

My most pressing quandary was that I stuck out like a sore thumb. My hair was mid-back length, my beard long and bushy. My clothes, after over six months cycling in Asia, were colorful and well-worn. Still high from my recent success I just stood and tried to take in the fact that I was in Red Square. I suppressed an urge to jump up and down and roar with laughter. I'd successfully snuck into Russia, so far quite easily. Maybe I was not taking things as seriously as I should have been, but it never occurred to me that I had done anything wrong except skirt around a couple of rules and regulations that were only in place to extract as much cash from your wallet as possible. I would be spending money in the local shops, and hopefully a locally-run, small non-*Intourist* sanctioned hotel. I decided to walk around first for a while before embarking on that adventure.

I had no desire to wait on lines to visit tourist attractions. I wanted to sit in small places and meet the locals. I began walking around, trying to look like I belonged – as much as is possible when you are wearing a faded pink tee-shirt and baggy Indian trousers. I stared at the minarets of St. Peter's for at least half an hour. I saw lines of people waiting to see the Kremlin, St Peter's Basilica and even a two kilometer line to eat in the first McDonald's in Russia. The Golden Arches had arrived. I enjoyed watching the entrepreneurial Moscovite children running up and down the line taking orders from those further down and then delivering them to their friends installed at the front of the line. Red Square was bustling in all the normal tourist ways, but I did not want to enter that world just yet, I was still feeling part of my own personal espionage movie! But now, time to find a place to sleep.

After an hour or so the hotel search was turning almost comical. I walked into places that looked like cheap hotels, which most were. If I had spoken Russian, life might have been easier (Chris's linguistic skills would have been handy), but I had to get by with hand gestures and lots of pointing. The outcome was usually the same, a pointed finger away from their establishment and the word "*Intourist*" on their lips. They were all well-trained and probably scared to let unauthorized foreigners into their hotel. To be honest, most of them had probably never had the experience of a large, hairy, non-reserved American turning up on their doorstep. After being turned away four or five times, I decided that the search for a cheap hotel was futile. I resigned myself to the sobering thought that I would be sleeping on the street, at least for one night. For some reason I was not worried. My experience to date was that things do work out. I'd seen some abandoned buildings, and thought that sleeping in one would not be awful. It was about two in the afternoon or so, and I was getting hungry. I was sitting on a cornerstone of a building, still feeling dreamlike about the whole thing and unable to believe my luck. I was just about to write in my journal when Andre walked into my life.

"Are you in some kind of trouble?" I heard a Russian accent speaking very passable English and looked up to see a goateed character with a small bag slung over his shoulder standing over me. The cautious side of me kicked in for a few moments, remembering the not so distant past in Vietnam, and I wondered what he wanted. Before I replied, I looked around. No official looking men in dark shades and black suits around. Then Andre spoke again. "Can I help you in any way?"

There was sincerity in his voice, so I replied, "Yes you can."

We started to talk and Andre took a seat next to me on the protruding cornerstone of the building. I was cautious at first but I could tell after just five minutes that he was going to be the man to help me out in Moscow. I asked him, "Think you can find me a cheap hotel for the night? All the hotels I've been to have sent me away to the expensive *Intourist* hotel. 'No foreigners' they all told me."

275

He was astonished and said, "This is my town, a new Moscow, *Perestroika, Glasnost*, a new Russia, come, follow me, I will find you a hotel."

We revisited one of the hotels I had just been in. I didn't say anything.

"What is your price limit?" he asked me.

"The equivalent of ten American dollars or so."

He looked at me and nodded almost as if to say that was a good budget, then said, "No problem."

I watched him go up to the counter and whispered loud enough for him to hear, "Good luck!"

I heard the murmuring of polite conversation before things got heated. Arms flailing and some pointing my way, and an irritated Andre came walking back my way looking dejected. I told him "Don't worry about it, it's not you or me, it's all about the money."

He said, "I explained to the guy you were my cousin from America, you didn't have much money and you wanted to stay in a local hotel. He kept on saying back to me, 'No Americans here, *Intourist*.' I kept on saying the *Intourist* was too big, too expensive, but he wouldn't change his mind."

I then told Andre I had been here and to three others, and the reaction was always the same. He was obstinate and kept on mumbling "*Perestroika, Glasnost*, a new Russia."

After the third hotel he was at his wit's end. He tried every ploy possible, but met with brick walls every time. Finally he turned and said to me, "You will stay at my place. My family is away in the south, you can be my guest."

I didn't expect that. I thought for sure he would find a hotel that he 'knew about' that would accept me without any paperwork. He hadn't managed that, but I could tell he enjoyed bending the rules. I reassured him he didn't have to do this, I was totally fine with finding a place to sleep – the train station or something – but he wouldn't hear of it.

"If my Russia will put you out on the street, that's their problem, I will not allow it. You will stay with me, that's it!" I wasn't going to argue too much. Sleeping rough for a week in Moscow might have been an adventure, but staying at Andre's was definitely going to be a more comfortable exploit.

We stopped in a café for some food. I would never have found it alone – it looked like an apartment block from the outside. Inside there were people chatting, smoking, drinking and eating. It had a real local atmosphere about it so that you felt you could turn around and see Trotsky sitting there, inciting revolutionary thoughts in all his friends at the table.

When it came out that my flight was the following week, Andre's response was his usual, "No problem." He added that I could stay the whole week at his place, his wife and child had just left; and would be gone for two weeks.

He was a doctor and lived in housing for the hospital workers on the outskirts of the city. His one request was that I wear some of his clothes and trim my beard a little so I didn't stand out that much. I was more than happy to comply.

We walked around town, and Andre showed me all of the construction sights and translated the signs for the coming Pizza Hut, and other fast food from America. I felt like apologizing to him, but like in so many countries in the world this is often seen as progress. I let my mind drift to the young guy I'd met in Mexico City who, after working a full shift in McDonald's, could not afford to buy a meal there. Capitalism. Exploitation. Why is it seen as progress? I had to bring myself back to the moment.

We got on the train to head back to Andre's. I got a few stares and even more as we headed out of the city center. The journey was about twenty minutes or so and took us to what you would imagine to be a suburb of Moscow; square ugly blocks of apartment buildings with some trees and brownish grassy lawns near the entrances. All of the streets were lined with more of the same. I would have to pay attention carefully to where Andre's building was because if I came back here alone, I'm sure it would take me hours of key-turning to find the right door to the right building.

As soon as we entered his apartment, I knew that I had met the right guy. There was black market stuff everywhere; stereo, television, VHS video player, lots of American movies crammed on overcrowded bookshelves, a Mr. Coffee machine in the kitchen, and who knew what was behind the bulging closet doors – the place just reeked of Andre and reminded me of his cool self-assuredness and summed up what Andre was about. We had a coffee, and afterwards I explained to him that I had the residual symptoms of what is known in traveler's circles as 'Delhi Belly'. He laughed, and handed me some black powdery liquid to drink that turned out to be charcoal mixed with water which is often effective in clearing up stomach upsets.

We had a simple dinner and spent the evening planning things to do. Andre worked four hours a day in a clinic but he could get out of his other work, so he could show me around Moscow. After getting to know him better, and sensing he'd like a challenge, I dropped the bomb on him.

"Andre," I said meekly, "I think I should tell you that I don't have a visa for your country. I snuck out of the airport, and changed my flight with none of the proper paperwork."

I'm sure I made his day, maybe even his week as his eyes lit up. His immediate response was, "Ah, you are a bad boy, I like it. Tomorrow we will sort out your visa!"

Simple as that. The conversation went on, and no more was mentioned about my visa. Andre was confident he could sort it out. We were in probably one of the hardest countries in the world to get a visa for an American, and Andre just matter of factly said we'd sort it out tomorrow. I told him about how in Southeast Asia we'd had to get special permission to enter Malaysia from Indonesian Borneo, how we were deported from Vietnam after sneaking half way to Hanoi, and the last adventure in India, needing to get hand-written permission to leave. This threw the final gauntlet down for Andre. "We will not fail with your Russian problem," he said with a smile while nodding his head and almost giggling, "You are a bad boy, I like that..."

The next morning was crisp and clear. I was dressed in Andre's clothes, which were a little more conservative than my Asian attire. I cropped my beard down a bit, and tied my hair back neatly in a pony tail. Off for morning battle with the authorities.

We took the train to the center of Moscow, and walked down dozens of streets, finally stopping in front of a place that looked like any other building. Andre proclaimed, "Here we are." I was getting used to that very quickly here. To my eye restaurants, visa offices, even houses all looked just the same; gray, square concrete buildings.

We walked inside and there was a long line. Not quite as long as the one at McDonald's, but I felt sure we were there for a while. Andre then said, "May I have your passport and plane ticket?" I told him I didn't want to leave this office without my passport. He nodded, and said, "Don't worry, I understand, your passport will not be left with these people."

I had every confidence in Andre. I watched in amazement as he went to the front of the line and started speaking to a woman behind the counter. Within minutes voices were raised, fingers were pointing my way but no one on the line seemed to notice, or should I say care. Andre was handed some forms and we filled them out together. The questions were mostly for Andre. After a few tense minutes on my part, he returned and said, "We must come back tomorrow morning for your visa," and handed me back my passport.

"That's it?" I asked.

He shrugged, "This is the old Soviet Union don't forget, but I do believe that it will be done tomorrow."

I had to ask, "Well, what did you say? What was all the yelling about?"

He told me, "That was not yelling, I simply had to raise my voice. When dealing with such official tedious people, this is how to get things done quickly and efficiently." I must have still looked surprised as he continued, "I told them the cousin story again. It didn't work with the hotels, but now I think it must have. You see the choices are few; they either had to simply charge a small fee and stamp a piece of paper, or else there is too much work involved. You are in Moscow, you have a place to stay and you have a plane ticket out. For them it is not worth all the fuss and bother to try and do things by the book. It would be too involved, and costly. They know that, but more importantly, we know that!" He gave me an Andre smile and we set off back through the rabbit warren of streets.

Again I had the feeling that everything was working out. It was that feeling of synchronicity that I had felt so many times in my travels. It was wonderful.

I had reached that space Ted Simon recounts in his book *Jupiter's Travels* – on a round the world journey, his motorcycle has broken down on the side of the road in India, not worried, he awaits confidently for his next adventure knowing everything will unfold slowly and shape the path of his journey. The tricky part was going to be holding on to that feeling when back in New York. Could I keep hold onto the magic I had uncovered over the past few years? Could I stay in my groove with a universe that was willing to provide? That, I knew, was the whole point of my movement towards the place I still referred to as home. For now, here was my Russian host, providing a bed, friendship, and my permission to stay, legally, in Moscow.

We stopped in a café for a celebratory hot drink. Andre had to go to work. We arranged a meeting place at two p.m. and I asked if I should eat, or would we eat together. He laughed and said, "Your Delhi Belly is feeling okay? I told you the charcoal would work. No, we eat together of course, I know of a good place," and he walked off.

I spent the day getting lost in the heart of Moscow – there was so much to see. I would stop in what I thought were shops, and stumbled into an area where there were street musicians entertaining passers by and artists doing beautiful sketches. I chatted with the musicians who gave me one of their tapes if I would promise to play it for my friends in New York. Their name was *Group The Loop* – a strange name I thought, but the music was good, and I did keep my promise.

I bought a beautiful charcoal sketch from a street artist, and still couldn't believe I was walking the streets of Russia's capital city. I stopped under a tree for shade to write down my thoughts, and it was one-thirty before I knew it. I tucked away my journal, and walked up the street waving to the artist, and nodding at *Group The Loop,* who were still fervently entertaining small groups of tourists.

Andre, true to form, was on time, and had a young guy who did not speak a word of English in tow. Andre introduced us, asking, "Do you mind if this young man joins us for lunch?"

"Certainly not," I replied. We followed Andre to yet another indistinguishable building and stepped inside to a lively looking bistro. Andre ordered the food, and promised it would be excellent. The young man – Mikhial – was from the Ukraine. It was his first trip to Moscow, and he was a real country bumpkin. He had come to see the sights of Moscow; Red Square, The Kremlin, St. Peter's Basilica, and McDonald's. I was taken aback that McDonald's was on the list, but Andre reassured me it was one of the premier tourist sights. It was a piece of America right here in Moscow. I wanted to cry and he must have seen it in my eyes because he added, "A small and far less interesting piece of America than you." Oh yes, Andre was a schmoozer.

Throughout lunch, which was excellent, I was feeling quite uncomfortable because Mikhial continued to stare at me, even as he ate. I finally said something to Andre who told me, "Mikhial is a country boy from the Ukraine. He lives on a farm, and this is his first trip to a big city; now he is sitting having lunch with an American who looks like a rock and roll star. This is probably the first and last time he will ever be so close to an American. Believe me, this will be more important than McDonald's when he goes back home, don't worry." Then Andre asked me if I had any memento I could give him. I had nothing except a dollar bill which, I signed my name on for him. Mikhial then signed a ruble and gave it to me.

The next morning it was time to visit the visa office. I was pretty confident, but had a small feeling in the pit of my stomach just the same – officialdom could often be tricky. We walked together straight to the front of the line, me taking the lead from Andre. The same person who had dealt with Andre was there looking just as unconcerned as yesterday. When he saw us, he handed Andre a small piece of paper. We opened it and there it was stamped on a not so official looking piece of paper – my week-long transit visa, which gave me permission to stay in the Moscow environs for one week. True to form, the visa expired the day and hour my plane left, not a moment later.

And so my week in Moscow officially began. In the mornings I would entertain myself, and in the afternoons I would meet Andre and he would take me somewhere interesting, or introduce me to someone he knew. One day he showed up with a young woman opera singer. She spoke Italian, and because it came out I spoke Spanish, he figured we would be able to communicate. The idea was good in concept, but in practice it didn't work all that well. With her 'opera Italian' and my rusty Spanish we gave communication a go, but it definitely had its limits. We went to a park on the outskirts of the city together. She was shy and I think uncomfortable in the situation. We all spent the day and had dinner together, and what I did not realize, which was why she was so ill at ease, was that Andre had arranged for her to sleep over. We finally all went back to Andre's place where he left us alone and went to bed.

There we were in his living room with one bed made up. I appreciated what Andre was trying to do. He thought: two young single people, a romantic night in Moscow – but the situation was extremely awkward – I do think she would have stared out the window all night until I took some bedding and went over to the couch. I reassured her I would sleep there, and she could sleep in the bed. I did, and assume she eventually did also.

The next morning was not nearly as uncomfortable. We ate together and Andre looked over at me with a raised eyebrow and asked if I had a good night. I just smiled back. They left together, and I was happy to be alone not struggling in Spanish/Italian to try to communicate. It was a fun day, and she was quite nice company, but I let Andre know, no more blind dates please.

The day that followed was probably the highlight of my week. After work, we met at the usual place and Andre thankfully showed up alone. We took a train a few stops out of town. Being a New Yorker, I always appreciate good inner city transportation and I enjoyed the Moscow subway system. The stations were so deep underground it felt like you were entering the bowels of the earth when you descended the stairs. They also doubled as nuclear fallout shelters. Each stop had me thinking we were pulling into a museum as they were filled with ornate statues and paintings.

We got off at a stop I couldn't pronounce if I wanted to, then walked into an ordinary-looking building. Again I wondered what was in store. We walked by a glass window, where Andre waved at the man sitting there reading. We were in a Russian bath house. This, I thought, I was going to enjoy.

I had been to bath houses in Japan and Korea. They are great places to relax, and the national identity shines through the steamy atmospheres they create. This bath house was definitely Russian. It just had that dingy feel that was quite atmospheric on the one hand, and almost off-putting on the other.

Andre introduced me to his friends and I think it was safe to say that not many swarthy, long-haired Americans frequented the place. We started with cups of hot tea from a flask. I was just thankful it wasn't Russian vodka! We then went to Andre's locker and undressed. Andre gave me a wool cap to put on and we entered a small room of very intense heat. I stood there naked with my wool hat on as two men on either side of me vigorously whacked me with branches from a eucalyptus-type tree. They did this until I was so hot I thought I would faint. Then Andre would yell at both his men and mine to stop before showing me a pool of freezing water and diving in. You stayed in until you could not stand it anymore, which was probably a matter of seconds. I took a deep breath and jumped in. The water was so icy I nearly shouted out and I was out almost straight away. Then it was back to the hot room for more beating. We did this a number of times, and Andre said that is why the Russians live so long.

There were some very-old-looking men there. I wished I could get into their brains – they must have had some stories to tell. I had to struggle through with a few pleasantries. I was then led to a room where a table awaited me. I lay on my stomach and two men worked on me with their hands and what felt like wire brushes. What I guess was meant to be a skin exfoliating session turned into one of agony for me. I had just finished cycling through lots of sunshine in Asia, so I think they took my sun-darkened skin for dirt. I put up with it to the point where I thought I was bleeding. I then called Andre over and asked him to tell the two gorillas to ease up as I would like some skin left. They laughed and apologized. After that we had showers, and drank some more hot tea. At last it was time to get dressed, and by this point I was starving. Andre was too, so we headed back to town to eat.

The eating experience took a few hours. We looked around for a place that was open that had atmosphere as both Andre and I enjoyed somewhere with a good feel. Everything here, though, to me had atmosphere; after all, I never forgot I was walking the streets of Moscow, although now it was beginning to lose its dreamlike quality and become more real. Only a few days ago I was just touching down in Moscow ready to take off again just a few hours later. Now here I was, a guest of Andre, getting to know the sprawling streets of this fascinating city.

We had a lunch of hot soup and a big green salad, accompanied by a heavy brown bread and very strong coffee. This time we didn't meet anyone Andre knew, nor did he pull anyone out of his magic hat for us to talk to so we just got to know each other. He was a doctor, and earned about $50 U.S. a week, housing included. It didn't sound like much to me, but he explained it was only part time, and he did other things in his spare time. He didn't expand on what the 'other things' were and I didn't probe, so they remained a mystery. I don't think they were too illegal; possibly black market buying and selling. He was more interested in New York than my travels as he had never been to America, nor did he think he ever would go. I explained to him about my neighborhood in The Bronx, and how it was the city, but to a New Yorker the boro of Manhattan was the 'real' city. I spoke of the nightclubs of my university days and waxed lyrical of the city I had not been in for over three years. He was like a sponge soaking up every word I said.

On the way home we stopped at a supermarket. The shelves were bare and I thought briefly of America where the choice in even the smallest store can be overwhelming. Andre had asked the lady at the checkout for milk, but she said there was none. He said something to her in Russian, and she disappeared to a back room and came back with a liter of milk. I asked, "Andre, where did she get that from?"

He said nonchalantly, "It was the liter she saved to bring home to her family."

"We don't need milk that badly, I'll have my coffee black," I protested.

"Accept it with a smile. This woman has probably never seen a foreigner before. This is a small suburb of Moscow, and now she is giving her milk to an American! This will be big news at her house tonight. Her family is used to many nights without milk. No milk tonight because she gave it to an American boy. This story will be her best!"

Was it Andre's way with words, or would she really be so happy to give up her liter of milk? With some misgivings I thanked her profusely, and she had the sweetest shy smile on her face. I'd never felt so good about depriving someone of their milk.

We dropped off Andre's shopping, then grabbed a bunch of empty plastic bottles and headed out for a long walk in the woods nearby. We were on a beautiful path, and came upon a spring with lots of people filling up bottles with fresh spring water. It was such a great scene. Everyone looked relaxed and was laughing and having a good time. Whatever the hard day threw at them, here in the woods, getting fresh spring water washed that all away. There were hikers, families, and older couples – someone representing most walks of life – it was something I did not expect to see a short train ride away from the center of Moscow. We waited patiently then filled up our own bottles.

"I love this place," Andre said with a twinkle in his eye. "It is one of the few pleasures in Moscow that is free, not controlled, and you do not need to fill out any forms to enjoy it! Can you see? That's why everyone looks so happy; deep down they feel they are beating the system."

I agreed with Andre; it felt great to experience such a good energy and even though we walked away from the spring loaded down with water, I felt very light. The day had been such a nice one and had shown me a whole different side to my stay. The bath house experience, the checkout woman and now this – it was great to see the inner glow of people emerge.

Over the next couple of days I took the subway in different directions and just soaked up the atmosphere walking around waiting to see what surprises Andre had in store. We met up at lunch time and would go to a shop or a gallery. I never joined any of the long lines to see The Kremlin, or St. Peter's. My penultimate day in Moscow I took a subway to a far-flung suburb, and just sat in front of a supermarket writing in my journal. It was nice to observe life passing by. I had been writing for a while when one of the workers from the backroom spotted me – I guess I stood out a bit. He invited me in to the stock room, which surprisingly enough had some stock! When they found out I was American the questions began. I didn't understand them, but we got by with movie English on their part, and hand signals and basic Russian on mine. Soon the fire water Russian vodka came out. Let me tell you, you'd never see this stuff for sale anywhere. When they were not looking I dumped as much of it as I could and probably killed a cherished pot plant. After a half an hour or so I bid my farewells, the few sips of Vodka I'd been obliged to have making my head spin. I stood up, took in a deep breath of fresh air and made my way to the subway station to meet Andre for our final day in Moscow.

No matter how hard I tried to spend those *rubles*, I couldn't manage it. That night Andre told me he had arranged a lift to the airport with a friend of his who had a car. The last day we just spent a mellow time together and went to the post office so I could send the few items I'd bought in Moscow home. Unfortunately the sketching and a Russian sailor's shirt that Andre had bought for me never did arrive, but fortunately I kept the music tape. I had snuck into Russia, and I would stride out, complete with a lift in a little red Lada.

We went out that night for a drink to officially end our time together. As usual the bar was hard to find, looking like anywhere else, but once inside I felt I stepped onto another movie set, but for a far different film than the one The Raj was in; the smokey room, and the men – some with jackets draped over their shoulders, cigarettes dangling from their moustached upper lips and dark sunglasses propped on their heads – had a very different script than the *saddhus* had. In either place, I was still far from the familiar.

Andre ran into some friends who all seemed to be well educated and spoke at least some English. Andre was obviously telling them of our little escapade. I received some looks and one of the beautiful young women came over and starting talking to me in near perfect English. She had never been to America or England, but she loved the language, and watched Hollywood films and read English language books. She knew more about New York City than I did – at least that was my impression.

The women of Moscow are quite pretty, but their prettiness came from a different place. It's hard to describe, but it felt like the make-up, tight-fitting clothes and curvascious figures came from a self love, not in a narcissistic way, but just in a way that made me think these women were not trying to be noticed, they were looking pretty just for the sake of it. Maybe after the years of no real free self-expression, expressing beauty was one thing that couldn't be controlled or monitored. There were no ulterior motives except that in this city of near drabness being dragged into an unknown future, the inner beauty of the human spirit could not be dampened. To express that beauty was easy, to have respect for yourself and how you present yourself to the world was something that was in your control, and the Russian woman of Moscow seemed to pull this off with great ease. Like the smiling happy people at the spring in the suburbs, they were unconsciously cheating a system that tried to cheat them. That was my take on it anyway.

We had a late night and managed to find Andre's apartment house in the dark on top of a few drinks – not an amazing feat for him, but I never could have done it alone! I was glad everything was sorted out for my lift to the airport. There was not much else for me to do the next morning except catch my plane to Frankfurt, albeit one week and an incredible experience later.

A coffee with some bread for breakfast and off we went to where the whole Russian dreamlike adventure had begun. I kept some *rubles* to give to my driver, and handed Andre what was left. I also gave him some American dollars for his hospitality.

Getting on that plane was a strange sensation. It was the same ten a.m. flight I would have been on the previous week. Did any of this actually happen? Even my visa stamped on a piece of paper didn't officially exist. I had snuck into the no-go zone, and now, almost too easily, I was leaving it. What a different week it would have been if Andre had not been out for a walk that first day and I had not been sitting there at that moment in time.

Two travelers, Kenji and me – Tokyo subway 1987

Yas Goto in his bike shop – Nagoya

Nabuoku, Simon, me, Phil – Mt. Fuji – 1988

Tibet-obsessed Neil

Akiko in Andosan's small *geishaku*

Mom and Aunt Mary adjust their sitting positions in a *minshuku*

Some Japanese kids decked out in traditional dress

Norm and me – Tasmania 1989

Noemi in New Zealand 1989 – Thank You in Kiwi speak!

Rugged New Zealand

Sharing the road in rural New Zealand – road/train bridge!

Aunt Jen, Den and mom – Australia 1989

Me and John Cottle – harkening back to the old days – Luke's house

Chris, John, Denise and Luke – an Aussie Barbie.

Bridge needs some work – Indonesia 1990

Road-side repair on beautiful Lombok – Indonesia

The boat crew and Rob – Carrum ready to play.

The tranquil Sea of Flores

A close shave for Rob – Nepal

Rob – Nepal 1990

Me and the *Sikhs* – road to Sri Badrinath 1990

Us with the *saddhu* and all the kids India

India stretched out before us

Rob surrounded by the lofty peaks – 19,000-foot Neellkunt

Me, Rob, The Raj – in the cave Sri Badrinath

The crazy line for McDonald's – Moscow 1990

Andre, Nadia, and me – Moscow 1990

Moscow 1990 – *Group The Loop*

# CYCLE THREE;
## The Land of My Ancestors
## - Rediscovering My Roots -

# Returning to the Familiar

As the plane touched down in Germany it marked the beginning of my first time in what is known as Western Europe. After alighting and finding my way to the center of Frankfurt, I became aware of the strange feeling that I was home. I couldn't explain why – maybe it was my being a second generation European – but something just felt right about treading on European soil.

Frankfurt had a lot more in common with New York than New Delhi did. I was glad to have some time to decompress on somewhat recognizable ground before diving into New York. I ate in restaurants where I didn't have to look at the whites of people's eyes. All the travelers looked so clean – hot showers were an everyday occurrence, not something to be savored every week or two. My last few months with Rob had been so intense, and now it felt as if I was on a cruise ship. It was a nice easy feeling but at the same time something was missing, plus the need to have my own transport was strong.

I saw many travelers had backpacks that were huge and stuffed full. I ran into two girls from Australia on a train lugging these monsters around and presumed they were camping. When they told me they weren't I was baffled as to what they could have in their packs. Just like my Canadian bus partner in Melbourne they were nearly dwarfed by the size and presumably building up good muscle bulk by carrying all the weight around. As they happened to be from Melbourne we spoke about the city which had now been the most recent place I called home – their accent bringing many other fond memories to mind.

We wound up heading to the same quaint village called Marburgh. It was a university town so had a good vibe to it; there were small cafés, lots of young people around, and a youth hostel. We walked together to the hostel and the girls noticed my small pack.

"Where's your other stuff then?" asked Shelley.

"This is it," I replied. "What you see is what you get."

"No way!" exclaimed Robin, the more effusive of the two. "There's no way I could fit half of what I need in there. How do you do it?"

I explained how I usually traveled by bike and you had to be pretty strict about what you carried. Handwashing in sinks worked a treat, and in Asia most things would be dry the next morning. Books usually took up more space than clothing, and over the past three years traveling light suited me, especially if I wasn't camping.

"Fair dinkum," Shelley concluded as she heaved her own huge bag into the foyer of the hostel where we had just arrived. "It would be great to not be carrying so much; I just don't know how I'd do it."

"Hey Joe," Robin nearly shouted, "I've got an idea. How about helping me cut down on my stuff? You seem like the guy to help me out. I'm tired of hauling this heavy pack everywhere."

I was happy enough to comply, and was secretly interested into what could be in the pack. When emptied, I couldn't believe what she had been carrying on her shoulders; three pairs of jeans, two wool sweaters, boots, sneakers and a pair of shoes, enough underwear to open a shop, mementos from her boyfriend – one in the shape of a flannel shirt – tee-shirts bought on the way, thousands of tops, and a toiletry bag with all sorts of things, plus a terry bath towel, full-size! It was incredible – it reminded me of Rob looking at my stuff when I entered Indonesia, but that was nothing in comparison.

"This is incredible Robin," I told her. "You could open your own roving boutique with all this stuff."

"You reckon? It's a bit much I suppose. What can I take out?"

After quizzing her on how long she had been gone (six weeks), how much longer she would be gone (two months), what she hadn't worn yet (most of it), we managed to get rid of a third of her clothes and cut her bulky towel in half. We tussled a little over some of the more sentimental trinkets but compromised by keeping a few of the smaller ones and making a parcel of the others to send home. Her bag was still enormous to my eyes but it was definitely lighter. To get rid of too much was foolhardy because the huge framed backpack would only compact down so much.

The lesson for me was one in stuff. I was heading back to the land of stuff and returning from the mind set of few possessions. I knew I needed to strike a balance. New York was going to be tough, but I needed to get a handle on a few things before I landed there. At the time everything I'd used for the last few years was on my back, or on a boat between India and America. There was more at home I would have to deal with, but I knew one of the biggest problems of western civilization was the accumulation of things and the misguided belief that all these things made you happy. The person who had just lived for more than three years with very little was on a collision course with the person I had left behind. How would they get on?

Before leaving Marburgh I did buy some transport. I decided with such a small pack, combined with the fact that I was heading slowly home; I didn't want to buy a bike, so settled on roller skates I found in a small open-air market. I thought I'd have a go at skating from hostel to hostel – maybe that would spice things up a bit. I just hoped I didn't run into Craig, as we both had a good laugh about the obsessed Japanese guy skating around Australia, I chuckled at the thought.

303

The skates were great for getting around on the river path but challenging in the more crowded areas. If I needed to, they easily came off and I could hop on trains and buses. The idea worked brilliantly and was certainly an icebreaker, meaning I met lots of interesting people, although my knees were starting to hurt a little. I skated along bike lanes and luckily I was in the flatter areas of central Germany rather than flying down the mountain roads of the Black Forest in the Southwest. Finding hostels was easy but the distances were hard to cover if I wanted to get further north. I had no destination, and after a week or so I decided to get on a train to continue westward and look up Richard, the Frenchman I had entered Guatemala with at the same time I met Alan. I took an overnight train to Strasbourg and gave him a call. Richard and I clicked and picked up where we'd left off years before. He had been to New York in my three-year absence, met my family, and stayed with my mom. He was glad to see me and I him.

From Richard's I had spoken to my mom who told me that Luke, from Australia, was at her house and heading over to England. We could meet up and, as I was getting low on funds, he could bring some well-needed money from my bank account saving me the cost of Western Union as I didn't have a bank card.

The rest of the week was spent exploring Strasbourg. It was nice catching up with Richard. He had a good job as a nurse where he worked one week on doing twelve-hour shifts, and one week off. I'd caught him on his off-week, and with some hiking through the beautiful French countryside, and a few dinner parties, I saw a nice side of Strasbourg. The surrounding countryside was accessible and the food a blend of German and French cuisine since the border had been moved several times thanks to the world wars.

My roller skates helped get me around town but my knees were now feeling painful all the time I was skating. I was looking forward to catching up with The Luke and was trying to find an interesting way to get across France. Rollerskating the whole way was not an option, at least not now. I had rollerskates back home so decided to donate my skates to a second-hand shop in Strasbourg. The experiment was good, but cycling suited me much better.

My trip was really about slowly heading home, not exploring Europe, but I decided that I would return in the future with my bicycle so I could properly explore this continent that was making me feel so comfortable. With a mix of hitchhiking and overnight trains I made it to Calais where I caught a hovercraft to Dover.

Entering England was an odd experience. They grilled me at the port in Dover, I thought it was maybe because of the way I looked, but people assured me that England was one of the tougher border-crossings of Europe – border being a relative term as it is an island. I was planning to look up Jezz and Sally – the couple Noemi and I had spent Christmas with in South Korea. We had kept in touch since, and they now lived in London. I had their address which was in an area called Wilsdern Green, but no idea where it was. I would find it no doubt, the language barrier being, for the most part, gone.

As the hitching went so well in France, I decided to hitchhike to London, but I wasn't the only one with that idea. There was a line of backpackers lined up on the road leading out of the port area. Decorum amongst the hitchers decreed that the last one out there was the last one in the line – I was about six back. All of the others had these huge backpacks just like Robin's, but mine was hardly even visible. We were spread out so as not to confuse any potential lifts on who was solo, and whose bag was whose etc.

I had been standing there about fifteen minutes with cars passing and no sign of a lift so far. At this rate I thought it could be a long wait. I pulled out my copy of *The Bhaghavad Gita* and was just about to get cozy when a red Porsche zoomed by. He gave a cursory glance at all of us lined up and as he passed me he looked twice, then stopped, backed up, and his window slid down.

"Is that your only bag?" he asked in English with a slight accent.

"Uh, yes actually," I replied.

"Where're you headed?" the driver asked.

"London," I replied.

"Me too, hop in."

I felt guilty jumping the line but their bags never would have fit in his small, two-seater Porsche. I shrugged and got in; after all it was his choice. Hans, as my chauffeur's name turned out to be, told me to throw my bag into the small rear space to give me more leg room.

What a coup I thought. Hans was from Sweden and did business in London every so often. He knew the city quite well, and what was a great lift got better and better by the moment. He drove his Porsche as it should be driven, fast. He didn't appear to be worried about speeding tickets and was confident behind the wheel. I had spent very little time in automobiles over the past few years, but now I was doing it in style.

I told him where I was heading and he seemed to know the area. I thought he would maybe drop me at a tube station, as London called their subway system, but not knowing London I just sat back and would just take what I was given.

After the speed of the open road we had to slow down once in the city. It was interesting to view it from the vantage point of a low-profile performance vehicle. After a while creeping along and making turns here and there with purpose, we pulled up to a street corner, and he said, "How's this?" I told him I didn't know London but was sure it was great if there was a tube station around. He said he didn't know where the tube station was, but this was Wilsdern Green. I thanked him, grabbed my bag, waved goodbye to him, and walked the 500 meters to Jezz's house. Incredible!

Catching up with Sally, Jezz, and meeting their friends was great. I spent a week there and was introduced to London pub life which was so different to the New York bar scene. Luke and I were going to meet up in a few days, and we would take a bus to Scotland where he had some family connections. We planned to rent a car and drive up to the highlands. It was a different way for me to travel, but it was now getting towards October and the weather was turning wetter up north. I was heading home now, so spending a little more on a rental car and staying in hostels every night was fine. I was still decompressing from Asia but felt on my final descent home.

It was good to see Luke, even though it had not been all that long since we saw each other. A lot had happened to me in that time, and he was thinking of a career change. That's why he was in Europe and had visited New York. He filled me in on my family and friends, he had even met up with my brother Larry, Kathy, his now wife, and Noemi at a dinner party my mother had given in return for his generous hospitality in Melbourne; everything felt as if it had come full circle.

He handed me an envelope with my money. I'd left New York three and a half years ago with a few thousand dollars that I'd saved working as a teacher, now I was coming home with more money than I ever had in my life, plus I'd had an unbelievable journey and it still wasn't over.

Scotland was beautiful – it reminded of New Zealand; remote with high mountains, friendly people and a nearly unrecognizable accent. Luke's brother-in-law's family was from Port Glasgow so we were off to meet them. In the busy pub with background noise I couldn't understand a word anyone was saying. I nodded a lot and wound up talking to a very attractive young woman. I knew we were speaking the same language even though most of what she said was indecipherable, and the whole scene made me feel as if I was almost, but not quite, back home.

Luke and I enjoyed staying in youth hostels, going to sheep auctions, and doing a whirlwind tour of Scotland in our rented car. It was soon time to head back to the south of Scotland where we parted once again as he was going to spend a little more time with his new-found family.

I headed to Edinburgh to look up Marie and Kathleen, whom I'd met in New Zealand. It was nice meeting up with familiar faces around the U.K.

and Europe. We caught up on what we all had been doing with our lives. The long icy walks and warm outdoor hot baths where we all first met held fond memories for all of us. We went to Edinburgh, what a beautiful city. The Royal Mile was some of the most attractive architecture I had seen in Britain but I was feeling excited to see the familiar, more modern skyline of New York. With all that had transpired since getting back from Asia to the relatively known world of Europe, I was still not on familiar turf, although feeling decidedly more at home.

I took the long bus journey back down to London where I was staying once again with Jezz and Sally. I bought a plane ticket to Italy thinking I still wanted to explore more of Europe; I thought it would be nice to see the land of my grandparents' birth before making it back home. I was not reading the signs properly – New York was a plane ride away but I was letting myself be drawn away from the most obvious decision to fly west over the Atlantic.

Sally and Jezz spoke highly of the southwest coast of England; it sparked some interest in checking it out. When I left their place we said our goodbyes and knew we would meet up again one day. I decided I would head down to the south of England to relax and wait for my flight to Italy. They said the coasts of Dorset, Devon and Cornwall were stunning. I was heading to the bus station to buy a bus ticket to Land's End, England's furthest point west jutting off into the Atlantic in the southwest corner – the closest I would have been to New York in quite a while. I didn't know why I was procrastinating in getting home, but I wasn't feeling ready to get there yet. Walking the streets of London was clearing my head, hopping on and off trains felt normal. While sitting on the underground – London's equivalent of New York's subways – I zoned out and forgot where I was.

With a plane ticket in my pocket and an idea of heading to the southwest of England in my head, I came out from the underground and was walking down the street to the bus station. On my way there I passed a travel agent that had a special in the window for New York. I walked in and asked when the next flight was. I was told it was in six hours time. The flight was cut-rate, and the spontaneity of it all felt right, so I scrapped any plans for the southwest of England or visiting Italy – not this time around Joe, maybe one day. I bought the ticket there and then, walked back to the tube station, and waited a few hours to give my brother a call. I was finally heading home!

# Hitting the Ground Running

It was great to see my brother Larry, who with his now wife Kathy, picked me up after three and a half years of us not having seen each other. We fell into easy conversation on the car drive back. Any lingering misgivings I had about my decision in New Zealand were quashed by their warm reception. We picked right up as if I had just come back from a week-long vacation in the Carribean. Time passing was so different with adults – I'd nearly walked by my unrecognizable nephew in Melbourne airport – but my brother and Kathy looked much as they did when we'd waved goodbye to each other with Noemi on the back of my motorcycle.

I had last seen my mom in Australia so Larry and I worked out a good way to surprise her now I was home. He called her to say he would pick her up from work the next day. She was delighted, always happy to see any of her children. A few blocks from her workplace, Larry dropped me off and continued on alone. The plan was I would pose as a hitchhiker.

I pulled my now very long hair out of its pony tail and started walking down the street. When my brother saw me he said to my mom, "I think I'll give this guy a lift."

My mom asked, "You're going to pick up a hitchhiker here?"

He replied, "Yeah, I know him from the neighborhood, might as well give him a lift."

She was surprised, but said, "If you say so."

As the car pulled up I had my back to it. My brother tooted the horn and I turned around and walked over to the passenger side window, "Can you give me a lift? I'm headed to Wickham Avenue."

My mom looked up, at first not recognizing me with the flowing hair and big beard, but it only took seconds for it to register and her eyes welled up with tears, as did mine. Silence and a hand clapped over her mouth before the scream, "Joseph! What are you doing here? Joseph! Larry, you knew!" Laughter interspersed with her tears, and there I was at last on the streets of The Bronx, feeling quite at home and reunited with my family.

It was great to see my mom on her home turf again, and to be back in the house of my childhood. I moved into the basement apartment which many of the kids from the house used as a place to live while in between houses, or at financially difficult times. For me it was the perfect place to be in the familiar, and to have my space. I put my few belongings in the basement and got used to the idea that I was now back where the long voyage all began.

On the lighter side of returning home it was always fun eliciting some good reactions from my sister Nancy. I'd popped into her health clinic after my return from Guatemala a few years back, and her co-workers had thought something was wrong as she'd laughed, screamed and sobbed behind her desk. This time back I thought I'd sneak around to her house without being seen, but she spotted me and answered the door pointing and saying, "You, you, you!" Tears, laughing and big hugs were in order. There were a few other surprises with friends, but by now people were getting used to my comings and goings, and nothing could ever match my mom's or sister's responses.

To meet up with my cousin Patty after my absence marked the time with a large stamp. Besides losing her mother – my Aunt Ida – and getting married, the last time we saw each other she was waitng tables working her way through the post-graduate law program at Brooklyn Law. We met up for lunch nearly four years later after I sat in a courtroom watching her prosecute a case for the Manhattan District Attorney, who she now worked for. Time had moved on for sure.

On a different level getting home in October 1990 was intense. Besides being thrown into the wedding party of my very good friend Vinny – who was getting married shortly after arriving – meeting my brother as a married man for the first time, watching my cousin at work and seeing my niece (who had been eight when I left) as a twelve-year-old, I walked into an America heading into war, and the realization that my life and my travels were now so intertwined that one formed and shaped the other. These were not just vacations; they were explorations of my innermost being and were letting me see myself from another perspective. For me they were better than any psychotherapy, clearing away familiar backdrops and mental clutter to let me know what the real Joe thinks and feels.

After being gone for so long, I came back to many changes. The American government's thirst for war was nothing new, but I felt in some ways we were entering a new paradigm. Iraq war number one put me face to face with friends, family, ideals and morals that I felt I had to face truthfully. I found it hard to keep control of my emotions and felt thrust between two worlds – I was glad to finally be home, but I wasn't given a soft landing. In many ways home had changed for me, it was somehow stolen by men in suits, or had it really been? Did I just come back with my eyes more widely opened and a different perspective? I truly didn't know.

Vinny and his soon-to-be-wife Valerie's wedding was a bonus. He had asked me to be in the wedding party, but as I was overseas, I'd had to say no. It happened to work out my original place as an usher was available a few days after my return. Meeting Val for the first time reminded me once again of how long three and a half years could be. Vinny and Val met shortly after Noemi and I left on our trip in 1987 so a good friend from my youth was marrying someone I'd never met before. It was the reality of my chosen lifestyle; I'd miss things, and be part of life in New York in a whole different way. I would have to make my time in New York with friends and family that more meaningful.

Being involved in the wedding party was excellent. It was a great way to catch up with so many friends in one fell swoop, but while there I saw an old friend from my substitute teaching days, Bobby. I hadn't heard he was dying of AIDS so when I saw him I hardly recognized him. He looked nothing like the Bobby of my memory. There was another teacher from those days I had been friendly with whose name was Gina. She was a nice woman and all she'd ever wanted was to marry, have children and lead a normal life, but there were other plans for her future. Unfortunately when Bobby and Gina got together he was already infected. They had been engaged to be married but everything ended and he had been diagnosed with AIDS. I met Gina for the first time since teaching at Bobby's funeral, and when I first saw her she didn't have to say anything for me to know she was HIV positive. With tears in her eyes she gave me a heartfelt hug and I returned it in earnest, not knowing what else to say. It was yet another lesson in life's fragility and the effects we all have on one another's lives.

My brother and I started doing some manual labor in the city for Tony – a friend of Bobby's who was also HIV positive. Now being thrown into a very intense awareness of issues surrounding AIDS, getting slowly drawn in to the politics of the ongoing push for war and joining the peace/anti-war movement I felt I'd hit the ground running. Each evening I sat tapping away letters of protest to George Bush and the White House. I'd started a relationship with Donna, Bobby's sister who I met at Vinny's wedding, but everything was put on hold while I tried to do what I could to stop another war from happening on the face of the planet.

The renovation project with Tony was coming to an end, but the war effort was heating up and I could not stay uninvolved. To fuel my passions further I came across an article which spoke of the murder of an American citizen in Guatemala who was living and working with the people in the jungle. He had set up a farm as a traveler's retreat and had been helping the poor of the area earn some money while trying to bring awareness of the Guatemalan's plight to the wider world. His murder might implicate the CIA as the manner of death had been a ritual killing to instill fear into the locals. The matter was not closed and his wife was in Washington making some noise.

The victim sounded eerily reminiscent of Bret, and all I could see were his idealistic bright eyes and remember his good energy permeating Phinca

Ixobella. The fond memories of sharing evening meals with fellow travelers cooked by the colorfully-dressed, friendly locals and the warm smiles in the hot jungles made me recall similar places in other parts of the world; leafleting, writing letters and talking to friends was not feeling like I was doing enough.

My bicycle frame and parts had arrived from India. While rebuilding it I was once again brought back to the images of disfigured children we had played volleyball with in Vietnam. Iraq was set to be the next place of human casualties and open wounds that would never heal. Agent Orange would not be used this time around, the terrain was different and times had moved on. Depleted uranium, used in armor-piercing ammunition, was now the weapon of choice. This poisonous substance pollutes both the earth and air with its toxic dust, and any human who comes into contact with it, if not killed, may suffer genetic mutations and pass it on to their unborn children.

I felt I had to do something more so came up with the idea of a personal grassroots protest against the war – to ride my bike from New York City to the Vietnam War Memorial in Washington D.C. – and named it *Pedaling for Peace*. It was my small effort to get an idea of what the American people were feeling and try to get my thoughts out there on what I had witnessed and why I personally felt this was the wrong move. It was getting close to the holidays, so I decided to do the ride the week before Christmas 1990.

I didn't plan my route too much; I spent time in the library doing some research, and got my niece and nephew to help paint the words **Pedaling for Peace** and **No Blood for Oil** on the front, back and sleeves of a sweatshirt. It was a contrast to the sheets they were handed in school with Saddham Hussein's face superimposed with a target.

I headed out on the bike which had most recently taken me up the Himalaya. I engaged people in conversations about the upcoming war and put myself out there in the line of fire. I slept in office buildings, halfway houses, renovation projects, or whatever else presented itself to me, plus there was always my well-used tent. I was met with lots of questioning faces, but as the war had not started yet, I was given a thumbs-up by most people. I helped fill in small gaps that hadn't made it to the American news media about our history with Saddham Hussein and that part of the world. I also threw in a few facts and figures from previous wars and shared some of the horrors I had witnessed in my years of traveling. I tried to have no expectations remembering what the *saddhu* had said to us not that long before in the same small tent which was now in the rear pannier of my bicycle.

My small protest ride didn't change the world, but it changed my world. I met and spoke to a wide spectrum of people and was humbled to stand at the Vietnam Wall in D.C. I was still full of everything I had learned since I had only been back two months.

After returning from my ride I threw myself headlong into the peace movement. I helped organize buses to D.C. with a coalition in New York City which was a powerful event for me. The peace movement got a lot of negative, unfair coverage in the media, and after being away from home for so long, my romantic homecoming was shattered with the reality of returning to the prospect of my home country at war.

Another issue that was being drawn in to the hype was the Israel-Palestine conflict, an issue never quite making the headlines it should. It is an emotive subject – especially in New York. Until my involvement in the peace movement it was also one I knew too little about. I did some research into the occupied territories, Israel's claim to an Independent state in 1948, displaced Palestinians, and thought how little I had been taught about it. I was being bombarded from all sides now, and had to try and siphon through what was pertinent at the moment. My sanity was challenged, but people were going to die, and it was American taxpayer's dollars – quite a lot of them – that would pay for it. I decided to unify my energies in the anti-war effort and learn more later on about other conflicts.

The peace movement dovetailed quite easily with the environmental movement – humanity constantly trying to annihilate itself on all fronts – and I started working for Greenpeace, although my waking moments were taken over by the war which started right on schedule – January 15th, 1991. I'd foolishly thought there was a chance of preventing it.

After the war began the American public was thrown into a weird space. There was certainly more anger towards protesters of any sort, and I was certain my bike ride would have been met in a whole different way. My feeling was that people were scared to demonize the soldiers as had happened in Vietnam. The peace movement was aware of this too and went to great pains to try and verbalize the fact that the soldiers were not to blame; it was the underlying powers that be. As the bombs had already fallen, the effort to prevent a war from starting had turned into one of trying to stop one which had already begun – a much harder task. Visions of Vietnam burned in my brain, and my passion started to turn to fury when I saw, first-hand, the manipulation of the media, and obvious control the people in power had over what we laughingly called the news.

One night I was eating dinner at my mom's. While she cooked, I was proofreading yet another protest letter to President Bush. She stopped cooking and sat next to me at the counter we had eaten on since I was a child. "Joe, can I say something to you?" she began.

312

"Yeah, mom, sure." I continued reading the letter, distracted.

"I have to tell you this because I love you and I want to help you."

I looked up from my letter surprised. "What is it?"

"It's becoming difficult to even be in a room with you at the moment. I understand what you're saying about the war but you're so angry towards everyone, even your family is finding it hard to have a normal conversation with you. I think you're going to start losing friends if you don't do something about it."

My mom and I had always had an honest relationship and had always felt it was better to discuss openly what was on our minds. Since my father's death we had been involved in some big arguments, from religion and drugs to sex. Over the years on our travels together, ours had matured into a good relationship. I respected her opinion and I knew she respected mine so those words hit home. I knew immediately that she was right – I could sense myself going over the edge, so I took to heart what she said, and acted.

I also tried to take heart the recent words of another wise person; "Just sit in silence, clear your mind, don't make it so difficult." Damn, I tried sitting in silence. I focused on a word then off I drifted to words and thoughts cluttering my head up. It was frustrating – up on that mountaintop it sounded so easy – back on the streets, fighting what I felt was 'the good fight' that presence of mind didn't come so easily. I knew I still lacked patience although there was one place I felt calm – it was sitting, but not still. Maybe I should try and explore the vehicle I loved so much on a different level.

I walked into a bicycle shop I had used to get some equipment for my 'Peace Ride' to D.C. and offered my services to the owner for the upcoming season. He asked if I had any previous experience so I explained about the last few years traveling by bike, and all my years in retail shops, how I taught the mechanics English in Japan, and in return learned basic bike maintenance. He asked me to build a bike so I did then and there with a few small mistakes and was hired on the spot. I told him I had to head out to California to ship back my motorcycle that was still in my aunt's garage. We agreed I would start in April.

I took my mom's advice and tried to detach myself a little from what was going on with the war. I didn't give up the fight, but thought it better to choose a better way that fit in with my life, and didn't turn me into a raving lunatic. I didn't want to lose perspective, plus all the calm I had tried to bring into my life would be thrown away if I didn't listen to loved ones. On the other hand the bicycle was something which allowed me a political voice, made a statement, and fulfilled a need in me for movement and adventure. I would now pursue a whole different side of the life of the bicycle industry.

I bought a ticket to California and sat on a train heading to the west coast. Not quite Woody Guthrie hopping on box cars, but I felt I was engaging the American population once again, and was very careful to keep the passion which had previously gotten the best of me in check. The train journey felt like a continuation of my 'Peace Ride' to D.C. I was able to talk to the people of America and see what was on their mind now that the country was at war.

My trip to Vietnam was still raw – less than a year before I'd been pedaling there feeling and seeing the devastation war leaves behind. I knew intellectually that wars don't just end and everyone goes back to normal – the wounds are deep and jagged often leaving years of infection in their wake. I had learned too much about the current war to be able to totally relax. My mind's eye was sent constantly back to a volleyball game played not long ago.

The train journey was three days across the continent. Sitting and sleeping in the seat which would become home for a few days was quite calming. I tried my meditation technique during the long silences heading to Albany. I acquired a seatmate there, and together we shared our cross-continental ride out west. It was a forced intimacy of sorts, and an interesting way to get to know someone. We talked long into the nights as the train rumbled west with America's vastness and natural beauty passing by just outside the window. I was already feeling calmer with all the recent moves I had made, plus I was writing in my journal which was helping to keep me sane.

After seeing my relatives in the San Francisco area I got somehow dragged in to the 'Free Tibet' scene with John Maier who'd worked for the computer firm with me in Los Angeles and headed off to Asia on his bicycle a few years back. John had headed to Tibet – his collision course with life was to take him on a path, a career change, and a realization about our world and our governments much as mine had. We talked about many of our similar experiences and now here we were campaigning for a free Tibet and against the inequalities of our world's systems. We were trying to talk to a government who had just declared war on Iraq and had a dubious hidden past in other parts of the world. Would they even listen? What about Guatemala, the Native Americans – so much deceit that John and I were not so proud to call the government 'our' government.

I saw myself getting sucked in all over again. We protested in front of the Chinese Embassy and put on a day of solidarity with the Tibetans of San Francisco in Golden Gate Park. Oddly enough this protest was picketed by Native Americans carrying signs about their forgotten cause. What a mess!

I found myself, through John, getting friendly with the founders of a fledgling organization called UNPO (Unrepresented Nations and Peoples Organization). Their main office was in The Hague in the Netherlands, with an outpost in San Francisco. They were up against a growing world where 'interests' were increasingly put ahead of people, or more to the point, as I'd learned on my travels, a world where it was coming to light that interests have *always* been put ahead of people. I knew I was here to calm down, and my journey west was to get my motorcycle and pull myself away from too much involvement. I thought, 'Okay Joe, you can do this – learn what you can, help out in your capacity, but stay calm.' I did, constantly checking myself to see if I could keep the balance. I survived the couple of weeks in San Francisco and was glad to have been a part of it all but now I had a job waiting for me in a small bicycle shop.

I bought a book with an interesting title to put me in a different headspace while on the train south, *The Lost Years of Jesus*, by Elizabeth Clare Prophet. It was a fascinating book about the possibility of Jesus's lost years in the Bible from age thirteen to thirty. The basic theory was that he traveled overland further east to India and wound up staying in a Buddhist monastery in Tibet where he was steeped in the inner mysteries of their tradition. He brought that knowledge back with him and incorporated what he learned into his teachings. The book was of course one of many theories, but seemed well researched and – with the many similarities between Hinduism, Tibetan Buddhism, and Christ's teachings – seemed plausible. I thought back to India, all the religions coming from that part of the world, and Jesus being known there as St. Issa – a name he was also known by in the Jewish faith. It was nice to be drawn back to that part of myself rather than remain constantly in my political activist mode. In San Francisco John Maier and I had spoken of Tibet and what had inspired him to change the course of his life. We agreed it is hard not to walk away from certain parts of the world untouched on a deeper level. I thought it would be intriguing to go to Tibet one day but it wasn't on the immediate agenda.

I sent my motorcycle back from Los Angeles to New York via a freight service, looked up some friends and relatives but was New York bound for the upcoming bicycle season. The return train journey to New York passed with a slow rocking movement through the southern part of the states that Gary and I had motorcycled across all those years ago. When I got back I was ready to chill out and fix some bikes. With my motorcycle out of storage I now had two modes of transport – they didn't feel like transport though – more like good friends.

315

Now it was also time to take care of the now healed gray blur on my arm. A friend, Maria, was a good artist, so she drew a 'medicine shield' that would fit nicely over the former snarling face of a panther. A medicine shield was something Native American boys would make when turning into a man and was a right of passage. The medicine shield would be made of pertinent objects for the young boy in transition, and it would shield him in the difficult times facing him. After all the pain and blood in Australia I hoped the new tattoo could be more pertinent to whom I now was and we tried to catch the essence of my life journey in the design. The general idea was freedom, nature, and a blending of eastern and western thought. I found an excellent tattoo artist near Woodstock, New York to do the job. Since it was a cover up it wasn't perfect, but I felt less self-conscious of it afterwards and if you looked close enough the old tattoo was still there underneath. That small part of my body has a story to tell, and in a weird way it is a reminder to me that no matter how far we travel or where we wind up in this world, we bring with us our old selves as well. We can never fully cover up what we were, and indeed, should learn from all our experiences. It was a hard, painful lesson to learn, but, like finding the path I wanted to be taking, it was a worthwhile exercise.

I worked from April to November learning more about the vehicle I fell in love with twice in my life, but this time I was getting to see the bicycle from another side. I saw the business side of it, and like everything in life, I had much to learn. I saw the goodness of the industry, and what an asset a bike shop is to a small town. Once again I had to try and strike a balance – bicycles were also part of the money making machine. In the past few years they had found a new popularity and the industry itself would be faced with many decisions regarding manufacturing, slave labor, and countless other sides of a multi billion dollar industry. At that moment, though, I enjoyed just being steeped in bicycles.

Jimmy, the owner of the bike shop where I worked, introduced me to a woman named Grace who was a keen cyclist, and worked in the local florist. We struck up a friendship, and would cycle home from work together. She was into boating, so her Sundays were spent floating in the Long Island Sound, and mine riding around the roads of Westchester County. She gave me another book by Robert Pirsig when she saw my tattered copy of *Zen and the Art of Motorcycle Maintenance* on my shelf. It was a book about him and his daughter traveling by boat down the Hudson River, then the eastern seaboard of the States – *Lila*. I found it much more accessible than his other book, and there was a sense of calmness about this journey on the water. Where his crossing America with his son was sometimes difficult and brought up many issues between them, this book brought me along with them instead of leaving me an observer. I'd also had a turbulent time, and in many ways was still being challenged by myself and the workings of the world. I needed to come to grips and live my life in a healthier manner, I had to try hard not to let the matters of the world affect my well being, physically or mentally. Books all came at the right time, as did people.

The bike shop had also helped to save me from myself. I was able to delve in, learn new skills, and get to appreciate its power as a political and environmental tool as well. The job in that shop saw me able to use my people skills in many different ways. I used my annoyance at the current affairs of the world to do what I could, and more importantly, kept myself in check so I did not lose my cool when the frustration got too much. I met the owner of a rival bike shop, Danny, and we became quite friendly. Jimmy was burnt out by the bike business, but me being fresh to it, loved it, so along with a young kid called Mike, we ran that shop the best we could.

I also discovered an organization called Transportation Alternatives. It was a great outlet for me to combine all of my loves; political campaigning, advocacy of the bicycle, caring about the planet and more specifically fighting for cyclist's rights in the city I was raised in and had a deep affection for. Joining in on bike rides or donating old bicycles to their various programs let me involve myself and the shop in being part of its altruistic ideals. I had found a way to integrate my two lives, and it worked quite well.

Along with my travels, the involvement in the many sided cycling world helped me find an inner peace and a love of the industry that had already given me so much. My life was taking a different path, and I was able to stay on it quite easily. It was easier than I thought it might have been, perhaps because I had found something that was so important to my being. I tried incorporating my mind-calming thoughts while working or riding – sitting in silence just wasn't doing it at the moment, but I was trying to work on that.

I had an amusing encounter with a good friend Larry. We had been friends for quite a long time and used to ride motorcycles together quite often. He became a cop, I became the traveler. I'd fallen out of contact with some of my old friends but Larry and I always managed to keep up our friendship. As teenagers we used to go to Cross County Shopping Center together, if we weren't on the 25 bus heading there, we were on our motorcycles or in one of Larry's many sports cars he owned over the years. Now, once again, we found ourselves heading to our old haunt. We stopped in B.Dalton Bookstore. He went his way and I went mine. I was drawn to the spiritual section, and Larry wondered off somewhere else. We met up at the register to pay for our purchases and as we looked at each other's books we laughed at how different we were. His book was titled, *A Thousand Ways to Become a Millionaire,* mine was, *Less is More, The Art of Voluntary Poverty.* It was prefaced by a man I had never heard of before, E.F. Schumacher. He writes about small economies and embracing simple economic policies not based on debt, a topic becoming more and more intriguing to me. It was great how many of the books I picked up or read led to others. It was nice that Larry and I were comfortable with each other and our choices. I thought that was what true friendship should be about, embracing the differences.

During that year my brother Larry and his wife Kathy had their first child – Kaela – in August and it was wonderful to be there for that occasion. I stood by her in a naming ceremony, as did Noemi. We had both missed the wedding but were there to welcome their first new addition to the world. We remained friends, and sometimes mixed in the same circles. Our years of traveling together had given us a special bond, but our romantic relationship was over.

Our circle of friends from the college days was much the same so it helped me stay in contact with those friends and feel part of what was happening with everyone I would lose so much contact with while traveling. I was making new friends through cycling and my political activities, but it was always nice keeping contact with my old buddies.

As Halloween approached the bike shop started to slow down. My birthday is the day before on October 30th but I had gotten used to spending my birthday away from home rather than surrounded by family and friends and I was planning to travel again soon after October ended so I wasn't too fussed about celebrating in a big way. Others, though, had a different idea.

Over the years my look had changed quite radically; long hair, a shaved head, a full beard or goatee, and now even my permanent tattoo had been changed. I felt like a chameleon, I even cut my hair short when I got involved more heavily with the peace movement so I couldn't be labeled a long-haired hippy and pigeon-holed. As Halloween approached there was talk of a costume party at my friend Ritchie's house. He had struggled with his own personal problems over the years, and had recently been discharged from the navy. A party at his house sounded a nice way to round out the last turbulent year before I set off again.

The build up to the party started to sound like a surprise party for me, but I went with it, and when I showed up at Ritchie's house, I was completely surprised. I was nearly moved to tears and had to laugh – there were lots of friends from varied circles; college buddies, cycling companions, bike shop co-workers, neighborhood cronies, my brother Larry his wife, Kathy and two-month-old Kaela too, my sister Nancy and

318

her husband Denis. They were all dressed up as me in different phases of my life and travels; motorcycle jackets, cycling outfits, long hair, bandanas, peace signs around their necks, and even a few creative gray blurred tattoos on some shoulders. It was nice knowing all my ranting and raving hadn't pushed them away, I felt so loved and understood. We had a great time, and I couldn't think of a better send off. My surprise party was a huge success, and touched me to the core.

What a diverse year it had been. I tried to connect to my young niece and nephew while busy coming to grips with myself. I spent some time with Dana, bonding and having deep conversations on motorcycle camping trips in upstate New York around the Woodstock area. I had a bond with Denis, who had visited in Australia, but with Dana, I saw she was searching, and her life growing up in the countryside which had been converted into another shopping mall suburb of New York, had stolen her independence as those places do in many ways. We talked about religion, poverty, war, and sometimes – to my mom and sister's chagrin – American politics. I just didn't want her to feel robbed of the other side of knowledge and tried to push open doors for her to at least look through.

My involvement in the anti-war movement and the environmental movement introduced me to groups of people I learned so much from, and after the party I knew I hadn't forsaken my old tried and true relationships. It was a good feeling.

I made connections in New York that I would get back to, but for now I was ready to go. I felt my relationship with New York had matured but I needed to continue on my path. The small taste of Europe a year ago had intrigued me – a bicycle trip there was waiting. This time I didn't procrastinate, I went out and bought a plane ticket as soon as the bicycle season ended.

# A Walk across Tunisia

In mid-November I flew back to Europe with my bicycle. One friend whose face had been missing at my surprise party was Jacqui who was now living in Heidelburgh, Germany, working as an editor for *Stars and Stripes* magazine. It was a job for the moment, but I knew Jacqui pretty well – she was a talented writer and wouldn't be editing that magazine for long. Since she was there I thought it was as good a place as any to start my journey and ended up staying a week to find my feet. We were pleased to see each other and, although she was a keen cyclist, she hadn't done any long-distance touring on a bicycle. She and her ex-husband had crossed France on motorcycle a year or so back and she enthused about her two-wheeled trip across the Alps. She was envious of the adventures which lay ahead for me as she was also an adventurous soul.

November turned out to be a tough time to start a cycle tour in Europe. My equipment was not made for the snowy cold damp cycling conditions, but I was finding lots of it about, realistically, what else could I expect? I fixed a few bicycles for the army personnel in the nearby American base. Jacqui was dating a guy in the army after the break up with her husband.

Between Jacqui and her friends' bikes I did enough repairs to earn a little pocket money, and bartered for some MRE's (military ready to eat meals). Not 'haute cuisine' by any stretch, but I knew they might come in handy on my journeys. They would store nearly forever, which was a tad scary, but I enjoyed working for exchange whenever possible.

I cycled for a few days in the sleet, and then started interspersing train travel. I was finally coming to realize that maybe I should park the bike and do something different till the weather picked up. Maybe it would be a good time to look up some family in the south of Italy. I decided to give the weather one more chance and found a hostel near the Italian/Swiss border. I used it as a place to do some day trips waiting for the weather to break. I rode up to a cyclist's monument at Madonna Di Ghisallo in the mountains near Bergamo not far from Lake Como, and it was absolutely stunning. The weather gave me a few days respite from the sleet and rain, and being the off-season the roads were not too busy. I bartered my stay in the hostel by offering to fix the owner's bicycle rental fleet after his last busy season. I tuned gears, adjusted brakes, lubed chains, and fixed a few flats. I enjoyed the newfound confidence I had working on bikes, plus was glad I carried a few more tools than were sometimes necessary. My recently-acquired skill of properly fixing bikes was coming in handy.

I cycled in snow and sleet with my breath forming icicles on my beard. I was spending a lot of money on cappuccinos and hot chocolates just to keep warm in various cafés. Camping certainly wasn't an option, and *pensions* – Italian bed and breakfast places – were eating through my funds quickly. I would be broke in no time at this rate, so I finally decided to head south.

I took a train that stopped in Naples, but put my bike on the cargo train heading directly to Bari. Near to my relatives in Rutigliano, and hopefully my plan would become clearer when I arrived.

When I started on my worldly wanderings I had headed off to the Far East before I ever set foot on European soil. I'd almost made it to Italy last year during my brief European sojourn, but this time I was determined to make it back to the land of my ancestors. My dad's sister Aunt Mary, who had visited me in Japan, had kept up contact with their side of the family and I vowed to look them up.

Joe Massotti was a distant cousin on my paternal grandmother's side of the family, but like true Italian Americans, we called him 'Uncle' which I believe had something to do with old traditions of respect from Italy. Every older male or female with the thinnest trickle of blood in their veins traceable to some common ancestry was called 'Aunt' or 'Uncle'. Aunt Mary and Uncle Lou kept up family contact with our relatives tucked up in Queens, which was where Joey and his family lived – he occasionally came over the bridge to give us haircuts up in The Bronx. He also had a house in Rutigliano, which he was waiting to move back to as he still loved Italy more than his adopted America. He lived in his own 'Little Italy' and Italian was the spoken language in his house. Even his daughters, who were born in America, spoke with Italian accents. We used to liken a visit to Joe Massotti's to an annual visit to Italy. We were under strict rules to touch nothing, eat everything that was served to us and not sit on anything that was wrapped in plastic. The strange custom of keeping a brand new couch pretty much permanently enveloped in clear plastic wrapping might not have spread to the wider world but it was quite prevalent in many of the Italian-American households I knew   needless to say, Joe Massotti's, for an eight-year-old, was not a fun visit.

When I first got to Rutigliano, a place I had obviously heard a lot about, I turned up with long hair that would have made Uncle Joe faint, and all my worldly possessions on a bicycle. I gave a call to Aldo, a relative I had never met before to warn him of my arrival. He sounded delighted on the phone, nearly tears in his voice when he invited me to stay, but I learned later on he slept with a knife under his pillow, even after checking out my credentials with the family back home!

A plan of action was forming as I had not planned my European trip well; I would visit for a few days, ask if I could leave my bike as I went over to Northern Africa to wait out the winter months, then return for a longer visit in early spring when I would continue on with my cycling. It sounded like a good idea to me, so I spent the first few days with the relatives stumbling through conversations as they didn't have more than two words of English between them. I was fed like a king, treated nicely, and blissfully ignorant of the knife under Aldo's pillow at that time. I felt my relatives found me hard to comprehend, and to their conservative southern Italian ways, my life was unthinkable. Thirty years old and not married to a nice Italian girl and working in New York? I was a freak. I was shown the house that Joe Massotti would one day re-occupy, and felt that somehow it completed my visit. I think we all breathed a small sigh of relief when I boarded a train heading to Sicily to catch a boat onward to Tunisia. Not to say my time there was awful, just a little awkward.

Bari, just a short ride from Rutigliano, is a handy place for ferries to Greece where I would start on my cycle trip, but not just yet; even Greece was getting snowy conditions. After wiping the tomato sauce from my beard and securing my bike in a heated garage, I was off to warmer climes with a small backpack and a sleeping bag.

I didn't give Sicily a proper visit, just took a week there walking through small villages conjuring up visions in my mind of Al Pacino in *The Godfather* secreted away in one of the many villas surrounded by stone walls dotting around the countryside. My objective in Sicily was to get a boat to Tunisia.

The boat was packed with Tunisians heading home for a holiday which didn't mean much to them. I was on a boat which would deposit us in the port of Tunis on Christmas Eve. Walking the streets of Naples and some of the Sicilian cities during the build up to Christmas was getting too much for me and I left Italy thinking North Africa sounded like a good place to pass a quiet Christmas and ring in the New Year. In Italy cheap Christmas trinkets and knick-knacks seemed to be everywhere. I was never one for Christmas commercialism, and some of my best Christmases to memory were spent out of America; Japan, South Korea – even Australia was low key – but I didn't know what to expect at all from a Muslim country. It was after all a moderate Muslim country, but it would be my first Christmas in the land of Mohammed.

There is something about arriving somewhere by boat. It gives you plenty of time to prepare for your arrival. I think it's also why my preferred mode of transport is a bicycle. You can ease yourself into a city or country at that slower pace. Leaving Sicily and heading down to Africa on a large ferry felt really special. I had a long time to think of where I was heading and why. Was it just to escape the cold, or was something else pushing me there? What sort of place would it be? How would I get beyond the language barriers? Would I miss my bike like I did in Germany the year before?

The boat felt like it shifted into a different mode as soon as we set sail. It cruised along in what seemed to my imagination a mellow African rhythm. Although I knew it was not a high speed ferry, I had to adapt to slothfulness and the smell of the diesel being pumped out of its two huge stacks. Even so, it would have passed the *Nusa Inda* like it was standing still; where the *Nusa Inda* turned a three-day ride into a seven-day debacle, this journey was supposed to be somewhere between eight and twelve hours long, depending on who you asked. The boat was just chugging along and everyone aboard were settling in for the ride.

The vessel had men and women sitting, laying down and tucked into every nook and cranny you could imagine. The distinctive smells aboard were definitely not European and if I closed my eyes I felt like I had already arrived. The boat was selling food although most people had brought their own snacks from home that were more North African than Italian. Although Sicily had begun the culinary transition from Europe to Africa, the boat was the final link.

The sea was calm, and luckily the boat was fairly stable. Even so, there were the usual few green faces around and I was just grateful that the weather had been good to us as we didn't have to tolerate worse in the form of vomiting passengers. For the most part the women took care of the children and the men sat and drank coffee and tea. The kids ran around and I didn't hear any other tongue other than French and Arabic. I made some conversation in English with a few people willing to give it a go. I had a few words in Italian, which sometimes worked but I knew I needed to get to grips with learning some French. I had a European phrasebook and a basis in Spanish, so it would not be like jumping in cold, but I knew that the key to getting the best out of the upcoming adventure would be to get a foundation in the language. I took a walk around the boat and noticed three people speaking English. I went up to say hi and discovered that they were American.

I do not like arriving in a new city under the curtain of nightfall, it makes things awkward. After clearing customs, we could have waited for a bus, but there were taxis waiting right there, and between all of us the fare, which we haggled for, seemed quite reasonable and got us into the heart of Tunis, Tunisia's capital city, with at least a half an hour of light to help us find a cheap place to stay. Two of the three were a couple traveling together so it worked out well; I roomed with Andy, who was the odd one out, and Jennifer and her boyfriend Tom got their own room. We quickly threw our backpacks in the room, took what was necessary and headed into Tunis to take in as much as we could before getting a bite to eat. We all had to change linguistic gears from Italian to French. The three Northern African countries known as the Maghreb, which were all former French colonies, have two official languages; French and Arabic. All of us were able to fake it in French, but were totally out of our depth in Arabic.

The confines of the Christian world had definitely been broken. Just a short fourteen hours ago I had been on a crowded Sicilian street being assaulted from every side – loud Vespa scooters in one ear, Christmas music in the other. The visual world was one of glitter, sparkle, wreaths, and gaudy model-sized street scenes of a white Christmas. Suddenly there was no more operatic, gesture-filled Italian being acted out on every street corner. A mixture of Arabic and French were now the languages filling our ears. The women were a beautiful mix of Black, Arabic and European – quite exotic, and pleasant on the eyes. Big brown brooding eyes meeting you with a smile that reached well up to the temples. The local men weren't as well turned out as the fashion-conscious Italian men. They ranged from casual dressers to robed men who appeared to have just alighted from their camels.

I'm not sure what I expected, maybe just a hint of Christmas floating over from Sicily a short way across the Mediterranean, where everything was so focused on Santa Claus and baby Jesus. Here there was nothing. Not one single trinket or melody or tree to even suggest that right over the water the major Christian/Commercial feast of the year was in full swing. For maybe five minutes it was confusing, but then I felt relief. It felt nice to be in a small country that held on to its non-Christianity so firmly and had not given in to the sheer commercialism of another reason to make money.

The next day was Christmas, but if I had been magically transported and not known anything of where I was, a quick glance at the *croissants* and *baguettes* in the bakeries and snippets of French conversation drifting by on the breeze could have almost fooled me into thinking I was on a Parisian backstreet on a warm autumn day. The more we explored the streets though, the more we realized we had truly left Europe.

We found a nice place to eat, and were once again eating *cous cous*, the dish which originated in Northern Africa and made it to Sicily over a thousand years ago when the small Italian island was actually ruled by Arabic people. It surprised me how prevalent the small spherical granules remained a prized meal there and a cultural reminder of the ties which existed between the two diverse countries. Food carried such a powerful link with our histories and it was nice to taste the subtle difference of flavor in this small restaurant in Tunis.

It made me happy to think of all the people coming home to see relatives, being able to sneak back to their homeland and spend a month or so in familiar surroundings, drinking cups of tea with friends within earshot of the call of the *muezzin* five times a day – exotic to my ears, but hopefully comforting to theirs – a brief respite from the unfamiliar markets of Europe selling their wares, or working as domestic help. It brought back the smiling face of Miguel returning to his family in Cabo San José all those years ago. Being in one of Africa's smallest countries it was hard envisioning the large continent spread out to the south stretching on for miles crossing many cultural and linguistic lines along the way.

So here we were, four Americans in a small restaurant in Tunis on Christmas Eve. We got to know each other better; Jennifer and Andy were studying in Florence, and were going to be there until the end of the school term in June. Jennifer's boyfriend Tom was just out in Europe for the Christmas holidays, so I think they were relieved I came along to take away any awkwardness they might encounter being three. Andy and I got along well. They filled me in on life in Florence, and it sounded wonderful. They were both art students, and Jen's boyfriend Tom was still at university in Santa Barbara California where they were all from.

Tunis by night was a lively place; women and men walking hand in hand, families out for a stroll, restaurants open, and lots of places to sit and have refreshing hot or cold drinks. It was not easy to guess you were in an African Muslim country, especially a tiny one which shared a border with the gigantic, much less moderate, Algeria which was in the middle of a military coup d'etat with the F.I.S. (The Islamic Salvation Front) which was quickly gaining popularity with the Algerian people, and the controlling F.L.N. (The National Liberation Front). The F.L.N. were worried about possibly losing the upcoming election, so, using rather unsubtle tactics, cancelled them. The army then moved in and took control – Algeria was in a mess, and the beginnings of a civil war were in the making. Islamic guerillas took advantage of the situation and now there were more 'Fronts', and acronyms vying for power in Algeria than you could count on one hand.

If people were nervous of their lumbering, volatile neighbor to the west, they did not let it show too much. Life was exuberant and lively in Tunis, the French language spoken on the street also added to the confusion of the geography for me. Most signs were in both French and Arabic, and thankfully none of the western food chains appeared to be here. There were a few copies of the originals, but usually with a handwritten sign out front. I guess an enterprising owner thought he might draw people in if he called his place McDonald's. It may have worked as he had a full restaurant, but a glance at the menu as we passed showed not a hamburger to be found!

The *medina* was the most interesting place for me in Tunis. The *medina* is the old part of town built by Arabs as far back as the ninth century. It is literally a walled maze of color, sound and smell. Nearly every sense is heightened in awareness. Anything could be bought from love potions to Madonna's latest musical endeavor and it seemed to be open any time of day or night. The white fabric draped over the frames of some of the stalls just added to the feeling that you were now in an underground world of shops, food stalls and who knows what else? It would take days to properly explore the *medina* in Tunis. *Souk* was a term used for the market places as well, and I wasn't sure if the words were interchangeable but they seemed to be. I had arrived in an entirely different place. It was not only the lack of Christmas music filling the warm scented air, it was more like a feeling, something permeating my whole being, something reminding me with every step that I was on a new continent. Every look I received was a look that said "You have arrived", and indeed I had.

I had noticed some women had their hands tattooed, I thought it was a class thing at first, maybe something like an untouchable in India. I would learn that the tattoo was a henna painting, or temporary tattoo. A woman would receive the intricate tattoos on her hands for her wedding day, as a beautiful elaborate ornamental part of the wedding attire, but it served a dual purpose. The woman would not do any house work until the tattoo faded. Great idea, I wondered if any clever woman got a real tattoo and turned the tide of women doing all the housework for a lot longer than a few weeks. I knew all too well how permanent tattoos were.

We all stayed for a few days in Tunis, mostly exploring the *medina* and sharing a Christmas meal the next day, complete with a dry wine accompanying it. Tunisia was moderate enough not to adhere so stringently to all of the laws of Islam, at least not in Tunis. We all were heading to different places in the south and southeast of the country, so I did some homework about trains, times and what there was to explore in the southern desert part of this small, but diverse country.

I had decided that I would take the train and a short bus trip to a place called Tatouine in the southern part of the country. I had no real plan, but I met a woman while in Tunis who was from England and working in a small town south of the city. The train stopped there on its way south so we made a plan to meet briefly on the platform so she could give me her guide book to Tunisia. She was leaving soon and had been to most of the places she wanted to see. She was very insistent that I have it. I normally liked having no guide books, but since I was in Tunisia with hardly any background information at all, I thought it would at least help to fill me in on the many missing gaps I had.

Our plan was vague; the early morning train would pass through the town where she lived at about ten-thirty and she would meet me on the platform while the train was stopped there. Often trains will stop for long enough to allow local traders selling snacks to walk through the train selling their wares so we figured we would have a few minutes at least to spot each other. She thought I would be easy to spot if I stuck my head out of the window. The students were coming as well, not going as far south as me, but we'd be together for most of the train journey. There was a possibility it might work.

The coolness of the morning was welcome before the daytime heat crept in. The train filled up in Tunis. It looked like there were twice as many people than number of seats trying to cram into the train. We found seats next to an Irish family traveling with two young children. It was something I never consciously thought about, but when you travel, you miss the innocence of children. You get to meet lots of children in other countries, but there are cultural and language differences. Sometimes those children are begging, sometimes they are just staring, but unless you are fluent in the language and tuned into the cultural customs, there always a distance between you and them. The two Irish children were about three and five years old and were friendly, chatty kids. They livened up the train car, and we immediately began interacting with them. It was like a breath of fresh air to hear a three-year-old's idea of what was going on. They were quick to tell us about the strange food and why they thought the train was so crowded. I think the parents were happy to sit back and listen to their daughters interact with a few adults. We all had language in common and enough cultural similarity to make for an easy, free-flowing exchange of ideas. The two kids happily filled us in on their trip with probably a bit too much information about daddy's trips to the toilet in their hotel in Tunis much to dad's embarrassment. That is one of the beauties of kids though; nothing is sacred, and they usually speak their mind.

Talking with the kids and then the parents passed the time quite quickly. They were heading to the island of Djerba so they would be getting off the train earlier than me. My student friends were also getting off before me in Sfax – I was on to nearly the end of the line. Although Tunisia is a small country, it felt as if I were heading into the bowels of Africa.

The station where I was to meet my English friend with the guide book came up quite quickly. I gave the two young girls an important job, I explained what she looked like, and I told them to look out for her on the platform. The kids were quite excited to be part of this great adventure.

The older one kept on asking what she was giving to me, and asked if it was mine, why she had it etc. We were all on the case, and quite honestly it was needed – the train platform, which was in a southern suburb of Tunis, seemed to be just as crowded as the one in Tunis had been. Lots of dark faces and hair were milling around the platform. The English teacher – Sarah – had short, cropped reddish hair and we were hoping that the color would help her to stand out a little. Thankfully the train wasn't too long, only about eight cars or so. As we approached the platform we all looked eagerly out of the windows. The three-year-old kept on saying, "There she is!" to every other person. The five-year-old was taking her job seriously and was scanning the crowd from her vantage point at the window.

It was actually Jennifer who noticed her first. Sarah was on her tip toes; book in hand, carrying a small bag as well. I shouted out her name when Jen pointed her out, and she came running alongside the train. The two little girls starting yelling, "Here we are, here we are!" I think this may have confused Sarah more than anything, but our mission was accomplished. As the train slowly came to a stop, we all had a quick reunion at the station. Very sweetly she gave us a bag of snacks for the train journey – the two Irish girls asked if it was sweets, but Sarah apologized and told them it wasn't. It was a bag of mixed nuts and salted fish; I think she was worried about us sweating too much. She also handed us a large bottle of water and when I tried to protest she said it was the least she could do as we had all had such a pleasant night together in Tunis the night before and she was leaving the next week for England. I gladly accepted and as the train didn't pull out for a while, we had lots of time to chat. The two little girls were introduced and thanked for their help in finding Sarah. They made sweet, coy responses of "You're welcome."

The train slowly departed from the platform which still appeared as crowded as when we'd pulled up. The train chugged along in the same slow motion as the ferry had. It was hot, but not stifling. Luckily it was December; so much of the heat was due to the number of passengers rather than the outside temparature. All the windows were opened, and if the train topped twenty miles per hour we were lucky, although the slight breeze did help. The little girls' energy faded, and they were both sleeping on their parents' knees within an hour or so. We all fell into a kind of hypnotic trance from the movement of the train, and sat in silence staring out of the window watching the countryside pass us by. I leafed through my newly obtained guide book reading all the history bits. It was quite interesting. I hadn't realized that the Romans colonized Tunisia. I had heard of Carthage but didn't realize it was so close. What an incredible empire, but like all empires, it was now gone, and reduced to the tourist trade for its income. It made me reflect on life once again, you name it – Mayan, Aztec, Egyptian, Greek, Roman, English, American – all just fleeting empires running around thinking themselves so important on the surface of this tiny ever-changing planet. We can all trick ourselves into thinking we, or the present balance of power, or even the earth itself will be around forever, but none of it will.

Back on the train we were slowly winding our way south through what was once a part of the long gone Roman Empire. The French also once colonized Tunisia, but now once again it was its own country in a part of the world where the dominant religion is now Muslim. Ah yes, the French language, that was something I needed to get a grip on. If I was going to travel here alone for a few weeks I needed to improve my nearly non-existent knowledge of that language. I had planned to stay in Tatouine for a few days and concentrate on studying French.

When all my fellow travelers got off, I was the only non-Tunisian in my car. It was still daylight but it was fading quickly. It was no surprise why what looked to be a relatively short distance on the map was going to take at least twelve hours, the train just idled along. I thought of how in France not so far away was the TGV (*train de grande vitesse* or high speed train) flying through the countryside at an average speed of nearly 200 kph.

Traveling in countries where the trains slowly plod along and buses are an adventure in themselves, a Western European or American would often find it frustrating. The locals don't even seem to notice. Are we somehow flying along and missing something? All the people on the train here seemed quite happy; children on their mother's knees, people chatting and exchanging pleasantries – they were all slowly getting to where they needed to go, and not minding taking the whole day to do so. The other passengers appeared to be enjoying looking out the window as much as I was. Life at a slower pace made more sense, but at the same time, I knew it was a matter of what we get used to. Just as the boat to Tunisia had lulled me into a slower pace as I crossed from Europe, this train ride was letting me drift further into a whole different mindset.

It was about nine in the evening when I arrived in Tatouine. Once again I had no choice but to arrive in the dark. My small backpack helped me not to stand out too much. I was as dark as some of the locals, and the shroud of night was also helping as I walked through the streets looking for a place to stay. I found a basic *pension*, the shower looked like it could electrocute me with several wires hanging dangerously close to the flow of water, but somehow or another it produced lukewarm water, and let me live to see another day.

After I had washed off some of the sweat of the journey, I went in search of some food and found a small shop which had some local delicacies. As I looked at the honey-soaked desserts on display, some with sliced nuts or almonds on top, and an omelette sitting next to some French fries in a small bain-marie causing the tiny display counter to mist up from the steam, my hunger hit me. The owner was a nice guy who was surprised to see me in his shop. I quickly called to mind the Muslim greeting Rob and I used in Indonesia all the time, and when I said, "*Salaam Allaaikum*," a broad smile came to his face. I felt instantly accepted. He had a big barrel of either buttermilk or *kefir* – something along those lines – either way I didn't understand the Arabic word he was using, and he didn't know the French word for it. It tasted like fermented goat's milk – not my favorite taste in the world – so I gulped it down quickly. He assumed that I liked it and I briefly thought of my first taste of *miso* soup all those years ago in L.A. when the same thing happened to me. I chuckled to myself knowing I would be drinking another. Sure enough, he quickly filled my glass up again, so I drank the next one slowly, which was not easy either, but much better, I thought, than a third! I had some kebab on flat bread with fried potatoes, and it was not at all a bad meal. Of course a sickly-sweet dessert was in order as well. He guaranteed me that my milk drink would make me strong, and, as always, in male-dominated societies, he assured me it would make me a sexual dynamo. Great, I thought, in a country where I probably could be arrested for just the thought, I needed a drink to stimulate my libido! He asked me to come by the next evening for dinner, and he would teach me some French.

Up till now, I had only seen Tatouine by night. It was the 30th of December the next day, and for some strange reason I decided to play a silly mind game with myself and not see Tatouine by the light of day until I had a better working knowledge of French. So I went off to bed, and decided I would stay in my room all the next day studying.

In the morning, light was coming through the one tiny window in my door which led to the hallway, but my room itself was windowless. The windows in the hall were so high up that I could not see out; just see light on the walls. I decided to stick to my silly idea from the night before. I didn't have any food, just the water bottle that Sarah gave me, and some salted nuts as well. There was a small table in the room, and a writing pad and pen, so I set up a little study area and started cramming. Of course I had no idea if I was saying anything correctly, but even if my pronunciation was off, I needed to get a good working vocabulary. Plus the owner of the food shop would help me out that night, and I would copy down some words and helpful phrases.

I didn't see a soul that whole day. I heard Tatouine below; cars going to and fro, the occasional shouts of people, but I fought the urge to go outside. I still don't know why I like playing these games with myself, but I enjoyed setting myself personal challenges. The light in my room was slowly changing from the bright midday sun to the oranges of sunset. I think if the window had been lower, it might have been quite a nice view. There was still the hint of sunlight outside, so I studied for another hour and waited for night to fully descend. I braved another quick shower then headed out into Tatouine for the second time in my life. I had remained indoors all day. I could now count up to a thousand in French, and had memorized all the words I would need to know in a market. I also felt more secure in my salutations. I set off towards the small deli-like place from the night before to try out what I had learned.

The owner, Mohammed, was actually waiting for me. He was pouring out a glass of whatever it was as I walked in and handed it to me with a smile. I wasn't sure whether to gobble it down or slowly savor it so as not to get two. Once it touched my lips, and I had a little taste of it, I couldn't help the urge to just get it down, so I did, much to Mohammed's delight. He poured me out a second glass which I did not touch until I had something to eat. The food was much the same as the night before but I chose to only have some potatoes even though I was quite hungry. I thought I would try and eat somewhere different later on. I slowly sipped my drink and had my French lesson. I was strangely growing to like whatever it was I was drinking, and with all the great side effects who could argue? After about an hour or so of French lessons and the most aggressive playing of dominoes I ever partook in – I lost every time – my new friend, Mohammed, made me promise to come back the next night.

I explored the now almost familiar dark streets, and was looking forward to seeing Tatouine by daylight. As I walked down the street searching out a place to eat, I saw some of the familiar faces from the previous night standing in front of their establishments asking if I needed a room or wanted something to eat. My day of study had definitely helped me out. I was able to respond, and even understand some of the basics so I felt my little game had paid off in a small way. I found a place to get some food, which was a thick omelet. It came with a few veggies on the side and was tasty, greasy, and salty. With that combination, how could it miss! To my amusement I ordered a drink from the menu, and when it came, it had a very familiar look and smell. I think I was growing accustomed to what seemed to be the national, or at least local, favorite!

I enjoyed just walking the streets feeling more confident in my French abilities, and also quite happy that I had a place to stay, because once I was able to convey that there was nothing I needed from the street hawkers, we could just relax and have a chat. I enjoy banter, and because my chosen life has been to travel, I am comfortable in most situations. Language barriers and cultural barriers aside, I usually wind up having quite a good time with people, and be it card tricks, jokes or language mistakes, I mostly have good memories of kindness and shared laughter with others.

That night I slept quite well, and the next day I would see Tatouine by daylight. As I woke the bright orange light reflecting off the wall behind my bed told me it was daylight, but how early was anyone's guess. Without Kenji's watch to tell me, I was still among the watchless of the world.

I headed out as soon as I got dressed. It must have been quite early because the small village seemed to be yawning and stretching itself awake. The dust lay still on the streets, some street sweepers halfheartedly shifting it around with long-handled brooms. None of the stalls were up yet. Then it dawned on me that it was New Year's Eve. I was sure that this day would also pass in an unremarkable fashion and I didn't mind at all. In our western arrogance we often forget that our year is based on a Christian calendar yet there are many other ways to count the date – Muslim, Jewish, Mayan, Japanese, and Chinese – just to name a few. The approaching year of 1992 though, was the date the world recognized as the current year, at least for purposes of international business. The cool morning air was refreshing; when the breeze blew in from the surrounding desert the dust rose up gently from the street. I watched a few large, van-like buses filling up. I'm not sure where people would be commuting to, and even though I've spent a lot of time in small towns and villages around the world, I still do not claim to know what or how things get done by a large percentage of the local population. An outdoor market, which no doubt would be buzzing in a few hours, was being set up and I'm sure I would later find myself walking through the stalls finding fresh fruit or local delicacies to enjoy. Outdoor markets are such a wonderful thing. Living in big western cities or towns you would not know that most of the world's population buys much of their dietary needs there. It keeps money circulating locally rather than creamed off to already rich multinational corporations and seems a fairer way to trade. It's also more real and keeps people in touch with where most of their food comes from. The lack of packaging and abundance of local foods to me is what our planet is calling out for.

Walking through the streets in the light of day was a whole new experience. The architecture was old and worn, and small bricks, the main construction material were apparent everywhere. The *Berber* influence in southern Tunisia is strong, and not far out of town were some ruins that sounded worthwhile seeing. I decided to explore Tatouine, search out some food, say hello to Mohammed in his shop, play dominoes, and get to know some of the locals.

I found a small stall to eat in on the outskirts of the market. The family running it was nothing but smiles – their eyes shone bright and weren't yellowed with jaundice or worse so I decided it was safe to eat there. Not a true health inspection by any stretch of the imagination, but smiles and bright eyes go a long way in my book. The meal was delicious. It was just eggs, potatoes and bread, but the yellow of the eggs were incredible, and the bread must have been freshly made that morning. I sopped up every last morsel of egg from the plate with the delicious warm bread, and after paying I had to stop myself from ordering another portion. I still carried my cyclist's appetite but had to remember I did not have my bicycle with me and was sitting on trains and buses a lot more. My French was working a treat, even though what I assumed to be Arabic or possibly *Berber* could be heard amongst the local workers and peasant stallholders.

I headed off to the shop for my morning fill of what was quickly becoming my favorite drink. My friend was surprised at my rapid improvement in French. He was quick to correct my errors, and it was endearing that he took me under his wing as his student. I told him of my plans to head out to the *Berber* ruins the next day, and he was very enthusiastic. He thought these were the greatest things next to the pyramids of Gaza. I have become used to this enthusiasm of local sights of interest. Mohammed, I was pretty sure, had never left Tunisia and he probably hadn't spent too much time out of Tatouine, judging from the hours of his shop. I daresay he hadn't spent much of his adult life too far from the area between his house and the shop. I say none of this in a negative way; I just mean to illustrate how it is all a matter of perspective. This man was proud to have these ruins on the outskirts of his small village in southern Tunisia that people from a city as famous as New York have traveled from to see. It is local pride in his area, and as long as that love of local places doesn't turn into a fervor or warped deception of the world and others it is quite nice to share in that energy.

As I suspected, New Year's Eve wasn't a big deal. Tatouine didn't appear to be building up to any sort of drunken fervor; in fact alcohol had seemed to disappear once I left Tunis. That was fine with me. Staying out on the streets till midnight would have been a lonely venture, so my New Year's Eve consisted of playing dominoes with as much bravado as the locals, and drinking fermented curd drink. I astonished the boys with a few of my card tricks, which were quite basic. After losing just about every game of dominoes I played, it was nice to have something to help me save face.

On the first of January 1992 I headed out to the bus station, and was surprised to meet up with a young French couple. Next to them my French didn't sound so good. They had just arrived in town and spoke very good English too. Their names were Alain and Pascale. Either laziness or embarrassment on my part let us slip into using English for our communication whereas any communication with locals was now done through the two French native speakers. I fell into the background – not in a bad way – it just seemed silly to struggle through a sentence when there were two people right next to me for whom French was their mother tongue. Anyhow, we really didn't have to do too much speaking. We bought our tickets to *Ksar Ouled Soltane*, the well-preserved ruins, boarded the bus and then fell to gazing out of the window as the desert passed us by. It was not true sandy desert, but rocky dry earth, accompanied by lots of dust. The bus ride out was about an hour or so, but after that we had to walk, then hitch a ride on the back of a truck. It was quite an adventure for what was probably only a thirty kilometer trip. We needed to be back for the last bus which was at four in the afternoon. We would have a good long time out here to enjoy the ancient remnants, and the quietness of the desert.

The three of us got on very well. They had been traveling for a few weeks, and, as it turned out, had been on the same train I had from Tunis. They had gotten off before me to visit another small town and had now come here to see the ruins. They asked what I had been doing in Tatouine for a few days. I opted not to mention my not-going-out-for-a-day game I played with myself as I didn't want them to think I was a complete weirdo, and just said I had been studying French and frequenting my little shop. They did not know of the shop or much else since they had only just arrived, so we made a deal to go in and have a drink with Mohammed.

We explored the ruins which were indeed quite interesting. The architecture down here was simple, and utilitarian. The multi story fortified grain stores called *ghurfas* were built to protect the village grains. These grain stores, or granaries, were built in the fifteenth century and were not too battered by all their time in the wind-swept desert, the living quarters built into the hillside blending in beautifully with the surrounding countryside. It was calm and tranquil now, but I could imagine a different story if marauding *Berbers* were out to steal your food. The small windows of the granaries and living quarters served many purposes; they kept heat and dust at bay, and also made the house much like a bunker if they needed to be used in that way – in case the next village over didn't have such a good grain crop I am presuming. There were a few food stalls, and we all decided that it was okay to eat from them. Alain and Pascale seemed to be adventurous when it came to eating from street vendors, and I was glad of that. It was delicious food, along the *tajine* lines once again and pepped up with plenty of the local spice *harissa*. The owner of the stall was quite happy to give us huge portions; spooning great ladleful's of it onto our plates as he told us of a tranquil walk out into the desert while gesturing enthusiastically with his ladle. He told us it was not far off the beaten track, but gave you the feeling of being in the middle of the Sahara. We took his advice and after lunch we walked out into the desert away from the modest crowds at the ruins.

The evening light was so beautiful in the desert giving everything a beautiful rosy orange glow. In January the weather was perfect; the days were not stifling hot, and the evenings nearing cold. Perfect for active days and comfortable sleeps. We wandered out only far enough for all of us to feel certain we would not wind up lost in the desert. Time and time again you hear warnings of people getting disorientated and lost only a few meters away from where they wanted to get back to. We sat on a rocky outcrop and got lost in conversation. They were on an extended holiday taking in the Northern African countries, before then heading back to France. They had explored quite a lot of Tunisia, visiting the north coast, and their descriptions made it sound wonderful. Of course, speaking the language is a big bonus. Here we were speaking together in near perfect English as well. If I ever come back in another life, I want to be a linguist – what a gift. I started too late in a silly education system that doesn't teach a foreign language until it is near enough too late. I need to study and struggle just to get a working knowledge of a language.

Anyhow there we were admiring the gorgeous colors of the changing sky when we realized simultaneously that those beautifully changing colors also meant it was getting quite late. We started to head back. None of us had a watch, and we were all bracing ourselves for a long walk home as we all kind of knew we had missed the last bus. The colors in the sky were too rich and reminiscent of evening for it to be only four p.m. As we got back to the ruins, our guess was proved correct. The food stalls and all the people had gone. It had only been an hour bus ride, but the bus had been driving very slowly, and stopped every ten meters or so. We knew it would be a long walk back, but possible. The only thing that worried us was that this far south, when the sun went down, it got inky-black very quickly.

We started heading out of the area, but then we saw two parked cars. They looked quite flash and on closer inspection they turned out to be Mercedes Benz. Beside them were a well-dressed family of mom and dad and their three children. The expensive cut and cleanliness of their clothes only served to emphasize the fact that we were quite the opposite – slightly grubby travelers. We heard the woman speaking French to her three

335

children and we smiled at them, offering a friendly "*bon soir*" as they noticed us approaching. The lady looked nervous, but we all decided we had to ask for a lift. There was only one road out of there, and even if they were not heading to Tatouine, they could get us well more than half-way there with more possibilities of lifts, or buses etc. Alain was the one we all picked to do the talking, he would approach the man and he had to do it quickly as they were getting in their cars. It was an awkward situation as it was obvious they were not going to offer us a lift, and it was also obvious that once they left we would be stranded, so it was really asking a question that had just one answer if they weren't heartless enough to leave us abandoned in the car park.

Alain approached the man and it was clear he was explaining our situation. The man kept on glancing over to us and then to his wife. We saw him nod, and Pascale and I breathed a sigh of relief. The three kids jumped in the car with dad, and Alain came over and said to me that I should go with him, and Pascale and he would go with her. I walked over to introduce myself and thank him, and was greeted by a strong handshake and faultless English.

I sat in the backseat with two of his three children, a young boy of about twelve and his daughter of about ten. The youngest sat in the front with dad. They didn't say much but their dad and I slipped into pleasant conversation. As it worked out he knew New York quite well and had lived there for a few years on business. He worked on 49th street, and we chatted about New York briefly, but he was much more interested in my thoughts on Tunisia and its people, the land, what I had seen so far of the country, the food etc. He was a man in his late forties or perhaps early fifties, and quite easy to talk to. His children were well-behaved and were able to add intelligently to the conversation when either I drew them in with a question or dad asked them to comment. As it worked out we got a lift all the way to Tatouine. I thanked him again, and he thanked me for answering so many of his questions and hoped we enjoyed the rest of our stay in Tunisia. Alain and Pascale came over to me with a big smile on their faces.

"That was pretty lucky, wasn't it?"

"It certainly was," Pascale replied. "You know who that was?"

"No, but he's obviously some sort of high-powered businessman."

"Actually," grinned Alain, obviously happy to fill me in, "he was the newly-appointed French Ambassador to Tunisia!"

It all made sense now; working on 49th street, speaking perfect English, and all the questions about Tunisia and its people. We all laughed at our luck, and even though it felt very late it was only about seven-thirty in the evening. Our stomachs were growling and we decided to go straight to a restaurant to get a bite to eat. Even a restaurant in this part of the world was affordable for travelers like us. We ate a simple meal, and all headed over to my local for a drink. The drink was definitely improving and we recounted the tale of our escapade, and hitching a lift with the ambassador. Mohammed wasn't as impressed with our story as he was with the fact that he had three foreigners in his small shop sharing a drink from his barrel of what I now knew was *kefir*.

I slept well that night. As I closed my eyes I had a giggle to myself about catching a lift with the newly-appointed Ambassador to Tunisia. I hoped I had satisfied his curiosity as I had had nothing but nice things to say about his host country.

I was in no rush to go anywhere the next morning. Alain and Pascale were heading off to the island of Djerba for some beach time. I was looking forward to a smaller village and getting back to practicing my French. If I stayed with native speakers I would never get anywhere with my language skills. We all saw each other the next morning to share a strong coffee, and exchanged addresses, something about the hitchhiking excursion from the *Berber* ruins had bonded us. They had plans to catch a bus but the excitement of getting the lift had whetted my appetite for something different. I bought some food in the market and filled up my water bottle so I was ready. I was going to head off to Medenine, which was a taxi drive away; about eight kilometers past Medenine there was a small village on the edge of the Sahara that looked to be off the beaten track. After arriving in Medenine with the sun still high in the sky and the weather perfect, instead of inquiring about buses or taxis to the unnamed village, I decided to walk. It was a decision that would shape my trip in Tunisia.

I had the up-to-date guide book that Sarah had given me, and even though I would have assumed there would be a place to stay in the smaller village, the book confirmed it and gave me a guideline price to work from. The guide book would also figure in to putting me on a great adventure across the Sahara. After walking the eight kilometers or so to the small village at the edge of the desert, I found the only hotel. The proprietor of the hotel, who was standing in front of his establishment, had seen me walk in to town. He was an off-putting man and even my best "*Salaam*" didn't warm him up. I asked if he had a room and he said yes, he did, and quoted me a price nearly double than the one in the book. The hotel looked pretty basic, and his whole attitude was not inviting in any way.

"Thirty *dinar* seems expensive for a hotel in the off peak season, do you have any less expensive rooms?" I asked.

He said in a surly tone, "Well just walk back to where you came from then, it is the only hotel in town, and that's the price." His sales tactics left a bit to be desired.

In a rash move I pointed out to the west in the direction of the desert and said, "I'll just walk to the next village that way."

He grunted, "If the wolves, scorpions and snakes don't get you."

I just smiled and went to the few small market sellers who had seen and heard everything. They smiled at me, and then gave a wave of their hand as if to say, "Don't pay attention to him." I immediately liked them all, and wished one of them owned the hotel. It was still early, the sky was blue, and it was warm but not hot, so I decided to make good on my threat. I asked how far the next village was, and received varying replies, just like my enquiries about the wolves, scorpions and snakes. My guide book was of no help now; it had got me into this mess, but now left me to my own devices. I filled my water bottle, bought some carrots, celery, nuts and bread, asked in vain once more about the wolves, snakes and scorpions, and was satisfied that I might make it to the next village alive. So without a lot of fanfare, just a nod and a wave, I set off to walk across the desert.

About thirty minutes after I left, I was surrounded by absolute silence except for the crunch of the rocky Sahara under my feet. The sun, just starting its decent towards dusk, threw a longer shadow than at mid-day, but I still had plenty of daylight, and a desert spread out before me. It wasn't uncharted territory – it was a dirt road of some sort. It gave me a guideline at least, because without it, I would have been coming back to stay at the hotel. I was pig-headed, but not willing to die for it. This felt right though; a small track, a lovely day, and an adventure. What could be better?

I walked on, always conscious of how much water was in my water bottle. I drank sparingly, and after a few hours I came upon a tiny village. The men looked at me with slight interest mildly surprised at me showing up on foot. They were all sat around drinking tea and I plopped myself down next to them and said hello in my best French, then pulled out my trusty "*Salaam Alaaikum*" and it worked a treat. Toothless smiles, hands brought together in greeting, and a small glass of tea was the reply. One of them asked many questions – curious about this solo traveler in his small part of the world. When he asked where I was sleeping I pointed to a corner of the courtyard on the flat rooftop, and gestured to my sleeping bag hanging from under my small pack. He wouldn't have it, but I thought he said something about waiting a little while. What else could I do? We sipped tea, made small-talk, and mostly sat around waiting.

To my astonishment, someone did appear. Somehow or another he knew my sleeping plans, and spoke very good English. "They will not allow you to sleep out in the night. It would not be correct. You will sleep at my house and eat with me and my family." It was the sort of invitation that was impossible to not accept, and markedly different to the greeting I had received a few hours back by the hotelier in town.

As it transpired, his name was Mustafa and he was originally from Tunis, but was working as the English teacher in the local school. He would only be here a few years then hopefully return to 'civilization' as he put it. I pumped him for as much information as I could about the road ahead, but he didn't know the terrain much further west than his tiny village on the edge of the desert. At that moment a big car zoomed through the village, kicking up dust and nearly killing a chicken that had been pecking about in the road. It came from the direction I was heading in and I wondered what it was all about. The English teacher looked at me almost in apology and explained that it was a local who worked in the tourist trade. He drove foreigners to the desert, but he didn't care too much for the local populace, or their chickens for that matter!

"Sometimes when the tour guides get the taste of money, they become this way. Not everyone is like that man," Mustafa gestured in the direction of the fading engine, "but there are a few like him around. It is not good...not good." Mustafa shook his head a little embarrassed that I had witnessed such a show from one of his fellow countrymen. As I got to know Mustafa better I saw that he had a true connection with his students and his temporary adopted home. He was a man who respected the ways of Islam and, for him, there were definitely right and wrong ways to behave.

Dinner that night was served in the traditional way; the women and children did not eat with the men but must have eaten before or off in another room somewhere. There was a communal bowl of food shared by the men, and it was served by his wife. The kids were quiet shadows sneaking glimpses of me when they could, but I never heard them utter a word. I ate with the teacher and his friend, finding out about his job, and what he missed about Tunis. It was funny to be talking to this native of the country's capital city and the way he spoke of it reminded me of the way I felt about New York City. He told me of the country people and their funny ways, and how backwards it was here. At the same time he liked it, but was a city boy at heart. He also thought I was crazy to want to walk alone across the south of Tunisia, but he didn't try to deter me, admitting that he had no idea what lay ahead. It was good to talk to someone from Tunis, as it made me conscious of the fact that I had been lumping everyone together under the collective heading of 'Tunisians'. Tunisia might be a small moderate Muslim country in the north part of the African continent, but Tunis and this tiny village, according to my host, had very little in common.

Even after my dinner and dialogue with the two men, I still found I was mentally putting the two into the one mixing bowl, and realized I had to stay aware of the differences that could be found within one country. I wound up staying the next day and we walked around the area. Fortunately he was off from school, or took time off to show me around. We met some of his students on the street, and they were very respectful of him and his American guest. It reminded me of the respect you were meant to show for your teachers back in my Catholic School in The Bronx. It was nice to see similarities in cultures that we are taught represent the enemy.

Emboldened by my success so far, I decided to keep on heading west and make it across Tunisia if possible. I shared a small simple meal again with Mustafa and his almost invisible family, slept in my own small room on a modest bed, and the next morning shared breakfast of bread and coffee with Mustafa, his wife actually joining us this time. I was given some food and water for my journey and I was certain that I would at least make it to another small village.

I set off – alone once again – the early start was chilly, but the weather was pretty dependable this time of year; cold nights, followed by fantastic sunrises and the gradual warming up to a nice comfortable walking temperature. The crunching of the small stones and the sand under my boots were the only sound I heard for most of the morning. I found myself taking about half an hour before I found my rhythm, being alone with just my thoughts for company. The days were just about an equal mix of nighttime to daytime. I could judge fairly well how much daylight I had left, and when the sun started to set it fell like a stone. Night would come quickly as though someone just threw a blanket over the sky.

I had been walking for a few hours and had not heard a car, but was still following something which did resemble a road. It was just a well-worn track in the desert, but if cars were to head east or west this would be the way they would come. I was being as frugal as I could with my water but, as nothing materialized along the track, my cockiness of the morning was slowly wearing off. I began thinking to myself that just maybe the hotelier in that small village near Medenine might still have the last laugh. The landscape was awe-inspiring though; vast and empty. The track rose and fell with the land, the huge blue sky stretching uninterrupted across the horizon. It is rare to be in a situation where you can actually see the curve of the land, but here, as I looked up from the track at the gentle arc where the sand met the sky, I was clearly aware that I was walking on the surface of the planet. I truly felt like a tiny ant and with all the same significance. From my perspective this small country might as well have been the biggest in the world; after all I was in one of the most well-known deserts, the Sahara! Borders did not mean anything here. I was not too far from Libya and even saw a sign for Tripoli. Pretty exotic, I thought.

Unfortunately there was no way an American was getting or even wanting to get a visa for Gaddafi's Libya at the moment, the relationship was tense to say the least. I was probably not even going to get a visa for Algeria; things were getting worse there as well. With the first Iraq war was just newly over, it probably was fool hardy for an American to be walking alone in a Muslim country. It helped that I didn't look your typical American, and with my dark skin getting darker by the day I was safe from looking North American at first glance. Not many people were asking to see my passport here, and I wasn't too worried. Tunisia was fairly moderate so if I was successful in getting my visa for Algeria, I'd have to see what I would do then. For the moment water was getting low, and I was getting hungry.

I had my small backpack on my back, a bandana around my head, a goatee beard, and my hair was getting long once again. As I rounded a small hillock, a young boy came running out of what looked like the middle of nowhere shouting "McGuyver!" and pointing at me. I quickly glanced over my shoulder to be 100 percent certain it was me he was pointing at, because if anyone could have been following me so quietly that I hadn't notice, it would have been McGuyver!

McGuyver was a character from a Canadian television program that had been popular in America during my youth, about a guy who could get himself out of any situation with a matchbook and a paper clip. The reruns obviously made it here. I checked quickly, but I was definitely the only person out here. The boy must have been about nine years old or so, and very enthusiastic for me to follow him, so I did. I walked up the hill, and there it was, in the middle of the desert – a small stand of olive trees. A donkey was tethered to a tree and a woman in full local attire complete with *burkah* (the Muslim veil a woman wears, also known as *hajib*) was up one of the trees with a stick. A second woman was cooking over a gas fired pot, and a man was spreading sheets out on the ground. Another small boy of about seven was there, and not as interested in McGuyver as big brother was. We greeted, "*Salaam Alaaikum*", and from then on they were convinced I spoke perfect Arabic – after all, McGuyver did! (The wonder of dubbing had fooled the locals!) Their French seemed to be about as good as mine, and my Arabic was pretty non-existent, so communication was a real challenge. I understood what they were doing, though, so I pitched in to help. The next hour or so I whacked olives off branches, spread out sheets and dumped olives into sacks. It was another surreal situation. A few minutes prior I had been walking alone worrying that I might have to turn back and now here I was picking olives in the middle of

341

the desert. The small boy was convinced I was McGuyver, but the most bizarre thing was that the man's sister-in-law, who was the woman up the tree, was flirting with me, and every time her hand came close to mine she would go out of her way to touch it, look at me from behind her veil, and flutter her eyelids. It was something out of a bad Hindi movie, which is where I'm sure she learned the whole eye-fluttering flirting technique. Her hands were pure leather, and although she might have been around my age, she looked to be ten years my senior. Even if she had been younger or more attractive, I was not going to risk any response to her open flirtations for fear of being dragged off and married, destined to inherit the family farm!

I was invited to join the small family for lunch which was, oddly enough, spaghetti and some bread, but unfortunately no olives. Olives need to be cured, and direct from the tree are pretty disgusting. The spaghetti was nearly up to the standard of the spaghetti on toast my nephew couldn't eat a few years back in Australia but for me it may have well been *Puglia's* in Little Italy. I tried not to look too ravenous, but man, was I hungry. The sister-in-law's flirting continued through lunch and I just returned her eye flutterings with a nervous smile. I don't know if anyone else noticed, or if she was always flirting and everyone was used to it, but I avoided eye contact with her as much as possible and just smiled politely when it seemed appropriate. I helped with the packing of the donkey after lunch and, what with one thing and another, I realized my walking for the day was definitely over. The sun was beginning to get low in the sky, and now I could make out the lights of a tiny village off in the distance. It was not on my road, but off a small track leading down and out of the hills. I had a couple of bandanas with me, so I decided to give one of them to the son who was still convinced I was McGuyver, even after spending the afternoon with me and me not doing anything very clever with my Swiss Army Knife. He was delighted, running off to show his mother. The father proudly showed me the lights of his village before leaving me a blanket and somehow or another conveying to me that I should leave it in the crook of the tree for the next day. They left me bread and some remnants of spaghetti. I also refilled my water bottle, and drank a lot of theirs. They were glad for the help, and I must say, I had worked hard. I silently wondered if they had expected to get that much work done in one day without help. I guess lunch had gone on longer than usual, but they obviously had plans to be back the next day. My plan was to be up early and out of there just in case the single sister-in-law had any other ideas!

I slept out under the stars wrapped up in the blanket and my sleeping bag. It was very cold and I found it hard to get to sleep. When I did sleep, though, I slept deeply, and before I knew it, a tiny diamond of light began

342

to split the black of the desert and the sky apart. I got up, left the blanket in the tree, and headed off into the now pale blue Saharan sky.

I was feeling very positive now – I still had the food that the English teacher had given me two days ago and I was getting further and further from where I had started. The further I got, the more impossible it was becoming to turn back. There were also a few smaller tracks leading off the main one down into tiny villages that were invisible during the day. They are more easily seen at night with the flicker of lights, but by that time, I would not want to be still walking.

I continued on, and picked a small sheltered spot to eat some breakfast. The morning was windy and overcast, but it did not look like rain. I kept eating down to a minimum so after a quick breakfast I walked on and felt inside me that everything was going to work out. My days were silent, and to be out here in the desert just walking with the barest of necessities, all alone, and with most of my family and friends not knowing where I was, was wonderfully freeing. I just focused on the scenery, and thought about my other travels and all the chance meetings I had had so far. I was far from thinking I was going to meet my end in the desert, but I did let my mind drift to those thoughts, and besides feeling sorry for family and all the hassle they would have finding where I was, I felt that personally I had had an interesting thirty years and it had all been worth while. This thinking was all quite matter of fact and not in the least panicky or suicidal but is probably a natural reaction to being in such a basic situation of survival; just me, the desert and a little food and water. I had nothing to hide the fact of my humanness here – no bills or obligations or duties to think of, my head was completely clear of anything other than that which was directly affecting my experience.

The first engine I heard since the reckless driver a few days back reached my ears over the wind. It was an exciting change in the monotony of the day. I tried to figure out where it was coming from. Was it a car approaching on the road I was walking on? Would I take a lift if it was heading my way? Would it be locals, or tourists in a four- wheel drive rented car? As my head formed these questions, the engine sound drifted in and out of earshot. One second I was convinced I would see the vehicle at any moment, then the sound would get lost behind a hill. Anyhow I did not have to make any decisions about lifts, or dive out of the way of a speedy driver, as the car never materialized. The noise in the distance simply faded into silence taking all of the possibilities with it. I just walked on, into the sun now that it was well past midday. My stomach must have been shrinking, because the amount of food I was existing on was nearly what I normally have for breakfast. I had stupidly left all my MRE's on the bike as I never imagined I would be walking across Tunisia. I felt so in the moment, all of my senses heightened; I could imagine now how a mountain climber must feel, being so in and totally absorbed by the moment and why it would be addictive.

My life was not in danger, but I had literally walked away from it all, and in a small way, the experience was peeling back the layers of me. At times my mind ran away with thoughts about my last year in America, and everything that had transpired there. I felt the anger and frustration come up as I thought of all the injustices in the world and of my specific experiences. Then, just as suddenly, calm would sweep through me and I felt the peace of rightness with the world. It was as if I was on a silent meditation, so different to any of the cycle touring I had done, and a world away from the motorcycle touring. I thought briefly my Indian *saddhu* would be smiling, his words still lingering in my head. This was something new, and it was what I had needed at this point in my life. It was my next step in trying to find a calmer side to my naturally passionate self. When I left America on this journey the last thing I expected was to be walking alone halfway across Tunisia but, as usual, it felt timely and perfect.

Back in the present moment I had reached the edge of a small town called Matmata where I stayed for two days. I didn't know of its *Star Wars* fame, but that night I found myself in an underground hotel having a drink in the same bar where Luke Skywalker meets Hans Solo amongst a host of other otherworldly beings. How appropriate, I thought, I already felt like I was on a different planet and here I was in a small village in southern Tunisia that had inspired some of the characters, costumes, and represented a different planet in probably one of the most famous sci-fi movies ever to hit the screen.

Where in the past few days I had been invited into people's houses and had picked olives with people, I was now being touted to come and experience life with the locals in a genuine underground house, of course for a fee. It made me laugh, and it was also sad that people made contact with others just to make a little money. At the same time, I thought, there are worse ways to earn a living. I didn't feel like getting involved and politely declined all the invitations. It was just a buzz to think that I made it to this place on foot, and now if I had to retreat and turn around, I wouldn't have to head back to Medenine. I kept wondering if that hotelier ever stopped to think what happened to the crazy foreigner who walked off into the desert.

After leaving Matmata, I was excited to be heading on. The bigger road which serviced Matmata was to the south and entered the village from a different way than I had done. I headed west on a continuation of the same road I'd been walking on previously. I walked out of town, being passed by a few cars and offered the odd lift here and there. I declined, and noticed a slight change in the landscape. The track I was on disappeared and the desert was not as rocky as it had been. It was getting sandier – not quite the high dunes and fine sand you associate with the Sahara – but more that way.

After a few miles the odd car stopped passing, and I was alone once again. It was hotter now, and the landscape was changing more quickly. Something was telling me maybe I should turn back although I didn't want to. I looked at my water supply, and I was already below the half-way mark. Matmata was still not so far away and I could still get safely back if I needed to. The track was getting more and more difficult to see so I gave myself a turning back point. I don't know what I was hoping to find in the middle of nowhere, but I said to myself, 'If I see nothing promising by the time my water is three-quarters done, I will turn back.' Needless to say I was being very frugal with my water – something in me wanted to keep going in the direction I was heading. I took a big swig of water and then heard what I thought was music. I stopped, tilting my head so I could hear more clearly, listening hard. Yes, there was the sound of music wafting over the sand. I could see nothing before the curve of the horizon, but now I was intrigued. I knew I had not passed anywhere since leaving Matmata and the road was definitely sandy and getting more difficult to back-track on. There was definitely music though – Arabic sounding. I briefly wondered if I was hallucinating but I felt normal, so I ruled that out. I was being drawn west, the sun was getting lower in the sky, and I knew I was taking a chance. Then I noticed something shimmering on the horizon. The music became clearer, and I was sure there was something out there. It had to be local desert people and my experience of Tunisian hospitality, except a certain hotel owner, had been nothing but warm welcomes so far. It felt too good a chance to pass up so I just kept heading towards the music and mirage-like shape on the horizon. I felt like I was the lead in the *James Bond* movie, when he lands in the middle of nowhere with a beautiful girl in the car, and says, "Hey, I know this great café in the desert." Okay, I did not have the car or the good-looking babe, but I was most definitely walking to a café in the middle of nowhere.

As I got closer it was getting stranger and I could not keep a huge grin from coming to my face. I even broke out into laughter, saying out loud, "I am walking to a café in the middle of the desert!" When I got there, there was one man sitting there squeezing and peeling oranges. We greeted each other and I just automatically sat down and started helping him make orange juice. He spoke to me in French and a smattering of English and asked if I would mind rounding up his goats so the wolves would not get them; he liked bringing them in before sundown. Of course, I thought, I bet that's what he asks all the strangers that roll up here after walking for days through the desert. I asked if he had a bed or a place I could put my sleeping bag for the night and he assured me it would not be a problem. It was all so nonchalant, like he was expecting me. I had a big refreshing glass of orange juice, and then went to round up his goats for the night. When I got back his wife and kids emerged, and he showed me where I would sleep that night. We never spoke of money, and I wasn't sure whether I should broach the subject so I didn't. He asked if I would like to join him and his family for supper and I willingly accepted.

I put my things in the small room, and had a quick lie down before heading off to dinner. I once again found myself thinking about the hotelier who had made all this possible, and then my thoughts drifted further back to other situations that had at first appeared unfortunate but had led to only good things; broken wrists, clueless travel agents, and now greedy hotel owners. If we can change our perspective, I suspect there's always some positive in most situations that can be found – we just need to look in the right places.

It turned out we would eat dinner all together. I was glad about that. I liked my new host, and the food was hot but I was not sure exactly what it was. It was food, though, and kindly offered – probably goat together with delicious *cous cous*. The bread was quite a heavy, unleavened type and made right there on the open fire. I was hungry, and enjoyed every morsel.

The night was remarkable. Millions of stars were out and equal in awe to the night skies of the high mountains; standing under them, making my neck ache as I just stared up at them almost made me dizzy. It was that ant feeling all over again. The desert is certainly impressive when it comes to big panoramic vistas by day or by night.

It gets cold in the desert night and I was tired so was happy when everyone began turning in fairly early. The room looked like a spare store room, but I had nothing to complain about; I was indoors with a full stomach and the prospect of a fairly comfortable night's sleep ahead. The man offered me the well for washing but I was so tired I said I would wash in the morning. Before bedding down we managed exchange names and I introduced myself officially to Ali.

I slept wonderfully, and, after waking to a brilliant sunrise, went over to the well and splashed some cold water over me. If I was just partially awake at the beginning of my wash, I was now fully awake and looking forward to what the day might bring. The family was already up, and some of the kids may have witnessed my feeble attempt at washing with the freezing cold water. Over our simple breakfast I brought up the matter of money. Ali had a very non-symmetrical face which made him look a bit sinister, but there was something about him that, although gruff, was sincere and he would not hear of it – I was his guest, and further more, I had walked there!

He told me that a German family was coming to his place that night in a vehicle. They were heading to Douz, and would give me a lift. The road from here on out was too sandy and dangerous for me to try and walk alone without proper equipment, compass, map etc. I was happy that he confirmed my own feeling from the day before. I found it hard to believe that a German family was going to show up here that night with a four-wheeled drive vehicle and whisk me off to Douz, but I trusted him, and his crooked face.

That day was spent walking out in other directions, and taking my sketch pad with me. I hadn't brought a camera with me to Northern Africa, so all of my memories are just snapshots in my head, and what I feebly managed to sketch. I wrote in my journal, peeled more oranges and herded the goats in and out of the place. The kids were intrigued by this long-haired American sleeping in the spare room and every attempt at conversation ended up in giggles. They followed me around and I liked having fun with them. I didn't show up for lunch that day and was not sure if that was rude or not, but I also did not want to think he was beholden to feed me all my meals. I had some food in my pack, and I knew I would be eating dinner with them that night.

No Germans showed up that night, but that didn't seem to bother my host. He was quite sure they were coming, and quite honestly, I was counting on their lift. A strange thing did happen that night though.

Our tiny café was at a vague crossroad in the desert. There was a nearly visible track coming in from the north, and the small path I had come in on crossed it from east to west. The Sahara was very sandy here, and you would not want to be driving in anything but a jeep or sturdy four-wheeled drive vehicle. I was in my beautifully dark room where I could not see my hand in front of my face. My mind was drifting off when in the distance I heard what sounded like a car stuck in the sand. The sound stopped and started. It couldn't be coming from Matmata – I had walked a good few hours from there. Where in the world could this sound be originating? I stayed in my room until my curiosity got the better of me. I came outside to a beautiful star studded night, and way off in the distance saw the headlights of a car. I joined Ali watching the progress of this car. It would get stuck, then move for a little while, then get stuck again. We both watched as the headlights approached. The car with two English guys, and two Danish girls had no option but to pull up to the café. They were heading somewhere south to a small town. Ali seemed concerned for them and offered them a bed for the night. I was playing translator, and told them of the offer. The driver, who was English, wanted to know if he could buy wine from the café. I felt silly asking the question, but repeated it. Ali looked confused and said no. I again repeated the offer of a free bed as Ali was concerned about them getting stuck, but the English guy asked me again where he could get some alcohol. I said I didn't know, and asked if he knew he was in a Muslim country on a desert road and being made a real offer of kindness. He knew, but didn't seem to care, they all wanted to get 'somewhere' and buy some wine or beer. They took off in the dark and Ali and I just stared at each other and listened to the car getting alternately stuck watching its tail lights disappear into the blackness of the desert night. It was probably even more bizarre to Ali than me walking here. I looked up at the sky, and was thankful that I enjoyed gazing at stars more than drinking beer or wine.

I woke up in the morning, and was wondering if what happened the night before was actually a weird dream, but as I saw their tire tracks being slowly covered up by the shifting sands I realized it really had happened. I hope they made it safely to where they were going, and I wonder if they might one day regret chasing a bottle of wine through the desert and missing the stars.

In the silence of the daytime I looked east to where the Iraq conflict happened not long before, and where the Palestine-Israeli one was ongoing. In the peace of the desert it was hard to imagine gunshots, bombs, and terrorism. I had been met with such kindness, and was pretty certain that Israelis and Palestinians would much rather be sharing their parcel of earth in some sort of compromised harmony, it was just that history is so hard to undo. I had read more about the Zionist movement and of course there was British and American interest in the whole mess. The lies told on all sides over the last few decades had spread enough hatred for both sides to have irreconcilable differences. How to find a solution?

My sitting meditations never became a reality, but I tried to incorporate them into my movements – the *saddhu's* words were not in vain; they helped me realize that inner calm was the key. Although I knew that yoga was a study which originated to keep your body and mind supple enough to be comfortable to sit in contemplative silence for long periods of time, for this point in my life walking meditation and hopefully – not too long from now – some riding meditation would have to suffice. I thanked my *saddhu*, picturing his beaming face and long beard, wondering where he was at this precise moment in time. Somewhere up in the high Himalya was my assumption. The thought pleased me.

I had to ask one more time if a German family was definitely coming to the café. Ali was sure they would arrive, but now not so sure which way they would be heading. I decided that I would stay one more day and see what happened. Sure enough, shortly after midday a 4x4 showed up with

Thomas Ullehman and his family inside. Unfortunately for me they had just left Douz that morning and were heading in the wrong direction. He said he would give me a lift to another café about fifteen kilometers west of where we were, where a road comes up from the south, and it would certainly be more probable to get a lift to Douz from there. He thought it would be too dangerous for me to walk alone. He was traveling with his girlfriend and his mom and dad. They found this café last year and were here for their holiday once again. They had called Ali to tell him they would be there the day before but got stuck in Douz because of some confusion with their rental car. They were a friendly family, and we spent the day together swapping stories, and forming a nice friendship.

This family was interesting because they were close-knit, and there were no strange feelings about a twenty-four-year-old son and his girlfriend traveling with his mom and dad. The dynamic was something I'd never encountered in America. They were all comfortable in where they were at as individuals, and as a family. It transpired that they were heading out into the desert for an adventure holiday. They enjoyed my story of how I wound up at this café on foot, and we all had a good laugh at the expense of Mr. Hotel man. I felt bad now; I was realizing that he had allowed me such an extraordinary travel experience. Although it had only been a short time, it had been an incredibly powerful experience. The synchronicity, the people I had met, the silence, the walk, the olive picking, the sheer challenge, and now sitting here in a café at the edge of the desert chatting with Thomas Uhlemann and his family, what an irreplaceable week. That night was like a party. Ali went out of his way for the Germans. I assumed they were paying customers, and the room they were in was a proper room, with beds, no boxes, and even a ceiling fan that didn't work! The meal was a proper feast, and I was invited by Thomas and his family to join them. Although we did not spend long together, there was something special about our bond, and when Thomas and I headed out the next morning in his 4x4, I knew we would meet again, and we did, twice in Germany, and many times over the years in New York.

The café owner in the next place seemed to be jaded and more the businessman, whereas Ali felt more like a friend right from the outset. In other ways it was perfect; there was a sweeping view over some high hills off in the distant desert with a road coming up from the south. I use the term road loosely but it was the most obvious road I had seen in the past week, and, although still unpaved, it was obviously more frequently used than where I had just come from with Thomas. I was certainly glad for the lift as it was proper sandy desert now, and besides so many possibilities of getting lost, just the task of walking through such a shifting medium would have been difficult enough.

I introduced myself to the owner and asked if many vehicles came by this way. He gave me a grunt, so I asked if I would be able to spend the night if no car came by. Another grunt. I wondered if he harbored anti-American feelings as the war in Iraq had just ended less then a year ago and Saddham was hailed as a hero. In Tunis I had seen some funny posters of Saddham dressed up as Rambo with the name ***SADDHAM*** written at the bottom. Any confrontation usually ended with a chuckle, but there was always an uneasy moment, or a comment about George Bush being my friend. I would be quick to reply, or make it known somehow or another that neither George Bush nor Saddham Hussein were high on my friend list, and I didn't care much for politicians.

Mr. Grunt had no way of knowing for sure that I was American so maybe he just didn't like foreigners in general; a silly business to be in if he didn't like people. Unlike Ali's café there were no goats to collect or oranges to peel and it didn't appear he was in a chatty mood, so I asked if I could leave my backpack while I headed out for a walk to the hills. Grunt was the reply along with a shrug that I took to mean yes.

I headed to the hills which looked much closer than they actually were, and it was a strenuous, but enjoyable walk there. I was not worried about food or water – if worse came to worst Mr. Grunt had food, I had a place to sleep, and I was confident that a car would pass, if not today, then tomorrow. It was not exactly the high tourist season, but I thought it should be. What perfect weather! The walk put things in perspective. I climbed to the top of the high hills and felt like a speck of dust. If I slipped and fell, that would be it. Mr. Grunt might grunt people in the general direction I had headed, but there was no identification in the backpack I left at the café, and everything else I had was on me. What a feeling. No one knew where I was. I looked out at the vastness stretched out before me unchanged by the modern world; no buildings, no skyline, the café out of sight, and the continent of Africa stretched out below me for thousands of miles. Europe was somewhere to the north, and America very far across the sea to the west, but from where I stood, none of that was visible – I could only see desert and could only feel the insignificance and profundity of life all in the same moment. Here I was, a small animal running around on the face of this tiny planet, just one of several billion people doing the same thing. On the other hand, my experiences were unique. I had broken bread, picked olives, and shared time with a handful of other human beings. The energy of human endeavor was tangible to me from up here on this small hill in a tiny corner of one of the world's biggest deserts in one of Africa's smallest countries. My life at once felt both tiny and insignificant as well as magnificent and wonderful. I was finding that life was full of these dualities and its great mysteries had never felt so close.

My walk across Tunisia was over. I was close to Douz now, but I would not be walking there, I would be catching a lift with someone. I felt it was going to happen. The past week had been nothing short of magical, so I could hardly wait to see what was in store.

I ate a small snack on top of my little mountain and envisioned biblical times. I realized that the scene I was now looking at was much like the landscape must have looked 2,000 years ago. There was nothing visible that spoke of modern times – not a telephone pole or electricity pylon in view. It was incredible and the feeling was so overwhelming that I just basked in it and let the sun and breeze wash over me. I felt Jesus could have appeared round the corner at any moment talking animatedly with his disciples, robes flowing as their leather-thonged feet kicked up the sand as they walked. My time on the road had been only a few months by this point, but what an incredible time it had been so far. There may often be moments in your life when you feel the perspective of the true reality – that we are all here for a glimpse of a moment that we call a lifetime and that our tiny, individual selves are only scratching around on the surface of the earth trying to make sense of it all and carve out a life of meaning – but these moments had come so thick and fast for me during the last weeks that they were permanently altering me. I would always carry these experiences with me – *as* me – and, as I had in India not so long ago, I could only wonder at how this would affect me once I got back to a 'normal' environment.

I dragged myself out of my own mind and started down the mountainside. I had built little stone towers to mark my way back, I definitely did not want to get lost here. I slowly headed back to the café, and as I approached I saw a 4x4 that had just recently pulled in, I could hear the engine crackling as it cooled down.

I went into the café and there sat four Europeans eating something. We greeted each other and they looked a little puzzled. I noticed another guy who looked like a local talking to Mr. Grunt, who he seemed to know. One of the people eating came over and spoke to me in Italian. I was able to answer him, but by my accent he knew I was not Italian so then switched to broken English. I asked where they were coming from, and they said they were on a packaged holiday – camel ride, camping out in the desert, 4x4 ride back to Douz. I immediately asked them if they were heading back to Douz now and if they had room for me and my backpack. No problem.

The other couple turned out to be French but of course they all spoke English. I could now fumble through pleasantries in Italian and French, so I tried to keep the conversation going in one of the two languages, but it was obvious that the two couples had been communicating in English with each other on their journey. We chatted about our respective journeys and adventures. Both couples agreed that there was plenty of room for me and my small backpack – since we all were heading to Douz, it was perfect. What a perfect ending I was thinking to myself. The French guy, Pascal, went over to tell the driver I was going to join them to Douz, but then a heated argument broke out and I was pretty sure I was the cause of it. Pascal was really riled up – the conversation was happening in French but way too fast for me to follow it. Pascal's girlfriend looked embarrassed – I think she knew I was the problem too. When Pascal came back over I said to him, "If it's a problem Pascal, I can wait for another lift, I don't want to cause any trouble."

He nearly turned on me as his blood was still boiling, "You are not the problem, not at all, he is the problem," pointing to the driver, then he continued, "you do not leave someone who needs a lift in the desert, I don't care. We have paid for this trip. This vehicle is ours until we get to Douz, and you, my friend will be in the car with us!"

I wasn't going to argue, I wanted the lift, and Pascal was absolutely fuming. The other three were with him as well. My mind drifted to that small village in the beginning of my trek and the Tunisian guy who nearly killed the chicken, I couldn't remember if it was the same car, but the attitude seemed to fit. The driver was outnumbered, and he didn't appear to care about the moral dilemma too much, or what these people felt about him, he just grunted as well, and sped off; now with five passengers. Mr. Grunt number one wasn't shedding too many tears on my departure. I could have let those two leave a bad taste in my mouth, but like my hotel man, I tried to let the situation be what it was. I felt a bond with the two couples, and we slipped into an easy conversation about our travels. We drove into Douz, and what a great feeling I had. I had made it! I had stayed my path, walked across a small portion of Tunisia, and set the tone for a wonderful year of cycle touring and self exploration which was still yet to come.

I went into my pocket and realized the original money I had taken out to pay for the hotel near Medenine had been nearly all the money I'd spent walking across the south of Tunisia. Matmata had been the only place where I had spent anything, all else had been given in kindness, or barter.

Douz, an oasis town on the edge of the Sandy Sahara Desert, was a great place to be ending my trip. To observe it from a distance coming out of the dry desert is a feast for the eyes – as the 4x4 bounces along the rutted dusty roads, a large swath of green appears on the horizon, and just gets bigger and bigger. As dry, dusty browns and sandy yellows are the colors you have been surrounded by for perhaps weeks in the desert, the green itself is as refreshing as the first tall glass of water after a long, hot walk. The trees – at first blurry – slowly come into view, you realize you are looking at a massive stand of date palm trees and you have arrived at the extraordinary reality of an oasis town.

The underground aquafilter of an oasis is amazing – it allows villages, towns, and thousands of trees to drink from its life-giving water source – and all survive in a symbiotic relationship. Dates were available to buy on every corner, just another gift from the oasis. This small town catered to all types of travelers from the hardcore overlanders from Africa to the well-heeled Europeans coming for a quick break. Then there were those who came specifically to Douz to begin and end their desert treks into the Sahara; some by camel, some four-wheel drive, and others a mix of both modes of travel. Everyone in Douz had their own story to tell, and mine was just another.

I spent a week there in a small hotel, shared with mostly budget travelers. Once I braved nearly getting arrested because I walked the streets with a pair of shorts on. It was not an act of defiance, but everything I had with me was in dire need of a wash, so I paid for everything to be washed and all I had left was a tee-shirt and a pair of shorts. I ran quickly to the laundromat, and put on my clean trousers there.

I wound up coming across the driver of the 4x4 in Douz nearly every day. He tried to play the hard man just staring me down. At first I felt I should have been the one to stare him down for his wanting to leave me in the desert. He was always out in front of the hotel he worked for, and although I could never summon up a "*Salaam*", I always said, "*Bonjour.*" On the third or fourth morning he finally relented and responded with a nod and we had a conversation. It was nothing earth shattering and we never brought up my lift or the argument in the café but every morning after that we would greet each other, and one day he invited me in for a hot tea.

"Why are you staying in Douz so long?" he asked.

"I'm resting after walking here nearly from Medenine." It was the closest we came to speaking about our first meeting.

"You walked here from Medenine? Alone?" He looked genuinely surprised.

"Yes, it wasn't anything like the sandy desert further south, I was able to find my way pretty easily, it was a long walk, but quite beautiful. The people of your country are very generous and beautiful, as is the scenery." I thought I detected an embarrassed look when I mentioned people's generosity as it was actually intended to make him think of our first meeting.

"When are you leaving Douz?" He asked.

"Probably tomorrow."

"Where will you go?"

"Back to Tunis," I replied, enjoying his turn around in attitude and curiosity.

"You are not planning on walking to Tunis, are you?" he smiled.

"Probably not, maybe I'll hitch." I felt much better now that we had a small connection, and it was hopeful to think that maybe, just maybe, I had found his soft spot.

The funniest sight I saw in Douz was with an English guy, Neale, who had spent nearly half his life traveling in Africa. We walked to the outskirts of town to where there were two big posh hotels, with a third earmarked for construction; hopefully someone in a tiny office somewhere will put a red dash through that possibility. These large watersucking monstrosities threatened any relationship Douz had with the natural aquafilter keeping it alive. These hotels were for the well-heeled tourist. We went into the lobby, and felt immediately out of place; women in dresses, men in casual suits, CNN in English on the three or four televisions dotted around the bars. Ah yes, the bars, we were on the doorstep of The Sahara desert but could have been anywhere in the world with those surroundings. It was incongruous. We left feeling dizzy, and Neale led me to an embankment far enough from the hotels, but able to see these two monstrous blots on the horizon. With a small turn of the head we were looking at sand dunes and desert as far as you could see. At the edge of the desert here were a lot of local men dressed in traditional clothes milling about, all with camels. I didn't know what was happening.

Neale nudged me, "Just watch this," he said with a grin. A big plush tourist bus pulled up in front of the hotel we had just left. The doors opened with a whoosh and people filed in. The bus filled up, drove about 200 meters, and then stopped. Everyone then was led from the air-conditioned comfort to a camel. There was a small performance as the well-dressed tourists were helped up into the saddles and then they lurched off into the sunset on their ships of the desert. My English friend Neale slapped me on the back laughing, "I come here every night to watch this. Sunset camel rides – these people pay a fortune for it."

"They do this every night?" I asked, amazed.

"Every night I've been here," he said and laughed his hearty laugh again. I laughed too at the craziness of the situation. If I'd had my camera with me, I would not have needed a wide angle lens to take a photo of where the people got on the bus to where they got off. I smiled, and felt a strange satisfaction that at least these locals had a steady income.

I wound up hitching halfway back to Tunis with a truck driver and his helper. It was strange to make it back so quickly. I found out that the Algerian president had been forced out of office while I was walking through the desert, now the military had taken full control of Algeria, and there was no way I was getting in with my American passport. I was disappointed, but my situation was nothing compared to what the people would now be forced to suffer there. I decided to book a flight to Morocco.

# Scared In Morocco

Getting off the airplane in Casablanca was exciting. I had seen the movie, and now here I was in this town made known to me by Humphrey Bogart. I walked the streets and perceived a distinctively more African feel than in Tunis. The women and men looked to be more from Black Africa, but the buildings and music seemed to have their own identity. Although Morocco was also influenced and occupied by the French, the presence of that culture didn't feel nearly as strong as it had in Tunisia. Morocco, on my first impression, felt more continental in an African way.

I opted to walk around getting a feel for the town and maybe something to eat before heading south. After strolling around I had to make some sort of plan. If I was going to head south, I needed to get moving. Casablanca was mellow, and I didn't experience any of the difficulties I had heard awaited me. After a few hours wandering its streets, I headed to the bus station to buy a ticket to Marrakech.

It was now February so I was still not in any great rush. I would enjoy what Morocco had to offer then slowly wend my way back to my bike. I would be hitting Greece and Turkey at the perfect time to start a long cycle exploration. I felt I needed to digest my trip in Tunisia and get back to Europe, but I couldn't pass up this chance to head down to Marrakech, then further south, and possibly do some walking in the Atlas Mountains.

I found myself in this interesting part of the world, but Morocco was having a problem with overzealous guides basically threatening you into taking them on as your personal escorts through the *souks*, city, or wherever else they could. They were aggressive in the selling of themselves, and I witnessed two guides coming to blows in the street vying for the custom of someone who had just gotten off the bus in Marrakech. I didn't plan on spending much time in Marrakech this time around knowing I would be back heading through once again on my way back from further south. I managed to sidestep all the guides plying their trade because of the ruckus caused by the fight. Finding a hotel was easy as there were many touts on the street bringing you to their 'Uncle's' or 'Cousin's' place. It was impossible to walk into a hotel without one of them following you in to try and collect their 'finder's fee' which was just a bit irritating. I was quoted prices including the fee for my unwanted shadow. Even the hoteliers were ruled by the leeches that were making life unpleasant, and matters were to get worse later on. I finally found a hotel which gave a decent price including the 'finder's fee'.

I was famished after a long day of travel and searched out some food. The Marrakech night food market is impossible to describe. There's food stall after food stall as you walk through the array of sizzling pans and steaming pots every dark smiling face beckons you to eat. Flames lick up from under huge vats of cooking soups, the smell of *tajine* instantly brings saliva to your mouth and *cous cous*, of course, is everywhere.

The choice of cakes was astounding; sweet cakes dripping in honey, macaroon biscuits, flaky pastries. There were also hot drinks, yogurts, cheeses, many of them as beautiful to look at as they were to eat. As if the display of foods were not enough, the surrounding street entertainers gave the impression that a circus caravan stumbled into the market and just decided to set up camp there – snake charmers, jugglers, musicians, singers, even dancing bears and other animal attractions. For me, just arrived from the solitude of the desert, it was major sensory overload. For the hungry traveler, it was impossible to choose which mouthwatering smell to be tempted by but inevitably someone's smile eventually brought me to their stall to sit at the makeshift table which would be gone in a few hours to be set up again the following night. I was careful to only order a savory dish – a delicious *tajine*, which I would eat quite a lot of in Morocco. I wanted to save my dessert for another stand, and go through the whole wonderful process of choosing all over again.

After satisfying my hunger, I walked around the heaving food market smiling at other westerners, and marveling at the humanity on show. Scammers were out, but I walked alone with no backpack and tried to look like I belonged. I didn't meet with any hassles and after a few hours and a hot drink at a stall slightly away from it all, I headed off to bed. Sleep came easily. I knew that I would leave Marrakech soon, I was being drawn to further south; I had not yet finished with the desert.

In Western Sahara they spoke Spanish. I thought that would be a great place to revisit the Sahara, and possibly get to know people on a deeper level since my grasp of Spanish was reasonably good. The next day I headed to the bus station but this time I could not get away unnoticed. There were more guides or ticket sellers milling around than buses. I was never sure if I was dealing with a bus driver, a scam artist or a policeman. It was unnerving – all I wanted to do was find out a time to La Ayoune, which I had seen spelt in several different ways, and I was finally able to find someone who looked vaguely official. I somehow managed to buy a ticket to La Ayoune and it was going to be a long ride on two buses, over eighteen hours! The price was reasonable, so I just held my breath till the morning hoping I had a real ticket for a bus that existed.

I spent the rest of the day taking in Marrakech. The architecture was exquisite; the Mosques were like towers, but not the typical dome shaped

357

mosques with the four minarets I associated with Islam. Marrakech was lively during the day as well, with a full-blown market taking over from the food stalls. Many of the acts that I'd seen the previous night were found there for sale now. If you fancied a dancing bear, or thought your new career could be in snake charming, then here was the place for you as it was possible to buy a snake complete with basket. It was an animal rights activist's nightmare as there were all sorts of animals in cages, or on the ends of chains being slightly abused in some way to perform tricks. I had lunch in a plain-looking restaurant and kept it simple – I was saving myself for the night's market.

I saw lots of travelers but at this point in time was still enjoying my solitude and looking forward to heading down to Western Sahara on my own. That night, with the moon hanging over the market place, the warm air enveloping me with delicious aromas and the constant  sounds of people assaulting from every side, I felt as if I were somewhere in the middle of the sprawling continent to the south. It was incredible to think that the narrow Straits of Gibraltar, not far north of here, were all that separated the two continents of Africa and Europe. Those small borders of separation divide continents, countries, cultures, lifestyles, and the rich from the poor.

The next morning I was up early and at the bus station before it was filled with thronging masses and their accompanying touts. I'm not normally too early a riser, but am always drawn to get up and watch a city or town wake up. It's like watching a young child wipe the sleep out of his or her eyes. This morning Marrakech was peaceful, the streets were almost empty, there were no market stalls, no guides, just street sweepers, and the call of the *muezzin* as the full warm sun ascended serenely into the morning sky.

At the bus station, I was glad to see a bus sitting in a bay with a piece of paper reading 'Agadir' in the window. This is where I had to change buses for La Ayoune. The bus was typical of the buses I had been on so far – old, but comfortable. I was glad of the seat space, and my early morning bus wasn't too crowded. I bought some bread and fruit for the ride, and thought it would be nice to get a window seat, and stare out, watching the desert pass by. My books and the view kept me occupied. I was getting excited about seeing the Sahara from a different side.

I had a two-hour wait in Agadir which was not a bad thing. I walked around and found a public toilet which was well-needed. My stomach was okay, but I had to be careful, the much longer leg of the trip lay ahead, and I would be sleeping in the next bus. I was careful of what I ate. Bread was easy to find and not too risky for my gut. I headed back to my seat on the bus which was now filling up, and spotted a western face in the crowd. He looked a few years older than me and when he saw the seat next to me was vacant, he asked with his eyes if it was okay to sit there. I answered also in body language that it was no problem. Neither of us assumed the other spoke English until he sat down and said, "Hello." When I said hi, he replied, "Oh, I thought you might be local, but you looked friendly enough." I took it as a compliment and detected nothing in his voice that feigned disappointment that my accent was American, as his was English. He asked where I was heading and when I told him La Ayoune, he seemed rather shocked and asked why I was heading there. I told him I spoke some Spanish and it looked like an interesting place to go. He said not many travelers made it down there, but he worked for the U.N. and had been stationed there for nearly three months. The next few hours I was enlightened to the inner-workings of a good ideal, gone wrong; yet another reason why I don't trust systems, and have lost faith in the accepted entities of government over my travels.

He was in La Ayoune along with about twenty others who were there to oversee a vote taking place in the desert to address some problems between Bedouin tribes of three countries – Morocco, Algeria, and Mauritania – as they all shared a common part of the desert. In the three months none of the issues had been addressed yet but my English friend had a local girlfriend, which he knew was a real no no in the local culture. He already had a wife in Southeast Asia, and he and all the other U.N. people stationed there had taken over the only decent hotel in La Ayoune which was now off-limits to locals. They were getting paid their normal salaries as well as seventy-five dollars a day overseas expense fee. Since they were away from home, heavy drinking was a nightly occurrence, and the whole process was costing the U.N. quite a lot of money. I liked my seat partner, I just didn't like the accepted way things got done in our world. I'm sure the U.N. has done great things, but like all systems, when they become too entrenched they need a shake up every so often to keep corruption and abuse at bay.

The bus journey was long and hot. As night approached the heat of the day slowly changed to the chill of the desert night. My sleeping bag kept me warm, and my seat buddy had his as well. After a fitful night's sleep the sunrise, even though seen from the cramped seat of an overcrowded smelly bus on unpaved roads, was glorious. The light had that special quality only seen in the hours around dawn and the fact that we were in the desert emphasized it. There's an incredible peace about that time of day. The colors are hard to describe as they move through the spectrum of black night shifting into the dark indigos and purples that herald the oranges and rosy pinks of the approaching daylight. Finally the sun pierces the horizon, and as it begins to rise lifts the tone of the colors into the more familiar hues of the morning.

Arriving in La Ayoune so early was nearly worth the overnight ride. La Ayoune was small, and it was weird to suddenly be able to converse with the locals. They had been occupied by the Spanish, but now were occupied by a nearer country. I was invited to go to the U.N. occupied hotel for a drink, but didn't feel I wanted to visit a hotel where the locals were banned. I found myself a nice, locally run place which was basic, the owner a humble guy, and the food quite nice. The bed, well, what can I say? It was lying horizontally, and I guess it's hard to handwash sheets to a perfect white, but I had my sleeping bag, and what La Ayoune offered in feeling off the beaten track was perfect.

What I learned over the next few days was that people in Western Sahara, who were also known as *Saharains*, were restricted to travel only in their own country; if they wanted to travel to Morocco they needed an I.D. card and did not have the right to a Moroccan passport. They were also becoming a minority in their own country and since the occupation, have lost control of its valuable resource to a Moroccan State-controlled company. So here was a country where apartheid was alive and well, and what did the western world know of it? Not much. Why? Because Morocco had marched in to Western Sahara in the mid-seventies, as the world turned a blind eye because of vested interests. Western Sahara was the world's largest producer of phosphates – very useful in the agricultural industry – and Morocco, through its now occupied territory in an unknown part of the world guaranteed the constant flow of these needed natural chemicals to the world at a good price. It was just one of the many subjects I tried to be aware of and bring awareness to, but my list was getting very long; with every encounter of beauty, kindness, and hospitality, the other realities of international politics and trade were not far behind, and seemingly extremely easy to uncover.

It was hard to miss the hotel with lots of U.N. four-wheel drive vehicles parked in the lot. I wondered how much would actually get done, and what would be the real impact on the locals after the vote was finally over, and the moving caravan left.

La Ayoune was tiny and walks into the desert were right on the doorstep. It was a basic place to live, and life was mellow to say the least. Even if these people were allowed passports, I doubt they could afford to go anywhere else in the world. Algeria was off limits, and I did not know much about the other country which lies to its south, Mauritania. A person in Western Sahara had few choices in their lives to make, obviously the extraction of phosphates was a big employer (becoming difficult unless you were Moroccan), but the few locals working the mines were not getting rich from that line of work.

Having said all that, the couple who ran my hotel were pleased to chat to me, and asked me to bring their story with me when I got back to America. I had so many stories and so many lives to carry with me that I had to remember personal balance. I knew I mustn't let frustration about the unfairness of life to so many throw me off center like it had during the Iraq war when I was last home. I used Mother Nature to keep my mind clear. One day I walked out towards the beach where the Sahara met the Atlantic. It was a beautiful long walk, and peaceful. I slept on the beach that night in my small bivvy and sleeping bag. It was in a secluded place and I felt I would be alright. Luckily I had my Tunisian experience behind me, and felt more comfortable sleeping in the open. I was used to a tent, but hadn't brought it with me. I was learning though that sleeping out under the stars was quite a beautiful way to spend the evenings as well.

I got back to La Ayoune and as there really wasn't much else to do but write in my journal, read, walk and eat. After three nights in my hotel, and one night under the stars I felt I was getting ready to start the slow journey back to my bike, and the original reason I left New York nearly four months previously.

Now I was heading to Marrakech once again. Despite all the possible hassles, I liked the place. On the bus, the driver tried to make me check my backpack. I didn't feel I needed to, it was much smaller than anything the locals were bringing on the bus, and for an overnight trip it was much handier to have it with me. The driver's assistant who was in charge of these matters also wanted to charge me for the inconvenience of putting my bag underneath. Some of the locals who were *Saharains* looked like they thought it was unfair too; my pack was small, but before things got into too much of a shouting match, I paid the fee, which was literally cents. To make a point that I felt it was just an out and out rip off, I took my bag with me. Once I had paid though, no one cared where my bag went. A few locals had a good laugh, and I had the convenience of having my sleeping bag, food, and reading material on hand.

I got off the bus before the main station and headed for the same hotel. The hotel man recognized me and gave me a smile as I managed to enter without any guides, interstingly the price was a tiny bit cheaper as well. I put my bag in my room and as I headed out to eat he told me another Englishman was staying in the hotel – maybe I would meet him the next day.

At the market the smells, faces and buzz were just as I remembered. I ate a big meal, had two sweet yogurt drinks, got back to my hotel and slept like a rock right through the morning call to prayer, which was incredible, because cheap rooms come at a price, which means that the speaker was right outside my window. By the time I woke up, Marrakech had clearly wiped the sleep from its eyes. I took a lukewarm shower in the communal shower room. I had missed breakfast time so decided for a big early lunch instead. The other Englishman, I was told, was staying another night but had already left for the day.

I took my sketchbook, found a place to eat that had a balcony and spent a few hours eating and sketching in my pad. I'm no artist, but had fun looking at the mosque in a deeper, more thoughtful way. I thought I would spend maybe two more nights enjoying Marrakech then head up into the mountains for a few days. When I got back to the hotel I saw a big guy in the common area who looked to be in his mid-fifties or so. He didn't look like a traveler, more like a traveling salesman. I assumed he was the Englishman so we struck up a polite conversation.

Graham had been traveling alone for a few weeks. He seemed genuinely friendly but just out of place here. Marrakech gobbled up people who were not somewhat street savvy. We went to the market together and ate at a place where I knew the food was good. Graham could eat, as could I, so we ate with gusto, and our stallholder was pleased – even spooning us more because he was having fun just watching us. I'm not what you'd call of small build, but Graham was big and quite bulky. After dinner Graham was on the search for dessert but we decided to walk off dinner a little first.

Just on the outskirts of the market a young boy came up to us and pointed at the floor, insinuating that one of us had dropped some money. Graham went to pick it up; my instinct told me to just keep walking. I said, "Graham, just leave it," but it was too late. He quickly put it down again and as we walked away the boy latched on to Graham and started to say something. We kept walking, but the boy got more agitated. "Mister, mister it's yours, you dropped it." We were both quite certain he hadn't, and kept on telling him to go away. Somehow or another it now became that we owed him money from some exchange we did and now he kept saying, "Ten *dinars*, you give me ten *dinars*." We just kept walking, but he wouldn't let up. He continued causing a fuss and soon a few more kids came around saying we took his money. I suggested going into a tea shop I'd been in before, assuming they wouldn't follow us in.

Once inside the owner refused to serve us and said we were causing a disturbance because of the boys outside. I tried to explain it was a scam and we just wanted a cup of tea, but he wasn't having it, and now even the customers were getting cross with us. How bizarre – was everyone in on this scam? We were forced to go back outside, and the group of boys stuck with us like glue. I was getting very frustrated but Graham was getting really nervous. We started heading back to our hotel which was a few winding streets away, but now the boys were getting aggressive. They were empowered by the fear, and the tea shop owner turfing us out. Under other circumstances it could have been seen as almost comical. At the end of the day, like most of the scams, it was a matter of cents, but scams are always annoying, and in this case it was downright unnerving. Graham broke into a run, and so did the kids who were chasing him. I ran behind and made sure Graham made it into the hotel. I stopped at the hotel next to ours as the guy who ran it was standing outside. He spoke English well, and we knew each other's faces. I asked if that was just a scam.

He said, "Yes, they all do it. No problem. They are just kids. If you pay them they will leave you alone."

"But they really worried my friend and, besides, we don't owe them anything," I countered.

"It's harmless. It's nothing to worry about." My hotelier friend brushed a hand into the air.

At that point I realized we must have been experiencing a major cultural difference as I felt it was anything but harmless. It had felt it was extremely invasive. I said goodnight and headed back to the hotel to find the kids still there. When I got there, they said to me, "Your friend, he owes us money." I protested that he didn't owe them anything, but they said they would stay there all night.

"Just do that." I went inside exasperated, thinking that maybe now we could just turn in and leave the kids outside to get bored and leave, but the man from the hotel came rushing up to me.

"Your friend is not well, go to his room." I hurried to Graham's room and when I got there he looked all sweaty and clammy.

"Great, he's going to have a heart attack," I thought, but was a little more compassionate with my words.

"Graham, its okay, just calm down, I spoke to someone outside, it's just a kid's scam."

"Please go and give them the money. Let's just get rid of them." Graham was jittery and had obviously been upset by the whole experience. I hesitated for a moment, not wanting to empower the boys outside, but decided that if fifty cents was going to keep Graham from a heart attack, I would give them the money. I went downstairs and the kids were still there talking casually to the two hotel guys. I really felt I was missing something in a big way here. These kids nearly gave Graham a heart attack as well as ruining our night, and all for fifty cents. The crazy part was that no one thought it was a bad thing, just kid's play. I guess growing up in The Bronx I did things I'm not so proud of either, but I'm not so sure that all the people from the neighborhood would have rallied around me and my friends saying, "Oh they only broke a few windows, and started a small fire in the lots. No problem. I did those things as a kid too."

I reluctantly gave them the money and off they ran. I told Graham they'd gone, and he looked relieved. He obviously wasn't up for dessert, and I felt bad about the whole thing. Was it partially my fault too, should I have just given into the scam from the beginning? After all, waiting ended up ruining the evening. It just didn't feel right. I went out and just out of interest went to the tea shop that had thrown us out thirty minutes ago. The owner smiled and showed me to a table but I declined and walked out and back into the food stall area. I had a yogurt and a hot chocolate to feel like I was acting normally. The moon hung in the sky at a funny angle, and the whole night just seemed to be out of kilter.

I decided I would head up to the mountains the next day. I needed to come to grips with what I was feeling about what happened as I couldn't shake the bad feeling it had left me with. The mountains were usually a good place to clear my head. Graham survived the night without a heart attack – I was genuinely glad about that.

I took a bus and shared a taxi to a place called Seti Fatma. I walked a little way and found an area nestled up near a river with the High Atlas Mountains stretched out before me. The mountain air was refreshing, and the feeling of being unnerved began to recede a little. I found a small place to eat, which also had rooms for rent. The spicy *tajine* was great, and after a few hours of travel, very welcome. I had a hot drink, declined smoking hash with the locals, and retired to my room. It was a cold, windowless room, quite big, with a bed looking out of place and almost floating in the middle of this cavern-like space. I wondered if the same guy who designed the cave Rob and I stayed in Sri Badrinath had also been at work here. I smiled at the memory and as soon as my head hit the pillow I was out like a light. Then something strange happened. I woke up after I didn't know how many hours of sleep. It was pitch dark in the room, and all I could hear was the few guys still smoking hash and laughing in the lobby. I was the only guest in the place, and my mind started running away from me. My body felt engulfed by fear, like flu or a fever and it just took over. I had a strange feeling in my throat and my body started shaking. I had never felt anything like it in my life. The laughter downstairs almost sounded sinister. Had I been drugged? No one in my family knew where I was. I'd had the same thought on top of the mountain in Tunisia, but now it was accompanied by this strange terror. Was it a reaction to the night before? Was Morocco getting to me? I couldn't stop my body from shaking. It was cold in the room, but I knew the shaking was from fright. Was it homesickness? Road weariness? I didn't know, and couldn't put my finger on it.

364

Up until then I had been enjoying the adventures. It's true that Morocco could be tough at times, but not life threatening. Perhaps I was just missing someone to talk to. I was so far from family, friends, Europe, my bike. I started to question everything, my lifestyle, my choices, what I was doing in this windowless room in a hotel in the Atlas Mountains alone with no one knowing where I was? Was this what I wanted out of my life? Was this where I wanted to be? I had a basic bathroom in the room, and my body was so tight with fear I needed to use it, and quickly. I thought I was going to be sick, but just had an explosion of diarrhea. I felt strangely better now, but still cold. I crawled back into my sleeping bag, and started to talk out loud to myself. I answered my own questions. I looked clearly at the road which brought me to this windowless room in the mountains of Morocco, and I thought yes, I do want to be here. Every choice, decision and move I've made has brought me right here to this place. I looked at all the suffering I'd witnessed, all the injustice in the world I'd seen, and thought that this was where I wanted to be. Some people didn't have the choice to be where I was. There are others I know personally who are stuck in lives not knowing how they got there. Their fear and mine might be the same – the difference was that I now knew that if I wanted to change my life's path I could, I was the master of my own destiny. I had brought myself here, I'd chosen to walk away from relationships, unfulfilling jobs, comfortable situations, the outcome being me alone in a cold room in Northern Africa, but I could board a plane in two days and be anywhere I wanted to be. Not many people have those choices.

I was on a road, it was an open road, but I had known somehow instinctively at a young age when I left the altar boys, quit little league, walked away from the teachings of the Catholic Church, bought a motorcycle and started on this journey, that it was my unique search. All of the labels I was born with were just labels; they weren't the essence of me. I was learning now that our world of borders, passports, religions, and careers has only been put in place by men no more truly important than me or anyone. We're all duped by the illusion that this is the only way it can be when there is actually no way it should be – only the way all six billion of us let it be. Each and every one of us is an energy which interacts with the others. Just because a certain system has been in place for one hundred or two thousand years doesn't mean that it has to be in place tomorrow. Our planet is moving, changing and growing. I've chosen a different path than most of the people I called friends and family, but it didn't mean it was better or worse – it just meant it was mine. I chose to be on my motorcycle crossing America, teaching in Japan, on top of that mountain, walking across the desert, in this damp room – my path, no matter where it's ending, is my path, and there's no other way for me but being right here in this moment.

I slowly started to stop shaking, still talking to myself and rubbing my legs. I then fell into a deep, dreamless sleep.

The next morning I woke up and remembered the trauma of the night before. I lay still for a few minutes just feeling my body and breath and mentally probing how I felt now. Although there was a slight anxiety around why I had felt so strange the night before, I knew that I felt much better – more like myself. I got up and ate a big breakfast, thinking that today I would walk up into the mountains to clear my head. I hired a guide to walk up higher into the Atlas.

We walked easily to a small village called Timichi. My guide was unobtrusive and we walked comfortably together, sometimes exchanging a few words of conversation. We spent the night there and I read the comment book from all other travelers who had passed this way on their journeys as well. It made me think how, no matter how long or short, any journey is worthwhile taking. I enjoyed being challenged, and even, in a strange way, nights like the previous one because it made me question myself. It kept real the reasons I traveled and also helped me to remember that I kept friends and family I love deeper inside the essence of what was me; my true home.

Snow had fallen unexpectedly and my guide told me that we would not be able to go on because we were not prepared for it. I was most definitely not prepared for snow and once again weather was pushing me to head a certain way. I experienced the same feeling as I had in India when I felt it was time to start heading back to a familiar place, I felt now I that I was ready to head to my bike.

I got back to Marrakech once again but this time it was just going to be for a night. I walked the food stalls and the *souk* where I had befriended a stallholder the last time and would go to his place to sit and have tea with him and watch humanity pass by. I told him about Timichi, and he knew of its outstanding beauty. It was nice to meet normal friendly people in Morocco; because I could leave thinking it was a country only full of scams, which I knew was never true of anywhere.

I was walking back to the hotel when I saw two young foreigners sitting having a cup of tea. I went over to say hello as there was something inviting about them that attracted me. They were two young American backpackers called Jeff and Mike. We wound up leaving Marrakech together, and took a night train to Tangiers. That journey was an overnight train and we blew it by buying third class tickets. It was the quintessential African or Asian nightmare train journey. We should have known – the tickets were so cheap they were almost free. It would have been worth the two or three dollar upgrade, but it was impossible to do once on the train, so we slept on the hard seats amongst the chickens, laying low beneath the fights, keeping out of the drunks way and tiptoeing through the puddles of urine swishing back and forth on the floor whenever we needed to move about. It was definitely not the romantic *Marrakech Express* Crosby Stills and Nash sang about.

We skipped Meknes and Fes and many places that I'm sure would have been wonderful. We took a bus to Ceuta for the shortest boat crossing to Spain. On the way through Tangiers a scam artist that Jeff and Mike had encountered weeks before was there once again. Meeting him and having to deal with his rudeness was almost a relief after that train ride. We were all glad to be going, and when we boarded the boat we saw other people who looked like they were also ready to get back on familiar ground. As we docked in Algeciras, with Gibraltar off to the right, it felt good to be back in Europe.

# Back on Track in Europe

Jeff, Mike and I were on slightly different schedules but decided that we would walk towards Cadiz, and say goodbye there. We bought some food, started walking west and found ourselves in unspoilt forest along the Straits of Gibraltar overlooking the continent of Africa a short skip away. We were confused as to why this prime real estate hadn't been developed with tacky hotels, and roads hugging the coastline. We never made it to a proper place to sleep that night – not a sign of a person or building anywhere – and ended up having to sleep out under the stars. It was incredibly beautiful waking up with the birds under the canopy of trees but we were perplexed as to where on earth we were.

The next day we came upon an army camp and realized that we had somehow stumbled onto private military land. The army personnel were as confused as us and weren't sure how to react. We obviously didn't have permission to be wandering around on military property but we didn't look like undercover agents on a mission either. We decided to play it as casual as possible so when we asked them for a drink, some food and directions. They handed us a beer, three sandwiches, escorted us to a large gate and sent us on our way. I'm not sure what could have happened, but the three of us looked like itinerant hippies, and I'm sure the paperwork for arresting three Americans trespassing on Spanish military soil would have been far more difficult than just telling us to scat.

After that we went our separate ways, Mike and Jeff caught a lift directly to Cadiz and I slept out under the stars for a couple of more nights. One evening I came across a party in a parking area overlooking the sea and was invited to eat and drink to my fill. When they all left that night, I was given the leftovers. Now with enough provisions stuffed in my backpack to keep me going for a day at least, I had one more night out before I would attempt to hitch to Seville to look at the stunning architecture, and the beautiful women.

Seville didn't disappoint on either front. I found a *pension*, strolled through the city gazing up down and sideways always casting my eye on beauty in both human and the architectural variety. Being back in Europe I was now close enough to feel like I wanted to be pedaling soon. March was approaching, the weather was getting better, and Aldo might have put away his knife by now.

I was running low on funds; I needed to think where I could get money wired to me. Now, back on a more familiar continent, I felt I could work my way around the system again. I hitched here and there, and after Seville took a long train journey towards Nice, in France.

All my hiking and lack of daily washing were taking their toll. I booked an overnight train, and found an empty compartment in the second class car. Perfect. Traveling out of season had its perks. I took off my boots and bedded down for the night.

I was sleeping soundly when the door to my empty compartment opened. I was awoken to the words, *"Oooh la la!"* and a French woman stepping out, sliding the door shut, looking as though she just discovered a wedge of *Camambert* cheese that had been in the back of the pantry far too long. I thought she was overreacting but when her husband came in and had a similar reaction I realized that perhaps new socks were in order. I gave a weak smile and a *"bon soir,"* but that didn't endear them to me enough to want to share my compartment. I was embarrassed, but what could I do? I turned over and went back to sleep vowing to wash my feet, buy some new socks, and somehow or another, air out my boots.

I showed up at Pascal and Sophie's apartment – they had invited me to look them up. He seemed genuinely pleased to see me but I felt she didn't share his enthusiasm. I remembered his fury at the driver back in the café and her embarrassment. I knew I would not stay long as I felt the unease of the situation already, my boots weren't helping I was sure. When I asked Pascal subtly if I was causing any problems, he waved me off and told me not to mind his girlfriend; she didn't appreciate travel the way he did. I didn't want to be a bother but he assured me it was no problem. I had my own room, and found out where a laundromat was.

I didn't bother washing my socks as there was no way that weeks of embedded grime were releasing its hold on them – I just bought some new ones. I also tried to air out my boots as best I could. My clothes washed up fine, and I felt nearly respectable. I decided I was going to try and get some money from a Citibank in Monte Carlo. I asked Pascal if it was okay to go to Monaco and then come back. He told me he was going on a ski trip with the school he worked for, so when I got back I could come as his guest for free. I didn't have to ponder long and hard to come up with a reply to that offer.

The Citibank in Monte Carlo felt somewhat unfriendly; backpackers getting money transferred did not seem to be their preferred customer. I didn't care; my travel funds were getting very low, and I would be paying for their services like everyone else. I enquired about wiring money and was told it would take a few days. I didn't want to push my luck with Pascal, but I was nearly broke. I called my mom, gave her the details to send my cash through, and started the ball rolling. If I had to, I could sleep out. I would get back, go skiing, and feel out the situation.

Pascal and I went out for a coffee. He told me about Nice and what a great place it was in winter, but the crowds of summer were awful for the locals who were not involved in the tourist industry. His commute time nearly doubled in time and the quietness of the off-season was gone till autumn.

We walked around the streets of 'Old Nice' and it felt quite mellow. Restaurants were open, but not all of them, and the cafés had a slight buzz about them; locals drinking coffee and wine, just soaking in the evening. It had a hypnotic effect – transporting me to a different world. Pascal told me that in the summer a lot of that charm was lost – the restaurants were jampacked, the cafés spilling out into the street, and the locals marginalized. The daytime brought crowds to the roads and the beaches – the game of *boules* (the French game which has relatives all over Europe, the big balls trying to get closer to the one small ball) we played on the beach two days ago would have been impossible without hitting a topless sunbather. Hmmm, I let my mind drift, it could be worse!

With that funny vision in my head I was snapped back to the present by the barking of a small poodle tethered to an impeccably dressed elderly woman with a face full of make up slightly smudged around her lips. She threw us a disapproving glance as if to say, "Please, you are causing my dog to bark!" As she tugged the small dog along passing us with a nearly audible grunt, I turned to Pascal and said. "I'm uncomfortable about the situation with your girlfriend, I really have the feeling I'm causing problems being here. I think I should stay in a hostel or find a cheap hotel when we get back from skiing."

"No, please don't worry, it isn't you, we are having problems. Our trip to Tunisia was supposed to sort things out, but it made matters worse. Believe me Joe; you are welcome in my apartment." He spoke with his usual passion, and continued, "It's good you are here, because it is showing the cracks in our relationship." I knew he was trying to make me feel better, but I insisted I should go. Now he sounded angry or maybe frustrated. "Really Joe you mustn't feel bad. Sophie doesn't like any of my friends."

I smiled when he said that, and he realized what he'd said and tried to backtrack. "I am not saying she doesn't like you...." he stopped midsentence and continued on a whole new line of thought, "I'm going up to Grenoble to see my parents the day after we go skiing, they live in a place called Valance which is in the countryside, I would like you to come with me. My parents are real travelers and you would get on well together."

I asked if he was just doing this because he was feeling awkward but he assured me he always went to visit, and in the winter he had a lot of time off. "So we go together to Grenoble?" He had a way of speaking and a great smile that brought out my own.

"Okay, let me take a look at the map, but what about Sophie?" I asked.

"She hates my parents!" He got a good laugh from that one, and I wasn't sure if he was joking or not.

I looked at a map, and thought it was a great opportunity, plus Alain and Pascale, the couple I shared the ambassador's lift with, lived in Grenoble so maybe we could all meet up for a coffee. Pascal thought that sounded great so we had a plan. I had enough money to get me through if I was careful. I never had a credit card, and it was interesting to be running so low on funds. Although I wasn't rich, I had some money right now traveling through the mystical ether of Western Union and coming to the district of Monte Carlo in a tiny city-state in Europe called Monaco. Two thousand dollars would be more than enough – I had left nearly a thousand hidden on my bicycle before I took off for Africa. I hoped $3,000 U.S. would get me through another year of traveling on my bike – it certainly would in Asia, and then some. For now though, I had thirty dollars worth of *francs*, and in France in 1992 that wasn't much.

Skiing in the Alps was almost surreal. I had skied in a few countries on my travels, and now here I was in the French Alps with barely enough money to afford a square meal, but I had skis, a lift ticket, and a lunch voucher in my pocket. Pascal had to look after the kids so he showed me the rental booth and told me where to meet him for lunch. I took off for the easy slopes. I can hold my own on skis, but I hadn't skied on snow since cross-country skiing with Alan in Australia, so I was a bit rusty. It didn't matter how much I fell, the views of the Alps Orientale (as they are known near the Med) from the lifts were worth every tumble. The next day we would be heading up to Grenoble, and who knew what was next? Pascal had had a good day but he was tired. The kids were from nine to twelve years old, and knew what they were doing on skis, but thirty kids with only two adults overseeing them can be hard work – I knew that from experience!

The next day we were off early and when we said goodbye it was the first time I saw a genuine smile on Sophie's face.

Pascal's parents lived in a rural suburb of Grenoble. They were quite a dynamic couple, and as his dad warmed up, and the stories began to flow, I saw immediately where Pascal got his travel bug from.

His dad had been a Merchant Marine and traveled the world on boats over a twenty-year period. His mom was the hardy type of woman who could survive the life of raising three children on her own with intervals of her itinerant husband showing up for the occasional whirlwind visit. As he spoke, Pascal would fall into a trance-like spell. We exchanged lots of travel stories and although his parents' English was quite passable I tried to make an effort at speaking French as well. We shared a delicious dinner, and the next day took a hike together. His parents belonged in the mountains and clearly loved them dearly. They had great knowledge of the area, and were keen skiers too. How strange, I thought, for a man who spent most of his working life on the open seas to seem so at home in the mountains. After the walk we sat outside in their garden and drank coffee, even though it was freezing. Luckily I had the loan of a coat.

We spent one more night and I called Alain and Pascale. It was very confusing, two Pascale's; one male, one female. They were going to be away till Monday but were keen to meet up. It meant I would be at a loose end for one night before their return but I had my sleeping bag, and wasn't worried about sleeping in the train station for a night. I didn't want to impose myself on Pascal's parents so fibbed that I would be meeting my friends later that day.

Once again it seemed like the universe was spinning its own story, and I was part of it. With Pascal gone I was now in Grenoble and not too sure what to do with myself. Grenoble is not as much *in* the Alps as it is surrounded by the Alps, and it was freezing. The cold air doesn't rise so it just hung icily over the town in a frosty haze. I hadn't brought warm clothes and layered nearly everything I had. I figured I'd find a café, write in my journal for a few hours, then have a walk around the town. Sleeping in the train station wasn't going to be fun.

I went into a bakery to get a *croissant* to have with my coffee. As I was leaving the bakery, I held the door open for a woman walking in and we smiled at each other and said, *"Bonjour."* I let the door close behind me and was looking up and down the streets wondering which way to go. I noticed a *2CV* – the classic timeless French car that looks like no other car on the road – its curved front end and roof nearly reminiscent of VW Bug, but not really, its insect eyes for front headlights, and door windows that fold in two instead of rolling down, the car just oozes personality – there was one in front of the bakery with another young woman in it who looked like she was probably waiting for her friend inside. She smiled too and I thought how friendly the people were on this bitterly cold morning. Just then her girlfriend came out, saw me looking perhaps a little aimless, and out of nowhere asked in French, "Where are you going? Do you need a lift?"

I surprised myself by answering in French without having to form the sentence in my head first, "No, I'm staying in Grenoble."

She then asked, "Where?" I was thrown by the straightforwardness of the question, and since I didn't have a place I was staying, and didn't know Grenoble very well, I just smiled and shrugged. She asked, "Would you like to join us for lunch?" I hesitated for a couple of seconds, surprised by such an unexpected offer, then accepted.

372

How incredible that a few minutes ago I was going to be café-surfing and spending the last of my *francs* on hot drinks and now I was heading who knew where with two French women for lunch. The driver, whose name was Anne-Laure, spoke some English and asked me if I had ever been to Grenoble before, I told her no, and made general small-talk with her and Jocelyn. I finally asked where we were going, and they told me that an American friend of theirs lived out in the countryside in a small village called St. Nizier and they were heading there for lunch. After about thirty minutes or so we pulled up to what looked to me like a real chateau. We parked, and knocked on the door.

A slight woman answered and to my ears spoke impeccable French. I was introduced. She smiled, looked at me – a complete stranger – and invited me into her house without hesitation. This, I thought, is what life is about. There was no forewarning, no phone call, just another face on the doorstep. The interior of the house was like a museum. The furniture was large, the chandeliers grand, and I almost expected a butler to appear discreetly at my elbow. We sat down for a hot drink and finally the French woman spoke to me in flawless English,

"So you're an American?" she asked.

I was shocked that she was the American the women had spoken of, and we fell into a conversation where I found out she had not lived in America for nearly twenty-five years. She had left for Canada during the Vietnam era and got involved with smuggling draft dodgers over the border. She was wanted by the U.S. government for her anti-war effort antics, and had not been back since. In Quebec she met her first husband, but in the seventies they broke up and she wound up in France where she met her second husband who was a composer, he had died a few years back and the house was testament to their life together – photos from around the world, awards on the mantelpiece, letters from heads of State's – fascinating! We went for a walk, and I told her of my trip to Vietnam, and how wonderful the country and the people were. She had no doubt although she had never been there. She was a true humanist and had given up her life, and even the country of her birth, for something she believed in.

We ate a typical five course meal and the conversation flowed as easily as the wine. I missed a lot of it when it was all in French, but I was drawn into the conversation from time to time in English. I tried my French skills now and again. At one point I was watching the sky turn from deep blue to a reddish orange, and thought wow, I have spent the whole day with these wonderful people, eaten great food, and all because of a smile. At one point Jocelyn asked me if I had to get back at any certain time. When I told her I didn't, she smiled and I think she knew then I had absolutely no plan

373

whatsoever. We left as the sun was going down. I thanked our host for a most enjoyable day, and she thanked me for sharing time with her in her tiny village. What a genuine, lovely woman.

Driving back to Grenoble I was thinking of the list of events all of the chance meetings in my life – those where I helped someone, or visa versa, and now here I was once again at the mercy of the universe, and it was proving to be a nice place. I also couldn't ignore the underlying serendipity as well. With Vietnam having been a powerful experience in my life, I met a woman – quite by chance in the middle of France – whose life had changed drastically because of that country.

In Grenoble Jocelyn asked me where I wanted to be dropped off.

"Oh, where we met today would me fine," I said airily.

"Where are you staying tonight?" she asked with a smile.

"Probably at the Youth Hostel," I told her, knowing I wouldn't be able to afford it, and would be seeking out the train station.

"Do you know where the Youth Hostel is?" she asked. I admitted I had no idea.

"You are staying at my place," she stated with finality and I looked at her with a sigh. The universe was treating me so well I didn't know how to refuse and, anyway, didn't want to.

She had a spare room and after getting everything settled I told her of my plans to meet with my friends the next day and how they were away for the weekend. This time she believed me, and said we'd call them in the morning. We talked about her mom and dad who lived in New Caledonia, which was a French Protectorate north of Australia. She said she had spent a few years there, and might go back, but for now the cold beauty of Grenoble was where she called home.

The next morning I woke to the smell of coffee and a warm *croissant*. We called Alain and Pascale who were back, so we made plans to meet up for lunch. Jocelyn was fairly new to Grenoble, but liked it very much. We stopped by Anne-Laure's place, and together we walked around the city.

Over lunch everyone hit it off wonderfully, it felt like a continuation of the previous day's warmth and companionship. After lunch Jocelyn gave me her number and we made plans to meet up later in the week. It also came out that Anne-Laure had to drive to Marseille and wondered if I wanted to accompany her. In that fantastic *2CV*, how could I say no?

Alain and Pascale filled me in on the rest of their trip, and I told them about my walk across the desert. They couldn't believe it, and we all laughed again about the Ambassador giving us a lift. Alain had prepared a slide show from his trip and a few friends were coming over to watch it. Did he think Jocelyn and her friend would like to come? I said I'd call and ask. The next few days were spent just taking it easy, and walking in the

374

countryside. Alain worked mornings, and Pascale was out of work for the moment. I luckily found a twenty dollar bill tucked away with my passport so I changed it for some *francs* in Grenoble. That would come in handy.

Thursday evening was an interesting mix; the house was full of people who knew Tunisia or had traveled extensively in other areas of the world. The slides were skillfully taken and evocative of that area. Jocelyn and Anne-Laure both came. I wound up going home with them that night because the next morning I would be driving with Anne-Laure to Marseille. The timing should be okay – I would get to Nice by Saturday, but that did mean two nights with Pascal and Sophie. I knew he would not mind, but I still felt uneasy knowing there was tension between them. Even if I wasn't the direct cause, I wasn't making things easier. I called Pascal and, true to form, he was fine with it. He said his brother was going to come over, and he was a funny guy. Pascal said his girlfriend was now fine. She was worried that he would want to go off cycling with me in Turkey if I stayed too long. We both laughed and I felt mildly better, not sure if he was fabricating the story a little because he knew how I felt.

The drive to Marseille was long in the little *2CV* which rattled all the way. Anne-Laure even wanted me to drive part of the way because she didn't like driving such long distances. It was a great French lesson for me as her English didn't stretch much beyond basic greetings. We laughed a lot, and she insisted on buying lunch because she had been dreading driving all that way alone and was happy to have me along. We had a simple lunch at a *routier* which was the French version of a truck stop – being French, it was very civilized. There was a three course meal including cheese, complete with a half-bottle of wine! She told me that these were the best places to eat when you were on the road; good food, lots of it, and at a great price. I kept that in the mental file.

We said goodbye at the train station and she made me promise I wasn't sleeping there. I laughed and promised I was heading to Nice to meet friends. She was satisfied enough to leave me there and I waved as the back of her *2CV* drove out of sight.

I had had another wonderful experience and once again was being wooed by the lure of living in the positive. For me it was another big draw of the road.

I made it back to Nice on the latest train possible so I could sleep on the move. I spent two more nights there and the energy had thankfully shifted. Pascal's brother turned out to be a natural comedian and had spent some time in New York. We had a great time spending the last of my money in Nice that night. I had tucked away my bus fare to Monaco and was hoping that the money being wired would be waiting for me.

Alas, when I got there I was told that no money had arrived. I was really bummed – Monte Carlo is not a place to be penniless. I asked the unhelpful woman to please check again, there must be some sort of mistake. She went into the back, and this time came out with a paper and what passed for a smile. She said it had just arrived that morning. I had to produce my passport, sign some papers, pay an extortionate fee, and was once again, flush. I didn't feel like spending over sixty dollars for traveler's checks. I had a money belt and felt confident enough to travel with cash on my person for the next year or so. I had done the same with my passport all these years, so why not?

I was finally on my way to my bike. I went back to Nice and treated Pascal and Sophie to dinner. I bought a train ticket to Italy where I would be getting closer to the next leg of my journey.

Since I was revisiting all of the people I met in Tunisia, I decided I would break up the journey to Rutigliano, which was going to be a long one, with a stop in Florence. I gave Jennifer a call once I was in Italy, and she said it would be great to catch up.

Florence itself felt like a living museum – The Duomo with its impressive dome in various shades of green and pink with white borders dominates the skyline, over thirty other churches, nearly as beautiful in their design, seemingly on every street corner, Piazza Santa Croce, the Pitti and Vecchio Palaces, statues vying for places to show off their beauty, the treasures behind the doors of the Uffizi Gallery and the list can go on. I not being much a museum going person walked the maze of alleys in slack-jaw dizziness. Hitler gave strict instructions to the Luftwaffe not to bomb any of the places of historical or art interest. That meant even leaving the famous (and tactical) Ponte Vecchio Bridge, built in the mid-fourteenth century, unharmed – hoping one day that all the treasures of Florence, and most of Europe, to be part of the Reich.

We picked a square to meet where I stood on the pedestal of a statue looking around for Jennifer; I had a strange feeling of being watched. Finally I saw her and when we hugged each other hello, I turned around to see Michelangelo's *David* had been right behind where I had been standing. I later found out that the original had been moved indoors, but the replica was what most people saw nowadays. At least it hadn't been me they were staring at.

Florence was a short stop – I was just breaking up the train journey and Jennifer was busy with art school. In Italy, the *kilometrico* train ticket was brilliant – it broke up journeys into kilometers, and was the cheapest way to get around by train in Italy. It allowed you to get off whenever you wanted and was quite convenient. I was also glad that my time traveling on

376

trains, buses and depending on lifts was coming to an end. I had done well without my bike for the past three months, but I was ready to ride.

I was off early the next morning – my train stopped in Rome where I roamed the streets for a few days discovering its secrets, the ancient capital of the fallen empire. After sidestepping the crazy drivers of that city, and living to tell the tale, I was two short train journeys from my bike. In Naples I had to switch trains, and then headed over the mountains towards the Adriatic Coast but not before making one more fateful stop.

# Finding Lost Relatives

Americans hold onto their ancestral roots strongly, my New York friends still refer to each other as Irish, Italian, German, Greek and more. It's true that we all eat different foods and some of our traditions around Christmas time do vary, but for the most part all of my 'European' friends are second or third generation New Yorkers, complete with Bronx accents, and a few remaining traditions from the 'Old Country'. We all have a Joe Massotti tucked away somewhere in one of the Five Boros, but in fact we're American, and more importantly, New Yorkers to the core!

We throw around the term 'Just off the Boat' meaning anyone with broken English, or who drank 'real black coffee', but very few modern day immigrants of European stock do get off a boat. Many of my friends have relatives who landed on American shores in the early 20$^{th}$ century, and were indeed, Just off the Boat. Unfortunately, for the most part, our European lineage seemed to stop there as well. Rarely did we have much contact with our relatives living on the other side of the Atlantic where many of our grandparents, or great-grandparents, got *on* the boat. I did have some connection with my relatives on the Adriatic coast, which was more than most of my friends.

My mother was a true New Yorker – she grew up in Harlem, raised her children in The Bronx and speaks with a strong New York accent. As children we never heard my mother utter a word of Italian. My dad would speak to his mom once in a while in 'the dialect', but that was it, until our visits to Queens. At Joe Massotti's most conversations between him and his family were in his native tongue. It was only then I would hear dad, Aunt Mary or Uncle Lou let loose with a bit of Italian now and again. I can only recall anything sounding vaguely like Italian passing my mother's lips when she was in a fit of anger, and her favorite was, "Don't you ever forget where your grandfather was from, *"Provincia di Potenza,"* like it explained everything. It would roll off her lips without the slightest hint of a New York accent. My brother and sister and I would roll our eyes at each other – "Here goes mom on about Potenza again." So when a train strike forced me off the train in a town called Melfi in the province of Potenza, I was inadvertently thrust into the land of my forefathers. While looking at the station sign and the other passengers on the platform, it occurred to me that I might be close to some living relatives up here in the mountains. I remembered Melfi being mentioned time and again, so why not turn an inconvenience into an adventure and head off to see if I could find any lost relatives. I had nothing to lose.

Some history is probably pertinent here. My grandfather moved to America with his Uncle Nick when he was twelve years old because his father (my great-grandfather) was kicked in the chest while working behind a horse in the fields resulting in his untimely death. When great-grandma decided to re-marry and not wear black for the rest of her life – as was tradition in those parts – it infuriated her brother and her son so much that they decided to leave Italy. The pig-headed southern Italian genes that I inherited were well at work here and I don't think my grandfather ever spoke to his mother again. He made a life for himself in New York, and, of his seven children, my mom was one. I never met my grandfather; he died a few years before I was born, but I was all too aware of where he was from.

It was a Sunday night and I went in search of a *pension* for the night. I wandered through the streets of this walled city watching the old men play *bocce* – another big ball coming close to the small ball game which *I* grew up playing. I walked and wondered if my grandfather as a small boy had watched his father playing this same game before that fateful day that changed so many lives, and, in a strange way, made me who I was. The setting sun made a beautiful scene over the city and the crisp air of the mountains was delicious and refreshing. After a while spent lost in thought conjuring up images of grandpa running to get black coffees for his dad and all the men playing a heated game of *bocce,* I needed to continue with my *pension* search.

I found one that was basic, inexpensive and welcoming. Melfi didn't appear to be a big tourist town, at least not in late February. I was well-treated in the restaurant I ate in, and slept very soundly in the first real bed in what felt like ages! The next morning was bright and crisp, and after a breakfast of strong coffee, a buttered roll and small bowl of cereal I strolled along the same ancient narrow, cobbled, winding roads and alleys that my ancestors must have. It was a good feeling just being able to visit these streets, and even if I did not find any distant relatives, it was more than worth one night to be privileged enough just to tread in the footsteps of my great-grandfather and grandmother.

I thought that my chances of finding anyone were very small. Melfi had swelled well beyond the walls of the original city now – no longer a small quaint mountain village full of peasants working in the fields, it had well and truly entered the 20th century complete with traffic and too much housing that was trying to swallow up the green fields of surrounding countryside. Snug inside the walled city you could still get a feel for the old ways of life. The houses were built so close to each other that neighbors could easily call across to each other. You could visualize man and beast working in the fields. The *paysans* of a generation or two back sweating to merely survive.

The strike was over, but I decided to head to the Municipal Office instead of the station. I would have to have one shot at finding some relatives, to say I tried if nothing else. I walked into the office which was packed full of people; mothers registering their babies, young couples making appointments to wed, and others registering recent deaths. It looked like I could be there all day but being an obvious foreigner in the office; a middle aged clerk asked me if he could help. I approached the counter and, feeling a little embarrassed at my pigeon Italian, I got my story across.

I explained who my grandfather was, the circumstances under which he left and guessed at the dates by doing some rudimentary math. The clerk rolled his eyes and said that there had been lots of earthquakes in this region and a lot of people died or left for America at that period in time. I smiled and nodded at him. He saw that I wasn't going to be easily deterred so with a sigh he opened up the phone book to the name Martino – my grandfather's surname – there were quite a few listed. He called one at random, and from the look on his face it was clear that the person on the other side of the phone line was not interested. He was nice enough to then take out an enormous tome of birth records. He asked me my grandfather's name again, and what his mother's name – my great grandmother's – had been.

I had done some homework by asking my mom the night before on the phone if she knew her grandmother's name. She had, and luckily I could give that information now. He opened up the big leather-bound book and turned each yellowed page with care. He found a Giusseppe Martino born to Maria Gallella in 1895. He wrote down the address on a sheet of paper and handed it to me with a look and a shrug as if to say, "That's all I can give you." I thanked him and realized he had already been helpful beyond the call of duty. I started to leave and he got on with his busy day.

As I was bending down to pick up my backpack an old man approached me and croaked in an almost undecipherable dialect, "My name is also Giusseppe Martino, I may know someone you are looking for." He beckoned me to follow. I turned to ask the clerk if I could leave my backpack in the office and off I went with my grandfather's name sake.

I did not understand much of what he said but I did recognize the first place we stopped – the local bar, for a quick drink to get the day going. Great, I thought, here I am following the town drunk on my journey into the past. I didn't know whether to be reassured by the fact Giusseppe wasn't the only one indulging – there were a few others doing the same – but it all seemed harmless enough in this enclosed city nearing the ankle in the boot of Italy. I followed Giusseppe through the tight tangle of the streets of Melfi. He kept on explaining something to me as I nodded appropriately comprehending very little.

I started thinking of my bike and how nice it was going to be to start traveling once again on my trusty steed that awaited me in another small village on the other side of these mountains, then we stopped suddenly at a very small house on a street which looked much like all the others. He knocked on the door and a small gray-haired woman dressed in black opened it. There was something vaguely familiar about her face but a lot of older Italian women share the same looks, and I'm sure there was a lot of ancient shared blood in this tightknit community.

Giusseppe explained something in dialect then they both switched to Italian for my benefit. I explained who I was and the whole story of my grandfather leaving for America etc. She looked somewhat interested, and then disappeared into the bowels of the house, which resembled an Aladdin's cave with furniture and knick-knacks in every nook and cranny. The walls were almost completely covered in mismatched frames with the obligatory gaudy mountain scenes or The Virgin staring down at you from a pedestal. The tiny woman in black resembled a small elf going into her magic cave.

Giusseppe and I smiled uncomfortably at each other then she returned a few minutes later with a black and white wedding photo taken in what seemed to be the fifties sometime. She handed me the photo, complete with the cracked glass, and on closer inspection I realized I recognized the photo. It was the wedding photo of my mom's sister, Jenny! My whole family right there staring out at me. I started pointing to people and saying in Italian, "My mother, my father, my aunt......" when I pointed at my grandfather I said, "My Grandfather" (*Mi Nono*) she looked up at me with tears in her wide eyes and said "*Mio Fratello!*" ("my brother!"). My knees buckled and I needed to sit down. I felt goosebumps up my arms and a smile came over my face. I could not believe my luck. Little Giusseppe had led me right to the very place I was looking for! I couldn't believe it. We had a cold drink – I declined alcohol and opted for water – Giusseppe had his second drink of the day, bid us farewell, and left me with my grandfather's half-sister, the product of my great-grandmother's second marriage!

When my grandfather found out that his mother had had another child with her new husband, he found he could hold no grudge against what was his flesh and blood half-sister so over the years he had sent her photos of his American life and there, sitting in my hands, was the photo of him at the last wedding he would make it to before his untimely death in New York in 1957. We went through everyone in the wedding photo and – true to the passions of the Italians – when I pointed to my aunt and my dad, who Maria had never met, and told her they were dead, she broke out into loud sobs. We managed to make it through without too many emotional outbursts and I was quite thankful she already knew her brother was dead and had been for nearly thirty-five years, for even that memory of the brother she'd never met brought a tear to her eyes. Emotions were running high for both of us.

After the shock of finding her lost relative, me, and realizing that my Italian was not up to the situation at hand, Maria made a phonecall and her son-in-law Stefano appeared shortly afterwards. He spoke some English and we started making plans for dinner, sleeping arrangements, meeting other cousins and a picnic in the mountains. In all the excitement, I nearly forgot my bag was still in the municipal office. I said to Stefano I'd better get down there to collect it so we set off together. On our way we stopped at the same watering hole as we had with Giusseppe – it was obviously the local favorite. Stefano was not as easy to say no to, especially now I had the status of *cugino* – cousin! He explained the story to nearly everyone we met with quite a lot of arm waving and back slapping going on. I eventually made it back into the office where the man who had helped me asked if I'd had any luck. When I told him I had and that I'd found my grandfather's sister his face erupted into a huge grin and the people in the office broke out into spontaneous applause. It was surreal, but then the whole two days since getting off the train had been surreal.

Getting back to Maria's house there was another cousin awaiting the American. This was Stefano's wife Vincenza so she was a blood relation, and warm hugs and tears were in order. Over the next few days I was treated like royalty. I had the privilege of drinking a coffee in the same room where my great-great-grandmother was born, and we took a wonderful trip into the mountains where my other cousin Gaetano took some video footage so I could send it back to America. I realized it probably was not a coincidence that Gaetano and Vincenza both shared names with my uncle and aunt in New York who were my grandfather's kids.

I also made a very interesting discovery having to do with food. As you can imagine I grew up eating a lot of Italian food. New York has many restaurants serving this wonderful fare but when all of your relatives are of Italian stock you would think that paying for Italian food would be silly, but to my surprise on the odd occasions when we did go out for meals, we usually chose Italian. The reason for this, I think, was to compare tastes. You might think that gravy, cheese and pasta can't differ so much, but oh, it can. Most of the food I ate was cooked by my mom. To eat at my mom's house or any of her four sisters' houses the food tasted practically the same. On the occasions when we ate at anyone from my dad's side of the family, it all changed. The taste wasn't the same; the tomato sauce – or gravy, as we called it – was thinner and less spicy, the eggplant parmesan had less cheese, and even the salad dressing was different.

Now, here in Italy, pretty far away from my childhood house, I found myself eating my mom's gravy. They were unmistakably her meatballs as well. Yes, even the salad dressing tasted vaguely familiar. Then it occurred to me that down in Rutigliano, I had been eating over at Aunt Mary's; more seafood, lighter sauce, and less cheese on the eggplant parmesan. Food had a lineage as well; it was passed down through your mom's side – in the female gene – filtering down through the generations. I wasn't sure exactly how this happened since my grandfather and uncle were the ones who'd left Melfi in a huff, but somehow, those recipes made it over with them. Was it so ingrained in their palates? I do remember my mom telling me about grandpa and Uncle Nick having some friends that helped them get on track in New York. I assume they were connections from Melfi and perhaps the recipes were safe with them. Who knows?

My time in Melfi turned out to be more positive than I had ever dared hope. My mother's cries of "Never forget *Provincia di Potenza*" had not all been in vain after all. I had found my lost relatives!

# Illiterate in Greece

After a brief stay with my relatives and a happy reunion with my bike, I was finally ready to pedal. First though, I found myself once again on a boat crossing to another country. I was leaving the shores of Italy for Patras, Greece. Not quite the long trip it had been to Tunisia, but the short crossing was still like passing from one world to another, even though the part of Italy I'd just left was part of the ancient Greek Empire – an actual borderline once existed between the two southern European countries somewhere not far from Bari. My surname, Diomede, hails from southern Italy, but is actually more Greek in its origins. With an 's' on the end it's the name of an ancient Greek King who was a friend of the gods on Mount Olympus. Legend has it King Diomedes was a great traveler and a favorite of Zeus and he finally settled in the part of the world I was now leaving. Maybe my desire to travel was more inbred than I knew. Now, heading to the country where my bloodline may have had its ancient roots, I was excited to be on my bike and entering a weather pattern which was a whole lot better than it had been three months previously.

Many people take their literacy for granted. Illiteracy is unnerving and can make you feel exposed. Imagine not being able to read road signs, make out the words on a package of something you are about to eat, find the date on a calendar or, in my not too distant future, pinpoint your location on a map written in another alphabet.

The saying 'It's Greek to me' kept on running through my head. In my months of hiking and taking the occasional train throughout Europe and Northern Africa, I would try and learn enough of the language of the country I was in to get by. The Latin based languages, although different, at least used the same alphabet. Even the two North African countries I had visited spoke French. With a fair grounding in Spanish, I had always been able to get through most situations so far, so it was probably not with a small amount of cockiness that I hopped on the boat between Italy and Greece without a working knowledge of the language or alphabet. I was laden with food given to me by my Italian family and on the boat I bought a map of Greece. The names of the villages were written in Greek and also Italian. I looked at the map, was able to figure out most of the place names and thought I couldn't go too far wrong. Oh, what bliss in ignorance!

The ferry docked at night so I rode a short distance to a field and free-camped there. Early the next morning I headed off to explore the Peloponese, the southern part of mainland Greece which is almost its own island only separated from the mainland by the Corinth Canal.

The Peloponese looks a little like a hand with three fingers pointing south through the azure blue of the Mediterranean Sea, and what could be considered a thumb hitching a lift east through a generous sprinkling of Greek islands towards Turkey.

The first few people I met spoke a little Italian and, since Italian was my default language at the moment, it worked out just fine. I had U.S. dollars and a few *lira* left over from Italy – no *drachmas*, which was the currency of Greece. The amount of *lira* I had wasn't much, but although luckily the first shop I went into accepted it since it was still near the port where arrivals from Italy often needed to offload some leftover Italian currency. It was a Saturday afternoon, and all the banks were shut. No big problem – I had some food left from my cousins, and camping in early March was free since all of the campsites were still officially closed. The weather was still unpredictable so I decided to head up into the hills for a few days and do some free-camping.

It was the weekend before Mardis Gras and the locals in Patras were really getting into the spirit of things. I was glad to escape without being sprayed with shaving cream, or come at the receiving end of any of the other pranks that seemed to go with the holiday. I sought out small roads as soon as I could and headed up into the mountains. Aaah! Peace, quiet, and no cars. I thought that this was heaven, my spirits were light and I whistled to myself as I headed up into my beloved mountains in a new country.

The first time I stopped in a tiny village I realized my mistake. I asked a local if he spoke Italian but he didn't. I could pass for a local, so he started speaking Greek to me. My only experience with Greek was when my friend Stan would speak to his parents or uncle back in New York. They usually spoke it in front of us non-Greek-speaking folk when they were having a huge fight, so the only Greek I knew were choice words or phrases that I probably wouldn't want to use to endear me to anybody.

I pulled out the map, pointed to a village name and followed my finger along a road using the universal sign language of shoulder-shrugging, pointing and a variety of facial expressions that I could probably market as 'the natural facelift facial muscle workout program'. My pronunciation was based on the Italian translation of the Greek name, which was obviously not Greek to him! I handed him the map and pointed to the name of the place I was heading to. It appeared that he couldn't read Greek either, or just couldn't see it with his old eyes, his tethered donkey looked just as confused, so there we all were; me lost, him uncomprehending and his donkey not too concerned.

We spent a few more futile minutes trying to make some sense out of the situation. In the end I just pointed to each road, and with my hands made the gesture of the road going up. He must have thought that nobody would want to go up with a bicycle that looked as laden as his donkey, so he would smile and point to the road I just came in on gesturing the downhill hand sign. I wanted to go up, he wanted to send me down and neither of us had any idea of what the other was saying or any way of figuring it out. After several minutes of this comical play acting that I would dearly love to be able to replay on some cosmic video recorder, he eventually came up with what was probably the best solution he could and poured me a glass of *Retsina*. Hmmmm. When in doubt drink wine.

I was all for going with the flow so I sipped from my glass for a few minutes to appear polite but when I got up to leave he motioned for me to stay put. I was just beginning the pantomime of trying to explain that I needed to go but then his son showed up. My friend smiled, pointing and nodding at 'The One Who Would Make All Things Clear'. As it turned out he did speak passable English, and although he didn't understand why I would want to do anything as silly as cycle my pack mule higher into the mountains, he showed me the road I wanted, asking me more than once if I was sure that was where I wanted to go, because, in his words, "There's nothing up there." I assured him it was where I was headed, and part of the reason was *because* there was nothing up there. He looked as perplexed as the old man who couldn't understand me. I said goodbye, and started my ascent feeling the wine in my body slightly. I was glad that, after spending time with my Italian relatives, I was able to handle the odd midday tipple.

The road did not disappoint; it kept going up but I was in decent shape after all my walking. The cycling, however, always awakened dormant muscles. The now familiar lactic burn in my thighs was a constant reminder of a different reason I preferred the bicycle to my former two-wheeled means of transport. I could feel it strengthening my body. Yes, there were frustrations and at some points the difficulty came to the fore, but like bouts of homesickness, confusion, or anything else, with the will to struggle through, you get stronger. The excitement of finally being on my loaded touring bike once again, destination unknown, made up for any of the small pains in gaining back my fitness which took a few days. The constant climbing and descending was hastening matters that was for sure.

It was heaven to once again have my own means of transport, to say nothing of my kitchen and bedroom whenever I needed them. To be free of train schedules, youth hostels or cheap *pensions* was liberating and as long as I had a few tools, a pump, a spare tube and a piece of rubber for possible tire gashes, I was truly independent. Here I was, penniless (once again), illiterate, and lost in an area that was not bursting with places to stay, that's if you didn't have a small tent. It was packed safely away in my rear left pannier and turned this area into a catalogue of unlimited choice; olive groves, empty fields, or small wooded areas offered a perfect night's sleep with uninterrupted views, and my stove afforded a cooked meal with a hot drink afterward.

The land was covered with a rambling jumble of small farms. The machinery harkened back to a lost time of small holdings and family farms. Large tractors would not have fit on the roads never mind into the fields. I know that my romantic vision of the past does not obscure the facts of how hard a life like that could be but as life has 'progressed', and I see people stuck in the loop of paying mortgages (which actually has Latin or Greek roots meaning death grip, or strangle hold!), insurance, car loans, kid's educations etc. I wonder, is it better to work hard and be in control of your life with the family small holding, or are we better off owned by the banks with our lives being lived out more like indentured servants to the machine called unbridled capitalism? Ah, but I digress as usual.

Each olive tree is nature's work of art; its ancient gnarled branches, beautiful old trunk, and small, matt, unique-colored leaves twisting and blowing in the wind. They were now devoid of all their fruits and leaves but I had seen, and even participated in, these magnificent trees being harvested in Tunisia a few months back, and I assumed the age-old harvesting tradition was much the same here – no mechanization on the smaller groves, a simple cloth spread out under the tree and the family or hired workers whacking the olives off their branches with a long stick. A beautiful harmony of harvesting that has been happening for centuries on the exact same trees! Now, much to my great fortune, I had seen the occasional stacks of pruned olive wood that had not been burnt during the winter months piled in many of the groves that I'd cycled passed. If possible I would ask permission to camp and have a small fire, but people were as rare as any type of motorized traffic. Just out of politeness I might ask a donkey in his field if he minded having a neighbor for the night. I'm sure I wouldn't cause any problems with the local population, donkeys or otherwise.

I'd cycled for a few hours since leaving my father and son duo and the perfect time of day was approaching. There was still some light in the sky, but as it was early spring, it was not too late in the day, and I could put up my tent, eat at a decent time, and have a good night's sleep before being awoken by the sun or the braying of a neighboring donkey. The evening was beautiful and I had enough water for a nice hot cup of tea after my meal of *focaccia*, sausage, and olives all imported from Italy – on the back of my bike!

Breakfast was the last of the Italian fare, which I didn't mind too much, now it was Monday, so I thought I should probably seek out civilization of some sort to get some money. I arrived at another confusing crossing with about six roads converging onto mine and by this time I had no idea where I was on my map. It was detailed, but had nowhere near the detail I would need to navigate the tapestry of tiny tracks and lanes. I passed through a small village with a tiny shop and walked in to ask if anyone spoke Italian or English. No luck. I hadn't had any opportunity to improve my non-existent Greek so I pulled out the map hoping to get directions to a bigger town that might have a bank or shop that would be able to change some money. The same stumbling block; the wonderful, toothless old woman with whom I was talking was undoubtedly a wise, hard-working woman judging by her well-lined face and leathery hands, but she could not read my map either. In that instant I would have traded for someone without so much character if they spoke a word or two of Italian, Spanish or English.

It was my fault I admit. How could I have forgotten something as basic as a dictionary and translation of the Greek Alphabet? After a few minutes of smiles and a tactful dodge of an early morning glass of *retsina* I was none the wiser of where I was or where I was heading. I was also still broke according to the local currency. I looked at the sun coming up over the horizon and headed in the general direction I guessed I wanted to be going. I cycled over challenging rolling countryside, the green-gray of the olive groves interspersed with rich browns of the fields that had been recently tilled and prepared for the spring planting. The continuous circle of the seasons also influenced the migratory movement of workers from Albania, Greece and many of the southeastern European countries coming to harvest, plant, pick, squeeze or whatever else needed to be done so the fields and groves from this small part of Greece could be a part of the food-producing areas of the world.

Greece was so different to the other European countries I had visited. It felt more like Northern Africa than it did Europe. I hadn't been to Turkey yet, but felt as if Greece was only in Europe by name. In my experience the language as well as the lifestyle was more akin to that in Asia than in Europe. The small cafés or teashops were normally only frequented by men. I'm sure the cities would prove different, but here in the countryside tradition ruled, and the lifestyle was one that seemingly hadn't changed in generations.

My bike and I were just enjoying the ride. A loaded bike with panniers not only feels wonderful in terms of self sufficiency, but if the load is properly divided, and the bike is balanced, although as heavy as a small motorcycle, it climbs and descends beautifully. It feels rooted to the road and quite safe.

As my body became more accustomed to the riding again I found my climbing legs, which meant I could ride without being aware of the effort it was taking to propel myself through the countryside. The hours passed quickly, and I stopped once to take a photo. As I regarded the scene I realized that I had just done a loop and was back at a familiar crossroads. It was a small loop, but now I knew which way to turn. Unfortunately, a big downhill. I wanted to stay up where I was but cycling in loops all day was not going to be very helpful. I started heading down, and passed a couple just sitting down to a meal. I was in two minds as to what to do. I knew I had ulterior motives – food! I pedaled up and asked in my near non-existent Greek if any of them spoke Italian, the answer in a bad Italian accent was yes, a little. That was a good start, but these people were definitely not natives, so my next question was "Do you speak English?"

"Yes, actually we are English." I tried to not show my hunger too much, but the bread, and salad, with the smell of fresh olive oil was nearly too much to bear. Fortunately, before I fell to my knees to beg for some food, they spoke again, "Where are you heading to? Stop and join us if you have time, why don't you?"

I need not tell you my answer to that question.

As it turned out, they were a nice middle-aged couple called Mary and Trevor who had moved down to Greece three years previously but didn't seem to be so happy with their decision. As we ate lunch the wine was flowing freely and they were glad to have someone to tell how they thought the Greeks were a backward race and that living here was not easy because of the way the country was run. As we progressed down what ended up being one and a half bottles of wine, the complaints got more vocal and vehement. I was obviously being used as somewhat of a sounding board but it was a small price to pay as they were very pleasant to me and the meal was quite sumptuous and delicious. They happened to be vegetarian and loved all the locally grown fresh veggies that were readily available.

Their story was interesting. They had moved to Greece to establish a guest house for vegetarians. They got down to their property and had to do a lot of work to the house, which was done to a high standard but not yet finished, all by themselves. They had a commanding view, right down to the sea, quite a far way down I might add, and they had cut all their ties with England. By all accounts though, they were still unhappy. It was another great lesson for me. Although they were lovely people; open, friendly and generous, their intentions were good in what they had envisioned for their retreat or guest house, but it seemed to me that the one mistake they made was one I made for years in New York. They hadn't settled whatever frustration they had in their lives in England, so it had just come along with them. Although the external space makes a difference, it's not only about that. Some of my most profound moments have been on the road, but I remembered again how, when I left New York truly happy, I felt freer to continue exploring.

After a couple of hours over lunch the conversation got deeper – I think the drink loosened tongues too. It was obvious that the drinking had got in the way after their move. Their house was nearly done, they had some money left over, and it was too easy to squeak out a simple life, drink the local wine, whinge about the Greeks and the backwardness of the area, rather than take advantage of their privileged position. The guest house was now put on hold. It felt like they were reaching out for someone or something to drag them out of their funk. My trip and outlook was hopefully a breath of fresh air for them as I was taken by the beauty of their home, their garden, the view, and told them time and again that I would love to stay in a place like this. I felt that if they kept up the energy that they must have had when they arrived here, great things would be possible. I knew it was a delicate topic but I casually asked if they drank this much every mealtime and they uncomfortably answered in a very circuitous way, offering me another drink, which I declined. Mary looked at the empty bottle shrugging, and giving a glance over to Trevor.

I would love to think that I may have been that small crack in the door they were looking for. I know they were what I needed at the time. Over all my years of traveling, before and since then, I believe that as every meeting and situation presents itself, we take away from those meetings as much as we're open to. As we are more open and willing, we are presented with situations from which we can learn. Well here was ours and hopefully we *all* benefited from our lunch in the Greek countryside.

As I was getting ready to leave I asked Trevor what he thought the possibility of changing money would be in the next town. He said not good; the banks were on strike till Thursday. Yikes, I thought, this was only Monday. I figured I'd be honest and let them know exactly where I stood. I explained my food situation and asked if they had any bread or cheese I could buy from them I would take their address and mail them some *drachmas* at the end of the week. As it turned out, they didn't really have much either. They shopped mostly every other day for their fresh veggies. They did have some cheese, olives and bread they could spare, but they wouldn't hear of accepting any money. They gave me a good tip about a great place to camp down near the beach, secluded in a stand of trees where they often went for its solitude. Just follow the road down, and I couldn't miss it. I'd been looking to do a fast downhill ever since I got back from Morocco so this was obviously my opportunity.

I found the place near the beach and, as promised, it was beautifully secluded. I pitched my tent and had to change my mindset. I would be here for three nights with little food. I did have a fresh water source which was a bonus, and I had just eaten a big lunch. I was grateful to my English hosts for everything they had provided me with; a home-cooked meal, some leftovers, a quiet place to camp, and most importantly lots to think about while I waited for the strike to be over.

I had made a few careless mistakes entering Greece; my fifty dollar bills were too large a sum for the tiny village shops to change, my lack of *drachmas* stupid, and having no dictionary or working knowledge of the language absolutely ridiculous. Nothing I could do about it now – here I was on a secluded beach in March, the weather was changeable at best, and I had been on this journey since November. Five months was not such a long time, my last journey had been nearly three and a half years and I had stopped and worked in those years, but I had been away from home, and anything familiar for that long. It is definitely life-changing and this trip so far had been quite magical.

My journal came out and became my companion for the next few days. I wrote a couple of letters and not since the High Atlas mountains in Morocco at a creepy hostel with not one of my friends or family knowing I was in that country had I felt so alone. I wasn't lonely, just had a good feeling of aloneness.

I was the only one responsible for where I was. I wasn't angry, I wasn't running from New York, or my friends or family there, but was on a journey, both physical and spiritual. I have always wanted to push myself to the abyss and look over it. I enjoyed looking at where I was in my life, and how I had gotten there. I enjoyed questioning the systems that kept our planet in just enough of a constant state of war to profit a few and care nothing of the rest. At the same time, the world I knew was a world full of beautiful open people. The world I traveled in for the most part was a place where people took you for what you were, not the passport you traveled with. Acceptance of others was directly related to their acceptance of you. Intolerance, I was learning, was why we were constantly at war with each other, but as I traveled and enjoyed lunches with friendly people like Mary and Trevor, living in what many people would consider paradise, I realized that we are all our own worst enemies. We need to get rid of the expectations we have, and it was much in this vein of thought that I spent the next two days and three nights.

My mood went from complete peace to homesickness. I was glad to be where I was; if I had been near an airport, felt strong enough to ride to a bus station or train station, and even had the money to pay for some things, who knows what I might have done in those moments of really missing home, friends, and companionship. It hadn't been my intention to go on this forced retreat, but once again, there was most definitely a positive side to it. The setting was idyllic and the weather changed as much as my state

391

of mind. I was comfortable in the fact that I was far enough from any high tides, as sometimes the wind and rain were quite strong. I wrote furiously in my journal, thinking about how lucky I was to have the strength to stay here with just me and my demons for company. After the third night I was hungry, but not famished. I had not been terribly physical in the past few days and was drinking lots of pure water from the stream feeding into the Ionian Sea. My food had run out a day and a half ago but soon I was going to be able to change money so I began to slowly pack up camp, conserving as much energy as possible as I did so.

I also had Richard Bach's *Jonathan Livingston Seagull* to keep me company. The tiny book lived in a plastic bag tucked behind a flap of my rear pannier. I often forgot it was there, but at certain times he found his way to the forefront; his journey always an inspiration. Even though my life was packed into six small bags I would often find something hidden away under my clothes bag, or squashed beneath my stove and cooking gear.

Packing my tent was a meditative exercise. It was a space I could be in without thinking. I would be able to go through the movements as I had done hundreds of times in the past few years; everything had its place and I would just pack, unzip and rezip panniers, stuff sleeping bags, put reading and writing materials into plastic bags then into certain panniers and before I knew it the bike would be ready to roll.

I was just strong enough to ride. It wasn't far and it was all relatively flat. I made it to the town I was heading for and, to add insult to injury, the bank was closed for lunch. Happily, the shop was open and the shop keeper was friendly. We spoke in about three languages and somehow or another I got my point across. He let me buy some food which I gobbled down while waiting for the bank to open. I must admit, until I saw the doors of the bank actually open, I wasn't totally convinced the strike was over. The shop owner seemed to be convinced though, and when he disappeared through the shop to emerge from the back door before crossing the small road to open the door of the bank, I knew why he was so confident. I changed enough money to see me through the next few weeks. I paid what I owed, filled my panniers with some more food that would serve as meals for the next few days, and off I went up into the highlands again.

The climb was a nice gradient – steep, but not too tough with enough switchbacks to allow me the view to constantly gauge my progress. It wasn't the same road I had come down on but it was heading back up into the same area. In my delight to be able to buy food, I'd forgotten all about asking for a dictionary so I was still going to be illiterate.

I made it up to a quiet farming area, and felt energized. Those few days lost within my journal and stuck on that small piece of secluded beach had sent me into a good mental space and I was ready to cycle both physically and mentally. I was heading east, discovering the Peloponese on the way before island hopping across the Aegean Sea to Turkey. I camped out on the outskirts of a small village that night, and the next day would be in glorious sunshine.

The weather looked as if it was making a turn for the better but the winter of 91-92 was a tough one for Greece and Turkey. I was waiting around for the more stable months of late April and May before heading into Turkey. I had a big breakfast of cereal and milk – I was getting used to the UHT milk which seemed to be the norm in Europe. I'd never had it before and at first thought it was undrinkable but like all things, it doesn't take long to get used to. I had a hot cup of tea, some bread and packed up while eating.

The last conversation I'd had was with the English couple – other than the few interactions with the shop keeper/banker. I hadn't had much human contact recently. My hair was getting long, and I was growing a beard. I hadn't thought of it but I probably hadn't had a wash since I entered Greece – a swim in the sea once, but it had been a short dip since it was freezing cold, and, other than a splash here and there, I was probably not very sociable once again.

As I cycled out of the field I noticed a lot of school kids coming down the road from the school I'd happened to be camping near, and they were as surprised to see me as I was them. They were young and happy to practice, "Hello, how are you?" and various other sentences in English. It wasn't exactly stimulating conversation but it was fun. One of the older students asked where I was from. I answered and spoke a few more words before his teacher arrived. She was a nervous-looking young woman, probably about my age or perhaps younger. I was aware that she seemed dubious of this character talking to her students.

She came up to me, and asked, "Parle Italiano?"

I answered "Si" without thinking as she then launched into perfect full-pelt Italian. It was polite but was beyond my comprehension level. She probably assumed I was Italian by my quick answer and Mediteranean looks. I stopped her and asked if she spoke Spanish. Till this day I don't know why I said Spanish and not English. When she said, "No", I asked, "English?" but by this time the interchange had gotten weird. From her viewpoint I was babbling, probably smelled awful, and looked a bit strange talking to her young students.

Her next move was to put herself between me and her class and shuffle them away from me. Instead of trying to explain myself, which I thought would make matters worse, I just laughed inside at the ridiculousness of it all. I got on my bike and pedaled away with a quick wave at the students, grateful that she hadn't called the police. What would I say? "Um yes, I have been camping for a week or so with no money, I just wanted to speak to someone in English so I told her I spoke Italian, then Spanish... blah blah blah..." I would have been put somewhere to babble and have a bath probably never to be seen again.

I headed out of the village and made a conscious choice not to ask any directions until I was well away from this village. I cycled along, one half of me feeling great, and the other half-feeling like a right fool. Sure I was on a path of discovery but I was also traveling in a world of languages and people. I needed to get a dictionary and someone to write out the Greek alphabet for me, and soon. I didn't want to continue feeling so insecure about my communication skills, especially if I planned on being alone for the foreseeable future.

When I got to the next village I stopped in a tea shop, had a cup of coffee and tried to look as respectable as I could. My confidence was restored when I was approached by a few locals. We shared a table and a rudimentary conversation about my trip in English. I asked if they knew of a place I could buy a dictionary and they told me Patras. I was certainly not going to head there as it was miles back to where I had come from, so for the moment, I was still illiterate, but at least I now had a plan. The next person I saw that spoke passable English I would get to write down the Greek Alphabet so I could at least read my map.

That person would come very soon. Heading out of town I heard someone shout, "Hello! Hello!" I turned to look, and saw a youngish, well-dressed guy waving to me. I cycled back to him and it turned out he was the teacher in the local school. He didn't mind my smell or looks, and invited me back to his school. Best of all he spoke English.

We walked back together to meet the students who were a lively bunch and a little older than the last group of kids I met. We went through all the, "Hello, how are you?" simple conversations before I told him I used to be a teacher in New York City. He translated for the kids and there were lots of, "Ooh"s and "aah"s, "New York City!" etc. I told him my alphabet dilemma and he got on the case. Although he didn't produce a dictionary for me, he did come up with a hand-written Greek Alphabet with all their sounds and some photocopied sheets from his students' English class. This marked the beginning of my becoming literate. I was getting into my stride and that night, before dinner, I vowed to myself to not go to sleep until I knew all the sounds of the twenty-four letters of the Greek Alphabet.

I was now feeling quite good in many ways. I spent a few hours with the class speaking of my travels, my life in New York, and they hung on every word I said. A small village in rural Greece, a tiny school, and this strange guy on a bike, who, in the students' minds, had decided to cycle to *their* village. I would get that question often; "Why did you decide to cycle to our tiny village from New York?" Sometimes I even had to explain that an airplane ride was also involved. Even some adults would ask how long it took to ride from New York to where we stood.

I was interested in them as well. I asked what their parents did, how they liked living where they did, and learned that most of those students had never even been to Athens and one of the younger ones had never been to the sea only a few miles away! It was a real peasant area in many ways – peasant in the real meaning of the word – person of the land. I also learned that not too far from the village was Olympia, the site of the original Olympic Games. Not to be confused with Mt. Olympus, home of the Greek gods, this was north of Athens on the Greek mainland. The town of Sparta was not far away either. All these ancient exotic names from my history classes in school were being brought to life.

I decided I would head for Olympia the next day. That night I would free camp and would have to retain my, shall I say, natural odor, for one more night. The day was drawing to a close and I realized I had spent most of the afternoon in the school. I waved goodbye to my friendly class and pedaled off. I spotted a camping sign and headed for the campsite. Maybe, just maybe, it would be open. When I arrived it looked as if it had not been open for quite a while, but looks can be deceiving. It does not take long for a campsite to look abandoned. Overgrown grass, untidy shower block, and no one around, all add to the feeling. I lifted my bike over the chain, with a sign hanging askew from the links, which I now knew said 'CLOSED'. The shower block was open so I went in to have a look, and luckily the water was still on. No hot water, that would have been too much to ask, but I needed a shower and a cold shower would have to suffice. Before I braved that chilly experience I decided to set up my tent. I got everything ready, took out some clothes that I hadn't worn since they'd been washed in Italy, and even treated myself to some underwear!

I took one last look around and when I was sure I was alone, I walked into the shower block, stripped down, and turned on the water. After a few choking gurgles a decent flow of water emerged from the shower head, but it was ice cold. I had gotten used to cold showers and, though I never looked forward to them, I knew that after the first minute or so your body got used to it. I forced myself to stay under the freezing stream of water for a few seconds, gasping and hopping, before I took out my soap. This was the scary part – once you soap up, you have made a commitment, because then you need to rinse off! I made the brave decision to wash my hair too and, after a nice soaping up and scrubbing down, I felt like a new man. The one good effect that cold showers have is making you feel a lot warmer when you step out and get fully dressed. It was a clear night, and a little cool, but I was feeling clean, hungry, and excited to have my Greek Alphabet and a few pages of words to learn.

I got back to the tent, crawled in and dove under my sleeping bag for a few moments. There is something about a tent that always makes me feel like a kid and I believe it's not only me as I have spoken to other adults who admit that, once they hear that rustle of nylon and smell that particular camping smell, they are also transported back to their youth and it's as much as they can do to not dive into the coziness that awaits inside. I was also hungry and after a few minutes of snuggling into the warmth of my tent and getting everything ready for my after dinner studies, I re-emerged from my cozy cocoon to cook up a meal of pasta, tuna and cheese.

What a transformation; clean for the first time since Italy, fed, and besides that unfortunate encounter with the first school teacher and her class, most of my interactions in Greece so far had been positive. My few days of fasting by the beach and my silent retreat of sorts had cleared my mind, the homesickness had passed and I now felt ready to see what was in store here in Greece and beyond. I stayed up quite late and, true to my word, knew the sound of every letter of the Greek Alphabet before turning in.

The next morning started out cloudy and windy so I packed up and headed for Olympia. It was not such a long day to get there and the roads were pleasant and quite devoid of traffic. When I arrived in the small village, it was obvious that the villagers and surrounding area made their living from the archeological site of Olympia. There was a small hostel in the village and I decided I would stay there. A bed, hmm that would be nice. It was almost a shame I felt so clean as there was even a hot shower! I was surprised to meet so many other travelers in the site. The hostel was pretty empty – there were a few backpacks around, but no other cyclists. Too bad, what a great part of the world to cycle travel – given about another month for the weather to settle, this would be cycling paradise.

The Olympic site was interesting and had the air of an archeological dig rather than a tourist trap. There was fencing around some of the parts where excavation was being done, and besides the few vendors selling postcards; I felt more like I had accidentally stepped onto a worksite, rather than one of the premier tourist sites of the Peloponese. As usual, I quite liked the lack of commercialization – maybe in the high-season things would be different, but like the campsites, it had a feeling of 'not just yet'.

The highlight of my stay was to eat in a restaurant, meet a few travelers and enjoy some free flowing conversation. Most people were traveling with rented cars and were older than me. I met one couple getting around by bus and they were interested in my bike travels – interested in the sort of way that it looked like they might even be thinking of that possibility for the next time they took a trip somewhere. They asked about equipment, logistics, difficulty, language problems etc. We wound up eating together; theirs were the two backpacks I had seen in the hostel. They were English – I was meeting quite a lot of English people on this leg of my journey. They were heading to Sparta the next day but I was feeling a pull to head down to the water. I still felt I was about two or three weeks ahead of myself as far as the weather was concerned. The hostel was run by a local family who were very kind. They made us all a hot drink and we sat in the common room until bedtime. Sleeping in a bed was nice, but not the treat I expected it to be – my sleeping bag and mat were serving me just fine.

The next morning breakfast was simple; coffee and bread rolls, perfect. The day was dry, but threatening. I said goodbye to the English couple, and as they headed off to the bus stop, I hopped on my bike and thought I saw jealousy in their eyes at the simplicity and freedom of bike travel. Maybe not, they also might have been quite happy to be getting on a bus on this blustery day in mid-March.

I had been told by my friendly school teacher two days back that over 10,000 English words had their roots in Greek, and I would learn during my time in Greece that by sounding out words I could figure out many of their meanings because of that link. My illiteracy was turning into a challenge and my working knowledge of Greek was improving all the time. All the niceties; hello, goodbye, thank you, you're welcome, also numbers and who, what and where questions too were all in my vocabulary now. I pedaled past a sign that said 'Camping Kyparissia' but didn't pay it too much attention.

I headed down towards the sea and after a few hours of cycling, I stopped for lunch and bought a loaf of bread to enjoy with a hot soup. After lunch the road was keeping near to the coast, but not hugging it. As often is the case for coastal riding it was up and down but pretty all the same. I saw a sign for the village Kyparissia. It looked like a good place to take a break. I found a *pension*/restaurant with a nice view overlooking the small harbor. I went in, ordered a hot drink, took out my journal and wrote for a little while. The owner was not over-friendly and was quite gruff in his dealing with me. I asked if there were any campsites around and he said no but he had empty rooms. At that point it started to rain. I didn't want to get into any discussions yet about a room, but didn't feel that I would like to stay in this place with just me and him; certain personalities do not suit running certain businesses. If he had been a nice guy, what with the weather being like it was, I probably would have considered staying the night, and even buying an evening meal.

Still, I was enjoying the view and my hot coffee. I looked off past the harbor and down the road a little further and saw what looked to me like a campsite. Immediately the faded blue and white sign on the outskirts of Olympia flashed across my internal eye – Camping Kyparissia. I went to pay and asked the owner what that was over there, pointing down past the harbor. He mumbled something about it being a campsite, but it was closed. I did not want to get into an argument, so I paid my bill, donned my wet weather gear, and cycled off. I headed towards the campsite, and when I was nearly there, I passed a small café. I stopped to look in when a big guy came out, saying in near perfect English, "Hey, are you American? You want a job on the campsite?" I was taken aback, but my answer, standing there in the pouring rain, feeling cold, was, "Yeah sure."

Theo was working with the three brothers who owned the campsite, getting it ready for the season which began in a few weeks. They needed a hand, and I looked big and strong according to Theo – a family friend who seemed more like the manager of the place. He figured I was American because who else would be nutty enough to be cycling around Greece in March? Not a Greek, he assured me. I didn't have a reply to that as this logic had led him to the correct assumption. We negotiated three meals a day, a bed in one of the small rooms they had on site, and if I wanted to stay on until the season, that would then become paid work. I said we'd take it a day at a time and he showed me to the room I'd be in. I put my bike in a small covered courtyard, unpacked what I would need and left the rest on the bike. I felt I had come a long way from feeling lost and illiterate just a week ago. What a whirlwind adventure so far.

I wound up staying for a little over two weeks although they were trying to tempt me to stay for the season. We all worked hard together; mowing lawns, pruning trees, lying slate floors after collecting the slate from a nearby natural quarry. The food was delicious as one of the brothers was a retired chef from Athens. Theo was the only one who spoke English to such a high standard. It came out that he'd grown up in Australia, and moved back to Greece when he was fifteen years old. He had a Bulgarian wife and an adopted daughter. I was taken in as one of the family and we all ate together. Although we worked hard, the workdays were not too long, after all, it still was Greece; late morning starts, long lunches, coffee breaks, stopping a few hours before dinner. The campsite was a labor of love for the brothers – no need to kill themselves.

Theo was like an adopted brother, and his command of English I am sure was invaluable for the season. That was why they wanted me to stay – I spoke English and decent Spanish and even though my Italian was poor it was better than any of theirs. A few campers came and went while I was there. The three that stick in my mind are a young English couple and a lone traveler from Norway. We stayed up late at night having philosophical discussions and I think they stayed on at the campsite longer than they expected because a nice vibe developed between us. The Norwegian guy recommended a book – *The Prophet* by Kahlil Gibran which I had never come across. I wrote down the name and have since always owned a copy or given it as a gift. Simple, poetic and enlightening is my unprofessional critique of its pages, and if my two weeks in the campsite only introduced me to that book, it was well worth it.

After they left the weather was starting to become warmer and more predictable. I had been having Greek lessons by immersion working with the brothers every day and had only been on my bike for a few weeks since I left New York in November. I was itching to get cycling again. Working on a campsite for the season in southern Greece was tempting but I wanted to be traveling. I let the brothers know I would be leaving after the next weekend and they were sad to see me go. They didn't comprehend my urge to cycle and explore but saw I was determined and not to be deterred. They invited me back to work there after the season was over as there was still a lot of work to be done and I told them I would think about it.

So from being lost, broke, illiterate and homesick in Greece, I cycled out of Kyparissia well-fed with a good working knowledge of Greek, heading into the spring and slightly more stable, warmer weather. I had made a few friends, learned a couple of building skills, and even had a standing job offer both for now, or in the future.

As long as the weather held I was happy. The cycling was getting easier – I was finding my cycling legs once again. The Peloponese is almost like a country unto itself. The area I had just cycled from was an olive growing area and quite beautiful. I was now vaguely heading for the port town of Monemvasia on one of the 'fingers' to catch a boat to a small island called Chios where I could continue on to Turkey. I found myself on the middle peninsula called Mani which is famous for its honey. That sounded good to me – honey was a nice treat, and the Greeks like pouring it on the top of their yogurt, and like Northern Africa, layered it thickly on top of pastry and nuts to create *baklava* and many other tantalizing desserts. I liked mixing it with peanut butter and spreading it on some fresh bread for a quick energy boost. Now I was unknowingly heading to one of the most celebrated areas in Greece famous for its apiculture.

On the Mani peninsula the wind had kicked up, but at least it was dry. My Greek – although far from fluent – was enough to get me by in most situations now, and I was feeling I could pedal all day. The days were slowly getting longer, and the flowers in this part of Europe were already in bud as were the trees. Spring is the time for the swarming of the bees, finding new places to build their hives, so the countryside is alive with the buzzy little fellows. I had no known allergies to their stings and felt quite safe cycling around the peninsula. When I was warned by another traveler I had met on his scooter that there were a lot of bees on the road I was heading out of town on I registered his warning but didn't let it worry me too much. He'd been traveling downhill on his small scooter, and it was true I would be pedaling up the hill and more exposed to a possible threat of stings but it was the only way on for me, unless I backtracked through Pirgos, the way I came. I decided to continue on.

I started out early in the morning with blue skies and a strong wind. The climb was going to be challenging, that much I knew. I had the benefit of the wind pushing me, and it wasn't too hot. I wouldn't fancy cycling in Greece in high summer. I had now timed the trip to be following the seasonal changes perfectly. I shouldn't get too hot, and would be in the more northern parts of Europe for the summer. I started out my climb with a light, long-sleeved jacket, but quickly stripped down to cycling shorts and a tee-shirt. My long hair was wet with sweat and the sweat on my arms from the hard work was quickly evaporating in the wind. I needed to drink plenty to replace the lost fluid. The occasional bee buzzed by, but it didn't seem threatening in any way and I was already used to more bees than usual on the peninsula. I looked up after about an hour and a half of steady climbing and saw what looked like a black line stretched across the road. I couldn't figure it out at first but soon realized that what I was looking at was a highway of bees crossing the road I was on about 500 meters ahead. I got nervous looking at the sheer number of bees there were. The English guy had said there were a lot more than usual, but this appeared to be millions – an unbelievable number of bees.

I continued riding for a couple of hundred meters and then actually started to hear the bees. I had no experience with bees and thought maybe I could cycle through them calmly and they would keep off me. I kept going and was under the 'highway' when a bee landed on me and stung me. I tried to keep calm but then a few bees got stuck in the curls of my hair and then I started to lose it. I got stung a few more times before really freaking out which, of course, is the one thing you should never do around bees. I started swatting the bees from my hair and now it felt like I was covered in them. I jumped off my bike, ran to the other side of the swarm, and ripped off my shirt. I tried to calm down thinking that the bees would probably be more attuned to my frightened body chemistry. I was making it all up as I knew nothing beyond the basics of 'don't panic' and I had already done that!

Thankfully I wasn't covered head to toe in bees, because, allergic or not, that would probably have been the end of my earthly travels. I made it to the other side, with my shouts of, "Help!" falling on barren ground. My cries were more a reflex reaction than a genuine plea. The buzzing in my ears was finally over, a few squashed bees lay around on the ground, and my heart was approaching its normal forty-eight beats per minute, rather than what I was pretty sure must have been closer to two hundred a few minutes ago. I assessed the damage and found I only had seven stings. I was out of immediate danger, but now I just stood there and stared at my bike lying directly under the obvious, black, buzzing highway. I tried to logically think of what I should do next.

What attracted the bees; my sweat, my smell, the fact I just got in their way? It was all just guess work. The one thing I did know was that I had to get my bike back. I wiped down my sweat and then tied my hair up with my tee-shirt, took a few deep breaths and kept on repeating to myself, "keep calm, keep calm" like a mantra. I knew I shouldn't make any sudden moves and start swatting bees again if they did land on me when I was so close to the swarm. The plan was to keep low, grab my bike, and drag it out from under bee highway. I was scared but tried to keep relatively calm. As I approached my bike a bee or two landed on me, right near my ears. I resisted the strong urge to swat it away as I grabbed the rack of my bike and pulled not caring if I ripped panniers or scratched bike parts – it was a matter of just getting the bike without getting stung. I pulled the bike far enough away to pick it up and wheel it. Once I was satisfied there was enough distance between me and the bees I swatted off the few bees which had landed on me and fortunately didn't get stung again.

After that unnerving experience, hearing the buzz of a nearby bee did make me tingle a bit more, and found I had developed an anxiety around them that I hadn't had before. Not in a big way, but it was there. I could understand how children develop phobias after any unfortunate experience with dogs, bees or whatever. I was glad I was leaving Mani rather that entering it. As I got up over the hill and made it to Gytheion as my stings were starting to swell a little. I bought some honey thinking I'd earned a nice big pot of it. The sting near my eye puffed up a bit, but it was my arm with four stings that was starting to feel tight. I ate some honey and yogurt, then made a peanut butter and honey sandwich. I was using the honey as an anti-bee sting serum. I'm not sure there is any science behind it, but it sure tasted great.

As I slowly pedaled in the countryside with my stings pulsing, I thought how that tiger I met in Carlos Castaneda's book all those years ago always popped his head out of the bushes to keep me in check. A few nights later in my tent in Monemvasia after my stings started to go down, I realized how dangerously close I'd come to something much more severe than a swollen face and arms. Years later, talking to friends in France who keep bees, and hearing horror stories of bee keepers dying from stings, and how common it can be among their ranks, I thought back to how lucky I was. Just like my young cousin riding on the road in front of his house in broad daylight, or any of the other freak accidents which happen every day to people just like us all, it is that thin line we walk every day, and the reason we should appreciate everyone of those waking moments in between.

However, fortunately I was alive and well. Greece had thrown up a few small hurdles but they had been surmountable. Traveling was about the whole journey, destinations are nice to keep in the back of your mind, but if it gets in the way of the voyage itself, then I personally wouldn't enjoy the open-ended travel. It's much like life – sure we have a vague idea of where we may be heading but I love savoring the moments in between. How often do things work out differently than we plan them anyway? In the end I had made it to my bike, briefly pedaled in Greece, but my boat was soon leaving for the tiny island of Chios for my last few days in Europe before entering Turkey. My trip so far had other ideas than a European cycle tour.

# A Turkish Experience

Turkey is a multi-faceted country with the Mediterranean and Black Seas lapping at its shores. Bulgaria, Iraq, Iran, Syria and Georgia, the ex-Soviet republic, are its land borders. The ancient Biblical cities of Ephesus and Antioch, and such wonderful natural wonders as Cappadoccia underground cave dwellings all add to the mix. The Black Sea Mountains, miles of coastline, and possibly a glimpse of the snowy peaks of Mt. Ararat in the southeastern part of the country, where rumor has it that Noah's Ark lies encapsulated in ice, make the country an outdoorsman's dream. According to some historical accounts even good ol' St. Nicholas, of Santa Claus fame, has traced his routes to a small village in the south western part of the country. With all this just waiting, how could I not be tempted?

The modern form of the language was something the father of the Turkish Republic, Mustafah Kemal 'Attaturk', loved by the Turks, and hated by the Greeks, had put scholars to work on shortly after the modern borders of what is now known as Turkey were established. It's an ancient language dating back to the 4th century B.C. and has linguistic roots in Arabic, Persian, Azerbaijani and Turkmen. The current Latin based written alphabet came into use in 1929 – six years after the founding of the new republic – replacing the Arabic alphabet. It's a contemporary, constantly evolving language for a modern moderate Muslim country which is trying to edge its way into the European Community. The language is much like the country, bridging the old and the new. Turkey spans many worlds; the modern and ancient, the moderate and conservative, the rich and the poor, Europe and Asia, Kurdistan and Iraq, The Bible and The Koran – a true crossroads of culture and history.

When I decided to head to Turkey from Greece, the warnings could not have been more dire. The Greeks, understandably so, have a huge grudge to bear towards the Ottoman Empire and history has unfortunately shown us that these grudges are buried deep and last for generations; many Greeks still refusing to call Turkey's most well-known city by its modern name, Istanbul, still refering to it as Constantinople. Healing the hurt is a slow process. I knew that I was somewhat removed from the emotion of it all but in many ways, with an American Passport in my panniers, I was still very much a part of the world's problems. Like Turkey, I also felt caught between two worlds. My bloodline somehow or another connected me on a deeper level to this part of the world, but on entering a village or town my bicycle and panniers instantly set me apart.

It was late March when I found myself landing in Cesme, on the East Coast of Turkey – a good place to start my Turkish experience – and I was raring to go, buoyed up by my recent cycling in Greece, the weight of my bike familiar beneath me and the content feeling of having almost everything I needed right there with me. It was strange to be on the far western borders of the continent where my current and ongoing love affair with bicycles had begun in a small country of islands called Japan. What a different part of Asia this was.

In many ways it felt as if I had not left Greece – the café culture and lack of women in those cafés seemed familiar. It was easy to see where the two cultures had blurry lines of division. The Orthodox Greek Religion and the Muslim faith of the Turks both had the Old Testament at their roots. The amount of Christian history in Turkey was astounding to me and it felt in many ways that I was on some sort of biblical pilgrimage.

The friendliness of the people was immediately appealing. In the tourist town of Cesme it was still easy to find real true Turkish hospitality. I was pushing my fully laden bike through the narrow streets of the sprawling market place when someone addressed me in English. "Do you want to buy a carpet?"

I laughed, looked at my bike, and made a face as if to say, "Does it look like I have room for a carpet?"

He didn't miss a beat in inviting me in for a cup of tea. One of those wonderful cups of tea which would delay my cycling in Turkey many a half an hour or hour before I realized I had to learn to say no or never make it very far. This was my first day – my first half hour even – and here I was sipping a delicious 'apple *chai*' in the middle of a carpet shop. How perfect!

After I declined the offer of buying any of their beautifully made, intricately woven carpets, it had transpired that, lo and behold, one of their cousins owned a *pension*. I tried to explain that I'd just arrived and wasn't ready to book any accommodation yet. I had my tent and would probably camp out. I wound up going to see their cousin's *pension* out of politeness, which was clean, airy and reasonably priced as well. I went on to explain further that I thought the *pension* was great but I wanted to spend a few months cycling the whole length of their wonderful country. I thought the price was very fair, explaining that I had unlimited time but limited funds and would rather not sleep in too many *pensions*, but put my tent up where possible. They were intrigued with the idea, and then looked at me differently.

"You want to do all this so you can explore my country?" one of them asked.

"Yes," I replied.

The man looked almost overcome, his eyes glistening. "You come and stay in my house," he said with sudden and unexpected force.

"No, no, no. Really, thank you, but no."

He was already opening the door to his humble dwelling to show me inside, my protestations falling on deaf ears. We passed through what looked like the entrance way to a long corridor with doors off to all sides.

"Put your bike here." Then he pointed to a bed that looked like it had been slept in the night before, "and you sleep here. If you are willing to cycle through my country at least I can be the first to offer you hospitality."

Now it was my turn to feel overwhelmed. My gut feeling was that this man and his friends were sincere but I had only been off the boat from Greece – where the warning of how terrible the Turks are had been ringing in my ears for days – for a little less than an hour. I was adjusting to a whole new part of the world and being given a bed in a stranger's house out of the blue was all a bit much. It must have shown on my face. My new friend put his hand on my arm. "Don't worry, everything is safe, you have my word. I may be a carpet seller and a businessman, but I am Turkish, and my words are spoken from my heart."

Feeling mollified, I thanked him profusely and went to my pannier for a bag that I would need for buying some food.

"Go," said my host, "enjoy our village, we will eat lunch together at midday. See you then."

I walked away a little dazed, thinking, 'Well, I guess this is Turkish hospitality.' I wandered through the town looking for food and must have been invited in for ten cups of *chai*. The gossip highway had been busy that morning and everyone already knew that I was the cyclist staying with Abdullah.

Lunch was a simple affair and, true to the Muslim way, there were no women around when we men all ate together. The food was delicious and I was fortunate that they all spoke English. They told me that the town had lots of tourists from Finland who were always drunk. Unfortunately during the couple of days I stayed, it seemed to be true. From daybreak to sunset I would see a lot of people staggering around town.

I ate lunch and dinner with Abdullah but every time I offered to give him any money he would never accept. I never saw anything else of the house except for the long room in which I slept and the modest bathroom through one of the doors off the hallway – we always ate in the back of the carpet shop. There were young kids around who stared a lot, but they must have either been on strict orders not to bother me, or some of the best behaved kids I met in Turkey. All the kids I met on the street were friendly and very inquisitive, eager to try out a few English words on me if given the chance. The kids in the house were always polite and displayed an obvious deference to me when they saw me. Maybe it was because I was a guest in their house? I never knew, and didn't want to ask in case I could not explain it well enough and got someone in trouble by being misunderstood. When I left, they all made me feel like I was their son going off to the wars. I had eventually managed to meet some of the women in the family and I was given a box of apple *chai* to drink at night when I was camping.

This was my entry into Turkey. The openness and hospitality was not to end there -although it came in many different shapes and forms. With only my instinct and experience from years of traveling alone to go on, I headed towards the east, a few days from Cesme on the bike, and found myself in a place called Ephesus.

Ephesus, of biblical fame, is one of the many places St. Paul spent much time while putting his indelible stamp on history. A man who never met Christ, and spent a lot of time crucifying early Christians, turned his fervor from wiping out the small fledgling group to spreading his interpretation of Christianity with an almost equal ferocity throughout Asia-Minor and Greece. Paul's zealous anti-female writings always rubbed me the wrong way. I remembered reading Nikos Kazantsakis' book, *The Last Temptation of Christ*. There's a scene where Paul meets Jesus and shrugs him off, telling him that his own preachings and interpretations of Jesus were far more powerful than Jesus himself ever was. That dialogue always makes me chuckle – Nikos and I were more on the same wavelength than Paul and I ever could be. Once again, as in Tunisia, I could imagine the Biblical times as I walked the ancient streets and wished I could have heard Paul speak for myself to see if my impressions were correct.

The old city is extremely well-preserved – to walk the cobbled streets of that city whose name was mentioned so often in the Sunday Masses of my childhood, "A letter from Paul to the Ephesians" – was almost eerie; the same walls, the same window frames, the same doorways; a mere shell of what they had once been. Many thoughts rolled around in my head about Paul and the spread of Christianity.

When I was younger I had bought the 'Greatest Story Ever Told', only because I wasn't ever told of any other one. Now I had witnessed and read too much to actually think that what Christianity had done in the name of God or Christ was always a good thing. How much blood had been shed – pillaging, murder and even genocide? How many cultures had been swallowed up – ways of life changed forever, all hidden beneath a mask called religion, or even more hypocritically, faith? After all, other religions existed and had their own mysteries. I'd read *The Book Of the Hopi*, and was surprised to see a story about a great chief who'd sacrificed his son's life to save his tribe from their evil ways – the parallels were astounding. As far as I could see, The Christian Empire and any other conquering, colonizing empire are all much the same. From what I had witnessed first-hand on my travels, any ideal spread by bloodshed, or sold under false pretenses isn't something to romanticize. That tack is fraught with danger, and just leads us down bloody road after bloody road throughout history.

As I walked through Ephesus pondering all this, I wondered; how far we have come as humans? We only need to look at our current wars, and obsessive need to control and conquer what is different to see the parallels with playground squabbles. We may yet be in the infancy of our race's development.

I spent an hour or so sitting on a wall, writing in my journal, contemplating everything running through my head, when a small boy with a big toothy smile of milk teeth asked me if I wanted to buy a postcard. I looked at his innocent face, big brown eyes, dirty skin, and bought a few. I stopped writing in my journal, looked around and grinned. Even though I was able to get lost in the depths of my mind I never lost sight of the fact that my life and travels had taken me to some of the most beautiful places on our planet. No matter what the media wanted us to believe, the world was still mostly good, and the people in it all just wanting the same thing; the ability to live a life free from fear and control and a basic level of happiness.

On this sunny day most people walking the ancient streets of modern-day Ephesus were from anywhere but Turkey. It was packed with travelers, tourists and people hawking everything from carpets to postcards. The crumbling walls and buildings were alive with history, but you needed to peep past the onslaught of modernity to sense it.

After hours of meandering through and taking in the atmosphere, I decided to cycle out of town and up the hill to a place called *Miriama* which was, according to local history, the last home of Mary, Jesus's mother. She supposedly lived there with John, the disciple told to spread the word of Christ in Asia-Minor. It was a tiny house with a spring which was said to benefit from holy powers. I was quite surprised at the lack of lines and craziness surrounding the place – visions of the nearly deserted Lumbini in Nepal came to mind. I felt almost alone and wandered over to the spring from time to time to splash my face with the cool water. I've heard stories of other such places – Knock in Ireland, Lourdes in France, countless sights in The Holy Land – where hotels, gift shops and crowds are the norm. I was glad it wasn't like that here.

I had now been in Turkey over a week and had slept in my tent only twice. In Ephesus there were enough backpacker hostels with dorm rooms and guest houses at cheap prices so I opted to stay in a guest house to meet some other travelers.

For some odd reason Selcuk, the closest town to ancient Ephesus to stay, seemed to be filled with resident New Zealanders – or 'Kiwis' – who either owned or managed these guest houses, and were even more talented carpet salesmen than the Turks. I wasn't quite sure why nearly everyone felt compelled to buy a carpet when in Turkey, but for me it was great to go to all the carpet selling parties. I would drink and snack for free, and watch the ingenious sales tactics of the Kiwis selling carpets to about 90% of the people staying in their cheaply priced lodgings. I even started getting pressure from the travelers who had bought carpets. The selling started mainly after everyone had had a few beers – free drinks being the main sales tactic. After the buyers had forked over the cash, or handed over their credit cards, the feeling changed, and then they would start to focus on the few who hadn't bought a carpet by saying things like, "C'mon you *have* to buy a carpet when you're in Turkey" or "Why aren't you buying a carpet? I did" etc. I didn't like the feeling and early on my second morning I mounted my bike – thankfully not laden with a carpet or *kilim* (much like a carpet, but woven flat) bought from a Kiwi salesman – and pedaled a few kilometers down the road to a small village called Cal.

Now Cal, I must admit, was not where I intended to stay for the night. It was a small, non-descript place about an hour from where there had to be thousands of tourists throughout the year. I assumed there would be some westerners walking around taking in a breath of fresh air away from the buy and sell feeling of the Ephesus/Selcuk area, but there were none.

There was a small market going on, and I stopped to top up on some food I might need for camping that night. I leant my bike on a wall and was about to get my lock out when an old bearded guy appeared and gave me a look as if to say, "No need to do that here, I will watch it." So I left it unlocked and he nodded at me and smiled. It was so nice to be back in that energy and I went off happily to the market which was bustling; vegetables, spices and many other household things on offer. I bought a few food items that would keep along with some cheese. When I got back to my bike, my wizened-faced old man was still there and he met me with smiling eyes saying, "You see, no problem!" He watched curiously as I packed my bike, and as I pedaled off he called after me, "*Allah hasmaladik,*" which translated roughly to "God be with you," or "God is good." I repeated it back to him enjoying that interconnectedness of the many salutations around the world recognizing a higher essence. It's also the Turkish way to say goodbye.

I was cycling out of the village when a small teashop appeared at the edge of town with a few men out in front. They beckoned me in for a cup of tea. I knew the day was young so thought, why not? A cup of tea won't hurt. It was the usual inside; smoke, the smell of coffee and tea, and no women. All the tables were full of men playing either cards or a tile game that looked something like *mahjong*. I couldn't resist doing a few of my best card tricks and this won over most of the men in the place. I had a few more *chai* and pretty soon it was nearing lunchtime. I motioned that I'd better get going but then was invited by one of the men to join him for lunch at a small place across the street. The teashop owner made me promise to come back to say goodbye.

I didn't have a big lunch because I hadn't done anything since that morning to work up an appetite. When we went back across the road so I could say goodbye, a different man came out from the café, and a thick Australian accent greeted me, "We would like it if you stayed in the village for the night, we think you're a funny guy and want to hear more of your stories."

Funny, so much for my magic tricks inspiring awe! It's true we'd all been having a good laugh together, but I slightly protested, "Well I need to get pedaling, I want to get out to the east." I saw that, once again, my protestations were falling on deaf ears.

"These guys think if you pedaled all the way from New York to their village, you might as well stay for a night," said the Australian.

Once again in this land of hospitality, how could I argue? Should I explain that it was impossible to cycle all the way from New York? I decided I'd save the geography lesson. "Is there a place I can spend the night?" I asked.

"Sure, right across the road. He has a room." It turned out to be even cheaper than the place back in Selcuk, and more authentic.

I unpacked what I would need from my panniers and headed out for a walk on the outskirts of the village. The surrounding countryside was gorgeous. It was lusciously green this time of year but there was still that feeling of early spring chill left in the air which made for nice cycling. For a few minutes I felt frustration that I wasn't riding but then other thoughts came in to my mind; 'This is exactly why you are cycling, to enjoy the people and see what life throws at you, your bicycle is merely a tool, you are traveling first and cycling second.' It was true for me, although I must admit I did love the riding. I enjoyed it more than any other mode of travel; the self sufficiency, the unlimited possibilities of small roads, the openness of the people you met. As well as all that, sitting on buses all the time didn't build up your appetite like pedaling did. It was wonderful to take guilt-free pleasure in sampling all the foods of the world, knowing that it was your fuel as well.

Another benefit of long-distance cycle touring is that it's usually far less expensive because you are getting into parts of the country that normally haven't been well-worn by other travelers and local prices are always far cheaper than the otherwise inflated prices in areas where travelers, backpackers or tourists are the norm. Locals are always interested when you pull in on your bike. It might feel overwhelming at first, but the more you cycle, the more it becomes a part of who you are, and the experience is something that gets better and better. Your fitness level on a long-distance tour becomes something you just take for granted; although my legs were building up their own muscle memory, sometimes the pain of finding the fitness reared its head. The weight of my bike became unimportant, and I grew accustomed – actually preferred the feel of my loaded down bike. I would just pick roads that look nice, or marked as scenic, not taking into account if they were mountainous or not. I'm not a proponent of overpacking, but since giving my camera away and traveling with my smaller Olympus, I have crammed other stuff into my panniers over the years, but always have room for extra samples of food that I find at open markets, but not enough space for a carpet!

I was now walking through the outskirts of Cal looking at the shacks which people called home. I thought my tent looked like it would have been more waterproof than some of the roofs I saw. All the children had smiles and the women looked away in an embarrassed shy way when I greeted them with a friendly "*Merhaba*" – Turkish for hello. The men were presumably working somewhere or playing cards and sipping tea in a nearby teashop. Walking out on the road made me excited to think of what lay ahead in this wonderful place. Hard to think that, if I really wanted to, I could keep on pedaling east and wind up in Pakistan or India. I felt that my trip wasn't going to take me that way, but did I truly know where I was heading? My trip was originally to be a tour of Europe, and here I was on mainland Turkey.

I walked on for a few hours and took some small paths off into the wooded areas. It was a beautiful part of the world with something gentle and serene about it. I walked back to town and at least felt I'd earned some dinner. There being only one place to eat in town, I thought I'd eat there rather than cook my own meal. Lunch had been nice, so I looked forward to another good meal.

I got back to my small room, wrote in my journal and read for a little while before heading down to eat. There were the same choices as before; *baba ganush, tsatsik*i, trays of eggplants fried up with other veggies, some roasted potatoes, tomatoes and a pita type bread. Everything looked fresh and tasted delicious. I filled up a plate, and, with a yogurt drink to accompany it, found myself quite sated. As night drew in, I went to the tea shop, had a few teas and played cards with my new friends. They made me promise I would come in the next day.

That night I learned that the Australian, who was from this tiny village originally, had moved to Australia when he was seven, but had come back to meet the girl he would marry – arranged marriages were still alive and well. So here I was talking to a Turkish guy who lives in Australia who has just flown back to marry a girl he'd never met, but he didn't think there was anything unusual about it. Whereas I could barely get to grips wih the concept.

Sunrise the next day was cloudy and there was a chill in the air, so I pulled up the covers and wrote some more in my journal. I dug my map out from my pannier and looked at the route I intended to take. I was trying to get a grasp of the language as well. It was becoming my routine to eat breakfast and study Turkish for an hour or so. I had learned my lesson from Greece and didn't want to be caught out like that again. My small vocabulary in Turkish was allowing me to make some connections with locals already. I couldn't get into any deep conversations but polite questions about people and their families as well as the usual encounters in the open markets were becoming easier every day.

I kept my promise and stopped in for a quick cup of *chai*. They were intrigued by me and my trip. I couldn't fully understand it – we hardly understood each other, and I lost most of the games I attempted to play with them – but when my Australian translator interpreted they hung on every word. The Australian guy was there and seemed genuinely happy to see me. All of the usual faces grinned a greeting to me and I wondered if any men in the village actually worked. The women were doing all the housework as well as looking after any young children not in school and the men were drinking tea.

I had coffee instead of tea but even the coffee was almost as sweet. It was the usual sludgy-bottomed cup of coffee most people associate with Turkish coffee. I got sucked into a game of tiles despite my continued protesting that I should head off soon.

The Australian guy's name turned out to be Mohammed. It was a little odd to hear this true Muslim name being pronounced with an accent that would be more associated with Sheila, or Bruce, but there you are – another curiosity of our world. I had met lots of Mohammeds in my travels – it supposedly being the single most popular name in the world. Anyway, my friendly Australian Mohammed asked where I was going, and if I had to leave today. I tried to explain that I didn't really have to be anywhere, but my vague schedule was to try and make it as far east as possible before heading up to the Black Sea and back towards Istanbul. I think they thought I was crazy. I tried to explain why I liked to travel, and the reason why I wanted to explore not only Turkey, but other countries as well. He was translating as I spoke and they were asking me lots of questions; where I had been, about New York, if I had family, how long would a trip take etc. It was a foreign world to them, just as living in a small village drinking tea and playing cards all day was to me. Although foreign, I was being privileged to witness their world from the inside. Here I was, only a week or so in Turkey, and I had been waylaid twice into staying in places I would have otherwise passed through. Each instance gave me a look into a world you rarely get to see as a tourist. In some areas savvy locals make a profit from people eager to make a connection with the local lifestyle and charge for time spent with a local family. I was having a wonderful insider's experience through my translator who was a local boy 'done good' by making a life for himself in one of the many 'Promised Lands' of the poorer peasants of the world.

As it was nearing lunchtime I thought I'd be staying for another meal, but wasn't prepared for what was coming next. Mohammed asked me if I wouldn't mind staying one more night because all of the locals liked me and some planned to close their shops the next afternoon so we could have a party out in the woods. The butcher had given them some meat for the occasion, two other shops would close, and we would all head out for a picnic at lunchtime. I could have said no but they were so sincere and warm-hearted and they had also organized a lower price for me in the *pension* I was staying in – nearly half the low price it already was. So another day of studying Turkish, walking in the countryside and playing cards it would be.

I headed out to one of the highest hills on the outskirts of town. I took a picnic lunch, my journal, Turkish phrasebook, and the book I was reading. The walk gave some spectacular views of the surrounding landscape. What better way to spend the afternoon. I could imagine the millions of stressed-out people all over the world who would give their left arm for a week of peace and tranquility in the countryside. I had filled my life with it and here was yet another moment to savor. I said to myself, 'Joe, here you are on the outskirts of a small Turkish village, a continent spread before you, nowhere to be but right here in the moment!' I was living the life of a rich man, but with very little money and a heck of a lot of time. I realized that not many people would want to be in my situation, it would probably scare the hell out of them. That was fine, because most of the lifestyles of the modern world scared the heck out of me.

Another day and night in Cal was actually good for me as it made me really want to get on my bike and ride. I hadn't even straddled the bike once since putting it in the foyer of my *pension*. I had done lots of walking, reading and writing and it had been an ideal place to get my Turkish up to par, to say nothing of enjoying the friendliness of the local people.

Before turning in that night I stopped in to see the boys and played a few games of cards only to get sorely beaten. Life was mellow in Cal, the men's lives were peculiar, and the women were shadows flitting around the periphery and presumably running the show. After an hour or so with the fellas I went for a little walk around the village, saw a few familiar faces, and retired back to my room to read. Sleep came easily and when the *mullah* called the devoted to prayer, I was awoken from my slumber to be reminded where I was.

The next morning was beautiful and I woke up feeling that life was one big exciting journey. Here I was for a very short period of time becoming part of these people's lives. I would soon be gone, leaving some part of me as a memory for them as well. I knew there were people and experiences for me around every turn and in every village. I was so glad to be able to get beyond the fear as I realized that it had played far too big a part in how our world was shaped. When I looked back on many of my journeys I saw that fear was the one big obstacle I had to overcome in myself. Once I overcame that fear, I was free. The human experience could be so wonderful for everyone if we all stepped through and beyond the hold of fear. It stops us from leaving jobs we don't like, moving to places we might want to move to, raising our children as our instincts guide us, and now with fear and the exploitation of it being so common a tool used by governments, we are even afraid to step out and say, "This is me, I disagree with you and your policies, and I will challenge them!" No, we fear being different by standing out or being outspoken. Many people's greatest fear is to be labeled different. Are we all becoming the Japanese nails being hammered back into the wood? I have faith and do believe we are slowly changing; waking up from our slumber, but we have a long way to go before we all embrace life and try to undo the mistakes of generations of following the status quo. Our planet is telling us though; time is running out.

My small room was comfortable, and I laughed to myself thinking back on what I had said to my first hosts in Turkey about wanting to camp. My tent had only made it out of its pannier twice so far. I knew I'd camp more as I made it further east, for now I was enjoying the small comforts of a room and bed.

I studied some more Turkish before heading outside into the day. I had a small breakfast of some food bought in the market, and stopped in to the tea shop to see the boys. They were all there playing cards and the tile game which I now knew was called *Okey*. I had a coffee, and got sucked into a quick game. I was asked to tell a few more travel stories, which were translated by Mohammed, and to do a few more card tricks.

The morning passed much in that way until about noon when a few new faces arrived in the shop, and before I knew it, there were a dozen or so of us cramming into two cars and driving out of town. If I wanted to let weird thoughts enter my mind I easily could have. I had all the cash that I had had wired to Monaco on me, as well as my American passport. My bike and all the camping equipment back at the *pension* was worth a bit too. All these thoughts briefly flashed through my mind as I got into the crowded car with a bunch of Turkish guys I didn't know, in the middle of nowhere, in a Muslim country not too long after the war with Iraq was over. This situation, despite appearing to be a classic, "What the heck are you doing?" situation, in reality wasn't – there was not a menacing face or inkling of bad feeling about it at all.

Another interesting thing I came across was Turkey's attitude to drinking alcohol; although a Muslim country, it brewed its own beer, and drinking it wasn't frowned upon – at least not in the western part of the country. The party was getting under way. A big fire was started; all the meat was taken out and being prepared along with lots of snacks, white bread, sweet drinks, and alcohol. I was not a big drinker, and definitely not a smoker. Most people I met while traveling understood me not smoking because of the cycling, but many people the world over had problems with my occasional decisions not to drink alcohol. I enjoyed the confused looks and outright disbelief if I was seen not drinking at a wedding, or party. I even had a Turk ask me, "You don't smoke and you don't drink? Why do you live?" This was a young man who had just been trying to convert me to Islam, in his words, "Just like Cat Stevens." I laughed as smoking, although not around in the Prophet Mohammed's time, was frowned upon in Islam, as it is deemed to harm your body – some Muslim scholars say it's forbidden for much the same reason. Drinking alcohol is also prohibited according to the Koran, but all was forgivable by Allah, especially after a pilgrimage to Mecca.

The party got into full swing and fortunately Mohammed was not a drinker, nor was the guy who owned the tea shop. A few of the guys got a little drunk but the food kept on coming, and I was glad I hadn't had a big breakfast and I wouldn't need to eat dinner either. The radio was on and soon the Turkish dancing began. It was quite fun and made for a pretty interesting scene: a bunch of guys in the woods, a few of them drunk, all doing some Turkish dancing, which resembles the Greek dancing I had been introduced to on my short stay in the Greek campsite a few weeks back. I had a go and we had a lot of laughs. To see these male friends together having such a good time was wonderful but my western eye found

414

the absence of their partners, or any female company, very strange. It was something I was getting used to; Tunisia, Morocco, Greece, now here.

The plan had been for me to get going after lunch, but of course, the afternoon drew out until nearly four in the afternoon. My bike was packed, though, and I had supplies. I was also well-fed and full of energy. To not use all that good food to propel me along would have been a shame. The day was perfect for riding and camping. We got back and spent ten minutes saying goodbye. With many handshakes and hugs I finally straddled my waiting bike.

I swung by to say goodbye to the first person I had met in Cal. He was sitting dutifully in his chair looking as wise and content as he had a few days before. His eyes twinkled when he saw me. A nod and a quiet *"Allah Hasmaladik"* was exchanged between us, this time I really was leaving, with the blessing of the town elder, I cycled east.

My entry into Turkey had been great, easing me in slowly and allowing me to get a handle on the language before I headed further east. Cycling through the Cappadocia area was the last time I stayed in an area geared at tourists. This area is full of small remarkable turrety-type towers that had been created thousands of years ago by a combination of volcanic activity and pockets of hard stone within the soft volcanic tufa stone. Over tens of thousands of years the Kizilirmak River and the wind have carved out an outstanding work of natural art. They made for a wonderful sight, especially seeing so many of them concentrated in one area. Early Christians had sought refuge in these odd shaped caves and carved out cities and underground dwellings while escaping persecution in the second century. Frescoes are to be found on the walls and in the entrance ways to many of the dwellings. The area since 3,000 B.C. had been inhabited by the Hitite, Assyrian, Byzantine, and Ottoman civilizations. Just riding and walking through the natural splendor of the area was enough and the history an added interesting bonus. Along with that beauty there were other natural phenomenon in the area; hot springs and lime deposits which made for milky white waterfalls as warm as a hot bath and had consequently become quite a draw for tourists. The *pensions* in the touristy areas usually had space in the back to pitch a tent at a fraction of the cost; it wasn't proper camping, but convenient and along with the use of a shower, very economical. It was heading east out of that absolutely beautiful part of the world that I felt I had unofficially entered a different country.

Now my tent was getting put to better use. Sometimes though, in the smaller villages away from the crowds, *pensions* and food were extremely inexpensive, and hospitality always forthcoming, but when the situation leant itself, I camped under the stars.

Camping wild was a good way to get lost in my thoughts and spend time alone writing or reading. I cooked simple meals and one night finally used one of the MRE's I had been given back in Germany which had since been buried in the bottom of a pannier. I gave a cry of delight on finding them and berated myself for not having remembered them when I was hungry in my tent those first few days in Greece. I wondered as I chewed my way through the rubbery contents of one, if perhaps I had been better off with my involuntary fast! I made a mental note to swap my bike fixing skills for army issue underwear next time. Still, they filled a hole after a long day's ride. I had a few left for moments of desperation, but for now they would remain shoved back to the bottom of my bag.

As I got further into eastern Turkey the people and dress became so different. Women were more covered up, and for some reason I felt more like I was cycling in a former soviet republic than in Turkey. The people were still friendly, but I was definitely much more of an oddity. Fear seemed to be prevalent here; fear of the Russians, of the Kurds, and also of the people in the next village. I can't remember how many times I was warned not to cycle through a certain village because the people there were mean or there were bandits in the hills. I admit it was sometimes unnerving but knowing about fear and closed-mindedness, I was able to cycle on and experience all the small villages and hear the warnings or amazement that I made it over that hill or through that last village. It was almost comical – I put it down to years of fear and control under Ottoman rule, a time when travel was unheard of or only undertaken out of sheer necessity, and robbery more common. Hopefully myself and other independent travelers were helping to break those generations of indoctrination although modern day media scare tactics wasn't being much of an aid.

My next experience was shaped by the fact that for some odd reason I have always been drawn to drums. I don't play them, but have always owned some kind of drum or bongo set. In Nepal I remember sitting and watching a drum maker make a magnificent drum out of wood and leather that would have been too heavy to carry and expensive to send home. So when I came across a small drum in a market one day, I couldn't resist. It was made out of aluminum, stood about a foot high and the 'skin' was made from a thick opaque bluish plastic. Perfect I thought; the weather would not affect it, and it was small and light enough to strap onto my back rack. I wound up using it as a camping table, bike prop, amongst other things and was always glad to have it with me, especially on one certain occasion.

As I left the small village market I was stopped by a white bearded man who spoke a little English and was curious about my route. I wondered what kind of warnings I was in for. He was a *hadji,* which meant he had been to Mecca and was considered to be absolved of all his sins. It's much like Catholic confession in that way. It's why the young Turks told me they could drink alcohol and smoke. They said they would wait to go to Mecca when they were older, but they would have to stop their indulgences after that. A trip to Mecca was something that, if you're lucky enough to do, happens only once in your lifetime, especially if you're not wealthy. Anyhow, this man seemed to be well-traveled and asked me why I did not take the big new wonderful roads of Turkey. I explained that, although they were beautifully paved, and yes, the quickest way to get to where you were going, on the bike it was much better to take the smaller forgotten about back roads which were still fairly good and quiet as the bigger vehicles were on the big beautiful newer roads. He laughed and actually got my point. I showed him the road I intended on taking heading towards the Black Sea coast road and the Georgian border. He agreed that it would be a beautiful road, but he warned me that on the following small winding road I would take from this village over the hills to the next town that there were some vicious dogs which might attack me. At least it was a new threat! Normally it was unsavory people and bandits; now it was dogs. It registered a little more with me just because he hadn't been so vehement in his warning, just said be careful and left it at that.

The road was sublime; empty, paved and full of gorgeous scenery like many of the others in this part of the world. This one had the added bonus of going up at a nice slow steady incline. It was now late spring so the weather was ideal; there was a gentle breeze at my back and my body was warmed by the sun. The road twisted and turned so much that I felt as if the wind direction was changing every few minutes. I was allowed a few glimpses of the road climbing towards the summit and thought that the climb would probably take about and hour.

I climbed steadily, enjoying the feeling of slowly propelling my loaded bike upwards. I stopped a few times for a photo or a drink. After a while I saw a field of sheep off to the right thinking that it was strange that there were no fences to keep them in. The top of the hill wasn't far off when all of a sudden two very big, hairy, scary-looking dogs came bounding towards me with a deep menacing bark. They were slavering – white froth dripping from their ferocious-looking teeth, upper lips drawn up, and bloodshot eyes regarding me with disdain. I kept on pedaling right up until the two dogs looked like they were not going to stop running and just mow me right down in their tracks. I leapt off the bike to my left so I had it between me and the killer dogs from hell. They were about twenty yards away now but had fortunately stopped tearing towards me and were now just standing, hackles raised, continuing to bark at me. The word bark doesn't do justice to the noise these two beasts were making – it was more of a growling snarl brought to a crescendo every few seconds. Even through my terror I managed to think, 'Hmm, well I was warned!' I didn't fancy going back down the hill, especially when the top of the climb was right there, maybe only 200 meters away. The dogs were obviously not happy about me being there – the road was narrow, and they seemed to be considering how they would deal with me. I was very, very nervous. There were two of them, and if they figured out they could come at me from opposite sides I would be in a real fix. My mind was racing. What should I do? I needed to decide quickly. If I chose to turn around and fly back down the hill it would need to be done with a lot of finesse as turning the bike around would be difficult.

I looked around at what could have, under other circumstances, been a beautiful picnic spot, and then noticed the drum on my rack. It lay on its side, the head of the drum facing out. I took a chance and gave it a quick tap. The sound stopped the dogs from their vicious snarling so I did it again. The dogs looked at me with tilted heads, saliva dripping from their, now silent, jaws. I did it again and took a few steps, which the dogs didn't appear to notice. I wished they would move with me as I did not feel like opening up the back of the bike to their eyes. Magically, they started to follow a little. I kept a slow steady beat on the drum, and they were transfixed – mesmerized by the hypnotic rhythm. The top of the hill was getting closer. The curve of the road was to my advantage; off to the right. I was slowly putting distance between the dogs and myself, and then the road flattenned out slightly. I decided that there was enough distance for me to chance it, so I made a sudden lunge onto my bike and started to pedal like mad. The thought of more dogs ahead never entered my mind, and luckily it wasn't the case. I never looked back and just pedaled as fast as I was able. I let out an adrenalin-releasing holler and just kept on speeding away. Till this day I will never know whether they were snapping close at my heels and following me as I was breathing heavily, my bike flying down the hill making the wind roar in my ears. When I felt I had pedaled far and fast enough I eased off and realized I had probably been a little overzealous in my escape, but boy was I glad to have purchased one of the most impractical things I'd ever traveled with. That drum had more than earned its place on my rack and it stayed there for the rest of my time in Europe.

The town I arrived at was fairly unremarkable compared to the surrounding countryside, but it looked like heaven. I had really been scared, and wonder if my *hadji* from the small village wonders if I made it over the hill alive. The dogs, I discovered were Anatolian Sheep Dogs, also known as Lion Dog and Wolf Dog. The proper name is the *Kangal* Shepherd Dog and they have a mysterious history. One rumor has it they were bred from lions and tigers during the Assyrian and Babylonian times – I believe it. They protect sheep on their own from thieves and wolves, and react ferociously to strangers, intruders and definitely cyclists! Fortunately, I survived without a scratch.

I was now cycling on another lonely stretch of road which was quite dry, with no sheep or dogs apparent, and still heading east. The road was rolling and I was now well on the other side of Ankara, where I bussed both in and out as I was only heading there to collect some mail and cycling in the capital held no real appeal.

I was a big fan of using the *poste restante* mail system which was an excellent way of picking up letters from friends and family, and keeping in contact. I found it to be a great pleasure on the road to walk into a post office, show my passport, and get in return a stack of mail or a few letters. What a buzz. It also meant you had to pick a certain destination once in a while, and to write your friends in enough time for them to get your letter, and for them to get one off to you. Imagine pulling into a totally unknown part of the world, leaving the post office with five or six handwritten letters from friends and family, and then sitting in a café, restaurant, or your tent and opening envelopes with familiar stamps on the well-traveled paper. The news is old, but current for you, and now it gives you the chance to write a return letter over the next few weeks or months. Sometimes there was disappointment of not getting a letter or bad news awaiting you, but it was all part and parcel of the world of travel, and without instant contact possible it made it feel more on a human scale. The few letters I picked up made the side trip worthwhile and the news from friends and family was all good.

The undulating road was slow going and the heat intensified by the semi-arid plain I was on. I kept on getting passed by the same truck. I would pass him on the downhills, and he would catch me on the ups and blow smoke in my face to the point where I would get on the outside of the truck just in front of the exhaust pipe and grab on to one of the many ropes that were dangling off the sides. I would hang on and hitch a ride to avoid taking years off of my life breathing in the toxic fumes. It was hard work to hang on with one hand leaving the other arm free to balance and steer the heavy bike but it was fun to get what felt like a lift up the hill. We played this cat and mouse, hitching a ride game for a while, when at the top of one of the hills he pulled over and asked me to stop. "Where are you going my friend?" He asked in broken English.

"Northeast," I replied.

"I am too. Come sit in my truck, put your bike on top," he insisted.

"I'm enjoying the riding, and occasional lift." I said and smiled.

"How far will you travel today?" he asked.

"Another fifty kilometers." From the map it looked like the road was going to continue much the same for a while. As I didn't need to cycle every millimeter of road and he was so insistent, I accepted his offer.

It was more trouble hauling my fully loaded bike to the top of the truck than it had been pedaling. The driver had a young assistant with him and together we finally managed to do it, heaving and pulling on my unwieldy bike. We tied it down with ropes and off we went. He said he had grain in the back and was heading to the mill that he worked for – seventy kilometers further.

He started speaking in disjointed, but comprehensible English, "It is a very dangerous area you are heading, The PKK are taking hostages, there are many troubles."

"Yes, I know, that's why I'm starting to go north. Why is there so much trouble?" I asked. I had heard something about it in Ephesus talking to some travelers, plus there had just been a major earthquake in an area called Erzurum. Eastern Turkey was in a mess; that put me a little ill at ease.

"The situation is not good my friend. You are German?" He asked it as a question, but seemed nearly certain.

"American." It could have been a dangerous statement in the wrong company, but it didn't feel that way.

"American! You are heading to the northeast of Turkey on a bicycle! Why?" He was pleased and perplexed.

I explained about my trip to date and it was hard for him to comprehend. I knew all too well the reaction. While most of the world's population struggles to eat, I was riding my bike aimlessly in Turkey. He went on to explain more of the situation happening not too far away.

Besides the world's obsession with wiping out ethnic populations, Kurdistan's other problems stemmed from water issues; The Tigris and Euphrates Rivers pour out from Kurdish populated Iraq (Kurdistan) then flow through Turkey before getting to Syria. The European money spent on damming and controlling the water for drinking and irrigation purposes was in the billions. Turkey controlled the flow into Syria which didn't amount to more than a trickle by then and that was contaminated by agricultural chemicals. International Treaties had been ignored, the world at large never truly informed and of course the finger pointed at terrorism and the threat to democracy. I wasn't in favor of terrorism, but Syria had been backed into a corner. What about ignoring treaties, controlling water, and having Turkey as an ally with NATO forces, and lots of European money being spent on its infrastructure? This created situation had many different viewpoints, and was not the black and white issue the news or governments would have everyone believe.

420

Too many stories in too short a time; Algerian Civil strife, Western Saharan Occupation, now here – these were just the ones that had sought me out. I knew I didn't need to search for more, they were easily apparent on my travels.

My driver didn't appear to be angry, and the fact I was an American seemed to make him happy. I asked if he was interested in politics and how he knew so much, hoping I didn't sound condescending.

"I am a highly educated man from Kurdistan," he said with some pride, then continued, "before the troubles I was going to be a professor. Now I drive a truck. I read all the papers, and speak three languages; Kurdish, Turkish, and Arabic."

I interrupted him, "Four. What about English?"

He laughed and waved his hand at me, "English, ha ha, you are so kind my friend, I do not speak English well, I just babble."

There I was struggling my whole life to reach a mere conversational level of any language, and my truck driver friend had a pretty good level of English and laughed it off as babble. Once again I stood – or rather sat – humbled.

I was now almost embarrassed that we had not spoken to his assistant so I attempted to strike up a conversation in Turkish with him. Nothing too deep, but good enough to keep the conversation flowing about where I was heading and where I was from. My driver praised my Turkish. I knew he was just being kind but was pleased at the small progress I had made. We arrived at the mill and managed to lower my bike down with no damage to his tarps or my bike for which I was grateful. I looked at this truck driver spending many long days driving and thought maybe he'd appreciate some MRE's. I showed him their drab green plastic casing, explaining how he could heat them on the engine of his truck while driving – the army designed them for this usage. He was so happy to accept them and impressed with the American Army issue stamp, that instead of keeping one back for myself I gave all I had to the both of them. It was a good exchange for the lift, and maybe in a pinch they would enjoy the beef stroganoff or spaghetti carbonara. On further reflection, as I thought about the delicious kebabs and other Turkish fare, I wondered if they would curse me once they took their first bite – but contented myself with hoping that they were *really* hungry when they ate them, or maybe just kept them as souvenirs!

I had been planning to mount my trusty steed and pedal on but my friendly driver insisted me meeting his boss who, he said, spoke English. As I was seventy kilometers ahead of myself with a village I could stay in not too far away, I figured, why not?

The mill was huge. If you were to see it from afar, you would guess it was a cement factory or something along those lines. I followed my driver dutifully inside to find the man in charge.

Once we found the boss, I thanked my driver and he vanished. We said hello and introduced ourselves in Turish, but my energy was slightly thrown for the moment. I wasn't sure why, but I thought something strange was afoot. Was he going to ask me for money for transportation? I didn't know, but his energy was confusing me. He was nice enough, and his command of English was much better than the truck driver's. My Turkish had its limits, so we switched to English quite quickly. Dressed in his casual attire, nicely shined shoes and his well-groomed hair he stood in stark contrast to the slightly heavy-set, sloppily-dressed truck driver who had just disappeared from view. He asked about my trip, then briefly told me about his operation, and how he supplies bread for much of this part of Turkey. It wasn't only a mill, but also a bakery where the bread was baked before being delivered to many small shops and restaurants. After my tour, I asked if he knew of an inexpensive *pension* or place to stay in town. For some reason, he didn't like me using the word 'inexpensive'.

"Sure, you come to my country and you don't want to spend any money, you're just like all the westerners, you treat Turkey like a cheap holiday resort!"

I was taken aback by his sudden anger. I replied by saying, "Would you prefer me to book a two-week holiday through a travel company, stay in an expensive resort where most of the money goes to the agents in the country where you make the booking, or would you rather me ride my bike in your country for months, stay in local *pensions*, campsites, and buy bread in all the small shops and restaurants I wind up eating in?" He was just looking at me, so I continued, "Sure I try not to spend a lot on a daily basis, but in the end, I will be here for three or four months, I will have met many local people, I will have a deeper understanding of your culture, some of the problems Turkey faces, and all of the money I spend goes directly to the shop owners, or *pension* owners, not some agent in England or Germany!"

He then countered with, "Americans are rich. My people cannot travel abroad as it is hard and expensive to get a passport."

I then asked him for some paper and a pencil and we made a chart. I wrote down the average salary of a 'Rich American' worker, and then an average mortgage or rent, car loans, insurance, two-week vacations, and then next to that a list for the average worker in his factory, expenses, etc. etc. When it was all written on paper, the Rich American was not that much financially better off than your average working Turk. They both lived in wonderful diverse countries which had coastlines, mountains and farm land. On top of that, at that time, only six percent of the American

422

population held passports, so a large percentage of Americans had never left their country either. We talked about the poor in both countries and the lack of a socialized medical system in the U.S. Traveling my way, cheap as it might be, probably gave more to the Turkish economy than he had thought. By the end of our conversation he had calmed down and seemed to see my point.

We shook hands and I repeated the question which had got us into this discussion in the first place. He told me to follow him on my bike, town wasn't very far, and he knew of a nice place to stay. I followed him as he drove a little too fast and I smiled to myself at his choice of car; a Mercedes. I managed to keep him in sight, and luckily we didn't have far to go. By now the sun was low in the sky, and I was getting hungry. He pulled up in front of a nice looking *pension* and went upstairs. When he came back down he said, "They have a room for you. It is very clean and not expensive." Then he smiled, thanked me for our time together and interesting conversation, shook my hand and was off. I waved goodbye and thought what a strange afternoon it had been.

I hadn't engaged in a conversation so deep in my mother tongue for so long that I had almost forgotten I could so it was difficult to switch back to Turkish. With my head still spinning, I asked the clerk at the *pension* if they had a room, and if I could also pay for a shower. The man looked at me quizzically and said, "Your friend has paid for a room and a shower already, here is your key." I was shocked and truly didn't know what to feel. I accepted his gift gracefully, although he wasn't there, and took it as a peace offering. I hoped that it meant that he had understood my viewpoint and had a better feeling towards people coming to visit his country. I went in to the room which was clean and basic, stripped off my dusty cycling clothes, and took a hot shower, silently thanking the mill owner as I stood under the powerful jet of water.

Turkey did look a big country, but it was surprising how the miles would roll by quite quickly. A few days earlier it looked like I had strayed too far south – Konya, Kayseri then Sivas – but I had found small villages, had some interesting experiences, and I now found myself crossing the Black Sea Mountains not too far from Artvin, near the Georgian border.

I had been in the border town with Batumi, and had toyed with the idea of heading into Georgia, but it was in the middle of a civil war and was deemed generally unsafe to travel there. There was an underlying hatred between the Turks and the Georgians here near the border, but the Georgians I had met in the markets or restaurants had been friendly and mostly intrigued to meet an American in this far-flung corner of Turkey. I was told of the war in their country but also of the beauty of their land. The Georgians here were refugees, and like anyone forced to leave the country of their birth they had a deep longing and love for their homeland. I was slightly tempted by the prospect of cycling there, but the lines at the embassies were always horribly long and this helped me to make up my mind not to bother.

I was treated like a king by both the native Turks and the displaced Georgians in this far eastern part of Turkey – not charged for food I ate, invited for lunch and dinner in places I walked past and, as always in Turkey, offered as much tea as my bladder could handle. Not many travelers came to these parts and people could not believe an American on his bicycle would pedal all this way to visit their humble part of the world.

"An American here in my restaurant! Please come back for dinner." When I went to pay they waved their arms and said, "No, it is my pleasure!" The unbelievable hospitality was turning out to be the absolute norm in Turkey rather than the exception.

The markets were fantastic; a combination of Soviet, Turkish, and Eastern European people – items ranging from imitation Levi jeans and old Soviet-issue army gear to shortwave radios dating back to what looked like 1940. The food was also great, and, if I left my bike behind, I did not stand out too much. As usual I was able to blend in slightly, but only when I did not speak. Space constraints meant I could not buy too much but I did manage to buy a small hand-crafted stainless steel bowl which is still part of my camping gear today. Anyhow, now being early June I thought it was the perfect time to head back towards the border with Europe.

Trabzon sounded as good a place as any for a destination in the western direction towards Istanbul. It was known as the 'unofficial' capital of eastern Turkey – a University town, right on the Black Sea coast. I was told that some women in university there were paid by less moderate Muslim thinking organizations or even bordering Muslim countries to wear their *burkha*. Some, of course, wore it out of choice. I was intrigued by this university town, but Artvin was a fair way from Trabzon.

The Black Sea Coast road was heavily trafficked with many trucks, and was a nightmare for cycling. I decided to head back over the Black Sea Mountain range once again to get away from the road's constant noise, dirty exhaust fumes and possible dangers. Once away from the more populated coast the small villages and the people were friendly enough, but I was definitely in a less liberal part of Turkey. I always tried to respect local custom but in the sweltering heat on empty roads I would sometimes take to cycling with no shirt on. The few times I forgot to pull a shirt on in a town, I was immediately reminded about it, sometimes nicely but more often than not with a frown. Comments were even made about my bare legs. I understood that my bare legs could be considered offensive in this area, but cycling with long trousers on was not a welcome option in the sometimes stifling heat. The slip-on trousers I would normally pull on had just fallen apart, so I had bought an imitation pair of Levis in a market. I had been introduced to the high-tech clothing world, but was back to Levis.

As I was getting closer to Trabzon I was on a gorgeous valley road following a river; high stony walls stretching up on either side of me. It was perfect cycling, amongst the loveliest I've ever done. It was a peaceful road, following the river in lazy meanderings. I slept in my tent, enjoying tranquil nights lulled to sleep by the river.

At a small worksite I came across a few workers playing cards, so I did my favorite card trick once again. The men were duly impressed, foisting tea upon me. I managed to leave before drinking too many and as I was leaving one of them mentioned something about my friend stopping here a few days ago. He was speaking in Turkish so I figured I was losing something in translation. When I asked him to repeat himself, he explained that there was a blond English guy on a bike who'd passed here a few days back. My ears perked up and I made sure I had not misunderstood him. When I felt certain that I hadn't, I waved them goodbye and thought about the stranger who was pedaling just a few days ahead of me. I was still on the land side of the Black Sea Mountains, and would be for another few days. The road that crossed the mountains back to the coast road was about one hundred kilometers away, leading out of a small village. After crossing the mountains again I would be about twenty-five kilometers east of Trabzon.

I made it to that small village the next night. The cycling was so pleasurable and the weather fantastic, so it was easy to spend long days in the saddle. I had been in Turkey for over two months by this point, had made lots of stops, and had seen quite a lot of the few worlds Turkey had to offer. This village was once again picture perfect with the Mosque dominating the skyline and the mountains not too far off in the distance giving a wonderful natural backdrop to the whole scene.

I found a *pension*, and by the time I'd had a wash and got something to eat it was dark. I was strolling around the maze of streets enjoying the balmy evening air when I heard loud music coming from somewhere. I followed the music to its source, and to my surprise came upon a huge street party. As I walked by, the person in charge of the music called, "American" and beckoned me over with a wave and invited me to dance. It was the same Turkish dancing I had participated in a few times before but this time there were women around. Interestingly enough they were not dancing with the men but everyone was having a good time.

The DJ who'd called me over spoke some English and told me it was a wedding. He explained it would be a full weekend of dancing and partying.

Being a less liberal part of Turkey, there was no alcohol or drunken people anywhere to be seen, just lots of smiling faces. I even had a quick dance with a woman, very quick I might add, with at least a foot or two between us. I was handed food and some sweets – all were home made, and delicious. I was having a chat with another of the guests who said these wedding feasts will usually last the whole weekend, when he also mentioned the other cyclist here two days ago. It had to be the same guy. The description sounded the same, and I was obviously heading the same way as he was. It was a little after midnight when I got back to my *pension*. Sleep came easily as I pondered on what a wonderful time I was having on my bike in this diverse, friendly country.

The next morning I got off early. The climb according to my map was about twenty-eight kilometers. Not too bad. I did not want to get caught climbing too much in the afternoon heat. Before I left I was given another special warning, this time about snow. It was now mid-June, and although I knew mountains could be unpredictable, snow seemed unlikely. I hoped it wasn't true. I had just given away my warm gloves and a few pieces of superfluous clothing to some poor kids in a village I stayed in a few days back. I had figured I didn't need them anymore since it was June and I was heading into a European summer.

The climb was at a nice gradient, but it kept on going. I was pretty hot as I cycled and stripped off a few kilometers out of the village. By the time I had climbed about twenty-five kilometers, the top still wasn't in sight and I was hungry. I'd had a nice breakfast, and had figured that a twenty-eight kilometer climb at this gradient shouldn't take too long. I was starting to realize that the map was wrong and the climb was going to go on much further. Then I turned a corner and thought I saw what looked like some snow. Uh oh, I thought, maybe that warning about snow was true.

I kept on going, and now it was starting to get colder; back on with my shirt. It was getting near forty kilometers of ascent with patches of snow appearing, and now snow actually began to fall. I had no choice but to keep on going. I had put on a few more layers of clothing, but had nothing warm for my hands. I couldn't believe it. I'd carried those gloves for ages and given them away a few days ago, and now here I was heading into what looked like a blizzard. As I approached a small village the snow was starting to fall quite heavily. There were snowdrifts on the side of the road, and I just stared in disbelief. I'd started the day a few hours ago with a sleeveless shirt and a pair of shorts. I now had on just about everything I had in my bags plus a bandana around my neck. I was also not well-prepared for food. I'd thought I'd be on the other side of the pass by now tucking into lunch. Once again I'd made the mistake of overconfidence. Fortunately I had some soup in a packet but nothing else. There was virtually no traffic, so I pulled over to the side of the road, left my bike on the other side of a snowdrift, grabbed my stove, water and soup packet, and found some shelter under the overhang of an abandoned house. It was bizarre as the town was abandoned. Was it always this deserted? After all it was summer, did the people move back in the winter? I couldn't figure it out, but it was true that there wasn't a soul to be seen. I didn't expect to find people out for a stroll in the middle of a blizzard, but the houses showed no signs of life, and some, like the one I was now sheltering by, were boarded up.

I fired up my stove, and then heard what sounded like an engine straining to get through the snow on the road. I looked out to see a truck coming the other way. It was a typical-looking Turkish goods truck with a big blue cab and an open back stacked high with who knew what, ropes holding all the tarps in place. I waved him down standing next to my bike in case he might have gotten nervous of a maniac jumping around for no reason in this small seemingly-empty village. With the snow it must have been hard to see me, but he finally did, and stopped. I asked him in my best Turkish how far it was to the top. "About four kilometers," was his reply. Then I thought to ask him if he had any food. After all he could have been transporting a truckload of bread. He wasn't, but he did have some on his front seat. He broke off some for me, and I offered to pay him. He waved it off and then asked "You have a cigarette?" I laughed, showed him my bike, and told him I didn't smoke.

"I saw your friend on a bicycle," were his next words.

Despite my distraction from being cold and hungry, I was surprised to hear that and asked, "When?"

"Oh, a few hours ago on the other side of the pass."

He must have slept on the mountain. If I could make it to the T-Junction at the coast soon I thought I might just meet up with this mysterious friend of mine. Right now I was just glad to have some bread to eat and only four kilometers to the top, great.

I devoured the packet soup and stale bread, being tired and cold in this empty village at the top of a pass in eastern Turkey, they sure did taste good. I briefly regretted giving away all my MRE's. Then I was reminded of my encounter with the mill owner wondering if the bread was from that mill. Who knew? I packed up my stove feeling warmer now, and just knowing that after four kilometers I would be rewarded with a long downhill right to the Black Sea brought a smile to my face.

The snow had let up a little, but now all I wanted to do was get over the top and start heading back down to summer. The road to the top was nearly flat now, and I was there in no time at all. I began to descend and the speed made my fingertips freeze. I had to stop every so often to warm up my hands under my armpits which didn't work that well as even they were cold. The road was still remarkably devoid of traffic. The only vehicle I remember seeing was that truck.

The snow made the route over the mountains so beautiful, I just wished I had been more prepared so I could have enjoyed it more. Once I got below the snow line it turned gorgeous and green. It was stunning. The road was so steep that I was leaning into the turns at incredibly fast speeds. There was no way I could descend like this all the way to the coast. My fingers were just beginning to defrost when I saw it; a small shack with smoke coming out of the chimney. It was a wonderful sight. I pulled up in front, threw my bike down, ran inside and started to hug the pot belly stove in the middle of the room. I laugh when I imagine the scene now. The place was full of men sitting having tea in their local, when a bearded, long haired westerner throws open the door, comes running in and starts hugging their stove like it is his long lost son, shouting, "*Chai!*" After they got over their initial surprise they welcomed me filling up my glass again and again until I had drunk about four hot teas. Then I was told my friend had been there about two hours ago. I had been in his wake about a week and was gaining on him but there was only twenty-five kilometers or so before the T-junction at the coast and, of course, I had no idea which way he was heading. It was funny because I knew all too well of him but he had no idea I was right behind him.

I left the tea shop very warmed now, with caffeine surging through my veins and singed patches on my windbreaker jacket. I was determined to catch this friend of mine if only to say hello so I started pedaling with a purpose. It was easy to do – the road kept on going down, and I was loving the warmth of the sun as I quickly left winter, cycled through spring and was now sprinting back to summer. A few more vehicles and towns popped up as I reached the flat. There was a taxi in front of me heading towards the coast road, so I flagged him down. I asked him to wait and I scribbled a note for the cyclist ahead of me. I wrote, "Hello there, you don't know it, but I've been cycling behind you for at least a week. If you get to the coast road and just wait a bit, we can at least have a chat, I'm an American guy cycling on my own, heading to Trabzon. Regards, Joe" I asked the driver if he could give this to my friend who was ahead of me. He said, "No problem."

I now had about twenty kilometers to go before I reached the coast road. I was in my high gear, and kept on pedaling. I'm not sure if I wanted to catch up with him more just for some company, or for the sheer coincidence of it all. Well I would soon see if it was going to happen. My energy was waning so I stopped somewhere to buy a snack and asked if they had seen my friend on the bike. A young girl said, "About one hour ago." I wasn't sure how her concept of time was, but if it was an hour there would be no way I would catch up with him. It was a matter of if he got the note, or if he just happened to stop at the coast road for a break. I kept up a good pace and it was great to be zooming along the road heading once more for the Black Sea coast.

When I arrived there it was pretty nondescript; just a road sign pointing to the left for Trabzon, and to the right for Batumi. Straight ahead there was a verge where I noticed a crowd of young boys gathering around someone; there's my friend the cyclist. I walked over to the small crowd of boys, and noticed a bike lying on its side. I spotted a shock of blond hair through all the dark-haired kids, and, as he was concentrating on doing something else, the cyclist didn't realize that some of the boys' attention had turned to the other stranger. I said, "Did you get my note?"

He looked up and shook his head in surprise, answering, "What note?"

So my taxi never made it. "Oh nothing, anyhow, my name's Joe. I've been cycling on the same roads following you for about a week or so."

He pushed himself up from the verge with hand extended, and in an English accent said, "Timothy, nice to meet you Joe."

The boys gathered around these two strange foreigners, both very different looking, with very different accents, but both right here on the coast on the outskirts of their tiny village. They giggled and laughed as Timothy and I got to know one another. We traded our stories and I told him about the workers who first told me of him. He was a photographer and into Georgian Architecture. He was combining that with a cycle tour of this part of Turkey. We decided we would head into Trabzon together, spend the night speaking English, enjoying each other's company and see what happened.

It was another twenty or so kilometers to Trabzon which was a sizable city. The traffic on the coast road was heavy and getting worse as we approached the city. As neither of us traveled with guide books we had to find accommodation the usual way you do on a bike – by cycling around for a bit. That was a nice thing straight off, we both agreed it was much more fun having our own trip rather than following someone else's. He had a book on all the Georgian architecture, but that was about it. We asked a few young people where a good area of town to find inexpensive *pension* would be and we finally made it to a place which was pretty centrally located, very affordable, and wound up being full of prostitutes from Georgia. The owner didn't know what to make of these two weird looking guys hauling their bikes up the stairs. The room was basic; three beds, a sink, shower down the hall, and one window facing the street. After unpacking what we needed and choosing beds we went off to explore Trabzon on foot.

We were walking around aimlessly, chatting about different things when we passed an ice cream shop. Our eyes lit up so we went in and were served by a giggling girl of about twenty or so. I think we made people nervous just because we were English-speaking foreigners.

Trabzon was an interesting place with a varied population. Because it was a university town there were lots of students, cafés and a certain amount of street life. Because it was eastern Turkey, it was caught between two Muslim worlds – the conservative and the moderate. We found a place to have a coffee, and later on a restaurant. Our *pension*/brothel showed us the paradoxes of this place. On the one hand walking the streets of Trabzon, women in *burkah*, the mosque calling the devoted to prayer five times a day, and on the other hand we would go back to our place with young ladies selling their bodies for money wearing tight jeans or short dresses. Every time we came in to the place we were winked at and asked if we wanted to indulge. We both knew that we would decline those offers which led to a whole different relationship with our fellow residents. We wound up staying in Trabzon for about five days and we got to know our housemates on a very different level. They may have thought we were gay, but they respected our decision. Every once in a while we'd get a come on, but for the most part, if the girls weren't working we would have chats about Georgia, and their life in Trabzon. It wasn't a pretty life, but the girls were genuinely nice, young, confused and living in a dream world of escaping to another life. By the look of some of them though, it was obvious that this world had taken its toll on them, and, if there was a promise of getting out of the pattern they were in, it most likely didn't lie here in Trabzon. I don't think their pimps liked us very much. It was reminiscent of Rob and me in Vietnam a few years back. They looked at us as a loss of income I'm sure, so we didn't take up too much of the women's time, we needed to keep a low profile.

One day we got back to the place and there was broken glass everywhere – a large window was shattered. We learned later it was a dispute with the hotel owner the young prostitutes' pimp. A fight ensued and a gun was fired – nobody was shot, but the large glass window which was now boarded up haphazardly was the largest casualty. Tim and I were glad to have missed the excitement. We also thought maybe we would not spend quite so much time talking with our friendly neighbors.

We found a café and it was there we met some students of Trabzon. We were engaged briefly in a conversation about Israel. Finding out I was American and Tim English, the assumption was we totally supported Israel's existence. The few articles and information I read back in New York was not enough to know about the whole situation, but could you ever? With every moment that the situation continued more gray blurred

430

the black and white lines that may have existed in 1899 or 1948. I surprised them with a little more knowledge about the disputed country close to a thousand miles south of us. I agreed about the wars of expansion being illegal and also Israel's dubious beginnings. I was glad to have done at least that little bit of reading up on the situation. My knowledge was not extremely thorough, but enough to engage a bit; Tim just sat quietly. It was an emotive issue. In New York many people didn't question the existence of an Israeli state, but here next to me the opinions were very much the opposite. The hardliners thought that its existence was an affront to every Muslim worldwide. All out holy war – *jihad* – and expulsion was the only answer. Some others fortunately had a more moderate approach, but the common thread was that Israel was an illegal occupying force backed by the Imperialist American regime. The conversation was getting heated between two of the male students as Tim and I watched it come to a near boiling point. One of the female students, who hadn't said much up to that point, made a comment quite forcefully in what sounded like Arabic, and nearly instantaneously the conversation ended.

If Turkey were going to move forward the future lay in the hands of strong opinionated women like the ones we spoke to. The men were happy to tow the party line and didn't mind things the way they were. The women, even those in *burkah*, saw everything as a means to an end. They had visions of a multi-cultural Turkey joining the EU (European Union) and moving ahead as a Muslim country, but also as a first world country, not just another developing nation. The woman who ended the conversation on Israel just minutes before told us she prayed for a fair solution to the issue in Palestine. We were impressed with her forthrightness, and actual power amongst even the males at the table. It was an intriguing glimpse of diversity of thought, particularly in a Muslim country.

The situation in the southeast was brought up briefly. I had a little history from my truck driver friend, but was conscious it was his side of the story; Tim knew a bit about it as well, and what he'd read coincided with my truck driver's information. The discussions were not heated, but informative; interestingly, much of what my truck driver said was seen as Kurdish propaganda – now there was the Turkish media at play. The Kurds needed to be demonized, those water damming projects were lucrative for the Turkish government, and kept much foreign money flowing into Turkey – even if it did stop the flow of water to Syria. It was agreed by one of the students that Syria was getting a raw deal, but many things were at stake here; one Muslim country mistreating another one, Turkish media hype, governments lying, and big money at work. At least we all agreed a way forward was needed and that terrorism and kidnapping really didn't help matters. Different stories from all corners; my truck driver had his, the students, Turkish media and government all had theirs too. Entering those types of discussions is always tricky; emotions run high, opinions obviously differ, media and governmental manipulation of the situation is hard to sift through, and personal connection with the area always adds to the complexity.

Back in the room Timothy's bike was in dire need of a tune up so we took it apart and laid everything out on the spare bed. We bought some gasoline and used that to clean all its parts. I don't think our room benefited very much from this so we tried to do a good tidy up before we left. My working in bike shops and carrying arguably a few too many tools came into its own once again. I was able to get Timothy's bike in good running order and it felt great to be able to do something for a fellow traveler. Even if it wasn't repaying kindness back to the locals I thought it was nice just to have the opportunity to be in the loop of giving. Timothy was heading southeast from here, and I was heading due west. We were traveling differently – Tim was on a study and photo journey of a particular architectural type and his days in the saddle were to get him to all the places he had heard about or discovered while traveling. It was an interesting way to do things, and he had taught me how to look at some of the buildings I was cycling past and appreciate the difference in a doorway or a roofline. His timeline was open, but his geographical limitations were local to the eastern area of Turkey.

I wanted to take a ferry on the Black Sea back to Istanbul as it sounded as though it would have been an interesting two-day journey but unfortunately there were fires in the docks in Istanbul, and there were no ferries expected to leave for at least six weeks. Even though, I enjoyed my trip back mixing up cycling and a bus or two to hasten my arrival to finally get pedaling in Europe.

My favorite memory of my last days in Anatolia – the Asian mainland of Turkey – is staying in an overcrowded campsite on the Black Sea. As I was unpacking my bike, someone noticed my drum and asked if I played. I feebly told him I didn't but used it as wild dog control. The joke was obviously lost on him but as it turned out he played the drum, and it got a good workout that night. It has never sounded as good since. We had a fun night of dancing, laughing and eating good food on my last night on the Asian part of this marvelous country. The next day I would cycle to one of the ferry ports and take a short crossing back to the European continent to explore Istanbul, ancient Constantinople, and see what that city had in store for me.

Istanbul is otherworldly; the skyline like no other modern city. The old and the modern rubbing up closely to each other, the Blue Mosque

432

dominates and immediately impresses you with its large dome and six minarets resembling rocketships ready to launch. I had never seen anything quite like it. While searching for a place to sleep I pedaled and pushed my bike through small alleyways my head constantly turning one way then the other. The wafting of smells and sounds at once European, and in the same instant Asian. It felt like a crossroads, and rightfully so. What an incredible journey I had been on for quite a while now.

Would I be cycling alone up through Eastern Europe? I had a feeling deep down that I wouldn't, so when I found the youth hostel in Istanbul, walked in and saw a bike leaned against the wall, I smiled.

After showering I found the common room, which was quite full, and looked around. The ease of finding the other cyclist was almost disappointing. There he was, hot drink on the table, and a map of Thrace spread out before him. I walked over and asked if that was his bike out in front. He looked up at me and said, "Is that yours leaned up over there?"

When I nodded he gestured me to have a seat at his table, and just calmly asked with a smile, "Which way do you think we should head up to Bulgaria?" I grinned and knew that we would have a good time together once I could come to grips with his Liverpudlian accent.

# Pedaling behind the Rising Curtain

We must have made a strange pair cycling together. John makes me laugh when he says that the first time he saw me he thought I looked like one of the wrestlers from the World Wrestling Federation; bib tights I cut down to shorts, bright pink shirt I wore for visibility's sake, and long unruly hair. John himself was clean-shaven and had short hair, with an accent I found pretty hard to comprehend at first. He was from Liverpool – which in local parlance was also known as a *scouser*. If I wasn't looking when he spoke, I could have sworn I was riding with John Lennon. He had been on a nine-month around the world cycle journey to raise money for the 'Queen's Children' – an English charity. John was on the last leg of his journey and was planning a faster pace through Eastern Europe than me but we hit it off so well together that we decided we would hook up at least for the moment and see how it went.

We were cycling the last part of Turkey before entering Bulgaria – the only vehicles passing us were army vehicles full of young boys cradling guns in their arms. Once again the features of war in a country where a smile came quickly to everyone's face and the gentle peasants working in the field were as quick to offer you a cup of tea as they were to show you their pearly (or not so pearly) whites. Surely these young people's time would be much better spent learning how to work the land and accept other people's religious and cultural differences. No matter how poor the country there always seems to be enough money to be found for tanks, guns, and damaging chemicals; my anti-war stance had never been stronger. When I saw youthful optimism – kids who should be filled with awe for our wonderful planet and its diversity – tainted at a young age from carrying a gun, dressing in drab green and learning not to trust, it saddened me. To my delight though the human spirit shines through – many of the soldiers were quick to wave, and would always glance back at these two cyclists getting lost in the dust their transport trucks were kicking up. I always tried to manage a wave and a smile. The smile had been a constant in Turkey; Attaturk was attributed with saying – when modern day Turkey was in its infancy after World War I – "It costs nothing to give away a smile." It was that legacy which Turkey left imprinted on my mind. With that small voluntary use of a few facial muscles, everything changes – a brightness, a connection; human contact at its finest and simplest. They may cost nothing to give away, but I was surely richer for having received them and keeping them now stashed away in my inner being.

We stayed in one last small town the night before we left Turkey and decided to enjoy the delights of a Turkish bath house. John hadn't experienced one yet. I had been to one other further east in a town called Nevshehir where the masseur had been pretty rough with me, throwing me around like a rag doll. Despite thinking I wouldn't be able to walk the next day, I had actually felt pretty good. Now I needed to work up the courage for another wrestling match with a strong Turkish masseur and this would be my last chance. We used up the last of our Turkish, money splurging on a good meal, a *pension*, and now a massage and a hot bath.

As we entered the steam hit us in the face. The marble slabs were hot to sit on and the big guy in charge looked surprised to see us two obvious-looking foreigners walk in. I let John go first to see if he survived. There were no loud screams of pain, and twenty or so minutes later a red-faced John walked into the room, throwing back his arms looking like he was ready to go the next round with Muhammad Ali. Maybe he just had. I laughed.

"So how was it?" I asked smiling.

"Great, now it's your turn mate. Good luck, I mean enjoy." He laughed his wide-mouthed laugh with a sinister glint in his eyes.

"No, really John, was it relaxing?" I probed.

Another smile, "Oh yes very."

John loved to joke, and it didn't matter, I was going for it either way – I just wanted to be prepared. The masseur appeared through the steam, nodding and grunting for me to come into the other room. I tentatively headed in, looking back at John who was smiling, and laughing as he said, "He wasn't too rough, just remind him of your bad back."

"Great," I muttered as I was handed a towel to wrap around my midsection. It started mildly at first, then the rubbing became more vigorous – he probably went to the same school of massage as my first masseur. My arms were stretched around my back and my legs coerced into positions that made my tight quads groan. I laid on my front, then my back, and the heat combined with the vigor of my masseur made me exhausted. I was in slightly less pain than I had been in Russia after seven layers of skin were scrubbed off by Andre's friends, but this massage's pain was born of stretching my abused tight muscles. I knew I would feel good the next day as I had in Nevshehir. After what seemed a lot longer than John's twenty minutes, I came out making the same boxing movements with my arms and shoulders. John was laying on a hot slab of stone, out cold. I went to the other side, lay down for a breather and quickly found myself in the same state.

We awoke, submerged our bodies in the hot bath for a few minutes just letting the water sooth our muscles. The few *lira* we paid for the whole experience was well-spent money indeed. We showered then dressed, and as we limped back to our *pension*, we both agreed it had been a unique massage experience, and both hoped we'd feel the benefits the next morning.

A good meal and dreamless night's sleep was just what the doctor ordered. The *mullah* awoke us for the last time as we packed up our bikes feeling suppler after our massages, and pedaled out of one of my finest cycling experiences. Now I finally felt as if my European cycling trip was beginning.

When we made it into Bulgaria it was handy to have the basic Turkish language skills I had picked up over the last few months. I hadn't realized how many people in Bulgaria spoke Turkish – remnants of arbitrary lines drawn on maps, and 500 years of the Ottoman Empire. The present is always a result of histories we think we know but are filled with subjective opinions and personal issues and handed down through the generations until we have a murky present filled with old hatreds, prejudices, class systems and civilizations founded on occupying other lands.

After a few days on the road and staying in the Black Sea coastal town of Burgas, we made it to a town called Bellene on the River Danube – which separated Bulgaria from Romania. We had missed the first bridge into Romania so would now have to cycle to the next crossing which we heard was a ferry. We were trying to avoid having to cycle into Serbia – the part of Yugoslavia which was in the middle of a bloody civil war – but we were being pushed in that direction.

In Bellene we met a character called Ivan Ivanovitch. He reminded me of the Bulgarian version of Andre who I had met in Moscow. We were trying to find a place to sleep and a phone as John had to call a newspaper in Manchester that was keeping track of his world tour. We couldn't find either in Bellene and when we were just about to give up, pedal out of town and camp under the cover of dusk, Ivan walked into our lives – jacket draped over his shoulders, cigarette dangling from his lips, sunglasses holding back his hair, and a moustache. He looked like something out of a bad spy movie, but was quite real. He bought us a coffee.

"You are riding your bicycles to Bellene for what reason?" he asked.

"Actually we're riding our bicycles as far north as Poland before heading west to England," John said.

"Poland? England? This is very far from Bellene, it is a long way to ride a bike, why do you want to do such a thing?" He seemed genuinely puzzled. I enjoyed the way he always referred to Bellene rather than Bulgaria. It showed to me that this was where Ivan was from, it was Bellene, not Bulgaria – he was a man of the town, maybe even the Mayor.

"I'm riding my bicycle around the world for a charity in England called The Queen's Children. Joe here is cycling around Europe because he likes to ride his bike, we will hopefully make it as far as Poland, and then I will ride back home to England, I'm not quite sure where Joe is heading after that." John looked at me and smiled. He was being deliberately obtuse and I could see that Ivan put his back up.

John was also still angry that he'd had to pay forty dollars for a visa to get into Bulgaria, and my entry was free. He had really lost it at the border-crossing. "I'm a European," he kept on saying, "*he's* the American. *He* should be paying!*" I was laughing but John wasn't too pleased. We thought Ivan might be an official of some sort, but like Andre in Moscow, he was a player. John then had the forethought to ask, "Is there a phone in Bellene? I need to call England and do an interview on the radio."

Ivan smiled and the gold frame of his front tooth twinkled. "I have a phone where you can call England from." I think before he invited us back to his house he wanted to be sure of who we were. After he was satisfied we were just two guys riding our bikes, he invited us to stay with him. When we got to his apartment, we put our bikes in the storage place in the basement, and entered Ivan's world.

Bulgaria was quite poor as it had only recently emerged from under the veil of the iron curtain. Bread was only to be found if you were on the line in time and could actually find the bakery, phones to the outside world were few and far between, if you did find one, they usually didn't work, food in restaurants was basic if there was any, and beer was the only beverage to be found in some places. Now, as we stepped into Ivan's house we saw that it was full. There was food of all description, nice furniture, and a phone hooked up to what looked like a computer of sorts. Whatever it was, John was soon talking to his newspaper. Ivan did have a family, but like Andre's they were mysteriously somewhere else at the time. I'm not sure if these were just coincidences, or if these men actually had families – there were photos on the wall which seemed to attest to the fact, but either way he didn't have to prove anything to us.

We went out that night to a bar for a drink. It was a hazy place full of smoke and the loud, nearly distorted words of *Winds of Change* by the Scorpions – which seemed to be the unofficial national anthem of Bulgaria – blared through antiquated speakers. The women all dressed in a fashion that looked like the oldest profession in the world was the only one available; very short skirts and no sign of the supposed ancient Greek innovation, the bra. It's unfair of me to make such sweeping rude statements, but it was my honest overall impression. Everyone was nice enough in a standoffish type of way. Ivan wasn't the Mayor but he might as well have been – everyone knew him and we were introduced to everybody as his guests.

The next day we met the real mayor and were interviewed by the local newspaper. In 1992 it was still a big deal for an Englishman and an American to come cycling through town. After the interview Ivan took us to a place called Pleven where he treated us to lunch. I had cow's tongue which was the local delicacy. John said he was vegetarian, which was the truth – and got away with a salad and steamed veggies. I thought back to my attempts at vegetarianism, "Maybe today would have been a good day to try again," I thought as the tongue appeared in front of me.

We stayed one more night in Bellene, and after a big breakfast and a small send off by the locals we headed on our way to a town called Nikopol from where we thought we could catch a ferry over the river into Romania. When we got to Nikopol, we were told the crossing was only for Bulgarians and Romanians. Damn, I wished I could stop doing that! We now knew that the only way we were getting out of Bulgaria was through Serbia.

We camped that night, and the next day cycled the 105 miles into the headwind which we'd picked up since cycling on the south bank of the Danube. Even with the wind, it was still an improvement over the day before. We pulled in, exhausted, to a place called Vidin from where we could cross into Yugoslavia, as it was still called at the time. We would have liked to stay in the Youth Hostel, but, like many of the hotels and hostels we had come across already; it unashamedly charged foreigners triple the local price, so we wound up camping. We found it hard to agree with the pricing system. Yes, we had access to more money than the locals, but at that point in our lives we didn't, and to pay three, four or even ten times as much for the same dingy room was a hard pill to swallow.

We weren't sure what to expect on the border, but it went pretty smoothly. It felt impossible that people were killing each other only 800 kilometers to the south of us in Bosnia. We stayed in Negotin and met some locals who were very eager to engage us in a conversation about Bosnia and all that was going on. John and I felt uncomfortable especially when one older guy who was drunk gladly boasted he was going down to kill the Croats who were deserving of everything they got.

We met another younger guy, who had just established a business after all those years under Tito, and now his exporting business to the U.K. was going to end, and if he didn't join the army he would lose all his benefits and any unemployment he was entitled to. He had done his time in the army already but the war had changed the rules. He had a wife and young child, and in another life he could have been John or I, but this time we were able to cycle out of the nightmare and he was going to have to join an army and fight for a cause he didn't believe in. He told us where he grew up was a mixed area, and the Croats and Serbs got along, sometimes you didn't even know if someone was a Croat or Serb – they were just your neighbor. I often wonder if that young entrepreneurial Serbian man is still alive, and if he is, what horrors did he witness or partake in just so he could feed his daughter and prop up another megalomaniac ruler of our sometimes insane planet.

On our arrival into Serbia the Yugoslavian *dinar* was just losing another zero or two off the face value on the notes. Inflation was making the current notes useless, and, as has been done in other countries, new notes were being issued with less zeros at the end. It's a good way to weed out black market and undeclared money but for us it meant total confusion. The old money was still circulating, but people spoke in the even older denominations which had been changed not long before. We were getting a mix of old and new notes and trying to translate the confusion of which money people were talking about. Ah, whatever happened to barter? Fortunately we did not need to change much as we were heading to Romania, and would be cycling in this country for just a few days.

After changing money and intriguing discussions over a hot drink, we cycled away out into the gorgeous countryside. It was the end of June and the land was wallowing in its fecundity; the earth was a rich brown and the sunflowers were in full-bloom. We camped out behind sunflower fields where we could keep a low profile and light a campfire to cook on. It felt too weird to both of us that, as we enjoyed the peace and beauty, people were killing each other surrounded by the same splendor.

The next day we were pedaling along enjoying the scenery when a bus passed us and pulled up in a cloud of dust about a hundred yards ahead. The driver jumped down from his seat and motioned us to stop. He then pulled out a bucket of fresh peaches, pointed to our panniers and, without saying a word, gestured to us to open them. He poured the contents of the bucket into our bags, gave us a big smile, got back in his bus and drove away. A short way down the road he swung in a wide u-turn to go back the way he had come. As he passed us he beeped, waved and continued on his way – not only was he generous, he had driven out of the way to be so. It was moments like these that every world leader should have. The amount of kindness over the years I had experienced was impossible to count up. If we nurture that side of ourselves that is what we would see more of, I was definitely convinced of that. The peaches were gorgeous, and we ate a few just to lighten up the load!

We made it into Romania and felt as if we'd been transported back in time. The Transylvanian Alps were cycling heaven; the gentle gradients, the spectacular scenery, the outdoor market places in every tiny village, and the car-less roads were fantastic. Every so often we would come to a big industrial town or city. They were grotesque especially after the beauty we had just come from. It was so hideous that it was something you could not dream up; the apartment blocks were square and soulless, the air was foul, billowing with black clouds and steam, and there was not a jot of color amongst the brown, gray and black that pervaded everything. The strangest phenomenon though was the wide piping that crossed the dusty roads overhead like some large supporting scaffold system. I never found out exactly what these pipes were actually for, but they graced the outskirts of every small town or village just adding to the ugliness of it all. Soot seemed to cover everyone and everything. It was like cycling from nirvana to hell and back.

They say Romania, after twenty-five years of despotic rule under Nicolae Ceausescu, suffered as much or even more devastation than if it had been involved in a full-scale ten-year civil war. From what we saw, it looked true. What must have been picturesque villages had been torn down and ugly austere blocks of concrete taken their place. What better way to control people and hamper their individuality than having them live in such ghastly places. Many atrocities had come to light after his overthrow and execution nearly three years previously, but Romania was still reeling. It was basking in a few new-found freedoms but there was a long tough road ahead.

Fortunately these hellish scenes were not far from the beautiful green rolling countryside. Our main road sharers were colorful gypsies in their horse-drawn gypsy caravans. It was like being transported to an age gone by to pedal past one of these and know that they were people's real homes.

We free-camped mostly and one strange night we found ourselves still cycling at dusk. We had stopped an hour earlier at a likely looking spot but we had heard lots of strange noises. We knew we were now in Transylvania and our imaginations must have run away with us, conjuring up images of Dracula and vampires. The tough Bronx boy and the *scouser* pedaled hastily off. We wound up pedaling through several small villages being chased by dogs in every one. It was quite unnerving until we came across a barman unloading beer from a delivery truck. We stopped to help him and had a beer as it was a warm perfect night. At about eleven in the evening the owner asked us where we were sleeping and we pointed to his front step. We then tried to explain what was happening with the dogs chasing us, and that we were tired. He may have understood some of it as he told us we would not sleep on his front step but we would be his guest at his house that night. He served us two more beers and as it approached midnight he kept on motioning enthusiastically to me and saying something. I realized that it was July third and he was telling me it was becoming July fourth. I smiled, thanked him, and thought it funny that this Romanian guy in the middle of Transylvania was buying me a drink to celebrate American Independence Day. I wish I could have felt as happy as he did about America. My travels and the current President George Bush the first made me a bit edgy about where the world was heading, who was taking it there, and why.

We went back to his house and much to our chagrin, he woke his wife up for her to cook us a meal. We protested, but he wouldn't hear of it. To make matters worse, in his tiny one bedroom house we were given the double bed and the only bedroom. It was extremely embarrassing but to fight it too strongly would have been an insult. So we ate a meal of fresh eggs, sausage and bread cooked by his smiling wife who appeared to be unperturbed that she'd been roused from her sleep to cook as well as give up her bed. Our guilt didn't keep us awake too long, we'd covered a lot of hilly miles that day and were not accustomed to the strong Romanian beer, so sleep came very easily.

We were awoken to another delicious meal, much the same as the night before, and now we could see his house and small courtyard in the light of day. I could not imagine where they had slept, but of course never asked. We were treated to what seemed to be a favorite morning drink among the peasants. Later in the day it was usually strong beer drunk from jars, but in the morning we were offered instant coffee and a coca-cola-like soft drink mixed up together, and man was the mixture lethal. Our heads were foggy from the night before and now our stomachs felt much the same. After saying goodbye to our gracious hosts and thanking them profusely, we decided that we would not be putting a lot of mileage in that day. We magically found a place that didn't charge foreigners ten times the price. We stayed in two separate cabins which cost us the equivalent of a dollar each.

The rest of our time in Romania was spent camping in scenic areas and pedaling into a stiff headwind all day. We didn't visit any big cities in Romania and even skipped the town where Dracula's Castle was. We were both winding down from a long bike ride and John was nearing the last leg of his journey. I was ready to get to Western Europe as my mom, sister, and niece were going to be in Switzerland on a pre-planned trip and I had it in the back of my mind that I might be able to meet them although it was still a month or so away.

We made it to the border town of Gyula where a violent thunderstorm saw us sitting in a café in Romania for the last hour spending our last few coins of local currency. We were right on the border and we both were eager to cross it.

Entering Hungary was, in many ways, like re-entering Western Europe. We treated ourselves to a hotel which had unlimited hot water – something that had been hard to find in Romania. It was not expensive and the comfy beds and our clean bodies allowed us to both sleep like babies.

John was enjoying the camping and the slightly slower pace – before we'd hooked up he'd never used a tent on his journey. I found it quite a compliment that now sharing mine he was enjoying the experience so much that he decided to start looking for one so he could continue using it after we went our separate ways. I was able to keep John's bike limping along but didn't quite have the tools for the overhaul his bike did need if it were to make it across Europe and back to England.

We decided we needed to push on to Budapest. The relentless headwind was still with us and we were still cycling pretty much along the Danube. The next morning we just put on our riding heads and, with pacing each other, cycled well into the night, covering over 200 kilometers into the wind with our fully loaded bikes. We slept twenty kilometers from Budapest on the lawn of a church in a small village on the periphery without even bothering to put up our tents. The church bells were our early alarm clock, and we awoke with dew settled on our sleeping bags and heads. Groggy-eyed I stumbled to a bakery, bought some bread and coffee, and we had breakfast on a bench looking and feeling like two homeless guys. Technically, at that point in time, I suppose that is exactly what we were.

The traffic started building up soon after we left the village heading towards the capital, Budapest. I'd never realized there were two parts of the city; the calmer less chaotic *Buda* side and the more commercial urban *Pest* side, the Danube being the dividing line. We decided to find an apartment share which was what the tourist office recommended. We went to an agency which we found through the tourist information, and wound up staying in an apartment with an older couple who could have been our parents.

They were a very nice couple, and were worried about us, me more than John – he was a little younger than me and clean cut with a girlfriend in England – I was in my thirties with long hair, a beard, and no prospects of a wife. Their conservative selves couldn't handle it, and of course John played right into it, nodding seriously at their worries, agreeing that, "Yes, it really is time he settled down," while I poked him in the ribs. We had lots of good laughs, with me constantly explaining to my Hungarian parents that I'd be alright.

We dabbled in the world of culture, and went to a modern dance called *Cristobal Colon*, a modern dance/opera based on the life of Columbus. It was pretty good but could have been an hour shorter. We ate in nice restaurants – after Istanbul it was the first big city we had been in, and the first time we felt we had come back to modern day Europe.

More importantly we found a bike shop and John got his bike sorted out – full tune up, new handlebar tape, and he was ready to go. My chain had broken once since Turkey, but besides it being a few links shorter, all else was in good order. At the dance show we'd met a pair of Danish sisters and spent the next evening with them. They were good fun, but 'mom' and 'dad' would never have approved of us bringing them up to our place! We felt as if we were getting closer and closer to home.

Czechoslovakia was officially divided into the Czech Republic and Slovakia now, and from Hungary we cycled into Slovakia. We had been speeding through many countries and things were getting blurry, but we still camped out and rode through the challenging countryside like we were on a mission. John was, and I was being sucked in. It was a change for me, I didn't mind it too much as I was enjoying the company and enjoyed riding. We were both in fantastic shape, the Tatra Mountains were coming up, and there we hooked up with a few Polish young lads on a cycle journey of their own. We crossed the high border from Slovakia into Zakopane, Poland, and what a beautiful ride that was.

Zakopane is a Polish tourist town, and quite rightfully so. Hiking and cycling in the beautiful Tatra Mountains is something many people around Europe travel there to do. It was easy to see why. With the help of the Polish lads we found a woman who accepted campers in her back garden for a small fee – it was the perfect place to spend a couple of nights, enjoy the food, and get ready to head due west for the first time in weeks. Our trip had taken on the aura of one of my first motorcycle journeys across America – we were covering ground quickly and two day's ride from Zakopane found us at the gates of one of the most infamous places of World War II – Auschwitz.

We had cycled to a place whose history was steeped in horror, another reminder of man's inhumanity to man. Vietnam to Germany and everywhere in between, I had witnessed the world's beauty and kindness traveling hand in hand with some of the worst atrocities ever committed towards human beings. All of my travels were showing me that the world was a good place – people were kind, and nature was forgiving and such a powerful force in all of our lives, but as we entered the eerie gates of Auschwitz, nature and beauty were cast far from the mind.

All the cycling, chance meetings and wonderment stayed suspended outside the gates as we entered the rooms of eye glasses, luggage, yellow-papered diaries – the personal belongings of all the humanity killed in the ovens – people unknowingly getting off at the last stop of the train, the last stop of their lives. The empty gas canisters glaring at us felt worse than a slap in the face. We see this and yet what do we do? Continue the madness. We had just cycled through war-torn Yugoslavia, Iraq was in shambles from the previous year, Algeria in a mess, the struggles were ongoing in Palestine – the list goes on, yet these places of grim reminders are there for all to visit. Can we still go blindly into the future knowing that this is our recent past?

We walked through Auschwitz in silence, our eyes opened once again to the ugliness that the human being is capable of. As we silently pedaled away from that most horrible reminder, we were glad to have our bikes to help us process what we had just seen. The comfort of our bikes and the peacefulness of the surrounding countryside was almost too strange to comprehend. There were small farms, farmhouses and villages so close to the camp. What did theses people think and feel? How deep had their fear been, or how much had they been able to close their minds to the reality of the situation surrounding them back in the thirties and forties? Had they simply processed and moved on?

I recalled again the war with Iraq and my mind shifted back to the experiences I'd had in Vietnam and all the other horrors I have been alive to witness. Had I done enough to try and prevent them from happening? Could I do more to prevent the powers that be from devastating our planet, stripping our resources, and killing its people? All my years exploring had revealed a deeper part of me that I had never known was there before, there was no turning back from it, and definitely no way to un-see or un-learn any of the things I'd had the privilege of seeing. I knew I would have to live these changes in my life from now on.

As we cycled on the small roads of the Polish countryside we saw a young local kid standing with a soccer ball in his hands and a bike on the ground turned upside down. With our phrasebook Polish we asked if he had a problem with his bike. He nodded yes, so we stopped, whipped off his wheel, took off his tire, found and patched the small puncture and put everything back together. We had completed the repair so quickly that the boy was still standing as we had first seen him with his ball in his hands. We turned his bike the right way up, placed his ball in his basket, and told him to have a nice day. We pedaled off as his confusion was slowly replaced by a big smile. We looked back to see him getting on his bike and cycling off with a whoop.

John's schedule was starting to play more heavily on his mind and our time cycling together was coming to a close. We enjoyed staying in some of the small villages and were glad to be behind what was once 'The Iron Curtain', newly opened to free travel. The curtain was now just a thin veil and in under fifteen years time this would be part of the wider European Union.

As we cycled west and re-entered the Czech Republic we decided that Prague would be where we would go our separate ways. When we arrived there, we found it to be truly breathtaking; reminding me of a fairytale village. The street musician's costumes and wonderful music transported us to a different era. The exquisite Charles Bridge, the colorful houses, the utter prettiness encapsulated us, and we were smitten by the city's charm. John felt that he ought to be walking the streets of this romantic town with his girlfriend Melanie – who was waiting for him in England – I didn't take it personally. I wanted to keep the image in my mind and return one day to soak up everything that Prague had to offer. I was reaching overload – not able to fully appreciate my experiences any more.

After John and I parted company I knew I was going to slow down, stick to the small villages, and find somewhere I could write, relax and process the last intense year of travel.

# From Prague to a Plan

We cycled out of Prague together to a small village where we camped out in our separate tents. John had his own now and he was ready to put it to good use heading back to England. On our last night we had a *Budvah Beer* to celebrate the past six or so weeks of sharing our lives together and knew we would keep in touch. After saying goodbye I headed on a small cycle path through the woods towards Germany not quite sure of my direction but knew that my mother and sister Nancy were coming to Switzerland fairly soon now. They would be traveling with my thirteen-year-old niece, Dana, sister to Denis who I had met up with at a similar age in Australia a few years earlier. I thought it would be a nice opportunity to meet up for a few days and save her from the itinerary of tours that my mother and sister had booked.

There was still time before they arrived and I found myself in southern Germany and decided to dip into Austria to enjoy the small picturesque villages there. Impeccably well-preserved homes resembled doll houses set into Tyrolean mountain scenery. What a stark contrast to Romania. On entering some towns the year of its founding would be inscribed on the welcome sign. Many of the places were older than modern-day America but seemed to age very well. Salzburg was more reminiscent of Prague in its beauty but it was still impossible to compare the two. I found Europe's history fascinating – when crossing America I could cover 600 miles where not even the scenery would change but here in Europe – both Eastern and Western – 600 miles brought me through more languages, cultures, religious influences, architectural differences and varied landscapes than most people would come across in their lifetimes.

Austria's beauty also hid some secrets in its past; the Austro-Hungarian Empire which nearly segued right into its annexation by the *Third Reich* and the Nazi regime – a history I needn't rehash here. I sought out Mozart's birthplace but didn't bother even wondering where Hitler was born, and very much doubted it would be a tourist attraction.

The German and Austrian campsites were organized, clean and expensive. After the somewhat disorganized adventures in Eastern Europe and Turkey it took some getting used to. Camping rough was possible but mostly forbidden. Any type of B&B or hotel was out of the question financially. Youth hostels were fine for the occasional bed, but the campsites were much more upmarket when it came to showers and other amenities and the price difference was negligible.

The food was meat-based, and although I still wasn't back to another try at a vegetarian diet, I was reaching sausage overload! The beer was always good and local brews could easily be found – the experience was so different to Turkey that it was hard to believe I had actually cycled from that reality to this; it was a world away, nearly as foreign as flying to Germany from my Asian adventures via Moscow, but not such a sudden shock. In many ways it was much the same as that flight. Although Turkey spanned both continents, on the larger mainland it felt more like Asia in its religious differences, poverty and openness. Austria wasn't unfriendly in anyway, but cyclists and tourists were more common, and arriving in shorts didn't cause a stir; the church bell's ring more familiar than the *mullah's* call five times daily.

The school holidays were winding down so the crowds were dissipating. I was having lunch in a scenic lookout on a mountain road one day when three cyclists pulled in on their loaded bikes. I nodded and waved and they came over to say hello. They were Austrian kids out on a three-week tour of Austria and Hungary. They talked about their trip; the beautiful scenery, beautiful villages, and how this was their second long trip together with more planned in the future. Their English was very good, which was a bonus, because my phrase book German was pretty limiting. They were heading back home now to Vienna and I was vaguely pointing my bike towards Innsbruck so lunch was all the time we'd share with each other. They looked young and when I asked how much time they had left in their travels they told me just under a week as they needed to get home for the beginning of the school term – the eldest of the trio was fourteen, the other two thirteen!

I cycled away from that lookout thinking of my upcoming meeting with my thirteen-year-old niece who had never taken the train with her friends from where she lived to New York City, just forty miles away! I definitely had to meet her in Switzerland to save her from the guided tour itinerary. Hopefully I was showing her another life was possible. I realized my sister and I were worlds apart but my niece and I could still bridge that gap.

Since John and I pedaled our separate ways I had slowed down my pace once again and was taking it easy with no real plan; if I was going to meet up with my family in Switzerland – which seemed more pertinent now – I needed to see how I would make that happen. I looked at a map and realized I was not far from Munich, where Thomas Uhlemann – who I'd met in Tunisia – was from, so I gave him a call.

He was glad to see me when I arrived and greeted me like a long lost friend. It was great to see him too and we enjoyed a couple of days together. Thomas was happy for me to leave my bike at his place while I hopped on a train to Geneva. I hadn't told my family I would meet them definitively in case it hadn't worked out but now I knew I'd get there.

I arrived at the hotel before they did, managed to talk my way into their room and was showered and rested before they arrived. It had been a nearly a year since I had seen them, and there were the customary screams, laughter and hugs before they calmed down – those Italian genes certainly are excitable!

We were all glad to meet up for a short visit. My mom and sister favored the method of fitting as many tourist attractions as possible into one day and Dana was getting bored of being dragged around with them. She and I just chilled out talking and walking around Geneva while the ladies did their tours. We had a close relationship and our motorcycling camping trips together in the past and our deep talks were starting to intrigue her young mind. She was starting to question and perhaps see things a little differently. I was glad to be part of that growth and add a different perspective to her suburban existence.

The next day we all took a boat together on Lake Geneva, otherwise known as Loc Leman – it was stunning scenery and we had a nice time catching up, it was clear though that our ways of traveling were solar systems apart. Theirs was a whistle stop tour as they had even squeezed in a day or two in England before heading home. However different I realized I was from the rest of my family, we had a close relationship and it had been an enjoying interlude.

Once back in Munich I stayed a few more days with Thomas and got to know the city a little. One day I was enjoying some busking musicians and found myself sitting next to an Italian girl. We started to chat and I discovered that she was traveling alone. I brought her with me to meet up with Thomas who was filming an African drummer that night in the countryside outside Munich. We all had a good time and Novella came back with me to Thomas's. A small romance was beginning between us and it was just what the doctor ordered.

She was heading to the Czech Republic, and I France, so we both altered our plans to spend more time together. We developed a creative way of traveling together along the *Romantickstrasse* – an appropriately named road leading from Munich to Augsburgh, passing through countryside and small villages. We would agree on a destination and then she would take a train while I would cycle to meet her there. We would meet at a train station then head off to a campsite, usually with me carrying Novella on my back rack. It was that way that we traveled all the way up into Nuremburg. It was beer festival time so every village or town had a party atmosphere – Novella and I joined right in. Drinking the occasional beer felt different here, more a part of the culture, whereas in Tunisia,

Morocco and Turkey I stayed clear of indulging at all. The Germans enjoyed their beer that was for sure.

Germany, for me, had reminiscences of Japan. The cultures were as stern in their rigidness as each other and that inflexible thinking also paved the way for alternative behavior which was just as extreme. Was it also possibly why their populations were able to be manipulated to such degrees? I didn't know, but thought their similar pre-World War II histories may have been more than coincidence. Individuality is something which is very dangerous to constrain.

I found Nuremburg creepy being the former seat of the *Third Reich*. Fortunately Novella and I decided to give Dacau, a concentration camp on the outskirts of Munich a wide berth, but it was eerie to be following Hitler's murderous trail – Auschwitz now Nuremburg I was feeling an odd energy somehow emanating from the city and its people. Novella, arriving by train a few hours later, actually felt much the same.

Our brief romance was perfect after so much time being alone or traveling with other men. The time finally came for Novella to continue with her original plan and head, funnily enough, to Prague, not on the cards for me even though the situation nearly called for it. She was from Florence, and I promised I'd look her up when I found myself back in Italy. We parted almost tearfully as Novella's train headed east.

After meeting up with family for a brief visit and my romantic break I was feeling rejuvenated. It was now early fall and the cycling was fantastic. I was now catching beautiful weather on the tail-end of southern Europe's recent heat-wave. In the middle of summer through the old eastern block it had been nearly stifling sometimes, but now with the coolness of autumn entering the weather pattern, it was ideal.

I cycled along the small byways and riversides of Germany into France. I only had a large general map of Europe, not great for cycling, but with the vast distances I was covering it would have been both costly and nearly impossible to have many detailed ones. It was years away from 'Google Maps' being available in every internet café.

A general idea of my destination combined with asking questions and having lots of time was working out well so far. I went with the roads that were small – winding through picturesque villages in a vaguely westerly direction. I was free camping, knocking on farmer's doors, setting up in fields, and in France the municipal campsites were fabulous; very cheap, and nearly every town or village had one. Now that the high tourist season had ended meant some sites were beginning to close. If I couldn't squeeze past the locked gates, or get in some other way, soccer fields served the same purpose. I was falling in love with France's roads. I was learning that, although famous for its bigger cities, it's mostly a rural country. If you can avoid the urban sprawl which is easy to do in such a large country, the cycling is fantastic.

One evening I was looking for the municipal campsite on a marked bicycle route when I saw a man jogging and rode up next to him. I started a conversation and we carried on chatting while he ran and I rode. When I got around to asking where the campsite was we were at a T-junction in the road. He pointed left and said, "The campsite is about three kilometers that way." Then he pointed right and continued, "My house is four kilometers this way. You can camp, or eat with me and my family and sleep in our guest room."

I was taken aback at first. Our conversation was in basic French so I did have to clarify. I was getting used to invitations but this one came so quickly and out of the blue. I laughed because I felt funny saying yes, but it was a sincere unprovoked invitation. I thought about it for a few seconds and asked, "How far to your house?"

He smiled as we both turned right and continued our conversation. His wife and children warmly greeted me as if they somehow knew I was coming, and an outdoor dinner was enjoyed under the setting sun. The guest room was perfect and the offer of a shower was also happily accepted.

The next day a simple breakfast was left out – his wife and kids were gone, and he was dressed for work. My host showed me how to shut the garage door before I left, and we said goodbye to each other. Their day started quite early as it was not even seven-thirty yet. It made me think back to Bob and Julie in Quebec all those years ago. Human kindness truly did straddle continents, and my travels were proof-positive of that.

I was now getting into the commuter belt of Paris. I drank down my coffee and since I hadn't unpacked much, was ready to head out and prepare for a more urban cycling experience. I made it to Paris through miles and miles of sprawl – what was I saying about sticking to the countryside? It was great to see Danny, my friend from New York, who was once married to my cousin Jennifer. I hadn't seen him since all those years ago in Los Angeles. Once again our paths were crossing and it was a long way from The Bronx for both of us. His French girlfriend – Catherine – was welcoming and spoke perfect English with a trace of a New York accent thanks to living in New York for nearly twenty years. My bike was hung up for a week's rest except for a short ride with Danny to Versailles to get a taste of real over the top opulence, Louis XVI style.

I took in Paris on foot by day and we enjoyed the café culture of that wonderful city by night. Both Catherine and Danny were artists. Their apartment was in the garment district of Paris, and in many ways it felt like a blend of New York, Asia, and Europe all rolled into one. As September was slipping away, I decided to start heading south. It was strange to once again be saying goodbye to familiar faces from home against another European city backdrop.

I had decided a few things while in Paris; firstly I called the brothers who ran the campsite in Greece to see if the offer to work there for the winter still stood – it did – so I would head there for the winter. Novella was in Florence and my Aunt Mary and Uncle Lou were going to be in Rutigliano in October, so Italy was on the cards as well. There would be no way I would be able to cycle all those miles in that space of time, but I now had a plan – enjoy France, cross into Italy over the Alps, and then start jogging south by train.

My Tunisian French was coming into its own and the weather was holding up nicely. I was in great cycling shape, meeting friendly people, and the French countryside was a pleasure to slowly soak in. On the outskirts of Annecy I was stopped by a Mercedes Benz, the driver flagging me down. He spoke English very well and asked me to join his family for lunch. I wasn't sure what was going on, I didn't look undernourished but people felt compelled to feed me. I wasn't complaining, and as it turned out, he was a cyclist and had seen me pedal by his house as his family was setting out the plates. We had a nice conversation over a three-course lunch – I was in no hurry – I had already decided I was treating myself to a campsite overlooking the lake which wasn't far off.

After a few glasses of wine, I wobbled off to find my campsite. I decided to splurge and go for a slightly nicer, more expensive campsite. I even washed my clothes in the washing machine on site. I was on my way to pick up my clothes when I heard someone say, "Joe?" I thought that there was no way someone was speaking to me, so I kept on walking, then heard again, "Joe, is that Joe?" definitely spoken in English. I turned around to see a familiar face from New York staring at me in disbelief. I walked over in amazement and said hello to Stephanie, my cousin, and Nick her British husband. They were living in the U.K. at that time and were on a camping holiday in France. I couldn't believe it, but then again, why not? Coincidences seemed to follow me around; out of the whole of France, we had met up by chance in this small campsite in Annecy.

We all spent one more night in the campsite than we expected so we could catch up with each other. I couldn't resist calling my mom and putting Stephanie on the phone to say hello. I thought how easily we could have missed each other even if we had been in the same campsite. It was another lesson in what a small, interconnected planet we live on. I felt less like I was traveling by bike but more like I was on an incredible voyage through life. The journey I was on had been nothing short of fantastic – all the invitations, chance and even planned meetings were making me feel

451

like sharing with the whole world all at once how wonderful life truly is, and how much better it could be for all of us. I had lots to give back to this wonderful place we called earth, and intended to find a way how.

A few days later I was cycling along a small lake on the outskirts of a village in the Alps when I saw a young guy obviously having some bike trouble. He had a flat and was unprepared to fix it. Punctures were one thing you learned to fix quickly in bike shops so, much like the young Polish boy with his football in his hand, and his mouth wide open in disbelief; I fixed this puncture just as quickly. He was excited to continue on his trip around the lake and invited me to dinner that night with the youth group he was working with there. More food!

That night, after finding the municipal campsite and showering, I went to spend the evening with the youth organization whose workshop was coming to an end. The group consisted of young people from around Europe and North Africa getting together to do some community development projects. It was great to see this melting pot of young people forging relationships; working together despite religious, cultural or language differences. That night was a farewell party, and what a party it was; true to French form, five courses, with a constant flow of wine or beer, main course of succulent meat and two vegetables, salad, bread, four or five different cheeses, and three choices for dessert. It far surpassed the exchange of fixing a flat tire!

I was invited to stay in the house the following night as there were a few spare rooms and I gave a hand where I could on the last day of the restoration of an old fountain that was fed by a mountain spring. I stayed two more days there and thought back on the wonderful memories the past year had for me. So many chance meetings, so much friendship, and such diverse countries and cultures, now for a few of my last days in France I was staying with young people from almost all of the countries I had cycled through. This could not be just coincidence. Maybe we had it all backwards. What if the things we call coincidence, chance meetings and synchronicity are actually the norm for us as human beings but because we have lost the way of going with the flow of life we have gotten used to a disjointed series of happenings that we consider normal. When we then somehow connect back to the way it should be we call it amazing or coincidental. I quite liked my new theory.

Climbing the last mountain pass in France, Italy came quicker than I expected. Once I crossed the border my increasingly good French got vaporized and I was forced back to phrase book Italian and hand gestures. These seem to be half of the system of Italian communication in any case so worked surprisingly well even with no words!

452

I made it down to Florence and met up with Novella. It was nice to be reunited at first, but she was now home with her mom, and our holiday romance didn't transfer very well to those living conditions. The spark we'd had in Germany fizzled out. It could have been me or her, or maybe we were trying to make something work that wasn't meant to be. After a few days of walking and riding those magnificent streets of Florence, we both realized that I was heading to Greece, she was staying in Florence, and our romance was still in Germany. Despite everything, Novella enjoyed seeing each other one last time. Time was running short if I was going to meet up with Aunt Mary and Uncle Lou. My bike and I left Florence by train, and I began heading back to Aldo and the relatives of the south.

Arriving – now for the third time – my relatives seemed to warm to me. It helped that my Aunt Mary and Uncle Lou were there to vouch for my sanity. They told me later on about the knife under Aldo's pillow but we kept it quiet that I knew. Privately we found it quite funny.

Aldo was such a character and had married our cousin Maria much later in life. He was a true caricature of a southern Italian; short and stocky in build, balding, always a cigarette hanging from his lips, a raspy voice, and black coffee on his breath constantly. He didn't talk to Maria as much as mostly yell in frustration, which, combined with his flailing arms and nervous manner made it feel like he was always waiting for two hit men to come bursting through the door. I didn't take the knife under the pillow personally, especially now I knew him better, but felt he'd probably just moved it from the bedside table drawer for quicker access! His nights could not have been full of restful sleep with all the nicotine and caffeine running through his veins. I even had a tough time sleeping just knowing he drank so much coffee at midnight. All the legal stimulants tearing around his brain probably increased his paranoia.

Uncle Lou, inspired by my finding lost relatives in the mountains, had decided he wanted an adventure of his own. Apparently he had some long lost relatives in that part of the world too – we decided to search them out.

My bike once again secured in the same garage, we took off to find *his* lost relatives. On the way we stopped by my mother's newly found relatives in Potenza and were treated like royalty. We were put up in a hotel for the night and tears were flowing as we left after only two days. My uncle and aunt's Italian filled in many of the gaps I had missed and we all reminisced and vowed to keep in touch.

Building bridges with Uncle Lou's relatives proved to be more difficult. We had an address for them which we were sure was correct but far from the royal treatment when we arrived, it seemed that his far-flung cousins were more wary than even Aldo. Maybe I looked a bit suspicious but Aunt Mary and Uncle Lou surely made us look respectable.

We knocked on the door to introduce ourselves and Uncle Lou explained who he was and gave our condolences for the recent death of Uncle Lou's cousin's father who we'd heard had died the previous week. That news came to us from some people on the bus we'd taken up to the village we were now in. The way the man who opened the door looked at us made us think that perhaps it wasn't true, and it was obvious we were not going to be invited in the house no matter what we said. Uncle Lou wasn't too wounded; we'd had a good laugh, stayed in a smelly hotel, had a train ride through the mountains, and even though we thought the house was the right one and we had indeed did found his relatives, no one in the house, or the village seemed to care too much. Maybe they thought we wanted to cash in on the deceased's estate. Whatever it was, the trip was an adventure nonetheless. Uncle Lou filled us in on the return journey that his family never got along anyhow!

My Italian family was nice once they'd warmed up, but their children were frustrated with their lives in a small town. They weren't much younger than me, but all they talked about was sex, and not in a healthy way, more in an obsessed, unnatural frenzy. My cousins' children who were in their twenties wanted to know if I'd had sex with girls and if so how many, when, where etc. It took me back to my high school days spent with teenage friends learning the ways of the world.

While staying there I'd met a girl, Patricia, from New Jersey who spent her summers with her relatives in Rutigliano and had done so since she was a toddler. She spoke fluent Italian and knew the town and its inhabitants pretty well. I met her on a few occasions and we spoke of our families and how we both wound up in this small village near the Adriatic Sea. When I knew her better, I felt able to broach the subject of the sex obsession that seemed to be all pervasive.

She chuckled, "No one has sex here without getting involved in the vicious sex obsession." She threw her eyes and hands to the heavens and feigned exhaustion. "The girls don't for fear of being labeled the town whore or '*putan*'. The boys all want to have sex but if they do, they brag about it which leads the girls who do being labeled *putan*." I was listening intently as she went on. "Few of the braver women who do go for it live with the label but have no chance of marriage locally. The men who are crazed by the age of twenty are willing to marry their virgin girlfriends just to have sex with them."

I stopped her and asked her if she had first-hand knowledge of all this. She laughed and said, "Oh yes, every time I come here I have offers of sex with everyone in town – married, unmarried, related or not. They know

I'm from America and things are different there. I'm so glad I grew up in New Jersey."

"What about all the young married couples with children?" I asked.

"Ah," she laughed again speaking with a certain authority, "those're the ones who marry too early and are usually frustrated by thirty. The men seek out the town *putan* or me for an affair. I don't get involved; I don't want to be part of the town gossip. I can have all the sex I want in Freehold!" She laughed then continued, "The women are equally frustrated, willing to have pre-marital sex, but don't dare in case they gain the honorary label, so they either get married too young, have kids, start repeating the patterns again, or risk being the town whore. Failing that, they do as they wish then leave town."

"I'm certainly glad I'm not involved. My family here is a bit crazy, but they think *I'm* nuts." I added.

Patricia smiled. "You?" she blurted out, "what about me? I'm nearly twenty-six, don't have two kids, and don't want them!" I smiled at her reaction and she admitted, "You'll never be accepted as normal either, that's for sure."

We met a couple of times in the village square, walking amongst the sex-starved or young married couples pushing strollers.

It was good to have gained some insight into one part of life in rural southern Italy, which seemed different from its northern counterpart. My cousins were heading down the traditional road and following, somewhat begrudgingly, their father's footsteps career-wise. No children yet, but their mother's dreams of grandchildren was unabashedly known. I knew why they thought Patricia and I were odd, but didn't care too much. Of course there were good sides to life in this small village near the sea as well, but our conversations made me think of my mother and aunt's comparisons of relationships in Japan to their grandparent's social structures in 19$^{th}$ century Italy, for Patricia and me, it all still seemed to be a generation or two behind. All the same I thanked my grandparents for leaving Italy and giving me the opportunities that growing up in New York had afforded me.

Sexual frustration, family dynamics, knives under pillows, caffeine and food overdoses aside we all had a real ball our last night together in Rutigliano. I was having a good time reading palms and telling fortunes, repeating back everything I'd heard Aldo, Maria and the rest of the family say over my past visits. They thought I was gifted but Aunt Mary knew me too well and we laughed till we cried, and ate till we dropped. Even Aldo let out a raspy laugh now and again which usually ended in fits of coughing. I always like being with people and this was capturing the essence of why I travel.

My bags were once again loaded with familiar Italian fare for my journey across the Adriatic. My Italian family thought I was crazy for heading over to work on a campsite in Greece and although they accepted me better with Aunt Mary and Uncle Lou around, I could tell they still thought I was nuttier than a fruit cake.

# Ian, Olives and *Retsina*

Cycling towards the ferry my head was spinning. On arriving in Europe for the first time I'd felt strangely at home, then getting back to an America at war after being away for so long I'd felt like a foreigner. Now after spending time with my relatives in Italy I felt oddly out of place once again. I truly felt like a man without a country.

In many ways Europe did feel comfortable; I enjoyed its history, the old streets and buildings, the traditions, the food, but on the other hand, I was from New York; my life growing up on the streets of The Bronx was filled with fond memories and had shaped who I was.

All this didn't allay the questions running around my brain about what an 'American' was. With the past year behind me, I had lots more to mull over. My life had shown me much more than I ever bargained for when I straddled that motorcycle back in 1983 for my first jaunt across America. Now I felt like a man without roots, European on one hand but an American through and through. Even that description didn't sit right; I felt more a New Yorker than an American – to me the difference was big, but hard to explain. To complicate matters further I had found some *Krishnamurti* speeches from the thirties in a few booklets in a small bookstore in Florence. I'd never heard of him, but they jumped out at me from a shelf and were all written in English. He questioned the whole labeling process and national identities in general. I'd been trying to pigeon-hole myself and I laughed as I realized that I also questioned those same ideas – but the labeling process is so ingrained within us that it is hard to shake off. The upcoming few months would be a well-needed rest for me. I was heading to a country once known as 'A democracy in a world of savages'. An interesting thought, despite being 2,500 years old; I wondered if we had come very far, or has the world's savagery just been better disguised?

A winter working on a campsite in the Peloponese, planting trees, doing some minor construction work and picking olives sounded a great way to relax; time to read books, write in my journal, filter through all of the recent and not so recent experiences I'd had. Many things, I was sure, would become clearer with some down time – they always did. I hoped I would even get to improve my feeble Greek language skills.

I arrived at the campsite with an English family I had met on the ferry crossing. It was mom, dad, and two boys traveling on their bikes. They'd spent a few years sailing and now they were trying it as land lubbers.

They were not your typical cyclists and were doing well considering what they were carrying; they'd packed their bikes as if they were still living on their boat. I was getting tired just watching them drag around all the extra weight. Mom was even hauling a pressure cooker! I promised I would give them a hand unloading to make life easier and we'd go to a small market to replace their glassware with some lighter plastic things. I must admit it had been fun camping out together in the abandoned campsites of Greece eating huge meals from china plates and drinking *retsina* from real glasses.

We arrived back at Camping Kyparissia and after the nine-month hiatus the owners were all happy to see me back. This time I would be helping out for a few months. They didn't mind that I'd also brought a family of four with me. Once October comes the bustling campsites in this part of the world either close down or are transformed into ghost towns, so any business was welcome.

A trip to the post office and the small local market the next day and the "Goodgames" were enlightened, by at least twenty-five pounds! They posted it all back by slow mail. With that deed done their bikes were in desperate need of some fine tuning; a few wheels, especially mom's, needed to look like a wheel again. I was once again grateful that I always carry more rather than less in the way of tools.

I was particularly enjoying the company of the two young sons. They were out of the ordinary kids with a colorful life behind them already. The boys and I enjoyed a few push up competitions. Matthew was nearly thirteen and we celebrated Patrick's 15th birthday on the campsite. Flo, their mom, trimmed my hair, and Mike, their dad, and I had some deep conversations about yoga, philosophy, and all things esoteric. We spent nearly two weeks together after which, with their wheels once again round, their bags twenty-five pounds lighter, and their bikes in decent working order, they were ready to roll on. Late-October saw the Goodgames heading towards Israel and more adventures further south. We said we'd keep in touch, and till this day, still do.

Kyparissia is a beautifully placed small village right on the Ionian Sea with a backdrop of hills behind and the seclusion that living on the Peloponese brings with it. The work that the Foundoukis brothers had lined up for the winter was planned out in that very Greek way – we got around to it when we got around to it. Some days were full of work, and most were full of *talking* about work. While this approach would not go down very well in America, it seems to work in Greece.

My thirty-first birthday passed without much ado and as November settled in, any small flow of people still coming through the campsite had all but stopped. By mid-November we were all into a routine. Each morning I would wake up, walk to town and get some fresh bread, buy some cheese, check the post office for mail, then head out to the dock and stare out across the sea towards Italy while I ate. Occasionally I would take long bike rides, but my bike was having a small holiday too. If I wasn't working I would spend the morning studying Greek or Italian and read anything I could get my hands on.

A box of books came from my mom, in it *The Prophet* – the book I had heard about for the first time on this same campsite – and another few books from John Cottle, another friend I kept in contact with from Japan. The physical work, interspersed with the mental workout of studying and reading, kept up a good balance. I had also found a Karate teacher in the small village. He was not my type of teacher but it was a fun way to pass a night of the week getting a good workout, plus it gave me something else to focus on. His home-grown thoughts on nutrition and smoking were definitely not founded in any of the Eastern traditions, but he was a Greek/Canadian, teaching Karate on the Peloponese, so what the heck. I had nothing else to do on a Tuesday night anyhow.

Living on the campsite was me and an Albanian guy named Alki. He was a hard-working guy, as were all the Albanians I had met in Kyparissia. We were doing some grunt work, and the brothers Foundoukis drank coffee. To be fair though, the brothers did mange a decent amount of work between the coffees. It didn't matter to me; I was getting two meals a day, hot showers three times a week, and a small room to sleep in on the campsite in exchange for a couple of days of work here and there. I thought it was well worth it. Alki, who I think was getting a small pittance, was grateful as well. He mostly socialized with his Albanian friends who were dotted around the area. I spent some time with the family who owned the campsite, and a lot of time reading and writing.

In late November I received a letter from my friend Vinny who was having a hard time beating his addiction to drugs and alcohol. We had been through quite a lot together over the years. I had given up alcohol for a year when I lived in California and later on in Australia but I didn't have an addiction to it so it hadn't been too difficult. I'd found it unusual how people would react to it though. Now here, where alcohol was such a part of every-day life, I decided I would give it up in solidarity with Vinny. I knew it would be a challenge especially as one of my jobs working at the campsite was being the occasional bartender with the perk of free drinks. Maybe I would get more of a clue as to how people do suffer when they have to give up drinking alcohol. I would stop drinking, not make a big deal of it, and just see if I could do it.

About a week later I was going to take a walk to town when a cyclist pulled into the campsite. I knew right away he wasn't local and from his dress knew he was traveling, but there weren't any panniers on his bike. He asked me, "Are you the American living on the campsite?"

I was surprised that someone was seeking me out. I admitted that I was and we shook hands, introduced ourselves and struck up a friendship from that point on. His name was Ian and he had cycled from England during the past year. He was now living a few miles out of town with a South African guy and his girlfriend and all three of them were working for a local farmer picking olives. We found we had lots in common and had cycled many of the same roads in the past year or so.

His work schedule was more intense than mine as olive farmers and campsite owners have quite opposite schedules; one set were busy in the summers while the others had a workload in the cooler months. I cycled up to Ian's place once in a while and he would come down to the campsite too during his time off. I would not get to see him and his friends that often but it was good having a like-minded soul not too far away.

As the weeks passed I also met another couple from England, Bas and Jan. They were potato farmers giving it a go in Greece. They liked their drink much like Mary and Trevor, who weren't too far north of Kyparissia. I sometimes wondered what transpired with their lives since we shared lunch all those months ago.I decided not to find out and fantasized their guest house up and running. With Bas and Jan I wasn't quite sure if their stories were based in truth, or an alcoholic haze, but nonetheless they were interesting to spend some time with every once in a while. It was easier not to drink with them at all because they didn't just sit for a glass of wine; once they were drinking it was a real event. Since alcohol, especially the ubiquitous *retsina*, was so easily available, and so universally consumed by everyone, I was finding my solidarity with Vinny quite difficult. It wasn't because I particularly wanted to drink, but my refusal always sparked a volley of protest and an argument that would be exhausting after the third or fourth time in a day. Apparently it wasn't easy for others to accept my not drinking.

The time passed by quite pleasantly on the Ionian Sea. Sometimes the wind would be so strong coming from the sea that I would be able to stand out on the rocks and let my body be propped up by the wind; the force of Mother Nature the only thing holding me back from plummeting down into the crashing waves.

The brothers had lots of family in Athens and some weekends the bar on the campsite was full of young Athenians. They all proclaimed how they loved to get out of Athens and come to the countryside. They would then spend the whole weekend drinking and smoking in the café from midday to midnight, with a break in between for dinner. I never saw any of them walk very far outside or get on a bike. Maybe it was just the knowing that there was peace and countryside outside rather than the chaos of the Athenian streets. They looked at me as if I were crazy for getting up early in the morning and going for a ride on my bike. They thought I was equally crazy for not indulging in as much coffee – if you could call the sugared, instant NESCAFE drink they loved so much, coffee – alcohol or cigarettes that I could get my hands on. We all wondered about each other's wackiness and I'm sure that we all had our strong opinions of how the other was wasting our life away. It made for good conversation.

They were mostly young students or working in Athens. They all had some command of English some were fluent. My Greek was getting better but not up to the heated conversations on how evil Turkey was. That conversation was the hardest for me. I do know there is lots of bad blood between Greece and Turkey but when I tried to tell these young people that the actual Turks of today were quite nice, they were all convinced of the opposite, even though I told them of having traveled alone from the Mediterranean to the Georgian border and back without incident and with mostly good experiences.

My enjoyable few months there meant nothing to a lifetime of stories about the war and occupation, etc. It was a fluke according to them. I tried to explain that we have to move on in life or there will always be enough hatred to fuel the powers of war, but they weren't having it. I suppose it was unlikely that they were going to take some tea-totalling, non-smoking cyclist who preferred freshly squeezed orange juice in the morning to a refreshing NESCAFE seriously. C'est la vie.

Life in the small village was colorful. Theo, the friend who had originally commandeered me to help, was also there with his family. They had a small olive grove and for a week I joined in the harvest. It was very hard work. After a day of whacking branches and collecting the olive fallings you knew you'd worked. As we ate out in the field, blessed with sunny days and views of the sea, I felt a connection with an ancient form of harvesting which couldn't have changed much in 2,000 years. I was reminded of my day doing the same in Tunisia, just about a year previously, and thought of all that had transpired since.

Theo and his family had lived in Australia but had come back to the homeland when he was eighteen and his sister sixteen. He looked forward to being back in Greece but his sister Anna came back kicking and dragging her feet. Theo had recently married a Bulgarian woman with an eight-year-old daughter and Anna had married a local boy that her mother and father thought would be a good catch; she was not a happy woman. She now had two kids, a small gift shop, and a constant longing for her long-forgotten life in Australia. Theo's wife was happy to be out of Bulgaria, but her eight-year-old daughter seemed to be withdrawn and distant. It was very difficult. There they were in a small Greek village, not speaking much Greek and with not much to do. There were lots of adjustments to be made. This though is life. Big city, small village, New York, or Athens, it's all about changing what you can, or accepting, moving on and trying to be happy.

Ian and I had made plans to spend Christmas day together. Ian – a true Englishman – liked tea, just like my other cycling English friend, Chris; I happened to like it as well and had some with me. We headed into town, bought some nice looking cakes, a loaf of bread, some fish and cheese and were off on our bikes to find a small piece of quiet paradise and have our Christmas dinner. The day was absolutely beautiful with a light breeze, blue skies, and empty roads. We explored for a few hours until we found a small beach sheltered from the breeze where we fired up my camping stove. With a cup of tea brewing, the bread and fish ready to eat, good conversation about traveling by bike, a mellow Christmas afternoon was ahead of us.

It came out that Ian would be leaving soon to head up north to pick oranges before he continued on his journey into Turkey, but he was having some bike trouble that had begun not long after leaving England. I told him I would try to sort it out for him if he brought it to the campsite. We chatted about various other things, enjoyed our meal, and then headed back to our respective temporary homes before nightfall. Getting back to the campsite, a chill had entered the breeze, plus it was getting late in the day and the strength of the sun had faded. I was glad there was hot water for a shower.

I was invited to the family house for dinner that night. Everyone was there; Theo and his family, the four brothers and their family, and me. The meal was a feast, the atmosphere was festive – the only thing amiss was that the guest of honor was the television. It remained on the whole time and not merely as background, it was the centerpiece. Playing non-stop was a cheesy game show, but the only two people not enjoying it were me and the eight-year-old Bulgarian girl. I commandeered some paper and pencils and we drew pictures of Christmas and had a pleasant time out of earshot – almost – of the television. I felt for this young girl. If I hadn't been there she would have been all alone, and maybe she felt the same for me because I was in the same situation.

Christmas passed and the time rolled on. Ian came by and I spent the day fixing his bicycle which made me feel good. He had been having the problem for ages and had failed to solve it. The experience of working in bike shops gave me the added bonus of more experience in maintenance. I looked back at all the past experiences of my mechanical skills coming into play; Italian bike rental fleets, American soldiers in Germany, John's bike, the Polish lad's, the Algerian kid's flat in the Alps, the Goodgames' bike fleet and other odd times I have managed to help out.

There was a standing offer for me to continue working on the campsite serving drinks in the bar. It sounded like an idyllic summer; crowds of Europeans having fun in the sun, volleyball on the beach, and everything else that went along with holidays. I had only ever been there in the off-season. The Kyparissia I knew was one of reading, good long conversations, quiet walks to a sleepy village, quirky Karate classes and no traffic. I decided I didn't want to give up that memory. I was currently helping out in the bar once in a while and I had the memory of working in *Donovan's* – the satisfaction of getting people drunk didn't approach the sense of accomplishment I had fixing bikes. When Ian's problem was sorted, it was easy to know what I wanted to do next. I gave the bike shop a call in New York to see if Jimmy had a mechanic sorted for the upcoming season. When he said he hadn't, I told him he could stop his search now – I would be back in April ready to start work. The decision felt absolutely correct, all thanks to Ian's faulty bottom bracket!

On January 6th the seldom-seen bearded priest appeared from the church carrying a crucifix surrounded by a small entourage. They followed him out to the pier where he threw the crucifix into the water. Then the young men of the village, who were standing shivering in their underwear, dove in to try to be the one to retrieve it. To be successful was to be a celebrity for the day and a great honor. It was a colorful event – quite rapid, I must admit, and to the point. I enjoyed watching the whole affair, glad I wasn't jumping into the sea on a windy day in the beginning of January. Ian and I happily sipped hot tea witnessing the traditional events commemorating The Epiphany – the Eastern Christian celebration of God's arrival on earth in the form of baby Jesus – a holiday in Greece on a par with Christmas.

Ian was due to leave on his orange-picking quest following which he had decided he would head through Turkey so we spent an afternoon poring over maps and I gave him some hints; roads I liked, villages that were interesting, I also gave him a photo of me and the boys in Cal, showed him where it was and asked him to deliver it for me. He agreed so I warned him to not stay too long in the tea shop and wished him luck. We had both enjoyed our short-lived friendship. He knew I had decided to go back to New York, and that he and his bike had played a major role in that decision. My life was all about these chance meetings and happenings, and had taken on many different shapes based on them. You have to take the moment, live it, feel right with it, and go from there. The universe does provide, you just have to have faith in yourself and be willing to take responsibilities for your choices. Once you realize that life is about the choices you make, you will take care and look at life in a way that will make it hard to have the attitude "that's the way it is" – it's not, life is what you make it!

With Ian gone and winter in full swing, life was getting quieter. With no more holidays coming up work on the campsite was pretty much on hold.

My mother and sister decided they would take advantage of cheap off-season air fare, and the fact that I was now living in a small village in Greece. They planned to come out in March and as I was now planning to come back to New York I decided not to tell them my plans and booked a seat on the same return flight as theirs. The one glitch was how to get the bike to Athens airport.

A plan of cycling to Athens in mid-winter across the mountains of the Peloponese was hatched. It sounded like a great idea. It would be possible – pretty cold, but what a great way to see all the small villages in the sleepy wintertime. I was getting more confident with my Greek too. So the vague plan was I'd cycle up to meet my mom and sis in Athens, leave my bike at the airport while we traveled a little together, and get on their return flight – a simple plan – and so far things were working out. The only thing I could not plan for was the weather. I'd have to wait and see.

Some work had come up at the end of February; a fence around the large campsite house needed to be sanded and stained. The job would take me perfectly into the first week of March and I planned to leave shortly afterwards. The weather on the coast was windy and billowy but we were still eating outside well into February. The wind then changed and began coming from the mountains – a cold stiff wind. The week I started to work on the fence was the coldest yet. I saw on the news that blizzards had shut down many roads in the mountainous areas and many smaller remote villages were cut off completely with some older people dying of exposure. My bike trip looked like it would have to follow the more circuitous coastal route to Athens. I was finding it hard to get psyched up to do the long cold ride alone.

I was lying in my sleeping bag in my small room one night when there was a knock on my door. That was indeed a strange thing for me. I don't think in all the months I was there anyone had ever knocked on my door, especially after night fall. I went to the door, which was never locked, to see who it was, or if I was hearing things. As I approached the door, I heard a familiar voice saying, "Joe, you there?" I opened the door to a bundled up Ian.

"Come in, what're you doing here?" I asked him in my surprise. I made a hot drink and he filled me in on his orange-picking experiences of the past seven weeks or so. I asked if he wanted to stay for the night as he had

464

a sleeping bag and there was an extra bed. He said that would be great but we had to wait until the next morning to continue our conversation because the hot drink, cold weather and warm sleeping bags sent us both nodding off mid-sentence.

As life would have it, Ian had taken the train back with his bike to collect some things he had left behind. He then planned to cycle up to Athens along the coast. We immediately agreed to go together and I told him of my mountain plan. Although he loved mountain cycling too, we had just been discussing the recent blizzards in the mountains so we laughed off the possibility. Since he was on a loose schedule, I invited him to help me with the fence job in exchange for two square meals a day and a place indoors for his sleeping bag and he was more than happy to take me up on the offer. The brothers did not mind one more worker to help with the job – it was a cold tedious task and, being close to completion, one more person would speed things up a bit.

Two days before we were planning on leaving, a strange thing happened – the wind changed and the sun shone brightly. We did not get our hopes up, but enjoyed working in the sunshine. That night we went inside the house we were working on to watch the news. The weather had broken all over the south. Each of the next two days got progressively warmer and it looked as though the ride through the mountains was on.

We left on a beautiful morning with the news talking about a freak heat-wave. We went the way the planet was pushing us to go, up and through the middle! I told the brothers I would see them in about two weeks to collect the few things I'd left behind and probably to stay a day or two with my mom and sis.

The riding through the mountains was superb. Since neither of us had done much cycling lately our cycling legs were waiting a few days ahead of us. The mountainous terrain was a challenge and we both paid for it in sore legs and increased heart rates, but now that I had a lot more miles and experience in gaining back fitness, I knew the pain was a passing phase, and I would soon be enjoying the riding without thinking too much about the climbing.

It could not have been planned better. The snow on the roads was melting but the mountains were still covered with their white shrouds. As it was olive tree pruning season the perfect place to camp out nightly was the olive fields. We would be guaranteed all the firewood we wanted to keep warm and a flat surface for camping.

All of the villages and villagers were quite happy to see two cyclists pull into town on their fully-loaded bikes in mid-winter. The almost hourly comment was, "What gorgeous weather – you should have been here a week ago." With each pedal stroke we each found our cycling legs again.

We also found that certain other something that can't be explained but is there deep down inside – unfortunately not used often enough in our daily lives. It's a confidence, a trust, a knowing, just something that becomes alive and engulfs you with strength. Some would call it religious, others spiritual – I'm sure humans would have many labels for it. My traveling and cycling have been an integral part of its growth and living in it – the groove.

  As for Ian, we fell out of touch. The day I said goodbye to him on the outskirts of Athens was the last time I saw him. Life is funny though, I don't count out ever seeing him again maybe one day on a long and winding road.

# Different Wavelengths

Before I headed back to New York, there would be eight days with mom and Nancy. I couldn't help but be slightly apprehensive about their visit. The last year had been very hardcore for me, my mom was getting older, and my sister lived a very different lifestyle to me even when I was in America. When I had met up with them briefly for the three days in Switzerland had been fun, but this time it was going to be just mom, sis and me for eight days in Greece in the off-season.

I met them at the airport and treated us to a night's lodging in a posh hotel called *The President*. It was a treat for all of us but there was a water shortage and brown out, so I couldn't wash my clothes which were in dire need of a clean. After a few months of only hand washing my clothes, living on the campsite, and sleeping in the same sleeping bag for well over a year, I had acquired a certain 'on the road' odor. Nancy let me know in the nicest of ways that I smelt like some of the homeless people she dealt with at her job in the health clinic in Peekskill so I decided to wash my clothes in the bath tub – probably not the best beginning for their trip.

With all of my clothes soaking in the hotel's shampoo, I was only able to wash myself over the sink. It was wet and warmish and fine for me but now I realized I had nothing to wear. I had to borrow a pair of my mother's sweatpants which, if you could see the size of my mother standing next to me – a tiny, bird-like figure next to my full-frame – you'd realize it really was an act of desperation. The sweat pants looked like pedal pushers, coming somewhere just below my knee, and my torso squeezed itself into one of her black sweaters – the sleeves reaching to mid-forearm. Now, where I didn't smell like one of the homeless people my sister worked with, I certainly looked the part. My sister and mom were practically doubled over laughing at me. The strange-looking threesome set off to look for some food.

Athens is a crowded city, and it was made all the more interesting by the lack of electricity. We found somewhere to have a good meal, and just enjoyed walking the city streets. I was hoping there was some heat that night so I could hang my clothes up to dry – my mom's clothes were fine under the shadow of a brownout at night – but I didn't feel like parading around in them in the full light of day. Thankfully when we got back I was able to wring out my clothes, which didn't consist of much anyhow, and hang them around the room to dry. My mom and sister were being good sports ducking under dripping trouser legs as they moved around the room. Even though we were in a posh hotel I had managed to lower the tone already!

The next day, mercifully dressed once again in clothes that fit, we did the obligatory visit to the Acropolis and Parthenon along with a couple of other famous Athenian tourist sites. My mom wanted to see some Biblical sights, so the next day we went to Corinth, to whose natives St. Paul wrote some more of his famous letters. Paul was my mom's favorite, and well, shall I say he made a good point of discussion for both of us. I seemed to be on a bizarre course following Paul – first Turkey, now here. It wasn't quite the Holy Land, but close enough for mom.

As I had always got so much more out of traveling in the non-touristy areas; I wanted to show them some of the real Greece. Nancy was not used to roughing it, and I on the other hand had been doing only the rough stuff for months. It took us a few days to find our level – Nancy wanted to see more tourist sights, and, in February on The Peloponese, the few of interest would not always have accommodation close by. I thought they would like to have a taste of real Greece down in Kyparissia but to tempt them down there I had to find a few other tourist things to do on the way.

We counted out going to any of the Greek Islands and took a train ride across the Peloponese instead – luckily it snowed again and coming over the mountains was magical. The train labored slowly up into the snowcapped mountains and from our vantage point we looked down at the glint of sunlight reflecting off the Ionian Sea miles off in the distance, framed by glistening peaks. It was truly gorgeous and I could not have ordered a more picturesque train ride. They were both surprised to have snow in Greece but thought it was a great adventure. As we headed over the other side of the mountains we descended down into the part of the land I knew better.

I had vaguely thought that they would share my room, but then realized that there was no way that was happening, especially since our experience a few nights previous. They had both balked at a hotel we had stayed in which I thought was great by my standards. Nancy had slept fully clothed with her hand on the radiator all night and, once again, I'd had to dig to deep to find some patience and to remind myself of what she was used to in her life, and after all, it was her vacation.

I knew that lodging in Kyparissia was going to have to be found. Sleeping in my cold boxy room would prove disastrous – that much was certain. Luckily there was a decent hotel down the road from the campsite, and it was open in the down season. That hotel saved the trip from disaster; the ladies had their nice room, I was right down the street, and we could meet up during the days where I could take them around to see some of the colorful friends and places I had got to know while living there; we were invited to Theo's parents' house – who spoke very good English because of their years in Australia – for dinner, we took beautiful walks along the water, went to the sight of the first Olympics, we even met up with Bas and Jan for lunch.

The time went by quickly. For me it was nice to share my short time in Greece with them and be a part of their exploration. I think my mom had a great time – she's easy to please – but it wasn't my sister's idea of a Greek holiday and I hadn't thought it was supposed to be. We were on completely different wavelengths. I thought they would both enjoy the experience of seeing life in a small village which they did up to a point, but I think Nancy and I were both a bit disappointed. It was a good experience in expectation. We'd both had our expectations of what each other wanted, and in the end, that set us up for disappointment.

Anyway, we all got over it and, despite a few uncomfortable moments, the trip was a success. It was a good time for me to be heading home – I was looking forward to working in the bike shop. I was still on my path, and knew that lessons came in a lot of different shapes and forms. The past few years of my life had showed me one thing for certain; life is what we make of it. Change is the only constant, and in these times of necessary change, we either have to embrace it or face constant disillusionment.

The time came for them to leave so I accompanied them to the airport and surprised them by being booked on the same return flight home. This trip had been nearly a year and a half but a lot had happened and I needed more time to integrate my experiences. The few months on the campsite had allowed me time to read, write and begin that process. Once back in New York I would continue to learn about running a bicycle shop while looking deeper into what happened to me on my journey in the land of my ancestors.

The Peace Ride – New York 1990

The cool ride – Vinny on his Harley

Come as Joe surprise 30th – good friends, good times.

Stefano, Enza, their kids, Zia Maria (grandad's sister) and me – Melfi,

Lost in Greece – neither man nor beast was of much help!

The Greek teacher and his students

The friendly carpet sellers of Cesme

Some of the men from Cal, Turkey

A line for the water – eastern Turkey

Me and John – Leaving Turkey 1992

Romanian Gypsies

Mom, me and Dana – a short reprieve from the bus tours – Switzerland

Me and cousin Stephanie – chance meeting in France!

Danny and Catu – ever the artists – Paris

Maria, me and Aldo (without his knife) – Rutigliano, Italy

With the Goodgames – Greece, 1992

Typical working day on the campsite in Kyparissia

The olive picking season – Greece

Mom, Jan the potato farmer and Nancy (roughing it) – Kyparissia

Ian after the blizzards – Greece

# CYCLE FOUR; A Collision Course
## -America and Australasia Revisited-

# Crossing Spokes, Crossing Wires

My working in bike shops back home was becoming a good way to earn enough money for my next adventure while giving me access to cycle equipment at wholesale prices. My life was pretty seasonal in the same way as the bicycle trade in New York. Unfortunately the basement apartment I had lived in the last time I was home was being used by my cousin who was going through a separation from his wife, but luckily my friend Andrea – who Noemi had had plans to travel across America with all those years ago – was now living with her boyfriend Charley. They had a big house with an unfinished basement and were enthusiastic cyclists so we worked out the perfect barter – I looked after their bikes and helped them refinish their basement in exchange for rent. Moreso it was in the village of Pelham – a short walk to work and a train line to Manhattan, perfect.

Working at the shop was an Australian guy named Jeremy. He lived in the city, and where I had an easy walk or very short bike commute he cycled seventeen miles each way, unless he took the train. He was a triathlete, and taught me a lot about road racing and proper cycling techniques. He saved my sore knees from getting worse by teaching me to use lower gears and spin more and I wound up buying a racing bike and riding with some local clubs. My love of bikes was deepening, and now I was becoming a bike geek!

I rode with a diverse group of guys; one ride was a mellow bunch of fellas out of City Island with a range in age from thirty to seventy-five years old. Then there was the racing training ride on the weekends known as 'The Gimbels Ride' which sped its way up Central Avenue and wound its way through lower Westchester County. It was a crazy ride, and quite large with sometimes up to 150 guys. The City Island group had a spin off called the 'Unemployment Ride' on Tuesday and Thursday mornings for anyone who was off from work at those times. I was getting sucked into the cycling world – all my touring mileage made me a strong rider and now helpful hints and club riding was helping me to become a good all-round cyclist.

Jeremy was a talented mechanic, he taught me how to build wheels – the meditative movements of crossing and fitting the spokes sat well with me and generally improved my ever-expanding love of the two- wheeled machine that was becoming such an integrated part of my being. An added bonus was that every once in a while Mike – the young guy I had worked with during my first season in the shop – would help out too, so we had a good crew and were building up the reputation of the shop.

Some friends thought I was actually putting down roots, suggesting I should go in on the bike shop, become an owner or offer to buy it from Jimmy. Even though I was making friends and enjoying the new side of cycling I was exploring, I felt deep down I was still traveling. This was just going to be a season or two at the most before I headed off again.

In the interim. I had found out my cousin Michael had Multiple Sclerosis and a weekend ride was coming up to raise funds for research into its causes and possible prevention. My friend Danny – who owned a rival bike shop – was organizing the mechanics for the ride, so I volunteered. What a great weekend it was. I rode the both days with my panniers full of tools, tubes, and a large track pump. I was still fairly fit from my touring and some guys on their racing bikes couldn't believe I was riding this heavy-looking machine loaded down with bags. It was light compared to my packing for a tour, and the hills in upstate New York were steep and challenging, but my legs had long memory; the Himalaya, the Black Sea Mountains, the Alps, who knew where next?

I also got back in touch with the organization Transportation Alternatives in the city and volunteered when I could; manning phones, stuffing envelopes or joining in on *crit mass* rides (a moving cycling protest) – a great way to raise awareness of cyclists needs in a big city choked with cars such as New York. I felt I was continuing to try and do my bit.

Besides the bike shop being a real source of healthy activity, a feel-good factor in serving the local community, it's also a sociable experience. You get to meet lots of people who are usually in a good mood – either excited to be shopping for a new bike, or buying one for their kids. It can become a social hub for cyclists who come in just to chat and hang out. Pelham Bikes was no exception and, as this was now my second season of working there, I had built up quite a network of friends and acquaintances. It was a good head space to fall into after my travels, and kept up my mechanical skills to boot.

This time around I got to know a local girl – Liz Napoli – and her father, who I only knew as Mr Napoli. He was a retired doctor who had got into cycling touring in a big way. I kept his steed finely tuned and he would come in to talk bikes with me and show me the latest itinerary for his cycle touring holidays. Most of his tours were with companies that specialized in Europe. Of course I knew that part of the world pretty well by now and many of the itineraries he showed me were in places I had been to and I would tell him how great it would be for cycling. Over the year he had done maybe three different trips in Europe, then one day he came in with a cycling Vietnam catalogue. I said, "Now there's a challenge for you Mr. Napoli, I only made it from Saigon to Denang before getting arrested back in 1990, but I'd love to hear how it is up around Hanoi in the north." I thought I saw him huff in frustration but didn't realize what the problem was.

Liz came in a few days later and we had lunch. We chatted for a while before she giggled and said, "Joe, you know you really piss my dad off."

I was taken back, but after that huff I thought I'd spotted, I was starting to think differently of our relationship. I asked why and she further explained, "My dad has worked his whole life as a doctor and as you can tell he's used to being the one in charge. Now that he's retired and found a love of cycle touring he has re-found a bit of status amongst his peers. Because he's in shape and does these two-week tours of European countries his friends put him up on a pedestal. He comes to the bike shop where the mechanic has cycled in all these places, and it really puts his back up. So now he has it in his head that you're lying!"

"Lying! Oh man, I probably shouldn't have mentioned Vietnam. Sorry Liz, I wasn't trying to piss him off. I thought he was looking for advice. I thought he looked frustrated or something last time I saw him." We had a good laugh about it, but the damage already had been done – we definitely had our wires crossed. Mrs. Napoli brought in his bike to be repaired the next time and although he did come in from time to time, our conversations were short and more about maintenance. I didn't bother trying to show him any photos to back up my stories, I almost found it funny.

After a few months in the shop, Rob – who I'd cycled with in Asia – gave me a call. We made plans to meet up in the autumn and hooked up for a cycle trip from Cortland, New York – nearly 300 miles northwest – back down to Westchester County. We hadn't seen each other since we parted company in New Delhi in 1990 and it was almost three years when we met at the train station. It was good seeing Rob and we filled each other in on what had been going on in our lives as we had both had intense trips the previous year.

We got caught in some snow blizzards near Binghamton. So we looked up Charley's sister Janet. It had been many years since we had last crossed paths. To confuse matters her boyfriend's name was also Charlie. We had a good time getting to know each other trapped in her house with twelve inches of snow piling up outside. Janet and Charlie were in a new relationship but didn't seem to mind us waiting for the freak blizzards to abate, which they finally did.

When we made it back to the New York City area, Rob met my friends and family. He had cycled in South America while I was in Europe and now he was heading back down to Brazil where a love interest beckoned.

His heading down to Brazil would have an affect on my next journey in a round about way, but that was a year or so away.

Personally it was great once again to be in New York to catch up with friends and family. We all picked up where we left off. This landing was much smoother than last time, and coming into the cycling world gave me a new circle of friends which allowed me to keep up my fitness while still keeping somewhat politically involved.

The world and its problems were continuing to show me how intertwined we all were. I was dating an English girl, Ruth. One night something had made the headlines from the Middle East and Islam was getting its usual slamming in the press. I thought back to all the hospitality shown me in the past – the Muslims of Indonesia, Malaysia, Turkey and Northern Africa had always been more than fair with me, and I tried to come to the defense of yet another anti-Muslim headline – unfortunately terrorism and Islam were interchangeable words in the press – when Ruth ferociously ended the conversation. I was a bit thrown until she told me of her personal connection with the airplane flying over Lockerbie Scotland in 1988. The bomb on the plane killed 270 innocent human beings, her younger sister being one of them. Her view of Muslims had been colored so differently than mine – terrorism struck a much deeper chord – with such opposing experiences how could it be otherwise? We didn't proceed further after she told me the story of her sister planning to visit her for the Christmas Holidays in New York, and never making it. Ruth was actually quite reasonable in her thinking, even after that personal horror, but we let the subject rest. On my way home from her house that night on my motorcycle I pondered how we're all our own worst enemies in this world – the hatred out there just gets fueled and re-fueled, the downward spiral continues, and unfortunately, the press runs with it and we get handed back to us the mess we have; fear of the unknown, unwillingness to change our thought patterns and prejudice against entire countries, religions or races. There must be a better way to live on this little spec of a planet spinning in space – tap into the good, and let it pour out. I was trying, and my travels were giving me a much broader scope of vision, but blowing planes out of the sky wasn't helping matters.

The good in the world was there, I just needed to somehow bring it to the fore and find my place in the puzzle. New York was the city of my birth, and I loved it, but still felt caught between many worlds and not ready to settle just yet.

# A Route Altering Root Canal

By February my feet were really beginning to itch once again. Cycling with Rob didn't help matters any and I thought back to the eye-opening trip with John behind the former 'Iron Curtain'. Continuing up into the northern part of Eastern Europe sounded an interesting continuation of that voyage. I decided to leave the bike shop at the end of May to go on my next cycling adventure. I had found my replacement and trained him for a month before buying a plane ticket to Poland.

Liz must have told her dad I was leaving as he came in to have a longer chat. I told him of my plans to head to northeastern Europe, and he told me of his next adventure. Now that I knew he thought I was a liar, it made me feel uncomfortable. I thought it was the last time we would probably see each other so we said goodbye and wished each other a good trip. It was too late for explaining – it was what it was.

Charley offered to take me to the airport – everything was set. Everything except for this niggling toothache I had. So on the morning of my flight I decided to get it fixed as I didn't fancy having to get dental work done in Poland. I went to the local dentist, and as he drilled happily away at the tooth, he informed me I had an exposed root, which meant I needed to get a root canal. Needless to say, I was not prepared for that bomb to drop; I had left the bike shop, my bike was packed, and my flight left in about eight hours! What to do? I needed time to think about this. My window for cycling in Latvia, Lithuania, Estonia, and Poland was short because of weather. I needed to make a decision quickly. The dentist put a temporary filling in my tooth and quoted me a price for a root canal and crown which was basically the amount of money I'd planned to travel with for the next few months.

I left the dentist's office thinking hard. The first thing I did was to cancel my flight – I was not going anywhere just yet. Once again life had different plans and I'd just have to see where it led.

I remembered once again Ted Simon in *Jupiter's Travels* eating his lunch in India on the side of the road so unperturbed, just knowing that the situation at hand would lead to some adventure or meeting with someone that would steer the course of his journey down certain roads that he never could have planned. I said to myself, 'Calm down, it'll all be okay.'

So there I was, jobless, flightless, but not worried – an adventure was lurking; I just had to find it. I saw Charley and told him, "Don't worry about driving me to the airport, I cancelled the flight."

486

Charley loved a good joke and went along with it, "Great, didn't feel like taking you anyway."

I saw he didn't believe me, "Seriously Charley, I cancelled my flight, I gotta get a root canal."

I wasn't freaking out, and was calm, but disappointed. He looked at me more seriously, "You're not kidding are you? A root canal! Man, that sucks. I'll drive you to the airport next week."

"I probably won't be going next week. I can't afford a root canal, and don't know what I'm gonna do about Poland. For now the flight's cancelled."

"Are you gonna ask Jimmy for your job back?"

"No, he's already hired somebody else. I'll figure it out." By this time I already knew what I had to do. I had a bad feeling about the local dentist – he was pushing me to get the root canal soon and with him. It didn't feel right.

My sister Nancy worked in a health clinic in Peekskill, so I gave her a call and booked in for an appointment. A couple of days later I met with a Latin American dentist who confirmed I had an exposed root, but if I was not in any pain he could put another temporary filling in but didn't recommend leaving it untreated too long. We were talking about prices for crowns when he said jokingly, "Get it done in Central America, it's a lot cheaper." My ears pricked up – this, I thought, sounded interesting. My bike was packed, I was ready for a nice long cycle tour, and now I just needed a destination. I asked him what he thought of me cycling with my temporary filling. He told me no problem but it could act up at any time, so stay close to home. Now there's a relative term, home. Didn't someone once say? "Home is where the heart is." My loaded bike had served as my home for many years now. Plan B was forming.

There are many defining moments in people's lives – some have to do with near scrapes with death, or the loss of someone significant; sometimes they force us to change our lives, or look at the bigger picture with a different perspective. My father's death made me look at the here and now in a different light, my first trip across America opened up a new side of me, a broken wrist helped me find a way to my life on the road, and now a root canal was altering my plans – pointing me west and south instead of east and north.

I had been in touch with John Cottle as he was working in the cycle industry as well. He was living in northern California and I called to say I'd see him in a few months. He wasn't surprised, maybe even jealous, as he was getting fed up sitting behind a desk selling cycle computers. Everything happened so quickly and before I knew it I had a plan to leave that Sunday to cross America. The only people who knew of this change were Charley and Andrea, with whom I was living, John, to whom I was vaguely heading to, and of course my family. I had said goodbye to everyone else, and now it was nearly time to go. My tooth seemed to be okay, my bike and equipment didn't need any tweaking, so Sunday it was.

There's a Parkway in New York called The Bronx River Parkway which is billed as America's oldest parkway. Ever since I was a kid seven miles of the parkway was closed to car traffic and opened for bicycles on Sundays. I thought that would be the perfect way to start off my self-propelled journey across America; go to my mom's house for a going-away breakfast, meet up with Andrea and Charley and cycle to White Plains on The Bronx River Parkway with them; when they turned back I would keep on pedaling west.

Sunday morning was perfect weather. Breakfast was delicious, my mom – who now was used to my comings and goings – gave me a hug, and her eyes welled up once again as she waved goodbye to her wandering son. She was somewhat glad I wasn't off to foreign lands this time – it was reminiscent of the old days when I used to head off on my cross-country motor cycle journeys. I met up with Charley and Andrea and we rode along with the usual crowds of families and people enjoying a relaxing Sunday ride. Many riders noticed that I had quite a lot of gear on my bike. I think Charley was more excited than I was – if someone made a comment about the amount of bags I had to go the seven miles to White Plains, Charley would chime in proudly and say "He's riding to California!"

White Plains is at the limit of the parkway closure – a social gathering place with the occasional entertainment and refreshments. We left our bikes and went to buy a cold drink. As we were standing there having a chat and saying our goodbyes, someone tapped me on my shoulder. I turned around and was face to face with a seventy-year-old man kitted out in his cycling gear looking as happy as a man could look. The only words he says to me are, "Poland? Lithuania? Estonia?" He chuckled then walked off as if to say, "Gotcha!"

I stood open-mouthed for a few seconds before starting to laugh. I was just so happy in the moment I didn't bother to run and get my loaded bike to show him and explain what happened – it would sound too made up anyway – so I just called after him, "See you Mr. Napoli, say hi to Liz."

Charley and Andrea were confused and asked, "What was that all about?"

I just shook my head and with a wide grin said, "It's a long story."

Besides one happy man, I did create a little confusion in New York amongst friends as I cycled across America. For me the situation was what it was; my tooth changed my trip and now I was on a cross-America cycling trip. I sent postcards from the hinterland and the recipients would be asking themselves, "Could this be Joe? I thought he was in Poland." One even called my mom to get it straight.

I decided to travel up through New York State and once again my brother decided to follow up and meet me at a campsite on the way. It was a different experience to the last time eleven years before – this time Larry came with his wife Kathy and their young daughter Kaela. We camped together in western New York State. After we waved goodbye in the sunshine I glimpsed, in my mind's eye, me leaning into the highway entrance on a cold drizzly day in August many years before. This felt a continuation of the same journey, but I felt somehow to have more direction, although it maybe didn't appear that way.

I had another visit in Binghamton with Janet and Charlie, now they were living together. It was good to pick up that relationship again although snow was not on the forecast this time as I cycled through an unseasonably hot spring.

I stayed with cousins in the Buffalo area arriving the same day O.J. Simpson decided to make a dramatic getaway after allegedly not killing his ex-wife. We caught up with each other while watching the drama unfold on the television. The ongoing case had America obsessed during the summer of '94. I personally didn't feel any other attachment with the big news event besides sadness for the young murdered woman and her lover, but passions were running high amongst many others. I was more interested in the Soccer World Cup being hosted in America that year. I fondly remembered the first time I heard of the world-wide championships while in Mexico eight years previously on the trip that would change the direction of my travels and life.

I had been on the road for a couple of weeks by now, and still was in New York State – in my motorcycle days I would have been nearly across the continent by that time. On my bicycle it took a week just to get used to cycling fully loaded. I had been riding racing bikes in New York, but nothing prepares you to lug such a heavy machine up and down river valleys or over mountain roads except of course doing it. Form comes back quicker each time you do, and now I knew Rob's secret from all those years ago in Indonesia as he laughed at me struggling – lots of years experience under his belt – as I now had.

There was one more familiar face to see before breaking the bonds with home; an old high school friend, Nick who had recently moved to the Buffalo area. I gave him a call and we met up for a drink over the Canadian border somewhere near Niagara Falls. He couldn't believe I had ridden my bicycle all the way. It was a long ride for sure, but I had a lot further to go.

It was good to see him – we'd been close in high school and stayed in touch through the occasional phone call. I knew he collected postcards so over the years I tried to send him exotic cards which also kept us in contact – but life had set us on different courses. Shortly after university he joined the New York City police force, but early into his career was involved in a gun battle. It had been a life changing moment for him and he decided then and there that, although coming from a family of police and firemen, it was not to be his career path. The decision was tough, but he made it. Around about the same time I was in Guatemala discovering my path, he was forging his way through the confusion which follows an experience which blasts you out of apathy and an unquestioned future. We had a good chat and, although our lives had been vastly different over the years, our conclusions were much the same – life is a precious gift, and too fragile to waste time just going through the motions because of family pressure, societal norms, or others' expectations. Money, status and career were secondary to the search for the inner true self. A bullet whizzing by your head can bring about quite profound changes in perception quite quickly – if you allow it to. His panther nearly attacked.

Since that fateful day he had been involved in different jobs and had moved around a bit. He was now involved in a barter system program which was by-passing the accepted monetary system. It was gaining popularity, and because it questioned the status quo and had potential repercussions for the American tax system, there was pressure coming from the government to end it. It was an innovative, wide-reaching alternative to the current flawed system and as such it had big enemies; the banks and the I.R.S. to name two. Nick filled me in on the ins and outs of the system as barter was something which definitely intrigued me – I had incorporated much barter into my lifestyle over the past few years. I was glad we'd had the brief time to meet up and, although we probably would not see each other again for a long time, it was fascinating to get a peek at an old friend's life path.

When I set off again the first people I met traveling by bicycles were a German couple: Thomas and Gina. I met them in the back of a pick-up truck provided by the highway authority as, with a breathtaking lack of forethought, the bridge that crosses from Canada into Michigan had no shoulder for cyclists. No bikes were allowed to cross and were obliged to use the silly truck system. Once back on normal roads we rode together and camped out for a few nights. Thomas was having rear wheel problems. I was able to keep him going, but he needed a new wheel. We called a mail order company and had the wheel delivered to the campsite. Thomas was appreciative, and once again I was glad to be in the right spot at the right time. Gina was struggling and after a day riding with her I thought it was strange that she should be going so slowly – she looked fit and they had been cycling for a few weeks by that point. Then I noticed she had practically no air in her rear tire as they had forgotten to pump it up after getting it off the plane. We all laughed, filled her tire up, and Thomas and I saw a lot of her back from then on.

I thought I would meet a lot more cyclists going across the continent. I was a member of an organization called *Bikecentennial* (now *Adventure Cycling*) – the newsletter telling of the thousands of cyclists crossing America each year. What I didn't realize was that the unofficial cycle trail across America started near Virginia and headed to Missoula, Montana where its headquarters were. There were a few other recommended crossings of the continent, but I hadn't been near any of them which was why I was greeted with such surprise by everyone I met. I assured the inquisitive people that there were plenty other people crossing America on their bicycles.

I was enjoying the miles slowly passing by. Crossing America by bicycle was proving to be a vastly different experience than my previous motorcycling experiences. If I had to choose a way to cross America – motorcycle or bicycle – I would be torn. My deeper feeling is that you can't compare the two, even though they do have some obvious similarities. To travel and explore is the most important choice in my estimation, the slowness of the bicycle as I had learned throughout the past years brought traveling down to a human scale in mileage, speed and distance. The motorcycle sucked me up into a different head space. Although I would never trade in my motorcycle journeys for all the money in the world, there's something special about self-propelled travel.

Many of the sights going across America looked vaguely familiar from all my cross-continental motorcycle journeys but from the saddle of the bicycle it all seemed different. This time I wasn't the college graduate looking to move to California, nor was I the inexperienced traveler looking to fit in somewhere. I had found my place within it all – the bicycle had found me in Japan and since then we had had many experiences together. On many levels I was a different person than I had been eleven years ago. I had packed a lot into those eleven years. This really hit home with me when I pulled in to a small town in Wisconsin and came upon a motorcycle gathering of Honda Gold Wing motorcycles, better known as a *Wingding*.

As I pulled up to a camp site with my fully loaded bicycle the man in the booth started to apologize that it was booked out to the *Wingdingers* when a big husky guy with a Midwestern accent clapped me on the shoulder and said, "You're welcome to camp here with us tonight, after all you're like a Goldwing without the engine." The guy in the booth smiled and I found a quiet spot to put up my small tent bought in Japan years back. I took out my stove as I was intending to cook my dinner when another friendly Midwestern voice said, "Put that away, we have more food in that tent than we know what to do with." I took that as an invitation to eat, and boy did I.

A few of the motorcyclists enquired about my trip, some saying that their wish was to cross America on their motorcycle. I somehow felt I shouldn't say that I had crossed America eight times by motorcycle with a trip to Alaska thrown in. Something about the way I was invited in, and the way they viewed my bicycle trip as a dream realized made me just keep quiet. Visions of a pissed off Mr. Napoli also made me cautious. We talked motorcycles and it came out that I owned and rode one as well. Everyone was friendly in that American way, and the food was great. I was glad I didn't mention my motorcycle trips as I didn't want to detract from any of their experiences or appear to be bragging. The whole experience was somehow better for it. One guy said he was planning on crossing America the next year and that I'd inspired him not to give up that dream. "If you could do it on a bicycle," he said, "I could do it on a Goldwing." I reminisced, remembering fondly my days traveling at seventy miles per hour – an average day's ride by bicycle. I left there the next morning with a full-American breakfast in me, and was glad of the hospitality.

Camping out alone in a State Park one night I had an encounter of quite a different kind. I pitched my tent in a wooded area and took a long walk after dinner. I was sleeping deeply, but the call of Mother Nature awoke me suddenly. I grabbed the flashlight and unzipped my tent. As I scanned the area my light caught two sparkles about ten feet away and I found myself staring into the eyes of a North American gray wolf. The initial rush of adrenaline and fear gave way to curiosity as the wolf made no move and just stood regarding me calmly. The urge to pee was strong so I walked cautiously into the surrounding brush to do my business. On my return, Mr. Wolf was still staring at me from the same spot. I moved the light back and forth to see if it was real and not some statue I hadn't noticed earlier. His head followed the light so, not knowing what to do, I said hello to him and got back into my tent. I started to read then felt the hair on the back of my neck bristle as the wolf start rubbing against the thin nylon which separated my head from him. I broke out into a sweat thinking I'd never get to sleep and attempted to write in my journal but was too distracted. I switched off my flashlight and the next thing I remember was seeing the early-morning glow of sunrise.

It was an intense encounter and felt significant in some way I didn't understand. His scent was now on my tent – maybe he was my protector for the rest of the trip. As I stuffed my tent I listened to the shortwave radio I had bought for this trip thinking how I could be in Poland. The weather was wicked to the south, and equally as bad to the north. I felt lucky to be in my corridor of good weather and heat.

Later on that day I passed a few girls on the road standing next to their cars. I smiled and they smiled back in their Midwestern loveliness. They passed me later on and gave a toot on their horns. I hadn't cycled a day under ninety-five degrees since I'd left home – last time it was the heat-wave in Europe, now I sweating across the flatlands of America. I passed a café, glancing in and wondering about a cold drink when I noticed the same girls from before. I decided to stop and when I walked in one said to the other, "You owe me a beer."

Not being shy I asked, "What was the bet?"

"When you cycled past I bet her you would stop in for a drink. Anne here thought you wouldn't," replied one of the girls.

"Well I stopped, be crazy not to, it's hot out there, and my water's as hot as tea. Plus I just earned you a beer."

She smiled and said, "Well you can have it if you want, Anne's buying."

"Can it be a tall glass of iced tea instead? A sip of a beer in this heat and I won't be going anywhere."

"Fair enough," she said, then called out to the man behind the counter, "A tall cold ice tea for….."

"Joe" I quickly added, she then completed her sentence with my name.

The three girls were from Minneapolis, St. Paul – a place I was headed to. I had the number of my sister's friend – now there were three more reasons! Anne gave me her number and said to call if I got a chance. "Maybe I'll show you the town by night," she said with a smile.

I liked the slowness of the bicycle, plus the American hinterland was quite friendly. It was this openness and traveling at a human speed that I fell in love with. Sure, meeting pretty girls was great and having a date in an unknown city was quite a nice option to be pedaling to, but it was the other invitations to camp out on someone's lawn, or join someone for lunch that happened more frequently on the bicycle. I had already experienced lots of hospitality around the world on my bicycle, and now it was nice to see America from that whole new slower perspective.

In the "Twin Cities" I stayed with Mick and Kathy who had four young kids; Sarah, Rose, Karen and John. It was exciting for them to have a cross-country cyclist staying for a few days, and it was nice for me to have a house to stop in to enjoy home cooked food and a bed. It was fun to spend time with the kids telling them travel stories and playing games. I enjoyed the company of bright eyed children. There is something inspiring about the look in a child's eyes that says, "Anything is possible." I struggle to keep this magic alive in my adult self, in the end I think we all do. If we lose that wonder, the belief in fairies, Santa Claus and all else magical, life becomes too scientific, we live too deeply in our minds and stop thinking that way. My travels had proven to me that if we stay on our path and live the life we want to live, then just maybe anything *is* possible and there *are* fairies in the woods.

Anne and I went out dancing one night – a nice diversion somewhere a third of the way across America. Mick and his family were also glad that I had someone to show me Minneapolis by night.

I was slowly making it across the middle of America. I cycled alongside buffalo in the 'Badlands' of North Dakota, and saw one of the last largest herds of these majestic animals. My mind drifted off to the once proud people who lived side by side with these wonderful beasts of North America. Where the plains were once full of buffaloes, now the last herd was a black dot on the imposing landscape. And the natives, well where were they?

I stayed in a campsite on the Missouri river and when I went to pay for my site, the ranger, Jim, refused the money. "I'm not going to charge you to spend the night. You're really doing it; all I see is people in caravans and Winnebagos. I want to introduce you to someone else." He then took me over to meet another young guy called Mark who was canoeing solo down the Missouri river from its source. We ate together that night, and Jim invited us both for breakfast the next morning. Breakfast was a feast, and Jim was over the moon to meet two guys on such adventurous journeys. His enthusiasm was infectious and I was glad we'd made him so happy.

Mark's canoeing trip sounded incredible; I had only done that canoe trip when I was sixteen with my brother's friend Kevin – Mark's trip was a lot longer, and on a different level. He was from that Midwest stock of people who just seem to live and breathe for the outdoor life. It always helped me through the boring days knowing that at the end of the day, there were other people looking up at the same beautiful stars on their own escapades.

The miles of eastern Montana slipped by – on my non-motorized crossing of Montana I was noticing the subtle changes; the undulation in the road, the change in flora as I headed further west, prairie dogs would pop out of their nesting holes in the earth. Those subtleties went unnoticed on my motorcycle, but now the prairies hadn't felt quite so boring. I didn't, and was quite glad not to, hear the rattle of the snakes that were supposed to be so common in this part of the world while camping out alone. Maybe my wolf was protecting me.

The Rockies were breathtakingly beautiful as always and brought back memories of my motorcycling days once again. Highway 2 was not that far

494

north of where I was now staying. As I got closer to Missoula, Montana, I started to meet a few cyclists. In Missoula I was surprised to find that the hostel I wanted to stay in, which was a specific hostel for cyclists, was full.

Scott and I pulled up at the same time. We were put on a waiting list, and told to call back at five. His loaded mountain bike looked like it could tell some stories. Scott raced mountain bikes, and knew a lot of the names on the racing circuit. We cycled around town and passed a bike shop where we stopped in as I knew I needed a new rim since my rear wheel had been cracking from the inside. I asked the owner if I could borrow his truing stand to re-build my wheel if I bought the rim from him and he said it wouldn't be a problem.

I got a helpful hint from a Belgian cyclist, who was staying in the hostel we were in, about re-building my wheel; taping the spokes together where they crossed, unwinding the nipples and re-fitting it all into the new rim. This was much quicker than taking out every spoke and re-lacing the whole wheel from point zero. It worked a treat, and my new wheel was set to go quite quickly.

Scott and I were getting along well so, although he was heading south to Denver, where he was from, he decided to head west a few days with me to Boise, Idaho. Out of Missoula we had a sixty kilometer gentle climb. At the top what we hoped would be a free-wheel for just as far turned into us pedaling downhill into a headwind – frustrating to say the least. We had each other to duck behind to benefit from a small windbreak and were exhausted at the end of the day. It was nice to have someone to share this part of the ride with. Scott reminded me of Gary whom I'd met in Oregon when I broke my wrist in what seemed two lives previously. He was glad to have some company – even in the wrong direction for a few days. He had been on the road for a while, and his trip was ending. He was a little younger than me, and he had the desire to travel further and wider. We had long talks about overseas travel, the possibilities of work, and talked about the deeper philosophical side of life as well.

Still feeling good, I was heading out west. It was in a very different world than it would have been had I stepped on that plane to Poland in May. I enjoyed relaxing, taking in the countryside, and being in a heat-wave. I didn't get wet but once.

I saw the storm in the distance sweeping across the horizon. It was one of those unmistakable inky blue-black smudges blotted on the clear landscape ahead. I saw I was on a collision course with the storm and tried to pedal faster in the hopes of missing it, but we collided. The storm was traveling from north to south and I was on an exposed road with no shelter to take, so I just put my head down and kept on pedaling. The moist smell of the rain on the dry earth came first followed by the side wind which made me tighten my grip on the bars, then the lashing of the rain coming horizontally from the right. My right ear was hurting from the force of the drops. It only lasted about five minutes then the sun came bursting back out. Unbelievably, the right side of my bike and body were drenched and my left side was bone dry. Not a drop of water on my panniers or my body. I have never experienced anything like it. While my right side was drying out under the hot sun, a guy in a pick-up truck pulled up from behind, opened his window, leaned out and handed me a cold beer.

"You deserve a cold one after that," were his only words before driving off with a wave and a toot. I sat in the sunshine on the edge of the empty road, half-wet, half-dry, and drank a cold beer. The weather, for the most part, was on my side – even the prevailing westerly winds which were at times very tough – were keeping me free from the constant nuisance of flies, so once again what could have been a bad thing was helping me out in a different way.

In the hot Oregon high desert I was thinking of the magical crossing I'd had all those years back when I met John and Louis on the other side of the mountains. Now the cycling was slower, and although I'd had a few nice encounters with cyclists, none were heading my way.

I pulled into a place called Dayville, Oregon where there was a church whith a backroom to accommodate cyclists on long-distance tours. Steve walked in when I'd just started cooking and we hit it off immediately. He was sunburned from long days on the road and had a strong English accent. We cooked together and bought a few beers in the small shop in the small village. He was heading east so the next day we decided to cycle together unloaded to the north of where we were. It was just a relaxing day of riding with no bags, and no destination as we knew we would be sleeping at the church that evening. He was a good person to chat away the night with. I always enjoyed the company of English cyclists on the occasions we met. He was headed to New York, so I handed him my address and phone number in New York.

My cross-country trip was coming to an end, one more mountain range to traverse. Ten years before I had crossed the same mountain range on my motorcycle. It all makes me feel as if time were not linear, the decade in between seeming to blur; stepping in and out of those two moments of my life, swirling in time. I can surely smell and feel the cool air whizzing by me at sixty miles per hour, my leather jacket zipped up, and my feet solidly on my highway pegs. I snap back to the moment – sweat pouring down my tee-shirt and cycling shorts. Ten years have passed, the person still me, but my experiences have certainly changed the perspectives of the twenty-two-year-old I'm reflecting on. I'm still being pushed to explore my inner depths; my vehicle has lost its engine, but the slowness of my now preferred mode of travel has given me so much. I'm revisiting many places on this trip, but seeing them as a different individual than I was a decade before. Balanced on my loaded bicycle melding in with the landscape I feel solidarity with the people I share our world with. The beauty that surrounds me never disappoints; the contrast of high desert meeting rainforest inspiring on either mode of travel, at any stage of life.

On the coast of Oregon I met with another cyclist named Jake, who coincidentally was also from England, a Geordie to be precise. The area in the north of England didn't mean much to me, but the accent was almost undecipherable to my ear. Whereas my scouser friend John sounded like John Lennon and Steve much like a proper Englishman, Jake sounded like he was from somewhere north of Finland. We cycled into California together parting ways under a large redwood tree as he headed for the coastal route to San Francisco, and I turned towards the the wine-growing areas of Napa and Sonoma counties to explore some unknown terrain.

This trip was over – another coast to coast ride; this time under my own steam. It was comfortable and familiar to arrive once again at Mary and Angelo's house. By this time I think they were convinced I was crazy.

I made it to John Cottle's house. The dissatisfaction with his job had grown and when I got out to California he was absolutely fed up with work, so the final push for him came from seeing my loaded bike. He didn't need much prodding to agree that riding down to see Rob in Brazil was a good idea, or at least a good excuse to get back on the road. We agreed that end of December would give us both enough time to take care of our mutual businesses; mine helping to pack the family house, his quitting his job and storing his few worldly belongings. Just in case he weakened, I left my bike at his place for a reminder.

For an added bonus, the bicycle show was in Los Angeles that year, so John and I went down together. The bicycle show was a buzz as always, all the new bike stuff to drool over, new inventions to see, and new directions for the bike industry. For the bike geek I had become, I was like a kid in a candy store.

I also looked up some old friends while down there and it was strange seeing Carina once again. We went out to dinner and she told me how she had succumbed to the Los Angeles partying scene, but it was getting boring and very difficult to break the bonds with its trappings. She was at a crossroads and our experiences since we last met had been quite different. Talking to each other we felt more like strangers rather than two people who used to be lovers.

I also caught up with my old college buddy John Nielsen. Like Nick, it was inspiring to meet friends who searched out their paths, and held onto their dreams. John and I had been in plays together in college and he'd always wanted to be an actor; for me it was a hobby, for him it was a passion – much like my traveling to me. After college where I went out to chase my dream so did he – his life took him from the small theatres in New York to Seattle, and now he was living in L.A. making his living acting. He worked hard at his chosen career, and was never awash in money, which never fazed him too much. Once in a while he landed small roles in Hollywood films, but his biggest coup at that moment in time was that he was making all his money as an actor; not painting houses, waiting tables or anything else that the struggling actor usually has to do to make ends meet. It wasn't to say one day he wouldn't be doing those other jobs to pay the bills, but for now he had made it. Our chosen paths shared many similarities; in order to travel I needed to do many types of work as well. It was part of the tapestry which created character and depth, two attributes well-needed to keep your sanity – in L.A. or on the road!

Like my first time in L.A. I felt it was a big city, but a place that unsettled me inside. I didn't know what it was, but unlike Paris, New York, or even Nagoya, it lacked cohesion. John was still a New Yorker deep down – a Brooklyn Boy – just like no matter where I lived, traveled or wound up, I felt like a Bronx Boy. Something about that bonded him and me and gave us that inner consistency that our chosen lifestyles couldn't give us from the outside. I spent a few days getting an insider's look into the Hollywood scene. It was peculiar being out there with him, the last time we'd seen each other was New York City, but something about us both being in our element felt quite good.

Before I left New York for this jaunt, it had been decided that our family house was going to be sold. All the children were gone, and The Bronx was changing. My trip across America had brought me into contact with some old friends, and now that I was heading back to say goodbye to the house of my youth, seeing these friends who all had history there too made it that much easier – we had all left the familiar comfort and surroundings of childhood, but took the memories along with us. I flew back home for a final few months in the house of my childhood.

Steve from Oregon came to spend a couple of days. I showed him my fair city and gave him a well-appreciated bed to sleep on. He was the last of many European guests and fellow travelers to stay in the house on Wickham Avenue in The Bronx while it was still our family home. I was glad to have this last chance to let the house show off its character; soon it would be occupied by strangers.

Thankfully my tooth hadn't acted up – the occasional twinge would remind me of why I was crossing America, not cycling somewhere in Poland or Latvia. Once back in New York I went to the clinic and got all the necessary work done and had a temporary crown put in. My next dentist's chair would be somewhere in Central America, where for a fraction of the price I would get a permanent crown fitted.

I earned what I had spent going across America, and added some more to the coffers for the upcoming Latin-American leg of my journey by helping a friend, Steve, make it through his first Christmas season in his new bicycle shop in New Canaan, Connecticut. Jeremy and I found ourselves working together once again, and Steve had a good opening season.

My Aunt Vi died while I was home, so it was good to have seen her before she passed away. She was the only one of my mom's brothers and sisters who had stayed in The Bronx, so I knew her the best out of all my aunts and uncles, she had been unwell for a few years, but always managed a smile. Like my Aunt Ida a few years back, cancer had taken her in the end. My mom had now said goodbye to two of her sisters, but much like my fahter's untimely death, and her younger son's worldly wanderings, her faith helped her through, and although we didn't share religious point of views, I respected her spiritual self, and felt in many ways to have that deeper connection to something unexplainable, my travels were helping me to see this side of life more clearly.

We had a street sale selling everything that couldn't be taken to the smaller places my mom, Aunt Mary and Uncle Lou were moving to. It was heartbreaking watching my uncle sell all the tools from his lifelong love of carpentry. I think it truly broke his heart even more to have to do it. He was never the same after that. Apartment life didn't suit a man who was used to working with his hands.

I wasn't too sentimental about the house – it held many fond memories for me, but like many phases and material things in our lives, it was time to give this one up. Much like the physical bodies we encapsulate, our truer selves are more than the flesh and bones we walk around in. The cadaver back in the funeral parlor was proof of the shell we all really are. The house was only a trigger for my memories – nothing could take away those days of running through the open fire hydrants, playing stick ball on the street in the hot sticky summer days, the barbecues in the backyard, the parties of my college days when mom was away, and later in my life all the visitors from my travels it bestowed its hospitality on. Those memories would always be there, it didn't matter if someone else was living in that house, as a matter of fact, it was a right of passage. It was time for someone else's family to enjoy that house and the neighborhood as much as we all had. I left New York for California on the 28th of December, and, for the last time, that house on Wickham Avenue.

# Northern Mexican Angels

The slow-moving train heading towards Arizona allowed us the time to take a deep breath and change our mindsets to travel mode after my three month interlude in New York and John's last two-year stint working in a job he didn't particularly enjoy.

We arrived in Tucson on New Year's Eve, and the next day the journey would begin. The Zapatista Revolution in Chiapas had begun exactly a year earlier on New Year's Day 1994 – the same day that NAFTA (North American Free Trade Agreement) – hailed as a great success by American, Mexican and Canadian politicians and big businessmen – was signed into law. In reality it was nothing but a further marginalization of the poor of the world, especially in Mexico which was losing more land, traditional livelihoods, and in some cases, their culture. For America and Canada it meant more manufacturing being moved south of the border, job losses in the north, cheap labor in the south – yet another move where big companies outsource their work, with skilled labor often lost forever. Profit margins do increase, shareholders make money, but the trickle-down-effect economics never surfaces, and there are many more losers than winners. So it was with a spark of hope when I heard of the revolution.

As we entered Mexico the *peso* took a huge crash and here we were on our bikes cycling through this beautiful country that was in the process of re-writing its history. It felt strange being so privileged to be able to do another long tour. Bearing witness to the struggles of the world made me realize that we in the richest countries can make that change if we truly wanted it, even when our life situations seemed impossible to change. I felt we must all strive to reach a place of happiness, because if those of us who were lucky enough to be born just across a border that separates complete poverty from extravagant wealth remain unhappy or unfulfilled, that is disrespect to life itself.

I was fortunate to work with people I could learn from, and when I worked in places where I could be a positive force, I would try to bring whatever I had learned over the years there. I remembered reading in the *Bhagavad-Gita* that if we worked from a place within ourselves, and truly enjoyed what we were doing, there was no need to think of the payment, for it would come. I've tried to always remember and incorporate this ideal.

I wanted, actually needed, to know the world I lived in – its people, cultures, religions and philosophies – it intrigued me on a deeper level and fueled my life force; and once again the unknown stretched out before me.

We had both chocked up lots of cycle touring miles in our lives. We knew that to be safe and enjoy the travel experience, it was good to respect local customs, and to get drunk or indulge in local drug cultures was a dangerous and possibly fatal game. As cyclists, most of our experiences were had during the day, and by the time night fell fatigue would set in, and sleep was usually much more important. If we stayed in some small village or town and got to know the locals, then an occasional drink or a night out could be a fun experience. In Mexico though, life out on the street was so vibrant that to experience night life it was never necessary to walk into a bar. Mexicans truly live life outside.

As most cyclists tend to do, we'd been poring over our map. We had crossed the border, and knew we were heading to Copper Canyon in Sinaloah State. It's deeper than the Grand Canyon in America – it's said you could fit five Grand Canyons into the same space. Copper Canyon was also home to the Taramuhara Indians, an infamous tribe of Indians who, legend has it, hunt deer by chasing them until the deer collapses from exhaustion. This explained their many successes in Marathons! I wasn't sure if they still hunted like that, but their broad flat feet looked tougher than the simple leather sandals soled with car tires most of the natives in the area wore and sold in the markets.

Further south and up in the mountains was home to the Yacqui Indians; Carlos Castaneda's *Don Juan* maybe still living amongst its magical splendor. Some say those books were all fiction, but true philosophy for me doesn't have to be based in anything but the mind, followed through by personal action and life experience. Richard Bach's *Jonathan Livingston Seagull* was fictional, but the metaphors drawn in that book are as powerful as any story, real or invented.

I'd taken a train along the canyon rim when I first came down to Mexico in 1986, but never made it to the traveler's destination sitting on the edge of the canyon, Creel. The small towns and villages we had pedaled through so far had dished out Mexican friendliness in large doses and refreshed my fond memories of America's neighbor to the south. Our map showed a tiny squiggle of a road that cut up and over the mountains between the towns of Tepache, and Sahuaripa. Two days cycling to Tepache, we estimated, then two or three days at most through the mountains to re-connect with the road we needed to Creel – a worthwhile detour.

Our map was pretty detailed, but the turning we found in Tepache seemed to be in the wrong place. We needed that tourist booth Norm and I had had in Tasmania years ago with a few locals saying, "Your map isn't wrong, the road you want is that way." That wasn't happening now, so we cycled a kilometer past the turning just to double check. No other road.

501

When we explained to one of the locals that we intended on going to Sarahuipa he nodded that it was possible to follow the small road over the mountains, but he seemed concerned at our decision to go that way. He beckoned us to follow him to his house where he ran inside, and came out with what looked like a side of beef, but was a big slab of smoked beef jerky – between us we were only able to fit half of it in our pannier space alotted for food as we had bought some other edible items in the last small *tienda* we'd seen. The helpful local looked over our map but remained unconvinced. It unsettled us slightly, but we had enough food for two days, and if the road led nowhere we could always turn back.

We also had these very cool water filters that we had picked up at the bike show in L.A. as one of the latest new products. They fit into our water bottle cages, and you could just dip into any water source and drink safely straight from the bottle. It didn't use iodine, so you could use it daily with no ill effects.

We were feeling confident in our equipment and strong and fit in our bodies – ready for a good off-road experience. It was nice that both of us were beginning the trip fairly fit. John had ridden lots before meeting up, and I had crossed the country and kept up my riding for the intervening three months in New York, although I noticed John struggling with his gearing. I was watching his riding style – a habit I picked up from working in the bike shop. I noticed he liked spinning an easier gear than me, especially when he climbed – much like Norm back in Tasmania. His 'granny gear' wasn't low enough on the steeper climbs – only thirty teeth, and wouldn't allow him that 'spin' – I remembered coveting Rob's twenty-six tooth chain ring cycling in Asia, and now that was my permanent dropout gear for the longer steepest climbs. I suggested trying to find a smaller front chain ring if we came across a bike shop, but it definitely wasn't happening soon. It was nice to have the expertise to help, and I enjoyed small challenges like finding chain rings in Mexico. My bicycle was about to throw a big repair challenge my way, but I didn't know that yet.

The first couple of miles of road were fine. It was a typical dirt road with a few ruts here and there, but rideable. The day passed mostly like that, up and down, and we thought we had it sorted. Our first night camping was beautiful as it always is in desolate mountains. We dug out our stoves, put up our tents and cooked up a small feast which we ate around a small camp fire. We still had enough food but didn't tuck into the jerky yet – we were being careful.

For a while it was just us and the star studded sky but later that night we were surrounded by howling coyotes. Even though you know intellectually they will not attack a human unless very hungry, it's a little unnerving to hear that howl not so very far from the place you are sleeping with only a thin piece of nylon separating you from them. John remembered reading somewhere that one female coyote would be designated to have all the babies and the whole group would work together to raise the young. With that knowledge I slept soundly figuring that with a hippy code like that keeping the group together, they wouldn't want to eat us and ruin our trip!

We survived the night and the morning was spectacular with a hint of coolness to the clear mountain air and beautiful blue skies, but the road just kept disintegrating. We found it was necessary to push our bikes every once in a while in the beginning. That soon turned into mostly pushing and riding our bikes only once in a while towards the end of day two. The dry earth, the smells of the mountainous high desert, and the absolute silence that is rare to experience in the modern world was mesmerizing. We pushed on although John suggested once that we turn back. I wasn't keen to go through some of those roads again, and, being the eternal optimist, felt sure we should push on. Whenever we saw any water source at all, we filled up all our bottles, and drank till we were full. We were now camped out for our second night, and weren't getting any closer to a town, village or road. Our friends the coyotes were keeping track of us, and we made sure that our jerky was well wrapped up and hung out of reach at night.

We were starting to realize that the jerky given to us by the concerned villager might be quite valuable later on and that his worry might have some foundation. The weather was with us though; cool mornings turned into hot days, but it was January, so it wasn't sweltering as the altitude was keeping the temperatures down. Our road descended and improved a little so we took advantage when we could and hopped on our bikes. We had been doing a lot of pushing, and we both thought how nice this leg of the journey would have been with just backpacks, but then again without our bikes we would probably have never found this place – a genuine 'Catch 22' situation. We eventually ended up cycling on a dry river bed so we made note of places to camp higher up on the banks even though it looked like a tempting flat camping surface. To camp out on a dry river bed is not a smart thing to do in case of torrential storms that cause flash floods. We camped out for a third night and by now turning back was not really an option as we had passed a few small dirt tracks leading into the dry riverbed which all looked similar to the one we had come down on.

The next morning was hard going, and we were both conscious of an underlying anxiety. We were still able to enjoy the landscape to a certain extent as well as the fact we had food and water to keep us going. We plodded onwards until about midday.

Gradually, as we pushed and cycled when possible, I began to feel a strange sense of calm, and when a warm breeze brushed across my face it felt symbolic and supremely peaceful. I had an overwhelming feeling that we were going to be okay and I told John so. Before having a chance to answer, John thought he saw some smoke in the distance and at the same moment a small road that looked like a dirt track leading somewhere appeared on the right. It was heading the way we thought we needed to go. Our map had lost its usefulness now – we were well out of its depth, and quite possibly ours!

"John, is that smoke coming from a fire, or a house?" I asked.

"Looks like a chimney," he answered.

We headed up the road, and to our bewilderment, there was a small house with smoke pouring from its chimney. We called and called, but no answer. We had turned off the riverbed to a road that was cyclable, so we rode on a bit, and saw another small house – this one looking deserted. It was a weird small cluster of houses which looked more like small holdings, but no one was around. We made mental notes of all the houses, and knew we could always go back later to the first house we noticed in this small enclave. Just as we were about to make that decision, we saw another small abode with a smoking chimney. We headed for it, and when we arrived there were two men sitting around the fire like something out of a film – quite surreal. They looked as though they were expecting us to show up and just nodded their heads in answer to our "*Buenas tardes.*" They were men of few words and seemed to like it that way.

John tugged on my sleeve and drew me back from the fire. "This is a *milpa,*" he said. The term was lost on me but he was a native Californian and knew more about the Mexican culture. He went on to explain that it was a farm out in the middle of nowhere (no kidding) where the farmers either drove or walked in and would stay for months at a time to work the family or owner's small holding mostly growing corn etc.

Now I was more informed, and very curious to know if there was a road that they drove in on as there was not a vehicle in sight. Anyhow, they got in here somehow, and we were pretty sure it had to be our way out. As hunger right now was surpassing our curiosity we decided that small-talk was not the way to go, and since these two men weren't brimming with things to say to us, we asked if we could eat with them. A nod was their answer.

It was a simple meal, but seemed a feast; tortilla, corn, beans, and plenty of hot sauce, all obviously home made – either right there or by their wife, employer or whoever dropped them in, who knew how long ago? We ate more than they did, but they didn't seem to mind. We finally dragged out of them that they were father and son and they lived there for four months at a time. Yes, there was a road, although a very rocky one, and a small river to cross, but we could get to Sahuaripa, which was about two to three days on foot. We pointed to our bikes, and they nodded, 'No problem.' After lunch we put our bikes out of the way as we didn't want to disturb their routine. We said we were going to go for a walk, and they let us know we could eat with them and sleep on the floor in the house if we wanted. We both felt relieved to be able to take a walk with a clear mind rather than pushing our bikes thinking, "Uh oh, where are we going, should we have done this?"

What a quiet, different way to live. The land was quite dry, but the corn and other crops were growing well in every conceivable corner possible. We had time to think as we walked through the silence and peace of this little known area. I fell to thinking how it was places like this where the quiet and isolation allowed time for contemplation and gave birth to philosophies such as Buddhism and Hinduism – I thought briefly of the high mountains and a certain bearded *saddhu*. Now here were two silent characters, but a world away from the Himalaya.

Monasteries of all religions are often built in hard to reach, isolated spots. Here the beauty and isolation was just as inspiring, but the spiritual practices and wisdom of the native religions and practices have all but been lost forever. It's hard not to be in awe of the beauty of the natural world when all that surrounds you is just that. So often in today's world we might spend days or even weeks without seeing more than a plant pot, so is it any wonder we forget about how the natural world is at the foundation of our existence?

John and I enjoyed a long walk, at times lost in our own thoughts and at others talking together. We had vastly different views on anything spiritual. For me it was easy and natural to believe in a deeper meaning underlying our existence – perhaps my mother's strong Catholic faith had helped in that. For John – the son of scientific, agnostic parents – everything had to have a scientific, rational explanation or it couldn't be. He longed to believe in things in a different way and was almost jealous of my easy faith, but he had been programmed this way since birth so it was almost impossible for him. We discussed this and many other things from the immensity of it all, to what was the best way to act at dinnertime with two of the quietest men we'd ever met.

We got back at what we thought would be a good time for dinner, judging it by the diminishing light. Clocks didn't seem to exist here, but then neither did electricity, or anything else pertaining to the century we were in. They were just starting the fire to cook dinner when we arrived, so we gathered some kindling, and tried to make ourselves feel useful.

The father was – in relative terms – a little more talkative, and worldy, than the son; John spoke to him about northern California, whereas it was possible that the son didn't even know he was living in a country called

Mexico. I'm not insinuating he was in any way mentally incapacitated, but if his experience was limited to this and another small village somewhere in the desert, he probably wouldn't be able to comprehend a world bigger than that. His life was a mellow existence but they both seemed happy enough, and compared to some of the places we had cycled through to get here – the buy and sell and general madness of any border town with the States, the truck stops and dusty road-side shanty towns – he could be doing a lot worse.

The star studded sky was the perfect accompaniment to the smoky fire and mouthwatering smells of fresh tortilla being baked. Washing up before dinner was a simple affair, bringing back memories of the simple washing a Muslim does before praying to Allah five or six times a day, or many other rituals witnessed in other distant lands that these same two bicycles had pedaled through. During dinner – the same basic meal as lunch – all was silent. We ate like true yogis, just concentrating on the simple food, chewing and being totally conscious of the well-needed nourishment entering our bodies. After dinner a neighbor dropped by to join us and we had what could be considered a chat by the dying embers of the fire. Sleep came easily, and the hard earthen floor of the kitchen was perfect with our sleeping mats and sleeping bags as the nights did get surprisingly cool.

Breakfast the next morning was fresh eggs, refried beans and more tortilla accompanied by plenty of water, and, oddly enough, Fanta Orange drink, which reared its head everywhere in Mexico. We ate to our fill, and were given some tortillas wrapped up in a cloth and a jar of spicy-looking pickled tomatoes. We thanked them, and they reassured us if we always took the main track leading to the left we would get to the river where the road became much more obvious.

Our spirits were lifted immensely. The synchronicity of it all had not been lost on me – all the years of coincidence and timing were proof to me that we just need to embrace life and our situations with a good heart and all will unfold as it should. John was just so excited to have actually stayed in a *milpa* that our conversation even entered the realm of spirituality related to these two men's existence. *Milpa*s were something he had studied in his youth so had ignited his schoolboy excitement. How great it would be if all school learning could be brought alive in this way.

We felt we were on our way, but knew we were not out of the woods yet, literally and figuratively.

'Keeping to the track to the left' is much easier said than done, especially when you are not familiar with the area and could easily confuse any of the hundreds of other small trails with a road.

"Was that a road John?" "Not sure." "What about that?" "Ummm…"

Our initial elation waned slightly as our quick foray into deeper conversations gave way to talk mostly about the dirt tracks which were now constantly appearing on our left. For a few hours there were many small off-shoots that deteriorated quickly from tracks to paths, but then we heard it – a river. We made our way towards the sound of flowing water. On the bank of the river though, our hearts, which had been briefly lifted, sank again.

It was a big, fast-flowing river, not something we could easily ford unaided. On the far bank was a pontoon hooked up to a cable for pulling yourself across. It was big enough to fit a car or two on, so now the mystery of access to the *milpa* with supplies was solved for us, but it was bobbing peacefully on the other side of the river. We both crouched down and looked silently across the river, contemplating how the residents of the *milpa* stayed there for four months at a time! Would we have to wait that long for someone to come and pull the pontoon across for us? It was an ideal place to camp, no shortage of water, and I guess we could always eat a coyote or two and head back to the *milpa*. I thought of jumping into the river and swimming across but luckily John put the brakes on that one. Not only was it fast flowing, but it was freezing as well.

So things weren't perfect, but, once again, I was in that lovely *Jupiter's Travels* space inside. We knew we wouldn't die of thirst or starve so we sat on the river bank and enjoyed the rush of the river. Our *Milpa* Angels, although silent, had saved the day once and maybe there were more lurking around? I thought of Ted Simon in northern India, and drifted off into philosophical thoughts once again.

We had some lunch, and were contemplating putting up the tents, when we saw movement on the opposite river bank. It was a shepherd or goat herder walking with his flock. I whistled and we shouted and waved our arms. He noticed us and walked closer to the river bank to hear what we were saying. We asked if he could get us across the river and in true Mexican form he treated the situation like it was a daily occurrence. Without missing a beat he hopped on the pontoon, unhooked it and started the hour-long process of getting it over to our side of the river. We were all silent, just living the moment as it happened. When he got to our side, we hopped on with our bikes, and he started off the whole process again to re-cross the river.

As our second Angel heaved and pulled the ropes we discussed quietly whether we should offer him some *pesos* for saving us from a possible four extra months in the mountains. We decided to see how it felt when we got to the other side. At our destination we felt that with the amount of physical effort, not to mention the time it took him, we should definitely offer something. He waved it off with a laugh saying that the keeper of the pontoon would have charged. He laughed again adding, "But he only comes every week or so."

Our pontoon pilot/shepherd was a bit chattier than our farmers at the *milpa* had been, and quite a likeable guy. We managed to persuade him to take a few *pesos* for the effort he put in and he thanked us and told us the way to Sahuaripa. The path was much more an obvious road now, but the 'stay on the main track to the left' rule still applied.

We cycled a little further then set up camp for the night. We tucked into our jerky for the second time and ate our tortillas smothered with spicy pickled tomatoes – we were splashing out more now that an end was most likely in sight. The terrain had definitely changed now; the better road surface meant that we would be cycling again, and the hills seemed to be higher.

In the morning we had a big breakfast figuring we would be in the small village that night. We cycled on and on deeper and deeper into the mountains. What an incredible feeling to reach the top of a climb and look out from a high vista over a sea of mountains spreading into the distance right to the horizon. I say incredible but it can also be incredibly scary when your food supply is nearly gone and water is scarce. We had only found one place to fill up our water filters which were literally acting as life savers. We had not passed any sign of humans all day; the only other life form we saw besides the man who took us across the river were buzzards, preparing for a feast – probably us! The cycling felt fantastic; although not paved it was the first thing that approached a proper road in ages. We were staying to the left but now the day was dragging on. They must be some fast walkers if they could walk this in two to three days. Then I remembered the Tarahumara chasing a deer to exhaustion and it made a bit more sense.

The miles were clicking by and the daylight was beginning to fade. Had we missed a turn? Were we on the right road? We felt we had to be but it was definitely a little unnerving. At the top of a small climb we hit a crossroads. One road went back on itself, the other headed off into the endless mountains, and the road to the left was a rocky rutted track. We decided to leave the bikes there and each walk for about a mile in opposite directions. We did this but I saw nothing to give me a clue that my road was the right one. I got back first thinking how I'd thought we had made it after being 'saved' twice up to this point. I looked around thinking, "man, we're screwed" – no water, just a last bit of jerky, and mountains, mountains and more mountains.

I looked around thinking, "Is this it? Does the road end here?" I knew I was being dramatic – we could always get back to the river if we needed to. The other side of me was enjoying a spectacular sunset over the sea of mountains in the high desert of northern Mexico. Then, suddenly, I heard an engine. It was an engine straining to climb and it seemed to be coming from the direction I had just come from. In the desert you can hear things quite a way off and I knew from my experience walking across Tunisia of how quickly those noises could disappear behind a hill. There was not even a glimmer of light coming from anywhere that would hint at a village out in those hills – nothing, just silent beauty, and the sound of an engine. I wondered if John could hear it as well, suddenly wondering, "Where is John?"

The engine noise was getting louder and it sounded like a van. I thought I saw a headlight when yes, there it was, the unmistakable hood of a VW campervan. It slowly approached and I realized I'd better be careful here, they might think I was a bandit or a crazed lunatic. It would be unbearable if they drove straight past me. I made sure our bikes were obvious, and with me in my cycling shorts it would probably take away any of their worries. Well, they still might think I was weird in my black lycra, but not dangerous! They saw me, I heard them downshift and they ground to a halt. It was a family heading up to their place in the mountains. They had the air of hippies, and again, true to form, treated the situation like they always gave directions to lost cyclists on this road. The Spanish words were music to my ears.

"Continue straight, just down the hill. In about three kilometers there's a place to camp, next to a river." then they added, "From there you're only six kilometers from the village."

"Can we cross the river with our bikes?" I asked.

"We just drove across it – it's wide, but not very deep. I think you can do it, but I would wait until the morning." I had every intention of waiting till the morning. Great camping near a river sounded wonderful, and we would finish off anything edible in our bags.

"*Gracias amigos*" I said, then added, "If you see a tall blond *gringo* with a red beard tell him you saw me and we aren't far from Sahuaripa." Curiosity got the best of me, and I asked before they drove off, "Where you headed?"

"We live 'off grid' with a few other families in the mountains in what is called a *milpa*, but we live there full-time."

The word I'd never heard before yesterday allowed me to picture exactly what they were talking about. In my mind I imagined an idyllic, yet tough existence working the land. They looked healthy and happy. The Zapatistas would be proud of their fellow countrymen questioning and doing something to get out of 'The System'.

"*Adios*, good luck," I shouted as they drove off in their noisy VW. As I said the word for goodbye in Spanish I thought of its wider implications, and the similarity once again with the Muslim words used for goodbye; *Inshallah*, meaning, 'If God wills it'. *Adios* literally means 'To God" and it is the same in Greek, Turkish and French. I thought once again of how it is a nice way to say 'goodbye', a term I used my whole life, but only recently heard that even that term was derived from 'God be with you'.

Our third Angel of northern Mexico drove off into the mountains and about ten minutes later John emerged. I ran to greet him asking "Did you see them?"

"See who?" he asked.

He had walked right up to the other side of the ridge and had not even heard the engine. I told him the good news, both of us now relieved of worry. We free-wheeled down to the river and ate the rest of our jerky. We even found half a bag of pasta in a pannier and drank a few bottles of water. We were now truly out of food, but we knew that we were back onto the road we wanted to be on and our Mexican Angels had helped us along the way.

We slept like babies, and early the next morning we forded a very wide shallow river, and finally cycled into Sahuaripa. We were looked at with amazement when we arrived. People could not believe where we'd come from, knowing the desolation that lay up there in the mountains. A knowledgeable local who knew the area very well had a look at our map and showed us the mistake. If, at the very beginning when we were searching for the road shown on our map through the mountains, we had cycled another two kilometers from Tepache, we would have found it and been on a decent dirt road all the way. It would have been a day or two at most through the mountains. The way we had come was not even shown as a track on the map and, our local assured us, was far more interesting! He asked if we had met anyone living in the *milpas*. We told him we had, and from our descriptions he realized that we'd stayed with his brother-in-law!

He owned the only small hotel in town, and besides giving us a reasonable price, he introduced us to half the village telling everyone where we had cycled from. He cooked us dinner, and wouldn't hear of taking any money for it – we supplied the beer.

We stayed two days in the welcoming village of Sahuaripa, and on the way out we saw the road we would have come in on if our map hadn't marked it in the wrong place. We were glad to have missed it!

We still had quite a distance to cycle from Sahuaripa to Creel across some hot desert landscape, but now we were more careful with our choice of roads. We found ourselves on a dusty road, but it was well-marked on our map. The dry dust had gotten the better of my chest resulting in a nasty infection that was making it hard to breath. Creel would be the place to stay and recuperate.

510

Camping out one night I decided to give my bike a once over. It had been making a strange creaking sound which was a tad unnerving. I was all too conscious that it was an older aluminum frame with lots of loaded miles on it, and they were susceptible to cracking. While washing the underside of my bike with river water I noticed a hairline mark on the chain stay – the tube going from the bottom bracket (where the pedal cranks meet the frame) to the rear wheel. I was hoping it was just dirt, but when I applied pressure the crack got bigger and made a creaking noise. Hmmm. What to do? Welding aluminum was a tricky business, and buying a new frame might be just as hard – we were not exactly in the middle of a big city, quite the opposite. I decided to ride carefully to Creel and see what happened there.

When we finally made it we found a drug store and a travelers' hostel, but no bike shops selling mountain bike frames. I bought some medication over the counter with the help of the pharmacist listening to my wheezing. I remembered having the same type of infection leaving the rainforest with Rob all those years ago. Over the years I'd turned my health around, learning much more about natural therapies, homeopathy, and finding other ways of preventing illnesses rather than always turning to pharmaceutical treatments. My travels had opened my eyes to other possibilities, as well as meeting the right people abroad and in New York who all seemed to be kindred spirits on alternative paths to health. Unfortunately now the cycling was becoming impossible, and my chest was far worse than it had been in Malaysia. I made the choice to take the medication which started to work extremely quickly. I attributed this partially to my body not being used to such strong drugs, so it reacted well when they were used. The food I was eating was good, and to sleep in a bed was a nice change. It felt like it was giving my body what it needed to recover. I was also eating two yogurts a day to try and counteract any ill effects of the antibiotics.

Often with cycling, when you get to a place like Creel where people are heading off to hike or take train rides – you are usually in the opposite mode of wanting to stay put. We had had a long couple of weeks getting there, and wanted to kick back and be still for a few days, especially me with my infected chest and cracked frame. We parked our bikes, read, and wrote in our journals. The hostel was a perfect place for a rest. Creel was a small place, well situated and full of travelers, mostly there to hike down into the Canyon.

There was a local who was trying to start a business doing mountain bike rides down into the canyon. I told him about my problem and he said he knew someone who might be able to help. We met the next day and I was introduced to an older guy who said he could weld my frame. I was a

511

little dubious as I knew that it was possible to make matters worse if you didn't know what you were doing. He looked confident, and he told me to come to his house after *siesta* time.

I looked around his backyard. Long ago comforting memories of the bicycle man came to mind. He turned my bike upside down, surveyed the crack, started sanding and cleaning then put on a welding mask and got to work. He was very quick, and fifteen minutes later he handed me back my bike with hot grease oozing out of the bottom bracket, and a big fat ugly weld. He said it was strong, and I gave him the equivalent of about seven dollars in *pesos* – a bargain. I got back to the hostel, re-packed my bottom bracket with grease, and thought no more about it.

A Swiss couple checked in to the hostel after we'd been there a few days. I overheard them tell someone they had come through a place called Sahuaripa. The guy was saying how nice it was, right near the mountains, but was hard to get to. He went on to say the man who ran the small hotel in the village kept asking them if they were friends of the two cyclists who were just there. The Swiss couple had no idea what he was talking about. Sahuaripa was pretty much off the beaten track and not somewhere you would expect to see cyclists so they assumed they were mistranslating something, and kept saying no. Then the Swiss guy saw our bikes leaned on the wall where John was fiddling with something. He kept glancing across then came over and asked, "Did you cycle through a village called Sahuaripa?"

John looked up, confused, as he hadn't heard the conversation. "Actually we did, just about a week ago."

The Swiss guy clapped his hands and laughed, "Well you are famous there with the locals and the man who runs the small hotel – he thinks everyone knows you."

"Great," John said with a laugh, "I always wanted to be famous."

"Did you cycle over through mountains to get there?"

"Yes, but not on purpose." John answered.

"That must've been beautiful – we camped out one night by the river," said the Swiss girl.

"So did we." John added. "It was beautiful but extremely difficult with our heavily loaded bikes. It took us five days."

They started talking about cycling, Sahuaripa, and getting there – as it happened they'd taken a bus there which sounded pretty treacherous too. I joined the conversation and we talked about our journey through the mountains, their route through Mexico. I was on the mend, so the next day we all took the train together a few stops and spent the day hiking on the rim of the Canyon.

I was soon able to eat more and breathe without coughing. Durango was our next big city, and with the right roads the cycling could be magical, with the wrong ones you were an inch away from death at every turn. We stuck to the smaller roads as much as possible, but never one as small as the road to Sahuaripa!

# The Letters

As in crossing America, it was a new experience to re-visit some of my favorite places in Mexico and Central America, by bicycle this time. We now pedaled on hard tarmac roads slowly winding our way south through the small villages. Friendly faces were our constant companions even though Mexico was having a rough time economically. It was never lost on us how fortunate we both were. The countryside as we left the high desert areas dramatically changed, and the crowded bigger towns and cities jolted us back to the reality most people in Mexico strive to live in.

We made a visit to San Miguel de Allende which had grown in popularity. There was now a Youth Hostel, and many foreigners in the dance clubs. It was interestingly recognizable and unfamiliar at the same time.

While there we met a midwife from America named Barbara and two other female medical students from America, all trying to help the plight of the Mexican woman in the face of staunch Catholic doctrine. They were trying to introduce birth control, break the rules of male dominated machismo and hand back some power to the woman. Their collective stories were disturbing. The amount of control the Church exerted over the lives of the population in this part of the world crept into all facets of Mexican life. The acceptance of its antiquated rules left no room for free thinking, and empowered the status quo – families bursting at the seams, the burden of survival being put onto the woman, and the all too absent man having affairs, drinking too much alcohol, and procreating at will. The ladies had their work cut out for them. Their success stories were what kept them going.

Another topic that came up was travel with children. Travel with children had never entered my thoughts although the occasional meetings with them on my travels brought a welcome new dimension when they happened. Barbara was traveling with her two little girls. They were speaking Spanish with all the children in the village while having an excellent opportunity to broaden their horizons. I asked her if she was worried about illness or food problems and our conversation went down the path of alternative medicines. She said her children ate well, and had never had any food-related problems. I asked about anti-malarials, which was for me always a tough decision. She said it wasn't a real problem in this part of Mexico, we agreed the side effects weren't worth it, but it was something that always needed to be re-assessed.

She also said her children were not vaccinated. Even though I'd been looking at alternative therapies in the past few years, I'd never even thought of questioning something as common and omnipresent as vaccinations. Many serums were coursing through my bloodstream injected into my body to prevent exotic diseases. Now I was conversing with a healthy woman, watching her two children happily playing with the others, talking about the possibility that even these were maybe not as straightforward as I had always presumed. She told me how it was a growing topic of debate in America, and we had a long involved conversation about pharmaceutical companies, side effects and drug efficacy – I was opened to a whole new way of thinking I never knew existed. Mexico was pretty good for challenging my life perceptions.

I showed her the Grapefruit Seed Extract which I traveled with, having been introduced to it by my friend Mike, a chiropractor who had gotten into traditional Chinese therapies and other alternative ways of thinking. It had become a running joke with John and me as I swore its unbearable taste staved off many possible bouts of *Montezuma's Revenge* and John was not so sure. She had made many informed choices after much thought, research and consideration, but said that she was always in the firing line of mainstream thought. I was learning that anyone who questioned the status quo was perceived to be a threat rather than an ally in bringing forth new ways to look at health, economics, politics or many other sides to life.

It was such a fascinating world and nothing I learned stayed static. New ways of thinking were coming to the fore time and time again. Sometimes it came in the shape of old friends such as Nick, new friends like Mike, or fellow travelers. I realized how many people were actually out there questioning everything and it was good to feel part of that club. Like a Russian doll, once you opened one doll, you were enticed to pull open the next, and one just naturally led to another. In the same way one question brought to light many others. Traveling I was able to see the direct effects many of our unquestioning ways had on a personal level, and in the world at large. My classroom was big, my teachers varied, and the subject matter – life – continually fascinating.

We left our bikes in San Miguel and opted to bus it into Mexico City; cycling there held no appeal at all, even with my love of cycling in big cities, John wholeheartedly agreed. We both knew we wanted to go to the big city, plus we hopefully had mail awaiting us.

John and I both availed of the *poste restante* system often on our worldly wanderings. In the capital we received mail and as always it was a welcoming stack of letters. We'd both told friends and family that Mexico City was a definite stop well in advance. It was worthwhile doing this because we both walked out with big grins and a small pile of letters each. We headed off to a café to have a hot drink and revel in our new treasures.

The hot drinks came as we looked at the letters before opening them. Some had familiar American postmarks, but others were more exotic; Japan, Namibia, France, England and Australia. My excitement quickly turned to confusion, then a sense of foreboding; in my pile on one of the letters postmarked England was a familiar surname – Edwards – that of Chris, our mutual friend from Japan. As I sat with the letter in my hand I had a bad feeling because it wasn't Chris's handwriting, which was a distinctive neat and tidy hand. The return address was in his sister's name, Clare. Why would Clare be writing to me? Even John was concerned at the peculiarity of a letter from Chris's sister. Why would she bother to write to Mexico unless there was something wrong?

We drank our coffee and ripped through some of the other letters. We'd save Rob's from Namibia for later; it was thick, which meant long and entertaining. My friends from New York surprised me every so often, and mom was pretty much my most solid correspondent. We left Clare's letter – with its weird energy – to the side.

"John, I really don't want to open this, why the hell is Clare writing to me? What d'ya think, bad news?"

"Well Joey, I think I agree, but maybe it's not, maybe she's forwarding a letter from Chris," he threw in hopefully.

"Johnny boy, we've been getting mail all over the world for years now, look at this thin letter, we both know that this envelope doesn't have a forwarded letter in it." He nodded in agreement. There was a pause, then I said, "Oh screw it, I'm gonna open it."

I slid my Swiss Army knife gently across the fold as it separated. If we could see auras, I'm sure many colors poured out of the slit envelope. For some reason I turned it over and read the closing paragraph aloud:

*I'm sorry to have to give you this news in a letter, but Chris would have wanted me to tell you. He considered you a good friend.*

An involuntary shiver ran down my spine. John just spontaneously said, "Oh shit!" My response was much the same. "Damn it, what the hell..." Then I turned over the letter and read it from the beginning. It told us that Chris had been killed.

Unbeknownst to us, Chris had a worsening mental illness which started rearing its head after he left Japan. It had been maintained in Australia, but back in England matters got worse and he had an unfortunate episode in the small village of Coggeshall – to where his family had moved back to from Australia. He hadn't taken his medication to keep himself even-

516

keeled and was acting out of his normal quiet character. He was arrested for his unruly behavior, put in a holding cell with a known violent criminal who had beaten him to death. We couldn't fathom it – Chris beaten to death in a holding cell. Tragic, crazy! What a terrible end for our mellow friend Chris. It was totally unbelievable – both of our memories of him were of a quiet guy who liked studying languages, reading anything from bicycle magazines to *War and Peace* (in its original language version), and of course cycling. His family was devastated and trying to come to grips with his death and at the same time trying to get to the bottom of the situation that ultimately ended his life in such a dreadful way – his face so severely disfigured it had been unrecognizable.

Clare also told us that at his memorial service his bicycle was adorned with flowers, and the Vicar spoke of how Chris's biggest pleasure in life had been riding his bicycle around the English countryside and further afield in America. That made both of us smile. We felt a big part of his cycling life. We knew where that love of long-distance cycling began – the same place it began for us as well.

We finished our coffee, packed away the other letters, both read and unread, into our small packs and headed out into the heat of late afternoon. The air felt that much heavier now. As I looked around the streets at the ethnic faces, the mixed races and sheer number of people, I reflected on Chris's horrific story. I felt it was made all the more pertinent for two reasons the first and most obvious being that we were his friends. The other reason was that in the part of the world we were in and entering countless thousands had vanished or disappeared in similar gruesome ways – their families and friends left with no answers, but economies needed to grow. What a grim thought.

We were glad to be with each other when we found out this sad news. Normally tearing open letters from friends was a great time to catch up with all the news, but this hurt badly. The vague plans of travel in Russia with Chris, which we mentioned in our letters from time to time, would never pan out now. While traveling you need to deal with many things thrown at you – bouts of homesickness, illnesses, indecision, confusion, the death of a friend or relative – there was no instant fix. The closest thing to that was the possibility of a phone call, but more often than not that was expensive and not available from everywhere. Sometimes you're alone and have to find a place inside to cope, but traveling in close proximity as we were, John and I had become a team. We were still at a loss for words but immediately wrote back to Clare not knowing what to say, but felt we must write just to tell her Chris would be missed. We thanked her for imparting this sad news and writing to us, knowing how difficult it must have been.

We both eerily remembered the last time we saw Chris in Melbourne, him thinking we were the ones going to die on our bikes in some unknown land. Now here we were and Chris was dead. It was difficult to come to terms with the terrible news and it hung there in our heads for weeks till the shock of it lessened and it became simply a sad fact. We were both glad to have known him.

Another less traumatic letter was the one from Rob. The postmark was Namibia because he was cycling with his Brazilian girlfriend. His trip sounded like it was spur of the moment, but his new girlfriend had never cycled before, so in true Rob fashion he figured a cycle tour through Namibia would be a good break-in trip. Some first date!

Our plans to meet in Brazil were now radically changed, should we meet up in Namibia? No, that was Rob's trip. We needed to re-think things. I personally was feeling the need to work, park the bike for a little while and make some connections with friends. Asia had always interested me since my last trip with Rob but John wasn't very sure how much longer he wanted his fair skin to be exposed to the hot equatorial sun. After those two letters our energy was thrown – we were enjoying each other's company but now felt at a loose end. Nothing too drastic to do yet, something might present itself.

We passed through Chiapas where the fledgling revolution was apparent in the smaller villages. Tension did exist; masked, armed rebels protected the limits of their *pueblos* or workers in the fields, but we were never bothered. Life in San Cristobal, though, seemed much the same as it was when I had been there before, but a larger presence of foreigners living there was definitely apparent. It was there where I started to open my eyes to a new world – my own private revolution. The young wanderer had had a baptism with fire, and Mexico and Guatemala would always be special places for me. The movement in Chiapas – where seventy percent of the people were poor, and nearly fifty percent of those faced near starvation and absolute destitution – was an inspiration to me personally – in the midst of a dark crisis, a beam of light.

The chosen symbol of the revolution – a snail – captured the true essence of change, taking time and thought. I knew all too well how hard change was, and how long it takes even on an individual smaller scale. To attempt to change the way society thinks and to break the systems that have been in place for a long time is a commendable task. The 'rebels' were starting to organize health clinics in small villages in the jungle to teach about traditional medicines or where to find and recognize the plants which most modern medicines are based on. Thus giving back to these financially destitute people a certain richness that comes with self sufficiency; growing your own food, finding your own medicines in the jungle, having a connection with your surroundings – all this in the face of a government wanting nothing else but for the Zapatistas to disappear, but thankfully, fifteen years later, these revolutionaries still soldier on. Who knows, one day the people of the world may very well be turning to these same people to re-learn what *we* have lost to make it through our next phase of existence.

Subcomandante Marcos, less a leader of a revolution but more a temporal, patient inspiration for the people fighting for their cultural survival, will be remembered in many circles as a visionary – whereas to the mainstream way of thinking he is simply considered an outlaw. Even his title – 'Subcomandante' – was meant to be ironic. I was glad of the red bandana-faced men and women we sometimes came in contact with – the red bandana another symbol of the uprising.

Besides Chiapas, for the most part Mexico and Central America were not standing still. Sometimes I was shocked at the progress; a paved road down to Lake Atitlan, new restaurants, a revolution! On the other hand some of the small places appeared exactly as they had been nearly ten years after my first visit. To cycle through the whole of the region and see a few new countries south of Guatemala was an added bonus. To be pedaling with John, whom I had done so much cycling with in Japan, made it even better. My bike's weld was holding up, and in a small bike shop we found John's chain ring. Luckily I had the tools to swap everything over, and it made a big difference to his cycling comfort. Two logistical bike problems sorted, and quite easily too. That was the simplicity of the bicycle which I enjoyed so much.

I finally got the ongoing tooth saga sorted out in a small village in Guatemala – for the equivalent of eleven dollars I had an off-the-shelf gold crown fitted. John looked on in astonishment as the dentist ground away at my tooth with what looked like handyman tools hooked up to a generator. John told me I was nuts to go through with it, swearing that he actually saw smoke coming out of my mouth, but I made it out alive, and with great care the crown lasted for five years before it disintegrated, but like my broken wrist, that tooth served its higher purpose.

Guatemala had meant so much to me and cycling through nearly a decade after my first trip triggered many emotions. I thought I was finished with getting tattoos, especially after the saga in Australia of getting one removed, but for some reason, I was moved to get another after I met a tattoo artist in Panajachel who worked with a single needle only doing customized designs. Yes, it was spontaneous, but the design was unique; a sun on one side, moon on the other drawn in a tribal motif which wrapped around my ankle. I checked out his studio – he was a visiting tattooist from Texas who also had a special place in his heart for Guatemala and spent his

519

life doing body art. His needles were all new, and cleanliness his priority, so I went for it. For me it was a small physical reminder to accompany all the wonderful memories and life-changing experiences Guatemala had etched onto my being. John again thought I was losing my head, firstly in a small dentist office, now in a tattoo studio – he was a more cautious character than I was, but it kept our travel relationship well-balanced.

There was one more memory from my first trip in Guatemala that niggled at my brain – the church in Chi Chi Castenango. I had told John much about my first trip to Guatemala, and over the years he knew that I leaned towards political and religious debate – we'd had quite a few of our own on our journey together. He didn't mind pedaling a little out of the way so I could re-visit this small church in a little village in a forgotten part of the world. To me though, it was anything but insignificant. If that church had undergone a full conversion, it would be a first-hand experience of something that had been happening for two thousand years. Many Christian churches in Europe were built on old Pagan sites, and Christianity had borrowed many rituals from these other far older traditions of worship. My curiosity was getting the better of me, the ten years in between had shed so much light on many other aspects of life. John was drawn in slightly although he didn't want to admit it.

Outside the familiar Catholic Church life looked much as it had a decade ago; colorfully dressed locals, a small market selling fresh produce, but my small old man was missing from his step. We walked into the church, and goose bumps immediately covered my arms. I felt strangely privileged at seeing an undying two-thousand-year-old tradition still re-enacting itself, and was actually able to bear witness to it happenning. The pews were in, the candles were lit in front of the Virgin looking calmly down from her pedestal, the saints were all in place, and adorning the walls around the church were the fourteen Stations of the Cross. Conversion complete.

I laughed inside at the complete absurdity of it all, grown men and women playing such silly schoolyard games; "He's my friend, not yours." "I'm stronger than you/better than you." From there it just carries on in a more grown-up fashion; "I have more nuclear weapons than you do." "I'm richer than you, so I'm more important." "I'm stronger than you, and nothing else matters." "My religion is more meaningful than yours, nya nya!" The next few countries we were to cycle in had those unfortunate ways of thinking living out their aftermath on the streets of the towns, cities, villages and countryside we passed through.

El Salvador almost comically translates into 'The Savior' in English, and had a dangerous feel to it. There were many guns around left over from the recent civil war and the towns and villages looked like they were battered, as did the people. It was probably the harshest country we cycled through, and hard to believe that through everything that had transpired in that tiny country, life went on; buses ran, and the roads – although full of potholes – actually connected one town to the next. We spent more time there than expected because John left his fanny pack in an ice cream parlor with all his papers, traveler's checks, and passport inside. On returning two hours later when we realized it, it was gone. Not John's smartest move, but it forced us to head to the capital city, San Salvador. Fortunately we were able to procure a new passport for John, and get most of his traveler's checks back from American Express. It cost John a few dollars, us a small hassle, but the ice cream that day was cold and delicious and almost worth it.

Crossing borders was very easy with our bicycles. Motorcycles and cars lined up for miles on some of the crossings but we just breezed to the front of the line, showed our passports, and, because we were not a motor vehicle, didn't have to buy any insurance or show any ownership papers for the bikes. It was quite costly to travel by motorized transport; levies, taxes and insurance were needed at nearly every border, adding up quite a lot if you crossed two or three international frontiers. The bicycle remained the best way to travel, and by far the most economical.

Passing whole families astride one bike was quite common and one particular day it was stifling hot, and we were stopped having a drink. We were passed by a bicycling family who smiled and gave us a wave as we had passed them a few miles back. Just ahead in the distance as we were mounting our bikes we saw a cloud of dust rise from the ground as their bike went down. Nothing too serious, there were no cars involved, so we cycled over to see if they needed help.

The young daughter who was sitting on the top tube of the bike had got her foot caught up in the front wheel. Her ankle was bloody and most likely broken, both the mother and daughter were sobbing. The two small boys on the rear rack were dusty, but not hurt. The father, who had flashed us such a wide smile not three minutes before, now looked so distracted that his whole demeanor changed. I gave him one of my water bottles with fresh cold water, and John gave one of his to the mother. A police car drove right past. John and I offered to help, call an ambulance, get the police or do both. The man's immediate response was a frantic wave of his hands – and a definitive *"No."* He apologized immediately for his abrupt negative reaction to our offer, then went on to explain that if the police got involved there would be some money to pay, and an ambulance would mean even more cost. We asked if we could help in some way, pay for the ambulance – anything – but downright refusal was the answer. He lived in the small village that was just ahead and would go to his brother's house there.

The mother and daughter had calmed down by now, and the young girl's stoicism was commendable as her white sock was turning a brownish red with the mix of blood and dust. We told them to keep the water bottles, and now a local with a large wheelbarrow came by, and we gently placed the girl in the makeshift stretcher. The police car had stopped and the two officers were having a cold drink not 200 yards away not even feigning any interest in what had transpired.

Everything looked under control at this point; the two young boys got back on the rear rack, dad cycled on slowly behind his injured daughter, and mom, holding back tears followed on foot. John and I watched the whole eerie procession with a feeling of dread. How awful to feel you cannot call a policeman for help, or afford to treat your injured daughter in a hospital. If the ankle went untreated it would, at best, heal with a small deformity. At worst, who knows? Sad to think that with the proper care it would be an unfortunate accident she would remember from her childhood days, but now it looked like it may be a limp or deformity she would carry with her always, a remembrance of hopefully what would become a dark time in Honduras's past when people could not trust authority, or use public facilities such as hospitals in such emergencies.

Oddly enough the arguments in America about health care at the same time were heated – President Clinton had gotten into office promising health care for all Americans. That fell through though – and with the spiraling costs of emergency room visits and ambulance rides, how far from a scene in Honduras was our own country? The broken wrist that changed my trip in Oregon only cost me seventy-five dollars but those days were long gone, even though it was not so many years ago. The system has been hijacked, and is just yet another way to make money rather than help people in need.

With the disheartening thought of that unfortunate little girl and her family in our minds, we pedaled on and hoped for the best possible outcome for her.

We left our bikes in the home of a Latter Day Saint (Mormon) Missionary we met on the street. He was just a young kid from Utah who was open to discussion and had no other experience of the world than the little village he was now working in, and Salt Lake City, Utah. The vehemence sometimes thrown at America's 'home-grown' religion didn't seem to faze him. All arguments of polygamy, deceit or worse surrounding the Mormons melted away. In a one on one human interface our young friend was quite personable, didn't try too hard to convert us in any way and didn't mind at all us leaving our bikes in his kitchen while we took a week off the bikes to head to Tegucigalpa – Honduras's Capital City.

Tegus, as it was referred to, had a lively feel to it, and a certain quality to its market that gave hope of a city on the rise; clothing, food, music, and smiling local faces mingling with the international faces making it to a part of the world often thought about only in terms of civil war. Back on the coast Honduras's beach resorts were starting to become popular with travelers, and it almost felt like a Caribbean Island holiday destination. There was hope for this tragic part of the world, and the entrepreneurial spirit of the locals was refreshing to see. Unfortunately the beaches and cities of Honduras were only two years away from a devastating hurricane which killed thousands and set that country's infrastructure back another twenty years. Would this part of the world ever get a break?

We met some friendly Peace Corps volunteers and I thought back to my close brush with joining that organization. I was glad I'd found my own way to travel, and although working in bike shops wasn't quite the altruism of the Peace Corps volunteer, it had given me so much, and enabled me to give back too. I realized not everything had to be on a grand scale to make positive changes. I tried to incorporate three A's into anything I did – Awareness, Activism and Advocacy and felt the trail I was leaving behind was a positive one. I always wrote letters, went to demonstrations or engaged in conversation when the moment warranted it. I donated money to causes or organizations like Greenpeace, Friends of the Earth and Amnesty International when I could afford to. The advocacy was mostly born of my love of the bicycle as a political and also a practical tool. I would try to seek out bike clubs or advocacy groups to try and inject my enthusiasm and experience or give free time if I could help in any capacity. I was trying to live by example rather than yelling in frustration – not easy but something to strive for.

An unwanted fourth A would always try and sneak in – Anger. I got angry at governments, big business, dictators, democratically elected officials, people disrespecting the environment, lies, genocide, and the list went on – most of all it was yet one more A that was the root of my anger – Apathy. When I saw injustice I would lose my cool, then quickly try to reel myself back in. My mom's helpful input from years back always lingered close to the forefront of my mind. I needed to be mindful of that side of me that was often not far from the surface. I was learning to put my passions to constructive use and making a conscious effort at trying to be positive.

Managua, Nicaragua looked as though the earthquake of the seventies had just happened a week ago; people living in half-tumbled-down buildings, drying clothes hanging from exposed steel reinforcement rods and tatty laughing children kicking around a ball of bundled up rags for a makeshift game of soccer. No matter how often you come face to face with it, poverty is always humbling. The people were always smiling, and where it lacked the liveliness of Tegus, it made up for it in gentle friendliness. There was no skyline to speak of except for one new hotel for the well-heeled tourist. The area we stayed in was an unassuming residential part of Managua comprising small apartments and houses. We hung our hammocks on hooks to sleep more comfortably in the hot humid nights, ate in modest yet noisy restaurants and walked the quiet streets of the city to a backdrop of broken buildings eerily silhouetted against the sunset.

Nicaragua's countryside was dotted with volcanoes, as was most of the isthmus, and the coffee plantations clinging to the lush green sides of those dormant giants made for exquisite scenery as we pedaled up and down the challenging roads. We decided to enter Costa Rica via a boat ride on Lago de Nicaragua – Central America's largest lake. The crossing was choppy at first, and many of the lovely dark complexions had turned a certain shade of green. John and I were leaning on the railing watching the land shrink away when all of a sudden our eyes started to burn. Wiping our faces in shock and confusion we realized someone on the upper deck had succumbed to the urge to empty the contents of their stomach over the side. The wind direction was not in our favor and we were in the firing line. The few other casualties around us twigged on at the same moment and, fighting back the urge to be sick ourselves, we ran inside. John and I threw water on our faces, and changed our shirts. Everyone was good-natured about the incident, and it bonded us in a strange way. After the brief flurry of activity we fell into conversation about our journey with the locals who were touched that we found their country and people so welcoming. Those of us who could manage it shared a snack of tortillas and hot sauce and, as the choppiness subsided, we all took our places on the floor to try and get some sleep for the night – far enough from the railing to be away from any other detritus being blown in by the wind! By the next morning we had been transported to a different world.

When we entered the relative calm and prosperity of Costa Rica, it was strangely familiar – more reminiscent of Europe than Central America – of Costa Rica's over three million inhabitants a startling 97% were of European descent, having to do with the Spanish colonization in the 1500's and the large influx of Europeans coming to work the coffee plantations in the late 1800's. Costa Rica, having such a large proportion of the population being non-native, I assumed meant that the Indigenous peoples had 'gone somewhere'.

Costa Rica, in 1995 was in stark contrast with southern Mexico and the rest of the region, where large indigenous populations and ongoing political problems were more apparent. This was due largely to its declared independence from the Central American Federation in the early 1800's. A successful nationalization of the banks miraculously happened in 1949 (escaping the communist purges of the fifties) along with a new constitution where blacks and women were given the vote. A few years ruled by dictators peppered its past, but in the main, democratically elected leaders ruled. The seventies saw some border skirmishes with Nicaragua, and it was nearly dragged into the Sandanista affair, but held on to its neutral stance which saved the day for Costa Rica.

So where El Salvador, Honduras, Guatemala, Nicaragua, and Belize to some extent, were just coming to grips with their recent bloody histories – civil wars, Sandanistas, Contras, border disputes, British occupation – Costa Rica was an enclave of American and European dropouts and was a good place for us to catch our breath.

Like the rest of the isthmus, it was a place of exquisite natural diversity, cloud forests, giant lakes, active volcanoes, and superb coastline (Costa Rica meaning the 'Rich Coast' – a name given by Columbus). Its capital City San José was actually a bit of a let down in its drabness, but the rest of the country's beauty easily made up for whatever San José lacked. We cycled within sight of an active volcano, and in the evening watched the bright orange and red lava flow slowly creep down the mountain's side, the explosions from its cone an awesome display from Mother Nature far outstripping any firework display we'd ever seen.

Throughout our journey so far the insect life and animal life was all alive and well; we cycled through jungle roads of noisy cicadas nearly reaching deafening crescendos as we passed. We hiked in a forest of Howler Monkeys unnerving us with their call and feeling as though they were surrounding us and closing in. We camped out at night amongst the frogs of the rainforest – let no one tell you of the silence in the jungle at night. My childhood memories in my bedroom in The Bronx were much more silent than any of the jungles I had ever been lucky enough to walk or cycle in. The bird life was always astounding. The elusive Quetzal bird which graces the notes of the Guatemalan money – aptly also named the quetzal – was even spotted once on our journey, and I'm sure much else of what we saw would make any bird watcher drool.

One meeting near the banana plantations of the east coast Costa Rica made me think of a quote by Levi Strauss, the philosopher, not the gold miner who invented the copper riveted jeans, "The rights of humanity end the moment they endanger another species."

Miguel was a native of the area and his ancestors had eaten giant turtle eggs for centuries. Leatherbacks – the giant turtles – were respected within the tiny indigenous population, and of course revered because of their majesty, and life-giving properties. They were occasionally killed and eaten, and eggs taken for food but, for the most part, the natives and the turtles lived in harmony with each other and the balance of their numbers was always respected. It wasn't until the coastal banana plantations started encroaching on the turtles natural habitats that their populations started to dwindle. On top of that the commercial fishing fleets of the last thirty years or so ended whatever traditional forms of fishing had lasted till then. The West's appetite for lobster, cheap seafood and bananas had transformed the area; the many poisons used to keep bananas alive on the unnatural monocultural plantations had caused severe health problems amongst the locals who then needed medical treatment which moved them away from their natural medicines, with the added burden of needing money to pay for the medicines. On top of that, international laws were passed to restrict the hunting of the dwindling sea turtle population and the eating of their eggs. Eating locally caught fish was almost seen as taking money out of your own pocket, so the locals were relying on imported foods more and another cultural and traditional legacy was on the verge of extinction. The human saga behind the plight of the turtles and banana plantations never made the news and of course the locals were depicted as uneducated natives hunting turtles to extinction which had never happened before the arrival of the Europeans. No alternatives were given, and now the workers on the plantations were yet just another discarded people in the annals of human history. I wondered if Mr. Strauss's thoughts included the many endangered indigenous humans in our world.

The mix of nature, culture, poverty and wealth made up so much of our cycle journey. At the end of any trip in a foreign land I am left with a renewed respect for the human spirit. John and I had the privilege in our lives to make choices that have widened our experiences. We challenged each others' view of the world, and even though we had been on similar paths since leaving Japan, it was good to see that we didn't always have the same conclusions. John's scientific way of looking at life was different; death in his mind was final, but in mine, it was a continuation. It made me able to look at Central America and the lives that people were forced to lead because of environmental devastation, commercialization, political upheaval or a combination of any of the above, in a different way. I was able to see the comical – almost farcical – side to it all. It was unfair to such a degree that it bordered on the ridiculous. To implicate America as a cause of many of the problems we witnessed made matters even more complex. In high school I nearly bought the great American story: how we are all created equal and what a great democracy we lived in, but always wondered about the slaughtered, marginalized Native Americans. Over the years my eyes were opened to a far wider problem. It would be too easy to only blame America, but it was far more complicated, and the globalization of the world made it nearly impossible to point a finger at any one culprit. Some of America's founding fathers and latter presidents warned against unchecked leadership and unbridled financial growth. Again you had to dig a bit deeper for that information.

Of course I still didn't have the answers. I remembered the emotional confrontation with my mother upon returning to New York and throwing my passport on the ground shouting, "How can I call myself an American when I don't even know what that really means? What have we done in the name of democracy, and why do we continue to do it?" Over the years I could easily have substituted *American* for *Human Being*. I'd found my niche in some ways of being that responsible American/Human Being I wanted to be when my head was reeling in the Central American heat alone on my first journey to this part of the world. So much had transpired since then. My mind threw up a vision of me nearly joining the navy all those years ago, then the Peace Corps. What a different path I had chosen from those possible ones. I discovered that there was so much more to being a world citizen. There is a lot more to the world than we find in the history books we learn from, the television we watch or the newspapers we read. I felt now that I was neither running from or to anything, I had found a lifestyle that suited me; the constant learning, the fulfilling work in small businesses, the combining of cycling, working and traveling were all part of the same continuous path I was creating. Yes it came with its own frustrations, but what didn't? I did feel something inside was changing – personal relationships seemed to be more of a focus and other fulfilling facets of my life were falling into place. This trip, although not over yet, was bringing me somehow to a new phase of my existence.

Of all the places I had cycled through in my life, when I compared them with the world at large – the microcosm to the macrocosm – none was ever as true as it was right there in Central America. Many harsh and beautiful images burned into our minds at the end of a day's ride; twelve-year-old boys covered head to toe in black sticky cane juice with machetes as tall as their legs emerging from the cane fields, families trudging through beautiful lush green jungle mountain tracks carrying bundles of goods to sell in the local markets – their cumbersome loads shared out between them all, small babies being carried by older but still very young siblings, villages devastated by natural and un-natural disasters sitting a stone's throw from stunning coastal beaches, and of course the young girl with her broken ankle. The realities of our planet could sometimes be harsh, but nothing compares with its natural beauty, cultural diversity, and universal hope for something better. I can't help but think there is more to life than science.

We were still enjoying the trip, but I felt that by Panama or perhaps northern South America somewhere, I would be in need of a break. John had also given up on Brazil as a destination, especially since Rob was no longer there, but he was fresher than me, and wanted to go on a bit longer. We would wait for something to present itself.

I had forgotten if I'd told anyone to write me in San José so was pleasantly surprised when I checked the post office to find one letter with an Australian postmark, the Luke, my old house mate from Melbourne. It was nice to have at least one letter, and it had been a very long time since I'd heard from him. That letter filled in my next destination.

Luke had written that he now owned a sandwich shop in a new mall in Melbourne. It was not the small café he had always wanted, but he and Jeff were now business partners, and along with a third partner they also owned a restaurant. They were new to the food business and I'd always worked with small retail shops, and had lots of restaurant/diner experience from my high school and college days. He hinted at the possibility of me coming back over and giving him a hand. There I was on my bike in Costa Rica, heading into Panama, but I knew that my next major stop would be Melbourne, Australia. Just knowing that I was heading to Australia gave me renewed energy. As we were in the northern hemisphere's summer, there was no rush to get to Melbourne yet. Late September would be perfect. John and I continued pedaling south.

John had some college buddies who worked in 'The Zone', as the area along the Panama Canal is known. It was quite a buzz for me to have actually pedaled most of the way from New York and very strange to be spending dollar bills once again, even though they were called *cordobas*. It was even weirder to meet up with John's friends who had grown up in the Canal Zone. It was as if we had landed in a small America here on the southern reaches of the Central American Isthmus. We had a real American barbecue with all the trappings of America bought in the PX, which was the small department store supplied by the U.S. Army for all its soldiers and workers in The Zone. I fixed a bike that was owned by one of John's friends who was a pilot on the canal. He explained to us that only a qualified ship pilot can maneuver any boat or ship passing through the canal. It was quite a responsibility; the captain of any vessel had to relinquish control of his craft to the pilot. There was a protocol to the proceedings – a bit of pomp and circumstance – but it was a fascinating world John and I knew nothing about. Pilots are well-paid and work long hours, but he enjoyed his work which might be in danger depending on what happened in the next year or two. He also loved his bike which was now tuned up and ready to roll. It always felt good to be able to help, but I made sure I wasn't given an MRE in return for the favor. A cold beer sufficed quite nicely.

It was strange speaking English and eating hamburgers with people who grew up in Panama, but looked more classically American than me. Their childhoods had passed on the streets of Panama, but their lives were as American as Apple Pie. It was a small sliver of American presence, but it was coming to an end as the American contract to run the canal was up, and the world was scrambling for the rights to one of the most expensive, busiest tolled waterways in the world. Bids were being made by the Japanese, Europeans and also the Americans. The newspapers were full of opinions as to who should and shouldn't run the canal and why. The Americans were slowly but surely receding from the scene and creating one of those situations which is not as cut and dried as it would seem reading about it in a newspaper.

The canal had run for all those years with Americans dredging it, lighting it, widening it, piloting boats through its locks and generally keeping it going. Generations of Americans have been raised on Panama's soil because of the canal. I was no fan of an American presence wielding its almighty strength everywhere in the world, and definitely not in Central or South America – the area still hadn't recovered from the past few decades and its legacy. There were problems, but nothing, I was learning once again, was black and white. There was always the human side as we had just been a part of. Open world markets, free trade and corporate interests were a world unto themselves – not a pretty one – and we were all in some way implicated in their web.

After nearly a week of Americana, even our own house to stay in, and the debate dominating the news and people's thoughts, we cycled off into a different reality – Panama beyond The Zone. Much like the rest of Central America, excluding Costa Rica, Panama had its apparent poverty, its civil strife, and crooked leaders taking advantage of the general population. Panama City was like a large, sweltering Canal Street in New York City; anything you wanted to buy was easy to find, the stallholders hawking and touting you to look at their wares, seedy characters beckoning you to purchase who knew what. It was a buzz, and in the light of day didn't feel dangerous, but we were pedaling out of its craziness and heat, heading further east.

We decided we would catch a boat to Colombia, which at this window in time, was available. John and I liked adventure, but neither of us felt the need to push our bikes through the Darien Gap – the malaria-infested jungle connecting the North American to the South American continent.

529

Many have done it, and even my Austrian friends, Hans and Ursula whom I met in Alaska all those years ago, somehow made it through on their motorcycle. On what felt like the tail end of our journey we thought it perfect that the boat was running and we were there to catch it. Heading on a fourteen-hour boat crossing, rather than a ten-day jungle odyssey, suited us quite nicely.

I remembered fondly all my past boat journeys; Canada, America, Mexico, Japan, New Zealand, Australia, Indonesia, Sicily, Tunisia and Greece, and most recently Nicaragua. All had special memories – chance meetings and sometimes life-changing conversations. There were more boat journeys to come, and right now in a place called Colon, Panama, a trip from one continent to another awaited us.

# A Subtle Shift in Gears

The boat resembled a small cruise ship. We didn't go for a cabin, sleeping out under the warm night air was a perfectly good, economical option. In the corner there was a table of Israelis having a heated argument with some new age travelers about Palestine. We had met some of the people at the table in a hostel in Nicaragua. John looked over to me when he heard the debate fueling up. I grinned at John and listened in but didn't get drawn into the action. We ate a hot meal of chili, rice, and tortillas, had a beer and staked out a place to lay out our sleeping bags.

"Hey Joey, why didn't you join in the conversation? Was right up your alley," John probed.

"Yeah John, I know you think I love to argue all the time, but that's only with you," I laughed. "Didn't feel like getting into it, the new age travelers like to argue about everything, don't you remember? They wouldn't even talk to you 'cause you didn't have any tattoos."

"Yeah, I'm not cool enough," he snickered.

"Now now John," I laughed.

We had met two of the new age travelers a few weeks back in Nicaragua. They were about twenty or so with dreadlocks, a few piercings and tattoos. They were young Americans out of college and backpacking around for a few months. Something came up about the revolution in Chiapas, and one of them – Joel – was saying that the revolution was a waste of time. It needed to be fought with more guns, more bloodshed – Subcomandante Marcos was a wimp. Others in the conversation didn't agree but Joel was ready to put everyone straight. I listened to his arguments and thought they sounded somewhat like the scenario for every other bloody revolution; quick change and nothing solved because the mindset was the same. My money was still on Marcos's approach. It was funny listening to him now argue with the Israelis about their occupation of Palestine. He was for a peaceful retreat and the Israelis just leaving the occupied territories – quite a switch in tack from his bloody Zapatista ideas – and also pretty unrealistic. Mostly, I was learning, simple solutions didn't exist, especially in situations as deeply seated as Palestine and Israel or the Zapatista Revolution for that matter.

On the boat our bicycles were put next to two motocross motorcycles fully loaded for traveling. The owners were a German couple. We were sharing a table with them the next morning over breakfast when one of them made me a generous offer to take his bike for a ride if we met up in Cartagena.

We wound up staying in the same guest house as the German couple where I took them up on their offer of a motorcycle ride. John sat behind me while the couple doubled up on their other machine. It was a strange sensation to be traveling so quickly on two wheels after pedaling at our human-scale pace for the past few months and in my case quite a bit longer. I remembered it like it was yesterday – getting off of Bruno's motorbike in Nagoya all those years ago and trading in the internal combustion two wheeled machine for the human powered one.

My mind drifted as we explored the countryside on the dusty roads, and I was surprised at how natural the downshifting, throttle twisting and powering into turns came. As the roads whizzed by, I remembered the reason I found myself being drawn to the bicycle, and those reasons still remained. I enjoyed the afternoon on the motorcycle, and appreciated the chance to zoom around but, like the slow arrival on our boat two days ago instead of a plane, something about the speeds possible on the motorcycle felt too fast. I was still glad that John and I had been traveling by bicycle throughout the past few months.

The walled city of Cartagena with its narrow alley-like streets and windows bedecked with colorful flowers reminded us of places on the east coast of Central America; a blend of indigenous, Spanish, and mixed Black races of the West Indies all living in a mélange of cultural diversity. It was colorful, the food was excellent and life seemed to pulse within the city's walls. The music coming out of doors and open windows reflected the rhythmic way people *Samba'd* through life in this small city on the Caribbean Sea. It was a perfect place to float into, and with all the horror stories of Colombia gracing the headlines, it was difficult to picture any of it being possible.

When we looked at our options for cycling to Bogotá, a small squiggle on the map through the Santa Marta Mountains enticed. It would be a challenging route, but even with the taste fresh in my mouth of the motorcycle a few days before, I preferred climbing up the long dusty roads under my own steam. That was the strange pull of the bicycle; the pleasure of having your body work hard, get stronger and sustain it. Plus the rewards of self propulsion in some of the most beautiful places of the world didn't go unnoticed. The high mountains and smaller rutted roads we chose to cycle on were difficult and no matter what shape you're in, after four or five hours of climbing, reaching the top is cause for a small celebration; a rest, a stretch and a swig of water.

The roads were mostly car free. We wove our way through green lush mountain scenery one minute and rocky barren land the next. The long arduous climbs in the heat were nearly stifling at times, but then we would be cooled by the altitude. The hard work uphill was actually easier than the downhills. On the descents we would need to keep our hands on the brakes, straining our fingers and building up the tension in our shoulders the whole time. Carefree free-wheeling was not an option because of the bad road conditions. We needed to pay attention and to swerve in and around ruts and potholes. We stopped more often going downhill than uphill. With all the physical challenges we still felt privileged to be able to do what we were doing; how many people would give anything to be where we were at this precise moment in time?

There were tiny towns and villages hidden away in these mountains, and it was always a welcome sight to round a corner and see a village which promised a cool refreshing drink, and, at the right time of day, maybe a place to spend the night. The ancient tobacco drying houses stood with their plants hanging on their inner beams, but the occasional brush with anti-guerilla soldiers – some of them just young teenagers with guns – reminded us of the cocaine culture, and the ongoing problems faced in this beautiful, varied country.

A drunkard stumbled off a bus on the outskirts of a small village just as John and I were cycling past. For some reason he laid into us about America getting involved in Colombia's affairs; he was right in our faces, quite angry and drunk. The bus didn't move as the driver looked concerned with the situation. A passenger came out of the bus and apologized to us and moved the drunk guy away who was flailing his arms and still shouting at the two rich Americans – us. I wasn't sure if he was berating us for America's involvement in political problems, arming the crooked government with helicopters and guns, or was it with the American-backed anti-drug campaign which ended many people's lucrative careers in coca growing in this part of the world. For some reason the latter seemed more likely, but that was a quick judgment made by me because of his drunkenness, and general scathing words and appearance. Who knew? The bus driver made sure all was calm before he continued on his way.

We both watched as the drunken man weaved his way into the overgrown verge disappearing into the green vegetation. It's always unnerving having such hatred aimed at you. As Americans we did represent a conflicting image; freedom, suppression, capitalism, democracy, and very dubious foreign policies in this part of the world. In his drunkenness he actually made quite an astute observation in thinking we were Americans. Who else – in his mind – would have the time, money or inclination to do something as futile as ride their bikes up mountains in Colombia? Getting food on the table was a much more pressing matter. We were privileged – that was never lost on either of us. It wasn't the first time I had such vehemence thrown in my face, but I understood it, and luckily was still alive to tell the tales. As we watched the bus bounce up the dusty road jolting its passengers along the way, we looked at each other.

"Hey Joey, what about that for local hospitality?"

"Yeah, heartwarming to feel so welcome." I said with a nervousness which betrayed an unease.

"Fucken downright scary is what it is, shit! I wonder where he's heading right now; a house, a shack, a guerilla stronghold in the hills?" John said shaking his head and pointing out to what looked like nowhere specific, but exactly where our friend had just disappeared to.

"Who the hell knows John? Pretty damn weird though isn't it?" I just shook my head, "You think other planets have this problem?"

John just laughed which lightened the energy a bit. We remounted our bikes, conscious that they represented at least a full year's income for any of the locals in these parts. As the dust subsided we started pedaling and a tail wind pushed us up the hill ever so slightly. The difficult climb put us both in our separate rhythms – John enjoying his new chain ring, me spinning my familiar gearing. We were off lost in our own thoughts nearly immediately, very glad to be on our bikes.

That night we found a field behind an old abandoned school. Close by there was a small bodega to buy some food and get some water. These locals were more than glad for us to camp, the proprietor even came out with a few beers later that night and we had a chat beneath the stars. The contrast of the interaction with two locals about thirty miles apart from each other was intriguing. We didn't get too deep into political conversation – he was born in these mountains, spent his life here, grew tobacco and owned his small shop. It was the reality for most of the region, just a simple peasant existence. The next morning was chilly. We cooked some porridge as we packed our bikes but there was no movement in the shop, he was probably out in his fields working.

We cycled off and I knew this leg of my trip was ending. Even though I wasn't in a relationship, I had an overwhelming feeling I wanted to save South America for travels with my family one day. A subtle shift in gears was happening. It was barely perceptible, much like the smallest chainring on my bike – comparing the rings at face value two teeth didn't look like much, but what a world of difference on the long, wearisome climbs. My patterns were becoming obvious to me, but hard to break out of. Would I continue letting visa problems seem real enough to dictate the length of my relationships? Was my whole journey going to be a solo ride? I didn't know for sure, but Luke's invite to Australia, made it feel like my life was slowly taking on a new direction.

John's idea was to head on to Ecuador. We had heard that the road from Bogotá to Ecuador was dramatic. I was tempted but had also learned to

534

listen to myself and observe how I was feeling. Even though I would be foregoing that part of the journey, like many times before, I knew I would never see everything there was to see, and would not want to anyhow. I felt more distracted about leaving John to cycle on his own to Ecuador. We both enjoyed having a cycling companion, and he was now going to lose his. Something would present itself – for now we were still enjoying our last week together.

One form of insect life we saw a lot of that sticks in my head were the ants. We saw ant hills as tall as small houses. It was incredible, and some of the biggest ants I had ever encountered. Nothing like the tiny ants Billy and I spent hours playing with as kids before discovering bicycles. At a side of the road refreshment stand we stopped for a cool drink. The water from our water bottles was constantly lukewarm and unsatisfying so the occasional home-made *horchata* – a sweet tiger nut drink found nearly everywhere – was a favorite for us both. It was usually served from big vats filled with ice – sickly sweet at times – but always refreshing and it supported the local economy rather than Coca-Cola or Fanta. With our cold drinks we ordered a salty snack, when the man said they were *ormigas* the word sounded vaguely familiar, but we didn't care what it was called. It was in a small bag, looked crunchy, salty and perfect.

We munched into our strange snack and drank a couple of cold drinks. I kept on repeating the word in my mind, and then started playing with the small black salty pieces on the table. When I put two or three pieces together the word clicked in my overheated brain. I said, "John, check it out, *ormiga*," then pointed to the finished puzzle on the table. We and the locals had a good laugh, and we continued eating our bag of very large, fried salted ants. What would Billy have thought? It wouldn't be the first insects either of us would have knowingly eaten; bees, *bhat* bugs (a large grasshopper type insect in Thailand), and many other delicacies throughout the world are derived from the insect world. We bought another bag feeling a little bad when we passed the huge ant colonies knowing we had their friends fried and salted in our panniers.

Bogotá was a big urban sprawl. We found a cheap crash pad to sleep in and explored the city on our bikes. The danger we had heard so much about may have been lurking, but we never encountered any. On our third day there we met up with four young English cyclists. They were heading to Ecuador, as was John, so having an older experienced cyclist join them eased some of their worries. It was perfect, and I felt a lot better knowing John had some riding partners as well.

What a great adventure it had been. I cycled out to the airport thinking of my circle of traveling friends; the idea to cycle through Central America and Mexico had been born with the vague plan to meet up with Rob who, at the time we left, had been in Brazil, but was now in Africa cycling with his Brazilian girlfriend. Two other friends we kept in contact with through the cycling world of Japan were Chris and Neil. Chris, we knew all too well of his fate, and Neil, who was now living in Taiwan, was attempting, for the third time, to cycle across Tibet. Such was the state of my friends in the long-distance cycling world as I attempted to take a breather in Australia, working.

Getting there though was proving to be just about impossible – the nearest embassy was in Venezuela, and flights were costly. So after shaking hands and saying goodbye to John I found myself on a plane heading back to New York to get a visa and a flight to Melbourne.

I thought customs in New York would be a nightmare with my shaved head, handlebar moustache and the fact I was flying in from Colombia. I watched people's baggage getting ripped apart in customs for drugs or whatever else they were looking for. As I prepared myself for the same experience I saw my bike – which had stickers from all over the world on the frame, six panniers on its three sets of racks, looking like it could tell a pretty interesting story itself – wheeled through a door by a custom's official. He called out in a deep familiar accent, "Who does this belong to?" I slowly walked over to claim it and when he saw me approaching he just said, "Okay, tell me the story with this." His New York accent was comforting and he was not in any way threatening.

"I left New York about fifteen months ago and cycled most of the way down to Colombia, now me and my bike are returning to New York."

He was still looking at the bike and sizing me up as we walked towards the doors which led out to the taxi stands and bus stops – him still wheeling the bike. He walked me through customs and out the door of the airport. As we parted he said, "I never heard that one before, welcome back to New York!"

I cycled out of the airport quite happy to have not had all my bags torn apart. Even though I had nothing to hide, it was one less invasion of my personal space which you get so often on the road. As I pedaled past the yellow cabs, crowds of people and shuttle buses I felt instantly back on familiar ground, right down to the hot sticky New York night.

Somewhere recently I had heard the news that O.J. Simpson had been found innocent of his ex-wife's murder. I had started this bicycle odyssey with her murder, and was now ending it with the news of his acquittal. It was about midnight when I made it to a train station. There was a group of black guys standing in the middle of the platform so I walked my bike over to them to talk. Much better, I felt, than cowering on the far side of the platform alone. My bike sparked their interest.

"Yo, man whachyu got, your life on that bike?"

536

"Yeah, basically, just got back from Colombia." I knew that would provoke an animated response, and it did.

"What's in the bags bro, got some good blow?" There was lots of hand slapping and laughing at the remark.

"Unfortunately no, camping gear, coffee and some dirty clothes."

"Oh man, that's whack, fucken' coffee."

The train pulled up and we all got on. As we all sat on the empty train heading to Manhattan, there was a lull in the conversation. I wasn't sure what the feeling was about O.J., so chanced a remark.

"Can you believe O.J. got off? If that was me or you we'd be doing time, that's for sure!"

Silence, then. "Oh man, he was innocent, whachyu talkin' bout, the brother was framed."

It was clear where these guys stood on the issue and I had to backtrack quickly, saying, "That's what I'm sayin' – if it was me or you we'd be doing time, but O.J. can afford the right lawyers, and get real justice." I didn't know quite how much of that I believed, but I didn't feel like being drawn into an argument about it in the middle of the night on an otherwise deserted subway with seven guys who obviously felt quite differently.

One was interested in my trip and I gladly changed the topic to the bike ride. He was impressed and said, "Man you fuckin' crazy." I told him he shared that opinion with a lot of people I knew and we both laughed. They got off a few stops later and I rode alone the rest of the way to Grand Central Station in time for a train to East Norwalk, where my brother and his family now lived.

That night I slept in their back garden in my sleeping bag with no need for a tent. In the morning my niece Kaela announced to her family, "Uncle Joey's back!" I laughed at myself, and thought how I was still finding myself sleeping in my siblings' back gardens un-announced even after all these years. How far had I really come?

It was unusual to not be heading down to The Bronx to stay for my short stopover. After leaving my brother's, I, for the first time, spent the night in my mom's new place. It was a nice sized condo in a purpose built complex next to a large shopping mall in Westchester, but a far cry from our family home. Mom was still settling in, she had not been there a year yet, but the smells emanating from the kitchen were familiar and welcome.

Timing, once again, was on my side. The following weekend my cousin Auggie was getting married, so I got to see my whole family in one shot, and had the ideal wedding gift for them; the bag of fresh Colombian coffee I bought before leaving Bogotá, perfect. At the wedding I overheard my mom telling some rich businessmen that I'd just got back from South America and was heading to Australia. They were rich Manhattan types and my mom was a true Bronx girl, so when they asked what business I was in I saw her suppress a smile as she told them how I'd ridden my bicycle to Colombia and I was heading to Australia to make sandwiches in a mall.

Later on she confided in me she was "Just having some fun!" My mom knew on a deeper level that I was happy and following my path. Her spirituality gave her strength, and I was the son who had helped her to see the world. Who knew where the next time we would meet up, or what new person would be knocking on her door to say hello? She embraced my lifestyle nearly as much as I did. I appreciated all those years that my mom stood by me. She told me with a laugh, "Joseph, I never worry about you, you have the right idea, you always did Joseph, you always did!" Those were empowering words for me, and I have her and that twenty-one-year-old kid who hopped on his motorcycle the summer after he graduated university to explore the country he was born in to thank. That journey, and all the others since, showed me what was important in life and what little material things have to offer us in the form of happiness.

My friend Steve needed someone to fill in for his mechanic at the now established bike shop in New Canaan. I showed Steve the ugly weld I had gotten in Mexico. He was astonished the frame hadn't burnt away when I told him how it was done. He had an old mountain bike frame in the back room which used to be his – a quality cromoly steel frame just like my original bike bought in Yas's shop. I remembered how beautiful that bike felt, and over the years I was recommended a steel frame over traveling with an aluminum one, so now the perfect frame found me. It was even the same color as my original mountain bike and a Bridgestone – the same Japanese make as the first quality bike Puerto Rican Phil got for me when I was sixteen. It brought back fond memories to look at the familiar logo as I swapped over the parts happily, while telling the young mechanic Chris all about my latest adventure. He enjoyed listening to my tales as much as I liked reliving them. The power of words and ideas so different to life in Connecticut were hopefully intriguing him; he looked as though he'd be spinning some tales of his own one day. The days passed quickly – all of us ensconced in our world of wheels, grease, tools, and bicycles. All the equipment fit perfectly on Steve's frame – which was now mine – and the size couldn't have been better. I smiled, and the feeling of the groove engulfed me. Steve was glad his frame would be off exploring the world, and I kept my old frame as a memento – all the stickers and miles we had done together fondly stuck and scratched into the frame adding to its personality.

As I was enjoying a drink with a friend at an outdoor bar in Manhattan, I was asked by someone at the next table about the tattoo on my ankle. I had nearly forgotten about it. I'd taken care to cover it and keep it from the sun as it was healing, but now it just felt it had been there forever. "Guatemala," I said with a beam.

"Guatemala, that's different, when were you there?"

"Just got back recently from a cycle trip throughout Mexico and Central America." The conversation continued about Guatemala, and we all got drawn into a small discussion about politics, poverty, and cycling. It was a dynamic discussion and after all those other years trying to talk about Guatemala and bring it into the conversation, my new tattoo had worked a treat as an ice-breaker. I looked down at my latest addition and was transported back to the warm smiling faces of the region.

While I waited to sort out plane tickets and a visa, I recouped some of the money I'd spent, replaced my broken frame, went to a family wedding, and four weeks later I was once again heading to 'The Land Down Under'.

Friends and family had no idea what to make of me. Those who didn't think I was doing something illegal must have thought I was independently rich. I wasn't either; I just was very creatively poor and didn't own much. It didn't bother me that I was thirty-three years old still traveling since beginning over twelve years previously. It still felt correct.

Touching down in Melbourne somehow felt like the final decent on my long voyage of discovery, a small nearly imperceptible change was taking shape. Helping The Luke out was just what I needed. I put my small business skills to use, made new friends, and caught up with old ones. It felt like a familiar place, and even though I had only lived there for seven months the last time, I had made deep connections with people. This time I met a young girl named Kelly, and we got involved in a relationship. We spoke of travel and living and working abroad. I knew she wanted to go to many of the places I had been, and many I hadn't. She was embarking on her own journeys and explorations. I admired her strength of purpose at just nineteen. I felt I'd entered her life at that time to re-affirm that the world was hers to explore. She helped me to realize the new phase I was entering; my feelings towards Kelly and our relationship forced me to look at relationships in a more serious way as I was sensing certain unknown feelings rearing their heads – not just wanting to travel with someone now and again – but feelings that I wanted to share my life with someone else on a deeper level. Where I was starting to mellow out in my travels Kelly was just beginning, and it was great to be a part of her life in that moment.

We did some traveling of our own in and around Victoria, and even took a week-long hiking trip on a tiny island called King Island that lies between Melbourne and Tasmania. It had nice rolling scenery – the small fishing villages and sheep reminded me of a cross between New Zealand and Tasmania. It was nice to see Kelly's enthusiasm for life. She was open to other modes of travel, and cycling appealed to her. I helped her find a bicycle in Melbourne – where she was studying in University – so she could get around more easily. She had plans to head up to Japan the following year. We had a lot in common, and even made a vague plan to meet up in Japan. We kept it open because she wasn't sure of making it there, and neither was I.

I spent most of my time working and enjoying the wider Melbourne area; I caught up with Alan once again and he seemed to have settled into life in one place, Mark and Pauline were a far cry from the footloose couple I'd met in New Zealand six years previously – they now had three kids a house and all that came with it – Jeff was now Luke's business partner, and his children had grown. Phil was still running the video shops, and of course once I was settled in I stopped by to see Rich at the Four Corners Travel Agency – I'd be seeing him again when I needed my next ticket out of Australia.

I had received the odd letter from Denise over the years; I had her new address, so we decided to meet for coffee. I told her the heartbreaking news about Chris – she was shocked – she also remembered the barbecue at Luke's all those years ago. We filled each other in on our news, as much as six years can be squeezed into an afternoon. Denise had fulfilled her desire to travel since we parted ways, funnily enough mostly in America. She had worked as a nanny in Colorado for six months, and had fallen in love with the mountains – I knew the feeling. She had been back in Australia for over two years now and her feet were starting to itch – another victim of the travel bug. She lived well on the other side of Melbourne and we only saw each other a couple of times.

Even Jeremy, from the bike shop and his American wife made it down from New York for a visit while he was visiting his parents in Brisbane – it was strange to show an Australian around Melbourne. I knew the city well, which happens easily when you explore a place by bicycle. Melbourne had changed quite a lot in the intervening six years. It now had a big gambling casino and two new shopping centers – one in the middle of Melbourne's Central Business District – where I worked – and the other on the bank of the Yarra River. It was growing up quickly, and in many ways it was quite nice to see such big changes in such a short time.

A new lottery game was now available everywhere and along with the new casino it was interesting to note how, along with those two legal institutions for gambling, came the social problems which usually follow. The phone booths were now filled with 'Gambling Anonymous' stickers and it was a hot topic for discussions on radio talk shows. On the one hand the 'lotto' was raising money for the schools, but raising money actually meant taking money from citizens' pockets – often the ones that could least afford it. It was not such a cut and dried debate, but unfortunately it was a situation that, although riddled with problems, was now hard to just remove by saying "Oops, sorry about that." In a smaller scale scenario like one's life, it's easier to make errors but then hopefully learn and move on or right the mistake, but when incorporated into societies they were much more difficult to retrieve. Be it occupied territories or gambling casinos, it isn't that easy to undo something on such a large scale. It was an interesting social experiment to be able to revisit places and see the changes. Sometimes it's harder to notice the implications when you're living there as the small problems creep up slowly. It's too bad that political leaders seemingly don't learn from the blunders of the past or those of other countries – I sometimes wondered if it was a prerequisite to ignore the lessons the world has to offer once you got elected.

There were so many micro neighborhoods in Melbourne and the food scene was excellent – you could choose to eat out in the Italian, Asian or Greek neighborhoods. I remembered my mom comparing Melbourne to New York. She was right they did share many similarities.

Another similarity with my hometown was Melbourne's large Jewish population. As in New York, the Jewish mother almost eerily resembled the Italian mother – food, family, and a bit of guilt kept things running smoothly in both traditions. I'd grown up in a predominantly Italian neighborhood, and hadn't had many Jewish friends in Catholic school. Here in Melbourne I had many; Luke's partner Jeff, Phil the video shop owner and another friend David, whose parents had numbers tattooed on their forearms – the mark of the holocaust survivor. Seeing the faded blue mark on this woman's arm, as she busied herself around the kitchen making a meal for us, was disturbing. It made those horrific events more real to me than even the stark images of Auschwitz had. What had her eyes seen as a young girl?

David interrupted my thoughts, and for some reason asked me what I thought about Palestine. I just looked at him, and then to his mother's arm, and realized where the question was coming from. He knew where I stood on other issues, and the conflict had been in the news recently.

"Well to tell you the truth, from what I read it seems to me that the Palestinians got a bum deal. It was a country in 1948, not just an empty piece of desert."

"Yeah Joe, but you see the tattoo on my mom's arm, do you know what the Jews have been through? My mom and dad went through hell and back. I think Israel needs to exist – it was meant to be there." He was pretty sure of himself on that opinion.

I didn't feel like getting into it, especially not then. I'd done some research into the whole ordeal in further depth since I first came across it in 1991. "David, I'll never understand what your parents went through. I've been to Auschwitz and it's a horrible reminder of such a human low point in history. But I've also done some reading up on the wars of expansion in the Sinai and the Gaza strip and well, it just feels that emotions cloud over what shouldn't be an emotional issue."

"Aw, c'mon mate, so what do you think, the Jews shouldn't have what was theirs historically?"

Oh boy we were going down a dangerous road here. "Look I don't know enough about the history before 1948, I read a bit about the Zionist movement in 1897, Herzl saying, 'A country without a people for a people without a country.' From what I have read, that wasn't the truth then, and has given the world yet another human catastrophe."

"What're you saying? What's the solution? Get rid of Israel?"

"No, what I'm saying is history repeats itself, and occupation is occupation no matter what you call it. Look, I have an idea, instead of arguing in your mom's house, let's pick a date, go to a restaurant and have a rational discussion. The Luke can mediate. Sound fair?"

"Yeah mate, sounds good."

What transpired was quite interesting. David went to the library, saw a book titled, *The Jews and The Arabs*, and gave it to me to read before our 'scheduled' debate.

"Read this," he said as he handed me the book, "it may fill you in on some history."

Luke was looking forward to it. He had lots of Jewish friends, and he knew both David and I liked a good debate. I started reading the book and was confused. The book was written by a Jewish author who had spent the first part of his life being a dedicated Zionist. He was a staunch supporter of Israel and decided to do research and come out with the definitive book supporting its existence. What had happened along his way was an eye-opening experience, and after years of research the book he ended up writing was in full support of the Palestinians. It was full of interesting information about Theodore Herzl –the founder of the Zionist movement – The British involvement, the Balfour Declaration, and continued on into the modern day wars of expansion, American support, and the mess we are faced with today.

When the day came for our discussion we sat in an Italian restaurant on Lygon Street in the Italian part of town, and enjoyed a great meal. Before we started our moderated debate I asked David if he had read the book he gave me. He admitted he hadn't, but thought from the title that it would be informative.

"Sure was informative David, the Palestinian issue has been recurring for the last few years in my life for some reason. I won't take the book as

542

pure fact, but man it was researched really well, and packed full of information."

"Good," he said. "Glad I could be of help."

"But, one thing, it's totally in support of Palestine, and written by a Jewish guy who used to be a Zionist and completely turned around after his research. So we can go on with the discussion, or you can just read the book and we'll have a quiet dessert talking about how great Led Zeppelin is, something we definitely agree on."

He was shocked but laughed at his folly. Luke was surprised at his mistake, "David, that's not like you mate, you armed the enemy!" He laughed, liking to rub it in a bit.

"Yeah yeah mate," David said to Luke, and then turned to me, "What d'you think about Zep's movie, *The Song Remains the Same*? Have you seen it?"

I laughed at their banter, and David's quick turn around. "Actually I haven't, is it good?"

"Great, mate." We did talk a little about the book, but didn't take the discussion too far, and the next time I saw David he still hadn't read it. I remembered not too long ago the Israelis getting yelled at by Joel on the boat, or the discussion in Turkey with the young students. I would try to follow up more in the future on the ongoing problems in that part of the world, but for now I was  considering heading to a very different place where, unfortunately, similar scenarios can be found.

I only saw David twice more as we were living on opposite sides of the city. I rode my bicycle nearly everywhere, trying to keep my fitness levels up; a long tour was on the cards and approaching quickly. I was also getting used to my new frame – it was feeling great. A long loaded tour would be its true proving ground.

My time there flew by and I was able to reflect on my next step. I didn't foresee long open-ended years on end in Asia this time around, it was more China. I had a desire to explore what I felt in many ways to be my political nemesis. I remembered being in San Francisco talking with the people at UNPO, and that day when the Native Americans came to the Free Tibet rally, I also remembered being in New Zealand when the Tianamen Square incident hit the news. I now felt I was finally heading there to take a look from the inside. I knew a little about China historically; its Dynasties, philosophies and architecture, but its modern history was more what intrigued me, and a trip there had been looming for a while. One day I was heading to the train station, and on a bus stop bench, just sitting there staring up at me with no one else around, was an aqua colored book, quite sizable and dog eared – *Wild Swans, Three Daughters of China*, by Jung Chang. I started reading the book on the train and hardly put it down for nearly a week. What a fascinating tale. Any indecision was gone, China it definitely was.

My back was behaving, and my general health was pretty good. Before the long cycle trip in China ahead, I decided to go for a massage. I was trying to take care of my back, but was never as astute as I should have been. My masseuse and I were also friends – not close friends, but we had met at a party and talked about alternative therapies. Intrigued by Barbara, the midwife in Mexico, I asked about vaccinations, their efficacy, and what she thought about them. She recommended looking into some alternatives to the vaccine regime I heard was needed for China. She was into alternative therapies; homeopathy, acupuncture and acupressure – much like Mike in New York – I felt comfortable with her recommendations. I did some reading up on the Yellow Fever and Japanese encephalitis vaccines. I decided to forego the two new shots and other boosters weighing up the side effects with the possibilities of actually contracting the diseases. I was happy with my choices and thought how, like so many other things on my travels, I would need to make decisions and back up what I learned with my own research – and quite quickly.

The issue of vaccinations and general health while traveling had nearly as many varied opinions as drug companies selling their cures and preventatives. Questioning these all-powerful, multi-national companies was nearly tougher than being a political dissident – you needed to be well-informed and well-intentioned, because everyone was willing to chime in with their opinions. It was a fascinating topic because of the emotion it would elicit. I also learned it was something not to bring up in casual conversation. I made the mistake of talking at a dinner party before I left about Barbara's kids in Mexico and my decision on not getting the Yellow fever vaccine. I realized then and there that medical topics were not to be discussed lightly; it was nearly as tricky as religion and politics.

I had received a letter from Nick telling me how external forces had finally shut down his barter system enterprise. What a shame that anything questioning entrenched systems were demonized, marginalize and finally propagandized out of existence. I found it odd because so many of the established ways of doing things had proven themselves to  sometimes be far worse; the gambling problems now facing Melbourne, the ongoing occupations and wars happening at any given moment and the financial problems currently facing the world. The slow paced revolution in Mexico needed to stay its path, the road ahead of them would be tough, but slowly the world was waking up to the realization that change was necessary, or at least I held on to that hope.

Kelly and I kept our relationship up until I boarded the plane to head into Manila. We didn't know if there was a future meeting in store, but we were enjoying the present. I felt China's pull, but also a slight trepidation creeping in. I needed to sit with those feelings. I knew I had to leave, that choice was made for me in the shape and form of visas. It still may have been a cop out, but although I knew I enjoyed my friends in Australia, it never felt like home, or even a possibility of being one.

Once again I was leaving Melbourne with my loaded bike as I had done six years previously. Rich, true to form, found me the perfect ticket to Hong Kong – a stopover in Manila that could have been for two hours, two weeks or two months. Noemi had given me the name of some of her relatives there, and it wasn't going to cost me anything for a look, even if it was only for a few days.

# China's Destinies

The Philippines was yet another country of spectacular diversity – politically, culturally and geographically. The 7,000 islands of the archipelago were dotted around the South China, Philippine, and Celebe Seas, some uninhabitable by humans, others bursting with a mix of Spanish and Asian blood which gave an exotic look to much of the population I came across and an interesting likeness to Mexico and Guatemala in many ways.

The Americans had put their stamp on this part of the world just about a century before ending Spanish colonial rule, then violently putting down a Nationalist movement for independence, ushering in nearly ninety years of American colonialism. The chaos of history revisited.

More recently the Marcos couple – with Imelda's farcical shoe collection – were forced to flee, and left behind the same damage as most crooked regimes do – a political, economic, human mess. Manila represented this quite well; a crowded city, masked pollution police pulling over trucks spewing out black smoke, and cars everywhere made for difficult, but exciting cycling. Staying with Noemi's relatives made logistics easier.

I cycled under polluted skies for my first full day's ride. My face was black, and I wondered how my lungs were feeling. When I blew my nose an alarming amount of black soot came out – the masked police had the right idea – so the next day, although with less traffic, I took to wrapping a moist bandana around my mouth and nose as a crude filter.

When I finally made it onto calmer roads, I realized I had no desire to head very far on the island known as Luzon. I had come across some literature about the dwindling populations of the Philippine Eagle – also known as the monkey-eating eagle because that's exactly what it does to the Macaque monkeys found in this part of the world. The eagle's quickly shrinking population saddened me and my romantic vision of possibly seeing one was slim. I remembered Rob and I cycling through this region my last time in Southeast Asia – the fascinating animal and bird life, and the human dilemma we came across in the Malaysian Rainforest – which was still disappearing. The jungles here were also experiencing the same fate. That was why not only one of the world's largest eagles was disappearing, but all the other animals of the jungles – humans included – unless they were the ones given no other choice but to enter the jungles with chainsaws to clear the lands for timber or growing crops.

546

I didn't want to just pedal for the sake of it. There were many appealing draws to the Phillipines, but instead of reliving my trip of six years back with Rob – which wasn't too far south from where I now was – or chasing the glimpse of an endangered bird, I felt I wanted to be heading to the mainland of Asia, to the place which intrigued me with its philosophies, history, geography, topography, human rights abuses and political ambiguity – China.

I enjoyed a few days in Manila with Lorna and Greg, visiting some of Noemi's cousin's – a glimpse of a possible different life for Noemi if her dad hadn't made the tough choice to leave the land of his birth with his youg family in tow all those years ago. One decision, so many lives changed. Noemi told me in Japan how much she appreciated the sacrifices made by her family after her visit back in 1989. I now knew the feeling. My bike and I though were being drawn just a short plane ride away, and off we cycled to board that flight.

Hong Kong was still part of the U.K. when I arrived, although the clock was ticking and there was just over a year left until it went back to China. There was an air of expectancy about the whole thing, but in many ways I could not relate to the depth of the feelings that must have been affecting everyone on the Island and in the wider Hong Kong area – the ex-pat community as well as the Chinese. I am sure that in the wake of everything that had happened a few years back in Tiananmen Square, emotions were high. I know they would have been for me if I'd been a part of it.

The plane felt as if it were actually skimming the tops of the skyscrapers as it swooped in a large u-turn to line up with the runway on the main island of Hong Kong.

I had the address of Jezz's ex-girlfriend who was living there, but for the first night I wanted to stay in one of the many hostels on Kowloon – the part of Hong Kong that was on the Chinese mainland.

When I had lived in Japan years before, many of my friends had cycled in China and Tibet. I'd never made it, opting instead for Southeast Asia, India and Nepal with Rob, but now my sights were set on the vast land of tea, rice paddies and Mao Tse-tung. I would take care of visas and boat tickets while I was in Hong Kong. There was something I was feeling inside the pit of my stomach and I needed to find out what that was. I felt there was something out there I was missing the sign for and it was perplexing me. I probed the feeling a little – thinking of New York, friends and family – but although it was in some ways similar to homesickness, that wasn't it. I was trying to tune in to what it was, but it was still eluding me.

I'd stayed briefly in the Chung King Mansions – a huge, infamous traveler hostel which was a city unto itself, I even met a guy who was living and working in there and hadn't been outside in nearly five days – but it wasn't ideal for me as there was no safe storage for my bike. On the second day I met an English guy working outside one of the many bars who told me of a hostel which was not nearly as big as the Chung King Mansions – it even had a storage place for my bike. I installed myself in The Victoria Hostel where I felt much happier – now I could explore the Hong Kong area by foot and public transport for a while. I walked around the streets knowing I was nearly in China, and took the boat back to the main Island of Hong Kong for a few days.

I looked up Jezz's ex, Imelda, who was still living there, and she took me around to the bars at night, and showed me some of the sights by day. I walked the Dragon's Back – a nature walk along a high ridge that offers spectacular views of Hong Kong. I met up with lots of ex-pats living and working in the financial world. In many ways, the nightlife in Hong Kong made me feel like I was in the U.K. I met Imelda's new boyfriend who was from New York, and he told me about some of his travels in China. The stories were not inspiring, and involved being either robbed or mistreated in some way. Those stories didn't help to allay any of the unidentified weird feelings I was having, but I told myself I wasn't him. I was feeling good, but had the pre-road jitters. Much like that journey to Alaska all those years ago, looking at the long road ahead made me question what I was doing, but I reassured myself that that trip had helped lead me to a path. Now, once again, I was nervous, but somehow I felt China was where I needed to head. I hadn't faced uncertainties like these in a while.

Relationships were still eluding me, or was I still dodging them? I had to keep a check on that. I'd felt a small, almost imperceptible, shift in my feelings around travel when that letter arrived from Luke in Costa Rica. I'd enjoyed my time in Australia working and settling in one place, now here I was, one piece of my brain saying go to China, another saying "What are you doing? It's over, head on home." Was that fear speaking? I didn't know, but I somehow didn't feel it was over. I remembered when I first came to Asia how right it felt to be traveling and the first time arriving in Europe when I felt that was home, but now I was confused. Where was I heading? What was I doing? I had none of the deep anxiety like I had felt that night in Morocco years back, and somehow it was strangely good to feel the nerves – it kept me in tune with the present moment.

Back in Kowloon I started the process of procuring a visa for China. If I used it, fine. If not, nothing lost except a few Hong Kong dollars. I had always been able to move on from a deeper feeling in my gut. I had to identify and cut through what was only fear, and look for the sign.

Something would always happen; a chance meeting or something to push me in the direction I needed to head. If I put good feelings and thoughts out into the universe, I felt I could siphon through the small haze of confusion that was now forming.

To distract my mind from wandering too much I searched out one of the many places to eat, and ordered a mixed vegetable soup. As I was eating I came across a cockroach in my bowl. I weighed up in my mind what to do. I'd eaten enough insect life over the years not to be freaked out by it but this was a matter of kitchen hygiene. I mulled over my next move, and decided to flick out the dead insect and keep on eating. After all, if I brought it back to complain I would certainly be served from the same vat anyhow. The food was so over-cooked; nothing too harmful could have survived. I laughed at the nonchalance of my decision, The Bronx Boy who nearly vomited tasting *miso* soup the first time. As I ate I was brought back to the small niggling I was trying to come to grips with.

I'd always felt blessed to be able to be on the road since the first time I straddled my motorcycle back in 1983 but now I felt that I was just one or two steps to the right of where I wanted to be. I knew I was thinking too much and decided that I would shut my brain down and go to an English-speaking movie playing in one of the many movie theatres in town after eating my soup, which, insects notwithstanding, was quite tasty. I walked by the place to buy boat tickets into China, but something said, "Don't buy it yet, head back to your hostel, and see what happens."

Like so many times in the past I started slowly to feel right, because I was now living through my feelings. I was trying to face them as they arose as I always had in the past, but feeling them and trying to hear what they were saying instead of trying to analyze them logically. I knew that I did want to cycle in China – I had always wanted to – now I was right here on its doorstep, a boat ride away. Maybe that was what was making me nervous.

I also did not purchase any boat tickets, but I made a positive step to get to China. I paid an agency a small fee and got my visa paperwork rolling – no waiting on the embassy line all day to be told you don't have the correct photo – the agency took care of it all.

Since being back on Kowloon I was feeling better about heading into China. Just being around the few travelers I had met, and hearing some of their positive stories was beginning to make me feel excited. The next morning I decided I would go get my visa.

I was coming back from the agency clutching my three-month visa. I felt ready now. Three months. Would I last three months cycling in China? As I turned a corner, I saw, leaned very low on a kickstand, a loaded touring bike right outside the Victoria Hostel where I was staying. I walked up the stairs of the hostel and saw a new face coming down – a young guy wearing cycling shorts.

Is that your bike outside the hostel?" I asked.

"Sure is," came the reply.

"Are you just coming from China?" I asked, figuring I'd get some good travel advice from another cyclist, as cyclists face different obstacles to those met by backpackers on buses and trains.

"Actually, I've just been living in Taiwan, but I'm heading into China tomorrow."

I felt a little jump of excitement. "I'm traveling by bike as well," I said.

"Really, where's your bike?" he asked, surprise in what I was now recognizing to be a Canadian accent.

"Up behind one of the walls in the hostel," I answered.

"Oh. Have you been cycling in China?" he asked with expectation in his voice.

"Not yet, just dragging my feet about getting a boat ticket, got my visa in hand though." I held up my small bag with all the necessary paperwork in it. "What've you been doing in Taiwan for the past nine months?"

"Studying Chinese, so I can enjoy my trip in China more. I cycled through Europe and didn't speak the languages that well. I felt I missed so much, so didn't want the same to happen here."

He seemed like a nice guy. "Would you mind some company cycling?" I asked.

"I'd love some company," he said quickly, then added, "I cycled alone a lot in Europe, but think it'd be nice to have someone else to ride with. I met this guy in Taiwan who attempted to ride from China across Tibet alone three times! Sounded pretty lonely."

Could that have been Neil he was talking about? Probably not, he wasn't the only crazy cyclist attempting that feat I was sure, although the last I heard from Neil, he was in Taiwan I'd ask Kent later about that, "What boat're you on?"

"Tomorrow morning leaving at ten from the dock right there." He pointed down the street.

"I'll get my ticket." I said.

I'd found the sign I needed and it came in the shape of Kent – a young Canadian from Saskatchewan. We both didn't mind having some company and now I felt my fledgling excitement for what China held in store grow larger and take flight.

We met up later that day and went out to eat. He told me about Taiwan and how it had some tranquil, off the beaten track beauty spots, but the industry was insane. He wasn't one for big cities but said he planned to go back as he had a girlfriend there.

550

We were both happy to have someone to break the ice with, and we could split up whenever we wanted. I was grateful that he'd given me the kick up the butt I needed to get into China as well as a travel partner – and he spoke Mandarin! It also came out that Kent *had* been speaking of Neil. I hadn't seen him since leaving Japan back in 1988 – he was another crazy Canadian like Rob. I'd had a few letters over the years and was delighted to hear that his obsession to cross Tibet by bicycle – from the Chinese border to Nepal – had finally been accomplished. How odd that Kent was the person to bring me that news.

Kent was working hard to study Mandarin, not only for his cycle trip in China, but for better communication with his girlfriend in Taiwan. I thought about Kelly, and about the new feelings I had about relationships. My attitude was changing and I felt more open and ready to explore this side of those feelings. Kent was sure he wanted to head back to his girlfriend, whereas my circle of cycle/travel obsessed friends, were still all single. Although Rob was somewhere with his Brazilian girlfriend, and I had just left mine, for the most part we were the non-committal types except in one facet of our lives – traveling and cycling – it had taken over. I didn't want to cycle around indefinitely and pointlessly, I always wanted – and up to now had always managed – to feel that my travels had a reason. In the Philippines it had felt as if I was just cycling for the sake of it, which was why I cut it short.

The Mandarin language is not easy; the spoken word uses five different tones for each vowel sound which makes it very difficult to be understood, especially by those who haven't grown up using a tonal system. I was impressed listening to Kent dealing with shop holders, making himself well understood.

I learned an interesting fact about the Chinese and Japanese written languages. I recognized a lot of the characters from Japanese and was interested to learn that the written language was introduced into Japan from China around the fourth century. The Japanese kept their spoken language, but used the Chinese characters – the symbols based on concepts, not actual phonetic sounds like in English – it's a very different spin on language than we have in the Latin based, or any alphabet-based written language, which is why the whole switch over process was even possible. Over hundreds of years both languages grew in their own separate ways, but there was still a lot of cross over in the written form. How uncanny that a Japanese person at a Chinese train or bus station could understand what was written on the information board, but if asked a simple question by a local, he would not be able to communicate. I also reflected on the lack of lateral thinking I came across while living in Japan which I attributed to the same pictographs stifling the logical process of combining letters to form sounds. All of it was part of the tapestry, and as hard as I tried to figure out things, or come up with answers, it wasn't possible. At least I felt I could pitch in a little, and, unlike Greece, I might even be able to look at a map and have a clue where we were.

We bought some good maps of China, although we were both pretty vague on where we were heading. We were hearing so many tales of people being turned back, and some visas from certain agencies not being valid, so we just showed up the next morning, sat on the boat for eight and a half hours and tried our luck.

The boat was a noisy hovercraft, and our bikes fitted nicely in the front of the vessel. It served as a commuting boat, and made pretty regular stops. Kent and I were the only non-Chinese aboard and were getting stared at, but more for our funny looking clothes than anything else. The people on the boat were used to *Guilo* – 'Big nosed foreigners'. Being so close to Hong Kong meant lots of Caucasian people came up and down this river, probably on this same boat, but on this particular day it was only Kent and I. We started wondering if we were going to have a problem getting off in Wuzhou – people had warned us about being sent back down the river after the long boat- crossing into China. The hovercraft just kept on noisily chugging its way up the river.

We eventually disembarked at a very basic dock where we were officially let into China by a disinterested official who gave our passports and visas a cursory glance. It was hard going pushing our bikes up the bank to the road where we eventually mounted our bikes for the first pedal strokes on Chinese soil.

We made it to town where our senses were assaulted with a streetscape that any cycle activist in New York City or London would love to see; bikes everywhere, bike lanes bigger than the car lanes with the cars so marginalized that they had only the odd traffic light, whereas the cycle lane, swelling with humanity, had its own police force standing at nearly every intersection. It was incredible – better than any *crit mass* ride I had ever been on in New York or Melbourne! I thought wow, this is fantastic.

I knew that China had its problems and that many of these people pedaling along with us at the moment would trade in their bike for a car in a heartbeat, but fortunately that wasn't happening – at least not yet. The cycle advocate in me loved it.

Kent and I cycled along gazing around us but receiving many returning stares along the way. People were on every different style of bike, but nothing quite looked like Kent and me on our fully-loaded beasts, with panniers in front and back. Even though a bit old and road weary, our bikes were far more technically advanced than most of the others around us. It didn't mean a thing at that moment though. Sit-up-and-beg bikes and ten speed mountain bikes were all vying for space amongst the crowded streets of Wuzhou. It had been a while since I had been in India – the country slowly catching up to China in population – that same feeling of humanity oozing out of every crevice immediately struck me once again. Incredibly, between the two countries alone they house 37% of the world's people, and it felt like it – feeling familiar at once with the crowds, the clanging bells, the indecipherable murmur of an unknown language in the background, the lack of motorized vehicles – I was happy just to be there.

Wuzhou was a small provincial town, but I'm sure there were at least a million inhabitants – just a sea of people. It was early in the day, and we were debating whether to stop in this town or head on further towards the more visited town of Yangshou. Now we had made it, Kent and I were keen to ride. The weather was not beautiful, but it was not raining so we decided to stay one night only, since it had been a long day already. We pedaled on and found a basic hotel which accepted us, and after putting our bikes in our room, we explored in the last few hours of waning sunlight.

The crowded streets and sidewalks were buzzing constantly. Outdoor markets were dotted around selling plastic junk, appropriately, 'Made in China', we both laughed at the familiarity of the items. We got a meal in a noodle shop. The stares were not full on yet; we were a novelty for sure, but life was moving on around us, and we were probably still on somewhat well-trodden territory by foreigners like us.

We wanted to savor the small towns and villages and didn't really care how far we made it into China. I still considered the bike a travel tool, but not my defining vehicle, and would still take other transport when the situation warranted it, but in that moment Kent and I were just glad that everyone's worse nightmare never became ours. We weren't turned back; we both had visas and a vague plan of heading west towards Tibet if possible. Our equipment and ourselves were fresh from long rests.

We were glad for our decision to stay the night in Wuzhuo, then start pedaling up to Yangshuo fresh in the morning – in the hotel we realized how late it was, and how tired we were.

It took about five days pedaling to get to Yangshuo, and it rained nearly all day every one of those days. We stayed in small villages, and one night slept in what looked like an abandoned house, the strange mountain landscape always off to our left. These mountains were so familiar to us from paintings that we had seen depicting China – gray-green layers of misty, other-worldly undulations.

So far China seemed so different to any other country I had ever cycled in. There were similarities with other Asian countries, of course, but the mentality of the people was unique. The people in the small villages were friendly in the same way that they are all over the world but one of the main differences came in the area of getting any kind of service. People were just not bothered. It didn't matter if you were waving money under their noses to pay for something that was plainly available under the glass of their counter – if they felt like sleeping under their hat then that is exactly what they would do, shouting "*Mei yao*" which means "we don't have it," or "no," something along those lines, but the way it was said it felt more like, "Go away, leave me be."

The other thing that struck me was the personal space issue. Most of Asia operates on a different norm of personal space than we do in the west, but in China it was accentuated. If I was discussing something with Kent, perhaps looking at the map, then there was no embarrassment from men who would come and stand a foot away just observing us talk, or perhaps peer over our shoulders, pointing and offering a few words of incomprehensible advice. And then there was the spitting. By spitting I don't mean a polite clearing of the throat and a discreet disposal of its contents in a tissue. I mean a whole-hearted, guttural, hawking certain to clear out any last foreign body from the whole lung area. It was not done by just the men either; you would hear a hearty sniffing and clearing from a street away and turn the corner to see a small, genteel old lady hawking a great glob of whatever right in your path, following it with an unembarrassed wide toothless grin. I don't actually think that embarrassment is an emotion that's recognized in China.

Yangshou was on the *Lonely Planet* guide book trail. What an incredible phenomenon that book was. The *Lonely Planet Guide Book* started in the mid-seventies by Maureen and Tony Wheeler while overlanding it from England to Australia. It was not even what you would call a proper guide book at the time – just stapled together information sheets – but it was a well-documented journal of places to see, things to do and restaurants to eat in as the independent travel scene was emerging. The popularity grew into the guide book series that has influenced a large percentage of travelers in all corners of the globe. The book itself is a great tool, and with its financial contributions throughout the world, is another positive example of what people can do to make a good change. The problem surfaces when the book reaches the status of an unquestioned authority.

I find it astonishing that the *Lonely Planet* series has reached biblical status amongst your budget/adventure travelers. I met people who would assume that if a village or town wasn't mentioned in a *Lonely Planet* book then it wasn't worth going to. If a town was mentioned for some historical reference, but didn't mention a hotel, it was then assumed there was not a hotel to be had there. For me it took the adventure out of adventure travel, although I did meet a guy once who said his way of using 'The' guide book was trying to never stay in a town or village mentioned in it! Maybe he was a bit extreme, but traveling by bike I had learned that you can find places to sleep nearly everywhere. If you had a tent with you, you could change that to *absolutely* everywhere. It might not always be perfect, but it would get you through the night. I also remember those two writers of guide books in Guatemala and South Korea. How much of that information is actually as first-hand as it comes across? Asking locals could be misleading and frustrating sometimes, but all part and parcel of the travel package. I'm not anti-guide book, they're a good point of reference, but when opinions start to define good places to stay, or the best food to eat, and the book starts to prescribe the whole travel experience, I get wary. Kent and I had a dictionary, a phrase book, a good map, and we found a book in Hong Kong pointing out places of natural beauty in China. I guess we may have missed things along the way, but I always felt you really couldn't 'miss' anything where everything was a new experience.

On a bike nearly everything was interesting and every small village you cycled through had something to make it unique. Every tea shop owner had a story to tell, and the architecture just oozed history. There was always the odd English teacher or person willing to fill you in on the local history and point the way to natural beauty spot. I felt the personal voyage, the people you meet, the weather you encounter, the stomach illness, or turning down the wrong road are what make up the patchwork of the whole experience.

Yangshuo was pleasant – a big town that catered to tourists as well as low budget travelers. Coming right on the heels of Hong Kong we didn't feel we needed that sort of break yet. It's usually great to pull into those places for a quick taste of the familiar after being away from it all for long periods, but there would be more towns like this ahead. After five days of wet cycling we decided to avail ourselves of Yangshuo's convenience while we waited patiently for the rain to abate, but after four days of eating Chinese versions of western food, and paying nearly triple for what we quickly learned to be the low rates for restaurants and hotels off the beaten track, we decided we needed to break out of our laziness and Yangshuo – the rain wasn't letting up anyhow.

In our guest house the last day we met up with a couple, Ignacio and Tracy, who had an interesting plan to head north and west. They knew they were going to spend lots of time on buses, but time is what they had a lot of, and they wanted to get off the usual trail in China. We assumed we would never see them again as we were on such different modes of travel. We had a nice chat over hot cups of green tea in a small tea stall as the rain pitter pattered on the canvas covering. The constant leak behind Tracy made me shiver picturing the water dripping down her back, but it was just an optical illusion, and me remembering the five wet days of riding to get to where we were. We wished each other luck on our separate adventures. It was always nice to meet hardy souls heading out on unplanned, open-ended excursions to the unknown.

The rain was relentless and we hoped that heading west and south might take us out of the swirl of low pressure hanging over us, so we cycled one more day in the torrential rain to Guilin to catch a long laborious bus ride to Nanning.

Nanning was similar to any other provincial Chinese town; lots of cement buildings, purpose-built as housing or shops, juxtaposed with ornate ancient architecture nestled in between. The market places were always full of life and great places to eat. Of course the bicycle ruled the roads. We stayed for three days, befriended a man who ran a food stall, and stayed in the cheapest, dampest hotel I had slept in for quite a while. We walked nearly everywhere like Pied Pipers with at least ten kids behind us. That, we would learn, was a small crowd. The rain though, did not stop – even thirteen hours on a bus had not gotten us out of it – we were getting wrinkled, nothing was drying, and I won't mention the smell of our boots. We were enjoying Nanning, but wanted to get on with some cycling. My lower back problem was not helped by all the damp, the tedious bus ride, carrying my bike up the hotel stairs, and the lumpy bed. It had begun to niggle a few days before and was now getting worse. We reluctantly looked into another bus to Kunming which would have been a thirty-six-hour ride, but on the way we fortunately saw something we had not seen in nearly fourteen days – a small patch of blue sky.

We watched with hope as the patch of blue got bigger and bigger. That night as we fell asleep we realized that the all too familiar sound of rain on the rooftop was no longer there. We decided to stay one more day in Nanning and see how it was without the obscuring lens of gray misty rain. It looked much the same, but the sound was different; our ears had been accustomed to the drops constantly splattering on the sidewalks, the rooftops, the stallholder's plastic coverings, us. We hung everything we had over railings, our bike frames, string tied between our beds, but the moisture was entrenched in the air and hung heavy in our room and clothes, sunk deep into our bones. We had only partial success and had to buy new socks just to feel the comfort of dry feet; our old socks were kept permanently out of our panniers in an attempt to save them from rotting away, or getting too fusty. After an obsessive day of sniffing clothes, looking up at the sky, and drinking enough tea for an army, we donned our warm dry socks and went to bed. The next morning, under a gray sky with blue patches, we cycled out of Nanning for our first semi-dry day in China!

556

After pedaling for an hour or so, we lost a lot of the traffic and the cycling became more tranquil; we were now able to cycle two abreast and talk as we rode. The relentless rain turned into an occasional shower, which was fine. My back was feeling good while actually on the bike, but it was not getting better and was slowing us up a bit. It was the pace I enjoyed in interesting parts of the world anyway but even Kent, who was used to spending more time in the saddle, was enjoying our stops and even commented that it was so nice to get to know the places and villages more intimately. Every evening, in the small characteristic villages along the way, I sought out a masseur or an acupuncturist. It became a nightly ritual, and quite an adventure. Very rarely was it a proper clinic or medical office, it was usually a small nondescript house hidden up a small alleyway or dark street.

We were getting quite good at picking out the ingredients for our meals – the people never seemed to mind us walking into the kitchen to point and nod at what we wanted, and whether it was *tofu*, fresh veggies or noodles and rice, it was always put together nicely and served in a large bowl. Unlike so many other parts of the world, we never worried about paying too high a price. We quickly learned the phrase for "no MSG" which was thrown on just about everything – "*weijin buyao.*" At first I thought the big bag of white powder in every Chinese kitchen was salt, but soon realized that it was the well-known addictive, chemical, flavor enhancer. The strange thing was that the food was delicious anyhow, but I guess the locals were so used to it that the food tasted bland without it. Luckily we missed eating about two pounds of it by always saying, "*weijin buyao,*" much to the delight of whoever was working in the kitchen. We would have huge crowds gather around us all the time at the usual distance of a foot or two. They were very hands off, but extremely curious about anything to do with us. We might have even started a no MSG craze, who knows?

It was frustrating finding hotels to stay in as we would be turned away because we were foreigners, or just by staff who could not be bothered to do any work despite the corridors of empty rooms. People in shops would sometimes run out in fear when we walked in – a lot of the places we were in had never seen white folk, and if they had, they were few and far between. The police nearly always burst into our rooms at midnight when we were comfortably sleeping, throwing open the doors and demanding papers like it was the most normal thing in the world. Sometimes we tried to block the doors so we would be pre-warned to their arrival by the rattling door. It was the rudest treatment I had ever encountered in all my years of travel, but rude might be another one of those words that doesn't exist in China. Officialdom is never easy, but China seemed to have fine-

557

tuned the system to be as awkward as possible. Besides the hotel hassles, though, our days were fine. We were getting quite used to eating with large amounts of people staring at us – it was a constant fight for privacy – so at the days' end it was always nice to find a room, close the door and just read, write or catch a little private time.

In Wuming two local girls just waltzed into our room and wanted to 'play' with us. Over the years of traveling in Asia and Latin America, I've befriended many prostitutes and enraged all of their bosses. Kent and I were on the same wavelength of not being interested. When he left the room I had a bit of banter with the two girls – not understanding a word we said to each other. I let them know, through sign language, that we wouldn't 'play' as they put it, but was interested in what they tried to say. I could have used Kent's translation ability but he was gone. The girls soon realized that Kent wasn't coming back and I was a waste of time if they were going to earn any money, so they left giggling, and maybe a bit perplexed.

We cycled on and, although the skies were not big and beautifully blue like the one we were tempted with on our penultimate day in Nanning, mercifully it wasn't wet. We stayed in basic hotels, ate excellent food in restaurants for three meals a day, and I was getting back treatment of one kind or another nightly.

Since we were off the *guilo* trail, and not yet in areas that were deemed closed, we were making good progress, and we could not believe how little money we were spending. I was never one to keep a daily budget, or count every penny spent, but I do remember asking Kent if we were actually spending anything, because it seemed that the money we changed in Yangshuo had not been used yet. Meals were averaging the equivalent of about fifty cents at the most, and hotels about a dollar each. I was still seeking out local acupuncturists in every small village, and was amazed that there always was one. They were usually old, wizened-looking characters out of story books, and ranged in price from free to a dollar.

One time the needles were hooked up to a wire attached to a car battery. Kent, much like John in the dentist's office in Guatemala, thought I was nuts, but my pain was getting worse, and, being all too well aware of how debilitating it could get from previous experience, I was willing to try it. The pain was stabilizing a little – walking was painful, riding was okay, but just lying flat was perfect. We decided to spend two nights in the first biggish town after Nanning which was Tiandong. It was great to explore these unknown Chinese cities with no tourist attractions to speak of – people were perplexed as to why we were there, but we were treated very kindly and the local police were hands off until their midnight visits. Kent's Mandarin was coming in handy, and I found I was able to decipher a few words here and there. Kent was teaching me a working knowledge for the time we would eventually split up.

The road was absolutely beautiful – when we reached the highpoint of a climb we would see the river we were following snake off into the distance. The area was such a lush patchwork of various greens, and if there was a patch of earth that was not planted, it was ploughed to a dark earthy brown, like an ad for rich luxury chocolate. Some towns were so small that we were put up in a local policeman's house for the night. Hygiene was getting interesting, and the toilet situation was nearing that of northern India. Toilet paper was something I had gotten very used to not using. It was an expensive item, and when you travel in such poor countries it doesn't feel right to spend money and waste space in your panniers for it. Water does the trick, and is a lot more hygienic, especially as showers become less and less frequent. Kent was getting used to it as well. He had experienced it before, but now saw the benefits of washing rather than wiping yourself. It works on the same lines as a *bidet* in France, letting the water do the work, with a towel or bandana for drying up afterwards; a definite shift in thinking after many years on the road.

We hopped a day-long lift to get us into Kunming quicker because we realized Kent's visa was actually only for two months. Time had ticked away and we had been in China for nearly a month by now. There was no absolute rush to get to Kunming, but we wanted get to Yunnan province and Kent wanted to know if it was possible to extend his visa. If not he would only have less than a month left in China. He wanted to try and make it further north and west of Kunming where things start getting a lot more interesting as far as cycling terrain and hill tribes, with maybe even closed areas to deal with. Kunming would be the place to chill out for a week, for me to sort out my back, possibly meet some other travelers and exchange information, and restock mental supplies for the push to the Tibetan Plateau, as it now seemed that became our unofficial destination.

By the time we arrived I was much worse, but the weather had really brightened up, spring had arrived and there were other westerners in Kunming. We found a youth hostel style place to stay with big dorm rooms where we met some interesting travelers coming from further west along with some teachers who were living and teaching there. For some reason the Chinese authorities were becoming intolerant of the amount of foreigners staying in peoples' houses and 'unauthorized' hotels. Many people were being herded to the two or three hotels and hostels in Kunming and it was worrying for the teachers and their students. It was reminding many people of the post Tiananmen Square times. It had been a few years since that situation, but every once in a while the police threw their weight around by reining in the foreigners. We had not had too many hassles getting this far, but we knew that from here to the west and north would be a different story. Kent and I both had things to sort out in Kunming, so I set off in search of an acupuncturist and Kent went to sort out his visa.

I hobbled off looking like an old woman who had spent too much of her life harvesting rice in the fields – I was bent over almost double to a position which gave me the least amount of pain. I was beginning to get a little more worried as the pain had been going on a while now and was not showing any signs of improving; instead it was worsening each day. I told Kent I wasn't leaving until I was sorted out. He said he didn't mind staying a few days or even a week to wait for me. We had been getting on well and complemented each other as cycling partners, both enjoying having each other to share the journey with. As well as that there were interesting things to see and do in the small city. With the added diversion of other travelers, bike lanes, spring weather, and cheerful colorful flowers everywhere, Kunming seemed like a good place to relax and heal. I was recommended a place for acupuncture and it was there I met my savior.

I walked down the road looking a sad picture; it reminded me of the time when the problem first reared its ugly head eight years ago in Japan. I'd hobbled down the street to an acupuncturist and masseuse who, after three visits, put me right. I also met the right duo in Australia, and was now hoping for the same miracle, although I knew that I now had a chronic recurring problem, usually brought on by my own negligence and something that wasn't right in my lower back. I walked into the clinic, and was greeted by the smiling face of a small elderly Chinese man who spoke near perfect English. I was ushered into his room, laid on my stomach, and his healing hands probed the inflamed tissues of my back as he told me that he had taught many students acupuncture from all over Europe and America. Wow, I'd found the right guy.

He prepared me an herbal treatment used for major wounds such as gunshot wounds. It drew blood to the area to help the healing process. I was told that, besides my muscles being in spasm and slightly damaged from the long travel and abuse they'd received recently; he also thought I had a herniated disc. He told me that if I was in America I would probably be having an operation done to remove the bulge and fuse two vertebrae together. He then explained why he did not think it was a good idea, and that I was very fortunate to be right where I was. I told him about our trip – where we'd cycled from and where we planned on going, and he was anxious to be a part of getting us back on the road. He made me promise not to ride my bike for two days, and come every day for seven days so he could treat me with acupuncture and deep tissue massage.

With the herbal treatment taped to my back I walked out of there feeling the best I had in ages. I told Kent of my luck, and he told me of his. He'd found out that he would be able to renew his visa for one more month, but it would be valid only from the day it was stamped. It sounded very Chinese, but it worked out well that we would not be leaving for at least a week so Kent could renew it at the last minute. The good news was he could renew it once more, but that would be the last time.

I stayed off my bike for two days as instructed, and spent every morning at the clinic. I was improving daily, and my mental state was lightening as well. I didn't realize how much my back had actually been getting me down – I was in such great cycling shape, but hadn't been able to enjoy it. By the fourth day I was nearly pain free. I was walking straight now, and even getting to enjoy Kunming on my bike. Kent and I were excited to get cycling again. Kent had only cycled with me and a hurt back, now the dynamic would change, and we would be heading up to the Tibetan Plateau.

In Kunming we met a French Canadian artist named Paul. He was fifty-seven years old and had given a lot of his time and energy to people in some unknown part of the world in rural India – his self-searching and study had made him hard on himself. We had some good conversations even though his English wasn't very good – he loved to laugh, and we nearly saw each other every day. We were good for each other; I lightened him up, and it was always inspiring for me to meet people who didn't fit into some small box of society's making. Although he was questioning his life choices, he had made conscious decisions and lived by them. It empowered me on my own path. Kent enjoyed meeting him too. Most of our time in Kunming was spent walking the streets enjoying each other's company. We parted ways with Paul, hoping one day our paths might cross again.

Although my back had slowed us down, Kent fell into the slower pace easily. His exploring seemed to be a soul search, not just a one-off bike trip around the world. I felt, after leaving The Bronx so many years ago, that I was slowly finding my place on the planet. Kent reminded me in some ways of that younger me. He was a good energy to be with, and I was glad we decided we'd leave Kunming together to head further west.

Fifty dollars and seven days of treatment later I was a new man. I couldn't believe it – my acupuncturist was true to his word – he gave me a stretching regime to follow as many alternative therapists had in three other countries. I guiltily tucked them into my pocket, and vowed to myself to be a better patient. I thought about Mike in New York, I still had the Grapefruit Seed Extract and it had been successful in helping my stomach and staving off many other illnesses, but I hadn't been doing the exercises he gave me as religiously as I should. The regime my small Chinese healer gave me looked vaguely familiar. I knew that I needed to be more attuned to my back but when there was no pain I ignored it – not a good thing to do. Hopefully I'd learned my final lesson. He told me to be thankful I was not in America where a sometimes unnecessary operation would have cost a lot more than fifty dollars. I must take my problem more seriously. I could be an integral part of my back's healing. I liked the holistic approach to health, but needed to be more pro-active as true health doesn't just happen without active participation.

Kent and I cycled happily out of Kunming right into some closed areas of Yunnan province – the Chinese tourist towns of Lifeng and Anning, near the Thai borders to the south. The hills in the area reminded me of northern Thailand. It was thick lush jungle with our small road piercing a way through the vegetation, and the hill tribes that lived there had not had much contact with foreigners like us. The crowds in China further east had been almost comical, but here they were approaching a whole new genre of ridiculous. It was impossible to walk, eat, fix our bikes or do anything without a hoard of people jostling and peering to get a look at us. Kids were constantly in our wake, and if I jokingly turned around and roared like a lion, or Kent made a funny face, the kids scattered, giggling and screaming in frightened laughter. We both liked messing with the kids who were a delight like kids all over Asia. The adults were just downright curious.

We were now used to having police coming into our hotels every night at about midnight to see our paper work – essentially our passport and visa – but one night we were faced with something I was all too familiar with from my Vietnam experience – greedy policemen!

We liked the feeling in Anning, and when we woke up on the second morning we decided to stay another night. The previous day we had met with the town's English teacher and he had invited us back to his house for dinner which was a fantastic opportunity. The meal was simple – the whole family eating together – and with his English and our (okay, mostly Kent's) Mandarin, we got along and they were all quite interested in our travels. The grandmother was very old, and I wish I could have asked her everything I wanted to about Mao's China, the Cultural Revolution, and all the things her eyes must have seen, but the English teacher was in control of the conversation and steered it more towards us and our travels. He was slightly nervous having two foreigners in his home so I didn't feel comfortable asking anything that might have been deemed inappropriate. We all ate under the watching eyes of Mao Tse-tung as he hung crookedly on the wall of their house, as he had in every other establishment we had been in. Mao seemed to be enjoying a resurgence which was scary as history can so easily be re-written, and in a place like China where you can buy a map which purposely puts some towns and cities in the wrong place, Mao could easily become a hero.

Kent wanted to explore near the river but the hills beckoned me to walk in them and, as I was feeling good now, my back had no twinges; we went our separate ways and said we would meet up later. Coming down from the mountains a few hours later I was picked up by a police car. In the back seat was the English teacher who, as soon as he saw me, subtly let me know that we had never met. He wasn't in trouble, but had been brought along to serve as translator for the two foreigners who had overstepped the mark.

At the midnight questioning the previous night we'd said we were leaving the next morning, so when we were still registered at the hotel for a second night a red flag went up. I was glad that I had dealt with similar situations in Vietnam, India and Malaysia, so I wasn't frightened and was ready to fight for a while.

The poor nervous English teacher was feeling awkward, translating the words of the police officer that I had "Crushed the Chinese law" and now must pay. Every time I said I would not pay, he would cringe and look at me pleadingly as if to say "Please, just make it easy and pay them." He would turn to the police office to repeat my words, but then hesitate and turn back to me. I would have to nod encouragingly and say, "Go ahead, tell him I'm not going to pay. " He would sigh and then turn back to repeat, as gently as he could, what I had just said, whereupon the Chinese policeman would begin bellowing at him again about disrespect for the Chinese Law, then say something about arresting me. I was feeling pretty certain that would have been a hassle for a small-town policeman to arrest an American citizen for cycling, so I put my wrist together, and nodded to the English teacher and said, "Tell him to arrest me." His eyes widened in disbelief, but I just nodded to him and said, "Don't worry, it's me speaking not you." I felt quite sorry for him but it was almost comical. After about an hour and a half of the same going back and forth the Police Chief came down to deal with me.

Now they both sat across from me, and told me again how I had crushed the Chinese laws by cycling in the closed areas, and they asked why we hadn't told them we were staying longer the night before at our midnight meeting. The Chinese mindset is so regimented that when I told them that we simply decided that morning to stay on, that spontaneity didn't seem to compute. Finally, so no one would lose face, they stopped talking about fines and wrote out a confession for me to sign. I remembered Neil telling me about falsely signing confessions all the way across China about eight years previously. I signed the confession Mickey

M. Mouse, hoping it was sloppy enough to get by. They looked at it, grunted, and made me promise that I would tell my partner in crime that we must leave town the next day. My translator looked relieved, and I could hear him sigh as he got up from his chair. I looked over to him and smiled, as we walked out of the precinct I whispered, "*Xei Xei*" (Thank you) and thought I saw him smile.

Kent was in the room when I got back to the hotel and I told him everything that had happened. He laughed and gasped a little at my audacity, saying he was glad he hadn't been there because he would have probably opted to pay the fine. We were not bothered for the next five days that it took us to cycle to the more visited town of Dali, even though we stayed on the same road, along the same river, and bought our food from the same tribal people who were from the hills all around the area.

I don't know for sure, but later on meeting up with other foreigners who did pay fines, it seemed they wound up paying them every night probably because the police telephoned to the next town to let them know there were foreigners with money on the way. For all the cycling time with Kent we didn't pay once, and I attribute it to the fact that I toughed it out and didn't pay in Anning. We weren't a good catch, and maybe the word spread not to bother.

We were now into the hilly areas and cycling longer distances. We both felt great, and it was the easiest I had ever slipped into cycling shape on my loaded bike. Maybe the comfort of the steel frame as compared to the harsher aluminum was helping as it definitely felt more supple. I was enjoying my new frame even though I missed looking down at stickers emblazoned all over. It gained its personality quickly though – the broken-in leather saddle helped immensely – and was now broken in perfectly to me or me to it!

Cycling towards Dali we started to leave the unmarked borders of China and head into Tibet. The faces of the local people were changing from Han Chinese to the darker, more Mongolian-type features of the Tibetans. The landscape was also changing, becoming more elevated and wilder. The road was hilly and the only traffic that passed us was an occasional bus. Little did I know that on one of those buses were four English girls with whom Kent and I would meet up in a few days.

The intervening days were fantastic – we stayed in tiny villages and slowly but perceptibly began to climb constantly. My new-found stretching regime was keeping things in check, and Kent's Mandarin was being put to the test as even English teachers started to disappear from the interesting palette of people we were meeting. We could have cycled for weeks on the empty roads, the green lush hills giving way slowly to higher mountains. Even the midnight visits stopped in our hotels which were more often than not small one or two roomed guest houses. In one place we were handed two boxes of green tea each after having an exquisite veggie dinner the night before, snacks of nuts laid out for us, and a delicious soup for breakfast. As we never asked for prices beforehand we thought maybe this was one place we should have, but were pleasantly surprised as the bill was not even the equivalent of two dollars – for both of us!

After making it to Dali we rested underneath an archway leading into the town. As we were talking and wondering where we should start looking for a place to stay, a Chinese guy on a bike came up to us and asked if we wanted a place to sleep. He had a nice face so we nodded and he jumped on his bike gesticulating ferociously for us to follow him. We cycled through the crowded inner village which was quite otherworldly. There was definitely a traveler feel about the place – more Yangshuo than Kunming which had been a big city. Dali was the smallest of the lot, and, being further away from Hong Kong, and quite a far-away destination by bus, only the hardier travelers made it up to here. We had to cycle quite quickly to keep up with our friend who was flying through the streets, keen to get his commission. We knew it would be all much the same, and following him seemed to be the easiest way for us to find a bed. When we pulled in to the courtyard there was a nice communal area, and we heard the voice of an English girl call out to her friend. She had dark curly hair and her back was to us, I turned to Kent and said, "Alright, maybe we can stay a few days!" He grinned as we went about finding our room and unpacking. We took all our panniers up to the room and left our bikes on the rack supplied by the guest house.

The first girl we met was Tonia who was traveling with three other girlfriends from England. We had a chat, and that night Tonia, Kent and I ate out together as two of Tonia's friends were having a tough time – one had a dodgy stomach and the other had twisted her ankle but the third friend was doing fine. Tonia and she had planned on doing a walk through a place called the Tiger Leaping Gorge. They were looking for some English books and I happened to have one. Tonia's friend Angie was also looking for the word 'tape' in Chinese. Kent wrote the characters down for her and I went to their room to deliver it along with the book. Angie was sitting on the bed, I smiled and handed her the book and the paper. I asked her about their plans for the Tiger Leaping Gorge, thinking it sounded like an interesting thing to do.

The next day I was sitting at one of the benches in the communal courtyard looking at the map and trying to figure out a way to head into Tibet. I wanted to head to a place called Derong – it was on a dirt road and looked hard to get to. I was poring over the map on the table next to the bike rack and Angie was there as well peering over my shoulder. "Where did you get such great maps?"

"We bought them in Hong Kong, we heard the maps available in China were rubbish." I answered.

"You're right about that, I love looking at maps and seeing where I've just been, or planning out the next day's journey, but it's impossible to find a good map here," she said with her soft English accent.

"We really need them because we're traveling by bike – some of the roads we've been on barely made these maps, we'd never have been able to do it with Chinese maps." Then I added, "I think that's actually the point of the Chinese maps, create confusion."

She smiled and nodded in agreement then said, "Oh, are these your bikes? I think we saw you coming into Dali, did you come in on the road from Kunming?"

"Yep, up through the hills, what an excellent bike ride, tough at times but beautiful. We haven't seen any other cyclists, so it probably was us you saw. How long ago?" I asked.

"Oh, about three days ago, we were on a thirty-eight-hour bus ride and I was looking out the back window when I saw you two pedaling up the hill. I said to my friends, 'Look, a couple of westerners on bikes!' We all looked as you faded into the dust the bus kicked up. Part of me was jealous, but I know I could never cycle up those hills!"

"I bet you could. It just takes getting used to, I know the feeling of the thirty-hour bus rides, and I'd rather be sweating up the hills for a few days." I think she agreed, but the thought of riding a bike seems daunting when you're not doing it. "For me it's the small villages that make it all worthwhile. Those villages you pass on the bus are the character of the countryside. You rarely get off the bus in the real small villages; it's always the larger places you wind up which are more used to seeing travelers. When we get to places like this, it's time for a blast of familiarity, make conversation with fellow travelers like you and your friends." I added, "It's still nice to explore whichever way you decide to travel."

"Yeah, I know what you mean. We try to get out into the countryside as much as possible, but after thirty hours on a bus, the last thing you want to do is get back on a bus the next day to get to a smaller village. Isn't China fascinating though?" As she spoke her green eyes lit up and I could see she enjoyed the adventure of it.

"Yes it's one of the most intriguing places I've ever cycled – completely and utterly frustrating sometimes, then some of the best cycling in the world." I laughed, just thinking of the last two or so months. "Where're you from?"

"I'm from the south coast of England, a town called Weymouth, in the county of Dorset. What about you, where you from?" She asked.

The way she said Dorset I could tell she liked where she came from, then I thought back to a conversation with Jezz and Sally, and their descriptions of the coastal counties in the southwest. I'd almost bought a bus ticket to that part of the world my first time in England. I looked at her and smiled my answer. "I'm from The Bronx, in New York."

It wasn't fair – her place was a secret, quieted away from the rest of the world and the mass media. My hometown was a constant subject in the news, or always depicted in movies.

"The Bronx, wow, and here we are meeting in Dali, China on the border of Tibet." She smiled, and there was something very nice about her smile. We continued the conversation over dinner that night with Tonia and Kent and thought we'd maybe do the walk together.

The start of the Tiger Leaping Gorge walk was nearer to a town called Lijiang. It was about a two-day cycle ride from Dali, but before getting there we decided we would meet up with Tonia and Angie in a place called Xaping.

Lijiang was a three and a half an hour bus ride from Dali, passing through, Xaping, where there was a morning market that many travelers in Dali took the hour bus ride to before returning after the market. I found it odd that many of the people heading to Xaping were going on to Lijiang, which was a few-hour bus ride past Xaping -passing through the very town they had been in the day before. All the to-ing and fro-ing didn't make sense to me – why didn't they stay at the halfway point and just continue on the next day? I put it down to the lousy maps – maybe people didn't realize they were doing that. At least that's what I hoped.

After dinner Angie and I talked about going to Xaping and I asked her why they wouldn't stay in Xaping for the night and continue on from there.

"There isn't a place to stay in Xaping." She said.

"How do you know? You've been there?" I probed.

"Well obviously no, but it isn't written down as having a place to stay in the guide book." She answered, realizing it sounded funny that a sizable town liked Xaping wouldn't have a place to stay.

"Ah." I laughed, *"The Lonely Planet* Guide has spoken!" She gave me a sarcastic smile, then I continued, "I've looked at the map, and from looking at the size of Xaping, I'd be very surprised if there isn't a place to stay. Why not have a little adventure? You and Tonia buy a one-way ticket to Xaping, and Kent and I will cycle there – it's only about forty miles. We'll leave early in the morning and meet you. If there isn't a hotel, you can get on the afternoon bus back here."

"I'll ask Tonia what she thinks. Are you sure there'll be a place to stay?"

"Not positive, but from our experience so far, a town that size always has a place to stay."

Tonia was up for an adventure as well, so the next morning Kent and I packed our bikes at first light, and were off. We pedaled hard trying to beat the bus and as it turned out we made it at just about the same time. It was a local bus, Angie said, and it stopped nearly every ten feet.

In Xaping about one p.m. all the foreigners disappeared back off to Dali, except, Kent, Angie, Tonia and myself. We had already found a place to stay, and all our gear was put into our two rooms. We walked around the village, and with the buzz of the market finished, we got a taste of what Xaping was like on a normal afternoon. Angie and Tonia loved it and were certainly glad they'd decided to stay. We sat down in a small café and had a drink. The hills on the outskirts of town were calling to be explored, so we packed some food and water and all four of us went for a small hike. We climbed up into the hills behind Xaping where we found a spot for a picnic with a great vantage point – we could look down and see the village in the distance. It was a magnificent view, and we all felt clearly that we were moving out of China – the terrain was different, the mountains higher, the land more rocky and rugged, the lines on the faces of the hardy mountain people and their dark skin set them apart from the Chinese race and something about the energy was changing.

Angie pointed down in the direction of our hotel. "Look!" We saw two loaded cyclists pulling into town. Kent and I were intrigued and when we got back later on we met up with the two cyclists. They were a Swiss Guy and a German girl – Stephan and Stephanie. They were heading into Tibet, and were a few days behind Kent and I. They had been having quite an adventure themselves. I looked over at Angie, but she didn't catch me looking at her. I had a memory flash of the French Canadian couple Noemi and I had met in New Zealand quite a few years back. Could this woman Angie and I be telling a similar story one day? I smiled at the thought then tried not to get too far ahead of myself and dragged myself back to the reality of the moment.

We decided to all have dinner together. Tonia and Angie had to sit through a bit of boring bike speak for a while until the conversation turned from bike gear to China and Tibet when they got involved too. Stephan and Stephanie were sad to have missed the weekly market, but were moving on the next day. They were hoping to make it to Lhasa, but Stephan was having a few small bike problems; his gears were acting up a bit, and oddly enough, he had a Brooks leather saddle – the same saddle from England I used. His had loosened up and he needed a special spanner to tighten it which I happened to have, so the next morning we made an appointment for a quick maintenance session. We all took a walk after dinner to enjoy the star studded sky and the quietness of the town. It was such a tranquil place, and the frenzy of the morning market and bus loads of people coming and going seemed so far away.

The morning bus heading to Lijiang left after we had had breakfast together. Angie said she would leave a note in the post office to let us know where they were staying. It was strange to be cycling to this unknown town called Lijiang to meet up with two British girls to walk along a place called The Tiger Leaping Gorge. It was going to be an interesting walk by the sounds of it. The girls had been in Thailand a month before at the beginning of their trip and Angie had met a girl who lived in China. Knowing they were heading there she asked the girl to recommend one thing to do in China. The girl did not hesitate to answer, "Walk along the Tiger Leaping Gorge!" So now here we all were heading to do just that.

We assumed it would take us a few days to make it there by bicycle and, although Stephan and Stephanie had planned to head out with us the next morning after we sorted out his bike, he unfortunately lost his bag which had everything in it – money, passport, and camera. He assumed it wasn't just lost, so they were going to stay in town and try to find it, if not, file a police report or whatever else had to be done. What a nightmare! At least I was able to help him out with his bike, and Stephanie had not lost anything. We said goodbye, and thought maybe we wouldn't see them again.

The road to Lijiang was challenging. The cycling had been hilly in the past few days, and now what was hilly at first had turned into mountainous. It was the sort of climbing I enjoyed. Kent and I were in good shape now, and heading up the long climbs put us in a good rhythm. We camped out for one night – what a feast for the eyes – as we were getting higher in altitude the stars appeared to be getting closer. I guess on the smallest possible scale it was true.

On the second day we met up with Stephan and Stephanie. We cycled the day with them; their bag mysteriously having shown up after a small 'donation' had been unwillingly extracted. Thankfully passport, traveler's checks and even the camera were still in the bag – it was almost a relief to lose only one hundred dollars. At a lunch break we ate together and exchanged our stories, laughing at the similar situations we had been in, but in different parts of China. They were not heading to Lijiang – at a fork in the road they headed on towards Lhasa, Tibet.

Getting into Lijiang the next day, we went to the post office, and there was a note waiting for us. Angie had drawn us a map to their hostel, but it

569

wasn't necessary – as we left the post office walking along the pavement there were Tonia and Angie. Angie greeted us with a big smile and she seemed genuinely glad to see us. My heart skipped a beat when I saw that smile and her green eyes – uh oh, something more was going on.

We walked together to the hotel, their two other friends having decided not to do the walk because of Julie's twisted ankle and Becky's bad stomach. They stayed in Lijiang for a few days, but were going to move on to Xian, to see the impressive Terra Cotta Warriors, the fake army cleverly placed to make it look like there were more soldiers than there were protecting the area. The Chinese have a history of making things seem not quite as they were, and it went back a long way. Tonia and Angie were going to catch up with them after the walk – at least that was the plan.

It was the last day of April, and I thought I was feeling something developing between Angie and me. I liked to hear her talk, and, although she was twenty-five and I was thirty-four, we seemed to click. We talked about her travels in Europe and Turkey, and how she loved Weymouth, the town where she was born and raised. The next night we went out for a walk together through an enchanted park with a river and lakes dotted throughout and kissed for the first time. Something was different about this, the way I looked forward to seeing her after we parted in Xaping, her genuine smile when she saw us walking out of the post office, now passionate kisses under a romantic moon in this far-off land. Just two passing ships? Hmm, not sure.

Getting to the small village near to the beginning of the Tiger Leaping Gorge was yet another adventure. We had to take a bus along rutted roads the sixty kilometers or so from Lijiang to the start of the hike then spend the night in a small guest house.

It had only 'officially' opened to foreign travelers in 1993, but in the eighties some intrepid travelers had made it there. Funnily enough my Tibet-fixated friend Neil may have been there on one of his aborted trans-Tibetan escapades. We were all still living in Japan and he'd returned describing the adventure of being carried with his bike down a track on top of a donkey in a state of delirium after having been bitten by a poisonous snake. He recalled, through the fog of his memory, an unbelievably beautiful gorge with steep sides dropping nearly 1,000 feet to a raging river. He was saved by one of the locals who had found him in a feverish state next to his bike. When, back in Japan, Neil described the place he'd been to us, it just sounded like a far-off exotic place I'd never get to see – 'wheeto sha' or something to that effect. When I saw a sign with the name of the gorge in Chinese – *Huitao Xia* – I kept mulling it over in my head. It was weeks later cycling on the backroads in Tibet, thinking of Neil's prior adventures and picturing the rugged terrain and steep drops to the river he spoke about that something just clicked. For some odd reason the place name remained in my memory banks, and I made the connection that, however improbable, we possibly hiked along the same place he nearly died.

The four of us walked along the rocky path high above the Yangtse River below – it was fascinating and beautiful. Angie and I fell into the same stride so we got to know each other more. Our twenty-two kilometer hike was bringing us closer together, and the backdrop of this wonderful gorge, staying in small guest houses with the local *Naxi* People native to the region, just made it that much better. The *Naxi* squeaked out a livelihood growing grain in this harsh environment and we would be passed by locals leading their donkeys loaded down with sacks, negotiating the rocky trails as if it was a ride in a children's petting zoo. It's always a humbling experience when the locals appear to do it all with such ease.

The ever-smiling faces were the same faces which greeted us at the basic guest houses at night – tiny rooms, no heating and a blanket stretched out on a simple straw-filled mattress. Our meager payment for the lodging and simple food helped raise their annual income – it was a symbiotic relationship that seemed to work well. It was too harsh a place to overdevelop, but coming under the Chinese government, who knew what was going to happen to the area.

We got to the narrowest section of the gorge, about 100 feet across, where legend had it a tiger had leaped across escaping a hunter, hence the name. It was an impressive moment – the frothing white water below looked as icy cold as the glacial lake, Gelandandong, which fed it from high above in the mountains. I imagined the unending flow of water far below, cutting through the rock for millennia to form this fantastic gorge. Mother Nature always impressed.

Mother Nature was also working her magic with Angie and I – after the three day walk, the bus rides, and guest houses, our first kiss had turned into a proper holiday romance, where would it go from there?

# Our First Date

About a mile from the top the lightning started. The steepest part of the climb lay ahead; four switchbacks with about a quarter of a mile stretch in between each one. It was hard, but now it was going to get worse. The day began hot and clear with us even splashing our faces in a river to cool off at one point. That all seemed far off as the hail started at about one turn from the top. With no other option available and nothing to shelter us on the stony desolate mountaintop pass, we pedaled on with our heads down to ward off the force of the hail. Off on the side of the road we could hear the flapping of the colorful Tibetan Prayer flags which usually marked the top of a pass. The hail turned into snow, and the lightning was beginning to scare us, charging the air until the hair on our arms stood on end. We crested the top of the pass but we knew we still had a few more miles to go. The snow was starting to accumulate when Angie turned to me and asked, "Are we going to die?" I'd never really thought about it like that. I guess I was so used to traveling alone or with others who were accustomed to the big risks involved in situations like these that, when in similar situations, the question would never be verbalized and somehow or another we had always survived. Angie was new to this and didn't realize that you shouldn't ask scary realistic questions to a guy who'd put her life in danger. I looked into her lovely green eyes, "I don't know," were the only words that came to my lips. I guess it wasn't the answer she was looking for, but it was the only one she was getting right now. The only way out now was down either way, so we kept on in our direction toward the unknown.

Such was our first date taking shape. Backtrack three weeks to the day we got back from our hike in the Tiger Leaping Gorge. We knew there was something deeper going on, but she was booked to leave China and fly home, I was headed somewhere into Tibet and Kent was now heading back towards Beijing – his time running short. We were looking at my map and I was showing Angie the small road following a river up on to the Tibetan plateau that I planned to take. She looked at the map saying, almost longingly, "I'd love to be able to do something like that. It looks fantastic."

The words were out of my mouth before I'd even thought them through. "Why don't you cycle with me?"

There was ever so slight a hesitation before she replied, "Oh, I couldn't. I've never ridden long distances, plus I don't have a bike.

I've surmounted that problem before, Vietnam coming to mind, but I felt that there was a bit more riding on this conversation, "Did I see you hesitate?" I asked.

"Me? No. Hesitate? What do you mean? I couldn't possibly cycle into Tibet, my plane leaves in two weeks."

I was sensing a willingness that just needed a slight push, "A plane ticket can be pushed back and not having a bicycle isn't a problem, we're in China!" I said emphatically. She laughed.

My mind was trying to work out all sorts of logistics as I tried to keep calmness in my voice. Do I really continue with this crazy idea of asking this young woman to head into Tibet with me? What if she pushes her plane ticket back and we hate each other? What then? What if she isn't up to it? Maybe I should back off. If I back off though, that would be it – she'd head to England, I'd head to Tibet, and all we would have is a great memory of our hike and short, but nice, romance. Her next words changed everything.

"Do you really think it's possible?"

Oh man, she's thinking about it. Can't back down now, it would all be remembered as just a silly conversation years from now and another quirky entry in our separate journals. "Yes definitely." Gulp, the die was cast.

"Do you think it'd be hard to change the dates of my plane tickets? What about a bike? Can we get one in this town?"

Wow, she was running away with the idea. Maybe she felt the same as I did. Do or die, take the chance or this all becomes a memory, an opportunity missed for both of us. "A bike, yes, there's a small shop selling cheap mountain bikes – I could take a look at them. Plane tickets – I'd guess maybe calling your mom would be easiest." Okay, here we go, everything hinges on her phone call and the ease of changing her ticket. I guess if her mom freaks out that wouldn't be perfect either. Can this actually work? Am I nuts? More to the point, is she?

"I can't believe I'm thinking of doing this, what am I crazy?" She read my mind – her nervous energy was apparent. I just smiled; what a huge decision for this twenty-five-year-old woman from Weymouth and what a large responsibility for me to take on. It could be dangerous, but I was caught up with the complete romanticism of the moment, and the improbability of meeting this young adventurous woman willing to head on a dirt road into nowhere with this otherwise complete stranger.

The mountain bike was cheap, but rideable. Her mom didn't freak out, and just asked if I was nice. How English is that I thought. "Is he *nice*?" I could just imagine her mom's English accent asking her daughter if this guy about to take her daughter into the wilds of Tibet was nice. I smiled, but to be quite honest, I was pretty nervous. I didn't expect it to happen, but now Angie and I were getting ready to go off on her first cycling trip, starting at over 5,000 feet above sea level, in as foreign a land as you could get from England or America.

The first day, as we began cycling I asked myself again whether I was doing the right thing. I remembered the other relationships I had seen over the years; the fervent cyclist and unwilling partner. This was different; I wasn't the pedal-every-inch school of cycling. Yes, I was in shape and had years of experience of this kind of travel under my belt, but Angie had been sitting on buses for the last few months and I was worried that, although she was generally in shape and willing, she wouldn't be able to manage the sheer physical effort of pedaling a pretty heavy bike up these badly-paved roads. There's something to be said for working up to a challenge, beginning perhaps with a nice weekend cycling together in the hills of one of our less challenging countries. But this was baptism by fire and we would certainly see fairly quickly if our trip, and even our embryonic relationship, was going to work out.

Angie told me later how, as she pedaled the first few feet of the rocky road – up, and into a drizzly day – that she was also questioning the wisdom of her decision. We both somehow knew though, that beneath all these understandable nerves, we were both excited and somehow confident that all was going to be well.

That first day out of Lijiang was rainy and had turned the road into a muddy surface with gullies carved out by the rain run-off. The surface wasn't great to start with because of the stony surface. It was all too familiar to me, having cycled for years on Asian roads but Angie was finding it difficult to choose the best line for her tires and kept skidding and slipping off stones which all made the bike more difficult to handle. She also had to stop to get her breath at fairly frequent intervals but didn't verbalize any complaints or worries and was generally upbeat about the whole experience. The road went up all day and, at last, we stopped for the night in a dingy truck stop. It was uninspiring at best and frustrating because we were the show, but Angie was done for the day and just needed to eat and rest barely noticing the Chinese men staring at her with interest.

The next day the road continued in much the same vein but it was no longer raining which was a blessing. We reached Qitaou which was the small village we had bypassed on the end of our walk through the Tiger Leaping Gorge because we had decided to ford the river instead. It had a nice feel to it, and we met a few foreigners coming back or starting their walk along the Gorge. After a two-day rest there we wound up cycling nearly sixty kilometers on a gentle climb to a place called Xiazhongdien. I was responsible for it being such a long day as I had convinced Angie that there would be somewhere to stay at a small village marked on the map at about thirty kilometers or so. When we got there it was nothing more than a few shacks clearly none of which were a hotel, the size of a village wasn't a fool-proof guide to finding places to sleep. We reluctantly remounted the bikes to continue on to the next village which was just a bunch of wood-clad buildings. Fortunately one of them had beds for us to sleep on. Angie could hardly walk after the day of constant uphill pedaling, so we stayed two days while her muscles and lungs strengthened. Being a physical therapist she showed me how to revitalize her aching muscles with massage. I gladly obliged, becoming more enthralled with this woman from Dorset.

We started getting into Tibet now and, although there was no official border, if there had been one, I thought it would be somewhere between Xiazhongdien and Zhongdien. We stayed in Zhongdien for about four nights, and it was interesting to be surrounded by a whole different race of people – smiling Buddhist Monks on bicycles, picturesque walks in and around the village, and the monastery on the outskirts with its commanding view over the village. We were still seeing the odd travelers here and there, and, somewhat surprisingly, we ran into Ignacio and Tracy. They were intrigued that my riding partner was now Angie and no longer Kent, so we told them our romantic tale. They were traveling slowly and stopping off in a lot of the small villages. Now they were just enjoying a familiar traveler atmosphere before heading off again, much as we were doing. They were getting ready for their long bus journeys and us for more cycling; our next stop being Benzilan, eighty kilometers away, on a challenging up and down dirt road – we were all leaving any sort of familiarity behind us.

Even my decent map seemed unsure of this wild terrain showing Benzilan to be on the wrong side of the river. We had to frustratingly backtrack twelve kilometers to cross a well-hidden bridge to the other side of the river we were following. A town called Bantou marked on the map also disappeared somewhere into the ether so we had to cycle a little further on to finally sleep on the kitchen floor of a truck stop. We were getting into tough terrain but it was fascinating. I had cycled in some pretty wild places before but this was wilderness on another level. The fact that people could actually scratch out a bleak existence in some of these villages boggled the mind. The word village conjures up the image of houses nestling cozily together with a few local shops and perhaps children playing in some communal space, but these villages couldn't be further from that. They were often just a few basic buildings (and perhaps that's too generous a description in some cases) with a few men standing around looking aimless, and as always an abundance of curious children. The fields managed to look productive and the women working those fields throwing us confused glances as we pedaled past. It was a world away from either of our homes that was for sure. There was also a lack of color to the whole scene; besides the traditional hand-woven cothing, everything seemed to be some shade of dusty brown. There was certainly some beautiful countryside between the villages, but it was clear that we were high in altitude with often a lack of trees and the whole impression was one of desolation, particularly as we pulled away from the river where life is always more vibrant and fertile.

Angie was finding a new fitness level and as she did so she was able to think less about how much her legs and lungs were hurting and begin to actually enjoy the hardship, and feel it was worth it. She was surprising herself and me at her increase in strength. After long bus rides where the closest she got to small unnoteworthy villages was a glimpse through a dusty window, she was now staying in those small places.

We'd been cycling in western Sichuan Province for a few days by now. The high elevations were slowly but surely getting higher. A pass at 11,000 feet was now commonplace. In America or anywhere else, the high passes would have had names, but here on the Tibetan Plateau, they just were part and parcel of the terrain. The early spring weather was beautiful. The air was crisp and clean and the lack of cars and trucks helped this immensely.

Angie had not been prepared for this sort of adventure; after all, the furthest she had cycled in recent years was from Weymouth to Dorchester in her home county of Dorset in the south of England. She reminded me that the return trip on that ride was fifteen miles, on paved roads! Here we were now seventy-five miles from the closest village on a dirt road in Tibet, breathing the thin air of this remote part of the world. The road's pavement had turned to dirt a lot further back than fifteen miles ago, and Angie and I had cycled every bit of it. I had a lot of mileage in my legs, and my lungs were used to the thinner air. Angie was now slowly acclimatizing and my initial fears were subsiding. She was up to it, and our romance was somehow blossoming.

Angie was finding it both hard and extremely satisfying pedaling her fully loaded Chinese mountain bike bought in that small shop in Lijiang. I'd had to rebuild it and custom make her some panniers out of two cheap backpacks we'd bought at a street market. I made the hooks out of teaspoons, and scoured construction sites for anything I could stiffen the back of them with to make them more functional. The locals were thinking I was crazy, and at the time I was close to agreeing with them. Angie was happy with the makeshift bags and appreciated their transformation. With her backpack strapped across the back rack, she was pedaling on some of the toughest roads of this leg of my journey. I was impressed with her staying power. We slowly pedaled on this dusty empty road – the view shared only by the occasional yak grazing or a few nomadic people near the river in their makeshift camps, the gypsies of the Himalaya.

Much as it felt like we were the only people to travel this road in the last year, it did serve as a route connecting the small infrequent villages of this lost region of the world. The occasional mail-truck would whiz by and kick up so much dirt we'd have to cover our eyes and mouths and stop to let the dust settle. Who could be writing letters to anyone out here in these remote places was anyone's guess.

We finally reached Derong, which was a beautiful village and almost tranquil after the harshness of the previous week's cycling. The white-washed buildings, the roaring river and the friendly people all made for a perfect stop for a few days. We met the English teacher in town who was one of the few Han Chinese people living here – the shop owners and those who ran the post office were also Chinese – but almost everyone else was Tibetan. It became clear that there was no love lost between the two races – another example of our world and the sad situations we create by occupying lands, and forcing one's values on others. Over on the main route we'd left behind near Zhongdien, the blue Chinese truck fleet was busy carrying out nearly every old-growth tree Tibet had, or so it seemed as these trucks just kept on thundering past. I shudder to think that this was, and probably still is, happening daily.

After Derong, we slowly cycled through the beautiful high plains. The next village, which existed on my map, was Xiancheng. We were getting lots of conflicting information as to where it might actually be, but everyone seemed to agree it was near enough to 160 kilometers away, meaning that my map was definitely wrong. The map was something of great interest to the locals. Some had never seen a map of the region, and many were surprised to see how far away Zhongdien was. The river was always nearby and where there was water, there was life: yaks, nomads, mail-trucks, and us. The nights were chilly but on the few occasions we did camp with my 'Friendship Shop' tent, we were just fine. Angie's ever increasing fitness level plus the awe factor of where we were outweighed the tough riding.

We did finally reach Xiancheng, lots of long climbs away, but fortunately nearer to 90 kilometers than 160. It was just a small village tucked away in the wilds of Tibet. There were no police checkpoints here, and we had been quite lucky not to get stopped the whole way so far as we were sure these areas were closed to foreigners. The occasional police visits to our room in some places elicited more questions about our bicycles than our paperwork. We stayed in a guest house which was a tiny room with four single beds. We slept in two of them, and our equipment took up the rest of the space. It was incredible walking through these villages; we were usually the main attraction. It would not be odd for crowds to get so big that I would find it hard to find Angie if I had walked away to buy something or find a room for the night. She would wave to me across the heads of the crowd, laughing at the ludicrousness of it all. The crowds sometimes worked to our advantage. My bike and gear weighed nearly eighty pounds, and to carry the bike up a flight or two in the typical ugly cement blocks the Chinese have graced this part of the world with was not a task I enjoyed, especially with my lower back problem. Needless to say, after pedaling all day neither of us were too keen on ending the day with a three flight carry up of our heavy, unwieldy load. This is where the crowds came in. The people wanted to see us; our bikes, my facial hair, Angie's green eyes, so what an opportunity for a few young strapping Tibetan boys to be invited to carry our bikes to our room. It always worked well, and in the end everyone was pleased. Our bikes were carried up, my back was intact, and a few local boys had first-hand experience with two foreigners.

From Xiancheng we then headed for a place called Sumdo. The road to Sumdo was incredibly desolate. We even slept on the earthen kitchen floor of another truck stop one night as there were fewer and fewer places for us to stay. The long days in the saddle going up for hours at a time made sleep come quite easily. Since Zhongdien, what rooms we did find were usually basic; a bed, sometimes two or three, and a bowl for hot water – that was it. The toilet was either down the hall (not usually), down the stairs (usually), or non-existent (rarely, but possible). In the last case there would usually be a communal village block of toilets, which were just holes in the ground with no doors between to separate you from the hole next door. In some places the maggot-infested excrement was actually mounding out of the hole – a far cry from a ten minute relaxation with a newspaper! The side of the road was usually a better bet if you could get the timing right. Showers were something we hadn't come across since Qiatou so we usually washed in sinks or the bowls with flasks of water that were usually provided now that sinks were becoming less common. I remember once braving the river but it was icy cold from the glacial runoff. The one shower we did come across was basically in the toilet – find a foothold and don't move – I guess they figured they'd save on drainage that way!

I was glad that Angie had already done a few months of traveling, although the sanitary arrangements must have been far worse than anything she had seen up to this point. I was lucky she wasn't too precious about needing high levels of luxury. Our relationship, however, was reaching levels of intimacy usually only reached after years of marriage –

578

there was nowhere to hide from each other – whereas it usually takes a few dates before you don't have to think about what clothes you might wear for example, there we were, no holds barred and sharing the world of squat toilets and non-existent washing facilities. If we could survive this then something special must be going on!

We had cycled quite a few passes by this time and now – confident that Angie's bike-handling skills were up to it – I showed her the little trick I learned in Turkey to save breathing in noxious fumes from the back of trucks which probably hadn't passed an inspection in years. It gave your legs a rest as well as saved your lungs, but was quite hard on the upper body as you had to hold the bike up with one arm while steering. It sounds more dangerous than it is, but I only chanced it on the occasional short pass where the truck and I were going at approximately the same speed. Angie was game to try so the next time we heard a truck grinding through its gears behind us, we looked back to see the telltale signs of black smoke spewing out the back, and a ball of dust behind it. Ahead of us there were about three or so kilometers to the top. I went over the details once again, and as the truck passed, Angie grabbed on like an old pro while I grabbed on to the other side. It was a little disconcerting not being able to see her so once in a while on a steep switchback I would be able to let go, fall back, and see if she was alright. She would nod – okay – with a deep look of concentration on her face. The truck took us near the top where it started going a bit too fast for our liking, so we let go having enjoyed our free-wheel up hill, now being that much closer to Sumdo.

After our short hitch, we had plenty of time to find our separate rhythms on the long arduous climbs in the thin air, and Angie was now getting used to her bicycle. What she couldn't get used to was me going up then coming back down to see if she was alright, and talk her up the hill. She let me know that what I thought was a nice gesture was frustrating her for two reasons; firstly, the last thing she wanted to do was talk up the hills – it took all she had to just breathe – and secondly, she could not believe that I was actually feeling good enough to come down the road a few hundred feet every once in a while. Once I found this out I stopped this tack and waited at the tops of little crests in the road at strategic places that would push her just enough to go a little further every time. I would usually have a snack or water bottle at the ready. It was fun, but extremely hard work for both of us. I thought this tack a bit better than the one Rob had used in Bali – laughing at me. It worked fine back then, but just knowing the amount of suffering she was going through, I thought better of the laughing technique, and quite honestly didn't think it was appropriate because she was truly blowing me away with her determination and new-found stamina. To say I wasn't finding it difficult would be an out and out lie, but with experience behind me, and the right gearing, my output of energy was a lot less for each mile, and I needed to constantly reassure Angie her state of mind was just as important.

The astounding scenery was a reward in itself. Angie, with her love of maps, would look to see how much ground we had covered, and realize that here we were a thousand miles from anywhere – just her, me, our bikes, the nomads, and the wild harsh countryside. It was that true feeling of freedom that few people get to experience and I knew it all too well – although slightly unnerving facing life so close up and raw – Angie was appreciating every minute of it. She said with such wildness and desolation for miles around, civilization and the world we had come from must have ceased to exist as it felt impossible that we were on the same planet with modern day inventions such as phones or computers. What a wonderful way to start out on our road together.

After breaking camp, still on our way to the elusive Sumdo, we pedaled on a damp road after waiting for a torrential rainstorm to stop. It was a mixed blessing; the slightly sodden road was slippery but would not kick up much dust if and when a vehicle did pass, and it was nice to hear the sound of the water trickling down through the nooks and crannies in the land. We both had kickstands on our bikes. It was one of those equipment pieces you rarely think about. I'd had one on my *mamasan* bike while living in Japan, but not since. When I met Kent he'd had one mounted on the rear of his bike, and it made a lot of sense. Each time we stopped Kent would be sitting down or doing whatever while I was still looking for a tree or rock to lean my bike against. It doesn't make sense always laying down a bike weighing eighty pounds; panniers get dusty, muddy or possibly ripped, or insects happily crawl inside your food bag. Plus what you want to get to is inevitably in the pannier lying on the ground. Our bikes were standing next to each other looking like two horses in a field. We had stopped so I could sew up a small gash I had in my tire. My wounded horse looked strange with its front wheel missing, but was stabilized by the low rider racks holding my front panniers on. I was sitting in the road with my dental floss, a small piece of rubber and my damaged tire, sewing. I always sewed with dental floss when repairing tires, or panniers, even my tent – it was a great strong thread, and also handy for flossing your teeth!

There must have been an unseen village or nomadic camp somewhere close by because a crowd had gathered from nowhere and were doing the usual unembarrassed viewing of the foreigners. Unfortunately some children leant on Angie's bike to get a better view of us and her kickstand just snapped in two. Oh well, we would have to try and rig something up for her but now that my tire was sewn and ready to go, I had time to play with the kids. I propped my bike back up on its kickstand, and the kids then leaned on my bike, and now both of our kickstands were gone – back to muddy panniers. I looked at the broken bits of both, and as they had broken in different places, I thought I would try to salvage at least one good kickstand from the both. Such was the practical side of cycling. With everything else going on, it was nice to have to do the occasional maintenance or side of the road repairs. It had always given me pleasure to help people and the accumulation of first-hand knowledge with small little intricacies like the practicality of touring with kickstands (of stronger metal than our cheap Chinese ones) has helped many a customer when I've worked in shops over the years.

I was glad that I'd failed to say anything to Angie about the Tibetan rebels that were meant to be in the hills the way we were going. Someone in Zhongdien had mentioned it to me, but I usually tried to underplay them as the stories were usually a lot worse than the reality. The rebels were supposedly robbing people for money, and not anything more. I figured that as cyclists we didn't stand out as good targets.

One day we had been pedaling along a river for hours and the cycling was quite meditative with the road only slightly rising. We suddenly heard the thundering hooves of a horse, and I looked back to see a majestic figure on horseback approaching. It was impressive and otherworldly; he wore a yak-skin vest, with his long dark hair pulled back away from his face, and some sort of traditional cap on his head. I didn't notice the sword or the plaits in his long hair until he had passed us. I said to myself, 'Okay, these are the rebels I was warned about, just be cool.' He rode past, kicking up a cloud of dust in his wake, then stopped his horse. Angie was dealing with everything we had had to put up with up to this point quite well, but when he beckoned us to stop, she didn't want to. She pedaled on slowly while I stopped to talk to him. He dismounted his horse, and Angie stopped about fifty yards away, looking back to see what was going to happen.

It was an incredible experience to be face to face with such a powerful looking figure from another century, if not another world. I was looking into the lined face of this nomad who must have had rank amongst his people judging by his appearance. His weathered face was framed by his cap and two large round silver fastenings at the base of each long plait. As I stared at him I realized that he was staring at me with the same amazement. He'd probably never seen a face like mine before either. I wasn't sure what was coming next, but after some basic sign language and broken phrase communication, he bent down to look at my toe clips which are the plastic or metal clips that keep your feet in a good position for optimum pedaling on the bike. He was intrigued by their design to the point that I thought I would offer them to him. At that point Angie came back because she had seen three more men approaching on horseback. She looked a little nervous but I told her he was only interested in my toe clips. It had been a hard couple of weeks, and the Tibetans gave you even less personal space than the Chinese. The other men had arrived by this time, and things were getting a bit claustrophobic. Imagine the scene of me, Angie, large Tibetan rebel chief plus three more Tibetan rebels all standing in a small circle of less than three feet in diameter. It was like some parody of the Hokey Pokey but Angie wasn't enjoying the party and tears welled up in her eyes. I think it was just tears of frustration rather than real fear, but those tears were even more intriguing to our Tibetan friend then the toe clips. He just stared at this green-eyed woman with tears streaming down her face. She wasn't bawling, but it was apparent she wasn't happy. The other men stared as well; we all stared at each other until Angie said to me, "Please, let's just go." This broke the spell of silence, and, if indeed these were Tibetan rebels ready to rob us, the combination of toe clips and tears had satisfied them and they were happy to let us cycle off. They mounted their horses, put their hands in front of their chests, nodded their heads and rode off from the direction they had come. How glad I was not to have mentioned the rebels to Angie, as it was lack of this knowledge that allowed her to be more frustrated than fearful. I eventually did tell her about the rebels, but not until a few weeks later.

We still had not reached Sumdo, from where we planned to continue on to a place called Litang, which was billed as the second highest city in the world. That wasn't why we were heading there, it was simply the next place that offered a bed in something other than a tiny village or a truck stop, which were usually tiny rooms with no privacy stuck in the back of a place to eat, and sometimes even a bed. There was usually just a wall of single plywood separating you from the next room, or the table where people ate. Another weird quirk was the occasional peepholes plugged up with small bits of paper – we'd be slipping into our sleeping bags so as not to come in contact with the dirty sheets (if there even were any), and then we would see an eyeball appear. We were the best show in town, but I could only assume the peepholes weren't for foreigners only, maybe to watch truck drivers sleep. Who knew? It wasn't the first time in Asia I had come across the peephole phenomenon, but it still baffled me. As we climbed to our fantasy of some privacy, and the largest town we would have been in for quite a while, the unremitting passes challenged our willpower. We would climb for an hour or so, turn a corner thinking we were near the top, and then see the lone road slither up in the distance over a looming peak. Angie was cycling with a baseball cap on and I would tell her in the times of her greatest frustrations to keep her head down and try not to look too much past her front wheel crunching relentlessly on the stony road.

The terrain was evolving from wild to desolate to high mountains. There wasn't any section of flat land apart from the thin rocky road we were on. The inhospitable mountainside wasn't giving in. As evening approached we were well aware we had not encountered anyone all day or anywhere for us to sleep. We decided we'd have to camp. There was nothing but the narrowest strip of mud next to the road that wouldn't have fit the tent even if we had felt confident in putting it there. As the sun dropped lower in the sky we continued our slow ascent scanning astutely for a camping possibility. What would we do if we couldn't find a place? There was absolutely nothing we could do except keep on pedaling until something presented itself. We were so isolated and cut off from anything resembling civilization – there was only the insistent ascent of the muddy rutted road before us. This time there was no truck stop to save us – even one of the dusty brown villages would have given us a small patch to put up our tent – but there was nothing. Eventually, as we rounded yet another switchback and Angie was on her last legs, we spotted two large boulders at the apex of the curve formed by the road and between it a tiny patch of relatively flat stony ground. We managed to squeeze the tent between them.

The next day found us climbing again with yet more desolation and wild mountain peaks. Surely, surely the road had to end soon? Suddenly, out of nowhere there appeared a truck stop. The Chinese women working there were more than pleased to give us some food. We ate with gusto and I'm sure that what would probably be a bad Chinese take out anywhere in either of our known worlds, 12,000 feet up, in the middle of nowhere, some greasy fried rice and *momos* were a veritable feast. One particular woman knew the roads very well. She told us the exact mileage to the top of what was the highest pass of these mountains. She warned us that we would go down a little then there would be another short climb before we headed down to Sumdo. I gathered all this without understanding a word she said. Paper and a pencil go a long way in the hands of someone whose whole written language is based on drawing characters with great precision!

Her advice was well-heeded. The climb was long, but now we focused more on the fact that we knew in twenty miles, albeit mostly up, there was hopefully going to be a place to stay. We yanked ourselves out of the warm truck stop and put on another layer each. I had started out with a sleeveless top and shorts. The weather was definitely getting cooler. The road seemed to go straight up after the truck stop. Then an absolutely otherworldly sound of female chanting hit my ears. I didn't know exactly what it was, but knew it was turning into one of those arm pinching moments – one that did not disappoint.

I was climbing ahead of Angie when, after I had been hearing the chanting getting louder for several minutes, I rounded a corner and saw a building of the most elaborate Tibetan architecture, painted in vibrant reds, pinks and blues with dragons winding their way around the supporting columns, ornate and beautiful. What a contrast to the square block architecture of the truck stops. The Chinese woman at the truck stop had failed to mention this slight detail. I arrived at the front of the monastery and peeped inside from the front door, to see about twenty Tibetan women with shaved heads chanting and walking clockwise around a centerpiece with prayer wheels attached every foot or so, spinning them as they passed. I stood and stared, transfixed. I didn't think they'd seen me as they were deep in a moving meditation so I moved back from the entrance way, and just listened and waited for Angie to appear from behind. I looked at the colorful monastery, dwarfed by towering mountain peaks all around, and, for not the first time in my life, felt how insignificant yet vitally important it all was.

Angie appeared around the bend in the road, looking quite in awe of the mountain majesty, and completely drained. Her own spinning wheels crunched on the road to herald her arrival as she finally heard the chanting; I knew because I saw her head cock to one side as one would do to try and focus on something heard. I put my finger to my lips and waved her on to hurry up and see this. By the time she reached where I was standing she had realized what the sound was, but when I turned around, I was faced with a shaven-headed nun, dressed in the wine colored robes of the Tibetan Buddhist, staring at us like we had just landed from Mars. The feeling, I can assure you, was mutual!

By the time Angie got off her bike the monastery was empty, and we were surrounded by giggling nuns, looking at our bikes and equipment. Then a hush fell over us all, and without a word said, one nun came out of the building with a bag full of *tsampa*, which is the barley flour used in most foods in this harsh part of the world, and simply mixed in with a yak butter mixture to make a dry doughy ball to eat. She then motioned for me to open one of my front high panniers, and deposited the bag inside. Great, just what I needed, a few more kilos to carry, I laughingly thought to myself, but on the other hand, much like a man handing John and me a side of beef jerky in northern Mexico, we accepted the gift gratefully, thanking them with a slight bow and our palms pressed together in front of our hearts. We communicated where we had cycled from and where we were headed to. Confusion came across their faces as their world was not one of wandering and outward exploration but of contemplation and stillness. We did not make any sense to them but we all smiled at each other anyway. We re-mounted our bikes, and as we pedaled off, we heard the chanting resume, as the road continued ever upwards towards the heavens.

"How incredible was that?" Angie said, and added laughingly, "I'm glad you are carrying the *tsampa*, might slow you down a bit."

I smiled and said, "Yeah, but I'm eating it all."

"I don't think so," she replied.

I thought it quite funny that we were joking about who gets to eat the *tsampa* with yak butter tea, something I don't think either of us would choose to eat under normal circumstances. I remembered forgoing the same yak tea years back with Rob in Kathmandu because of its rancid smell and taste. The goal posts had now changed, we were in a different part of the world and *tsampa* and yak butter tea were important – indeed, it was pretty much all that was available. We had even grown to like the yak cheese – the only cheese to buy in the open markets of all of the past villages. A restaurant and some food in Litang sure sounded good.

About another hour and a half passed after that, and we could see the top of the climb, or so we hoped. It appeared close, but as we learned from experience we knew we were looking at at least the same amount of time again in our lowest gears just pedaling away slowly but surely. Now, though, some ominous-looking clouds were moving in and we had to make a choice. Head back down to the truck stop, and re-climb all that we had just done tomorrow, or push on. We didn't feel like doing the climb all over again, so we pushed on.

As the blizzard swept in matters looked pretty bleak. After Angie asked me if we were going to die, the lightning stopped, but the snow kept falling, accumulating quite quickly. Angie's question had shifted all my thoughts. Had I finally met a woman I knew deep down inside I could be with forever, just to have both of us die of exposure on some unknown road in Tibet on our way to a village that had not even made it on my fairly detailed map? All we could do now was pedal on. I'd look back and smile at Angie to reassure her we would be fine. I just had to hope her mind was so engrossed with the matter of pedaling that it couldn't wander too much, and if it did, I hoped it wandered to the scene of the female monks giving us *tsampa*, and the chanting.

We were descending now, but going up was preferable as far as frozen fingers were concerned. The mental lift of heading down to a small village was reassuring though. My fingers were getting so numb that I had to stop and use Angie's armpits to warm them up every few minutes – mine weren't doing it. Angie had put on all the spare clothing we had, which wasn't much. We saw something in the distance – a shelter of some sort

585

that looked dilapidated. Daylight was an issue, but we knew the sun gets lost in the high mountains long before the sky turns black with night. We were still good for about two hours at a push, but we had to get moving.

Through the snow and wind we smelled smoke coming from what looked like an uninhabitable ruin, so we leaned our bikes on the wall and rushed inside. There were a few young lads huddled round a tiny fire in a room with no panes of glass in the windows, and a roof that kept out only some of the falling snow. We warmed up by the sad flame with the young Tibetans; their toothless grins making them look sinister. They asked us questions not accounting for the fact we didn't understand, and would start to giggle if we even tried an answer.

We knew it would be a long night if we were to stay there. Our decision to leave after we had thawed out was made very difficult by the wind and snow blowing in swirls, but we needed to mount our bikes and carry on; daylight was fading. We thanked them for their fire and warmth, and walked back out into the snow. We slowly pushed our bikes to the now invisible road, and started to pedal. I think I said, "Hi would you like to see a movie?" or something you would say on a normal first date – Angie wasn't smiling. Although it sounded like a suicidal decision, we both knew staying there for the night wasn't a preferable option. We now had the slight uphill the lady at the truckstop had warned us about, then it was down to Sumdo. We knew we had made the right decision – we were warmer and drier, with our spirits lifted. We put a lot of faith in our little hand-drawn map.

With the lightning gone, it was just a blizzard. I wanted to answer Angie's question now and say, "No we aren't going to die," but I thought better of it and just stayed right next to her as we pedaled up the hill impossibly slowly; and soon were quite cold and wet again. Riding was sometimes impossible as the snow was drifting deeper than our axles. It's not easy pushing an eighty pound beast at the best of times, but through two-foot snow drifts with a blizzard swirling around your ears and your fingers numb from cold, it becomes a whole lot harder. We made it to the top and were once again descending in about zero visibility when it appeared.

We were still about five miles from our destination, but there it was – a big building, in good repair, with smoke coming out of the chimney. It was surrounded by a high fence with locked wrought iron gates, so we banged and shook the gates to get the attention of the tenders of that fire. Finally a Chinese woman came out and saw us. She ran inside and got the key, we must have looked a sorry sight. We walked our bikes to the doorway, leaned them against each other and stumbled inside. We were greeted by a pot belly stove, four adults playing *mahjong,* and warm cups of tea. Outside it was dusk.

We were in another truck stop. I couldn't understand it, there were all these truck stops, but in the last few days all we had seen were three trucks. We weren't going to question it, and we gladly drank three or four cups of Chinese green tea as we were never offered yak tea in Chinese establishments. It was like the two worlds – the Chinese and Tibetan – lived side by side in the same area, but never recognized each other's existence.

After grunting through whatever Chinese we had picked up in the past few months, we went back outside to put our bikes under cover, and Angie was now smiling. We were then shown up to a room with a bed; it had one window out the back and was pretty stark but at that point in time room service at the Essex Hotel could not have been better. We went back downstairs, and after watching our hosts play *mahjong* and drinking more tea, we settled in, and the tension of the last few hours gradually left us. An hour or so later we were eating with our hosts – steaming hot vegetable-filled noodle soup – then they continued playing. There were a couple of kids who came out from somewhere when it was dinner time, so I entertained them with a few of my trusty card tricks. They were about four or five years old and not as impressed by the tricks as they were with us.

Sleep came easily in our small room upstairs – no peepholes, and a mosquito net around the bed giving an air of extravagance to the otherwise simple room. The next day we woke up to a magical scene. It must have snowed all night. The window of our room looked out to mountains as far as the eye could see, and they were all gleaming white. About 200 yards from our window was a nomadic tent encampment complete with a herd of yaks. With the fear of dying of exposure on the mountainside past, and the absolutely incredible scene in front of us, I said, "Not a bad first date after all." Angie turned around with a smile and nodded in agreement. We then went downstairs where we were met with smiling faces, tea, and a warm fire.

They probably didn't get too many foreigners on bicycles stopping in to wait out blizzards, and it was obvious we were not going anywhere soon. That was alright with us, and it also seemed not to worry our hosts too much. We ate two meals a day with our saviors in the mountains. We spent time in our room reading, writing, and cuddling to keep warm. We went out for a few walks, and even managed to draw a crowd up there in the middle of nowhere. It was a small crowd, but we had drawing power, that was for sure. We soaked in the absolute splendor of where we were, and both thought how incredible it was that we had actually cycled to this place.

After two days the snow disappeared from the main part of the road. It was a five kilometer descent to Sumdo, and we would be glad to see it after heading there for so long. It didn't even make it on my map, but once it was mentioned to us, it became a place to focus on. From there we would have to make up our mind on what to do next. For now, it was time for us to go.

We were now faced with the tricky part. At no time had we discussed money with the people who ran the truck stop. We could have thought "No problem they saved our lives, let's just give them the equivalent of twenty bucks each." I would have had no problem with that – three nights, two full days, plus food, on top of that the small matter of saving us a freezing night out in the snow, or possibly worse. But I also had traveled in the aftermath of well-intentioned travelers handing out aspirins, sweets, or pencils to the poorer natives. It can do some good, but it can also wreak havoc and create beggars where none ever existed. It can condition people to look at westerners as an endless supply of such items and the same can happen with overpaying. The balance is hard to strike and I did take the matter seriously. After cycling for over three months in China, I knew that a meal in a restaurant was about fifty cents, a room in a hotel anywhere from one to three dollars equivalent. Offering too much money might belittle the human side of things, whereas offering too little might offend as well. We came up with a price we thought fair on all accounts – a bit high, but not extortionate.

I called over the man who'd mentioned payment the night before and handed him the money (which in the end was about ten dollars American in local currency for both of us). He accepted it in a discreet manner bordering on embarrassment. He looked at the money briefly without counting it and gave us a big smile. We felt we did the right thing as we left that place which would always hold a fond memory for both of us. After we took a photo – the adults and children standing in front of the the big gate on which we had banged three days ago – I promised to send it to them. They wrote the address down for me on a small envelope. Normally I wouldn't expect any mail to make it to an isolated building like this, but since it was a truck stop, and most of the trucks passing us on this road were mail-trucks, we thought the odds were pretty good they would one day get it.

The experiences of the last few days were some of those special moments you cann't plan for, and no amount of money could buy. There had been a real connection with other human beings, and a push to the outer margins of fear that kept us so focused that all life and its details become the present moment.

The decent to the village was thrilling. There was still some snow around and a chill to the air, although now the road had completely disintegrated. Sumdo, in fact did exist; it had a small market where we could buy some yak cheese, and get a cup of warm yak butter tea – the rancid flavor a comfort now. As we pedaled away from the village, we realized it was probably small enough to be one of those few villages that might not have had a place to stay, but now it didn't matter. We were well-rested and fed, it was early in the morning, and we had a two-day ride to "The second highest city in the world" – although that might have been according to our Chinese map only!

# The Rutted Roads to the Invisible Border

I hadn't known when I first met Angie, but her dad was very ill and as we were on our way to Litang he was in Weymouth battling a cancer that would eventually take his life. Tonia had told me that Angie's mom didn't want to make her feel guilty about heading off with me, so she'd played down the severity of his declining health. I thought that was a moving gesture, and who knows what would have happened if Angie had decided to head back to England as planned with her friends. Would that door we'd both walked through never even have opened? It is hard to answer these questions with our choices now lit up by hindsight.

It was for this reason though that I lost my cool in Litang with a post office worker when Angie was trying to call her mom This was the first place we'd been in that had a telephone since we'd left Lijiang. The woman at the post office would not let Angie get through on the phone, and Angie came back to our hotel room looking distraught. I returned with her to the post office and started yelling at the woman who was another non-interested Chinese worker. Getting hotel rooms or something to eat was akin to pulling teeth sometimes because often the workers were so apathetic. Now seeing Angie nearly in tears, I was furious – there was no reason for it, just lack of interest. I grabbed the phone from behind the counter and tried to use the calling card I had used in other towns to call New York or Australia but she wasn't having any of it. Every time I dialed, the woman would somehow make the line go dead. I reached into her little cubicle behind the glass, grabbed a sheaf of papers, and threw them all up in the air swearing. The Tibetans in the post office had a good laugh – they didn't mind seeing someone lose their cool with the Chinese. China illegally annexed Tibet as the world watched in 1949, and they have remained exploiting the people, their religion, customs, culture and resources ever since. I remembered the small enclaves of displaced Tibetans Rob and I had come across in India all those years ago living in hope of returning to their unoccupied homeland one day. Now here I was on their native soil, but it was still occupied. Maybe it was this knowledge fueled my temper.

Litang was a wonderful place in many ways, surrounded by gorgeous scenery and lofty peaks, the town itself a tad over 13,000 feet up. Our map billed it as the second highest city in the world it didn't matter to us – we had made it, we were washed, and now it was time to find somewhere else that would enable us to get in contact with Angie's mom.

On our search we happened upon a market which made us feel like we were on a movie set – I kept waiting for the director to shout "Cut." There were Tibetans with their long glossy black plaits, dressed in a cross between a medieval and a cowboy outfit, selling yak cheese and serving us hot tea. The costume and makeup department had worked hard to create their wonderful faces with deeply etched lines on their brown leathery sun-worn skin.

Angie looked at me, "It's hard to believe that my other life exists. Are there people in Weymouth walking to the shops or going to the pub to have a pint?" It was a humbling thought. Here we were on the other side of the planet – we had cycled to a place with no quick connection to anywhere. To get out of Litang in any direction was a long and arduous journey over the mountains. Furthermore, we had cycled to this place from somewhere that had itself taken months to reach. Was there any other life going on? Was there a modern world with televisions and toasters, or was the world all just yak cheese and *tsampa*? In the future, back on the streets of Weymouth or New York, how real would this scene be to us? Right now it was our only reality. We could now put faces to the people we were supporting when we stuck a 'Free Tibet' sticker in our window, but how do you keep experience alive? It seemed unlikely that just because we were in the middle of Tibet, England had ceased to exist.

Our hotel ended up being the answer to our phone problems. Angie noticed a phone behind the desk, and the receptionist agreed that we could use it to make a phone call, so Angie finally got through to her mother who let her know all was okay, her dad was the same, and yes, Weymouth still existed.

Litang was supposedly the second most important city in Tibet to Lhasa. The newer architecture was austere; the block cement buildings were in a strange contrast to the beautifully ornate Buddhist Monastery – built in the 1500's by the third Dalai Lama – which overlooked the town. It was also one of the main armed resistance areas to Chinese occupation in the fifties. I wouldn't want to be messing with those rebels, armed or not! The Wild West came to mind on entering Litang, and its history was telling of a past to fulfill that image.

We weren't sure whether it would be classified as a city or a town. In England the difference between a town and a city is often the existence of a cathedral and sometimes it's up to a population count. Kent and I came up with our own system in China; if it was big enough to have a Friendship Shop, it was a city. The Friendship Shops were department stores. It was where I'd bought the tent I was now carrying since I'd left my original tent in Hong Kong not thinking I'd be out here in the wilds. When Kent and I realized we were heading further west than we both planned, we knew a tent would be necessary. You could get just about anything you wanted in a Friendship Shop – the array of items available was impressive; radios, tents, tools, electrical goods, kitchen appliances, furniture, and the list goes on. They were like an old-fashioned Five & Ten store on steroids. Angie and I liked looking around these shops, and once in a while you could almost think you were somewhere familiar. Unfortunately the 'Made in China' labels were to blame for the demise of our own countries' stores in the same vein – at least it almost made sense in China, but being in Tibet added an extra sting to the label's meaning. I had always tried not to purchase things made in China because that could mean made by 'prisoners of conscience' languishing behind bars because of political or religious beliefs, many of them right here, close enough to touch. We didn't buy much in the bigger shops and couldn't have carried more even if we had wanted to – right now all we needed was available in local markets. When possible we tried to support the local Tibetans selling their products in small market stalls.

It was nice traveling on a bike with someone I deeply cared for, and being newly involved. With Rob, John, Kent or any of the other guys I traveled with over the years it was different – we all had experience and knew what we were in for. Noemi and I had been involved as a couple before we took off on our journey; it was an incredible time then, and we had explored much together, but something up here on this high plateau surrounded by mountains pushing towards the heavens felt different. Firstly, in many ways Angie had no idea what she was in for. On top of that, it was some of the most isolated, toughest cycling I had ever done and we were in it together no matter what. Whatever Angie's private thoughts were on the wisdom of her decision, she was living with it, and so was I. We'd made it so far, and the adventure was far from over.

On another level I felt a responsibility for her which I deserved. I'd asked her to come along, and now here we were in the middle of nowhere, with some risky moments making it this far. "Was I nice?" I'd like to see what Angie's mom would think now. To be fair to myself, though, I suppose I was just clueless to the other realities of our world. I had embraced adventure from the first day I had set out on my motorcycle many years ago and my reality was one that was not shared by most people. I once read an interview with the musician 'Prince' where he said, "Life is death without adventure," and I agreed wholeheartedly with those sentiments. Now Angie and I were in this together. Her 'yes' had been a 'yes' to adventure, which also meant risk, but we were embracing it and it was wonderful, dangerous, and exhilarating simultaneously. I thought back to the book I'd read about Jesus's time perhaps spent in a monastery hidden in these far-off mountains, John Maier's life-changing experiences,

Neil's exotic death-cheating tales. I'd thought how I'd like to visit Tibet one day. Have a thought, let it come alive, believe it, work towards it and let it happen. Now here I was cycling in Tibet with a woman who had been adventurous enough to let go of fear and do it with me. My head was in the travel and we had to be astute – we were in foreign, unknown territory on two levels. I liked the feelings we were sharing; since life was being lived so close to the edge our guard was down, we were opening to each other quickly, and I was falling into the deeper end of the feelings about relationships that had been rearing up from time to time over the past year or so.

There was a magic to this place, our meeting, and to what was happening between us. If we had met in a local bar what would our first few weeks have been like? We'd never know that answer, our meeting had been synchronous and we were going with it all the way. Where it was going to go from the Tibetan Plateau was something we couldn't even guess at, life right now was too intense – we needed all of our faculties to live through the experience as it was arising. Litang and miles of mountains in either direction was our present reality. We might as well have been married for ten years as nothing was sacred; our bodily functions, our feelings or our fears. To ride all day in this stunning beauty, then cuddle up at night together in our small hard bed was an added bonus, but strangely foreign. When she spoke with her English accent I would be snapped into the awareness that I didn't really know this woman, her mother, her friends or her family – I barely knew where she came from. Now we were on a honeymoon of sorts, never even having had the wedding, and not knowing if there was ever to be one. It put a whole different spin on this part of the journey, and it made every experience we were having that much more special, for no matter what became of us after we left this place, we had cycled into some of the remotest regions of the planet, had crossed some of the highest mountains in the world, eaten amongst the nomads and locals, and that would always be our special connection. It was something people only dream of doing, and here we were weeks into our relationship doing it together. Wonderful!

Angie's yoga practice had brought her an awareness of the philosophies of this part of the world and we were now challenged to face the issue of Occupied Tibet up close. 1996 was an auspicious year for us to be cycling in this part of the world. The Chinese government had waged war against the *Dalai Clique*, which referred to Tibetans wishing to see the Dalai Lama return to Tibet one day, along with the eventual freedom of their country. To the Chinese they were considered to be dangerous radicals. As we were pedaling along gawking at the beauty and wonder of where we were, the Chinese were putting into force the 'Strike Hard' campaign. What this

593

meant was the Chinese government had strict control over the nunneries and monasteries of Tibet, and had appointed committees to oversee the re-education of their inhabitants. Oaths had to be sworn – under extreme pressure – to denounce the Dalai Lama, and oppose the idea of an independent Tibet. Numerous people had been arrested, and even shot if they refused to comply with the embargo on photographs of the Dalai Lama.

Not only were we kindling a relationship with each other, but also redefining one with our world and its issues. For years since I'd started to be more aware of the world I lived in, I had always supported a Free Tibet, and it was incredible to be here and see the reality. Angie felt much the same. The last few months of travel in Southeast Asia with her friends had opened her eyes as well.

*The People's Daily* was the 'official' state newspaper you could find in bigger cities and we found an English language version in Litang. Reading through the pages of the Chinese patting themselves on the back for building roads into the outer reaches of the TAR (Tibetan Autonomous Region) bringing electricity, and modernizing these backward villages made me cringe. What they failed to mention was that those same roads had fleets of trucks constituting an almost non-stop traffic jam of flatbeds laden with trees, many of which were at least a meter in diameter. This deforestation was having repercussions not only in Tibet, but on the Indian sub-continent as well. Trees, especially big old-growth trees, have the ability to absorb and hold back quite a lot of water, and as Tibet had slowly been deforested over the past fifty years or so, the lowlands of northern India and especially Bangladesh now suffered from major flooding on nearly a yearly basis where tens of thousands could perish in one flash flood. Besides this little side blip of environmental disaster being wreaked by these 'wonderful' roads civilizing Tibet, plus the ongoing civil strife caused by the 'Strike Hard' campaign, there was also the problem of the Chinese trying to hijack Tibetan Buddhism.

The Chinese were trying to get their own handpicked, reincarnated Panchen Llama into the ranks of the ancient, very traditional religion. The Tibetans were refusing, and had long been searching for a reincarnated soul of the last Panchen Llama. *The People's Daily* had a small article talking about the ongoing process but had glossed over the fact that the week before about thirty kilometers from where we sat, there had been riots where Tibetans had been killed, and many arrested in clashes with the government over the whole affair. In a monastery in a place called Ganden, just about when Angie and I were having our first kiss, Chinese security forces shot three monks, and arrested eighty more for refusing to comply with the photo ban. The journalist's sarcastic credo – "Don't let the truth get in the way of a good story" – had been taken to heart by the Chinese.

We only heard about the bloody clashes because of my shortwave radio. I'll be the first to admit that propaganda exists on all sides; left wing, right wing or mainstream media is far from perfect. I found small publications and news stations over the years in America and elsewhere trying to present a different side to the news, such as *The Nation* or *Pacifica Radio,* but sitting here with a blatantly one-sided press reporting on everything, the feeling was definitely one of frustration. It was so difficult to do anything about what was happening.

We were constantly asked for photos of the Dalai Lama – the Tibetans were not complying with the 'Strike Hard' campaign – but unfortunately we didn't have any. We also both noticed the size of families. In China it was normal to see the typical Chinese family: mom, dad, and one child. Here the one child rule didn't appear to apply and we saw many Chinese families with two children. It intrigued us, and it was later on when we got to Chengdu we were told that it was overlooked in many of the 'Autonomous Regions' in China – it built up the Chinese population quicker, and made the indigenous people of these areas a minority in their own lands. These past few weeks on the bicycle we had pedaled into yet another new reality.

It was nice to have a rest in a bigger town for a few days. We just walked around to get a feel for the place. We visited the monastery that sat, imposing, on the skyline – a constant reminder of the culture we were in. Some of the young monks were giggly young boys of about eight like you would find anywhere in the world. The older monks were soft-spoken, but their chanting truly otherwordly; eerily vibrational bass tones underlying what sounded like a symphony of creatures from another planet having a heated discussion. We fortunately found one monk who spoke some English. He was about sixty years old, and spoke sadly of what he had seen during the past half-century. He was optimistic though, and very glad to speak to an American and an English woman. He hoped we would talk about Tibet fondly in our homelands. It was very touching to speak to him. I can still see his lined face, and the smile that reached his eyes. How incredible is the power of a strong spirit? I would think to myself. Here was a man who has witnessed the slow environmental rape of his country, the breakdown of his culture and religion, an occupation by a foreign country and the temporal and religious leader of his homeland forced into exile for nearly a half of century, yet he was hopeful. He gave us hope too. Unfortunately I'd met so many people across many lands with the same hope. I daren't tell him it was becoming harder and harder to find goods in the west which were not made in China, serving to strengthen his country's oppressors.

We went up to the monastery a few times to listen to the chanting transporting us to another time and place, but not quite helping Angie get any closer to Beijing for her flight home. The imposing high peaks surrounding Litang started to make us question how we were going to head out of town. We would have to try to figure out if we were going to brave the road heading east out of Litang. The reality was that my visa was running out, and Angie's flight from Beijing was on June tenth; it would take a remarkably long time to make it out of this place on bike, and we needed to get to Chengdu within the first week of June. It was now nearing the end of May.

In a restaurant we ran into the two mail-truck drivers we had hitched a short ride with on our way to Litang. The road had been in a bad state, and we hadn't realized that the distance from Sumdo to Litang was another 230 kilometers. On our way with them we had stopped two or three times to do some fishing – our mailmen dragging out a bucket stuffed with nets which was also, worryingly, the same place they shoved any letters they picked up. It made for an interesting contrast to the blizzard, truck stops and disintegrating road conditions we were cycling through.

Here they were again, joining in with the other customers spitting bones and grizzle happily onto the restaurant floor which was disgusting. We tried not to judge the eating habits too harshly, but it was an assault on western eating sensibilities. Besides eating all sorts of animals it was difficult not to look at the chicken bones scattered everywhere and not cringe. Where Japan had put me back on a meat eating diet, China had unknowingly pushed me back to being a vegetarian, it just came so naturally not to eat meat; where in some countries eating local buffalo intestine soup, cow tongue, or snake felt like a courteous endeavor, here in China it just felt indulgent and wrong eating owls, dogs, or anything that flew crawled or walked. Plus the amount of fresh vegetables available was astounding, not to mention delicious fresh *tofu*, so why bother?

I'd caught a few colds in China, and it was no wonder. The hygiene, especially the spitting, crossed the whole continent, from Guilin to where we now stood. We walked into the kitchen, ordered a plate of veggies with *tofu*, and asked for no MSG, which still brought smiles from the cooks. Our mail-truck drivers offered us a ride to a town the next day which would put us well on our way towards Chengdu. My visa, Angie's flight, and the worsening roads meant we decided it would be prudent to go with them.

We told them where we were staying, and agreed that we would meet them at six the next morning. If we were going to make it to Kangding on these treacherous roads, an early start was necessary. When someone knocked on our door at two a.m. we were rudely awakened thinking it was the police, but it was our truck drivers ready to go. Luckily we had packed the night before anticipating an early start, but this early we didn't imagine. We had agreed a price already so there was no haggling, which was a relief. We just had to put our bikes in the back and go. It wasn't going to be that easy; there were two other hitchers with us and no room in the cab, so we were all put into the back of the truck – the mail, our bikes, and four passengers.

The truck threw up an incredible amount of dust from the rutted road which poured in through all the cracks. Each bounce just tossed it about even more resulting in a constant dustcloud inside the truck. We had to get our bandanas out to try the filtering technique. It cut out a certain amount but we still found ourselves choking and coughing constantly. Getting comfortable was impossible. The bottom of the truck was solid ridged metal that would not have been easy to sit on even at rest. The roads meant we hit a pothole every second or so, actually tossing us physically off the bottom of the truck, landing only to be tossed up again the following moment. The same thing happened when we lay down but the shock of the landing was eased minimally through our whole body. The worst thing about it was that it was absolutely relentless – not a moment's respite from the tossing and bouncing. It was impossible to move about or even alter position other than changing sides. We faced each other, not even able to talk for all the noise and dust, praying for the journey to be over and to get back on our bikes once more. Needless to say, it was a long, difficult ride.

The two Chinese guys in the back with us had settled themselves on some mail bags and managed to fall immediately into a sleep. I was jealous. Since it was impossible to talk, we both had to be left alone with our own swirling thoughts. Sleep came in fits and starts, and we could not see if it was still dark outside. Miraculously, after what seemed like ages, the engine stopped, and the back doors swung open. Blinded by the light, it was incredible to see how bright it was. The scenery framed by the truck doors was fabulous. We were stopping for breakfast, and through one of our fellow passengers who spoke some English, he let us know we still had eight more hours to go. It was eight a.m. now, so we somehow had braved six hours already. We couldn't focus on anything but eating. If we thought about eight more hours of the same, we would be too depressed.

We wanted to get breakfast over with and get back in the truck. We didn't want to be tempted to ride as we knew that even Kangding was still quite a long way from Chengdu, and there was definitely nowhere between where we were and there where I could renew my visa, and Angie get a flight to Beijing.

We climbed into the back of the truck, looked at the dust, the mail bags, our bikes, and resigned ourselves to eight more hours. We needed to live in the moment, which was exactly where we didn't want to be. The engine shuddered into life, and off we went.

We spent the next eight hours in a state of half-sleep, half-pain, breathing through our damp bandanas. We stopped for a toilet and a snack, but fortunately our driver was as keen to get there as we were. This was a mixed blessing; we were moving faster but the speed meant the bounces were bigger and the landings were harder. At this pace we should arrive with some daylight left which would be a bonus.

Liberated from our truck, we cycled around and took in the wonderful atmosphere. Kangding was a beautiful place surrounded by high mountains – much greener and lusher than the higher, drier Litang, with a large swift flowing river creating a cool breeze constantly. We were on the eastern borders of Tibet which was clear from the growing number of Chinese faces amongst the Tibetans. Kangding was an ancient trading post between the Tibetans and Chinese, but that history had long since changed. There were still monasteries to be seen, but we were definitely on the 'officially' non-existent frontier.

Kangding at only 8,000 feet, made the mountains surrounding the town look much higher from our new perspective. It was awe inspiring – like an advert in an outdoor magazine. It's true that the beauty was highlighted by the fact we were no longer being thrown around in the back of a mail-truck sucking in dust with every inhalation.

We ate a big meal, and even ordered a third serving each. I felt almost hungrier than if I had pedaled all day. I also felt an annoying niggle in my throat, cold number four was coming on, time to break out the Grapefruit Seed Extract once again. I felt it had been helping keeping my colds from turning full-blown.

The next morning we had an exhilirating sixty kilometer downhill following the raging river. It was awesome to be flying through these surroundings and making such progress. It wasn't a total free-wheel, but almost! Even though my cold was progressing, nothing could put a damper on the day's ride. The only thing to slow us up was the rice or barley that had been cut and laid across the roads to let the trucks cars and buses do the work of threshing out the grains. This was no problem for an automobile, but with the bikes it was different – the stalks would get caught up in our derailleurs and we would have to stop to pull them out and disentangle them. After the first time we learned to free-wheel through then pull out the stalks before they got too entrenched in the gear system. If possible we would skirt around them, but sometimes they covered the whole road, and it was easier to just pull out the stalks. It only happened a few times, but it gave us the feeling of being somehow involved in the harvest.

Luding, our next stop, was a Chinese tourist town, and it was here we realized we had miscalculated the date hence losing two days somewhere since crossing the invisible yet apparent border back to China. After gliding into town, securing a place to sleep and eating a well-deserved meal we went to the bus station to find out how much it would be for a bus to Chengdu, as we now were a bit more pressed for time because of our mistake. The drivers were unhelpful to the point of being rude. It put us off so much that we decided to cycle out of town and try to brave a ride on another truck.

The next morning, bright and early we headed off. The weather was beautiful and my cold was getting better. The road, which had been in pretty good repair from Kangding to Luding, started to deteriorate once again and climb, climb, climb. The downhill we had enjoyed the day before – which we thought we'd have for a few days – just ended. Now we were on roads going up all over again. We were deep in the mountains. Angie enjoyed the riding, but the hill just kept on going up. She wound up getting on a small open tractor-looking vehicle with a few locals in the back. They beckoned me to get on but I was feeling good, and assessed that I could probably keep up with its slower speed, and if I needed a rest, just hang on to the side. We all had a good laugh with me clowning around pretending to fall back and get exhausted and then speed up alongside them. For about twenty kilometers we went on like that, but then the ride ended at a place to eat. We took advantage of that, and it looked as good a place as any to try and hitch a lift.

After we ate, we saw a truck pulling out, and we flagged him down. We thought it was only about 250 kilometers to Chengdu, so we'd be there by evening. We could not have been more wrong. The truck was one of the many blue trucks leaving Tibet on a daily basis. It was confusing as to what all these trucks were carrying, the trees were obvious, but the other trucks like the one we would now be on were covered with tarps, and were all trundling eastwards with their mysterious loads. The driver pulled back the canvas, and now our bikes were two more pieces amongst the cargo. We all squeezed into the cab, and off we went. Wow, we thought, this was going to be great. We might even be able to spend a few days in Chengdu at this rate.

After about thirty or so kilometers he just stopped. As soon as he pulled off to the side of the road, he instantly put his head down on the steering wheel and was asleep. It was so comical we just looked at each other thinking maybe we missed something. It was almost as if he was going to sit up again and say "ha ha, gotcha." But no, he just slept. Not long after another two trucks pulled over and our driver just popped open his eyes. He got out and joined the other two drivers as they opened the hood of one of the other trucks, and all three of them went to work on the engine. We just poked around, and I looked over their shoulders to see what they were doing – changing the air filter. After about an hour they all jumped in their trucks and off we went again. We felt that we were finally on our way but after about ten more kilometers the same thing happened again, and the same two trucks soon joined us. Our driver slept while he was waiting, and they started working as soon as all three men were reunited. Angie and I were perplexed, but when we stopped the third time, it was to fix *our* truck. There were always trucks stopped fixing something. Maybe it was the 'Made in China' quality rearing its ugly head. Whatever it was, it was comical, but hugely frustrating. Angie and I would be practically holding our breaths while we were driving along, just notching up a few more kilometers, before the inevitable happened – the driver would swing off the road and we would let our breaths out with a groan. Sometime it would only be two or three kilometers after we had started off, at which we would get the giggles through our frustration. We had to keep telling ourselves that we were still moving faster than we would have done on our bikes.

Then the road somehow just went from mildly bumpy, with potholes here and there, to just the opposite, potholes everywhere with the occasional piece of road. There were a couple of close shaves near to the sheer drop offs at the side of the road. Who knew what our mail-truck went through while we were being choked and bounced half to death in the back? The truck traffic had built up, and now there were lines of trucks miles long, and when the traffic stopped moving, our driver would turn off the engine and just go to sleep. The whole day went like this, and then when night was approaching we pulled up to a place to eat. He made a hand gesture of eating, and we thought great as we were hungry. After we ate, we assumed we were getting back in the truck, but he locked the doors, and said the word for sleep, which sounds very much like the word for eat. "Shway jow" is how it sounded to our ears. We were totally confused now, but it looked as if we were here for the night. Our bikes were under cover, we had grabbed our bags with passports and money, paid for our meal and a room, and – a bit baffled – went to go to sleep.

Now did these truck drivers get up early? The mail-truck drivers certainly did in Litang, my friend Stan was a truck driver, and was the sort of guy to wake up before the sun. I had my shortwave radio which had an alarm on it, so we set it for seven a.m. We slept quite well, and for the very reasonable price we paid, it was clean with no peepholes, and the toilet just down the hall.

We woke to the inky blackness of seven a.m. but there was no sign of any of the truck drivers to be seen awake. The trucks were all out front ready to go. We saw a woman and ordered a hot drink and some bread for breakfast. We waited for nearly two, long, frustrating hours, then our truck drivers emerged from their rooms and ate while walking around. Maybe they were affected by China's weird time zones – everywhere being linked to Beijing time. We finally all piled into the trucks, and off we went. Stopping within meters of the truck stop, the hood of our truck was up quickly, and they started to disassemble something else. It had gotten so ridiculous that we didn't know whether to laugh or cry but we felt committed to our lift now. I peered over at what they were doing. They were making what looked like a gasket of some sort out of cardboard. You had to admire their ingenuity and resourcefulness – how many western truck drivers could knock up a head gasket out of cardboard? We toyed with the idea of just getting our bikes off the truck, but we always thought that any minute we would be leaving. Finally, about an hour later, we were off.

Our truck driver seemed to be a nice guy, he never asked us for money. We bought him and his other friends hot drinks once, and now we were moving and praying that there were no more side of the road repairs. It was hard to judge how far we had covered with all the stopping. Our speed was a mystery too, since nothing inside the truck – including the speedometer – was working, we could never tell if it was ten or thirty kilometers per hour we were traveling at; with the constant rattling it always felt like seventy. At midday we arrived at last in Ya'an, and with his usual indifference our driver just hopped out of the truck, climbed up the back, and started to unstrap the bikes. Although not in Chengdu yet, we hoped, as we'd done several times by now, that we'd be there soon.

# Saying Goodbye in Chengdu

It was now the sixth of June and we had a lot to do in a few days. We caught a local bus to Chengdu which was as bumpy as the truck journeys had been, but at least this time we had seats. Our bikes were strapped up on top in the usual Asian manner of transporting anything that didn't fit inside the bus. I loved that casual and practical approach to things like that in a world that was yet to become completely wrapped up in red tape brandishing the words, 'Health and Safety'.

On the bus we met a woman doctor who spoke English and was quite concerned that we didn't know where we were staying that night. She insisted on walking us to a hotel, and negotiated us a room. She left with a smile, happy that she had done her good deed and found these two grubby looking travelers a room for the night. Thankfully she would never know what happened in the next few hours.

We left our bikes in the lobby, unhooked our panniers and trudged up to the room with them. It was almost like being transported in time to a whole new world. The prices seemed reasonable for a big city and such a clean hotel – it was about twelve U.S. dollars for both of us, and after the last few days we were more than willing to stretch to that much for the night. The room even had its own bath and shower, which we hadn't had since, well, I couldn't remember. The water was hot, we were filthy and it was divine. To feel that clean was incredible and our bodies were a few shades lighter now. We had noticed an outdoor food market across from the hotel. Now that we were clean, food was the next thing on our agenda.

As we were walking down the stairs, a young girl from the hotel stopped us and said, "Go back to your room, we bring you food." We tried to say that we were going out to eat but she was very insistent that we stay. We weren't quite sure what was going on, had the doctor paid for all of this? We hoped not. A few moments later two steaming bowls of soup were brought up to the room. We ate and couldn't believe our luck. Angie looked clean and relaxed. We talked about the last few weeks, and now that we were out of the highlands she was more certain that life existed elsewhere. It had been an incredible trip. I had never expected to cycle into Tibet when Kent and I left that boat over three months ago. I definitely didn't expect to be in a hotel in Chengdu with a woman I thought I quite possibly might spend the rest of my life with, but life was unfolding nicely and the beds with clean sheets looked so inviting. A clean double bed with a proper mattress! This was going to be a well-deserved, comfortable sleep, or so we thought!

There was a knock on the door then a tentative voice in halting English said, "Hello, can I come in?" Before we had the chance to say yes in walked the same girl who'd told us to go to our room to eat. "Was the food was alright?"

"Yes, fine." My radar was up already, I glanced at Angie who had the same quizzical look in her eyes, knowing all too well what China could throw at you when you least expected it. We sensed something was up. She looked nervous, and it was now about eleven p.m. We were tired, and the clean sheets were calling.

"I'm so sorry, but you are not allowed to stay here tonight." I thought I must still have bath water in my ears. She saw our confused looks so she repeated, "Foreigners can not stay in this hotel, I'm sorry."

We both asked in unison, "Why not?"

"Foreigners can not stay here; it is for Chinese people only."

Oh no, Kent and I had been through enough of this already. "Look, we took a bath, we ate your food, just don't tell the police, and we'll leave early tomorrow morning."

"I'm sorry, it is not up to me. Can you please come downstairs."

I smiled a very sarcastic smile at Angie. "Here we go again." I said over my shoulder, "I'll be back, unless you want to come." Angie wisely opted to stay back. I was sure she would take advantage of those clean sheets even if it was only for a few minutes rest.

In the lobby the manager was on the phone with someone. He handed me the phone, and the voice on the other side of the line cracked in immediately and to the point, "I'm with the tourist police. It's illegal for you to stay in the hotel. We have found a hotel that will accept foreigners in the same area. Could you please go to that hotel." His monotone voice conveyed little compassion for the situation.

"My wife and I" (I decided it would be less of a hassle saying 'wife') "have already taken a bath. We have eaten here, and it's very late. We'll go to that hotel tomorrow."

The robotic toneless English continued, "I am sorry, you cannot stay in that hotel. If you do, we will come and you will have to pay a fine."

"Is the other hotel the same price?" I asked.

"It's more expensive because it is for foreigners. It is a much nicer hotel." Visions of *Intourist* in Moscow, being thrown out of Vietnam, and all the previous hassles in China came flooding back. I knew there would be no winning this battle, not even at this late hour.

"So you're asking my wife and me to leave the hotel in a strange city near midnight, is that correct?"

"Yes, we have found another hotel for you and your wife." Then 'click' as he hung up.

I was absolutely fuming. As it turned out the other hotel was forty dollars for the night. There was no way we were going to pay that, just on principle. I was so frustrated by this time that I was seeing red. Then the hotel manager turned to me and asked for money for the food with not a hint of apology in his voice. I just walked away and went upstairs to break the bad news to Angie.

I opened the door, and she was dressed to go, seeming to know the situation already. We slowly packed up everything into our bags. We checked the bathroom and the bath had a ring around it the size of Saturn's. Normally I would have cared, now I was just pissed off. We went downstairs, and put the bags back on the bikes. I went up to check the room one more time – nothing was left but half the dust of Tibet in the shape of a dirty bathtub ring – a small gift from the occupied territories I laughed to myself. Back downstairs the girl was apologetic and I felt bad that she was caught in the middle of all this. She was just a student who spoke English; she didn't even work for the hotel. There was no way I was paying for the food or the use of the shower. Let the 'Tourist Police' pay I thought. We started to leave, but the manager stopped me at the door.

"You must pay for the food," he demanded.

I really lost it and then exploded. "You want me to pay for food that I didn't even ask for? You're throwing me and my wife out on the streets of Chengdu at midnight for the crime of being a foreigner, and you want me to pay for food? No fucking way, let the fuckin' Tourist police pay! Now get away from my bike, because we're leaving!"

Angie had the good sense to be outside already. She'd seen me lose my temper in Litang, and although I'm not condoning my behavior, there was something about China that pushed me to the limits of my patience. Maybe I was finally feeling justified in reacting to all the injustice. I know the hotel manager didn't deserve to get the brunt of it but I don't think he took it personally. The Chinese were pretty good at not getting too upset over things. He yelled back something I didn't understand and together with a few of the young staff they surrounded my bike. I wasn't backing off – I was bigger than them, and a lot angrier. After a few more angry words and me telling them in no uncertain terms to get their hands off my bike, they finally backed away. They had probably not understood a word I said, complete with a few New York expletives, but the tone of the conversation gave them the general idea – the meal was on the house, as was the bath and few hours of comfort.

"Well Angie, nice meal and a shower wasn't it?" I said jokingly as I emerged from the hotel lobby.

"Great, now what?" she replied as we pedaled off into the night air as it is meant to be in June, warm and balmy. We were both clean and fed, the

604

night was clear, and there was still some life on the streets. I wondered if the Tourist Police were going to come zooming around the corner, but we pedaled off without incident.

We tried to find a hotel or guest house that would accept foreigners but there were none to be found. We ran into a young student on his bicycle who spoke some English and was concerned about what we were doing cycling the streets at one in the morning. I guess we could have asked him the same question. When we told him of our problem he was determined to find us a place to stay. We did find one hotel – it was expensive and therefore accepted foreigners. Now that it was so late, it would have been pointless to spend that much money for a few hours sleep, especially when we didn't even need or want a shower. Our student found some interesting places, but none of them would accept foreigners. It reminded me of the situation with Andre expecting *perestroika* to have solved the Soviet Union's problems all those years ago in Moscow. He was frustrated then; our Chinese student was frustrated now. Angie and I, feeling clean and fresh, were actually enjoying it all. After a few more failed attempts at installing us for the night, it was getting late and we started to feel bad for our self-appointed guardian. We reassured him we were going to pedal back to the expensive hotel and stay there for the night. It was a lie, but it let him off the hook, and now we could start looking for a place to sleep on the street. We were both so tired by now that any place started to look good. Such a different night than the one that might have been.

We came across an enclosed area near a gazebo on the river with chairs put up on tables. We had to squeeze by a fence with our bikes, but it seemed quiet enough, and instead of sleeping on a comfortable bed in each other's arms, we were in our sleeping bags, under a table on the cold hard ground.

We woke up after a fitful night's sleep to find we were not the only ones sleeping under the tables. The workers were up before us and when we crawled out from beneath our evening's residence we were met with smiles. They were already busy sweeping and getting what was a restaurant ready for the day's trade. Angie and I were glad we hadn't spent money on a hotel now that the night was through. I was enjoying Angie's company very much, and we'd already had quite a few interesting adventures in our short relationship. What to do next – visa, flight or find a hotel that would accept foreigners that was not extortionately expensive? First some food.

We found a place to eat, and in one of my panniers I did have a few torn pages from the visa information section of a guide book about Chengdu. It was a pretty straightforward affair; I went to the prefecture office, showed them my passport, told them as little information as I could, and received a one-month extension on my visa. Sometimes I was shocked at what was simple to do and what wasn't. Trying to extend visas can be a nightmare in many countries but here in China, where we were forced to sleep under a table because finding a reasonable hotel to accept foreigners was nearly impossible, I took care of my visa in less than fifteen minutes! After that we just rode around the streets, enjoying being in a city filled with bicycles. It reminded me of Nanning; bike lanes everywhere complete with policeman directing the bicycle traffic – this fantastic infrastructure in place and working wonderfully, which has since been slowly undermined since by the hard sell on the car.

Getting a plane ticket would be easy. We could find a place selling tickets by just looking – we didn't need a guidebook for that. We took our time soaking in the atmosphere, and if anyone wants to tell you that Tibet and China are one and the same, we now knew from experience that they could not be more different.

Angie bought her plane ticket on China Airlines, an airline notorious for accidents. It was the only internal flight she could get to Beijing on the day she wanted, so it would have to do. She figured she'd cheated death once already, so why not try again? Now we had to find a hotel. The nicest and most expensive hotel in town was the Chengdu Hotel – this was for the well-heeled traveler. We figured if we got there someone was bound to speak English, and then we could find out where the backpackers stayed. The plan worked.

The sights and sounds of Chengdu were thrilling; outdoor markets, covered markets and thousand of places to eat, or so it seemed coming from where we had just been. With all its frustrations, China was still a fascinating place to travel. The people were usually standoffish, but polite. When you did get to have a one-on-one experience with someone there was usually some mutual interest. It was the general apathy that would drive me nuts, or the officialdom that was a nightmare, unless of course it was getting a visa extension. The only thing that had changed things for me and Angie was our brief time in Tibet. It was something that was always a known in both our lifetimes – The Chinese occupation of Tibet. Although our two governments would try to make believe it didn't exist, it well and truly did. In Hong Kong someone told me if I was thinking of heading to Tibet, Chengdu was a must. We'd done it backwards and found ourselves here *after* our Tibetan adventure, and now having just been there, and witnessing first-hand what that occupation meant, it made it that much more difficult to deal with the things that drove me crazy from an unprejudiced point of view. It felt the same as when I had just got back from Guatemala.

Now back in China, after 'officially' never having left, I could not help but see the monasteries that had been destroyed, the Chinese families of four walking around, and the trucks – the thousands of trucks – carting away Tibet's largest natural resource, its trees. I had to try and let those thoughts fade. I was in China for another few weeks at the least, and the common man on the street was just a consequence of a huge powerful propaganda machine. I had to take everything down to a personal level, much like I had done in the country of my birth. It wasn't individuals that were the problem; it was the largeness of government, and the faceless corporations. As individuals, on a completely human level, we all held the real power, if only we could somehow figure it out. Between here and Beijing there were some interesting things ahead to do, and more people to meet. In the short term, Angie and I had to get a place to sleep, and enjoy our last few days together.

We cycled to the backpacker hotel near the station and when I walked in saw the lobby full of westerners, I knew I had the right place. I negotiated a private room for our final nights together and had to pay a little extra because it was the last room and it had four beds. With that settled, I went out to tell Angie we were sorted. It was strange to come out and see her and our bikes, but no crowds. We actually had to carry our own bikes, rather than pick out a willing helper from the crowd. It wasn't so bad, just a two story carry up. After getting settled, we took showers and found some clean clothes in our bags. There was a laundry service, so since we were on 'treat ourselves' territory, we even paid for a load of washing to be done. Luxury!

We took off all the bags from our bikes, knowing that Chengdu would be best discovered by bike. It was big enough to warrant riding around, and small enough to explore quite a bit of it while doing so. We headed off into the lobby just to soak in the atmosphere of being around a few travelers. We hadn't been in a place like this since Lijiang. It was also interesting to see how many of the travelers were turning the pages of their *Lonely Planet* guide books.

We overheard some conversations of people who were heading into Tibet, or just coming back. The preferred route was into Lhasa – Tibet's capital city. It would have been nice to make it there, but the road sounded riddled with police checkpoints, lots of fines to be paid, and Angie's time would not have permitted it. Our trip into Tibet was our special little foray. Even though it was a closed area and fines were supposed to be paid, any encounter we'd had with police were minimal, and the twice we had stayed in an official hotel on our few weeks in Tibet, the police would come to our room to fine us, but would get so sidetracked by our bikes that it would turn into a show and tell session. Besides nearly being arrested with Kent in Anning, the worst luck on my whole trip had been right here, in Chengdu, the night before. The few times we did speak to other foreigners about what had happened it was hard for them to believe, as Chengdu at face value seemed such an open town.

Angie was tired, but I wanted to write in my journal. She took herself up to bed after dinner while I stayed downstairs and wrote. As I was leaving to head upstairs, I heard someone say, "Joe?" and turned around to see Ignacio and Tracy once again. Warm hugs were in order, our paths crossing now for the third time. After catching up briefly with each other, we said we'd meet the next day for breakfast.

I told Angie of meeting up with them, and she couldn't believe it. The next morning after a dreamless sleep we were excited to hear about their last month of travels on the long bus rides Angie had left behind. They had covered a lot more ground traveling on those buses, so we had lots of interesting stories to swap. As we had met for the third time we decided to exchange addresses. They lived in Ignacio's home town of Madrid, but Tracy was English. They had been on the road for six months and China was their most interesting, frustrating leg so far – we all knew about those frustrations.

They had done a loop up to the northwestern provinces, and said it was quite an interesting part of China, the people being so different than the Han Chinese. The country was more a large land mass of annexed autonomous regions which had been incorporated into the larger picture known as modern day China – we all had just left two of their more recent conquests.

As they headed further west and away from Beijing it felt unnatural how the days were divided up – the whole of China being on Beijing time the sun would come up quite late in the morning. The people adjusted their lives accordingly, but it was hard for Ignacio and Tracy to get their heads around it. Angie and I being removed from bus schedules, and not having watches, didn't notice as much.

Their furthest bus ride had taken them to the capital city of Urumqi in Xianjang province. There they felt they had entered a northern Asian country more akin to what they thought the ex-Soviet republics to be like, especially being predominantly a Muslim region in what is vastly a large desert province. We all agreed that arbitrary lines were just that, and the colorful cultures, different languages, foods and religions were still surviving, although severely marginalized. The break up of the Soviet Union, Yugoslavia, and fall of the Iron Curtain countries was all new historically, but for some reason China was still expanding – Hong Kong soon to be back in the fold. We swapped some of our stories, expounded our theories, and solved the world's problems over steamed rice buns and

608

hot tea. It was nice to have made the connection with them. We felt that one day we might all meet up again.

The next few days were just Angie and me exploring Chengdu. It had the feel of a frontier land – the end of the line before you got into the regions further west and isolated from the rest of the world, the paved roads of Chengdu giving way to the rutted potholed dust-choked tracks high up through the mountains we'd recently arrived from. The wood-clad temporary buildings with tin roofs on the outskirts of the ever sprawling city encroaching with its concrete structures, the mixed races walking the streets looking like misfits astride their bicycles, instead of horses as they were a few hundred kilometers away, the displaced country folk at the markets mingling with the Han Chinese, uncomfortably rubbing shoulders and sharing street space with the race that has slowly encapsulated their country. I realized I probably was looking at it with biased eyes, but facts were also facts.

As the frustrations of our hotel experience faded, we were lulled into thinking that it was actually more relaxed in Chengdu. The rules did seem to be more lax out here in the west, but only a few days ago we knew differently, it was just better hidden here. Now that everything was taken care of, all that was left was saying goodbye, which wasn't going to be easy.

While cycling Angie to the airport on the outskirts of town, I was confronted with many visions of past present and possible futures, too many times before relationships had just slipped away and turned into fond memories or life-long friendships. Did I want that once again? Digging deeper into my thoughts and looking back on the feelings I had been having over the past year or so, I was coming up with a resounding, "No." I wasn't going to let myself slip into the pattern I had been in, the comfort zone of non-committal. If I let this slip away, what was the sense? I had learned a lot from Angie taking that risk of saying yes to come to Tibet. As she told me a few days into our cycling journey, "What if I let this opportunity pass, would I always regret it?" As I glanced over at the homemade panniers, the cheap mountain bike, and the adventurous woman cycling next to me, my mind was turning over those same exact questions. What happens now? Once Angie boarded that plane into her known world and saw that it actually had continued to exist while we were in the wilds of Tibet, would I also become a question of existence in her mind? 'Did it all really happen?' The occasional glance at her bike would be hard evidence that it had. But don't we all look at small reminders of the past, back to something which happened years ago which brings a smile or tear to our face? Time has a way of smoothing the edges. All my journeys had shaped me, but already time was doing its magical work; crossing

609

America, cycling throughout Central America, Chris's brutal death, living in Australia, my relationship with Kelly – the sharp focus of the emotions of those times has faded. Yes, I smile recalling most of those memories, but listening to that bicycle crunch the gravel next to me, looking at Angie's face, and sensing a smile on mine, I knew that somehow the most recent memory of cycling in Tibet meant something more.

After a tearful goodbye with lots of hugs, kisses and awkward moments, she was gone, and everything was thrown into a funk – all those previous thoughts now a hard, cold reality. What would I do?

Back in Chengdu I busied my brain with checking out the bike to make sure everything was okay to go on. I even mended the kickstand I found in my panniers and had nearly forgotten about. It was good to be doing some maintenance, and not thinking of Angie heading back into her known world. I was still thinking of heading to Japan or Taiwan to teach English, but neither option was filling me with enthusiasm. I wrote a letter to Kelly in Australia telling her about Angie, which put an end to any of our future plans to meet up. I had written to her from China a couple of times keeping her abreast of the cycling trip; now that things had changed, I hoped the honesty was better than making up other excuses. I always found no matter how awkward the truth might be at first, it far outweighed the small untruths and lies we sometimes rely on in such situations.

I was so sure that something between Angie and me was different than any of my past relationships. I hoped I was not going to let it slip away. A few more weeks lay ahead to sort out the confusion. I was in Chengdu, but my plan was to get to Beijing, have some time to think about all that had happened, and, as I have always done before, adjust my plans accordingly.

# The Three Rivers Gorge

As I pedaled away from Chengdu, my mind was mulling over many possibilities. I tried to focus on the present and not get caught up in thinking too much about England, Angie or what I should do. I focused on getting to Chongqing, and catching a boat down the famed 'Three Rivers Gorge' to Wuhan. I had heard that it was a worthwhile boat trip, and as the Chinese were building a huge dam in the area, many of the places the boat would pass through would cease to exist in the not too distant future. It was an opportunity I wanted to take advantage of, and I did enjoy boats.

Little did I know that Chongqing – the town I was heading to for the start of the boat trip – was earmarked to become one of China's biggest cities as all of the displaced people from the dam project would need places to live. Officially, hundreds of thousands were going to be displaced, in reality much more was at stake. China's balance of urban to city dwellers was just over a decade away from tipping in favor of the latter, a scary thought.

For the first time in quite a while I was pedaling alone. My head lost in thought as I cycled along in the hot basin of China. The shimmering mirage-like images being formed by the mid-day heat reminding me of many other hot places I had cycled in my life. My journal was the perfect companion as I scribbled away in the small hotel rooms, the obvious question coming up again and again. What would I do next?

My Chinese was basic, but Kent had taught me well, and for all the frustrations I found the Chinese easy to travel among. They were interested without being too pushy, always asking questions and I was often given a free cold drink or a beer. It was a change from Tibet where the culture was so different. I found the Tibetans much quicker to touch, or fiddle around with something curious on the bike. China was easier in some ways, more frustrating in others. I wasn't in any officially closed areas and finding cheap hotels, or *laguan* as they were called, which would accept me was tricky, but easier than before.

I still had plenty of Chinese currency – *yuan* – *dong* in local terminology, and my visa was already ticking away. The villages were typical of small town China; crowded, lots of concrete apartment buildings giving way to the smaller dwellings on the outskirts of the villages. To see a woman with a long rod balanced across her head with a bucket swinging on either side emerging from the toilet blocks was common. She would walk out into the field, and then disappear beyond the horizon. The waste would be left to decompose and break down to be used as fertilizer, or 'humanure' as I have heard it since coined.

It had been airless and hot under the relentless sun since I'd pedaled out of the haze of Chengdu. I think I had turned a permanent shade or two darker in the past decade, my skin constantly darkened from so many hours exposed to the sun. I tried to wear silk shirts rather than slapping on potentially dangerous creams all over my arms and face daily, but the sunbeams were relentless in their search for my melanin.

. I was cycling next to, and occasionally under a brand new major roadway – The Chengyu Expressway. It was eerily empty and it would have been a lovely road anywhere in the world, especially the areas I had recently been. Just for the heck of it, I took a bus for the last fifty kilometers into Chengdu to experience its smooth surface. The bus was unmistakably one of the nicest I had ever been on anywhere. The seats were made on a smaller scale, but I'm not too tall – someone over six feet tall might not have enjoyed it so much. I shared the bus with one other person, he was dressed quite well, and off in his own world, not very interested in this sweaty *guilo* who had just stepped onto his empty bus. He didn't make eye contact, so I sat far enough away not to encroach on his private space. I watched the highway and countryside roll by, interspersed with a Chinese adventure movie and even complimentary drinks. Only China could pull off such a feat of contrasts.

Angie and I had mail coming to Chongqing as we both thought we would be getting there together and never bargained for so long in Tibet. We had also thought that Chongqing was much smaller than it actually was. Trying to find our mail was a nightmare. After being sent to three different post offices, and in the third being sent back to the first, I knew our mail was lost forever, and had to chalk the disappointment up to one of the possible frustrations of the *poste restante* system. Besides that disappointment, Chongqing was hilly and the most bicycle unfriendly place I had cycled in China. No bike lanes, and too many cars. It was a quick glimpse at the future China was heading towards and was disheartening to think that this was considered progress. There was building going on everywhere. I had originally thought it might be nice to stay a few nights, but quickly decided I'd rather be on a boat. Try as I might, I couldn't help but think of Beijing, and what possibilities could lay ahead in England.

I made it to the docks and negotiated a ticket for a five day, four night ride down the Yangtse. The tout who was taking me to the ticket office somehow got separated from me as we were boarding one of the small boats to get there and I ended up in a local crowd to pay for my ticket. I handed over too much *dong*, because the price quoted was more than the locals' price and fortunately only my hands were seen at the counter. When my ticket came back for one person and one bicycle, I was pleased

612

to see that more than half my money was returned as well, and I had ended up paying just two hundred and twenty *yuan*, the local price. I slowly walked away, grabbed my bike, found a place to store it for the five-day journey, and got settled in my bunk.

All the rooms were bunk rooms as far as I could see, eight in a room where I was. Maybe there were more expensive rooms elsewhere, but at least on the two lower levels every room appeared to be shared. There were a few boats in the dock, and while the boat was filling up I took in the scene for a while then pulled out my journal and started to write. I thought about the book Grace gave me years ago when I returned from my first time in Asia; *Lila*, by Robert Pirsig. I felt that calmness a little more, although I had lost my temper in China a few times, and was nowhere near perfect, overall I felt an inner peace. I felt something in me had shifted as a person. Just as Pirsig's journey with his daughter down the Hudson was quite different to his travels with his son, I felt a new phase of my life's journey was approaching. Floating down the Yangtse was not exactly the Hudson, but both were rivers formed by glaciers, and at times I could drift back in my mind to a more primal state, where only the moment mattered and only survival was the focus. Not much had changed since then, but like many times before I realized that as humans we have forgotten that survival is an animal instinct, and no matter what we surround ourselves with in material wealth, we are all still primarily animals surviving on this tiny planet called earth. I drifted off in my journal and wrote with the gentle rocking of the boat.

I noticed there was another westerner on the boat, and from a distance he looked like a guy called Pete we had met in Chengdu. He was English and not a bad sort, but always had a beer in his hand. Not my preferred company on a long boat ride, but I figured some time in the five days which followed we would run into each other so didn't go out of my way to find him at that point.

I had no idea what to expect from this trip. I was looking forward to the unexpected as we began to float east, my mind drifting away as I fell asleep on my bunk in the hot mugginess of the bunk room. The ceiling fan stood motionless above me, and the air clung to my skin.

As we drifted down the river any residual worry of someone realizing that I'd paid the local fare left me. It was nice to feel that for once I had just paid the same as everyone else. It was one of those occasions where I didn't feel exploited because I was a westerner, even though it was an accident.

The beginning of the trip was ordinary, nothing of striking beauty to make my jaw drop. It was the basin of central China, plus it would have been hard to beat some of the Tibetan scenery I'd spent weeks in. The three-day hike through the Tiger Leaping Gorge had been fantastic, hard to believe I was now floating down the same river, although it was quite a bit wider, and soon to be dammed. The damming of this river would have far-reaching consequences. Even though downstream by hundreds of miles from the small town of Qiatou, where Angie and I had stayed for a few days in the beginning of our cycle journey through Tibet, that small vibrant village would possibly be flooded out and displace the *Naxi* people as well. I read years later an interview with a few people from Qiatou, there were protests from that village and petitions signed against that probability, the water levels are still being fiercely opposed till this day, and the dam, now completed has been replete with both human and environmental repercussions. I constantly remind myself that the people can truly have the power if they want it. A small wooden doll from my childhood which stood on the windowsill in my cousin's house downstairs from ours always empowers those thoughts of the strength of the people. It said, "What if they threw a war?" then you pushed down its head, and another quote popped up saying, "AND NO ONE SHOWED UP!" I liked that, and it has always stayed with me.

I didn't move from my bunk much on the first evening. I had come prepared with some snacks and I figured I would have plenty of time to walk around. My room was full of young students who were traveling together. They stayed put mostly, playing cards and eating junk food. The rest of the boat was full of Chinese tourists, and there was a business trip going on. I bumped into Pete later on the following day, after offering me a beer he complained how he thought the boat was a rip off, and six hundred *yuan* was too expensive for the crappy eight bunk room. I didn't tell him what I paid for the same room, but just nodded in agreement that the rooms weren't the best in the world. We had a chat about his trip in China and when he asked where my wife was, I smiled to myself. In the six weeks I'd known Angie, she was referred to already twice as my wife, once by me. I told him more about us and as we mellowed into each other's company it turned out to be nice to have someone to talk to once in a while.

Pete lent me his *Lonely Planet* guide book to read and I read some tidbits of where I had been, and where we were now heading. I took down some mental notes about Wuhan being a university town, and was just reading the guide book on the fore deck when a young Chinese student started yelling something at me. I looked up at him from my spot on the floor, and yes, he was definitely pointing at my book and yelling. I didn't know what his problem was, but he seemed to be pointing at the back cover, and for some reason he was furious. I told him in Chinese that I did not understand what he was saying. He blurted out in broken English, "Tibet is part of China, your map is wrong."

614

I then looked at the back cover of the book, which indeed showed China and Tibet in different colors. I asked, "Have you been to Tibet?"

He said, "No, but Tibet is China, your map is wrong."

I wasn't into a political discussion, especially as the subject seemed to be closed already in his mind. I then said in very slow precise English, "If you have never been to Tibet, maybe you should go there. I was just there, and it is very different to China."

He didn't like that, and just kept saying, "Tibet is in China."

I wasn't too bothered, and was surprised at his vehemence. I said, "Just leave me alone, I want to read my book about China and Tibet."

One of the many businessmen on board came to my rescue asking me if I was enjoying China and where did I come from. Fortunately the annoying student soon disappeared.

The days and nights blurred. We stopped in a few small towns where it was possible to take boat excursions up smaller tributaries, or just walk around the villages on the banks of the river. Pete took an excursion up a river known as 'The Minor Three Gorges' where I opted to walk around the village. I met a classic-looking Chinese man with a friendly face and thin wispy beard. When he smiled at me I went over to see what he was making. They were intricate, hand-carved stamps. His daughter translated for us, and I asked him to make me a small stamp that said Joseph Loves Angela. I didn't know what use it would be, or if he could even do it in Chinese characters, but thirty minutes later he produced a simple, but wonderful, stamp. It was a prism of clear plastic and on the bottom there was an intricate-looking array of characters with a nice fat heart in the middle. It was a small gesture, like something you write on the back of your notebook in high school, but in that moment I knew I was heading to Beijing to fly to the U.K. The stamp somehow made me realize I would be foolish not to – it made me think of Angie, our time in Tibet, walking along another much narrower gorge on the same river as the one I was currently floating on. I smiled thinking of her English accent and green eyes. Unfortunately that man, his family and his small business were one of the many to be displaced by the Three Gorges Dam project.

There were some beautiful high gorges at one point of the ride; the names of the actual three gorges were Qutang, Wuxia, and the Xilong. The boat ride was about 120 kilometers long. Some of the high precipices were quite wonderful to look at and it was hard to believe that the murky water below me now, at times as wide as the Hudson River in New York, was the same raging glacial fed river I had walked far above a few weeks ago with Angie, Tonia, and Kent. We floated past the dam project which was underway but not even half-done at that point.

On the last day of the journey I stayed in the room with the students, and we shared card tricks, and played games. They were interested in my travels, and seemed a lot more open to matters of Tibet and China than the other young student was. We docked in Wuhan that night, and were not allowed to get off the boat. We were obliged to stay aboard one more night. I didn't mind, although it was just a scam to get more money. It was gratifying to be in a room with feisty students when, at midnight, a rude woman came in to collect sixteen *yuan* each for the extra night's accommodation. She was met with a barrage of complaints and refusals from my roomies. It was supremely satisfying to watch the argument unfold, but this time I could just sit back and watch it done for me. After all those months of nightly barge-ins by the police, it was great to listen to this rude woman get yelled at for coming in so late. When she left in a huff, I gave the thumbs up to them all, and they gave me a smile and a thumbs up back. When I saw Pete to bid him farewell he was cursing the Chinese, disgruntled about the thirty extra *yuan* for the night. I just nodded, shrugged and smiled.

# Slow Trains, a Fast Plane and a Big Change

Now that I felt I was heading to England, I was excited. I knew that pedaling to Beijing wasn't on the cards as it was too far and now I'd made my decision I wanted to act on it. I was sorry not to have taken a train journey in India all those years back as I'd heard so much about them, so now Wuhan to Beijing seemed to be a perfect train ride.

We were off the boat quite early, and I cycled happily from the dock to the train station, my mental space clearer with the knowledge that I would soon be leaving China. Kent and I had done a fair bit of cycling together through quite a large chunk of China and Angie and I had had such a memorable experience in Tibet that I was ready to stop moving for the moment. This trip had started with a surprise root canal radically changing my northeastern European tour and had snowballed into something much bigger. I sifted through the memories as I rode; a solo ride across America, John and me cycling to Colombia, living in Australia, the Philippines briefly, then traversing China into Tibet. Now I was heading to a train station to buy a ticket once removed from hopefully the final ticket I would buy in China – the one to England.

After getting off the boat with the sun rising and Wuhan just waking up, I found a place to get some breakfast. Like a child I was filled with excitement to finally be making it to Peking, now commonly known as Beijing. Big cities are great fun to cycle in, see a few sights, maybe catch a movie, and more importantly buy an airplane ticket.

I made it to the station in time to catch the ten-thirty train. Eighteen hours later I would be in the capital city. Bikes normally traveled as cargo in China, so, after purchasing my ticket, I took off all the bags, went to a counter that looked like it was for baggage, and wheeled my bike to the desk. My Chinese was far from perfect, but coupled with sign language, and showing the clerk my ticket to Beijing, I was happy enough that I'd got my point across, "I'm going to Beijing, this is my bike, can you send it on to Beijing as well?" With a nod of agreement, and quite a big smile, I received a ticket for my bike. I said goodbye to it thinking we'd soon be happily reunited in Beijing.

I found my hard sleeper – an open non-private slab with two people below me. The whole compartment was hard sleepers and was like a large dorm room on wheels. The train was crammed with all the variables of humanity and was home for the next eighteen hours. I threw my bags out of sight and explored the train as it slowly pulled out of the station. I noticed the sign at the station said, Hankou not Wuhan, so realized I must have been at one of Wuhan's smaller stations. Not that it mattered so much, or so I thought.

The train was typical of what I'd expected; the hard sleeper afforded me a tiny modicum of privacy when perched upon it, but privacy was a long forgotten luxury I'd left behind somewhere in another life. I had a half-read novel to get me through the long journey. The scenery was much the same as I had cycled through during the days before the boat ride, and the passing rice paddies were pleasant and calming to look at. In the past few weeks I'd felt less like a cyclist with all the different modes of transport I had been using; trucks, buses, boats, now a train, I felt more like a traveler with a bike. All the mini-journeys on other modes of transport felt like exciting adventures in their own right, and I was glad that after all the years I had lived on my bicycle I was still able to enjoy them. Every time I sat on a bus or a train, though, I knew I was missing all the small villages and experiences that were to be had while pedaling along, but I had a fair share tucked away in my memory banks forever.

I smiled and stared out of the window watching the countryside pass me by, thinking back to the unbelievable cycling that had taken place in the past few months. As the train chugged along I fell in and out of sleep, and was glad to have the time to travel in this way. I felt I had found my balance as a cyclist/traveler, and from that first trip in Australia, my love affair with the bike had grown and developed. I thought about the past thirteen years of traveling I had done and how it had shaped me as a person. I'd made plenty of mistakes, met lots of great people, and learned so much. In the years since I'd taken to the road I had been involved in a few different relationships, and I could only hope that the honesty which I always tried to live by hadn't left anyone hurt. I had been confused in many of my relationships, not only relationships with women, but also those with travel, my life, my family and friends, and my country. I was always trying to find a place I fit in as a human and tried to incorporate all my learning on a spiritual, intellectual, and romantic level, and put it to use in my everyday life. When I looked back on all those years, it brought me right to my present circumstance; almost flat broke, thirty-four years of age, on a train heading once again into an unknown future. Somehow or another it all felt correct. I tried to listen to my heart – I wasn't always successful, but attempted at least to be honest with myself and everyone in my life.

The train rocked slowly, and I fell asleep thinking of calling Angie when I got to Beijing. I was getting nervous now. Would she want me to come to her part of the world? Had the few weeks she'd been home snapped her into a new reality? Would she want to be involved with this itinerant New Yorker? Maybe it *was* just a holiday romance. I had to be prepared for whatever she said as well. Now eighteen hours seemed too long to wait to hear her response.

The day rolled by, the novel I was reading was something I'd picked up in Dali, nothing great but it helped to pass the time. I'd also found Richard Bach's *Jonathan Livingston Seagull* tucked away in a small hidden part of my pannier as I was looking for something else. I had forgotten it was there, and was quite happy to rediscover it. I had a funny relationship with that book. During my travel years I usually had a book on a deeper level to refer to. I smiled thinking that I had read so many other books by the same author before I read what was probably his best known book. I remembered the day it found me.

Rob and I used to go to a book shop in Nagoya which had English language books. We would read entire books in the shop – it was a bit naughty, but English language books were expensive. One day Rob saw *Jonathan Livingston Seagull* and asked what I thought of it. I said I'd never read it, and he couldn't believe it. He handed it to me and I read it right there, sitting on a step, in two hours. After I'd finished it, I went up to the counter and bought it. It was that same water-stained, slightly damp copy wrapped in a plastic bag shoved in the back of a pannier which I was glancing through now. I smiled reading its pages. What an inspirational, simple book.

As I drifted off I could hardly believe how swiftly night fell. I thought of my bike traveling in a different part of the same train and looked at my ticket stub. Suddenly I had a question about my bike making it to Beijing. I didn't know what it was, but, thinking back, something seemed wrong about the luggage area where I'd left the bike. I got up from my bunk and went in search of someone to reassure me that my fears were ungrounded. I saw a few students chatting and asked if they spoke English. One of them did, and we had a chat. I then showed him my ticket, and asked if I would be able to collect my bike with the ticket in Beijing. He looked at me quizzically, and said, "Yes, you present this ticket and you can get your bike."

I asked again, "In Beijing?"

He deftly avoided saying in Beijing, and said, "You just give them this ticket and you will get your bike."

I was now worried. I knew all too well the trait of not wanting to tell someone something they did not want to hear, Japanese society had accustomed me to it, and traveling in Asia over the years had fine tuned the feeling to know when it was happening. That moment was now, I just felt it. It was obvious I'd made a mistake. The young student had seemed uncomfortable and evasive and I hadn't managed to get a straight answer out of him. I had a deep feeling of dread in the pit of my stomach that I'd done something really stupid. I thought back to the lady handing me my ticket with a big smile on her face. At that moment I had been a little tired and maybe too cocky after my boat trip coup. I had also been feeling excited and keen to get going to Beijing. I felt now that I hadn't fully clarified the situation and wasn't at all sure that my bike was trundling along only a few carriages away. With no one to talk over my fears with there was nothing to do but head off to bed. Feeling like an idiot I opted to finish my novel instead of reading more of Jonathan soaring to previously unreached heights. Sleep finally came, but for some reason, before I forgot the name of the train station, I wrote in the back of my journal, 'Hankou Station'. With that thought in mind, I fell off to sleep.

The train ride, which was supposed to be eighteen hours long, lasted nearer twenty so we arrived in Beijing at about seven a.m. which was a much better time to arrive than five a.m. I would have loved to get my bike, ride out of the station and look for a place to stay, but it wasn't to be. I searched out the cargo area, and handed my ticket over to someone there.

He looked at it and said, "Not here, you go to left luggage."

Off I went to left luggage, the feeling in the pit of my stomach a little heavier with each step. I handed him my ticket, "Yes, this is ticket for left luggage, you go to Hankou station, give them ticket, and they give you bike."

The lead in my stomach hit the floor and that small seed of doubt which had sprouted the night before now blossomed into a fully-blown nightmare. Here I was in Beijing, and my bike was in left luggage eighteen hours back. I wanted to scream, and then I wanted to cry. I was so frustrated. I blew it big time. I found one of the dreaded tourist police who had been responsible for turfing us out of the hotel in Chengdu. I didn't expect too much help, but I briefly formed an idea of him calling Hankou left luggage, and getting them to send on my bike to Beijing – a feat that would probably be hard to pull off even in America. I went through the motions anyway – I wasn't ready to face the inevitable which was to either say goodbye to my bike forever, or board a train back. It was now seven forty-five. I looked at the train board after the helpful policeman repeated, "You go to Hankou, give them your ticket, you get your bike." I knew what I must do. Leaving my bike in a train station left luggage just didn't feel like a fitting end for my buddy. Even though the frame was new, I felt that its familiar logo from all those years back had re-found me, all the equipment had been with me for a long time, and it was a perfect fit. We had developed a bond in our short time as a pair. We hadn't done so much traveling together, but the last few months in China and Tibet were enough for me to realize the comfort of the steel frame suited long-distance touring perfectly. My decision was made – the next train to Wuhan was at one p.m.

I was feeling like a complete jerk, not a well-traveled person who didn't do stupid things like that. It was a good lesson in humility. I felt bad for the feelings I'd had towards Pete when he was paying the high prices on the boat. It must have been instant *karma*. I remembered something from many years before on a ferry, crossing the Georgian Bay with my motorcycle in the bow of the Chi-Cheemaun ferry. It was something Paul had said; "When you think you have it all figured out is when you realize you have so far to go." I believe that that can apply in most situations in life, but right now it felt like it had been written for me.

My trip in China had gone pretty smoothly. I'd met Kent who spoke Chinese, and then I'd met Angie. So many coincidences and chance meetings have filled the past thirteen years of my life and there I was feeling smug on a boat in China because Pete paid the tourist price. I now apologized to Pete in his absence and laughed at myself. I thought back to Paul and all the intervening years of travel. What a stupid thing to do. I left my bike in left luggage and took an eighteen-hour train journey, only to have to return the same day. Yes Joe, instant *karma*!

It was still too early in England to call Angie so I purchased my return ticket, and now had to sit and wait. I walked around and just absorbed the atmosphere. Here I was in Beijing train station. The city was just there a few steps beyond, waiting for me to explore, but it would have to wait another frustrating thirty-six hours or more! I could only laugh, because if I thought about another thirty-six hours of train journey just to get right back to where I stood, I would be tempted to cry. To add salt to the wound, I had finished reading my novel so it was just me and *Jonathan*. I walked over to left luggage with all the gear I wouldn't need to lug back with me, and hoped the worker didn't remember me from earlier and think I wanted to send them back to Wuhan! I left my bags at left luggage and asked twice if I could collect my bags from there the next day. He looked at me like I was crazy, and repeated himself again, "You give me ticket, I give you bags, yes."

I took a walk outside and ran into some young Norwegian travelers who were looking nervous. I greeted them, and asked if they were alright. They said their friend had gone to change money when they arrived, but had been gone for two hours and they were frightened that something might have happened to him. They were young – maybe in their early twenties – and were freaked out enough that they were contemplating calling his parents. The time difference would have meant waking up his parents in Norway very early in the morning with the news that their son was missing. A big mistake I thought. I advised them to hold off on calling as there was nothing his parents could do. He may have just gotten lost or the banks and exchange places may not have opened yet. I persuaded them to sit down and have a hot drink. We all sat together and I told them of my stupid mistake. It felt good for all of us to be having a good laugh on my account. I went off to check the time but it was still too early in England to call Angie. It would have to wait until I got back. I couldn't stand the suspense. If I called would she say, "Thanks, but no thanks, maybe we'll meet again one day." I didn't think so, but it was possible that maybe my next flight wouldn't be heading to England. My silly move with my bike had me questioning my self assuredness, but I was letting my mind drift too much.

The time was ticking by so slowly. I wanted to be heading southwest back the way I'd come, to at least begin the process of getting back on track. I walked back outside the station and saw the Norwegian group with an extra member. They waved me over with a smile. "Here he is he got lost. Thanks for your advice." I was happy for them and thought of how pleased the parents would be to not get that phonecall. We chatted for another few minutes, and they asked when I was heading back to Wuhan. I told them soon. We waved goodbye to each other, and I wished them a good travel in China.

I finally boarded my train and hadn't purchased a hard sleeper this time. I figured I'd save the extra expense for the return journey. I should be arriving in Wuhan the next morning.

It all looked too familiar to me; the countryside, the train, so I started reading the same novel again. It got boring quickly, so I pulled out *Jonathan*.

There he was soaring ever higher, proving all the naysayers wrong – even though I had read that book several times, every time I could extract something different. I thought back on my life to that point. Had I reached lofty heights? Had I pushed myself? I felt I had worked on my inner self, but at this point felt there was so much more work to do. Angie and I had had some deep conversations during our travels in Tibet. She had pushed herself in saying yes to coming with me on a bike to Tibet. She said it was out of character but felt if she passed up the chance she might regret it for the rest of her life. Who is to know? How many of those same situations slip by almost unnoticed, but also how many people's dreams and waking thoughts are plagued with 'What ifs?' It reminded me of another book by Richard Bach called *One* – about all the different paths we can take to create our life. Each decision changes everything. There was now no one to speak to and my brain was running around in circles – Angie, England, Wuhan, train rides, left luggage, life pathways. It felt like some doors open wider than others. Over the past thirteen years I had tried to be a conscious creator of the path I was treading. The next thirty-six hours or more gave me lots of time to think and sometimes too much of that is dangerous. As

622

the light came through the opened window of the train I just zoned out for a good bit of the daytime.

I searched for the left luggage ticket. I looked at it and laughed again at my stupidity. That little piece of paper represented my bicycle sitting in a train station in the middle of China. Don't lose it I thought to myself, that's why you're on this silly train! I was weary now, I read a few more chapters of the small blue book, dog-eared and damp, but couldn't focus or stay awake. I closed it, shoved my left luggage ticket between the pages and put it in the top of my small backpack.

We had passed a nuclear reactor the night before and I was glad to have left it safely behind – now we were passing it again. I didn't like its proximity and I knew I would have to pass it one more time. When the journey was half over, I began to feel a little less frustrated – at least I was closer to forward progress now. Once night came I would sleep and we would be getting there near first morning light.

I flitted in and out of sleep. With no working lights it was useless to try and read to pass the time. I bounced around uncomfortably in a dreamless unrelaxing sleep. When first light arrived I felt in a state of delirium from too much train travel and too little rest. Let me see what Jonathan was doing. I pulled out the book and was actually able to stay awake to read it.

The train slowed and stopped, we all watched passengers alight onto the platform. I was staring out in an unfocused way, just drifting in and out. The usual unintelligible announcements were made then I started to speak to some of my fellow passengers. They all knew I was going to Hankou, not the Wuhan main train station, which was twenty minutes beyond Hankou. I happened to look out the window noticing that it looked vaguely familiar. It seemed too early for it to be Hankou but when I asked my travel companions if this was indeed Hankou, they all said yes. The door closing bells were just beginning to ring so with no time to think I quickly grabbed my backpack and just made it onto the platform as the doors shut. I didn't know what to make of it as they had all known I was going to Hankou. I looked around, and indeed it was the right station.

I was standing bewildered on the platform. Why hadn't anyone told me it was my station? I didn't understand it, and after all the months traveling here, I was still as perplexed as ever as to the Chinese mindset. As the train started to leave the station, I was snapped back to the present moment. I then had a vision of my book lying on the window ledge where I had been seated just minutes before. In my hurry I'd put the book down, grabbed my pack and run off the train. "Shit, my left luggage ticket was tucked in its pages," I nearly said aloud, or maybe even did. My heart sank. I looked at the slow movement of the train and started to chase it, cursing myself and my lack of sleep. I didn't have time to beat myself up too much before I heard a loud whistle, and looked up to see someone throw something out of an open window pointing at me. I saw my book and a small yellow ticket flutter to the ground. I ran over to snatch the ticket before it was wafted away by the moving train. I quickly pocketed it, then looked down at the faded picture of a seagull staring up at me. I shook my head in disbelief at my carelessness and yelled to the slow moving train, "*Ni hao mah* – Thank You." Man that was close Joe, wake up.

I walked over to the left luggage booth and there was the same lady. I wanted to blame her, I wanted to be angry and have a good yell, but didn't. I was just so relieved on many levels; half the journey was over, I had my book and ticket back, and life was feeling quite nice on this small platform in the middle of China for the second time in my life. She was so pleased to see me, nodding and smiling as she asked for my ticket that I just laughed. I handed over the small yellow paper and thought to myself, small disaster averted. She ran to get my bike and proudly wheeled it to me. I then paid for the privilege of having had my trusty steed kept safely in the small left-luggage room, and walked my bike over to the large timetable near the ticket counter.

The next train to Beijing was in five hours, and I was told again that I would not be able to travel with my bike on the same train. I did not feel like waiting in that station for five hours, or trying to explain how important it was that my bike and I travel together. I needed to get to another station. I pedaled out into the crowded hot streets of Wuhan. A strange feeling of déjà vu engulfed me. Oh yeah, I've been here already. I cycled off, not particular about the direction. My bike wasn't abandoned and now that I was here riding him again I was glad I hadn't left him in left luggage for the rest of his days. I still wasn't looking forward to the long train ride and even toyed with the idea of a flight – too expensive though and none available for that day. I got to see more of Wuhan at any rate. It wasn't a bad place. The Yangtze River flowing through it made it feel open and I crossed a bridge that had a nice view of the river. There was a lot of traffic here, though, and I much preferred the other towns and cities of southern China where Kent and I had cycled months before. Had I been in China that long? It was time to go. Get to a train station and get the next twenty or so hours over with.

Wuhan main station was twenty kilometers away and when I arrived the next train was due to leave in a half an hour. There was no way I could get my bike on it so I opted to wait. The next train the ticket clerk could get me and the bike on together was eight-thirty that evening. It would get me into Beijing at one the following afternoon. No sleeper was available but it was the best he could do. It was going to be a long day. I cycled around and saw much more of Wuhan than I'd bargained for. It was a big sprawling city.

I cycled around aimlessly drinking and eating out of boredom more than hunger and thirst. I decided to head back to the station for the remaining few hours. The stifling heat was sticking to my skin in droplets. June was hot, and I was glad cycling wasn't in the plans. Two thirds of the train journey was now done, and here I stood only twenty kilometers from my starting point. What an ending to my time in China, comically frustrating, like many other situations in the past few months.

In the station I met an American woman who was doing a manic two-week tour of China – train stations, airports, bus stops, translators at every stop, and very expensive. She was nice enough and blown away that I had just been here for over three months exploring mostly by bike. She didn't think open travel like that was even permitted. I told her a few stories, and she took it all in. She had a great time laughing at herself and the extortionate prices she was paying. She didn't seem to mind, and her clothing and mannerisms reeked of the well-heeled traveler who would be staying in the nicer hotels in the bigger towns and cities. We had a good laugh about my latest blunder, and I felt much better about it now that it was nearly over.

We passed a couple of hours chatting while she waited for her train heading west. Unfortunately she didn't have a novel to trade with me, but I gave her mine anyway and she was appreciative. When she left I wrote in my journal for what seemed like an eternity. Finally my bike was taken away to be put on the baggage car which I was assured was on the same train I was. Fortunately, my American companion's translator stayed an extra few minutes to help me get everything absolutely straight and give me peace of mind that all was as I thought. It was almost over.

I then noticed a phone – at last I can call Angie. The phone rang a couple of times before Angie's mom answered. She quickly gave Angie the phone. It was so nice to hear her lovely accented tones. I had to get round to the point quickly as I didn't have too long on the phone. I asked what she thought about me coming out to England and us living together. She drew a breath in and said, "Let's give it a go, I'll try to find a place for us." Music to my ears.

The time slipped by quickly now that I had spoken to Angie. I arrived in Beijing the next afternoon, picked up my bags in left luggage, and cycled out into the heat and haze of Beijing. I found a place to stay where there were backpackers and one other cyclist who had a folding bike – what a great idea. When he heard of my foul up with the bike, he nodded knowingly. His journey was exploring mostly the eastern part of China. He had limited time, and thought one day he'd love to head to Tibet and further west. I hope my descriptions inspired that possible journey to become a reality, for no matter how difficult, it had been extraordinary.

I cycled in the crowded bike lanes with what felt like the whole population of Beijing. I visited the Great Wall, The Forbidden City, and met other travelers who I enjoyed swapping stories with.

I met a couple from the U.K. who thought it was a bad decision to go to England with so little cash. They said I should stick to my plan to teach English in Japan or Taiwan, and then go to England when I'd saved some money. Jobs were tough to find, etc. I told them it wasn't for the work I was going there. It was mostly to see if Angie and I would work out as a couple. I also met an American named Harvey, and we went to The Great Wall together. He thought my story was incredibly romantic, and no matter what the circumstance I should head to England – I liked Harvey.

I briefly threw around the idea of taking the Trans-Siberian Express across Russia back to Hungary. My bike could only go cargo, and wasn't guaranteed to make it to Europe. After all I had just been through to get reunited with my bike, I thought better of it. I thought back to all the Japanese bikes I'd saved from being thrown away all those years ago, but my bike had personality and we'd formed a bond. I know I was probably becoming too attached to worldly possessions, but he was my trident, and had a lot more journeys left in him. I thought that ending up on a Chinese scrap heap wasn't a fitting end. I almost thought my bike was sensing my thoughts so I patted his well-worn leather saddle, and reassured him we'd be in England together. After nearly sixty hours on a train already I probably wasn't up to a ten-day epic train journey across Siberia, although on many levels it was quite tempting – maybe another time.

Over two years earlier when I left New York, I'd never dreamed the five thousand dollars I had to my name would see me this far. I knew I'd need to do something in England if I was going to spend time seeing what was to become of my relationship with Angie, but all that would become clearer once I was walking the streets of Weymouth. Something told me that my travels as a single man were over. They had begun by throwing my leg over that motorcycle thirteen years ago with my college buddy Gary – starting me on my synchronous voyage of discovery. It wasn't ending; it was just taking another route. The subtle shift I'd felt on my way to Bogotá – coming back to South America with a family – flashed before my eyes and I just knew that Angie and I were starting something special. When I'd told Kent this after that second night in Lijiang he'd thought I was crazy, but I couldn't deny that something just felt right.

I checked the *poste restante* in Beijing. Three letters were waiting for me; one from Angie, one from mom, and another from John Nielsen – my actor friend in L.A. I read Angie's first; she filled me in on her journey home, her dad's deteriorating health, the problems she had with her bike in London, and how strange it was to be back in Weymouth with summer just kicking in – Did Tibet exist? She'd only been back a week or two and was still feeling unsettled. She hoped we would see each other again, it was sent and written before our phone call obviously, but it still made me feel warm and fuzzy.

Mom's letter caught me up on what was happening with my family and how she was settling into her new house and getting used to life in the suburbs after spending her whole life in New York City – quite a big adjustment to make. She also forwarded a letter she had received from England, inside was a photograph of a bicycle adorned with many flowers and a large wreath. At first I was confused, then I turned it over and saw written in an unfamiliar hand;

*"Chris's Bicycle, thanks for being such a good friend to our son."*
*Audrey and Paul Edwards.*

With the emotion of Angie's letter still fresh, now this; I felt a lump in my throat. We can all affect others' lives in a positive way, and the thought of my friend on his bicycle made me smile.

John's letter told me of how he had landed a great part in a television series on a cable show. He was excited, and his perseverance had paid back in dividends. He wasn't sure where it would take him but it felt great to have reached that part in his career. I thought how we both had just seemed to reach a new level in our lives; my traveling wasn't ending, but with the feelings I was having about Angie, England and the future, it had definitely taken on a new and deeper level. All three letters made me happy, and feel heartened to be part of the great adventure called life.

I enjoyed my last week in China. Maybe those strange feelings in Hong Kong had been preparing me, telling me to keep awake and look for the signs; a door is going to open and I should walk through it. Every bus ride and pedal stroke that led Angie and me to meet in that small hostel in the middle of China were results of conscious choices we both made. The outcomes of those choices were what lay ahead. Visas and other logistical problems were not going to be obstacles or excuses, but challenges.

I can now say the most important thing I did in Beijing was to buy that plane ticket to England. When we were reunited in London, my future wife and mother of our two beautiful children gave me a hug and a kiss. Thirteen years and many more adventures later, our journey still continues....................

Charley, me and Andrea – Bronx River Pkwy 1994

Kathy, my brother Larry and Kaela – meeting me in a campsite

Me, Gina and Tom – Michigan

Midwest charm (Anne and me in the middle)

What, no wheels! Mark and me in North Dakota

The storm approaches

Me and Steve – hot and dry in Oregon – 1994

Johnny C. waving goodbye to the Wickham Ave. house – The Bronx

John and the quiet boys in the Milpa – northern Mexico

The better of the roads from the Milpa – stay left John!

The local girls dressed up in Nicaragua

The anti-guerilla soldiers and me – Colombia 1995

The challenging road in the Santa Marta Mountains – Colombia

Friendly German couple and their mean machines – Cartagena

John's companions to Ecuador – Bogotá

Saying goodbye to John – Bogotá, Colombia

Kelly on the runway – King Island

Drawn into China – the road to Yangshuo

Some friendly Chinese folks

Kent with a small following

Angie at the Tiger Leaping Gorge – western China – 1996

Angie with her Chinese mountain bike and Tibetan prayer flags

Angie and a Tibetan Nomad

Small village – Tibetan Highlands

Me and a Tibetan monk – Litang – 1996

The stamp maker and family – Three Rivers Gorge – China

A Chinese Junk – Three Rivers Gorge

Harvey and me – The Great Wall of China

My bike – finally made it to Beijing – still rolling!

Weymouth still existed – Angie and me at her mom's house.

# Epilogue

In my travels I came face to face with environmental devastation, occupied land, destitute poverty, the after-effects of war, colonization and religious intolerance walking side by side with open friendly faces, optimism in the face of wonton destruction, idyllic small villages that were as close to paradise on earth as you could find not a day's cycle ride from a living hell, rainforests disappearing with the saws of smiling faces working to feed their young ones, once proud nations living on reservations ripped away from their land and heritage to live in squalor, factories manufacturing junk of no use to anyone standing in fields which used to grow enough food to feed the surrounding villages. These images still burn in my mind, sometimes they make me laugh at the same time I could cry.

If I thought every time I drank tea, ate chocolate, rode my bicycle, or pulled on a piece of clothing, about the unfairness behind it, I would certainly drive myself mad, and there have been times when I nearly did, but I would then remember the *saddhu* who walked into the tent, "Try and get rid of expectation." I realize that yes, because of an accident of geography I am one of the planet's privileged, but I make every effort to look past the harsh realities and, like so many I share the planet with, see the beauty which keeps the world hopeful. This life is tough for many, but do we have other experiences awaiting us? I like to think so. I can look around with hope and say to myself; possibly in some unknown future we all may know something other than this.

"We are here, but they are there," never felt correct to me. How could we not all be interlinked? Do we need to know that everything in existence can be proven? For me, knowing that it all *can't* be is the mystery that helps me go on. Existence, I feel, can not be merely substantiated. The lives we are all living right now may hold something different in a not too distant future. It feels more realistic to feel part of it all, endeavoring to improve the problems from within. Live in harmony with ourselves and not let the anger take over; there already is too much of it out there. In the end it may bring about some changes, but does it do anything for the greater good?

I try not to use these beliefs to hide behind. I still question authority and consciously make choices. The difference is I don't kid myself that no matter how hard I try, I'm still involved in someway with the whole world and its problems. I have learned though, every day I walk amongst the planet's diversity and beauty that we are all truly blessed, we just need to shout it from the mountain top and share it with all of the inhabitants of our home.

When I get angry, make mistakes, feel frustrated in the face of apathy, I know I still have more to learn. I still shake my head in disbelief of how much further we all need to go so we can accept and celebrate our differences. Can some people be capable of such needless destruction of nature, and killing of his fellow human beings knowingly, and not be evil? Does evil actually exist? These answers elude me, and I know that I am not the one to judge, but the more I see, read, learn and watch our world move into the future, I am perplexed, yet remain optimistic. The world's consciousness, I feel, is changing.

At times, my travels enabled me to disconnect from anything familiar, I was allowed to find deeper meaning in the mundane, enjoy the many people and places of the world and remove myself from the every-day pressures too many of us face, be it in the richest or poorest countries of the world. My travels have meant so much to me, and writing this book has been a catharsis. In writing, reading and re-reading these stories my wife and I have realized what a gift our life is, and the marvel of our children and every phase of their development is wonderful but also ordinary. It is shared by billions of others, and all anyone wants is to see their children grow and become adults.

Our choices as human beings are much more powerful than our choices as Americans, British, Italians, Mexicans or whatever other label we can use to define our diverse race scurrying around on the face of planet earth. Our world is constantly showing us we are all one interconnected unit. I read books about men like Greg Mortenson who wrote *Three Cups of Tea,* he turned his mountaineering endeavors and travel experiences into a lifelong pledge to better the world by building schools for the poorest of the poor. I can't help but be inspired in the power that one person really does have to make a change.

I hope that my stories – saved from dozens of journals – ties a thread through each and every one of us and that by sharing them with a wider audience, I helped to put a human face on problems we see as existing elsewhere. There is no elsewhere, we are all here.

I discovered that the gray areas make life complicated, but to draw everything in black or white makes it too simple. How could this small planet spinning around at a thousand miles per hour one hundred million miles away from the life-giving sun be that simple? The gray areas, I'm only beginning to realize, are not gray at all, they're all the colors of the rainbow. The difference in our religious beliefs, the way we dress, the music we listen to, the love we share, childbirth, thunderstorms, vibrant sunsets, the oceans crashing onto the shores, fruit growing on trees is all just ordinary, but even the most ordinary daily occurrence is quite magical. That is the wonder of life on earth!

Throughout my travels I always kept in touch with young people, if not in a classroom teaching or fixing bikes for the local populace, I would occasionally give talks in schools of various ages. I spoke at a few high schools, and I knew everything was worthwhile when I received a letter from one of the students a few weeks after I spoke to his high school class. I will enclose that letter here:

*Dear Joe,*

*Where ever you are in the world today, hello and thank you. I have met many people in my short yet interesting 17 years. It is on a rare occasion that any one of these people made an impression right off the bat. I have realized and learned and relearned so many things in my senior year. The most important realization though was triggered by your visit. I'm not a very happy guy. I am not going in the direction I want to. The harder thing is that I don't even know what that direction is. That is to say, I cannot read the compass correctly. To stand my ground is what I would like to do but I always, time and time again, back down. I'm not saying physically, I'm talking emotionally, mentally.*

*The other day, I was telling my girlfriend about you. Her comment was that you had no life. This disturbed me. I look up to you, a lot. Your life is your home. Your home is your life. Your home, which you do have, is as large as the world and as awesome as the human mind. That is to say you live at home wherever you go. You seem to keep your home in your head. You find joy because you live. This is what everyone is searching for, yet few know they are. I feel it is time to let myself know where I am going. The time has come for me to take that responsibility.*

*I am going to college soon. In the mean time, my 'significant other' is going to be left behind. I'm going to college around here. But as you said, it is an entirely new world. This frightens me. You have helped me to face my fear. I learned a lot from you. I wish you the best of luck in your travels, in your life. Thank you for sharing.*

*Sincerely, Peter*

Thank you all for coming on my journey with me. Peace, Joe.

# About the Author

Joe Diomede lives with his wife Angie and two children, Louis and Francesca, in the stunning beauty of Southern France where the majestic Pyrenean Mountain chain secrets away small hamlets and villages from the modern world.

Cycling is still a big part of his life, and besides riding bikes with his family, Joe co-owns two small-scale bicycle shops serving local communities in England and Ireland. To supplement a low-key lifestyle their back garden produces (or tries to) much of the food they consume as a vegetarian family.

Although his open-ended travel has changed with the arrival of children, his love of life, passion for social justice, and trying to keep his life simple is a constant challenge.

Coming from The Bronx in New York City, he struggles between his love of nature, and the 'buzz' of a big city, but manages to maintain the balance.

Writing short stories and articles have always been a hobby for Joe but this book is his largest writing endeavor to date.